Research Anthology on Artificial Neural Network Applications

Information Resources Management Association
USA

Volume II

Published in the United States of America by
    IGI Global
    Engineering Science Reference (an imprint of IGI Global)
    701 E. Chocolate Avenue
    Hershey PA, USA 17033
    Tel: 717-533-8845
    Fax: 717-533-8661
    E-mail: cust@igi-global.com
    Web site: http://www.igi-global.com

Library of Congress Cataloging-in-Publication Data

Names: Information Resources Management Association, editor.
Title: Research anthology on artificial neural network applications /
  Information Resources Management Association, editor.
Description: Hershey, PA : Engineering Science Reference an imprint of IGI
  Global, [2022] | Includes bibliographical references and index. |
  Summary: "This book covers critical topics related to artificial neural
  networks and their multitude of applications in a number of diverse
  areas including medicine, finance, operations research, business, social
  media, security, and more, covering everything from the applications and
  uses of artificial neural networks to deep learning and non-linear
  problems,"-- Provided by publisher.
Identifiers: LCCN 2021034008 (print) | LCCN 2021034009 (ebook) | ISBN
  9781668424087 (hardcover) | ISBN 9781668424094 (ebook)
Subjects: LCSH: Neural networks (Computer science)
Classification: LCC QA76.87 .R47 2022 (print) | LCC QA76.87 (ebook) | DDC
  006.3/2--dc23
LC record available at https://lccn.loc.gov/2021034008
LC ebook record available at https://lccn.loc.gov/2021034009

British Cataloguing in Publication Data
A Cataloguing in Publication record for this book is available from the British Library.

The views expressed in this book are those of the authors, but not necessarily of the publisher.

For electronic access to this publication, please contact: eresources@igi-global.com.

List of Contributors

Table of Contents

Section 2
Development and Design Methodologies

Section 3
Tools and Technologies

Section 4
Utilization and Applications

Section 5
Organizational and Social Implications

Section 6
Emerging Trends

Preface

Intelligent technologies such as artificial neural networks have played an incredible role in their ability to predict, analyze, and navigate different circumstances in a variety of industries ranging from medicine to education, banking, and engineering. Artificial neural networks are a growing phenomenon as research continues to develop about the applications, benefits, challenges, and impacts they have. These statistical modeling tools are capable of processing nonlinear data with strong accuracy and are an effective and efficient problem-solving method. Helping to solve real-world issues, the advantages of artificial neural networks are difficult to ignore, as more and more businesses begin to implement them into their strategies.

Staying informed of the most up-to-date research trends and findings is of the utmost importance. That is why IGI Global is pleased to offer this three-volume reference collection of reprinted IGI Global book chapters and journal articles that have been handpicked by senior editorial staff. This collection will shed light on critical issues related to the trends, techniques, and uses of various applications by providing both broad and detailed perspectives on cutting-edge theories and developments. This collection is designed to act as a single reference source on conceptual, methodological, technical, and managerial issues, as well as provide insight into emerging trends and future opportunities within the field.

The *Research Anthology on Artificial Neural Network Applications* is organized into six distinct sections that provide comprehensive coverage of important topics. The sections are:

1. Fundamental Concepts and Theories;
2. Development and Design Methodologies;
3. Tools and Technologies;
4. Utilization and Applications;
5. Organizational and Social Implications; and
6. Emerging Trends.

The following paragraphs provide a summary of what to expect from this invaluable reference tool.

Section 1, "Fundamental Concepts and Theories," serves as a foundation for this extensive reference tool by addressing crucial theories essential to understanding the concepts and uses of artificial neural network applications. Opening this reference book is the chapter "Fundamental Categories of Artificial Neural Networks" by Profs. Arunaben Prahladbhai Gurjar and Shitalben Bhagubhai Patel of Ganpat University, India, which provides an overview on the various types of neural networks like feed forward, recurrent, feedback, classification-predication. This first section ends with the chapter "A Journey From Neural Networks to Deep Networks: Comprehensive Understanding for Deep Learning" by Profs. Priyanka P. Patel and Amit R. Thakkar of Chandubhai S. Patel Institute of Technology, CHARUSAT University,

India, which discusses deep learning fundamentals and the recent trends and mentions many advanced applications, deep learning models, and networks to easily solve those applications in a very smart way.

Section 2, "Development and Design Methodologies," presents in-depth coverage of the design and development of artificial neural networks for their use in different applications. This section starts with "Artificial Neural Network Models for Large-Scale Data" by Prof. Vo Ngoc Phu of Duy Tan University, Vietnam and Prof. Vo Thi Ngoc Tran from Ho Chi Minh City University of Technology, Vietnam, which proposes algorthims to process and store big data sets succesfully. The section ends with "Artificial Neural Network (ANN) Modeling of Odor Threshold Property of Diverse Chemical Constituents of Black Tea and Coffee" by Prof. Jillella Gopala Krishna of NIPER Kolkata, India and Prof. Probir Kumar Ojha from Jadavpur University, India, which develops an artificial neural network model using odor threshold (OT) property data for diverse odorant components present in black tea (76 components) and coffee (46 components).

Section 3, "Tools and Technologies," explores the various tools and technologies used in the implementation of artificial neural networks for various uses. The section starts with "Tool Condition Monitoring Using Artificial Neural Network Models" by Prof. Srinivasa P. Pai of NMAM Institute of Technology, India and Prof. Nagabhushana T. N. from S. J. College of Engineering, India, which deals with the application of artificial neural network (ANN) models for tool condition monitoring (TCM) in milling operations in order to develop an optimal ANN model, in terms of compact architecture, least training time, and its ability to generalize well on unseen (test) data. The section ends with "A Novel Prediction Perspective to the Bending Over Sheave Fatigue Lifetime of Steel Wire Ropes by Means of Artificial Neural Networks" by Profs. Tuğba Özge Onur and Yusuf Aytaç Onur of Zonguldak Bulent Ecevit University, Turkey, which focuses on a novel prediction perspective to the bending over sheave fatigue lifetime of steel wire ropes by means of artificial neural networks.

Section 4, "Utilization and Applications," describes how artificial neural networks are used and applied in diverse industries for various technologies and applications. The section begins with "Literature Survey for Applications of Artificial Neural Networks" by Profs. Pooja Deepakbhai Pancholi and Sonal Jayantilal Patel of Ganpat University, India, which discusses the major applications of artificial neural networks and the importance of the e-learning application and presents an investigation into the explosive developments of many artificial neural network related applications. It ends with "Forecasting and Technical Comparison of Inflation in Turkey With Box-Jenkins (ARIMA) Models and the Artificial Neural Network" by Prof. Erkan Işığıçok of Bursa Uludağ University, Turkey and Profs. Ramazan Öz and Savaş Tarkun from Uludağ University, Turkey, which predicts inflation in the next period based on the consumer price index (CPI) data with two alternative techniques and examines the predictive performance of these two techniques comparatively.

Section 5, "Organizational and Social Implications," includes chapters discussing the impact of artificial neural networks on society and shows the ways in which artificial neural networks are used in different industries and how this impacts business. The section opens with "Comparative Analysis of Proposed Artificial Neural Network (ANN) Algorithm With Other Techniques" by Profs. Deepak Chatha, Alankrita Aggarwal, and Prof. Rajender Kumar of Panipat Institute of Engineering and Technology, India, which develops robust edge detection techniques that work optimally on mammogram images to segment tumor area and presents output results of proposed techniques on different mammogram images of MIAS database. It ends with "Forecasting Automobile Sales in Turkey with Artificial Neural Networks" by Profs. Aycan Kaya, Gizem Kaya, and Ferhan Çebi of Istanbul Technical University, Turkey, which aims to reveal significant factors which affect automobile sales and estimates the automobile sales in Turkey by using artificial neural network (ANN), ARIMA, and time series decomposition techniques.

Section 6, "Emerging Trends," highlights areas for future research within this field. The final section opens with "Artificial Neural Networks in Medicine: Recent Advances" by Prof. Steven Walczak of the University of South Florida, USA, which examines recent trends and advances in ANNs and provides references to a large portion of recent research, as well as looks at the future direction of research for ANN in medicine. The last section ends with the chapter "Convolutional Neural Network" by Prof. Mário Pereira Véstias of INESC-ID, Instituto Superior de Engenharia de Lisboa, Instituto Politécnico de Lisboa, Portugal, which focuses on convolutional neural networks with a description of the model, the training and inference processes, and its applicability and provides an overview of the most used CNN models and what to expect from the next generation of CNN models.

Although the primary organization of the contents in this multi-volume work is based on its six sections, offering a progression of coverage of the important concepts, methodologies, technologies, applications, social issues, and emerging trends, the reader can also identify specific contents by utilizing the extensive indexing system listed at the end of each volume. As a comprehensive collection of research on the latest findings related to artificial neural networks, the *Research Anthology on Artificial Neural Network Applications* provides researchers, computer scientists, engineers, practitioners, educators, strategists, policymakers, scientists, academicians, and students with a complete understanding of the applications and impacts of artificial neural networks. Given the vast number of issues concerning usage, failure, success, strategies, and applications of artificial neural networks in modern technologies and processes, the *Research Anthology on Artificial Neural Network Applications* encompasses the most pertinent research on the applications, impacts, uses, and development of artificial neural networks.

Chapter 24
Application of Multiple Regression and Artificial Neural Networks as Tools for Estimating Duration and Life Cycle Cost of Projects

Brian J. Galli
https://orcid.org/0000-0001-9392-244X
Hofstra University, USA

ABSTRACT

Project managers face complex challenges when planning project stages because contract durations and project costs are difficult to predict accurately. The purpose of this study is to investigate statistical tools and concepts that can be integrated in the second phase of the project life cycle: the planning stage. Furthermore, this study aims to compare the accuracy of multiple regression and artificial neural network models, as well as the application of simulation in construction models used in predicting project duration and cost. This paper will also discuss the industry's current estimation methods, the use of statistical approaches, simulation, and the relationship between the application statistical tools and project success. Thus, this review identifies the trending statistical tools used by scholars to develop regression and neural models to solve the complexity of cost and duration estimation. The findings indicate that although the industry needs more accurate predictions and estimating tools, and regardless of the investigations and advancements made with integrating statistical tools, implementing these statistical approaches is faced with barriers.

DOI: 10.4018/978-1-6684-2408-7.ch024

INTRODUCTION

In the field of project management, the life cycle of a project is composed of the following phases or stages: initiation, planning, execution-monitoring, and project closure. The focus of my investigation is concerned with the planning stage, namely cost estimating and duration estimation. This paper intends to provide an understating of the application of statistical methods and concepts used in the forecasting of cost and durations in construction projects.

The project life cycle, as described previously, lacks the phase of project implementation or post-occupancy planning. Construction projects, such as power plants, treatment plants, buildings, dams, factories and other types of structures, undergo a period of implementation. This paper explores the application of statistical tools for forecasting the running cost for operating and maintaining completed projects. In the context of this paper, operation and maintenance is treated as the last phase of the project life cycle prior to retiring the asset or terminating an initiative.

Furthermore, this paper reports on existing literature, concerning the application of statistical models by industry professionals, to determine duration of contracts, manage cost, and estimate cycle costs. Additionally, we will discuss the steps involved in developing regression and the neural network model. We compare the view of researches and results of regression and neural networks, as well as the advantages and disadvantages of each method.

The literature appears to share the same concept of significant items. Cost significant items refer to elements of the work that influence cost and duration when compared to others. The identification of these items is essential for developing models of high accuracy. Researchers have developed models for various project types, but implementing statistical principles to determine project cost and duration during the planning phase remains low among professionals.

The difficulty of estimating project cost and durations accurately results in a dilated schedule; longer durations will require additional resources, and project cash flows may be impacted. Nonetheless, computer technology advancement and the integration of applications and software have made statistics helpful in estimating project success factors, such as cost estimating, duration, and scheduling. The wide implementation of statistical approaches to estimating is hindered by cost of technology, skill level, and awareness.

Scholars agree that cost is a life cycle constituent of great importance. A poor estimate can make the difference between success and failure, so the accuracy of cost estimates and monitoring is essential to avoid cost overruns (Chew, 2017; Burnes, 2014; Galli, Kaviani, Bottani, & Murino, 2017). As a response to this problem, the industry is adopting modern simulation tools that are gaining ground, as computing power can handle large amounts of data and can perform advanced mathematical and statistical analysis.

A typical construction contract is coupled to a construction schedule that is legally binding. The duration of projects is determined by the owner and consultants. Once the contractor is selected and the contract is awarded, then the contractor must finish on or before the stipulated date. This research will report on the quantitative data processing methods and techniques, such as stepwise regression, multiple regressing, and artificial neural networks. Researchers agree that regression and neural networks are viable methods for estimating project cost and project duration (Adjei-Kumi, 2017; Marcelino-Sádaba Pérez-Ezcurdia, Lazcano, & Villanueva, 2014; Schwedes, Riedel, & Dziekan, 2017).

The current method of estimating durations represents a risk to the contractor, as there is a high probability that the project duration determined by the owner is not reasonable, which makes the contractor liable for penalties and liquidated damages (Jin, 2016; Zwikael, & Smyrk, 2012; Todorović, Petrović,

Mihić, Obradović, & Bushuyev, 2015; Medina & Medina, 2015). Furthermore, unplanned durations increase litigation and compromises construction quality. Similarly, if duration is overestimated, then the client will incur damages, so the difficulties of projects are unique and require high-level customization.

Deviation from planned duration in developing parts of Africa ranges from 51% to 92%. This affects building and transportation projects that are reported to deviate from the stipulated completion date by 20%. Stakeholders, project owners, the government, and construction professionals will benefit from more accurate project durations (Mensah, 2016; Galli & Hernandez-Lopez, 2018; Easton & Rosenzweig, 2012; Brown & Eisenhardt, 1995). Overall, there is consensus in the literature that the duration of projects is strongly related to the quantities of work, rather than to the project cost. Popular scheduling computer programs are based on the Gant Chart, the critical path method. The Gant Chart illustrates the project schedule and the dependency relationship between items of work, and cost is not influential. Developed countries, such as the U.S Japan, Hong Kong, and countries in Europe, have developed models for estimating the construction duration of bridges, roads, and buildings (Ahmadu, 2015; David, David, & David, 2017; Galli & Kaviani, 2018; Hartono, FN Wijaya, & M. Arini, 2014; Parast, 2011).

Moreover, the literature improves the analysis of the quantities of work for non-significant items to be identified. Only the most important items are considered for study. Also, this paper will report on statistical significant work items that impact the duration of bridge construction projects. The completed activities will be the independent variables, and the goal is to understand significant work activities that greatly influence contract duration. This study aims to understand the development of models using regression and artificial neural network methods.

In addition to discussing the application of regression and neural networks for estimating duration of projects, we also explain the application of these statistical tools for the estimation of the life cycle buildings (Whyte, 2014; Sharon, Weck, & Dori, 2013). The literature emphasizes the common notion that the initial capital cost of projects represents a fraction of the operating and maintenance cost. A cradle to grave or whole-life approach is required to capture future expenditures accurately.

The concept of life cycle cost is important because decisions regarding elements of construction during design development will be selected based on operation and maintenance cost, rather than on the initial cost. Moreover, cost savings can be identified and applied before the project goes into the execution phase (when the implementation of design changes is costly).

According to PMBOK, the project life cycle is broken up into phases to make the project more manageable. Therefore, the design or planning phase creates the roadmap to a successful project completion and implementation. The estimation accuracy of a project's life cycle cost is heavily dependent on the amount of information that is available during the design phase.

The planning phase provides the opportunity to identify areas of waste, to enhance the design by improving specifications, to foresee challenging construction tasks, and to plan for efficient operation and maintenance once the project is implemented. Researches attribute the increased importance of life cycle cost to the development of simulation software, which allows the inclusion of estimating and managing facilities into the model.

The unique nature of construction projects makes them good candidates to benefit from the enhanced accuracy of statistical estimating tools. Primarily, the cost estimation of projects is reliant on the accuracy of the estimation of labor and material, and the cost estimate is subjected to the specification provided by the design or planning team (Whyte, 2014; Parker, Parsons, & Isharyanto, 2015; Nagel, 2015). Inaccuracy in cost estimates continues to affect the industry; estimators fail to recognize factors that affect accuracy and continue to rely on the aggregate value of estimates by generating estimators for various elements of the project. Effective methods for cost forecasting must be developed for the design intent to be met with reduced delays, and life cycle cost is estimated with greater confidence (Yamn, 2009; Papke-Shields & Boyer-Wright, 2017; Milner, 2016).

Clearly, the significance of the planning phase in project management is supported by research, primarily the cost estimation component. Authors state that cost estimation provides significant amounts of useful information in decision-making, regarding planning, resource allocation, and monitoring. The sophistication of construction systems and the request to reduce running cost drives the market to look for innovation. This is often found in digital estimating tools that can handle the large range of variables found in construction projects.

Ultimately, the goal of developing such estimating tools is to help solve the challenges of cost prediction. Researchers argue that simulation and statistical tools can be used to develop models that close this gap (Cheng, 2010; Svejvig & Andersen, 2015). Regression models are gaining popularity for determining the impact of significant factors on cost estimation. To select the most appropriate regression equation, the relationship between significant factors and cost estimation must be established. The literature indicates that modeling methods can address prediction problems in construction cost estimating (Whyte, 2014; Xue, Baron, & Esteban, 2016; Zhang, Bao, Wang, & Skitmore, 2016).

Artificial neural networks propose to solve estimating challenges by formulating the relationship between variables, but formulating or mapping the relationship between data points is challenging. Therefore, methods for identifying activities that are strongly related to cost factor must be applied. Interestingly enough, the Pareto rule is present in construction cost estimating, which contains about 80% of total construction cost that can be contained in 20% of construction activities. In developing the models, significant activities and non-cost activities will be applied.

This literature review focuses on the application of regression analysis and artificial neural models to predict the construction duration and life cycle cost of construction projects. Also, this investigation seeks to demonstrate the use of statistical models during the planning phase of the project to predict durations and cost. The selection of appropriate variables and simulations models in cost management will be discussed. The research papers reviewed for this report relate to the use of statistical tools in public works and commercial construction, but topics related to project life cycle apply to all project environments.

Background

Typically, the duration of construction projects is estimated poorly, with methods that are antiquated and unable to handle the complexity of modern projects. The critical path method is the prevailing tool for construction scheduling and activity planning. Unfortunately, the development of estimation models is delegated to teams that do not account for all factors. The type of equipment used, weather conditions, labor force, cash flows, the availability of materials, issuance of required permits, and other unforeseen conditions affect duration. Similarly, cost estimating is performed without accounting for significant cost factors, leading to profit loss for investors. In the traditional method, an estimator performs a quantity take-off to which a unit cost is assigned. The product will constitute a bill of quantity item, and the sum of the line items is the project cost. In this method, the project is subdivided into multiple sections, and each section is estimated individually by individual estimators. Then, all of the estimates are added to arrive at a project cost. Both durations and cost are difficult to estimate because the condition of each project is unique, and projects are customized.

Previously, research has been done to predict the lowest bidder for public schools. The studies concluded that for accurate results to be achieved, the appropriate number of significant factor must be used (Whyte, 2014; Xue, Baron, & Esteban, 2017; Winter, Andersen, Elvin, & Levene, 2006a; Von Thiele Schwarz, 2017). Also, the building sector applied the multiple regression method to develop a model to estimate the duration of housing projects (Jin, 2016; Yun, Choi, Oliveira, Mulva, & Kang, 2016). The research indicates that neural networks can minimize uncertainties when estimating building systems and some authors have conducted studies that demonstrate that the neural networks are more accurate than regression techniques (Elkassas, 2011; Xiong, Zhao, Yuan, & Luo, 2017).

Additionally, scholars in Nigeria and Kuwait have developed regression models to predict the duration of building construction. Duration models were constructed using buildings characteristics or elements of construction as the major determinants (Jarkas, 2015; Shenhar & Levy, 2007). Nonetheless, neural networks cannot show the relationship between the predictor with the outcome, and regression cannot assist in selecting a cost model that fits the variables to an established level of accuracy (Wheaton, 2009; Usman Tariq, 2013; Sutherland, 2004).

However, scholars in Bosnia, Korea, Vietnam, have developed artificial network and regression models to predict construction duration (Petruseva, 2013). Probabilistic models have also developed models to predict risk and its influence in public works. The sample size used for developing models was greater than 30 in all cases. If the sample size is sufficiently large (n>30) and the sample data is approximate the normal distribution, then sample measures and data description will closely approximate that of the population.

In the United States, the Department of Transportation of North Carolina analyzed over 400 bridge projects to determine the duration of the design development phase. The researcher determined a number of factors that had an influence in the duration of the engineering phase (Liu, 2012; Ahern, Leavy, & Byrne, 2014). Of the factors identified, four were significant: 1) geographical location of project, 2) environmental requirements, 3) scope of work, and 4) team in charge of assembling environmental documents. The study was validated using a sub-sample drawn from the larger sample. The result was a set of regression equations that the DOT can use to estimate the duration of the engineering and design phase.

Governments and administrations can benefit from statistical models to more accurately estimate duration during the second phase of project life cycle, the planning stage. An accurate prediction of project durations minimizes completion delays and maximizes the use of project resources. Other research points to Neuronal networks as a more accurate method, and it is argued that neural models can predict construction cost without detailed drawings. This notion deviates from current practices; projects must reach a high development level for an accurate estimate to be generated (Arafa, 2013; Al-Kadeem, Backar, Eldardiry, & Haddad, 2017a; Andersen, 2014).

Overall, this research review contributes to the understanding of effectively integrating statistical concepts into construction project planning. The body of this paper is framed to study the integration of statistical models in the construction industry against the background of current estimating methods.

Problem Statement

Project managers in the construction industry are faced with challenges in the second phase of the project life cycle: planning. The planning phase includes three vital parts: 1) estimating the durations of projects, 2) project cost, and 3) the cost of running buildings after completion. Traditional methods prevail in the industry, but these methods are being displaced by statistical models that can make predictions more accurately. This is an area of concern to investors and managers because it directly impacts profits. Also, the planning stage of a project is vital because it sets procedures for monitoring the execution of the project. Hence, the ability to accurately estimate duration, project, cost, and operating cost is vital for project success. This paper seeks to shed light on the benefits of statistical tools, as well as to provide a background and practical examples of regression and neural networks.

Research Hypothesis

Statistical models can be effectively integrated into a project life cycle. Artificial networks, regression, and modeling will be explored to confirm the effectiveness of statistical models applied to project planning. Regardless of the poor performance, traditional methods continue to be widely used. If the findings reveal that statistical models are more reliable in estimating durations and life cycle cost, then the industry should consider investing in resources that would allow the adoption of statistical models.

Research Objective and Research Gap

For the most part, literature addresses how these variables, concepts, and models are necessary in project management and performance, but certain information is not addressed. There can be more literature on why these variables, their concepts, and models ease the progression of project management and performance. Thus, a research gap has developed. The variables, concepts, and models will be assessed to find what they share and what they do not. As a result, this will allow for a universal framework that features their best aspects. In this study, there are evidence-based answers for primary questions about these variables, their concepts, and models, such as how to maximize on them for project management and performance objectives. This study can act as a reference for future research, as well.

Originality

The originality of this literature review is expressed to explore the reach of statistical estimating methods in the construction industry. In addition, the existing literature does not mention the traditional method and anecdotal approaches to estimating. This paper heavily focuses on the application of statistical models, but it also touches on traditional estimating methods and drawbacks. Furthermore, this literature review aims to synthesize research performed on the topics of 1) statistical models, 2) traditional methods, and 3) simulation techniques.

This study will contribute more literature to expand on the effectiveness of these variables, their concepts, and models and their likenesses and differences. Studies that have tested this paper's hypotheses contribute information, as well. This study uses a design-science-investigate strategy, and it then approves a valuable growth reveal to apply reasonably and hypothetically. In the end, this study provides an assessment model for these variables, their concepts, and models. The evaluation instrument is emphasized as responses to the examination question, and the instrument is reviewed with an explanation of the approach to the outline and results of the meetings. The conclusion features primary findings and ideas to arrange investigative limitations and future studies.

Contribution to the IE/EM/PM

Clearly, this paper contributes to the field of project management and engineering management because it explores non-traditional methods for estimating cost and duration of construction projects. Also, this study introduces the combination of statistical tools and simulation techniques for better duration and cost estimation. These research findings show the benefits of these variables, their concepts, and models. However, this study depicts the detriments of not addressing performance and sustainability. This study also highlights the need for real-life examples, as it features examples to apply these theories to the real world.

Managerial Relevance

Engineering managers must always make decisions, which will become even more important in the future of project management and engineering. This study addresses such a future and the role of the engineering manager and the engineering management field. Furthermore, the implications are addressed within different organizational levels, such as corporate level, managerial level, and project team level. Also, an engineering management practitioner can utilize the conclusions to capitalizing on these variables, concepts, models, and their relationship within project environments and operations. The variables, their concepts, and models will be assessed to propose a framework that will fill a research void in pre-existing literature. Many different business subjects can be enhanced by this study, as it contributes to each body of knowledge with novel approaches for future research.

Paper Organization

This paper begins with section two, which features the literature review of literature in these fields of research. The research methodology is presented in section three, and the findings and analysis are in section four. Lastly, the implications are outlined in section five for practitioners, but it also features ideas for future research, limitations, and general conclusions.

LITERATURE REVIEW

Multiple Regression Cost Prediction Application

Construction projects present complex estimating challenges. There are many variables or factors that can affect the outcome of a project, as conditions are unique and products are personalized. The diversity of challenges in construction projects makes it difficult to predict durations and costs. Hence, to find a practical solution to the estimation of project duration and running costs, an equation that can handle multiple variables is required. In this case, we are interested in the variables that influence the mean duration and running cost of projects.

Before we introduce research information on multiple regression, basic definitions and concepts should be discussed. The multiple regression model is an extension of the simple linear regression analysis. The linear regression only uses two variables: a dependent variable, such as cost, and an independent variable, such as building type. We say a regression is linear when the relationship between the independent and dependent variable is linear. With this technique, we try to explain the variation in the dependent variable.

Now that we have explained the basic concept of linear regression, we can discuss multiple regression. We will begin with introducing an experiment performed by a researcher to determine the operation and maintenance cost using 20 construction projects. The data was taken from three separate sources. The significant cost factor affecting the cost of operation and maintenance had been established from previous research (Whyte, 2014; Arumugam, 2016; Badi & Pryke, 2016). Furthermore, the parameters of the experiment indicate that 11 cost significant items were identified as most influential, and these items applied to all buildings.

We will also introduce the definition of neural network, as the following example will compare the accuracy of both methods. Artificial neuron network models are nonlinear and find the complex relationship between inputs and outputs. Artificial networks differ from regression models, in that they employ the concept of machine learning to reach the desired outcome (Ontepeli, 2012; Besner & Hobbs, 2012; Cova & Salle, 2005; Detert, 2000).

Existing publications indicate that the running cost of building is approximately 70% of the building's life cycle cost. This measure is the result of an 18-year study done on the operation and maintenance cost of buildings. Also, 7 non-cost factors that are reported as having an influence on the estimation cost are also established by an existing study.

Overall, eight factors will be used as the input for the multiple regression model. These inputs are the nodes that will be linked to the hidden layers via weight connection. We will later perform the same experiment, but by using the neural network method. The multiple regression model equation for the mentioned outputs will be constructed as follows:

$$Y = a + b_1 x_1 + b_2 x_2 + b_3 x_3 + b_4 x_4 + \dots b_n x_n + u$$

Where:

Y= The variable that we are trying to predict (DV)
X= The variable that we are using to predict Y (IV)
a= The intercept
b= The slope (Coefficient of X1)
u= The regression residual error

In our equation, *a* is the intercept b_1-b_n. The R-squared value is a measure of how close a data point is to the fitted regression line. R-squared value of 0% indicates that the model cannot explain the variability of the data around the mean. Similarly, p-values are key for the evaluation of the model. A p value $< .05$ means you can reject the null hypothesis. Also, if a predictor has a low p-value, then it is most probably a significant addition to the model.

Resuming our model, the R-squared values indicate the percentage cost variability. If our R-squared value is close to or equal to 1, then there is a strong correlation between the model output and the actual value. Moreover, p-values were used to determine if changes in the predictor resulted in changes in the response variable. Those variables that were not deemed significant were eliminated. Thus, the research argues that variables with a p-value less than .05 should be included in the model (Ontepeli, 2012; Eskerod & Blichfeldt, 2005; Galli, 2018c).

In regression analysis, we have the option to bring all possible independent variables into the model in one step using full regression, but the case selected for illustration utilizes a stepwise method to identify significant variables. In this method, we determine the p-value for each of the eight variables originally identified. Any variable with a p-value greater than .05 is eliminated until only the significant variables are remaining.

At this stage of the experiment, we move on to regression validation to decide if the results are acceptable descriptions of the data. Validation can be done by determining the aptness of the model (Sosmez, 2010; Galli, 2018a; Galli, 2018b). However, our research utilizes the cross-validation method. From the 20 projects, 17 are used to develop the model and 3 are used to validate the model. The model performance will be measured using the mean percentage error. This value is the calculated average of all percentage errors by which the predictions differ from the actual value. For this calculation, we use the difference of the actual output and the predicted/model output.

Neural Networks Cost Prediction Application

As discussed earlier, neural networks utilize a hidden layer called the black box, as the relationship between the variables is determined. The inputs are selected and are processed through the back box; the model value is then generated. In this section, we will consider the same scenario presented in the previous regression model, where 20 construction projects are being studied to estimate the operation and maintenance cost.

In our model of 20 projects, the goal is to optimize the model and to reduce the neural network weighted error to zero. To reduce the weighted error, the weights will be adjusted from input to black box and from black box to outputs. A neural model can be trained to predict outcomes. Optimizing one node at a time can turn into a daunting task, so the process of training begins by guessing or selecting a random weight. The process is then allowed to run, and the resulting deviation is the analyzed and then weights adjusted. Finally, the process is repeated.

The number of hidden layers can be calculated using traditional parametric methods. As previously mentioned, during the training process, the weights and hidden number in the black box are adjusted to find a model that will result in the lowest value of mean percentage error and root mean square. The sigmoid curve is used to analyze the neural model.

Similar to the regression model, the 20 projects are divided in two sets, while 17 projects are used for model development and the remaining set for testing the procedure. It is worth emphasizing the importance of the training the model for the best arrangement of the neurons to be identified. One must keep in mind that acceptance of the model is judged based on the root mean square and mean percentage error values.

In this section, we will talk about the connection weight method that is used to determine the importance of the input. Our inputs will be the eight variables, which are also called predictors, and our outputs are the running cost (Olden, 2014; Gimenez-Espin, 2013; Hoon Kwak, & Dixon, 2008). In this step, we calculate the sum of the products from the output to the hidden node and then from the hidden node to the output. We determine the importance of a node based on how large the sum of the products of the weights. Also, a larger number means the more influence on the corresponding input value.

Considering both the regression model and the neural network models are the same, a paired test was conducted to compare the accuracy of the two estimation methods. The rules were set up as follows:

H_0: No accuracy difference between the two methods
H_1: There is difference in accuracy between the two methods

The comparison indicates that neural network models are more accurate than regression models. The neural network model is argued to predict the cost of operation and maintenance with high accuracy, while the regression model is less accurate. The difference may seem insignificant, but we must pay attention to the minimum number of variables required to develop a model. The lowest number of variables required mans that the technique would be more useful for practitioners during the planning stage of a project. Accurate estimates generated early during planning will transcend and have positive impacts on the project outcome.

Regression and Duration Estimation

In this section, we will demonstrate the application of multiple linear regression and artificial neural network for the estimation of project durations. For the development of this model, a sample of 30 completed bridges was taken. From these projects, the bill of quantities was collected. Information on the bill on quantities will be used to determine the items that can potentially affect the duration of projects (Czarnigowska, 2014; Labedz & Gray, 2013; Lee Lapira, Bagheri, & Kao, 2013).

The work items that were selected as inputs are elements of construction and characteristics of the bridges, and these elements of construction represent work activities that have been billed. Overall, 11 activities were selected and analyzed statistically, while the items selected from the bill of quantities represent the independent variables and are analyzed. Then, descriptive statistics of mean and standard deviation are calculated. For the purpose of the analysis, the scheduled and actual completion data were secured. These parameters will be used to compare calculated predictions.

Multiple regression analysis is gaining popularity among practitioners, but scholars use it to advance models to predict project durations. The formula for the duration estimation is identical to the regression formula used in cost prediction in the previous example. In this case, the cost of maintenance will be replaced by the "T" for time duration:

$$T = a_0 + a_1 x_1 + a_2 x_2 + a_3 x_3 + a_4 x_4 + \ldots a_n x_n + u.$$

"X" represents the independent variables, and "a" is the regression parameter.

The literature explains the effects of multicollinearity and how to determine if the model appears reasonable. Multicollinearity can be a problem when two independent variables provide duplicated information to the model. When highly correlated independent variables are part of the model inputs, then the regression results can be negatively impacted. The standard error of the regression coefficients is increased and impacts the accuracy of the regression model (Jarkas, 2015; Loyd, 2016).

Although there are disagreements, some researchers argue that if the inflation factor is greater than 10 between two pairs of independent variables, then these are regarded as high correlation or multilinearity. In the analysis under study, a variable inflation value exceeding 2 is enough evidence of multicollinearity. The model under examination consists of 30 completed projects to develop project duration models; the regression model designated 80% of the projects for model development and 20% to validate the model (Irfan, 2013).

For the 30 projects, four models are developed using stepwise regression to identify the significant variables. The process identified four significant work items from the bill of items. Also, the model selected will be the one with an R-squared value closest to 1, which indicates the most accuracy in predicting duration (Nani, 2017). This result, if less than zero, would suggest that our best model has a percentage of variance between predicted value and actual value. The R-squared is the proportion of total variation in the significant variables.

Conversely, the R-squared value would indicate the percentage of variation of the dependent values that are accounted for: 1) material transportation and handling, 2) cast in place concrete, 3) weight of structure, and 4) underlayment subbase. For the standardized coefficients of the model to be considered significant, their respective p-values must be lower than .05. The variance inflation factor in good models, according to scholars, should be lower than 2. This process will confirm that multicollinearity between variables was removed during the stepwise regression process. Also, the R value of the model selected must be checked, as it indicates the relationship significance between the predicting variables and the duration of construction. The result is a mathematical expression to estimate time, "t":

T= Standard Coefficient + Bata Coefficient X (bill of quantity)

Neural Networks and Duration Estimation

Artificial neural networks, as mentioned earlier, are mathematical models that use nodes as processing units in the form of layers. A simple model would contain three layers: the input layer, the hidden layer and the output layer. Also, all layers of nodes are connected with weights (Afrifa, 2013). The node value and the weights are adjusted until the desired outcome is achieved. The significant quantities observed during the regression analysis will be entered as the input layer, the hidden layer, and internally will represent the issue at hand. Lastly, the output layer will provide the time duration prediction.

The artificial neural network described its termed multilayered perceptron, and it is characterized by comprising three layers of nodes. Furthermore, all nodes, except the input layer, are neurons that employ a non-linear activation function. In this perceptron, the quantity of hidden layer is determined by trial and error during the model training phase. The neurons in the hidden layer, also called the black box, are activated by a predetermined function and generate an output (Ahiaga-Dagbui, 2013).

The artificial neural network is sensitive to the amount of data used for training. Researchers agree that the ability of the model to accurately make predictions is affected by training data. The accuracy of the model can be assessed by calculating the mean absolute percentage error, MAPE. The proportions for training and testing are consistent with proportions used by previous scholars in developing neural models. In the case illustrated in this paper, 22 projects will be used for training and 8 for validating the model. This represents 75% and 25% respectively.

The hypotheses developed for comparing the regression and artificial neural model are as follows:

1). H_1: There is no significant difference between actual mean and predicted duration
   $H_{11:}$ There is significant difference between actual mean and predicted mean of duration
2). H_2: There is no significant difference between the planned and actual duration means
   $H_{22:}$ There is significant difference between the planned and actual duration means

The artificial neural network was developed using 22 projects, and 8 projects were used for validation. As in the regression model, four independent variables were used: material transportation, cast in place concrete, weigh of structure, and underlayment subbase material. A total of five models are developed, while the R, R-squared, MAPE, and average accuracy are calculated to compare the accuracy of the artificial neural model (Nani, 2017). R-value indicates the strength of the relationship between the variable and the outcome, and the R-squared value the determination. The selected model should have the highest accuracy level and the lowest mean absolute percentage error (MAPE) (Asiedu, 2017).

Simulation Techniques

Simulation methods involve mathematical and logic models that rely on 1) equations with known and specific output values and 2) random variables. The result is a graphical representation of construction activities (Chew, 2017). Simulation is used to study the influence that variables or uncertainties have on project planning. Also, simulation can be a powerful tool during the planning stages of a project, namely duration estimation, scheduling, cost estimating, risk assessment, and resource loading (Jahangirian, 2011).

Currently, the construction industry relies on commercial computer software, such as Cristal Ball, Innovaya, Monte Carlo, Revit, and Bentley (Liozou, 2013). These programs are used to model uncertainties and to help construction professionals make decisions. The Monte Carlo simulation technique is one of the pioneering simulation tools applied in the construction industry. The simulation is based on probability distribution, and statistical sampling.

Furthermore, this method uses uncertainties as inputs and will then predict different scenarios of risk by randomly selecting inputs to estimate outputs that represent the desired solutions (Grinstead, 2013). In the planning phase of construction, this method can be useful to estimate construction cost and/or durations. Monte Carlo relies on random sampling to calculate values that are plotted to form a uniform distribution. In our study, construction project variables are used to generate values for the variable, and a computer will repeat this process multiple times to determine the distribution of the project (Potts, 2011).

Another simulation method used in construction is 4-diamentional. The 4th dimension in construction modeling is the schedule, allowing the construction to be simulated before actual project execution. The literature states that although cost values cannot be linked to the model, the simulation of time provides further insight to managers during the planning phase of the project. The modern computer aided drawing allows the creation of multi-layered models that display the different building systems, such as plumbing, electrical, and mechanical (Latiffi, 2013).

RESEARCH METHODOLOGY

Literature Review Research Approach

Two steps went into the literature review. Step one involved searching for relevant information, which included inputs from keywords. Step two was more structured, as it involved the use of databases and search strong for the review process. The tables of contents were also searched through, as two journals were applicable.

Part 1: Explorative and Unstructured Literature Review

This study aims to reconsider certain keywords, so publications that reflected the keywords were assessed. This led to 31 applicable journal articles and 7 books. With the 38 publications, the keywords were studied to be search terms in the structured review.

Part 2: Structured Literature Review

In general, this step involved a structured and systematic approach to conduct reviews, which was taken from other literature. Four phases went into this step, as phase one entailed preparation and scoping. Phase two was the review planning, and phase three was the search, evaluation, and selection of literature. Phase four entailed evaluating the literature.

The phase (1) review scope was based on key concepts on projects, marketing, and strategic planning. This phase promised to result in adequate data from journals that would contribute to the study.

To gain more information, phase (2) involved connecting other concepts to the keywords. Other concepts were the keywords and their relationship and interaction. Some concepts were too vague, such as success, evaluation, and impact because their results were not practical.

Then, phase (3) began with a successful compilation of applicable results from many databases. Some databases included ProQuest, Business Source Complete, EBSCO, and ScienceDirect. As a result, 15 conference papers and 25 results were found that reflected the journals. Overall, 40 results were compiled, which featured conference papers and the journal entries.

The search ended with looking through the tables of contents for tier 1 and tier 2 journals. These journals were academic and practitioner-based, as any pertinent article was applied that may not have matched the keywords. Below, Figure 1 illustrates that there were three streams to the search and selection phase: the explorative and unstructured search, the structured search with search strings, and the tables of contents search.

Applying the three streams condensed the results to 42 publications. With the selection process, between 24 and 18 results were collected with a concentration on results from academic journal articles, literature reviews, conference papers and proceedings, and books. Triangulation methods were utilized, while the first selection should indicate a link between the resulting publications and the keywords to the project research. Also, the evaluation was executed with inclusion and exclusion criteria that highlighted the abstract, as some publications used the introduction or the entire paper.

For phase (4), the collected information was organized into an inductive and deductive analysis. This was then documented with a software package, as the deductive analysis involved documenting the author's university and country. To indicate the research genre, empirical research, theory development, research essays and literature reviews, or the category of "other" were used. With proof that the publications utilized theoretical frameworks, the deductive coding was added. Such frameworks included a research-based perspective and contingency theory. Lastly, there was an indication if the publication had a model.

A grounded theory approach was utilized for the inductive analysis to code publications with open and selective codes. Since the annual number of citations was the basis of most of the selected publications, older aged publications were balanced out. Vital literature reviews were applied, as well as some current publications that contribute to the keywords research.

Furthermore, phase (4) involved the creation of certain key themes by studying the list of open codes. These would then be collected into axial and selective codes. Throughout April and August of 2018, parts 1 and 2 of the literature review took place. Also, there was a final evaluation performed during this time for pertinent data and how they overlap.

Figure 1. Research approach for literature review

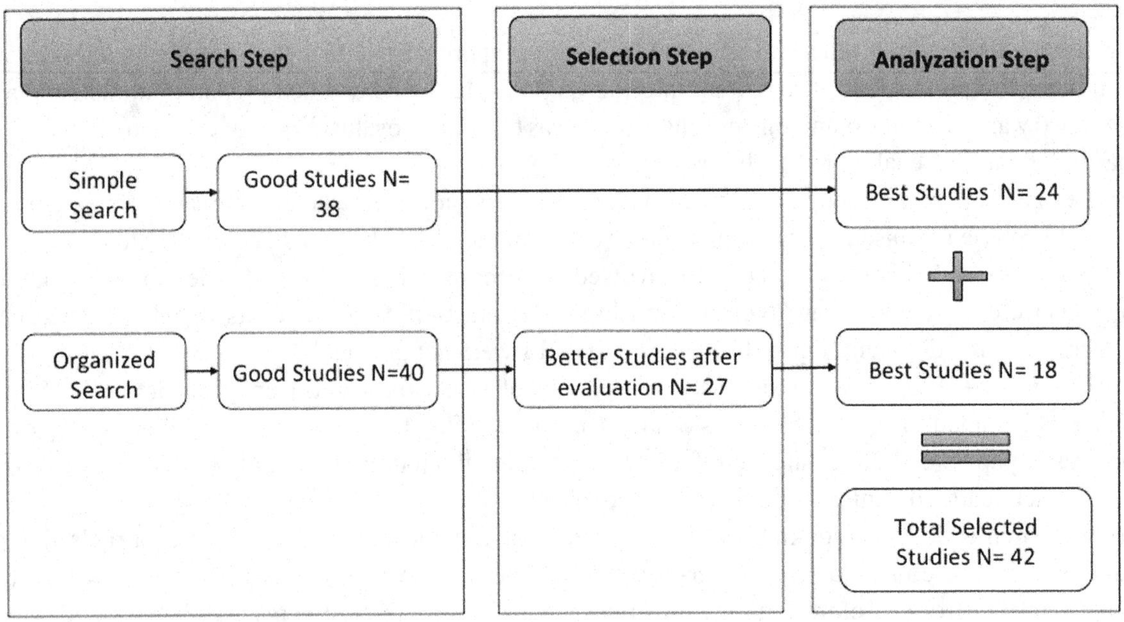

The collection of these papers has revealed that there are some key themes shared between the variables, concepts, and models. By performing a statistical analysis and investigation of other variables or factors, this study's research conclusions were given more weight. The following section includes Table 1, which includes the 42 studies and key themes.

Assessing the 42 studies showed that the literature evaluated the keywords with many statistical methods that took relational and causal perspectives. This added significance to the research conclusions, as well. In Table 2, the statistical methods for the 42 studies were summarized. Additionally, Table 3 summarizes the factors or variables that were assessed in the journals.

The subsequent section features the findings of the research methods. These findings are rooted in the themes and topics that are featured later within this study.

FINDINGS

The findings section will be formatted in the corresponding order with the sections and topics covered in the literature review section of this paper. Multiple regression and neural networks modeling techniques were applied in construction cost estimation; regression and neural models were to estimate project durations, and then there was simulation for cost management.

Table 1. Identified studies from research approach by theme

Theme #1	Theme #2
Adjei-Kumi (2017) Ahern, Leavy, & Byrne, (2014) Arumugam, (2016) Cova & Salle (2005) David, David, & David, (2017) Eskerod & Blichfeldt, (2005) Galli & Kaviani, (2018) Galli et al., (2017) Hartono, FN Wijaya, & Arini, (2014) Jarkas, (2015) Xue, Baron, & Esteban, (2016) Xue, Baron, & Esteban, (2017) Andersen, (2014) Schwedes, Riedel, & Dziekan, (2017) Petruseva, (2013)	Afrifa, (2013) Al-Kadeem et al., (2017a) Badi & Pryke, (2016) Irfan, (2013) Liu, (2012) Medina & Medina, (2015) Milner, (2016) Parast, (2011) Parker, Parsons, & Isharyanto, (2015) Sosmez, (2010) Sharon, Weck, & Dori, (2013) Shenhar & Levy, (2007) Yun, et al. (2016) Gimenez-Espin, (2013) Kwak, & Dixon, (2008) Sutherland, (2004) Wheaton, (2009)
Theme #3	**Theme #4**
Ahiaga-Dagbui (2013) Arafa, (2013) Cheng, (2010) Detert, (2000) Easton & Rosenzweig, (2012) Elkassas, (2011) Galli, (2018c) Galli & Hernandez-Lopez, (2018) Grinstead, (2013) Jin, (2016) Liozou, (2013) Svejvig & Andersen, (2015) Todorović et al., (2015) Labedz, & Gray, (2013) Olden, (2014) Ontepeli, (2012) Lee et al., (2013) Potts, (2011) Usman Tariq, (2013) Von Thiele Schwarz, (2017) Yamn, (2009) Zwikael & Smyrk, (2012)	Ahmadu, (2015) Asiedu, (2017) Besner & Hobbs, (2012) Brown & Eisenhardt, (1995) Burnes, (2014) Chew, (2017) Czarnigowska, (2014) Galli, (2018a) Galli, (2018b) Jahangirian, (2011) Latiffi, (2013) Xiong et al., (2017) Winter et al., (2006a) Loyd, (2016) Marcelino-Sádaba et al., (2014) Mensah, (2016) Nani, (2017) Nagel, (2015) Papke-Shields & Boyer-Wright, (2017) Whyte, (2014) Zhang et al., (2016)

Before discussing the results of the literature review, the data collection methods and the instruments for collecting data will be discussed. The experiments and studies reviewed for this report collected sample data from 1) bill of quantities and 2) costs index data. There are also two inherent problems with the source of the data: 1) inaccuracy of quantity initial estimate and 2) price indexes estimated probabilistically.

Construction estimates are not accurate, and the quantities recorded on a bill of quantities differ from the actual values. The final cost of projects can be predicted with more accuracy than the components of the total cost. Literature indicates that construction estimates are incorrect 17% of the time (Jarkas, 2015). Thus, collecting and using poor data quality affects the variables and inputs that are selected for the regression and the artificial neural network.

Table 2. Systematic analysis results by statistical analysis method

Statistical Method	Number of Articles (Frequency)	Author(s)
Regression	17 (22.97% of total articles)	Adjei-Kumi (2017) Asiedu, (2017) Chew, (2017) Cova & Salle, (2005) David, David, & David, (2017) Detert, (2000) Easton & Rosenzweig, (2012) Elkassas, (2011) Galli et al., (2017) Gimenez-Espin, (2013) Irfan, (2013) Loyd, (2016) Nani, (2017) Petruseva, (2013) Sutherland (2004) Xue, Baron,& Esteban, (2017) Zwikael & Smyrk, (2012)
ANOVA	13 (17.57% of total articles)	Afrifa, (2013) Ahern, Leavy, & Byrne, (2014) Ahiaga-Dagbui (2013) Brown & Eisenhardt, (1995) Cheng, (2010) Galli, (2018b) Galli, (2018c) Latiffi, (2013) Nagel, (2015) Papke-Shields & Boyer-Wright, (2017) Potts, (2011) Xiong et al., (2017) Yun, et al., (2016)
Q-Test	13 (17.57% of total articles)	Arumugam, (2016) Badi & Pryke, (2016) Czarnigowska, (2014) Grinstead, (2013) Kwak & Dixon, (2008) Jarkas, (2015) Jin, (2016) Labedz & Gray, (2013) Olden, (2014) Parker, Parsons, & Isharyanto, (2015) Schwedes, Riedel, & Dziekan, (2017) Usman Tariq, (2013) Von Thiele Schwarz, (2017)
t-Test	15 (20.27% of total articles)	Ahmadu, (2015) Andersen, (2014) Arafa, (2013) Besner & Hobbs, (2012) Burnes, (2014) Eskerod & Blichfeldt, (2005) Galli, (2018a) Winter et al., (2006a) Hartono, FN Wijaya, & Arini, (2014) Lee et al., (2013) Sharon, Weck, & Dori, (2013) Shenhar & Levy, (2007) Sosmez, (2010) Yamn, (2009) Zhang et al., (2016)

continues on following page

Table 2. Continued

Statistical Method	Number of Articles (Frequency)	Author(s)
Chi-Square Test	17 (22.97% of total articles)	Al-Kadeem et al. (2017a) Galli & Kaviani, (2018) Galli & Hernandez-Lopez, (2018) Jahangirian, (2011) Liozou, (2013) Liu, (2012) Marcelino-Sádaba et al., (2014) Medina & Medina, (2015) Mensah, (2016) Milner, (2016) Ontepeli, (2012) Parast, (2011) Svejvig & Andersen, (2015) Wheaton, (2009) Whyte, (2014) Todorović et al., (2015) Xue, Baron, & Esteban, (2016)

Table 3. Systematic analysis results by number of variables studied

No. Factors Studied	Number of Articles (Frequency)	Author(s)
1	14 (18.92% of total articles)	Andersen, (2014) Arafa, (2013) Besner & Hobbs, (2012) David, David, & David, (2017) Galli, (2018b) Grinstead, (2013) Latiffi, (2013) Lee et al., (2013) Medina & Medina, (2015) Nagel, (2015) Papke-Shields & Boyer-Wright, (2017) Sutherland, (2004) Von Thiele Schwarz, (2017) Yun et al., (2016)
2	14 (18.92% of total articles)	Afrifa, (2013) Ahiaga-Dagbui (2013) Ahmadu, (2015) Al-Kadeem et al., (2017a) Brown & Eisenhardt, (1995) Cheng, (2010) Elkassas, (2011) Galli & Hernandez-Lopez, (2018) Jahangirian, (2011) Jarkas, (2015) Shenhar & Levy, (2007) Sosmez, (2010) Petruseva, (2013) Xue, Baron, & Esteban, (2016)

continues on following page

Table 3. Continued

No. Factors Studied	Number of Articles (Frequency)	Author(s)
3	17 (22.97% of total articles)	Arumugam, (2016) Badi & Pryke, (2016) Chew, (2017) Czarnigowska, (2014) Eskerod, & Blichfeldt, (2005) Galli et al., (2017) Gimenez-Espin, (2013) Irfan, (2013) Liu, (2012) Loyd, (2016) Marcelino-Sádaba et al., (2014) Mensah, (2016) Nani, (2017) Svejvig & Andersen, (2015) Usman Tariq, (2013) Winter et al. (2006a) Zhang et al. (2016)
4	11 (14.86% of total articles)	Adjei-Kumi (2017) Ahern, Leavy, & Byrne, (2014) Detert, (2000) Easton & Rosenzweig, (2012) Galli, (2018a) Hoon Kwak & Dixon, (2008) Labedz & Gray, (2013) Parast, (2011) Potts, (2011) Todorović et al., (2015) Zwikael & Smyrk, (2012)
5	9 (12.16% of total articles)	Asiedu, (2017) Burnes, (2014) Cova & Salle, (2005) Galli, (2018c) Jin, (2016) Liozou, (2013) Sharon, Weck, & Dori, (2013) Wheaton, (2009) Xue, Baron, & Esteban, (2017)
6	10 (13.51% of total articles)	Galli & Kaviani, (2018) Hartono, FN Wijaya, & Arini, (2014) Milner, (2016) Olden, (2014) Ontepeli, (2012) Parker, Parsons, & Isharyanto, (2015) Schwedes, Riedel, & Dziekan, (2017) Whyte, (2014) Xiong et al., (2017) Yamn, (2009)

Estimates in construction and other project-based industries continue to be estimates and not exact predictions of cost and duration. Traditionally, estimators add a safety factor to the estimate as contingency, but this contingency is based on the estimators experienced and not on actual project cost records. This precisely is the problem that statistical tools and concepts aim to solve for the construction industry.

Similarly, cost data indexes are probabilistically determined. Costs are determined based on representative samples. Sampling errors are inherent in probabilistic methods of estimation, so there is a measurable level of uncertainty in the variables selected for model development. Since the same data samples were used to develop the regression and neural network models, the effects of standard error will impact the predictive accuracy of both models.

The main results of the literature review, related to the hypothesis statement, indicate that statistical analysis tools can be successfully integrated into the planning life cycle stage of construction. There are disadvantages found in random sampling, such as sampling bias, in which some data points are less likely to be selected during sampling. Nevertheless, statistical tools can be applied to engineering management and project management fields.

Furthermore, in the literature review, the authors demonstrate the leading statistical methods used in construction for cost and duration estimation. Moreover, the authors demonstrate the performance of each modeling technique and rank the predictive accuracy of each modeling techniques. The literature argues that artificial neural models have superior predictive accuracy over multiple regression.

The inability to explain or to trace the steps of the hidden layer creates skepticism among practitioners, which affects the acceptance of findings, its implications, and the practical application in the field. The hidden layer can approximate the statistical algorithm or function, but the link between the weight and the node, or the axon and the neuron, cannot be studied. Thus, no insight is gained concerning the relationship between the input variables and the outputs. Two distinct artificial neuron models can produce the same result, but there are different connection weights. The inability to produce a formula or equation that will always produce the same result is problematic. Below, Table 4 and Figure 2 show the calculated accuracy of the cost estimating models developed:

Figure 2. Multiple regression vs. neural networks

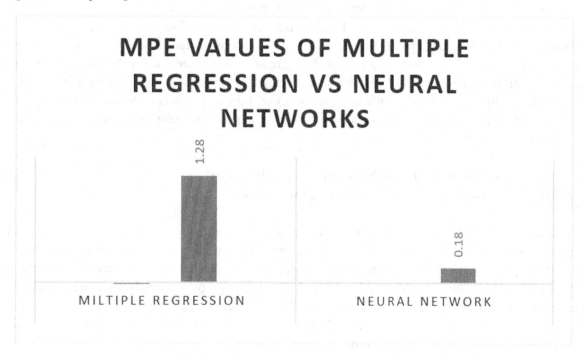

MPE VALUES OF MULTIPLE REGRESSION VS NEURAL NETWORKS

1.28

0.18

MILTIPLE REGRESSION   NEURAL NETWORK

Table 4. Accuracy of cost estimating models

		MPE	Standard Deviation
Multiple Regression	Training	-0.02	1.67
	Testing	1.28	1.77
Neural Network	Training	-0.01	0.38
	Testing	**<u>0.18</u>**	0.31

In our cost prediction studies, the mean percentage error in the testing stage for the neural network was significantly lower than that of multiple regression. The mean percentage error for regression is 1.28 compared to 0.18 of the neural model. It is demonstrated by this literature review that artificial neural models not only work well in predicting cost, but they also display higher predictive accuracy. In our study, the neural network can predict cost with an accuracy of 99.8% (Whyte, 2014).

In the literature review, we discussed the importance of ranking the independent variables, such that only cost significant items are selected as inputs. Given the accuracy of the developed model, the literature demonstrates cost items selected as significant are influencing the output values. In other words, presumed cost significant items influence the life cycle cost of buildings.

In the regression model, the stepwise method was applied to the input variables to select those influencing the model. Also, the aim of the stepwise method is to optimize the model. The p-value for each variable is determined, and the value of coefficient of correlation is calculated to determine the relationship strength between variables. A low value means a low association. Also, a value that is greater than zero means that the variable is both significant and positively associated to the outcome. As the value of the independent value increases, the value of the output is also affected.

Consequently, the best regression model is identified. The literature indicates that the most accurate regression model has a mean percentage error of 1.28, compared to the same statistic for the neural network model, 0.18. This result tells us that the regression model can predict the life cycle cost of buildings with an accuracy of 98%. Despite the evidence that artificial neural models are more accurate than regression model, the results confirm the adequacy of statistical models in the prediction of project costs. Therefore, the null hypothesis is rejected, as there is a difference in the predictive accuracy of the two models.

H_0: No accuracy difference between the two methods - REJECTED
H_1: There is a difference in accuracy between the two methods

Overall, our study constituted four models for the multiple regression analysis and five models for the artificial neural network analysis. The stepwise method was used to determine the accuracy of the regression models. After the process, regression model four was selected, as it has a calculated R-square value of 0.71. This value is higher than models 1, 2, and 3, and it represents the percentage of variance that is explained by the model. The selected model also has a calculated R of 0.84, while the calculated R-value confirms the significance of the predictors used to build the model. Thus, the input variables do influence the duration of projects. Table 5, below, summarizes the R-squared values for each of the models.

Table 5. Summary of R-squared values for each model

Model	R-Square
1	0.36
2	0.47
3	0.58
4	**0.71**

The four regression models under consideration have a mean and median R-squared value 0f 0.53, which means that on average, the level of accuracy of the four models considered is approximately 50%. The standard deviation is 0.15, which represents the extent of deviation for the group of models. The model with the least accuracy has an R square value of 0.36, and the highest was the selected model, model four.

The difference between the actual value and the predicted value show no indication of autocorrelation, as the study shows that the variation inflation factor for all models was less than 2. Variation inflation models with values less than 2 are assumed to have no collinearity, and that predictor is not influencing each other. A model where collinearity between variables exists will exhibit a high variance. Variables found to have a linear relationship were eliminated from the model during the stepwise process. Table 6 highlights the R-squared descriptive statistics for this model:

Table 6. R-squared descriptive statistics

R-Square Descriptive	
Standard Deviation	0.15
Mean	0.53
Standard Error	0.08
Median	0.53

In the case of neural network models, five models were developed. The aim is to select the model with the MAPE closest to zero and the highest percentage of accuracy. The MAPE score was as follows: 6.6, **4**, 4.6, 5.8, and 7.9 for models 1, 2, 3, 4, 5, respectively. Also, the validation test was 26.8, 26.0, **27.7**, **27.7**, and 26.1 for models 1, 2, 3, 4, 5, respectively.

From the results, we can see that model two has the lowest MAPE score, so it was selected. However, models three and four indicate a higher percentage of accuracy, while model two is selected based on MAPE criteria. The selected model has an R value lower than the other four models considered. This indicates that variables in models not selected have a stronger relationship with the outcome value.

DISCUSSION

Implications to the Field of Engineering Management and Project Management

Cost and duration estimating has always been a challenging task in the planning phase of construction projects. Poor estimates lead to cost overruns, and the dilation of project schedules impacts project success and investor's profits. Planning is the roadmap to project success, but if planning is not done properly, then the roadmap can lead to project failure. Also, resource management is particularly impacted by poor duration and cost estimation.

The industry has systems and methods in place for scheduling and estimating project costs. Large amounts of time and resources are allocated to scheduling and estimating projects. However, the results obtained through such methods lack the accuracy needed for capital budgeting and investment decision-making. Investors, owners, end users, and managing teams are affected by the inaccuracy of project schedule and cost estimates.

This literature review demonstrates that the industry can benefit from utilizing statistical tools and concepts in estimating cost and duration of projects. Multiple regression, artificial neural networks, and construction simulation are models capable of predicting construction cost and duration with high levels of accuracy. The literature demonstrates that regardless of neural networks superior predictive accuracy, both methods perform well and provide high-level confidence estimates and accurate predictions.

Furthermore, the literature provides step-by-step instructions on how to build working models for managers and administrators. The literature presents the two specific methods for collecting input variables, namely bill of quantities and cost significant items. The bill of quantities can be obtained from cost records of completed projects, and surveying construction professionals and project teams can procure from published cost index data or the significant cost items.

One issue that construction companies face is poor data collection and record keeping. Companies typically dispose of project records after completion, and the records kept during the project are not always representative of real conditions and costs. Prices are typically set based on negotiations or the estimator's experience, rather than quantitative mathematical approaches. This culture, coupled with antiquated estimating methods, has a negative impact on the accuracy of duration and project cost.

Furthermore, the accurate estimation of quantities has its set of challenges. An accurate estimation of quantities is dependent on the quality and level of development of the design documents. Although there are commercial computer programs dedicated to construction estimation, the implementation of these programs remains low, due to cost and level of skill required and culture.

In the literature, the authors illustrate methods and techniques for designing a predictive model. The stepwise concept and Durbin Watson's statistic to address issues with correlation and multicollinearity are covered. The advantages of developing an equation that can be used for estimating cost and project duration can be of strategic value. Predicting events accurately during the planning phase is vital for projects to achieve milestones and targeted budgets, which will optimize resource allocation and investment planning.

The models studied in this paper can be used by project managers for predicting the duration and cost of construction projects. The literature demonstrates that project durations stipulated in contract documents deviate significantly from the actual duration. The scholars recommend using the estimated quantities once the project is ready for bidding. However, the problem with inaccurate quantity take-offs and unit prices can affect the inputs used for model development. Nevertheless, the research demonstrates that statistical methods are effective and can be integrated in the planning phase of project life cycle.

The multiple regression model appears to be the most user-friendly choice, since once the model is developed, then only the values for significant items are needed for a prediction to be made. The application of neural networks requires the use of a computer and an operator to enter the significant items and to run the simulations until the required project duration is created. Multiple regressing is a more accessible tool, and the results are very similar.

Scholars suggest that regression models be replaced by artificial neural network models because for higher accuracy. Also, neural models can handle a larger number of inputs, whereas the regression model equation may become too complex with an increasing number of cost factors. Moreover, the relationship between variables must be analyzed prior to designing the model, adding to the complexity of the problem if a large number of variables are being handled.

The study demonstrates that both models are capable of identifying the significant variables affecting cost and duration. The important factors identified by the authors in the papers reviewed match those identified by other researches in previous studies. The literature also points out the opportunity estimate of a project's life cycle, taking into account taxes, inflation, and other non-cost factor that influence the total life cycle cost of the asset. An accurate selection and specification of materials during planning stage can translate into future savings accrued during the life of the asset.

Additionally, the implications of this study in project management are profound. Effectively integrating statistical tools and concepts into the planning phase of the project life cycle can change current practices. The implementation of statistical models in cost and duration estimation can help in the optimization of project management and delivery. Thus, statistical models will increase the capacity of managers and firms to handle more complex projects. Good planning translates in the effective use of resources, namely time and materials.

Organizational Implications

Through studying the acquired skill and management strategies from these variables, concepts, and models, it is seen that they are useful tools for business projects and project management. Furthermore, they encourage teamwork skills to better achieve company goals, so they are more valuable than current technology for projects or management. Within the results, it is emphasized that strategic planning is important. This includes a top-down and bottom-up approach from leadership, especially with project management, operations management, and process improvement elements.

Also, this study indicates that current organizational problems are derived from poor leadership skills, as only having a bottom line focus can be damaging. Long-term problems can arise by only focusing on profits and costs. Thus, the necessary tools and information is needed for supervising project management and operational performance. Having only a financial focus is not as beneficial as managing multiple business elements, such as operations, project management, financials, performance, strategy, and human resources. As a result, multiple organizational elements will improve, including performance, profits, and costs.

Managerial and Team Implications

The primary implication from this study is that the results evaluate the variables, concepts, models, and their relationship in a novel way. This new approach aims to fill a knowledge gap in research by evaluating how the variables and their relationship affect each other and outside elements. A business' performance and effectiveness can be impacted, so using these variables in the best way is important.

Secondly, an outline can be derived from this study for business projects and performances. Having a better understanding of the relationship between these variables can yield better management performances. Business leaders can then generate more comprehensive constructs to mentor teams to find their shortcomings and performance gaps. Thus, teams can find ways to avoid these shortcomings for better performances.

Thirdly, this study reveals how businesses can benefit from a more comprehensive training program to improve projects, performances, and overall effectiveness, especially for project teams, project leadership, and organizational leadership. In this study, they can find ways to evaluate the performance of a team, project, or business, so as to measure them against standard and industry accepted models. Also, leaders can find ways to better manage teams and projects to reveal how teams and projects influence overall performance and effectiveness.

Applications to the Field of Engineering Management and Project Management

The techniques and methods discussed in this paper have many applications to the field of project management, particularly in the planning phase. Of the five phases in the project life cycle, planning and monitoring are of great importance. Two components of the planning phase that were investigated in this literature review were cost and duration estimation. These topics were selected because they play an essential role in the success of projects.

Project managers face challenges when developing project duration schedules and cost estimates, so they typically rely on reports and advice from consultants. However, these scheduling and estimating consultants are not contractually bound to the accuracy of their estimates. Estimates are reported to be 30% off target the majority of times. To account for this variation, contingency money is added to the estimate. In the case of duration estimates, consultants arbitrarily determine the duration of projects.

Furthermore, project managers and other practitioners accurately estimate the cost and duration of projects with multiple regression and artificial neural models. They can do this by developing equations and models for each project type. Managers have the necessary tools to identify significant cost factors that can be used as inputs for preliminary experimentation.

Independent variables can be obtained from the project's schedule of values; this schedule provides a breakdown of construction cost by category. Also, these categories are taken from the construction specifications institute and are related to construction components of a project, such as metals, thermal protection, conveying equipment, and earthwork. These sections can be used as starting points for selection dependent variables.

Once variables of interest are identified, managers can begin experimenting with cost and duration models. The stepwise process variables that are not significant contributors to either cost or duration can be eliminated. The literature offers techniques, such as the stepwise method, to determine how much the input variable has on the output variable. To perform this step, managers need to calculate the p-value for each variable. If the value is higher than .05, then the variable is considered non-significant and is eliminated. Overall, the resulting model should be a working model that can be used by project managers to predict cost and duration.

For the traditional construction firms, I suggest the use of the multiple regression modeling technique because it can be computed and programmed using excel or a basic calculator. Once an equation is developed, then adjustments can be made as variable change over time. For a more sophisticated firm, I suggest using neural network model. Also, for the implementation of these models, computers and a program are needed to perform the iterations produces an output.

Construction simulation is a technique reviewed in the literature. There are commercial computer programs available for construction simulation. This can be a powerful tool for designers, managers, and builders, as it allows teams to execute the project virtually and to gain insight about constructability issues. The tool is currently used for estimating, logistics planning, and risk analysis.

The simulation approach can be useful in communications management because it allows stakeholders to visualize the construction process. This visualization can provide stakeholders with the information required to make project decisions. Improved decision-making during the design phase can reduce the cost of construction errors and rework. The simulation of construction can have a positive impact on construction and site management. Also, the benefits of simulation can be shared by designers, owners, and builders, as simulation creates a platform for collaboration.

Engineers require more attention, as well. The job of engineers used to involve problem-solving with math and technology, but they now provide stakeholders with economically viable solutions. These variables, their concepts, and models are undoubtedly vital for engineering decisions, as a product must be created on economically sound manufacturing to succeed. Business management and maturity models can help engineers to find technical knowledge that can help their investors.

According to research, these models can identify certain project elements from a business perspective. This study takes an engineering perspective to also address pure engineering filed techniques like budgeting, equipment, and purchasing material. The IE/EM profession and research field heavily relies on project management and operational performance, as lean thinking is not always the answer. As a result, these variables, their concepts, and models are best used to create different environments in this profession. However, the structural orientation of a scope can make those within IE/EM create the required scopes of interest at each level. A strategy can only come from applying the concentrations needed for every interest level.

Also, stakeholders, such as system engineers, project managers, and others within industrial engineering and engineering management, can find information on applying maturity to project management. Stakeholders will also be guided to capitalize on the roles of system engineering and project management, so their success rate will increase.

CONCLUSION

Recommendation for Future Research

These research findings should be done to implement predictive models in construction. Also, research should investigate the degree of variance in construction quantity estimations. This is important because estimated quantities and cost will then become inputs for predictive modeling, so the quality of the independent variables is essential. For future research, it can be studied how these variables, concepts, and models relate within other environments, such as other industries and managerial settings. This can reveal any benefits, detriments, impacts, outside influences, and outside perspectives. Future research can also assess the organizational, strategic, or cultural perspectives on this topic to find how culture, strategy, human resources, and operations influence these variables.

Limitations

The primary limitation of this research is the quality of the data used for developing the models. The errors in the data collected are not accounted for in the experiments. Further, the findings of this study pertain to commercial construction, primarily in the public sector. A secondary limitation is the limited availability of relevant literature. Although the findings can be applied to any project-based company, the literature review applies to construction projects and to the life cycle cost of completed projects. Hence, this study is somewhat limited to the prediction of cost and duration of commercial construction projects.

Additionally, this study is limited by a small sample size that only addresses key factors within them. Thus, there is bias and validity that could be avoided with a larger sample size. Since the study only assesses certain key factors and their relationship from a project environment, then the conclusions and analysis can only apply to project environments. The findings are also not applicable to supply chain management, operations management, strategic management, and more. As a result, the findings cannot be deployed to other industries or managerial settings.

Conclusion of Research

Decision-making becomes difficult when there is limited information. Predicting the operating cost of a building will impact the choice of materials and specifications for the project during the planning phase. The first step towards developing a model is the identification of significant variables. Also, regression models cannot select the most accurate design model and can become complex with an increasing number of input variables. On the other hand, neural networks can handle many variables. Although the results identify the artificial neural network as the best model, multiple regression can be more practical for project management.

Furthermore, the stepwise method is critical in developing a regression model because it helps the estimator to rank the input variables in order of importance. The goal is to identify the predictors that will be used to develop the model. The implementation of the models discussed in this literature review is recommended to project managers, designers, and owners. Also, the resources referenced in this study can develop methodologies for real-world scenarios. Statistical tools may require a level of understanding that has not been observed in construction firms. Construction planning can benefit from applying statistical tools, as information can be gained in cost estimation, project duration, constructability, and risk analysis.

Overall, project management professionals are ambassadors for the implementing new technologies. The best way to promote innovative estimating techniques is to use them within forums and professional organizations. Thus, stakeholders can greatly benefit from statistical tools and simulation during the planning and monitoring phases of the project life cycle.

REFERENCES

Adjei-Kumi, G. N. (2017). Duration estimation models for bridge construction. *Journal of Engineering, Design and Technology*, 754-777.

Afrifa, R. A.-A.-A. (2013). Artificial neural network model for low estrength RC beam shear capacity. *Journal of Science and Technology*, 119–132.

Ahern, T., Leavy, B., & Byrne, P. J. (2014). Complex project management as complex problem solving: A distributed knowledge management perspective. *International Journal of Project Management*, 32(8), 1371–1381. doi:10.1016/j.ijproman.2013.06.007

Ahiaga-Dagbui, D. T. (2013). A neuro fzzy hybrid model for predicting final cost of water infrastructure projects. In *29th Annual ARCOM Conference*, (pp. 181-190). Association of research in construction management.

Ahmadu, H. I. (2015). Modeling building construction durations. *Journal of Financial Management of Property and Construction*, 65-84.

Al-Kadeem, R., Backar, S., Eldardiry, M., & Haddad, H. (2017a). Review on using system dynamics in designing work systems of project organizations: Product development process case study. *International Journal of System Dynamics Applications*, 6(2), 52–70. doi:10.4018/IJSDA.2017040103

Andersen, E. S. (2014). Value creation using the mission breakdown structure. *International Journal of Project Management*, 32(5), 885–892. doi:10.1016/j.ijproman.2013.11.003

Arafa, M. a. (2013). Early stage cost estimation of buildings construction projects using artificial neural networks. *Journal of Artificial Intelligence*, 63-75.

Arumugam, V. A., Antony, J., & Linderman, K. (2016). The influence of challenging goals and structured method on six sigma project performance: A mediated moderation analysis. *European Journal of Operational Research*, 254(1), 202–213. doi:10.1016/j.ejor.2016.03.022

Asiedu, R. F., Frempong, N. K., & Alfen, H. W. (2017). Predicting likelyhood of cost overrun in educational projects. *Engineering, Construction, and Architectural Management*, 24(1), 21–39. doi:10.1108/ECAM-06-2015-0103

Badi, S. M., & Pryke, S. (2016). Assessing the impact of risk allocation on sustainable energy innovation (SEI): The case of private finance initiative (PFI) school projects. *International Journal of Managing Projects in Business*, 9(2), 259–281. doi:10.1108/IJMPB-10-2015-0103

Besner, C., & Hobbs, B. (2012). The paradox of risk management; A project management practice perspective. *International Journal of Managing Projects in Business*, 5(2), 230–247. doi:10.1108/17538371211214923

Brown, S. L., & Eisenhardt, K. M. (1995). Product development: Past research, present findings, and future directions. *Academy of Management Review*, 20(2), 343–378. doi:10.5465/amr.1995.9507312922

Burnes, B. (2014). Kurt Lewin and the planned approach to change: A re-appraisal. *Journal of Management Studies*, 41(6), 977–1002. doi:10.1111/j.1467-6486.2004.00463.x

Cheng, M.-Y. T.-C., Tsai, H.-C., & Sudjono, E. (2010). Conceptual cost estimates using evolutionary fuzzy hybrid neural networks for projects in construction industry. *Expert Systems with Applications*, *37*(6), 4224–4231. doi:10.1016/j.eswa.2009.11.080

Chew, A. M. (2017). Simulation techniques for cost management and performance in construction projects. *Built Environment Project and Assessment Management*, 534-545.

Cova, B., & Salle, R. (2005). Six key points to merge project marketing into project management. *International Journal of Project Management*, *23*(5), 354–359. doi:10.1016/j.ijproman.2005.01.006

Czarnigowska, A. a. (2014). Time-cost relatinship for predicting construction duration. *Archives of Civil and Mechanical Engineering*, 518–526.

David, M. E., David, F. R., & David, F. R. (2017). The quantitative strategic planning matrix: A new marketing tool. *Journal of Strategic Marketing*, *25*(4), 342–352. doi:10.1080/0965254X.2016.1148763

Detert, J. R., Schroeder, R. G., & Mauriel, J. J. (2000). A framework for linking culture and improvement initiatives in organizations. *Academy of Management Review*, *25*(4), 850–863. doi:10.5465/amr.2000.3707740

Easton, G. S., & Rosenzweig, E. D. (2012). The role of experience in six sigma project success: An empirical analysis of improvement projects. *Journal of Operations Management*, *30*(7), 481–493. doi:10.1016/j.jom.2012.08.002

Elkassas, E. M. (2011). The neural network model for predicting the financing cost of construction projects. *International Journal of Project Organization and Management*, 321-334.

Eskerod, P., & Blichfeldt, B. S. (2005). Managing team entrees and withdrawals during the project life cycle. *International Journal of Project Management*, *23*(7), 495–503. doi:10.1016/j.ijproman.2004.12.005

Galli, B. (2018a). Application of system engineering to project management–How to view their relationship. *International Journal of System Dynamics Applications*, *7*(4), 76–97. doi:10.4018/IJSDA.2018100105

Galli, B. (2018b). Can project management help improve lean six sigma? *IEEE Engineering Management Review*, *46*(2), 55–64. doi:10.1109/EMR.2018.2810146

Galli, B. (2018c). Risks related to lean six sigma deployment and sustainment risks: How project management can help. *International Journal of Service Science, Management, Engineering, and Technology*, *9*(3), 82–105. doi:10.4018/IJSSMET.2018070106

Galli, B., & Hernandez-Lopez, P. (2018). Risks management in agile new product development project environments–A review of literature. *International Journal of Risk and Contingency Management*, *7*(4), 37–67. doi:10.4018/IJRCM.2018100103

Galli, B., & Kaviani, M. A. (2018). The impacts of risk on deploying and sustaining lean six sigma initiatives. *International Journal of Risk and Contingency Management*, *7*(1), 46–70. doi:10.4018/IJRCM.2018010104

Galli, B., Kaviani, M. A., Bottani, E., & Murino, T. (2017). An investigation of shared leadership & key performance indicators in six sigma projects. *International Journal of Strategic Decision Sciences*, *8*(4), 1–45. doi:10.4018/IJSDS.2017100101

Gimenez-Espin, J. A.-J.-C., Jiménez-Jiménez, D., & Martínez-Costa, M. (2013). Organizational culture for total quality management. *Total Quality Management & Business Excellence*, *24*(5-6), 678–692. do i:10.1080/14783363.2012.707409

Grinstead, C. a. (2013). Introduction to probability. American Mathematical Society, 1554-1602.

Hartono, & Wijaya, & Arini. (2014). An empirically verified project risk maturity model: Evidence from Indonesian construction industry. *International Journal of Managing Projects in Business*, *7*(2), 263–284. doi:10.1108/IJMPB-03-2013-0015

Hoon Kwak, Y., & Dixon, C. K. (2008). Risk management framework for pharmaceutical research and development projects. *International Journal of Managing Projects in Business*, *1*(4), 552–565. doi:10.1108/17538370810906255

Irfan, M. K. (2013). Planning-statge estimation of highway project duration on the basis of anticipated project cost, projext type and contract type. *International Journal of Project Management*, ●●●, 78–92.

Jahangirian, M. E. (2011). Simulation in manufacturing and business. *European Journal of Operational Research*, 1–13.

Jarkas, A. (2015). Predicting contract duration for building construction: Is Bromilow's time- cost model panacea? *International Journal of Project Management*, 1–8.

Jin, R. H. (2016). Application of case base reasoning for estimating duration of building projects. *Journal of Construction Engineering and Management*.

Labedz, C. S., & Gray, J. R. (2013). Accounting for lean implementation in government enterprise: Intended and unintended consequences. *International Journal of System Dynamics Applications*, *2*(1), 14–36. doi:10.4018/ijsda.2013010102

Latiffi, A. M. (2013). Building information modeling applications in construction. *International Journal of Construction Engineering and Management*, 1-6.

Lee, J., Lapira, E., Bagheri, B., & Kao, H. (2013). Recent advances and trends in predictive manufacturing systems in big data environment. *Journal of Cleaner Production*, *3*(10), 45–55.

Liozou, P. a. (2013). Risk and uncertainty in development: A critical evaluation of using monte carlo simulation method as a decision tool in real estate development projects. *Journal of Property Investment and Finance*, 298-210.

Liu, M. R. (2012). Predicting the preliminary engineering duration of bridges. *Construction Research Congress*, 505-514. 10.1061/9780784412329.051

Loyd, N. (2016). Implementation of a plan-do-check-act pedagogy in industrial engineering education. *International Journal of Engineering Education*, *32*(3), 1260–1267.

Marcelino-Sádaba, S., Pérez-Ezcurdia, A., Lazcano, A. M. E., & Villanueva, P. (2014). Project risk management methodology for small firms. *International Journal of Project Management, 32*(2), 327–340. doi:10.1016/j.ijproman.2013.05.009

Medina, R., & Medina, A. (2015). The competence loop: Competence management in knowledge-intensive, project-intensive organizations. *International Journal of Managing Projects in Business, 8*(2), 279–299. doi:10.1108/IJMPB-09-2014-0061

Mensah, I. A.-K., Adjei-Kumi, T., & Nani, G. (2016). Duration determination for rural roads using the principal component analysis and artifical neural networks. *Engineering, Construction, and Architectural Management, 23*(5), 638–656. doi:10.1108/ECAM-09-2015-0148

Milner, C. D., & Savage, B. M. (2016). Modeling continuous improvement evolution in the service sector: A comparative case study. *International Journal of Quality and Service Sciences, 8*(3), 438–460. doi:10.1108/IJQSS-07-2016-0052

Nagel, R. (2015). Operational optimization: A lean six sigma approach to sustainability. *Proceedings of the Water Environment Federation, 3*(4), 1–12. doi:10.2175/193864715819556688

Nani, G. (2017). Duration estimation models for construction projects. *Journal of Engineering, Design and Technology*, 754-777.

Olden, J. D. (2014). An accurate comparison of methods for quantifying variable importance in artificial neural networks using simulated data. *Ecological Modelling*, 389–397.

Ontepeli, M. (2012). Conceptual cost estimating of urban railway system projects. *Journal of Construction Engineering and Management*, 1017–1028.

Papke-Shields, K. E., & Boyer-Wright, K. M. (2017). Strategic planning characteristics applied to project management. *International Journal of Project Management, 35*(2), 169–179. doi:10.1016/j.ijproman.2016.10.015

Parast, M. M. (2011). The effect of six sigma projects on innovation and firm performance. *International Journal of Project Management, 29*(1), 45–55. doi:10.1016/j.ijproman.2010.01.006

Parker, D. W., Parsons, N., & Isharyanto, F. (2015). The inclusion of strategic management theories to project management. *International Journal of Managing Projects in Business, 8*(3), 552–573. doi:10.1108/IJMPB-11-2014-0079

Petruseva, S. Z.-P. (2013). Neural network prediction model for construction project duration. *International Journal of Engineering Research & Technology (Ahmedabad)*, 1646–1654.

Potts, K. a. (2011). Construction cost management. *Engineering, Construction, and Architectural Management*, 224–237.

Schwedes, O., Riedel, V., & Dziekan, K. (2017). Project planning vs. strategic planning: Promoting a different perspective for sustainable transport policy in European R&D projects. *Case Studies on Transport Policy, 5*(1), 31–37. doi:10.1016/j.cstp.2016.08.006

Sharon, A., Weck, O. L., & Dori, D. (2013). Improving project–product life cycle management with model–based design structure matrix: A joint project management and systems engineering approach. *Systems Engineering, 16*(4), 413–426. doi:10.1002ys.21240

Shenhar, A. J., & Levy, O. (2007). Mapping the dimensions of project success. *Project Management Journal, 28,* 5–13.

Sosmez, R. (2010). Parametric range estimating of building cost using regression models and bootstrap. *Journal of Construction Engineering and Management,* 1011-1016.

Sutherland, S. (2004). Creating a culture of data use for continuous improvement: A case study of an Edison project school. *The American Journal of Evaluation, 25*(3), 277–293. doi:10.1177/109821400402500302

Svejvig, P., & Andersen, P. (2015). Rethinking project management: A structured literature review with a critical look at the brave new world. *International Journal of Project Management, 33*(2), 278–290. doi:10.1016/j.ijproman.2014.06.004

Todorović, M. L., Petrović, D. Č., Mihić, M. M., Obradović, V. L., & Bushuyev, S. D. (2015). Project success analysis framework: A knowledge-based approach in project management. *International Journal of Project Management, 33*(4), 772–783. doi:10.1016/j.ijproman.2014.10.009

Usman Tariq, M. (2013). A six sigma based risk management framework for handling undesired effects associated with delays in project completion. *International Journal of Lean Six Sigma, 4*(3), 265–279. doi:10.1108/IJLSS-05-2013-0028

Von Thiele Schwarz, U. N.-H., Nielsen, K. M., Stenfors-Hayes, T., & Hasson, H. (2017). Using kaizen to improve employee well-being: Results from two organizational intervention studies. *Human Relations, 70*(8), 966–993. doi:10.1177/0018726716677071 PMID:28736455

Wheaton, W. a. (2009). The secular and cyclic behavior of true construction cost. *The Journal of Real State Research,* 1-25.

Whyte, A. A. (2014). Estimation of life cycle cost of building: Regression vs artificial neural network. *Built Environment Project and Asset Management,* 30–43.

Winter, M., Andersen, E. S., Elvin, R., & Levene, R. (2006a). Focusing on business projects as an area for future research: An exploratory discussion of four different perspectives. *International Journal of Project Management, 24*(8), 699–709. doi:10.1016/j.ijproman.2006.08.005

Xiong, W., Zhao, X., Yuan, J.-F., & Luo, S. (2017). Ex post Risk Management in public-private partnership infrastructure projects. *Project Management Journal, 48*(3), 76–89. doi:10.1177/875697281704800305

Xue, R., Baron, C., & Esteban, P. (2016). Improving cooperation between systems engineers and project managers in engineering projects-towards the alignment of systems engineering and project management standards and guides. *Proceedings of Joint Conference on Mechanical, Design Engineering & Advanced Manufacturing, 24*(2), 23-40.

Xue, R., Baron, C., & Esteban, P. (2017). Optimizing product development in industry by alignment of the ISO/IEC 15288 systems engineering standard and the PMBoK guide. *International Journal of Product Development, 22*(1), 65–80. doi:10.1504/IJPD.2017.085278

Yamn, H. a. (2009). A building cost estimation model based on functional elements. *ZITU Journal of Faculty of Architecture*, 73-87.

Yun, S., Choi, J., Oliveira, D. P., Mulva, S. P., & Kang, Y. (2016). Measuring project management inputs throughout capital project delivery. *International Journal of Project Management*, *34*(7), 1167–1182. doi:10.1016/j.ijproman.2016.06.004

Zhang, X., Bao, H., Wang, H., & Skitmore, M. (2016). A model for determining the optimal project life span and concession period of BOT projects. *International Journal of Project Management*, *34*(3), 523–532. doi:10.1016/j.ijproman.2016.01.005

Zwikael, O., & Smyrk, J. (2012). A general framework for gauging the performance of initiatives to enhance organizational value. *British Journal of Management*, *23*, S6–S22. doi:10.1111/j.1467-8551.2012.00823.x

This research was previously published in the International Journal of Applied Industrial Engineering (IJAIE), 7(1); pages 1-27, copyright year 2020 by IGI Publishing (an imprint of IGI Global).

Chapter 25
Single–Channel Region–Based Speller for Controlling Home Appliances

Praveen Kumar Shukla
National Institute of Technology, Raipur, India

Rahul Kumar Chaurasiya
Malaviya National Institute of Technology, Jaipur, India

Shrish Verma
National Institute of Technology, Raipur, India

ABSTRACT

The brain-computer interface (BCI) system uses electroencephalography (EEG) signals for correspondence between the human and the outside world. This BCI communication system does not require any muscle action; hence, it can be controlled with the help of brain activities only. Therefore, this kind of system is helpful for patients, who are completely paralyzed or suffering from diseases like ALS (Amyotrophic Lateral Sclerosis), and spinal cord injury, etc., but having a normal functioning brain. A region-based P300 speller system for controlling home electronic appliances is proposed in this article. With the help of the proposed system, users can control and use appliances like an electronic door, fan, light, system, etc., without carrying out any physical movement. The experiments are conducted for five, ten, and fifteen trails for each subject. Among all classifiers, the ANN classifier provides the best off-line experiment accuracy of the order of 80% for fifteen flashes. Moreover, for the control translation, the Arduino module is also designed which is low cost and low power-based and physically controlled a device.

DOI: 10.4018/978-1-6684-2408-7.ch025

INTRODUCTION

People suffering from neuromuscular diseases like brain stroke and Amyotrophic Lateral Sclerosis (ALS) have very limited muscle-based control capabilities; hence they are heavily dependent on secondary caregivers. For such patients, Brain-computer interface (BCI) is a useful approach for interaction with the outside world. This technology provides communication between the human brain and the external environment. BCI systems acknowledge the subject's intentions and convert these brain patterns and signals into control command (Mak & Wolpaw, 2009). Once the signals are converted into control commands they are used in a wide range of applications such as controlling a wheelchair, 2-D cursor, keyboard, mobile robot, home appliances (Hoffmann, Vesin, Ebrahimi, & Diserens, 2008), etc. BCI-based home appliances control system is an important application that will give an easy life to a patient who has a neuromuscular disease. Moreover, BCI also reduces the cost of care and dependency on others. The use of Brain waves for controlling the support system has been an active research and development area for about the last 10 years. Some of the major contributions in BCI are now described.

Brain patterns are analyzed by acquiring electroencephalography (EEG) signals. Both invasive and non-invasive techniques are used to acquire EEG signals (Ramadan & Vasilakos, 2017). Non-invasive methods are more popular for BCI as do not require surgical implantation of the devices. The ease of access along with the painless acquisition of EEG signals inspired the author to use the noninvasive method. There are six types of signals generated from the scalp which is dependent on the frequency band. A P300 potential is one of the most important components of EEG which works on the principle of odd-ball paradigms (Farwell & Donchin, 1988). It is used to transfer subject intention into input command. For EEG-based BCI, several other signal patterns are used. These include steady-state visually evoked potentials (SSVEPs) (Zhang, Yu, Jiang, Wang, & Qin, 2019), motion-onset visually evoked potentials (MEPs) (T. Ma et al., 2017), motor imagery (MI)(Jais, Mansor, Lee, & Fauzi, 2017), hybrid signal (Masud, Baig, Akram, & Kim, 2017), etc. BCI-analysis is a useful approach for clinical applications like understanding the need & requirement of totally disabled patients in hospitals. Many paradigms like single character (SC)(Pan, Li, Gu, & Yu, 2013), row/column (RC)-based (Farwell & Donchin, 1988), region-based (RB)(Fazel-Rezai & Abhari, 2009), checkboard (CB) (Townsend et al., 2010), rapid serial visual presentation (RSVP)-based (Acqualagna & Blankertz, 2013) have been investigated using BCI analysis.

Controlling home appliances using EEG-signal based approach in a real environment is a complex task due to various difficulties like the cost of software and hardware, stability in system performance, convenience for users, and technical challenges that occurred in real life. Some of the real-life examples for BCI-based home appliances control systems are wireless BCI-based system especially P300 and SSVEP based signal translation, Bluetooth-based wireless transmission of EEG signal, infra-red (IR) technology, TCP/IP communication and UPnP (Universal plug and play). But limitation these systems are that they depend upon the availability of the internet and many times they are not capable to interact with many devices at a time. Several research publications discuss about single appliance control, for example, fan device (Wang, Lv, Wen, He, & Wang, 2016), TV (Hsieh, Sun, Yeh, & Pan, 2017a), cooling system (Hsieh, Sun, Yeh, & Pan, 2017b), door (Alrajhi, Alaloola, & Albarqawi, 2017), buzzer and music system (Chowdhury, Kashem, Hossan, & Hasan, 2017; Tseng, Wang, Lin, & Hsieh, 2012). Some researchers proposed multiple appliance control (TV, Fan, AC, Door, light, etc..), virtual reality-based (Holzner, Guger, Edlinger, Gronegress, & Slater, 2009), microcontroller-based (Alshbatat, Vial, Premaratne, & Tran, 2014), FPGA-based (Belwafi, Ghaffari, Djemal, & Romain, 2017), infrared-based

(IR) design (Corralejo, Nicolás-Alonso, Álvarez, & Hornero, 2014), Bluetooth-based (Lin, Lin, Lin, & Chang, 2014), web server-based (Aydın, Bay, & Güler, 2016) have been implemented.

Some attempts have been made to control home appliances through eye blink signals. (Wahy & Mansor, 2010a) proposed a design to control light bulbs using eye blinks. (Uma & Sheela, 2017) used a graphical user interface-based system to control the left and right direction of wheelchair and home appliances. (Usakli & Gurkan, 2010) suggested a design to operate the keyboard control system through eye blink detection. (J. Ma, Zhang, Cichocki, & Matsuno, 2014) proposed prototype for robot control using different eye movements and ERP-based. (He & Li, 2017) suggested a single channel-based EOG speller using eye blink for character recognition. (Khushaba, Kodagoda, Lal, & Dissanayake, 2011) have been proposed to extract numerous cognitive signals like eye blink which are used to detect drowsiness from the driver. The reduction of eye blink kind artifacts from EEG signals is an important preprocessing step in designing of EEG-based home appliances control system to enhance the efficiency of these systems. There are various methods are used for detection and reduction of eye blink artifacts from EEG signals which are following: Detection of eye blink artifacts, using a discrete wavelet transform (DWT) (Tibdewal, Fate, Mahadevappa, & Ray, 2015), suppression of eye blink artifacts by cross-correlation and empirical mode decomposition (EMD) (Patel, Janawadkar, Sengottuvel, Gireesan, & Radhakrishnan, 2016), regression (Hillyard & Galambos, 1970), blind source separation (BSS) (Sweeney, Ward, & McLoone, 2012), principal component analysis (PCA) (Casarotto, Bianchi, Cerutti, & Chiarenza, 2004), wiener filtering (Somers, Francart, & Bertrand, 2018), sparse decomposition (Donoho, 2001), hybrid method- wavelet and ICA (Pesin, 2007), EMD and BSS (Soomro, Badruddin, Yusoff, & Jatoi, 2013).

Motivation and Requirements

In India, 2.21 percent of the total population is disabled (Velayutham, Kangusamy, Joshua, & Mehendale, 2016). According to Census 2011, in India, 20% are having movement disability, 19% are with the disability in seeing, and 8% have multiple disabilities. The brain-computer interface communicates with those people, whose motor cell is damaged and who are unable to perform any muscle activity. Therefore, by using BCI, they can interact with the external environment and access their daily needs like a wheelchair, home appliance, 2D-3D cursor control, etc. BCI-based home appliances system can solve the above-mentioned problems of disable and elderly people. Following are the design requirements and objectives of such BCI based system:

- To design a signal acquisition system for BCI-based home appliances and control system.
- To select accurate classifier and design a suitable and quick response hardware module.
- To make a cost-effective system that can control the maximum number of devices.

Proposed Work Based on the State of Art

In this study, a BCI-based control system for home appliances is proposed. In the proposed system classified signal is converted into a command signal. The control interface includes two different stages namely 1) BCI interface and 2) Control translation. BCI interface normally has four stages namely, data collection, preprocessing, feature extraction, and classification. In this proposed work, a novel data acquisition system is designed, dedicatedly for paralyzed people. In this state-of-art proposed work, an eye blink based home appliance control system is designed. The proposed system uses Arduino-UNO based hardware module to make the proposed system cost-effective. The system can handle a maximum number of appliances that include compatibility with electrical devices. Moreover, in this paper, a region-based speller system is proposed, which can control appliances like fan, light bulb, electric heater, etc. using eye blink signals. The region-based speller contains 2-panel menus on which the required option can be selected through an eye blink signal. In the subpanel menu, there is a back option that is selected through eye blink; with this option, the user can come back to the main menu. The proposed system will help to reduce the dependency of the paralyzed patient on caregivers at low cost and enhance their lifestyle. Furthermore, we have also implemented an eye blink artifact removal method to enhance the performance of the proposed system. The proposed block diagram of such a BCI-based system to control the home appliances as proposed is shown in Figure 1.

The rest of the article is structured as follows: The next section explains about material and methods and classifiers. Then the data acquisition section explains, preprocessing steps, feature extraction methods, and proposed system architecture. Afterward, the result section represents the evaluation of the proposed method. The discussion and future scope section are dedicated to the discussion and finally concludes the study.

Figure 1. Block diagram of BCI-based Home environment system

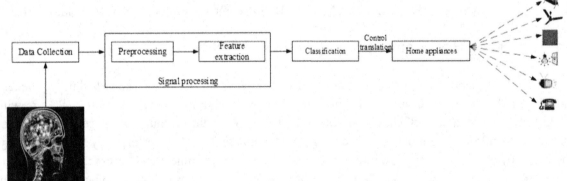

MATERIAL AND METHOD

The working principle of the proposed BCI–based home appliances control system has five subtasks viz data collection, preprocessing of the acquired EEG signals, classification of blink and non-blink signals, correct target appliance detection and finally appliances connected to the hardware instrument. The working principle of the proposed approach is shown in Figure 2.

Proposed Region-Based Paradigms for Controlling of Home Appliances System

Generally in region-based paradigms (RBP), there is the main screen that is connected with user and again the screen subdivides into many sub-regions where the item to facilitate the user. For the selection of the target icon from the main panel, RBP operates on two levels, the former is called the main panel

Figure 2. Working principle of BCI -based control of home appliances system

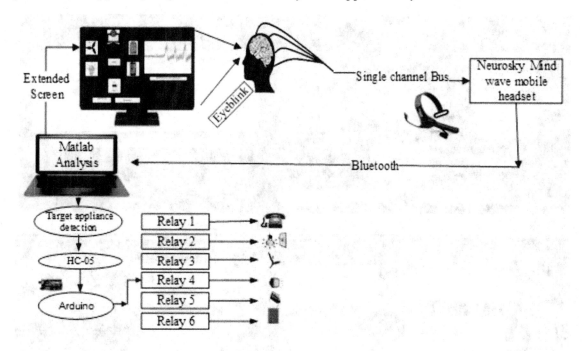

and the scatter is called a sub-panel. These panels are used for the selection of stimuli presentation and target selection. The main panel consists of many options for the selection of various home appliances like TV, door, mobile, light bulb, fan, electric heater, etc. Figure 3 shows the proposed GUI for the region-based speller system. The upper screen shows the main menu and down one display sub-regions. Once a selection is made from any of the 6 options through eye blink, the display is redirected to the selected sub-panel menu. Depending on the detected appliances, the main paradigm will be redirected to one of the 6 possible paradigms to control mobile-phone/TV/door/light-bulb/electric-heater/fan.

Figure 4(a) shows the paradigm to control mobile that contains forward, backward, the main menu, call orientation, call termination and hash button. Figure 4(b) shows the paradigm to control door that contains door close, door open, key inserted and key not inserted, door locked, door not locked. Figure 4(c) shows the paradigm to control a fan that contains fan on, fan off, fan running on speed 0-3. Figure 4(d) shows the paradigms to control the light that contains Tub light on/off, night bulb on/off and light bulb on/off. Figure 4(e) shows the paradigms to control heater that contains on/off, heater ignition started, and heater full ignite, temperature low/high. Figure 4(f) shows the paradigms to control TV that contains TV on/off, volume up, volume down channel up, channel down, and mute options.

Classification of acquired signals helps in predicting blink signals in the target region. Blink and non-eye blink signal prediction is a binary classification task. Considering the challenge of classification in the region based (RB), we are applying artificial neural network (ANN) classifier, support vector machine (SVM), and Linear discriminate analysis (LDA) classifiers KNN and Bayes classifier.

Figure 3. Proposed region-based (RB) paradigms for the home environment

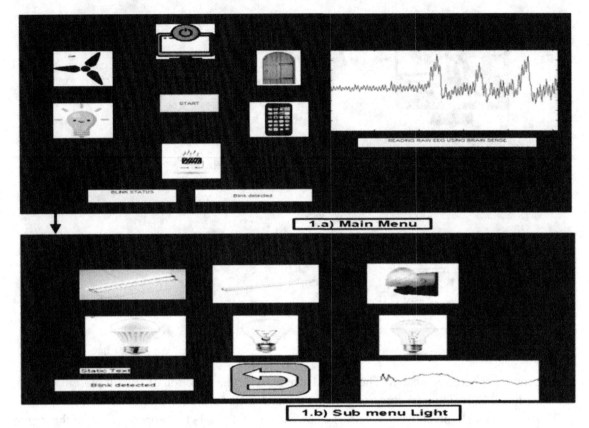

Figure 4a. Sub-regions

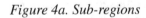

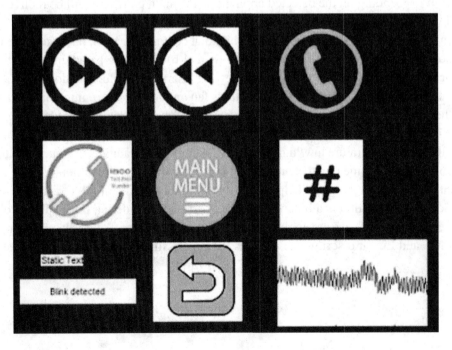

Figure 4b. Door control

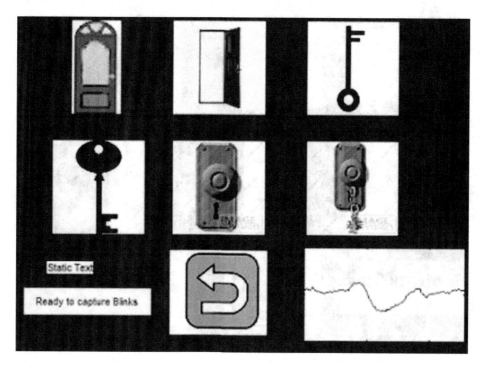

Figure 4c. Fan control

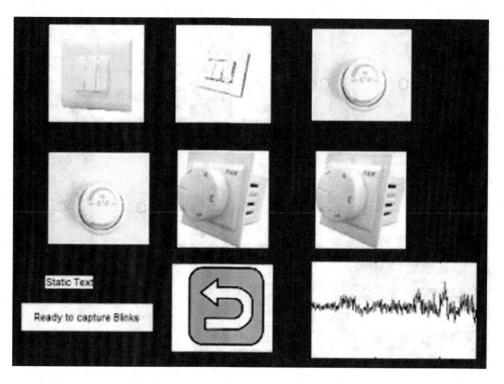

Figure 4d. Light control

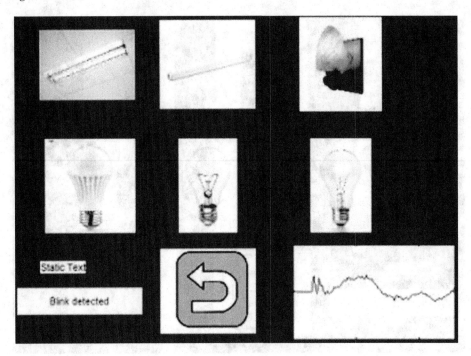

Figure 4e. Heater control

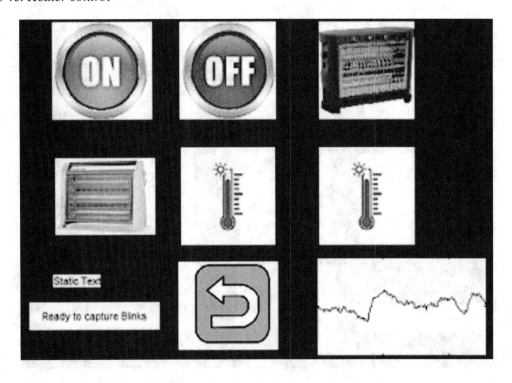

Figure 4f. TV control

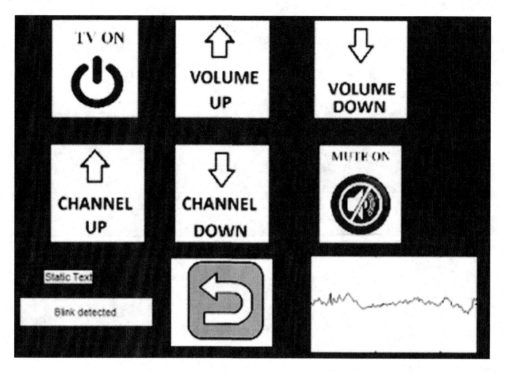

Artificial Neural Network (ANN)

Figure 5 shows a commonly used model called the multi-layered perceptron (MLP). it comprises one layer of input and one layer of output and a hidden layer between input and output (Mitra & Pal, 1995). Each layer uses multiple neurons and each neuron in a layer is linked with distinct weights to the neurons in the neighboring layer. Except for the input layer, each neuron gets signals from the prior layer's cells linearly weighted with neuron-to-neuron interconnect values.

It is presumed that a total of N sets of training data will be accessible. Inputs $\{X_1, X_2, X_3, \ldots, X_N\}$ are fed to the input layer. The ANN is trained to respond to the corresponding target vectors $\{Y_1, Y_2, Y_3, \ldots, Y_N\}$ on the output layer. The training goes on until a certain stop-criterion is met. Training is typically stopped when the average error is less than a predetermined threshold between the desired and actual outputs of the neural network over the N training data sets. The weights of the network $\{Wij\}$ are adjusted to decrease the output error according to the difference between the generated and the actual outputs. A node's activation function determines the neuron's output given input or an array of inputs.

The output of neuron k, Y_k connected from the input of neuron layer j is:

$$Y_k = f\left(\sum_j w_{kj}.O_j\right) \tag{1}$$

Where w_{kj} is interconnection weight, O_j is the output of a neuron in previous layers and f is sigmoid function $f(a) = \dfrac{1}{1 + e^{-a}}$.

Figure 5. Artificial neural network

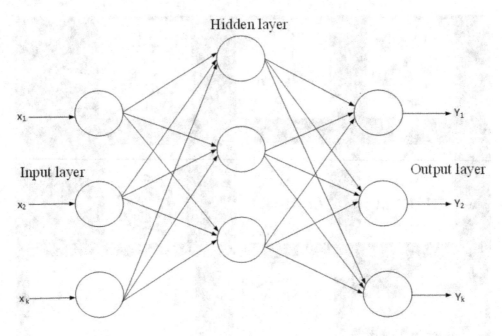

The loss function can be defined as:

$$E\left(w_{kj}\right) = \frac{1}{2}\left(y_{true} - y_k\right)^2 \tag{2}$$

Where y_{true} is the correct output for the input x_i.

Weights of the final layer are updated by the gradient descent algorithms (Qian, 1999):

$$\frac{\partial E}{\partial w_{kj}} = \frac{\partial E}{\partial y_k} \cdot \frac{\partial y_k}{\partial a_k} \cdot \frac{\partial a_k}{\partial w_{kj}} = -\left(y_{true} - y_k\right)y_k\left(1 - y_k\right)O_j = -\delta_k O_j \tag{3}$$

Where $\delta_k = (y_{true} - y_k)y_k(1 - y_k)$ and a_k is input for sigmoid activation function (Han & Moraga, 1995)

So weight change is:

$$\Delta W_{kj} = \eta.\delta_k.O_j \tag{4}$$

Where η is the adaption gain.

Error in the hidden layer is given by

$$\delta_j = O_j\left(1 - O_j\right)\sum_k w_{kj}.\delta_k \tag{5}$$

And again weight change is given by:$\Delta W_{ji} = \eta \bullet \delta_j \bullet x_i$ (6)Where x_i is input to the hidden layer.

Support Vector Machine (SVM)

SVM classifier provides good generalization capability. If the data is linearly separable, then SVM classifiers are in two hyperplanes such that separation margin's is maximized between two classes of the used dataset. The function involves optimizing the separation margin and managing error point, which is allowed in the process called stack variables, for the non-linearly separable dataset. This issue is considered an optimization problem and is resolved by Lagrange's multipliers. As a result, for novel data points x consider a linear, discrete function as shown in equation (7).

$$F(x) = \sum_{i=0}^{n} y_i \, \lambda_i (x.x_i) + b \tag{7}$$

Where x_i, i=1,2......N are trainning data points with $y_i \in \{-1,1\}$, i=1,2...N, λi i=1,2....N.

It is observed that by replacing dot product (x,x_i) with a Kernal function K (x,x_i) this equation (7) converted into equation (8) which is called radial basis function (RBF) (Dhanalakshmi, Palanivel, & Ramalingam, 2009).

$$K(x,x_i) = \exp(-\frac{\left\| x - x_i \right\|^2}{2\tilde{A}^2}) \tag{8}$$

Linear Discriminant Analysis (LDA)

LDA's concept is to discover a hyperplane maximizing the distance between means of two classes and minimizing the variance of the interclass. Classical LDA aims at optimizing the conversion by minimizing the distance between classes and maximizing the distance between classes at the same time, thus reaching maximum discrimination. By calculating the Eigen decomposition on the scatter matrices, the ideal transformation can be easily discovered.

DATA ACQUISITION

All participants involved in this study suffer from motor impairments disease. The details of all nine participants are shown in Table 1. Data were acquired through a single-channel Neurosky headset as shown in Figure 6. In this screenshot, the subject wears a single channel neurosky mind wave mobile headset. This device permits associations with apps like BCI2000, Mat lab and digitized forehead brainwave signals. This device is able to measure multiple states of the mind simultaneously. The data were recorded with nine subjects ages range 21 to 40 at the research lab of the national institute of technology, Raipur India. The data samples collected for a time period of (0 to 600) ms, with a sampling rate of 512 Hz. MATLAB software was used for designing of region-based paradigm.

In the main panel, six appliances (icon) are presented which are shown in Figure 3. Icons were shown in random order to the subjects for a fixed amount of time. The subject was asked to do a single eye blink for activating the device. Once the subject selects a device according to his needs, its sub-panel will be open. In subpanel there are 6 icons for selection, users can select according to their needs by a single eye blink. In the subpanel, the icon was also shown in random order. Subpanel practiced the same method as the main panel. After that subject can select the 'go back' option for going back to the main menu by using a single eye blink. Here, the appliance status in the main panel menu was the same as previously. The subject can change device status through selection, using a single eye blink. The experiments were performed in a silent room. In training sessions, the subject was requested to complete 18 tasks (36 selections) for both trainings as well as testing sessions. In the testing session, classes were not defined. The multi-trail analysis was carried out in this study. We collected data into 5, 10 and 15 trails. The time required for completion of 15 trails is 27 seconds (15*6*300ms). To switch between levels the speller needs 2 seconds of time. Total time needed in 56 seconds for completing the task.

Figure 6. Screenshot of the participant wearing Neurosky headset

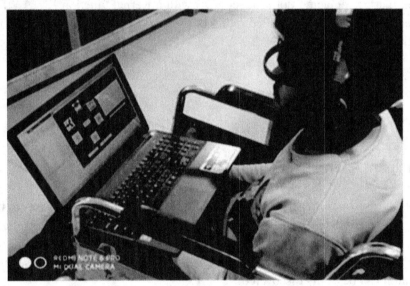

Artifacts and Eye Blink Detection from EEG Signals

EEG plays a significant role in recognizing brain activity and behavior. However, the electrical exercise recorded is continually contaminated with artifacts and affects the EEG signal analysis. There are various types of artifacts that come from the body itself (eye blink, muscles, and heartbeat) which are categories as intrinsic artifacts. There is an external artifact that comes from experimental error (electrode misplacement, cable misplacement) which is classified as extrinsic artifacts. In some instances, eye blinking artifacts are noises because EEG information collected with open eyes can be delivered with such artifacts. In this research, however, the eye blinking is the necessary parameter to activate the home appliances control system.

During the experiment, the data were saved by single-channel (Fp1) while the user intentionally caused an eye blink. Since we are collecting frontal region data, this portion of data is best suitable for blink detection. For the detection of eye blink signals, we have applied the thresholding method. Typically, eye blinks are defined by peaks with comparatively high voltages. They are often situated by setting a limit for all activities which exceed the threshold value and classifying it as eye blinks. There is also some variation in the amplitude of a particular individual's peaks, more variability among distinct subjects. Eye blinks can be categorized as small blinks if the blink period is less than 300ms with a limit value of ± 4 µV. The detection and removal of small blink are necessary to maintain the peak amplitude of EEG signals. In the proposed RB home appliances control system, once eye blink signals (for example: single, double and triple) detected to the corresponding region particular appliances will activate.

Table 1. Summary of all participants

Sub.no	Patient	Age	Sex	Diagnosis	Time since Injuries (Months)	Motor impairment degree
1.	Subject 1	30	M	SCI	11	A
2.	Subject 2	35	M	SCP	5	M
3.	Subject 3	40	F	SCI	16	S
4.	Subject 4	25	M	LD	20	M
5.	Subject 5	25	M	LD	25	M
6.	Subject 6	30	M	SCI	5	S
7.	Subject 7	35	M	SCP	10	S
8.	Subject 8	33	M	LD	15	M
9.	Subject 9	32	M	SCI	20	M

SCI: Spinal cord injury, SCP: Spastic cerebral palsy, LD: Locomotive diseases
Motor impairment degree: absent (A), minor (m), modest (M), severe (S), profound (P)

Preprocessing, Feature Extraction and Classification

Filtering

EEG signals are extremely weak and are affected by various types of noise and impairments that must be carefully removed. Differential amplifiers are used to reduce the effect of common noise on the electrodes. Each electrode is connected to the input of a differential amplifier. A standard device reference electrode connects the other input of each differential amplifier. Such amplifiers, with extremely high peaks, are very low-noise amplifiers. There are various common filters, for example, low pass, high pass, band-stop, bandpass, notch, comb and all-pass filter which depends upon frequency responses. There are some linear filters, for example, Chebyshev filter, Butterworth filter, Elliptic filter, and Bessel filter are commonly used filters for EEG noise removal. The collected (EEG signal) was transferred to the PC by using Bluetooth at a baud rate of 57600. A built-in notch filter in the neurosky mind wave headset removes the noise in the 50-60 Hz band. But we need filtering to remove known noise frequency such as heartbeat and noise from muscles. Subsequently, an 8-order Chebyshev bandpass filter was used for filtering purposes of each extracted signal with a cutoff frequency range between 1 to 10Hz and the data was decimated.

Segmentation

The data (EEG signal) collected from a single-channel neurosky mind wave mobile headset was segmented into one second time window for each stimulus. A feature vector was extracted for determining the target region using eye blink. After segmentation, six feature vectors namely X1 to X6 were created (shown in Figure 7). After the extraction of feature vectors, classification of eye blink (class labal+1) and non-eye blink (class label-1) was performed. In binary class classification problem one class belongs to blink signals and the other five classes belong to non–blink signals.

Figure 7. Segmentation of features

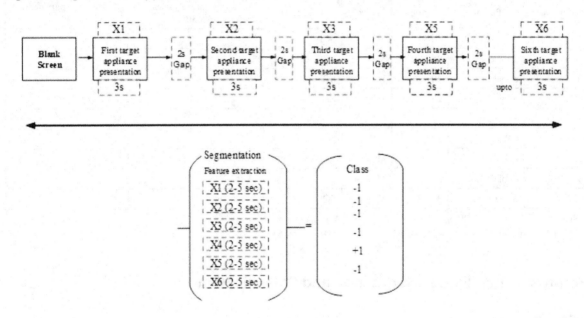

Training of Acquired Data

Training of ANN Classifier

The multilayer feed-forwards with three hidden layers with a sigmoid activation function was used in this proposed classification task. This presented study used three hidden layers (256, 5 and 2 neurons based on mean square error) and was chosen as the basis for the trial and error.

Training of SVM Classifier

In the proposed classification problem SVM classifier is trained with full training data set using the RBF-SVM classifier. The technique of 5-fold cross-validation was used. To summarize, in the RBF-SVM, C and σ parameters need to configure for better classification performance. The parameter of C and σ (for this experiment C=26, σ=28) were applied to get the best results.

Training of LDA Classifier

In the proposed classification task the hyperplane separation is obtained by maximizing two classes distance of their means and minimizes the interclass variance. Fisher's LDA assumes that data having a normal distribution with equal covariance matrix between the classes.

Target Appliance Prediction and Hardware Design

After segmenting and classifying the blink and non-blink signals of the training session, we have applied classifiers to classify targeted home appliances. Ideally, as a result of classification, we should have two features vectors of blink (class + 1) and non-blink (class -1). But the data is too noisy to get the correct target appliance from just one trial. So we used a multi-trial approach to reduce this issue. We added +1 to the score of detected in class +1 after each trial. Therefore, after n number of trails, the highest score was listed to represent the desired appliance.

After the detection of a target appliance, signals are transmitted through a Bluetooth module (HC-05) to the Arduino module. Specifications of the HC-05 module are, voltage range = 4V to 6V (Usually +5V) and current can flow up to 30mA. The Bluetooth module is working with serial communication and follows the IEEE 802.15.1 standard protocol. The collected signal is transmitted to the Arduino board using a Bluetooth module HC-05. The module supports a baud rate of 57,600 that can be selected using the AT (attention) commands. Signals received by an HC-05 Bluetooth module that is directly attached to the Arduino module. Arduino UNO board is working as a microcontroller board based on the AT mega 238. Figure 8 shows a screenshot of hardware design in real-time. It supports 16 MHz crystal oscillator. It has 16 digital inputs and output pins, six pins are used for the PWM outputs, 6 pins are analog pins one pin is used for USB connection, a power jack, and one pin for ICSP heater. Figure 9 presents pin configuration of Bluetooth–based Arduino module. Once a blink signal detected, it is transmitted to a relay board that switched the suitable device accordingly.

Proposed Algorithm

Figure 10 shows the flow chart of the proposed work. In the proposed design, the neurosky mind-wave mobile headset was used for data acquisition. Speller was shown in front of the subjects for data collection. In the speller, flashes are changed in random order. The subject can select any of the appliances according to his/her needs using eye blink. Once the eye blink and target appliance detection are complete, it will give translation command to the Arduino board which is connected through the HC-05 module. Once Arduino gets the command related to the particular target appliance, it will pass command through a relay and activate the targeted appliance.

RESULTS

The resulting segment is divided into three parts. The first one presents the results of the blink and non-blink classification using three ANN, SVM, and LDA classifier. The second presents target appliance detection accuracy results with 5, 10 and 15 sequences of the signals. The third part shows the results obtained with the statistical analysis of the data. The performance of classification has been assessed in terms of accuracy. Figure 11 displays the flow chart for the classification process.

Figure 8. Screenshot of hardware design in real environment

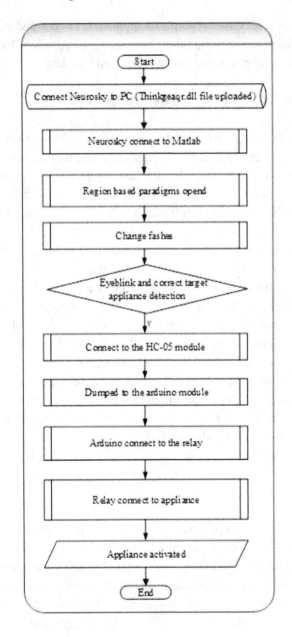

Result of the Signals for Blink Classification

For eye blink detection, LDA, SVM, and ANN models were trained and evaluated using 36 target appliances dataset. The results of the blink classification for 36 target appliance detection subject-wise and trail wise shown in Table 2.

The average accuracy of subject wise and trails wise are shown in Table 2. In the case of blink detection using SVM classifier, the achieved average accuracy in 5, 10, and 15 trails are 59.00%, 67.77%, 75.77% respectively.

Figure 9. Pin configuration of Bluetooth- based Arduino control module

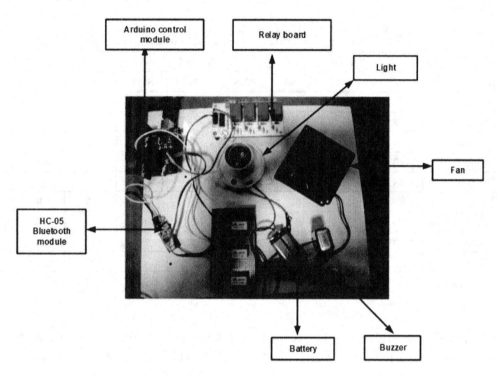

Figure 10. Flow chart of the proposed algorithms

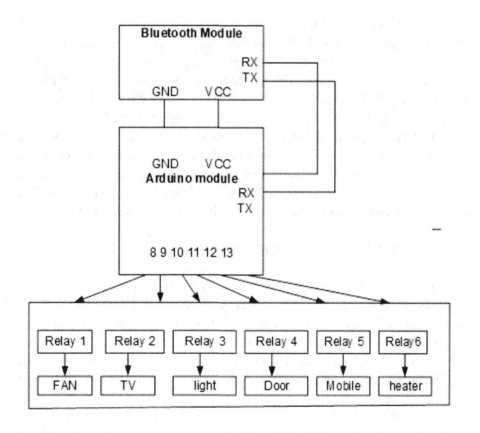

Table 2. Result obtained using the single channel with 5, 10 and 15 sequences of the signals for blink classification

SUB. NO.	User Number	Classification accuracy for different subject								
		5 Trails			10 trails			15 Trails		
		ANN	LDA	SVM	ANN	LDA	SVM	ANN	LDA	SVM
1	Subject 1	59	56	53	70	65	68	80	71	77
2	Subject 2	58	52	56	70	62	66	76	71	74
3	Subject 3	61	51	59	71	66	67	77	69	76
4	Subject 4	63	57	53	71	65	69	76	70	76
5	Subject 5	64	62	58	72	67	66	78	68	73
6	Subject 6	65	63	62	73	69	69	82	74	75
7	Subject 7	60	65	63	71	68	66	84	72	74
8	Subject 8	68	56	65	70	66	70	83	71	78
9	Subject 9	67	59	62	73	65	69	79	72	79
	Average	62.77	57.88	59.00	71.22	65.88	67.77	79.44	70.88	75.77

In the case of SVM classifier, subject wise highest accuracy is achieved for subject 1 in 15 trails and the lowest accuracy was achieved by subject 9 in 5 trails. Subject S8 and S2 attained the largest average accuracy and the smallest average accuracy of 65.33%, and 71% respectively. The reduced observed accuracy from 15 trials to 5 trials in percent are S1-24, S2-18, S3-17, S4-23, S5-15, S6-13, S7-11, S8-13, S9-17% respectively.

In the case of blink detection using the LDA classifier, the average accuracy in 5, 10 and 15 trails are 57.88%, 65.88%, and 70.88% respectively. Subject 6 was achieved in 15 trails and subject 3 was achieved the lowest accuracy in 5 trails. Subject 2 and attained the largest average accuracy of 69% and subject 6 attained the smallest 62% respectively. The reduced observed accuracy from 15 trials to 5 trials in percent are S1-15%, S2-19%, S3-18%, S4-13%, S5-6%, S6-11%, S7-7%, S8-15%, S9-13% respectively.

In the case of blink detection using ANN classifier, the average accuracy in 5, 10 and 15 trails are 62%, 71.22%, and 79.44% respectively. Subject 5 was achieved in 15 trails and the lowest accuracy was achieved by subject 2 in 5 trails. Subject 2 attained the smallest average accuracy of 68% and subject 6 attained the highest accuracy 74% respectively. The reduced observed accuracy from 15 trials to 5 trials in percent is S1 -18%, S2-16%, S3-15%, S4-13%, S5-9%, S6-10%, S7-14%, S8-10%, S9-12% respectively. The result shows that for blink classification ANN classifier gives a better result than others.

Target Appliances Detection (In Region-Based)

Target appliance detection to the corresponding blink classification is detected for a different number of trails. The results of the 36 target appliance detection classifier wise shown in Figure 12, 13, and14. Blue line shows 5 trails, the red line shows 10 trails and the green line shows 15 trails.

In the case of the target appliances detection to the corresponding blink classification using SVM, an average of all subject 19.5 24, 23.5 target appliances were detected correctly out of 36 in 5, 10 and 15 trails. However, Subject 2 has the highest appliance detection among all subjects. Subject 9 performs the lowest correctly appliance detection. However, when we lowered the number of trails from 15 to 5, the amount of target appliance detection incorrectly categorized increases. The average accuracy for target appliance detection in 5, 10 and 15 trails 54.1%, 66.6%, and 65.41% respectively.

Figure 11. Shows the flow diagram of the classification process

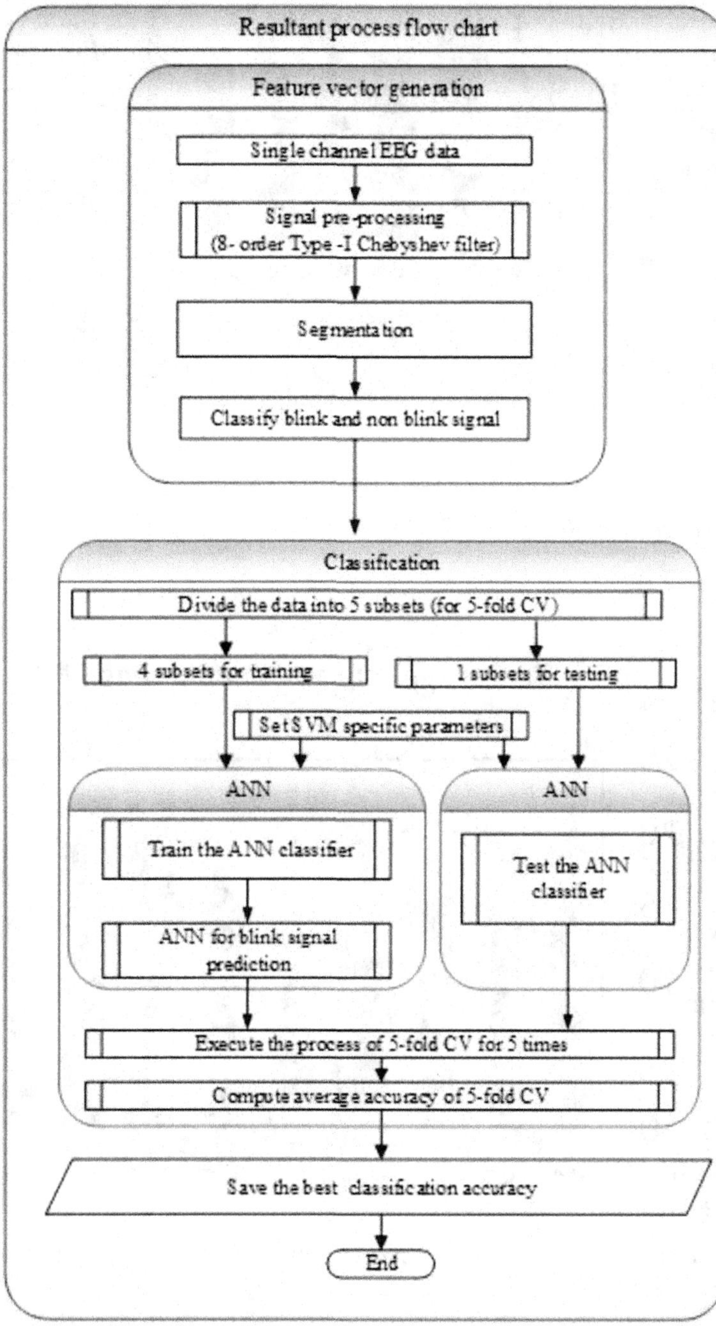

Figure 12. Target appliance detection using LDA

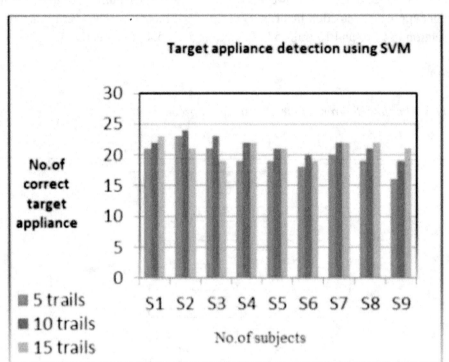

Figure 13. Target appliance detection using SVM

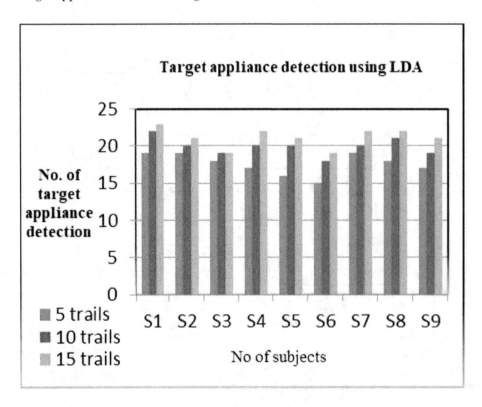

Figure 14. Target appliance detection using ANN

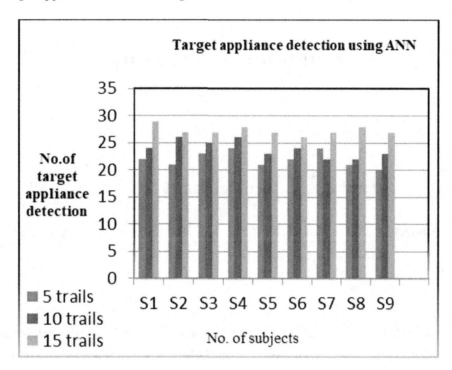

In the case of the target appliances detection to the corresponding blink classification using LDA, an average of 17.5, 20, 21.1. Target appliances were detected correctly out of 36 in 5, 10 and 15 trails. However, Subject 1 has the highest appliance detection among all subjects. Subject 6 performs the lowest correctly appliance detection. However, when we lowered the number of trails from 15 to 5, the amount of target appliance detection incorrectly categorized increases.

In the case of the target appliances detection to the detected blink classification using ANN, an average of 24.5, 26.55, 27.33 target appliances were detected correctly out of 36 in 5, 10 and 15 trails. However subject 4 has the highest appliance detection among all subjects. Subject 9 performs the lowest correctly appliance detection. However, when we lowered the number of trails from 15 to 5, the amount of target appliance detection incorrectly categorized increases. The average accuracy for target appliance detection in 5, 10 and 15 trails 68.00, 73.77, and 75.9 respectively.

Figures 12, 13 and 14 show the achieved results using different classifiers on 9 subjects for 5 trails 10 trails and 15 trails. Table 3 shows the average accuracy of nine subjects in 15 trails using all used classifiers. Among all classifiers, ANN classifiers performed better than others.

Statistical Analysis

The Friedman method was used for statistical comparison of various algorithms. It is the non-parametric method chosen over repetitive ANOVA analysis. This test can be said to be similar to repeated ANOVA analysis. The basic principle of this experiment is that various methods of classification are evaluated according to their ranking. Rank 1 rate the best performing system the second one rank 2 and so forth (Figure 15).

Figure 15. Shows the results of the post hoc analysis for all three models

Friedman p = 0.01564

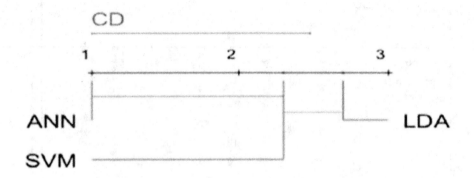

The Friedman method is used according to the average ranks obtained from the different approaches. A null hypothesis for the p-value is evaluated. A p-value refers to a confidence level. The assumption is that if the p-value is higher than the confidence level then there is no distinction between subjects, the answer will be rejected. The post hoc Nemenyi test is used in this situation. The next criterion is that if the p-value approaches the confidence level, then there is a rank difference between a pair being greater than the critical difference (CD) at a certain confidence level, the performance will be significantly different in this case. The Friedman method was implemented across all nine different subjects with three different classification methods (ANN, SVM, and LDA) (obtained using 15 trails). The estimated P-value according to the experimental outcome was 0.01564 lower than the confidence level. The null hypothesis was rejected by rule and the Post Hoc test was used. The CD value obtained is 2.5135 more than the p-value of 0.05.

Table 3. Average accuracy of all nine subjects in 15 trails

S.NO	Classifier	Average accuracy
1	ANN	80.00%
2	SVM	75.77%
3	LDA	70.88%
4	KNN	68.77%
5	Bayes	60.55%

DISCUSSION AND FUTURE SCOPE

Table 4 demonstrates the comparison between the proposed and existing BCI–based controlling home appliances. We compared the accuracy as well as hardware design (cost of the system, convenience of the users) of the existing model

Table 4. Comparative analysis between existing and proposed BCI- based home appliance control system

Author	Subjects	Types of Paradigms	Classifier	Total selection	Average Accuracy (%)	Session	Signal	Disability
Hoffman et al. (Hoffmann, et al., 2008)	4	3x2 images	Set wise-LDA, Fisher-LDA	24(2)	100.0	2	P300	Healthy
Rebecca Corralejo (Corralejo, et al., 2014)	15	10 matrices images R/C	SLDA	134(3)	74.4	3	P300	Disabled
E.A.Aydin (Aydin, et al., 2016)	5	Main menu 6x6, Submenu 6x6	LDA	20(2)	95%	2	P300	Healthy
S.F.Anindya et. al	4	-	SVM	-	83.26%	-	SSVEP	Healthy
D.Achanccaray (Achanccaray, Flores, Fonseca, & Andreu-Perez, 2017) et al.	8	Matrix 2x3	ANFIS	-	Above 80%	-	Eye blink (EEG/ EOG)	Healthy
M.Uma(Uma & Sheela, 2017).	5	GUI based menus	ANN	-	90%	-	P300	Healthy
U.Masud (Masud, et al., 2017)	3	Matrix 4x6	Random Forest	-	87%	-	-	Healthy
Proposed	9	Main menu 2x3	ANN	36(2)	80%	2	Eye blink (EEG/ EOG)	Disabled

Comparison Study Between Proposed Vs Existing Controlling Home Appliances System

Regarding existing studies related to BCI–based home appliances control system applications, Hoffman et al. (Hoffmann, et al., 2008) tested a P300-based BCI system for 5 disabled subjects having distinct pathologies and 4 healthy subjects simulating a paradigm for environmental control. Four of them achieved 100% classification accuracy. Nevertheless, a quite distinct P300 paradigm was used to carry out this research. One stimuli matrix was used, consisting of six pictures flashing one by one. In addition, four sessions were held, each consisting of six single item selections. In the proposed BCI design system contains 36 items from 6 menus or matrices, stimuli were distributed over the intended area, and 2 assessment sessions are performed consisting of at least 36 single item selections. Rebeca Corralejo et. al(Corralejo, et al., 2014) increases 113 items from ten menus or matrices, 2 assessment sessions are conducted consisting of at least 42 choices of single items. But overall average accuracy 74.4% achieved. In our proposed BCI system based on the ANN model achieved better accuracy than existing. E. A. Aydin et al. developed a home automation control system based on a web server that achieved good accuracy by 95%. The existing home automation control system based on the webserver requires constant internet access for activation. The proposed systems need not internet access consistently. (Belwafi, et al., 2017) designs a system using FPGA model, which is a critical design for the users. Our proposed design system easy and economical for the users. (Wahy & Mansor, 2010b) also developed a 3-eye blink signal system (four seconds long) using a microcontroller (PIC16F877A), but the proposed system was designed for single appliance only. Our proposed model convenient with an electrical device and control multiple appliance control systems. (Uma & Sheela, 2017) designed a home appliance control system model using eye blink for a healthy person. This design did not talk deeply for signal analysis and target appliance recognition and achieved 90% accuracy for a healthy person. The proposed model deeply analyzes blink classification; waveform detection and target appliance recognition for completely disable patients and achieved 80% accuracy for completely paralyzed patients. The proposed system achieves the highest eye blink classification accuracy with subject 5, which has the locomotive disease. Furthermore, highest target character classification accuracy is achieved with subject 4, which has SCI. This model not only performing good in terms of accuracy but also has robust hardware design. The system is very economical, easy to use, and makes life easy for paralyzed people.

Figure 16. Performance of different device (In terms of time)

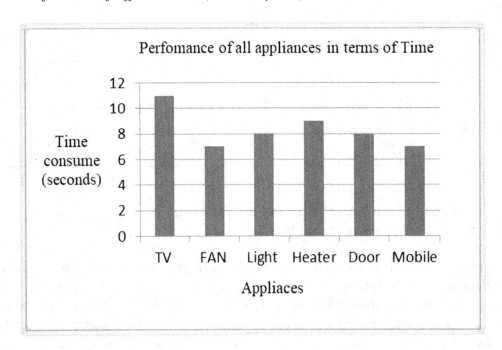

The different device takes some time for activation. For evaluation, average activation time for all devices was calculated and all devices were analyzed with respect to this average time. Light and fan take minimum average time for activation. The TV appliance takes maximum average time for activation. Heater and door take above average time for activation. Figure 16 shows performance of difference appliance (In terms of time).

From the presented results and discussion, it is evident that further research and technical enhancement is required on EEG-based control systems for them to be publically accepted. We assume that seeing the potential of this area, the managers, government bodies and policymakers will start to focus on this in the very near future.

Open Issues and Future Scope

There are many issues and challenges in the development of BCI-based technology. These challenges are categorized based on usability and technical requirements. Non-linear behavior of the brain, correct data acquisition, noises and high dimensionality of the data comes under technical challenges. Information transfer rate (ITR) and the average time for selection comes under the usability challenges. RC-based paradigms are having many challenges like adjacency problem, crowding effect (Chaurasiya, Londhe, & Ghosh, 2016), and task difficulty. Proposed work can significantly resolve such challenges. The integration of more devices will further improve the usability and performance of the proposed system. The inclusion of different kinds of disability into existing and collected datasets will make the proposed dataset more robust for the training of the proposed system. Additionally, the application of the Internet of things (IoT) with the proposed method will enhance the usability of the proposed system.

CONCLUSION

In this proposed article novel region-based paradigms for BCI-based home appliances control system. This design is very helpful, for people who are unable to move or unable to communicate verbally because of complete paralysis. In proposed designed an RB-based speller that contains 36 options which are generally used in daily life. These options can be selected with the help of just an eye blink. Moreover, EEG signals data were collected from paralyzed patients using a neurosky mind wave mobile headset for feature extraction to segment blink and non-blink signals. Different filters were applied to segment and classify blink and non-blink signals. After that, for target selection classification different classification methods like SVM, LDA, ANN, KNN and Bayes were applied. The highest achieved average accuracy through ANN classifier is 80% which is higher than (Corralejo, et al., 2014). For the blink classification, with ANN classifier, proposed system achieves subject wise highest accuracy from subject 5 in 15 trails and the lowest accuracy from subject 2 in 5 trails. In the case of the target appliances detection using ANN, an average of 24.5, 26.55, 27.33 target appliances were detected correctly out of 36 in 5, 10 and 15 trails. It is observed that the newly developed system is cost-effective and necessitates only little effort to select the target. A statistical analysis reveals that the ANN classifier is outperforming SVM, LDA, KNN, and Bayes classification methods. The Arduino-based hardware module of the proposed system is easily available and very cheap.

REFERENCES

Achanccaray, D., Flores, C., Fonseca, C., & Andreu-Perez, J. (2017). *A p300-based brain computer interface for smart home interaction through an anfis ensemble.* Paper presented at the 2017 IEEE International Conference on Fuzzy Systems (FUZZ-IEEE).

Acqualagna, L., & Blankertz, B. (2013). Gaze-independent BCI-spelling using rapid serial visual presentation (RSVP). *Clinical Neurophysiology, 124*(5), 901–908. doi:10.1016/j.clinph.2012.12.050 PMID:23466266

Alrajhi, W., Alaloola, D., & Albarqawi, A. (2017). *Smart home: toward daily use of BCI-based systems.* Paper presented at the Informatics, Health & Technology (ICIHT), International Conference on. 10.1109/ICIHT.2017.7899002

Alshbatat, A. I. N., Vial, P. J., Premaratne, P., & Tran, L. C. (2014). *EEG-based brain-computer interface for automating home appliances.* Academic Press.

Aydın, E. A., Bay, Ö. F., & Güler, İ. (2016). Implementation of an embedded web server application for wireless control of brain computer interface based home environments. *Journal of Medical Systems, 40*(1), 27. doi:10.100710916-015-0386-0 PMID:26547847

Belwafi, K., Ghaffari, F., Djemal, R., & Romain, O. (2017). A Hardware/Software Prototype of EEG-based BCI System for Home Device Control. *Journal of Signal Processing Systems for Signal, Image, and Video Technology, 89*(2), 263–279. doi:10.100711265-016-1192-8

Casarotto, S., Bianchi, A. M., Cerutti, S., & Chiarenza, G. A. (2004). Principal component analysis for reduction of ocular artefacts in event-related potentials of normal and dyslexic children. *Clinical Neurophysiology, 115*(3), 609–619. doi:10.1016/j.clinph.2003.10.018 PMID:15036057

Chaurasiya, R. K., Londhe, N. D., & Ghosh, S. (2016). Binary DE-based channel selection and weighted ensemble of SVM classification for novel brain–computer interface using Devanagari script-based P300 speller paradigm. *International Journal of Human-Computer Interaction, 32*(11), 861–877. doi:10.1080/10447318.2016.1203047

Chowdhury, A. M., Kashem, F. B., Hossan, A., & Hasan, M. M. (2017). *Brain controlled assistive buzzer system for physically impaired people.* Paper presented at the Electrical, Computer and Communication Engineering (ECCE), International Conference on. 10.1109/ECACE.2017.7912988

Corralejo, R., Nicolás-Alonso, L. F., Álvarez, D., & Hornero, R. (2014). A P300-based brain–computer interface aimed at operating electronic devices at home for severely disabled people. *Medical & Biological Engineering & Computing, 52*(10), 861–872. doi:10.100711517-014-1191-5 PMID:25163823

Dhanalakshmi, P., Palanivel, S., & Ramalingam, V. (2009). Classification of audio signals using SVM and RBFNN. *Expert Systems with Applications, 36*(3), 6069–6075. doi:10.1016/j.eswa.2008.06.126

Donoho, D. L. (2001). Sparse components of images and optimal atomic decompositions. *Constructive Approximation, 17*(3), 353–382. doi:10.1007003650010032

Farwell, L. A., & Donchin, E. (1988). Talking off the top of your head: Toward a mental prosthesis utilizing event-related brain potentials. *Electroencephalography and Clinical Neurophysiology, 70*(6), 510–523. doi:10.1016/0013-4694(88)90149-6 PMID:2461285

Fazel-Rezai, R., & Abhari, K. (2009). A region-based P300 speller for brain-computer interface. *Canadian Journal of Electrical and Computer Engineering, 34*(3), 81–85. doi:10.1109/CJECE.2009.5443854

Han, J., & Moraga, C. (1995). *The influence of the sigmoid function parameters on the speed of back-propagation learning.* Paper presented at the International Workshop on Artificial Neural Networks. 10.1007/3-540-59497-3_175

He, S., & Li, Y. (2017). A Single-channel EOG-based Speller. *IEEE Transactions on Neural Systems and Rehabilitation Engineering, 25*(11), 1978–1987. doi:10.1109/TNSRE.2017.2716109 PMID:28641264

Hillyard, S. A., & Galambos, R. (1970). Eye movement artifact in the CNV. *Electroencephalography and Clinical Neurophysiology, 28*(2), 173–182. doi:10.1016/0013-4694(70)90185-9 PMID:4189528

Hoffmann, U., Vesin, J.-M., Ebrahimi, T., & Diserens, K. (2008). An efficient P300-based brain–computer interface for disabled subjects. *Journal of Neuroscience Methods, 167*(1), 115–125. doi:10.1016/j.jneumeth.2007.03.005 PMID:17445904

Holzner, C., Guger, C., Edlinger, G., Gronegress, C., & Slater, M. (2009). *Virtual smart home controlled by thoughts.* Paper presented at the 2009 18th IEEE International Workshops on Enabling Technologies: Infrastructures for Collaborative Enterprises. 10.1109/WETICE.2009.41

Hsieh, K., Sun, K., Yeh, J., & Pan, Y. (2017a). *Home care by auditory Brain Computer Interface for the blind with severe physical disabilities.* Paper presented at the 2017 International Conference on Applied System Innovation (ICASI). 10.1109/ICASI.2017.7988473

Hsieh, K., Sun, K., Yeh, J., & Pan, Y. (2017b). *Home care by auditory Brain Computer Interface for the blind with severe physical disabilities.* Paper presented at the Applied System Innovation (ICASI), 2017 International Conference on. 10.1109/ICASI.2017.7988473

Jais, A. A., Mansor, W., Lee, K. Y., & Fauzi, W. (2017). *Motor imagery EEG analysis for home appliance control.* Paper presented at the 2017 IEEE 13th International Colloquium on Signal Processing & its Applications (CSPA).

Khushaba, R. N., Kodagoda, S., Lal, S., & Dissanayake, G. (2011). Driver drowsiness classification using fuzzy wavelet-packet-based feature-extraction algorithm. *IEEE Transactions on Biomedical Engineering, 58*(1), 121–131. doi:10.1109/TBME.2010.2077291 PMID:20858575

Lin, C.-T., Lin, B.-S., Lin, F.-C., & Chang, C.-J. (2014). Brain computer interface-based smart living environmental auto-adjustment control system in UPnP home networking. *IEEE Systems Journal, 8*(2), 363–370. doi:10.1109/JSYST.2012.2192756

Ma, J., Zhang, Y., Cichocki, A., & Matsuno, F. (2014). A novel EOG/EEG hybrid human–machine interface adopting eye movements and ERPs: Application to robot control. *IEEE Transactions on Biomedical Engineering, 62*(3), 876–889. doi:10.1109/TBME.2014.2369483 PMID:25398172

Ma, T., Li, H., Deng, L., Yang, H., Lv, X., Li, P., Li, F., Zhang, R., Liu, T., Yao, D., & Xu, P. (2017). The hybrid BCI system for movement control by combining motor imagery and moving onset visual evoked potential. *Journal of Neural Engineering, 14*(2), 026015. doi:10.1088/1741-2552/aa5d5f PMID:28145274

Mak, J. N., & Wolpaw, J. R. (2009). Clinical applications of brain-computer interfaces: Current state and future prospects. *IEEE Reviews in Biomedical Engineering, 2*, 187–199. doi:10.1109/RBME.2009.2035356 PMID:20442804

Masud, U., Baig, M. I., Akram, F., & Kim, T.-S. (2017). *A P300 brain computer interface based intelligent home control system using a random forest classifier.* Paper presented at the 2017 IEEE Symposium Series on Computational Intelligence (SSCI).

Mitra, S., & Pal, S. K. (1995). Fuzzy multi-layer perceptron, inferencing and rule generation. *IEEE Transactions on Neural Networks, 6*(1), 51–63. doi:10.1109/72.363450 PMID:18263285

Pan, J., Li, Y., Gu, Z., & Yu, Z. (2013). A comparison study of two P300 speller paradigms for brain–computer interface. *Cognitive Neurodynamics, 7*(6), 523–529. doi:10.100711571-013-9253-1 PMID:24427224

Patel, R., Janawadkar, M. P., Sengottuvel, S., Gireesan, K., & Radhakrishnan, T. S. (2016). Suppression of eye-blink associated artifact using single channel EEG data by combining cross-correlation with empirical mode decomposition. *IEEE Sensors Journal, 16*(18), 6947–6954. doi:10.1109/JSEN.2016.2591580

Pesin, J. (2007). *Detection and removal of eyeblink artifacts from EEG using wavelet analysis and independent component analysis.* Academic Press.

Qian, N. (1999). On the momentum term in gradient descent learning algorithms. *Neural Networks, 12*(1), 145–151. doi:10.1016/S0893-6080(98)00116-6 PMID:12662723

Ramadan, R. A., & Vasilakos, A. V. (2017). Brain computer interface: Control signals review. *Neurocomputing, 223*, 26–44. doi:10.1016/j.neucom.2016.10.024

Somers, B., Francart, T., & Bertrand, A. (2018). A generic EEG artifact removal algorithm based on the multi-channel Wiener filter. *Journal of Neural Engineering, 15*(3), 036007. doi:10.1088/1741-2552/aaac92 PMID:29393057

Soomro, M. H., Badruddin, N., Yusoff, M. Z., & Jatoi, M. A. (2013). *Automatic eye-blink artifact removal method based on EMD-CCA.* Paper presented at the 2013 ICME International Conference on Complex Medical Engineering. 10.1109/ICCME.2013.6548236

Sweeney, K. T., Ward, T. E., & McLoone, S. F. (2012). Artifact removal in physiological signals—Practices and possibilities. *IEEE Transactions on Information Technology in Biomedicine, 16*(3), 488–500. doi:10.1109/TITB.2012.2188536 PMID:22361665

Tibdewal, M. N., Fate, R., Mahadevappa, M., & Ray, A. (2015). *Detection and classification of eye blink artifact in electroencephalogram through discrete Wavelet Transform and neural network.* Paper presented at the 2015 International Conference on Pervasive Computing (ICPC). 10.1109/PERVASIVE.2015.7087077

Townsend, G., LaPallo, B., Boulay, C., Krusienski, D., Frye, G., Hauser, C., Schwartz, N. E., Vaughan, T. M., Wolpaw, J. R., & Sellers, E. W. (2010). A novel P300-based brain–computer interface stimulus presentation paradigm: Moving beyond rows and columns. *Clinical Neurophysiology*, *121*(7), 1109–1120. doi:10.1016/j.clinph.2010.01.030 PMID:20347387

Tseng, K. C., Wang, Y.-T., Lin, B.-S., & Hsieh, P. H. (2012). *Brain computer interface-based multimedia controller.* Paper presented at the Intelligent Information Hiding and Multimedia Signal Processing (IIH-MSP), 2012 Eighth International Conference on. 10.1109/IIH-MSP.2012.73

Uma, M., & Sheela, T. (2017). Analysis of Collaborative Brain Computer Interface (BCI) based Personalized GUI for Differently Abled. *Intelligent Automation & Soft Computing*, 1-11.

Usakli, A. B., & Gurkan, S. (2010). Design of a novel efficient human–computer interface: An electrooculagram based virtual keyboard. *IEEE Transactions on Instrumentation and Measurement*, *59*(8), 2099–2108. doi:10.1109/TIM.2009.2030923

Velayutham, B., Kangusamy, B., Joshua, V., & Mehendale, S. (2016). The prevalence of disability in elderly in India–Analysis of 2011 census data. *Disability and Health Journal*, *9*(4), 584–592. doi:10.1016/j.dhjo.2016.04.003 PMID:27174073

Wahy, N., & Mansor, W. (2010a). *EEG based home lighting system.* Paper presented at the 2010 International Conference on Computer Applications and Industrial Electronics. 10.1109/ICCAIE.2010.5735107

Wahy, N., & Mansor, W. (2010b). *EEG based home lighting system.* Paper presented at the Computer Applications and Industrial Electronics (ICCAIE), 2010 International Conference on. 10.1109/ICCAIE.2010.5735107

Wang, M., Lv, Y., Wen, M., He, S., & Wang, G. (2016). *A Fan Control System Base on Steady-State Visual Evoked Potential.* Paper presented at the Computer, Consumer and Control (IS3C), 2016 International Symposium on. 10.1109/IS3C.2016.31

Zhang, F., Yu, H., Jiang, J., Wang, Z., & Qin, X. (2019). *Brain–computer control interface design for virtual household appliances based on steady-state visually evoked potential recognition.* Visual Informatics.

This research was previously published in the International Journal of E-Health and Medical Communications (IJEHMC), 11(4); pages 65-89, copyright year 2020 by IGI Publishing (an imprint of IGI Global).

Chapter 26

An Integrated Model of Data Envelopment Analysis and Artificial Neural Networks for Improving Efficiency in the Municipal Solid Waste Management

Antonella Cavallin
Universidad Nacional del Sur, Argentina

Hernán Pedro Vigier
Universidad Nacional del Sur, Argentina

Mariano Frutos
*Universidad Nacional del Sur, Argentina &
CONICET, Argentina*

Diego Gabriel Rossit
Universidad Nacional del Sur, Argentina

ABSTRACT

In the last decades, integral municipal solid waste management (IMSWM) has become one of the most challenging areas for local governmental authorities, which have struggled to lay down sustainable and financially stable policies for the sector. In this paper a model that evaluates the efficiency of IMSWMs through a combination of Data Envelopment Analysis (DEA) and an Artificial Neural Network (ANN) is presented. In a first stage, applying DEA, municipal administrations are classified according to the efficiency of their garbage processing systems. This is done in order to infer what modifications are necessary to make garbage handling more efficient. In a second stage, an ANN is used for predicting the necessary resources needed to make the waste processing system efficient. This methodology is applied on a toy model with 50 towns as well as on a real-world case of 21 cities. The results show the usefulness of the model for the evaluation of relative efficiency and for guiding the improvement of the system.

DOI: 10.4018/978-1-6684-2408-7.ch026

INTRODUCTION

The ways in which waste is disposed reflects many relevant features of a society. The differences in garbage production may arise from the corresponding differences in the industrial structure, the physical distribution and the health considerations among districts (Gören, 2015). Municipal Solid Waste (MSW) disposal has become an increasingly serious problem in many parts of the world. In general, a greater economic prosperity and a higher percentage of urban population leads to a larger amount of production of waste (Aziz & Abu, 2016). The amount and type of waste generated is largely influenced by geographical and socio-economic factors. These factors include the population, the size of households, the age structure, the distribution of income, the type of dwelling, the geographical location and the time of the year, as well as the average standard of life. Furthermore, it depends on the frequency of collection and the characteristics of the source area (Chatsiwa, Mujere & Maiyana, 2016). In this work, the efficiency of systems of Integral Municipal Solid Waste Management (IMSWM) is analyzed and evaluated. In the context of resource shortages, either technical or budgetary, and in the face of an increasing rate of garbage generation, the correct management of the IMSWM is one of the main challenges for local governments that, no matter the size of the cities, aim to a path of sustainable development (Schejtman & Cellucci, 2014). Municipal Solid Waste Management (MSWM) is defined as the class of independent and complementary activities that constitute the process of dealing with waste in order to reduce the impact on the environment and the quality of life in a city. IMSWM encompasses in an integrated way activities as garbage generation, collection, transport, treatment and final disposition. The objective of the IMSWM is to enhance the appreciation of municipal waste, i.e., the transformation from waste into resources without endangering human health or the environment. These activities are carried out in suitable processes that cut down the amount of waste that ends in final disposition and, additionally, reduce its impact on the environment. Environmental management policies are aimed to prevent pollution, preserve natural resources, and reduce environmental risks while creating an environmentally friendly image for different stakeholders. Effective waste management methods reduce the consumption of natural resources and lower the ultimate needs for waste disposal (Kasemsap, 2017). MSWM has become an integral part of the urban environment to ensure safe and health human while considering the application of sustainable economic growth technology.

To run a successful IMSWM system, it is necessary to define and apply adequate indicators of performance. Although the activities of the system consume time, human resources and money, they should be considered more as an investment than expenditure. This becomes obvious upon the realization that the current increment in the Municipal Solid Waste (MSW) generation rate is not sustainable in the long run, not only because of budgetary limitations but also because of the limited amount of land that can be used for landfills, i.e., with the proper chemical conditions for dealing with garbage. Adequately designed indicators are useful for identifying the drawbacks of the systems and the adequate ways for improving them. Additionally, they are crucial for raising social and governmental awareness on how the incorrect handling of MSW affects human and environmental health (Inter-American Association of Sanitary and Environmental Engineering, 2005). In this way, social pressure can force governments to invest in improving the sustainability of MSWs and enhance the general welfare of urban areas. Indicators can also help to distinguish those cities that run efficient MSW systems. They also help to detect the connections between different environmental variables, facilitating the anticipation of risky situations for water supplies or wildlife. As it is usual in the design of indicators, IMSWM ones are generated combining straightforward parameters: frequency of garbage collection, size of the vehicle fleet or number of trips between the dwellings and the landfills, among others (Government of Chile, National Commission for the Environment, 2001).

In the analysis of IMSWM systems, Data Envelopment Analysis (DEA) has been used in numerous applications, leading to the design of indicators of efficiency. DEA is receiving an increasing attention as a tool for evaluating and improving the performance of manufacturing and service operations (Miidla, 2013). Another strand of techniques draws on tools that are based on the imitation biological knowledge-acquisition and processing systems, the so-called *Soft Computation* approach. Among these techniques aiming to provide robust solutions, Artificial Neural Networks (ANN) play a salient role, being data processing systems inspired in the behavior of nervous systems.

In this work the analysis of the efficiency of IMSWM is addressed through a model that combines DEA and an ANN. The procedure has two stages. In the first one DEA is applied to classify municipal administrations according to their efficiency in the management of the MSWM system. Then, they are compared to detect where inefficient IMSWM systems can be intervened to improve them. For this purpose, an ANN is designed to yield the actions that can boost the efficiency of a MSWM, optimizing the use of the resources assigned to the system. In contexts of multi-output (or multi-input), the ANN treats each output independently in terms of efficiency. Therefore, it is possible to conclude that one unit can be deemed efficient with regard to some outputs but inefficient for others, facilitating the adoption of specific strategies for sections of the system and thus tailored to each case. Our results show the convenience of a combination of DEA and ANN in the evaluation of relative efficiency in the area of IMSWM and its potential for orienting the management decision towards sustainable development.

MOTIVATION

Sectoral policies of IMSWM have been focused on carrying out integral investments aimed at increasing both the coverage and quality of service. The adoption of sustainable development practices has political and social impacts. Many countries are facing a conflict between, on one hand, economic growth and, on the other, the protection of the environment. Unfortunately, sometimes the choice implies to neglect the environment and consequently harm the decision-makers in an indirect way (Salman, Tarkhan, Mohamed, Farouk, & Kamal, 2015).

An integral way of managing solid waste require to make deep environmental, economic and health-related changes, that have to be taken into account in the planning and implementation cycle (Acero, 2012). Guidelines have to be laid out for the assessment and control of the process and results of the system, starting from the generation to the final disposal of waste. The technical schemes implemented must be economically sound and sustainable in time. In their design, all the stakeholders (national, district and municipal governments, sectoral leaders, users, firms and service providers) must be actively engaged. This is the only way that transversal and dynamical high quality schemes can be implemented.

This chapter is intended as, on one hand, a survey of the literature on DEA and ANN techniques applied to MSWM. On the other hand, we introduce here a concrete model that can become a tool for policy-making in the field of these systems. The model is tested in order to show its accuracy and usefulness, while at the same time posing new questions to be answered in the future.

BACKGROUND

In the last years, the rise in the consumption of disposable products, the rapid obsolescence of consumer goods along with the urban development in many cities has increased not only the volume of generated waste but also its composition, including now an increasing variety of materials. According to an Argentinian report (Secretary of Environment and Sustainable Development of Argentina, 2014), in 2012 the MSW production rate for Argentina was 1 kg per capita per day. A national law (25919) provides the incentive to find innovative ways of dealing with this problem. Municipalities started to implement different procedures according to their needs and the current state of their respective IMSWM, e.g., closing "open-air" waste dumps, constructing landfills, promoting garbage sorted recollection and recycling and installing waste treatment facilities. The improvement in some cities was remarkable, whereas in others the inefficiencies of their MSW systems remain. Another national report in Argentina (Secretary of Environment and Sustainable Development of Argentina, 2016) reveals that in some Argentinian provinces the collection system has improved and the coverage surpassed the 80% threshold. The national average percentage of final disposition in landfill covers 61% of the population. However, the distribution is quite unequal since in provinces like Neuquén, San Juan, Tucumán, Misiones and Gran Buenos Aires this percentage is above 80%, whereas in others it is as low as 20%. For example, in the province of Buenos Aires, the potential focus of this work, almost 85% of the municipalities have an adequate final disposition of their waste. With respect to waste classification facilities, the garbage generated by 37% of the Argentinians and 76% of the citizens from Buenos Aires is processed by them.

On the other hand, along with the development of sustainable initiatives, every IMSWM system has to present a monitoring plan in order to measure the performance of the system and assess its strengths and weaknesses. Therefore, measures to reduce environmental pollution, save fuel and other resources, develop cogeneration, and use large-scale renewable resources acquire a pressing importance (Zharkov, 2016). To achieve this goal, in the last years many indicators measuring environmental sustainability have been developed yielding information about the relation society-environment (Chávez, Armijo-De Vega, Calderón-De La Barca, Leyva-Aguilera & Ojeda-Benítez, 2011). These indicators provide empirical and numerical-based assessment of environmental problems, gauging the environmental impact of human activities and helping decision-makers and stakeholders to define targets for sustainable development (Rodríguez Solórzano, 2002). Specifically, in the area of IMSWM, indicators arose with the aim of monitoring and controlling the operation of the system in order to improve the quality of the service provided by the public or private institutions and companies that run the system. Since the 1960s, many and varied mathematical models have been developed for the evaluation of different policies and assisting in the decision making in the field of IMSWMs (Huang, Baetz, Huang & Liu, 2002). The approaches in this literature are manifold, including the analysis of landfill location problems, the evaluation of the ensuing vehicle routing problems, the prediction of the composition of waste and the problems with its generation (Pires, Martinho & Chang, 2011), among many others.

In relation to the management of MSW, DEA has been used in several papers with the objective of comparing the operating efficiency of the MSW collection systems of cities in different countries. Ali, Yadav, Anis & Sharma (2015) integrate DEA to the hazardous waste management in USA. Baba, Purwanto and Sunoko (2015) and Villavicencio and Didonet (2009) evaluate the efficiency of the systems in different towns in Graha Padma and Catalunya, respectively. In the latter work three models, assuming output generation with constant returns to scale, are used to evaluate 48 municipalities. In the first one two outputs are considered (amount of waste collected and number of inhabitants per municipality) and four desirable outputs (amount of collected organic waste, glass, paper and packaging). The second one only considers the number of inhabitants as an input and the amount of waste that ends in the landfill as undesirable output. The third model integrates the inputs and outputs of the previous models, inverting the undesirable output (raised to -1). The three models indicate that only two MSWs are efficient among the entire group under study.

ANNs have been extensively used in different areas like engineering (see, e.g., Esfe et al., 2014), economics and finance (see, e.g., Feng & Zhang, 2014), medicine (see, e.g., Amato et al., 2013), emerging energy technologies (Cebi, Kahraman & Kaya, 2012), etc. In the specific case of IMSWM, many papers use ANNs in the prediction of the amounts generated by MSWs, as in Jafarzadeh & Hashempour (2015) and Batinic et al. (2011) predicting also the composition of garbage according to the socioeconomic indicators. Zade & Noori (2007) propose a model for the prediction of the amount of waste generated weekly in Mashhad (Iran), a touristic city that has variable conditions during the year. Jahandideh (2009) focuses on the generation and composition of hospital waste, in fifty hospitals of the city of Fars, Iran. ANNs have also been used in the analysis of recycling as in Liu, Liu, Wang & Liu (2002), where a model assesses the recycling potential of a product based on the opinion of experts. In Mazhar, Kara & Kaebernick (2007), the authors used an ANN to predict the degradation rate of recyclable products.

Closer to our objective, there exists a literature integrating DEA and ANNs in different ways and contexts. One of the first contributions is the work of Athanassopoulos and Curram (1996) that determines that DEA and ANNs are comparable and potentially complementary models for the evaluation of performance and the measurement of efficiency. Wu (2009) developed a hybrid model using DEA, an ANN and a Decision Tree (DT) to evaluate the performances of different suppliers. The model has a first module, where DEA is applied to discriminate between efficient and inefficient suppliers, and a second one, that takes the information of the first module to train an ANN and a DT to evaluate future markets and possible providers. In Çelebi and Bayraktar (2008) an integrated model is also used to evaluate suppliers. However, in this model the ANN is used first for determine performance indicators, which are then applied in a DEA evaluation of the efficiency of providers. In Kuo, Wang & Tien (2010) performance indicators are also generated to be later used to measure efficiency with DEA. In Kuo, Wang and Tien (2010) criteria for selecting sustainable suppliers are defined using the Delphi[1] method. Through an Analytic Network Process (ANP) they develop an indicator weighting up the different criteria. After that, they train and predict the performance of each supplier through an ANN. Later, these outputs are combined with DEA, resulting in a model called ANN-MADA that makes a final evaluation of each supplier. In Mostafa (2008) and in Wu, Yang & Liang (2006) the efficiency of Arab and Canadian banks is evaluated, respectively, comparing the performance of each technique. In Sreekumar and Mahaoatra (2011), two DEA models are used to measure the efficiency of Indian business schools: CCR and BCC. Then, with the output of that evaluation, an ANN is trained to predict the outputs of those DMUs (Indian business schools) from which the authors do not have complete data. In Kwon, Lee & Roh (2016) a similar model is applied to evaluate Japanese electronic industries, and the ANN is trained to predict the required resources in larger hypothetical industries.

Methodology and Techniques

In the following a short theoretical introduction of the techniques used in the hybrid model is presented.

Data Envelopment Analysis

DEA is a method that supports a decision-making process by measuring the relative efficiency among so-called Decision Making Units (DMU). A DMU is a homogenous decision maker entity that consumes inputs in order to produce outputs. The relation between the consumption of inputs and the production of outputs is a measure of the efficiency of the internal process in a particular DMU. The higher this relation the more efficient is the DMU deemed (Dyson, 2001). It is possible to maximize this relation by either minimizing the inputs or increasing the outputs. Note that this technique does not require knowing the production function. The optimal weights correspond to units where the weights add to 1, also called best practice units (Moghaddas & Vaez-Ghasemi, 2017). The model can be thus said to be input oriented or output oriented, respectively. Three kinds of efficiency can be distinguished:

- **Technical Efficiency:** Reflects the ability of a DMU to obtain the maximal production level under a given use of resources.
- **Assignment Efficiency:** Reflects the ability of a DMU to use the resources in optimal proportions (given their prices).
- **Scale Efficiency:** It is defined according to the operation nature or scale of the DMU.

For determining the technical efficiency, DEA may consider two models: Constant Returns to Scale (CRS) and Variable return to Scale (VRS). The results of the DEA technique are obtained on the basis of the non-parametric linear programming model developed by Charnes, Cooper and Rhodes (1978), (CCR model). The model yields, in an input oriented approach, a value usually called θ, which is equal to 1 when the evaluated DMU_0 is efficient in relation to the other DMUs since it is not possible to find another DMU or a linear combination of DMUs that yield at least the same output as DMU_0 using less inputs. On the contrary, if $\theta<1$ DMU_0 is considered inefficient. Similarly, orienting the model to the outputs, a particular DMU will be efficient if $\theta=1$ and inefficient if $\theta>1$. Considering Figure 1, four DMUs can be identified (A, B, C and D), each one yielding an output (Y) using two inputs (X_1, X_2). The production plan is shown (X_1/Y, X_2/Y) for each of the mentioned DMUs. The identity isoquant of efficient DMUs is II'. Therefore, DMUs that are above this curve are inefficient. In this way, the capacity of the DMU to yield the maximal output from the given inputs is obtained comparing the observed value of each DMU with the optimal value located on the production frontier. In the figure, it can be seen that units B and D are technically inefficient since both could reduce the consumption of inputs and keep producing one unit of output. The inefficiency of these DMUs is given by the distances B'B and D'D, respectively. On the contrary, units A and C are technically efficient since they operate above the efficient isoquant. When a DMU has $\theta=1$, it is said to have *Farrel efficiency*. However, it can happen that in the solution process residual or slack variables may appear, indicating the presence of inputs or outputs that can be reduced or increased, respectively. A DMU is said to have *Pareto-Koopmans efficiency* when $\theta = 1$ and the value of slack variables is zero, and to be inefficient even if $\theta=1$ but the slack variables are nonzero. Figure 2, in which two inputs (X_1, X_2) and one output (y) are considered, intends to depict this situation. The DMUs labeled as A, B, C and D are technically efficient according to the condition of Farrell efficiency, since their corresponding θs are equal to 1 while DMU E is inefficient ($\theta < 1$). However, only DMUs B and C are technically efficient according to the Pareto-Koopmans condition, since A and D present slacks. The first one in input X_2 and the second one in X_1, indicating the amounts in which A and D should reduce their use of inputs. None of the DMUs present slacks in the output.

Figure 1. Farrel efficiency in data envelopment analysis

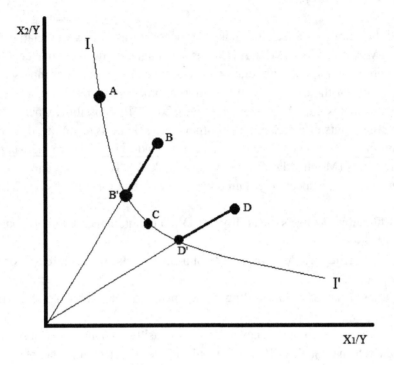

Figure 2. Pareto-Koopman efficiency in data envelopment analysis

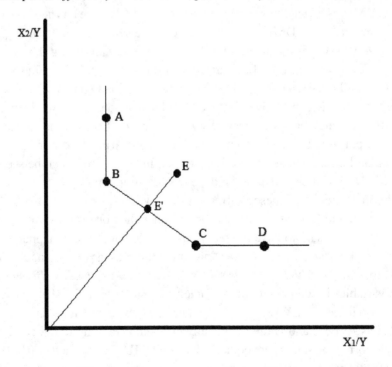

Artificial Neural Networks

ANNs are data processing systems inspired in biological neural networks, which are able to process information and learn from this. However, ANNs are, in practice, useful tools for signal processing and statistical analysis with independence of its original biological inspiration (Kar & Das 2016). Their main application is in the approximation of functions that are either unknown or too complex to be approximated with other methods (usually due to their strong non-linearity). A basic scheme of a neural network is shown in Figure 3. It consists of a network of highly interconnected units, called "neurons", which are grouped in layers (Olmeda, Bonilla, & Marco, 2002). In this kind of neural network three types of layers can be distinguished:

- **Input Layer:** It is the initial layer of the network, receiving the input data that will be processed by the network.
- **Output Layer:** The last part of the network yielding the output of the system.
- **Hidden Layers:** The inner layers where data is processed. They do not have connection with the outside. There can be one or more hidden layers depending on the complexity of the network (see Figure 3).

Figure 3. Composition and operation of an ANN

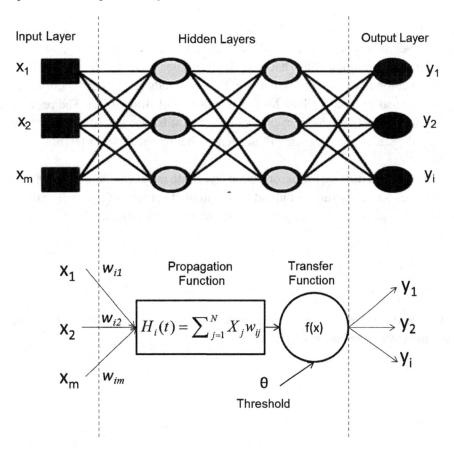

The number of neurons at each layer depends on the type of network, the complexity of the information to be handled, the decision of the designer and the function that the network will perform. All the neurons from one layer are connected to neurons in the next layer, every one of them receiving information from different source neurons. However, depending on the design, some networks can be connected with the predecessor layer (*feedback*) or with themselves *(recurrent)*. But even in the last case, output of each neuron is finally sent to the following layer. This flow of information is weighted by different synaptic weights: each w_{ij} relates neuron i with neuron j. All the information that arrives to a neuron is added up according a propagation rule. The most common propagation rule is the synaptic potential $H_i(t)$ (García Estévez, 2002) defined according to the following equation.

$$H_i(t) = \sum_{j=1}^{N} X_j w_{ij} \tag{1}$$

where:

$H_i(t)$ is the synaptic potential of neuron i at moment t.

X_j is the information obtained from source j.

w_{ij} is the synaptic weight of the source X_j and received by neuron i.

The synaptic potential is compare with a threshold value (θ). If the synaptic potential is equal or larger than (θ) the neuron becomes active and the information is passed to the following neurons after being modified by a Transfer Function. That is, if $Hi(t) \geq_\theta$ then $Yi(t) = f(H_i(t))$, where $Y_i(t)$ is the output information of neuron i at moment t. There are different kinds of transfer functions, being the most common step, linear and sigmoidal (Sanz Molina & Martín del Brío, 2006). The result of the transfer function on each neuron of the hidden layer is its output that is sent to neurons in the next layer. The configuration and the size of the network will influence directly the time for learning and the accuracy of desired results.

In a neural network with just two layers, one input layer with m entries (X1..., Xm) and an output $laye_r$ of n neurons, with the identity as transfer function, the output of neuron i (Yi(t)) will be the sum of weights times the entries plus a parameter μ that gives additional freedom to the model. See equation (2).

$$Y_i(t) = \sum_{j=1}^{n} w_{ji} X_j + \mu_i, \text{ for i} = 1, ..., m \tag{2}$$

The error will be the difference between the actual output of the network and the desired output. In a finite sample, the error is (equation (3)):

$$E\left(w_{ji}\right) = \frac{1}{2} \sum_{r=1}^{N} \sum_{i=1}^{m} \left(c_i^r - y_i^r\right)^2 \tag{3}$$

where:

c_i^r, is the desired output, the one that the network should obtain for the r –th pattern.

y_i^r, is the output value of the network for the r –th pattern.

The weights w_{ij} that minimize this error function should be chosen.

Designing an ANN

There are two phases:

- Training **Phase: A set** of training data or patterns is used to determine the synaptic weights of the neural network. They are calculated in an iterative manner, according to the training values, minimizing the error between the actual output and the desired output of the network.
- Testing **Phase: It is** possible that the model is overfitted to the training patterns, lacking the ability to predict new cases. To avoid this, it is advisable to use a second data source different from the training one, to control the learning process.

Neural networks are usually classified in terms of their corresponding algorithms or training models: on line or off line weights networks, unsupervised or supervised training networks.

The Hybrid Model

The hybrid model integrates DEA and an ANN to evaluate the efficiency of DMUs and propose alternative assignations of resources in order to make them more efficient. From here on, the model will be called DEA-ANN. A general scheme of our model is shown in Figure 4.

Initial Considerations

To select the inputs and outputs, the results in the literature on the development of sustainability indicators for IMSWM systems are summarized, classifying them according to their range of application. That is, some indicators can only be computed for consolidated IMSWM systems while others can calculated for systems with lower complexity. Indicators are classified in basic, intermediate and advanced as can be seen in Table 1.

Table 1. Classification of indicators

Classification of Indicators According to the Degree of Development of the MSW System	
Basic	Applicable to any MSW system.
Intermediate	Applicable to MSW systems with frequent recycling process of waste.
Advanced	Applicable to MSW systems with recovery, treatment and sale of recyclable materials.

This classification addresses the variety of approaches in the literature. For example, some of the oldest papers like Bahia (1996) and the criteria of the Environment Ministry of New Zealand (2000), just consider the amount of waste generated by a MSW system. On the other hand, in more recent documents, like (Secretary of Environment and Sustainable Development of Argentina, 2014) the indicators considered are the composition, the generation rate per capita of the MSW, and other basic and elementary indicators. In this chapter this is taken into account, considering the different municipal situations. There are towns that still use outdoors dumps for the final disposition of garbage whereas other municipalities already integrate the MSW system with recycling facilities. This way of classifying indicators can help municipalities, firstly, to assess the degree of development of their MSW system and, secondly, which strategy they should adopt for generating a sustainable development of their system. It is important to note that the absence of indicators for a municipality could indicates not only the lack of control of its system but also, worse yet, even the possible inexistence of that system.

We will focus on a model that can be applied mainly in municipalities that are at a basic level of development. Therefore, the parameters and indicators that are used are the ones present in the Basic classes, which are described below:

Inputs:
- **MSW Collection Vehicle Capacity (C):** Number of trucks that are used to perform the collection. A homogeneous size truck is considered for all the DMUs.
- **Collection Staff (S):** The amount of time needed to perform the collection of MSW, expressed as the sum of working hours in a week.
- **Frequency (F):** Number of times that MSW is collected in one site per week. It is related to the awareness and commitment of the society since it takes into account if the citizens take out trash in the right time and day, contributing to the organization of the collection through the minimization of the frequency.

Output:
- **Amount of Collected MSW (R):** Kilograms of MSW collected in a week.

Operation

The hybrid model DEA-ANN has three parts. Part 1 starts using DEA for determining the efficient DMUs. In this case a DMU is a municipality. The inputs are those indicated above: Collection capacity (C), Collection Staff (S), Collection Frequency (F) while the output is, as said, the amount of collected MSW (R). According to Dyson (2001) the amount of DMUs to be considered has to be equal or larger than the double of the number of inputs times the number of outputs, as shown in expression (4). Therefore, the minimal number of DMUs will be:

$$\text{Numbers of DMU} \geq 2\big(\text{Number of inputs}\big)\big(\text{Number of outputs}\big)$$
$$\text{Numbers of DMU} \geq 2\big(3\big)\big(1\big) \tag{4}$$
$$\text{Numbers of DMU} \geq 6$$

Figure 4. Hybrid model

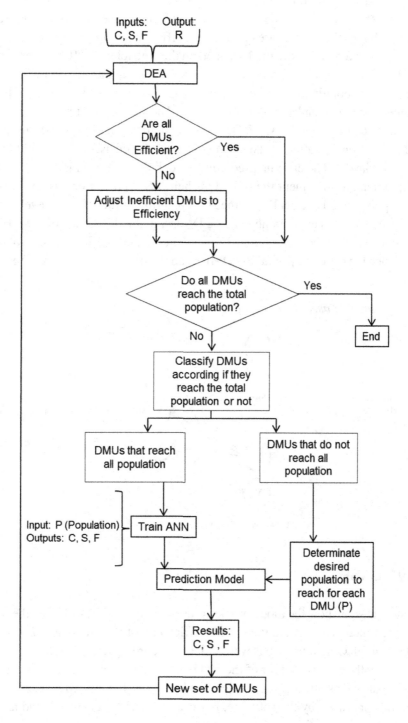

It is important to note that instead of DEA, ANN can be used to evaluate relative efficiency. However, DEA was chosen because in preliminary tests it produced more coherent and practical results. Other authors arrived to a similar conclusion (Tsai, Lin, Cheng, & Lin, 2009 and Athanassopoulos & Curram, 1996).

The CCR-CRS model was used because we assume constant returns to scale in the resources. The input orientation is used in order to reduce the amount of inputs used to collect the same amount of waste. According to the results, DMUs are classified in efficient and inefficient units. Then, the necessary adjustments suggested by DEA are implemented on the inefficient DMUs. After that, in the second part of the DEA-ANN model, each efficient DMU is analyzed taking into account whether the collection system reaches the whole population or if the municipal government is planning to expand the service, the extra requirement of the extended collection system. The systems that reach the whole population are considered as training units for the ANN. On those, desired population (P) was used as input and as outputs C, S and F. The configuration of the network (Figure 5) consists on one input layer, one hidden layer and three output layers. The ensuing prediction model allows estimating the necessary resources for the DMUs that intend to increment the spread of their MSW collection system. It is meant that up from the desired population (P) of each DMU, the ANN determines the efficient level of the variables C, S and F. Therefore, new DMUs are obtained. These DMUs, in the third stage of the DEA-ANN model, are analyzed again to evaluate their efficiency, using again the DEA technique and following the cycle of the procedure. Once the efficiency of all the DMUs and the desired spread is reached, the cycle ends.

Figure 5. ANN configuration used for our model

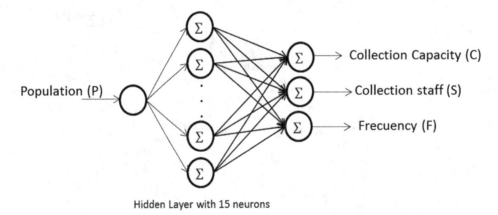

Hidden Layer with 15 neurons

ILLUSTRATIVE CASE

In order to validate and show how the model works a case of fifty DMUs, well over the minimal number of six DMUs, is presented. To evaluate the relative efficiency of the units the *DEA-Solver Pro 5.0* of Microsoft Excel was used. Only four DMUs were efficient according to the Pareto-Koopmans condition. Tables 2, 3 and 4 show the results for four of the 50 DMUs that were analyzed. Table 2 shows that only DMU 2 has been identified as efficient with value $\theta = 1$. The inefficient DMUs were corrected according to the indications produced by the software. For example, DMU 21, which had as initial values C = 19, S = 30, F = 10 and an initial $\theta = 0.62$, has to decrease its resources to C = 12, S = 15 and F = 7 in order to be efficient (Table 3). After that, the spread of the MSW collection system was analyzed identifying the DMUs that have an expansion project. The efficient DMUs without expansion plans are used to train the ANN. In the example of Table 3, these DMUs correspond to DMU 1 and DMU 2. For the design and evaluation of the ANN MatLab® with the Levenberg-Marquardt transfer function was used. In the learning and training process of the ANN, the offline weights and supervised method were used. Considering that fifty DMUs are not enough to produce coherent results in an ANN, noise was introduced on the amount of inputs. Therefore, the network ends up evaluating 500 DMUs, yielding better results. Out of the group of efficient DMUs that reach all the desired population, 70% was used for training, 15% for validating and 15% for testing the network. The number of neurons at the hidden layer was sixteen, a number obtained after numerous tests, seeking to minimize the Mean Squared Error. As was mentioned before, larger numbers of neurons in the hidden layer give the network more flexibility because the network has more parameters it can optimize. An important thing is to increase the layer size gradually. If the hidden layer is done too large, might cause the problem to be under-characterized and the network must optimize more parameters than there are data vectors to constrain these parameters.

The network underwent several training phases until the MSE could no longer be improved. Each training phase was stopped at one thousand iterations or when the validation error of the network (threshold) reduced below 0.01. The results can be observed on Figure 6 and Figure 7. In the first one can be seen how the MSE is reduced until epoch number 580, iteration at which the validation performance reached a minimum (MSE = 0,003202). The training continued for six more iterations before the training stopped. This figure does not indicate any major problems with the training. The validation and test curves are very similar. It is important to know that if the test curve had increased significantly before the validation curve increased, then it is possible that some overfitting might have occurred. The Figure 7 shows the relationship between the outputs obtained with the trained ANN (output values) and the targets values (original outputs) for each subset. The three plots represent the training, validation, and testing data. The dashed line in each plot represents the perfect result – outputs = targets. The solid line represents the best-fit linear regression line between outputs and targets. The R-value is an indication of the relationship between the outputs and targets. If R = 1, this indicates that there is an exact linear relationship between outputs and targets. If R is close to zero, then there is no linear relationship between outputs and targets. For this example, the training data indicates a good fit. The validation and test results also show R-values that greater than 0.97. The scatter plot is helpful in showing that certain data points have poor fits.

After this, the values of resources necessary for DMUs with projected expansion were predicted. According to our example, DMUs 14 and 21 intend to grow 25% and 18% respectively, obtaining the values of C, S and F shown in Table 3. Finally, with the new values for the projected DMUs, the efficient evaluation with DEA was repeated. The values are reported in Table 4. The efficiency parameter of the DMUs with projected expansion is higher to 0.9 (DMU 14).

Table 2. Data obtained from the tests at stage one, corresponding to the DEA model

DMU	DEA-CCR-CRS				
	Input			Output	Efficiency
	C (Units)	S (Hours)	F (Times per week)	MSW (Kgs per Week)	
1	16	864	5	3492	0,65
2	12	528	5	5379	1,00
14	12	1104	9	4562	0,70
21	19	1440	10	5615	0,62

The cycle of the model has to be repeated until all the efficient DMUs considering their potential for expansion are reached. For example, the next step is to correct DMUs 1 and 14, analyzing their potential for expansion and, in case that this is not intended, the cycle ends.

Table 3. Data used and results at stage two (ANN)

| DMU | Artificial Neural Network | | | | | | | | | |
| | Output for Training | | | Population | Projection | Input for Training | Input Prediction | Output Prediction | | |
	C (Units)	S (Hours)	F (Times per Week)					C (Units)	S (Hours)	F (Times per Week)
1	8	384	4	4656	1	4656	-	-	-	-
2	12	528	5	7172	1	7172	-	-	-	-
14	9	768	7	6083	1,25	-	7899	10	432	8
21	12	720	7	7487	1,18	-	8835	5	816	10

Figure 6. Evolution of the mean squared error

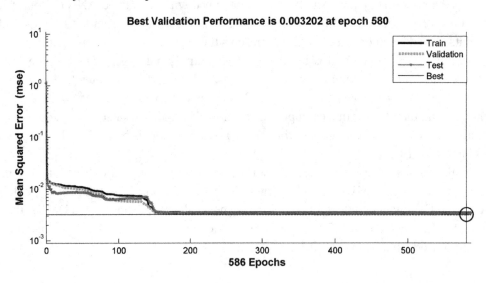

Table 4. Results of the application of the stage three of the model

| DMU | DEA II | | | | |
| | Input | | | Output | Efficiency |
	C (Units)	S (Hours)	F (Times per Week)	MSW (Kgs per Week)	
1	8	384	4	3492	0,88
2	12	528	5	5379	1,00
14	10	432	8	5924	0,92
21	5	816	10	6626	1,00

Figure 7. Correlation between the original outputs (target) and the outputs obtained by the ANN trained for each subset

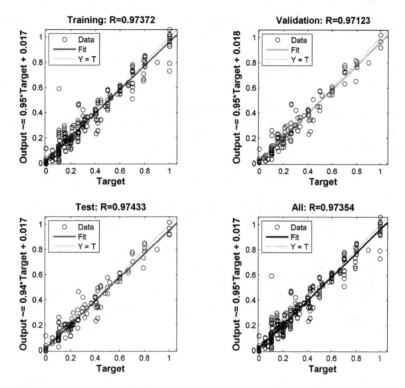

APPLICATION CASE

While the previous section considered a toy case that provided a testbed for the model, now a real-world case is considered that intends to analyze the efficiency of 21 MSW systems in the Southwest of the province of Buenos Aires in Argentina. Having not been authorized to disclose the names of the respective municipalities, numbers to distinguish them are used instead (Table 5). The relative scarcity of data points is a reflection of the rather low degree of development of these MSWs. The respective municipalities are currently updating their data collection systems in parallel to the upgrade of their waste disposal systems. The data for the first stage of the procedure (the C, S and F variables) are approximated, collected in interviews or through e-mail inquiries to the people in charge of the MSWs. As it is to be expected, the current systems do not respond to any quantitative optimization analysis. They are the ad-hoc result of decisions made on the basis of the expertise of the people of the towns under consideration.

The DEA-ANN model is run again starting with the assessment of relative efficiency through a DEA analysis using MS Excel DEA-Solver Pro 5.0. From the 21 DMUs the only Pareto-Koopmans efficient ones are DMUs 4 and 7. Figure 8 shows the relation between the number of inhabitants in a town and the degree of efficiency of its respective MSW system. It can be seen that smaller (population wise) DMUs are more inefficient. Moreover, the efficiency of the MSW system tends to grow with the population it serves. The relation between the output and the population for DMUs of efficiency 1 yields 6.3 and 6.02 kg per inhabitant per week for DMUs 4 and 7 respectively. Notice that these amounts are not the highest in the lot, which are the yield of DMUs 2 and 18 (6.7 kg.). The efficient DMUs use large amounts of resources (C, S, F), being most noticeable the frequency of collection of 17 times a week in DMU 7. Finally, it can be noted that 14 DMUs (66.7% of the group) are highly inefficient, with θ less than 0.45: DMUs 8, 14, 20, 5, 13, 11, 1, 18, 16, 15, 6, 19, 9 and 3.

Figure 8. Efficiency vs. population: stage one of the procedure

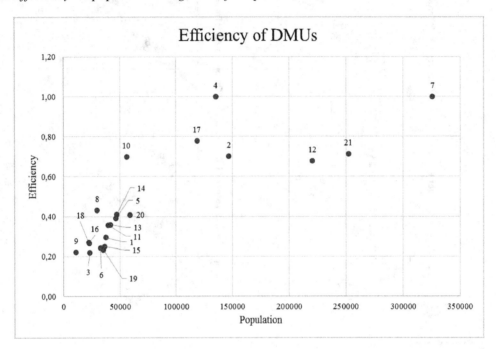

After obtaining the aforementioned first results, inputs were adjusted in order to train the ANN (Table 6), using again MatLab® and a Levenberg-Marquardt transfer function. Introducing noise to increase the number of DMUs 168 artificial DMUs were generated. From those, 70% are used in the training phase, while in the next phase 15% of the DMUs are used for validation and the rest in the test procedure. The number of neurons in the hidden layer of the ANN, obtained through tests aimed to reduce the quadratic noise, is 20. Each of the rounds of error reduction involved more than 1000 iterations unless the error fell below the threshold of 0.01. Figure 9 shows the reduction of MSE and Figure 10 the regression between the original output values (the target) and the results of running the trained ANN for each of the rounds. Again, the R- value is around 0.9.

The values for DMUs with expansion plans are reported in Table 7 and with them at hand the DEA analysis is run again. Unlike in the toy example, the degree of efficiency in these DMUs is quite irregular, from $\theta = 1$ (DMUs 3, 9, 11, 12, 13, 16, 20) to $\theta = 0.71$ (DMU 8), arguably as a result of the scarcity of DMUs. Figure 11 shows the efficiency degrees in terms of the population in towns were the municipality is planning an expansion. Both variables seem now rather unrelated albeit the lower efficiency values seem associated still to less populated towns.

The variability in the requirement of resources can also be detected. For instance, DMU 2, to achieve a 20% growth in the coverage of its MSW has to use one truck more and run a Schedule of 14 collection rounds a week, without increasing the total number of hours, achieving an efficiency rate of $\theta = 0,93$ in stage three of the procedure. On the other hand, for DMU 20 to increase a 20% its coverage, it needs only an additional truck, getting a total amount of waste of 68431kg a week and $\theta = 1$ in the third stage of the procedure.

Table 5. Application case: inputs, outputs and efficiency at stage one of the DEA-ANN model

DMU	DEA-CCR-CRS				
	Input			Output	Efficiency
	C (Units)	S (Hours)	F (Times per Week)	MSW (Kgs per Week)	
1	8	720	7	216800	0,29
2	11	2112	12	986967	0,70
3	7	960	5	138180	0,22
4	13	1440	6	853209	1,00
5	5	1056	8	273362	0,39
6	5	864	10	170060	0,24
7	14	1920	17	1959872	1,00
8	3	384	8	168740	0,43
9	2	384	4	62200	0,22
10	7	384	11	273714	0,70
11	5	720	8	250047	0,36
12	15	1920	17	1327350	0,68
13	5	768	12	251215	0,36
14	7	672	9	281971	0,41
15	5	672	8	171139	0,25
16	3	432	9	111573	0,27
17	10	1536	8	770264	0,78
18	4	768	8	150932	0,27
19	5	912	8	163641	0,23
20	6	864	12	342151	0,41
21	15	1824	15	1253236	0,71

Table 6. Application case: stage two of the DEA-ANN model

DMU	Output for Training			Population	Projection	Input Training	Input Prediction	Output Prediction		
	C (Units)	S (Hours)	F (Times per Week)					C (Units)	S (Hours)	F (Times per Week)
1	2	192	2	37770	1	37770	-	-	-	-
2	8	1008	8	146870	1,2	-	176244	9	1008	14
3	2	192	1	23500	1,1	-	25850	3	192	1
4	13	1440	6	135430	1,15	-	155745	13	1440	8
5	2	288	3	46490	1,3	-	60437	4	288	3
6	2	192	2	32830	1,3	-	42679	2	192	2
7	14	1920	17	325560	1	325560	-	-	-	-
8	2	192	2	29760	1	29760	-	-	-	-
9	1	96	1	10970	1,4	-	15358	2	96	2
10	2	288	3	55860	1,1	-	61446	4	288	3
11	2	240	2	39690	1	39690	-	-	-	-
12	10	1296	12	220490	1,2	-	264588	10	240	15
13	2	240	2	41730	1	41730	-	-	-	-
14	2	288	3	47390	1,15	-	54499	2	288	3
15	2	192	2	36490	1	36490	-	-	-	-
16	1	96	1	22770	1,4	-	31878	2	96	2
17	8	960	6	118320	1	118320	-	-	-	-
18	1	144	2	22460	1	22460	-	-	-	-
19	1	192	2	35420	1,1	-	38962	2	192	2
20	3	336	3	58890	1,2	-	70668	4	336	3
21	10	1296	11	252160	1	252160	-	-	-	-

FUTURE RESEARCH DIRECTIONS

In order to improve the results in the analysis of the application case further work is needed. For instance, the number of DMUs needs to be increased, by collecting data from more municipalities. For several reasons this is complicated, both for the institutional limitations in provincial towns and the lack of appropriate social contexts for the improvement of wage management systems. Another extension involves the addition of alternative methodologies, like Zellner & Huang (1962) Seemingly Unrelated Regression (SUR) or Second Stage of DEA, in order to associate the variation in operating efficiency with various exogenous variables capturing features of the operating environment which are not under the control of the management of the system. This incorporation allows decomposing operational inefficiency into an environmental component and a residual component reflecting managerial inefficiency, as recently prescribed in the literature (see Khan, Khan, Zaman & Arif, 2014; and Fu, Sharma, Wang, & Tang, 2017). Along these lines, other factors can be considered, like population density, the state of the collection routes, and the willingness of citizens to collaborate. Moreover, the application of the Sto-

Figure 9. Application case: evolution of the mean squared error

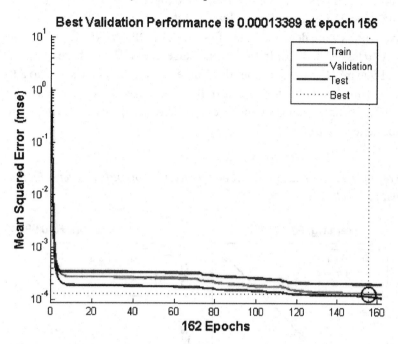

chastic Frontiers approach (Kumbhakar & Lovell, 2003; Griffiths & Hajargasht, 2016: Vidoli, Cardillo, Fusco & Canello, 2016) can contribute to the analysis of the results, identifying potential causes of the inefficiencies be they due to incorrect management decisions or other conditions. Besides, if data could be collected in real-time, Dynamic DEA could be applied (Fare and Grosskopf, 1996; Tone & Tsutsui, 2014; Cui, Wei & Li, 2016) in order to evaluate the overall efficiency over the entire observed period, the dynamic changes in efficiency and the dynamic changes of divisional efficiency, among other features.

CONCLUSION

Social and governmental interest on the management of MSWs has grown in the last years. This is mainly due to the large amount of resources that governments spend dealing with these systems and the high risks involved, for the society and the environment, in their incorrect management. Data Envelopment Analysis (DEA) and Artificial Neural Networks (ANN) are two useful and practical tools to evaluate efficiency and to predict values that cannot be approximated by simple functions. In this chapter a hybrid model for the evaluation of the efficiency and the prediction of better ways of spending resources in IMSWMs is presented, using in a combined way DEA and an ANN. The procedure, called DEA-ANN, has three stages. The first one classifies Decision Making Units (DMUs) according to their efficiency by running a DEA based on a constant returns model (CCR-CRS). The second stage adjusts the inefficient DMUs to latter use them jointly with the efficient DMUs in order to train an ANN. This ANN predicts the resources needed by municipalities in order to expand their IMSWMs. The last stage consists on evaluating the efficiency of new generated DMUs, resulting from the prediction of the ANN. This workflow has to be repeated cyclically until all total efficient DMUs, even considering potential expansions, are gathered. In this work an illustrative example of 50 DMUs was presented as well as a real-world case involving 21 towns in the southwest of the province of Buenos Aires, Argentina. In the latter case, 2 efficient units were detected in the first stage of DEA-ANN as well as 14 with a rather low degree of efficiency (θ less than 0.45). In the second stage, the training phase of the ANN yield reasonable R and Minimal Squared Error values, but the scarce quantity of DMUs lead to a lack of accuracy in the predicted values. This was in the third phase of the procedure, since the relative efficiency obtained is low (around $\theta=0.7$). The intention is to improve over these results by gathering more information and applying more precise techniques.

Figure 10. Application case: correlation between the original outputs (target) and the outputs obtained by the ANN trained for each subset

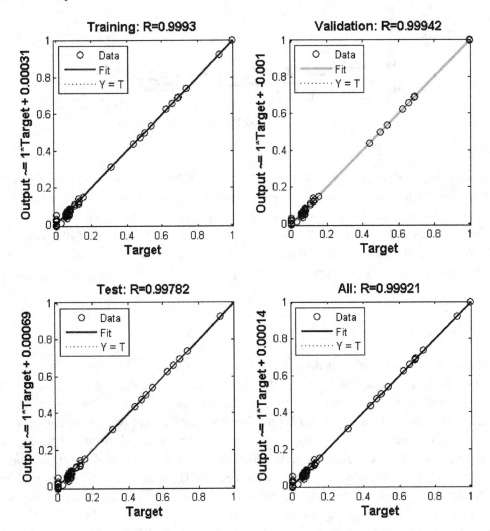

Table 7. Application case: stage three of the DEA-ANN model

DMU	DEA II				
	Input			Output	Efficiency
	C (units)	S (hours)	F (times per week)	MSW (Kgs per week)	
1	2	192	2	216800	0,91
2	9	1008	14	1184361	0,93
3	3	192	1	151998	1,00
4	13	1440	8	981191	0,88
5	4	288	3	355371	0,97
6	2	192	2	221078	0,93
7	14	1920	17	1959872	0,99
8	2	192	2	168740	0,71
9	2	96	2	87080	1,00
10	4	288	3	301086	0,82
11	2	240	2	250047	1,00
12	10	1296	15	1592820	1,00
13	2	240	2	251215	1,00
14	2	288	3	324267	1,00
15	2	192	2	171139	0,72
16	2	96	2	156203	1,00
17	8	960	6	770264	0,94
18	1	144	2	150932	0,93
19	2	192	2	180006	0,76
20	4	336	3	410582	1,00
21	10	1296	11	1253236	0,94

Figure 11. Efficiency vs. population: first stage of the model

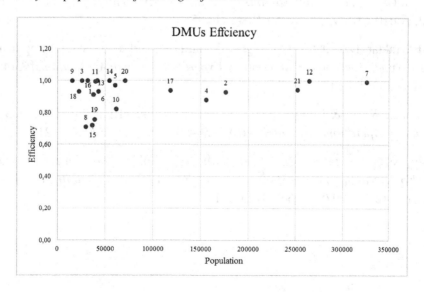

REFERENCES

Acero Albarracín, R. (2012). Formulación de los criterios para la evaluación de planes de gestión integral de residuos sólidos en Colombia [Bachelor's thesis]. Universidad Libre.

Ali, M., Yadav, A., Anis, M., & Sharma, P. (2015). Multiple criteria decision analysis using DEA-TOPSIS method for hazardous waste management: A case study of the USA. *International Journal of Managing Information Technology*, 7(3), 1–17. doi:10.5121/ijmit.2015.7301

Amato, F., López, A., Peña-Méndez, E. M., Vaňhara, P., Hampl, A., & Havel, J. (2013). Artificial neural networks in medical diagnosis. *J Appl Biomed*, 11(2), 47–58. doi:10.2478/v10136-012-0031-x

Athanassopoulos, A. D., & Curram, S. P. (1996). A comparison of data envelopment analysis and artificial neural networks as tools for assessing the efficiency of decision making units. *The Journal of the Operational Research Society*, 47(8), 1000–1016. doi:10.1057/jors.1996.127

Aziz, H. A., & Abu Amr, S. S. (2016). Introduction to Solid Waste and Its Management. In H. Aziz & S. Amr (Eds.), *Control and Treatment of Landfill Leachate for Sanitary Waste Disposal* (pp. 1–23). Hershey, PA: IGI Global. doi:10.4018/978-1-4666-9610-5.ch001

Baba, S. J. O., Purwanto, D. E. A., & Sunoko, H. R. (2015). Evaluation of Municipal Solid Waste Management System (Case Study: Graha Padma Estate, Semarang). *Science Journal of Environmental Engineering Research*.

Bahia, S. R. (1996). Sustainability indicators for a waste management approach. In Proceedings of Congreso Interamericano de Ingeniería Sanitaria y Ambiental, 25, 1-11.

Batinic, B., Vukmirovic, S., Vujic, G., Stanisavljevic, N., Ubavin, D., & Vumirovic, G. (2011). Using ANN model to determine future waste characteristics in order to achieve specific waste management targets-case study of Serbia. *Journal of Scientific and Industrial Research*, 70, 513–518.

Cebi, S., Kahraman, C., & Kaya, I. (2012). Soft Computing and Computational Intelligent Techniques in the Evaluation of Emerging Energy Technologies. In P. Vasant, N. Barsoum, & J. Webb (Eds.), *Innovation in Power, Control, and Optimization: Emerging Energy Technologies* (pp. 164–197). Hershey, PA: IGI Global. doi:10.4018/978-1-61350-138-2.ch005

Çelebi, D., & Bayraktar, D. (2008). An integrated neural network and data envelopment analysis for supplier evaluation under incomplete information. *Expert Systems with Applications*, 35(4), 1698–1710. doi:10.1016/j.eswa.2007.08.107

Charnes, A., Cooper, W. W., & Rhodes, E. (1978). Measuring the efficiency of decision making units. *European Journal of Operational Research*, 2(6), 429–444. doi:10.1016/0377-2217(78)90138-8

Chatsiwa, J., Mujere, N., & Maiyana, A. B. (2016). Municipal Solid Waste Management. In U. Akkucuk (Ed.), *Handbook of Research on Waste Management Techniques for Sustainability* (pp. 19–43). Hershey, PA: IGI Global. doi:10.4018/978-1-4666-9723-2.ch002

Chávez, A. P., Armijo-De Vega, C., Calderón-De La Barca, N., Leyva-Aguilera, J. C., & Ojeda-Benítez, S. (2011). Diseño de un instrumento de evaluación para los programas de manejo de residuos domiciliarios. *Investigación ambiental Ciencia y política pública, 3*(1).

Cui, Q., Wei, Y. M., & Li, Y. (2016). Exploring the impacts of the EU ETS emission limits on airline performance via the Dynamic Environmental DEA approach. *Applied Energy, 183*, 984–994. doi:10.1016/j.apenergy.2016.09.048

Dyson, R. G., Allen, R., Camanho, A. S., Podinovski, V. V., Sarrico, C. S., & Shale, E. A. (2001). Pitfalls and protocols in DEA. *European Journal of Operational Research, 132*(2), 245–259. doi:10.1016/S0377-2217(00)00149-1

Esfe, M. H., Saedodin, S., Bahiraei, M., Toghraie, D., Mahian, O., & Wongwises, S. (2014). Thermal conductivity modeling of MgO/EG nanofluids using experimental data and artificial neural network. *Journal of Thermal Analysis and Calorimetry, 118*(1), 287–294. doi:10.100710973-014-4002-1

Fare, R., & Grosskopf, S. (1996). *Intertemporal production frontiers*. Dordrecht: Kluwer. doi:10.1007/978-94-009-1816-0

Feng, L., & Zhang, J. (2014). Application of artificial neural networks in tendency forecasting of economic growth. *Economic Modelling, 40*, 76–80. doi:10.1016/j.econmod.2014.03.024

Fu, L., Sharma, R. P., Wang, G., & Tang, S. (2017). Modelling a system of nonlinear additive crown width models applying seemingly unrelated regression for Prince Rupprecht larch in northern China. *Forest Ecology and Management, 386*, 71–80. doi:10.1016/j.foreco.2016.11.038

Garcia Estévez, P. (2002). Aplicaciones de las Redes Neuronales en finanzas. *Documentos de trabajo de la Facultad de Ciencias Económicas y Empresariales*, (5), 1-42.

Gören, S. (2015). Sustainable Waste Management. In U. Akkucuk (Ed.), *Handbook of Research on Developing Sustainable Value in Economics, Finance, and Marketing* (pp. 141–156). Hershey, PA: IGI Global; doi:10.4018/978-1-4666-6635-1.ch009

Government of Chile, National Commission for the Environment. (2001). *Indicadores para gestión municipal de residuos sólidos*. Chile: Santiago de Chile.

Griffiths, W. E., & Hajargasht, G. (2016). Some models for stochastic frontiers with endogeneity. *Journal of Econometrics, 190*(2), 341–348. doi:10.1016/j.jeconom.2015.06.012

Huang, Y. F., Baetz, B. W., Huang, G. H., & Liu, L. (2002). Violation analysis for solid waste management systems: An interval fuzzy programming approach. *Journal of Environmental Management, 65*(4), 431–446. doi:10.1016/S0301-4797(02)90566-9 PMID:12369404

Inter-American Association of Sanitary and Environmental Engineering (AIDIS) & International Development Research Center. (IDRC). (2005). Directrices para la gestión integrada y sostenible de residuos sólidos urbanos en América Latina y el Caribe. Sao Paulo, Brasil.

Jafarzadeh, S., & hashempour, s. (2015). Optimization and forecasting of urban solid waste management by artificial neural networks. In *Proceedings* of *International Conference on Management and Humanities 2015*.

Jahandideh, S., Jahandideh, S., Asadabadi, E. B., Askarian, M., Movahedi, M. M., Hosseini, S., & Jahandideh, M. (2009). The use of artificial neural networks and multiple linear regression to predict rate of medical waste generation. *Waste Management (New York, N.Y.)*, *29*(11), 2874–2879. doi:10.1016/j.wasman.2009.06.027 PMID:19643591

Kar, P., & Das, A. (2016). Artificial Neural Networks and Learning Techniques. In P. Samui (Ed.), *Handbook of Research on Advanced Computational Techniques for Simulation-Based Engineering* (pp. 227–251). Hershey, PA: IGI Global. doi:10.4018/978-1-4666-9479-8.ch009

Kasemsap, K. (2017). Environmental Management and Waste Management: Principles and Applications. In U. Akkucuk (Ed.), *Ethics and Sustainability in Global Supply Chain Management* (pp. 26–49). Hershey, PA: IGI Global. doi:10.4018/978-1-5225-2036-8.ch002

Khan, M. A., Khan, M. Z., Zaman, K., & Arif, M. (2014). Global estimates of energy-growth nexus: Application of seemingly unrelated regressions. *Renewable & Sustainable Energy Reviews*, *29*, 63–71. doi:10.1016/j.rser.2013.08.088

Kumbhakar, S. C., & Lovell, C. K. (2003). *Stochastic frontier analysis*. Cambridge university press.

Kuo, R. J., Wang, Y. C., & Tien, F. C. (2010). Integration of artificial neural network and MADA methods for green supplier selection. *Journal of Cleaner Production*, *18*(12), 1161–1170. doi:10.1016/j.jclepro.2010.03.020

Kwon, H. B., Lee, J., & Roh, J. J. (2016). Best performance modeling using complementary DEA-ANN approach: Application to Japanese electronics manufacturing firms. Benchmarking. *International Journal (Toronto, Ont.)*, *23*(3), 704–721.

Liu, Z. F., Liu, X. P., Wang, S. W., & Liu, G. F. (2002). Recycling strategy and a recyclability assessment model based on an artificial neural network. *Journal of Materials Processing Technology*, *129*(1), 500–506. doi:10.1016/S0924-0136(02)00625-8

Mazhar, M. I., Kara, S., & Kaebernick, H. (2007). Remaining life estimation of used components in consumer products: Life cycle data analysis by Weibull and artificial neural networks. *Journal of Operations Management*, *25*(6), 1184–1193. doi:10.1016/j.jom.2007.01.021

Miidla, P. (2013). Data Envelopment Analysis in Environmental Technologies. In *Industrial Engineering: Concepts, Methodologies, Tools, and Applications* (pp. 625–642). Hershey, PA: IGI Global; doi:10.4018/978-1-4666-1945-6.ch036

Ministry of Environment. Wellington, New Zealand. (2000). Environmental Performance Indicators. Confirmed indicators for waste, hazardous waste and contaminated sites, Signposts for sustainability. Wellington, New Zealand.

Moghaddas, Z., & Vaez-Ghasemi, M. (2017). Ranking Models in Data Envelopment Analysis Technique. In F. Lotfi, S. Najafi, & H. Nozari (Eds.), *Data Envelopment Analysis and Effective Performance Assessment* (pp. 265–311). Hershey, PA: IGI Global; doi:10.4018/978-1-5225-0596-9.ch007

Mostafa, M. M. (2009). Modeling the efficiency of top Arab banks: A DEA–neural network approach. *Expert Systems with Applications*, *36*(1), 309–320. doi:10.1016/j.eswa.2007.09.001

Olmeda, I., Bonilla, M., & Marco, P. (2002). *Redes Neuronales Artificiales: Predicción de la Volatilidad del Tipo de Cambio de da Peseta (No. 2002-08). Instituto Valenciano de Investigaciones Económicas.* SA: Ivie.

Pires, A., Martinho, G., & Chang, N. B. (2011). Solid waste management in European countries: A review of systems analysis techniques. *Journal of Environmental Management, 92*(4), 1033–1050. doi:10.1016/j.jenvman.2010.11.024 PMID:21194829

Salman, D., Tarkhan, F., Mohamed, N., Farouk, A., & Kamal, D. (2015). How Can We Achieve Sustainability?: Lessons from Developed Countries. In U. Akkucuk (Ed.), *Handbook of Research on Developing Sustainable Value in Economics, Finance, and Marketing* (pp. 205–217). Hershey, PA: IGI Global. doi:10.4018/978-1-4666-6635-1.ch012

Sanz Molina, A., & Martín del Brío, B. (2006). *Redes Neuronales Y Sistemas Borrosos* (p. 436). Madrid, Spain: Ra-Ma, Librera y Editorial Microinformática.

Schejtman, L., & Cellucci, M. (2014). *Gestión integral de residuos sólidos urbanos. Políticas municipales que promueven la sustentabilidad. Serie Buenas prácticas municipales.* Buenos Aires: CIPECC.

Secretary of Environment and Sustainable Development of the Argentine Nation. (2014). Sistema de indicadores de Desarrollo Sostenible (7th ed.). Ciudad autónoma de Buenos Aires.

Secretary of Environment and Sustainable Development of the Argentine Nation. (2016). *Mapas Críticos Gestión de Residuos.* Ciudad autónoma de Buenos Aires.

Sreekumar, S., & Mahapatra, S. S. (2011). Performance modeling of Indian business schools: A DEA-neural network approach. *Benchmarking: An International Journal, 18*(2), 221–239. doi:10.1108/14635771111121685

Tone, K., & Tsutsui, M. (2014). Dynamic DEA with network structure: A slacks-based measure approach. *Omega, 42*(1), 124–131. doi:10.1016/j.omega.2013.04.002

Tsai, M. C., Lin, S. P., Cheng, C. C., & Lin, Y. P. (2009). The consumer loan default predicting model–An application of DEA–DA and neural network. *Expert Systems with Applications, 36*(9), 11682–11690. doi:10.1016/j.eswa.2009.03.009

Vidoli, F., Cardillo, C., Fusco, E., & Canello, J. (2016). Spatial nonstationarity in the stochastic frontier model: An application to the Italian wine industry. *Regional Science and Urban Economics, 61*, 153–164. doi:10.1016/j.regsciurbeco.2016.10.003

Villavicencio, G. J. D. & Didonet, S. R. (2009). Eco-eficiencia en la gestión de residuos municipales en Catalunya. *Revista de Administração da UFSM, 1*(2).

Wu, D. (2009). Supplier selection: A hybrid model using DEA, decision tree and neural network. *Expert Systems with Applications, 36*(5), 9105–9112. doi:10.1016/j.eswa.2008.12.039

Wu, D. D., Yang, Z., & Liang, L. (2006). Using DEA-neural network approach to evaluate branch efficiency of a large Canadian bank. *Expert Systems with Applications, 31*(1), 108–115. doi:10.1016/j.eswa.2005.09.034

Zade, M. J. G., & Noori, R. (2007). Prediction of municipal solid waste generation by use of artificial neural network: A case study of Mashhad.

Zellner, A., & Huang, D. S. (1962). Further properties of efficient estimators for seemingly unrelated regression equations. *International Economic Review*, *3*(3), 300–313. doi:10.2307/2525396

Zharkov, S. (2016). Assessment and Enhancement of the Energy Supply System Efficiency with Emphasis on the Cogeneration and Renewable as Main Directions for Fuel Saving. In P. Vasant & N. Voropai (Eds.), *Sustaining Power Resources through Energy Optimization and Engineering* (pp. 1–25). Hershey, PA: IGI Global. doi:10.4018/978-1-4666-9755-3.ch001

ENDNOTE

[1] The Delphi method consists in collecting data from a panel of experts and finding a consensus through questionnaires and exchange of information among them. In this particular case, the experts are acquisition managers.

This research was previously published in the Handbook of Research on Emergent Applications of Optimization Algorithms; pages 206-231, copyright year 2018 by Business Science Reference (an imprint of IGI Global).

Chapter 27
Prediction of L10 and Leq Noise Levels Due to Vehicular Traffic in Urban Area Using ANN and Adaptive Neuro-Fuzzy Interface System (ANFIS) Approach

Vilas K Patil
Sardar Patel College of Engineering, Mumbai, India

P.P. Nagarale
Sardar Patel College of Engineering, Mumbai, India

ABSTRACT

Recently in urban areas, road traffic noise is one of the primary sources of noise pollution. Variation in noise level is impacted by the synthesis of traffic and the percentage of heavy vehicles. Presentation to high noise levels may cause serious impact on the health of an individual or community residing near the roadside. Thus, predicting the vehicular traffic noise level is important. The present study aims at the formulation of regression, an artificial neural network (ANN) and an adaptive neuro-fuzzy interface system (ANFIS) model using the data of observed noise levels, traffic volume, and average speed of vehicles for the prediction of L10 and Leq. Measured noise levels are compared to the noise levels predicted by the experimental model. It is observed that the ANFIS approach is more superior when compared to output given by regression and an ANN model. Also, there exists a positive correlation between measured and predicted noise levels. The proposed ANFIS model can be utilized as a tool for traffic direction and planning of new roads in zones of similar land use pattern.

DOI: 10.4018/978-1-6684-2408-7.ch027

1. INTRODUCTION

In recent times, there is an exponential rise in the number of vehicles on the roads which leads to an increase in the vehicular traffic noise levels (Choudhary & Gokhale, 2018). The high noise levels have been appeared to influence the health and prosperity of an impressive segment of society, particularly those living in the nearness of highways as well as urban roads (De Coensel, Brown, & Tomerini, 2016). In India, the transportation part is developing quickly and the quantity of vehicles on Indian roads is expanding at a quick rate prompting overcrowded roads and noise pollution (Konbattulwar, Velaga, Jain & Sharmila, 2016; Leung, Chau, Tang & Xu, 2017). The traffic situation is regularly not the same as different nations because of the prevalence of an assortment of bikes which has multiplied in the most recent decade and structures a noteworthy lump of the heterogeneous volume of vehicles (Shukla, Jain, Parida & Srivastava, 2009). The distinctive kinds of vehicles handling on the Indian roads incorporate bikes, three-wheelers, cycle rickshaws, animal trucks, autos, trucks, transports and horticultural tractor trailers (Ramírez & Domínguez, 2013). The presence of a wide range of vehicles on the roads, topology of the roads and crossing points, pavement surfaces, driving propensities for individuals and (Givargis & Karimi, 2010) huge number of vehicles because of the regularly expanding populace make the traffic conditions and traffic attributes very extraordinary and impossible to miss to the Indian sub-landmass (Chang, Lin, Yang, Bao & Chan, 2012; Rajkumara & Gowda, 2008). The noise pollution principles have been characterized by the administration of India under 'the noise pollution (direction and control) rules'. Numerous scientists have detailed diverse noise expectation models for various nations, in view of traffic flow data and field estimation of different roadway noise descriptors (Delany, Harland, Hood & Scholes, 1976). Albeit, distinctive specialists have created diverse noise forecast models to suit neighborhood traffic conditions, due to heterogeneous nature of traffic flow on Indian roads same model can't be utilized as it is for Indian traffic conditions (Nedic, Despotovic, Cvetanovic, Despotovic & Babic, 2014).

This record contains the endorsed noise level limits in various business and private zones amid day and evening time (Di et al., 2018). Additionally, the kind of vehicles, synthesis of traffic and type of road surface and status of the road surface can vary from nation to nation (Dai, He, Mu, Xu & Wu, 2014). Nashik city has been announced as one of the quickest developing urban areas in India (Brown, & De Coensel, 2018). The fast development of the city has resulted into an expansion in the vehicle populace (Cho, & Mun, 2008). In this work, three diverse soft computing methods have been utilized for model development, by considering the factors (Kalaiselvi, & Ramachandraiah, 2016) as traffic volume, the percentage of heavy vehicles and average speed of vehicles in Nashik city, accepting it as a representative set of the traffic conditions in India (Steinbach & Altinsoy, 2019). The experimental values of these variables along with the equivalent continuous sound pressure level (Leq) values establish the data set that has been utilized to build up the models and to approve them (Patil & Nagarale, 2015). The present examination expects to build up a dependable and precise ANN and ANFIS model for noise prediction of urban zones by considering regularly utilized noise descriptors, for example, Leq, L10 as a yield parameter (Zhao, Ding, Hu, Chen & Yang, 2015). The paper is structured as follows: section 2 explains the existing papers related to road traffic noise prediction with different simulation models, section 3 explains the existing problems related to vehicular traffic noise prediction models, section 4 portrays the proposed prediction modeling, and section 5 describes the results and discussion. At last, the conclusion part is described in section 6.

2. LITERATURE REVIEW

In 2014, Kumar et al. proposed Multilayer feed forward back propagation (BP) neural network and it has been trained by Levenberg– Marquardt (LM) to build up an Artificial Neural Network (ANN) model for predicting thruway traffic noise. The created ANN is utilized to foresee 10 Percentile surpassed sound level (L10) as well as Equivalent persistent sound level (Leq) in dB (A). The results demonstrate that the rate distinction is substantially less utilizing ANN approach when contrasted with regression analysis.

In 2011, K. Kumar et al. have created road traffic noise forecast display for Indian conditions utilizing regression analysis. Data gathered has been analyzed and contrasted with the qualities anticipated by Calixto model. After correlation of results, it was seen that Calixto Model could be agreeably applied for Indian conditions as they give acknowledged outcomes with a decent esteem.

In 2016, vehicular traffic noise forecast models were exhibited by Singh et al. Four distinctive soft computing strategies, to be specific, Generalized Linear Model, Decision Trees, Random Forests and Neural Networks, have been utilized to create models to foresee the hourly identical continuous sound pressure level, Leq, at various areas in the Patiala city in India. The execution of the four models is thought about based on execution criteria of the coefficient of assurance, mean square error, and precision.

In 2018 Debnath and Singh examined the spatial qualities of road traffic noise at different interims viz. morning (6– 9 Am) and (9 Am– 12 Pm), afternoon (2– 5 Pm), evening (5– 8 Pm) and night (8– 11 Pm) hours at various road networks of Dhanbad town by utilizing Sound Level Meter and furthermore noise shape maps were created by GIS to view the observing areas. The checked outcomes showed that the most noteworthy and least average noise levels (LAeq) were 87.2 dB(A) and 71.3 dB(A) at evening and night respectively.

In 2017 Hamad et al. utilized the Artificial Neural Network (ANN) system to model road traffic noise in a city with known hot atmosphere, specifically Sharjah City in the United Arab Emirates. Toward this end, field data were gathered from three distinctive road destinations which brought about in excess of 420 hourly estimations of noise level, traffic volume and grouping, average speed, and roadway temperature. By and large, an aggregate of 16 feed-forward back- propagation ANN models with one and two hidden layers were embraced and the outcomes demonstrated that ANN models outflanked the regular models.

In 2012 Arora, J.K. and Mosahari, P.V., clarified single layer Artificial Neural Network (ANN) modeling of noise because of road traffic in Agra-Firozabad highway. 95 dataset has been utilized by estimating the noise force crosswise over different focuses along the Agra-Firozabad Highway at customary interim of separation. In the ANN approach, the arrangement of trials resulted into the execution assessment, considering 20% data for testing and 20% data for cross-validation at 1500 Epoch with 0.70momentum. The Levenberg-Marquardt (LM) algorithm was found as the best of BP with a minimum mean squared error (MSE) for training as well as cross-validation.

3. RESEARCH GAP

An overview of the accessible literature on traffic noise indicates that the main interest of various researchers was establishing of different highway noise descriptors and criteria; assessment of highway noise, undertaking traffic noise survey, establishing of different parameters influencing traffic noise and formulation of mathematical models, etc. (Kalaiselvi & Ramachandraiah, 2016). The existing prediction models like decision trees, Random forest (Singh, Nigam, Agrawal et al., 2016) and ANN (Hamad, Ali

Khalil & Shanableh, 2017) can predict the noise levels with high accuracy for the particular region, but cannot be used as such, in a region where the road traffic conditions are significantly extraordinary. Also, the collection of a huge amount of data for formulating the reference energy means emission level (RE-MEL) equations (Zhao, Ding, Hu et al., 2015) for different vehicle types remains a big challenge. Based on the survey of the above literature, it was seen that many scientists have endeavored to model urban noise, but the results have not been as good as expected because of the reduced number of variables. In order to conquer these issues, the methodology presents an innovative model for predicting traffic noise.

4. METHODOLOGY

The traffic load on Indian road is also increasing day by day, with the presentation of varieties of new vehicle models. This methodology is aimed to develop a more relevant and precise free-flow traffic noise prediction model for highways in India i.e. a model which predict the output precisely by accounting the input traffic parameters as the traffic volume, percentage of heavy vehicles and average vehicle speed in Nashik city. In view of the experimental values of these variables, Equivalent continuous (A-weighted) sound level, Leq and Percentile exceeded sound level, L10 is predicted by the simulation models like regression, ANN and ANFIS.

4.1. Site Location

Being one of the quickest developing urban communities in India, Nashik (Maharashtra) has been taken as a case study for the improvement of the noise prediction model. In the wake of completing a surveillance of different areas in the city, a segment of the road near the civil hospital was chosen to gather the essential data for the formulation of the model. Since the chosen area is close to the Central Bus Stand, traffic jams are a typical situation. This issue is fundamental because of the unlawful traffic development by bikes and auto rickshaws.

Estimations of various noise parameters were taken utilizing Sound Level Meter (SLM) 100, which continuously shows the Sound Pressure Level (SPL), Equivalent sound level (Leq), Maximum and Minimum sound pressure level and the Sound Exposure Level (SEL) integrated over the period of operation. Noise levels were estimated in range two and in fast mode to get the peak values of sound levels due to blowing of horns. Recordings of A-weighted sound-pressure levels were made at an interval of one minute at the time of the morning, afternoon and evening hours of the day between 8 a.m. and 9 p.m. The SLM was placed at a distance of 15 m from the focal point of the carriageway and mounted at a height of 1.2 m from the ground.

4.2. Assessment of Variables

The different highway noise descriptors and traffic noise parameters are described in the below section.

4.2.1. Traffic Noise Parameters

The noise that may result from vehicular traffic on highways is more intricate due to the fact that, riding quality of the highway may not remain same throughout its alignment that influences the propagation of noise. The factors like type of vehicle, the presence of a number of heavy vehicles in traffic stream and an average of speed of the vehicles are taken into consideration.

4.2.1.1. Traffic Volume (Q)

The noise level near the highway relies on the number of vehicles. The noise level increases with the increase in traffic volume. The number of vehicles plying per hour or during any selected period is called as traffic volume. When different classes of vehicles are found to utilize the regular road route offices without isolation, such flow is called mixed traffic flow and is expressed in terms of Passenger Car Units (PCU). To convert the heterogeneous traffic into homogeneous traffic, the equivalency factors recommended by Indian Road Congress (IRC) are shown in Table 1 the vehicles are classified into five categories in a specific car, bus, truck, two-wheelers, and auto rickshaws.

To get a genuine portrayal of traffic, characterized traffic volume is recorded at various hours of the day i.e. during morning, afternoon and evening hours. Manual vehicle count survey is conducted and traffic volume is expressed as vehicles per minute. It is generally accepted that over an extensive variety of traffic flow, the variation of L_{10} with flow rate can be represented by a logarithmic relation. So the traffic volume has been considered in logarithmic form in the present paper.

Table 1. Recommended equivalency (PCU) factors for various classes of vehicle on urban roads (Source IRC: 106-1990)

S. No	Vehicle Type	Equivalent PCU Factors % Composition of the Vehicle in the Traffic Stream	
		5%	10%
1	Two-wheeler, Motor cycle, scooter	0.5	0.75
2	Passenger car, peak up van	1.0	1.0
3	Auto Rickshaw, Light Commercial Vehicle	1.2	2.0
4	Truck, Bus	2.2	3.7

4.2.1.2. Percentage of Heavy Vehicles (P %)

The proportion of a number of transport/trucks to the aggregate number of vehicles is taken as the percentage of heavy vehicles. % of heavy vehicles is processed from the minute perceptions of traffic volume, and the equivalent is consolidated in the model.

4.2.1.3. Average Speed of Vehicle, (V)

In heterogeneous traffic, diverse vehicles are moving with various speeds. Hence, the speed of the traffic stream has been considered as the average speed of the vehicles. In a chosen stretch of the road, the time taken by the vehicle to cross a known distance is recorded. Delany, Harland, Hood et al. (1976) have examined that the commotion yield of a composite vehicle stream can be approximated as a logarithmic capacity of speed. In this way, the speed of the vehicle is indicated as Log V in the model.

4.2.2. Highway Noise Descriptors

To represent the ear's response to different levels of noise, measuring channels are utilized while estimating the sound level. The weighted sound level is concocted to address a people subjective response to the variety of sound all the more absolutely. The A-weighted sound level, estimated in decibel (dBA), is, for the most part, satisfactory scale for estimating sound level in highway transportation. The different highway noise descriptors are Percentile Exceeded Sound Level (Lx), Equivalent Continuous (A-weighted) Sound Level (Leq), Day-Night Average Sound level (Ldn), Traffic Noise Index (TNI) and Noise Pollution Level (NPL). Out of the above noise descriptors, L_{10} and Leq levels are broadly utilized in numerous nations to describe the highway traffic noise.

4.2.2.1. Equivalent Continuous (A-Weighted) Sound Level, Leq

The energy equivalent continuous noise level expressed in dBA is the average rate at which energy is received by the human ear during the stipulated period.

4.2.2.2. Percentile Exceeded Sound Level, L_{10}

L_{10} is a descriptor of the highest sound levels i.e. those well above the ambient level, but neglecting levels occurring for less than 10% of the time and provides a better measure of intermittent or intrusive noise, i.e. traffic noise.

4.3. Simulation Modeling

With the utilization of these experimental data, the output parameters such as L_{eq} and L_{10} are predicted by using the soft computing techniques like regression, ANN and ANFIS with a minimum error rate for the three input parameters. At the selected location, totally 732 samples of input as well as output were collected, out of which 512 (nearly 70%) samples were used for training and remaining 220 samples were used for validating and testing of data. Sample observations for regression are shown in Table 2.

Out of the accessible data sets, 70% data is utilized for training of model and staying 30% data is utilized for testing of the model. Regression, ANN and ANFIS models have been shaped utilizing three input parameters as log Q, P % and Log V and L_{eq} and L_{10} as output parameters.

Parameter Normalization: To enhance the accuracy in prediction, normalized datasets are used while training and testing of ANN and ANFIS models. The input parameters utilized in the model are in normalized form and in the range of 0 and 1; this is essential when dataset contains two input parameters of extensive variable range produce the same amount of variation, then the network may disregard the smaller input because of the significant contribution of the large input parameter. The condition utilized for the normalization of data is as given underneath:

$$Normalized\ value = \frac{\left(Data\ po\operatorname{int} - Minimum\ value\ of\ Dataset\right)}{\left(Maximum\ value\ of\ Dataset - Minimum\ value\ of\ Dataset\right)}$$

Table 2. Sample observations for regression, ANN and ANFIS model formulation

Sample No.	Input Parameters			Output Parameters	
	Log Q	P%	Log V	Leq (dB)	L_{10}(dB)
1	1.81	16.73	1.70	71.7	72.8
2	1.76	11.40	1.66	70.3	72.6
3	1.71	16.82	1.66	70	72.3
4	1.65	19.53	1.69	68.3	70
5	1.77	25.70	1.69	71.4	73.3
6	1.65	14.47	1.70	68.1	69.9
7	1.57	11.60	1.55	66.1	68.4
8	1.63	15.40	1.59	67.8	70.2
9	1.71	29.81	1.66	70.6	72.1
10	1.65	19.64	1.68	68.2	69.8

4.3.1. Regression Model

Regression is utilized in a wide variety of applications in finance and accounting to analyze how the value of a single dependent variable is influenced by the values of one or more independent variables. Using the observed data, the correlation among the variables has been studied to discover the strength of association of dependent variables with independent variables, and among independent variables. Using Microsoft excels spreadsheet multiple regression analysis is carried out to obtained equations for the prediction of L_{eq} and L_{10} noise levels. The parameters used for regression are Log Q, P % and Log V. The equations obtained are:

$$L_{eq}(dBA)= 9.5658 + 36.8233 \text{ Log Q} + 0.04264 \text{ P} -2.3177 \text{ Log V} \qquad (1)$$

$$L_{10} (dBA) =11.8190 +36.9698 \text{ Log Q} + 0.04510 \text{ P} -2.6031 \text{LogV} \qquad (2)$$

4.3.2. Artificial Neural Network (ANN)

A neural network is a structure of at least two neurons in a layer with a weighted association between the neurons, which are frequently nonlinear scalar changes. The network design includes an input layer with input parameters, two hidden layers with hidden parameters in every one of the hidden layers and the output layer:

- **Input layer:** This layer is in charge of accepting (data), signals, highlights, or estimations from the outside condition. These data sources (tests or examples) are generally standardized within the limit values created by activation functions;
- **Hidden layer:** The Hidden layer of the neural network is the middle of the road layer among the Input and Output layer. Activation function applies to a hidden layer on the off chance that it is accessible and the weights in the hidden node need to test utilizing training data;

- **Output layer:** The nodes in this layer are dynamic ones. This layer likewise made out of neurons and is in charge of creating and also displaying the last network outputs, which result from the processing performed by the neurons in the past layers.

4.3.2.1. Training of ANN Algorithm

After the neural network model is developed, training of the neural network is the basic step of the prediction model. Training of neural network is an iterative procedure of nonlinear enhancement of the parameters like weights and bias of the network. Backpropagation is a systematic technique for training multi-layer ANN. The Levenberg– Marquardt method has been utilized to refresh weights in back-propagation algorithm.

Levenberg-Marquardt (LM) algorithm: The Levenberg-Marquardt curve-fitting method is a combination of two minimization methods: the gradient descent method and the Gauss-Newton method. In the gradient descent method, the sum of the squared errors is reduced by updating the parameters in the steepest-descent direction. Simple steepest descent method to minimize the following error function:

$$R = \sum_{t=1}^{l}(S_t - C_t) \tag{3}$$

where S is the target, C is the actual output for the pattern of the neuron, R is the error function, l is the total number of training patterns.

The weight update vector ∇N is calculated as:

$$\nabla N = [J^T(N) * J(N) + \varepsilon I]^{-1}J^T(N)R \tag{4}$$

The LM algorithm involves calculation on the Jacobian J (w) matrix at each and every iteration action as well as the inversion associated with JT (w)J(w) square matrix and the R is a vector of size.

The accuracy of prediction using the ANN model not only depends upon input and output parameters but also relies on the selection of a number of neurons in the hidden layer. The optimum number can be arrived at by changing the number of hidden layers and the number of neurons in each layer during performing various iterations for training and testing of the model.

4.3.3. Adaptive Neuro-Fuzzy Interface System (ANFIS)

Adaptive Neuro-Fuzzy Inference Systems (ANFIS) is a class of adaptive networks that are functionally equivalent to fuzzy inference systems which represent the Sugeno Tsukamoto fuzzy model and it uses a hybrid learning algorithm. ANFIS is a combination of two soft-computing methods of Artificial Neural Network (ANN) and fuzzy logic. Unlike ANN, it has a higher capability in the learning process to adapt to its environment.

The procedure involved in the ANFIS model:

- **Structure Initialization:** Initialize the input parameters as percentage of heavy vehicles and average speed, total traffic volume. These parameters are represented as:

$$V = \{V_i\}, \text{ where } i=1,2 \text{ and } 3 \tag{5}$$

- **Fuzzification:** In the fuzzification procedure, the initialized input variables i.e. the crisp variables are changed over into fuzzy variables or the linguistic variables using the MF. The fuzzy membership grade of each crisp input is evaluated by the following equation:

$$D_i^1 = \mu M_i(V_1) \text{ where } i=1,2,\ldots3 \tag{6}$$

where S is the input to the node $i=1,2,\ldots3$, M_i is the linguistic variable associated with this node function μM_i is the membership function of M_i.

- **Rule Generation:** This layer includes fuzzy operators; it uses the AND operator to fuzzify the input sources. They are named with Π, indicating that they perform as a simple multiplier. The output of this layer is known as firing strengths of the rules. The rules are based on the IF-THEN rules. For each rule, its weight computed as the product of the input membership values as:

$$D_i^2 = w_i = \prod_{i=1}^{3} {}^* \mu M_i(V_i) \tag{7}$$

where w_i indicates the weight of the rule generated layer, $i=1,2,\ldots3$ is the number of input parameters considered in the vehicular traffic noise prediction.

- **Defuzzification:** Each node in this layer is a fixed node. The nodes are also fixed nodes named by N, to show that they assume a standardization part to the firing strengths from the past layer. The yield of this layer is known as normalized firing strengths and it can be represented as:

$$D_i^3 = \bar{w}_i = \frac{w_i}{\sum_i w_i}, \, i = 1,2,\ldots3 \tag{8}$$

The normalized firing strengths (weight) of the structure are trained through the Neural Network, to alter the input parameters and to minimize the errors. The output of every node in this layer is evaluated as the product of the normalized firing strength and a first-order polynomial:

$$D_i^4 = \bar{w}_i P_i \tag{9}$$

From Equation (9), $P_i = a_i(V_1) + b_i(V_2) + c_i(V_3) + d$ and a_i, b_i, c_i, d are referred to as consequent parameters, i^{th} indicates a number of rules.

- **Output Layer:** The final layer is named as an output layer where the nodes are fixed one. The output is evaluated as the summation of all incoming signals:

$$D_i^5 = \sum_i \bar{w}_i P_i \qquad (10)$$

By using the simulation model regression, ANN and ANFIS, the traffic noise level are predicted in terms of Equivalent Continuous (A-weighted) Sound Level (Leq) and Percentile exceeded sound level, L10.

5. RESULT AND DISCUSSION

This section discusses the results of regression, ANN and ANFIS prediction model of Nashik city traffic noise level. This simulation process is implemented by MATLAB 2016 a with 4GB RAM and i5 processor. The validation tests between the predicted results and the actual results for the number of testing data are presented.

5.1. Sample Used for Simulation Modeling

The sample observations used for testing the model are shown in Table 3.

Table 3. Sample observations for validation of regression, ANN and ANFIS model

Sample No.	Input Parameters			Output Parameters	
	Log Q	P%	Log V	L_{eq}(dB)	L_{10}(dB)
1	1.80	10.29	1.65	72.1	74.4
2	1.61	00.00	1.56	67.1	70
3	1.85	21.34	1.60	74.7	76.7
4	1.82	6.65	1.62	72	74.6
5	1.81	6.72	1.59	71.9	74
6	1.90	16.56	1.67	75.1	77.4
7	1.88	5.75	1.66	77	79.2
8	1.77	7.31	1.72	71.4	74
9	1.76	11.26	1.73	70.4	72.8
10	1.72	24.92	1.71	70.5	72.7

5.2. Performance Evaluation

The criterions used to check the validity of the model are, correlation coefficient, mean square error and root mean square error:

- **Mean Square Error (MSE):** MSE is the capacity to minimize the errors and it is characterized as:

$$MSE = \frac{1}{n}\sum_{t=1}^{n}\left(z_j - \hat{z}_j\right)^2 \tag{11}$$

where N is the total number of prediction, z_j is the first time series and $\hat{z}_j$ is the predicted time series.

- **Root Mean Square Error (RMSE):** The root-mean-square error (RMSE) is a frequently used measure of the differences between values predicted by a model or an estimator and the values actually observed:

$$RMSE = \sqrt{\frac{1}{n}\sum_{t=1}^{n}(e_t - \hat{e}_t)^2} \tag{12}$$

where 'n' is the number of data points, e_t is input attributes.

- **Correlation Coefficient (R):** Correlation is a measure of the linear relationship between two sets of data. It is defined as:

$$R = \frac{\sum_{i=1}^{n}\left(a_i - \bar{a}_i\right)\left(b_i - \bar{b}_i\right)}{\sqrt{\sum_{i=1}^{n}\left(a_i - \bar{a}_i\right)^2 \sum_{i=1}^{n}\left(b_i - \bar{b}_i\right)^2}} \tag{13}$$

where a is the observed value, b is the predicted value, $\bar{a}$ is the average of all the observed values, $\bar{b}$ is the average of all the predicted values and n is the number of sample data points.

Table 4 discusses the observed and predicted values (regression, ANN and ANFIS) of two output parameters Equivalent Continuous (A-weighted) Sound Level (Leq) and Percentile exceeded sound level, L10. The Leq and L10 are examined for the 10 number of samples which are collected from the Nashik city.

5.2.1. Comparative Analysis

The parameters such as Equivalent Continuous (A-weighted) Sound Level (Leq) and Percentile exceeded sound level, L10 are compared among three simulation models and the observed values. The analyzed three simulation models are a regression, ANN and ANFIS. When comparing the noise levels, ANFIS model is more superior when compared to output given by regression and ANN model.

Table 5 explains the training and testing data of ANN architecture for L_{eq} output parameter. By varying hidden nodes in ANN, three measures are analyzed in terms of correlation coefficient, MSE and RMSE. The best solution is attained in the case of 20 hidden nodes, the values are 0.9750 correlation coefficient, 0.0001984 MSE and 0.0141 RMSE for the training samples and 0.9581 correlation coefficient, 0.0005682 MSE and 0.0238 RMSE for testing samples. Similarly, the nodes 4, 8, 10 and 25 are depicted in Table 5.

Table 4. Comparison of observed and predicted values of output parameters for data used for validation

Sample No.	Experimental		Regression		ANN		ANFIS	
	Leq(dB)	L_{10}(dB)	Leq(dB)	L_{10}(dB)	Leq(dB)	L_{10}(dB)	Leq(dB)	L_{10}(dB)
1	76.60	79.10	79.67	81.79	77.68	79.49	78.66	80.92
2	76.30	79.00	77.19	79.31	77.60	79.40	77.99	84.72
3	69.90	72.20	74.71	76.82	70.09	71.73	68.25	74.59
4	72.10	74.00	69.89	71.98	71.47	73.13	70.81	78.60
5	76.10	77.60	76.21	78.35	76.39	78.17	77.63	85.37
6	71.80	73.60	71.34	73.46	71.19	72.85	70.24	77.94
7	81.30	82.90	71.73	73.84	82.43	84.35	81.67	87.29
8	76.30	78.90	78.56	80.70	77.20	79.00	77.24	85.00
9	73.80	76.80	72.85	74.97	73.02	74.72	73.46	81.46
10	69.80	71.40	74.03	76.14	69.62	71.24	68.52	74.01

Table 5. Comparison of training and testing data of ANN architecture for L_{eq}

Hidden Nodes (N)	Training			Testing		
	Correlation Coefficients (R)	MSE	RMSE	Correlation Coefficients (R)	MSE	RMSE
4	0.9748	0.0002003	0.0142	0.9497	0.0005156	0.0227
8	0.9718	0.0002234	0.0149	0.9488	0.0004829	0.0220
10	0.9732	0.0002125	0.0146	0.9563	0.0006616	0.0257
20	**0.9750**	**0.0001984**	**0.0141**	**0.9581**	**0.0005682**	**0.0238**
25	0.9742	0.0002047	0.0143	0.9544	0.0005995	0.0245

The training and testing data of ANN architecture with a different number of hidden nodes for L_{10} output parameter is illustrated in Table 6. The correlation, which shows the linear relationship between two sets of data, for all the methods, and the values are given in Table 6. The highest correlation coefficient with minimum error rate is accomplished in the case of 10 numbers of hidden nodes when compared to another set of nodes.

The training and testing performance of ANFIS prediction model for the parameters Equivalent Continuous (A-weighted) Sound Level (Leq) and Percentile exceeded sound level, L10 are depicted in Table 7. For Leq, the MSE rate for training samples is 0.0002384, RMSE is 0.0154 and correlation coefficient is 0.9698. For L10 the MSE rate for training samples is 0.0002544, RMSE is 0.0160 and correlation coefficient is 0.9668. Similarly, these measures are analyzed for the testing samples.

5.2.2. Error Analysis

The percentage error between observed, Regression, ANN and ANFIS output result for samples used for training the model is shown in Table 7. Noise level Leq predicted using regression; neural network and ANFIS model for testing data set. The values for correlation coefficient (R) of 0.846, 0.9129, and

0.9668 were obtained using s regression, neural network, and ANFIS model. Also, values for root mean square error (RMSE) of 2.2246, 0.0257, and 0.0200 were obtained using regression, ANN and ANFIS model respectively. These values indicate that highly satisfactory prediction of Leq is given by the ANFIS model. ANFIS model can be used for noise prediction for other cities after training these models.

Table 6. Comparison of training and testing data of ANN architecture for L_{10}

Hidden Nodes (N)	Training			Testing		
	Correlation Coefficients (R)	MSE	RMSE	Correlation Coefficients (R)	MSE	RMSE
4	0.9671	0.0002529	0.0159	0.9239	0.0007734	0.0278
8	0.9713	0.0002206	0.0149	0.9292	0.0007151	0.0267
10	**0.9722**	**0.0002134**	**0.0146**	**0.9129**	**0.0007450**	**0.0273**
15	0.9696	0.0002362	0.0154	0.9350	0.0005028	0.0224
20	0.9636	0.0002878	0.0170	0.9284	0.0008534	0.0292
25	0.9646	0.0002979	0.0173	0.9168	0.0012	0.0349

Table 7. Performance of ANFIS for L_{eq} and L_{10}, training and testing

Parameters	L_{eq}		L_{10}	
	Training	Testing	Training	Testing
Mean Square Error (MSE)	0.0002384	0.0003996	0.0002544	0.0004884
Root Mean Square Error (RMSE)	0.0154	0.0200	0.0160	0.0221
Correlation Coefficient (R)	0.9698	0.9535	0.9668	0.9091

6. CONCLUSION

The paper presented a vehicular traffic noise prediction model for highways in India. Three different soft computing methods are utilized in developing the models for typical road traffic conditions in the Indian city of Nashik. The traffic noise prediction models are developed, with equivalent sound pressure level, Leq and Percentile exceeded sound level, L10 as the output (dependent variable) and the traffic noise variables: hourly traffic volume, the percentage of heavy vehicles and average speed of vehicles, as the independent variables. Among the three approaches, a high correlation coefficient and less percentage error difference between experimental and predicted output are achieved in the ANFIS prediction model. The proposed prediction model can encourage urban organizers and traffic engineers in the design of suitable moderation measures like re-routing of traffic, installing traffic calming measures, making flyovers, slip-roads and road networks. For future work, the diverse traffic conditions with the inclusion of time as a variable input, this can be predicted by the neural network model along with the optimization algorithms.

REFERENCES

Arora, J. K., & Mosahari, P. V. (2012). Artificial neural network modelling of traffic noise in Agra-Firozabad highway. *International Journal of Computers and Applications*, *56*(2).

Brown, A. L., & De Coensel, B. (2018). A study of the performance of a generalized exceedance algorithm for detecting noise events caused by road traffic. *Applied Acoustics*, *138*, 101–114. doi:10.1016/j.apacoust.2018.03.031

Chang, T.-Y., Lin, H.-C., Yang, W.-T., Bao, B.-Y., & Chan, C.-C. (2012). A modified Nordic prediction model of road traffic noise in a Taiwanese city with significant motorcycle traffic. *The Science of the Total Environment*, *432*, 375–381. doi:10.1016/j.scitotenv.2012.06.016 PMID:22750184

Cho, D. S., & Mun, S. (2008). Development of a highway traffic noise prediction model that considers various road surface types. *Applied Acoustics*, *69*(11), 1120–1128. doi:10.1016/j.apacoust.2007.06.004

Choudhary, A., & Gokhale, S. (2018). On-road measurements and modeling of vehicular emissions during traffic interruption and congestion events in an urban traffic corridor. *Atmospheric Pollution Research*.

Dai, B., He, Y., Mu, F., Xu, N., & Wu, Z. (2014). Development of a traffic noise prediction model on the inland waterway of China using the FHWA. *The Science of the Total Environment*, *482-483*, 480–485. doi:10.1016/j.scitotenv.2013.06.019 PMID:23810035

De Coensel, B., Brown, A. L., & Tomerini, D. (2016). A road traffic noise pattern simulation model that includes distributions of vehicle sound power levels. *Applied Acoustics*, *111*, 170–178. doi:10.1016/j.apacoust.2016.04.010

Debnath, A., & Singh, P. K. (2018). Environmental traffic noise modelling of Dhanbad township area – A mathematical based approach. *Applied Acoustics*, *129*, 161–172. doi:10.1016/j.apacoust.2017.07.023

Delany, M. E., Harland, D. G., Hood, R. A., & Scholes, W. E. (1976). The prediction of noise levels L10 due to road traffic. *Journal of Sound and Vibration*, *48*(3), 305–325. doi:10.1016/0022-460X(76)90057-2

Di, H., Liu, X., Zhang, J., Tong, Z., Ji, M., Li, F., ... Ma, Q. (2018). Estimation of the quality of an urban acoustic environment based on traffic noise evaluation models. *Applied Acoustics*, *141*, 115–124. doi:10.1016/j.apacoust.2018.07.010

Givargis, S., & Karimi, H. (2010). A basic neural traffic noise prediction model for Tehran's roads. *Journal of Environmental Management*, *91*(12), 2529–2534. doi:10.1016/j.jenvman.2010.07.011 PMID:20678858

Hamad, K., Ali Khalil, M., & Shanableh, A. (2017). Modeling roadway traffic noise in a hot climate using artificial neural networks. *Transportation Research Part D, Transport and Environment*, *53*, 161–177. doi:10.1016/j.trd.2017.04.014

Kalaiselvi, R., & Ramachandraiah, A. (2016). Honking noise corrections for traffic noise prediction models in heterogeneous traffic conditions like India. *Applied Acoustics*, *111*, 25–38. doi:10.1016/j.apacoust.2016.04.003

Konbattulwar, V., Velaga, N. R., Jain, S., & Sharmila, R. B. (2016). Development of in-vehicle noise prediction models for the Mumbai Metropolitan Region, India. *Journal of Traffic and Transportation Engineering*, *3*(4), 380–387.

Kumar, K., Katiyar, V. K., Parida, M., & Rawat, K. (2011). Mathematical Modelling of Road Traffic Noise Prediction. *Int. J. Appl. Math and Mech.*, *7*(4), 21–28.

Kumar, P., Nigam, S. P., & Kumar, N. (2014). Vehicular traffic noise modeling using artificial neural network approach. *Transportation Research Part C, Emerging Technologies*, *40*, 111–122. doi:10.1016/j.trc.2014.01.006

Leung, T. M., Chau, C. K., Tang, S. K., & Xu, J. M. (2017). Developing a multivariate model for predicting the noise annoyance responses due to combined water sound and road traffic noise exposure. *Applied Acoustics*, *127*, 284–291. doi:10.1016/j.apacoust.2017.06.020

Nedic, V., Despotovic, D., Cvetanovic, S., Despotovic, M., & Babic, S. (2014). Comparison of classical statistical methods and artificial neural network in traffic noise prediction. *Environmental Impact Assessment Review*, *49*, 24–30. doi:10.1016/j.eiar.2014.06.004

Patil Vilas, K., & Nagarale Prashant, P. (2015). Mesurement and Analysis of Noise at signalized Intersections. *Journal of Environmental Research and Development*, *9*(3), 662–667.

Rajkumara, H. N., & Mahalinge Gowda, R. M. (2008). Development of a Road Traffic Noise Prediction Model under Uninterrupted Traffic Flow Conditions. *International Journal of Sustainable Development and Planning*, *3*(1), 45–56. doi:10.2495/SDP-V3-N1-45-56

Ramírez, A., & Domínguez, E. (2013). Modeling urban traffic noise with stochastic and deterministic traffic models. *Applied Acoustics*, *74*(4), 614–621. doi:10.1016/j.apacoust.2012.08.001

Shukla, A. K., Jain, S., Parida, M., & Srivastava, J. B. (2009). Performance of FHWA Model for Predicting Traffic Noise: A Case study of Metropolitan City, Lucknow (India). *Transport*, *24*(3), 234–240. doi:10.3846/1648-4142.2009.24.234-240

Singh, D., Nigam, S. P., Agrawal, V. P., & Kumar, M. (2016). Vehicular traffic noise prediction using soft computing approach. *Journal of Environmental Management*, *183*, 59–66. doi:10.1016/j.jenvman.2016.08.053 PMID:27576153

Steinbach, L., & Altinsoy, M. E. (2019). Prediction of annoyance evaluations of electric vehicle noise by using artificial neural networks. *Applied Acoustics*, *145*, 149–158. doi:10.1016/j.apacoust.2018.09.024

Zhao, J., Ding, Z., Hu, B., Chen, Y., & Yang, W. (2015). Assessment and improvement of a highway traffic noise prediction model with Leq(20s) as the basic vehicular noise. *Applied Acoustics*, *97*, 78–83. doi:10.1016/j.apacoust.2015.03.021

This research was previously published in the International Journal of Business Data Communications and Networking (IJBDCN), 15(2); pages 92-105, copyright year 2019 by IGI Publishing (an imprint of IGI Global).

Chapter 28
Vocal Acoustic Analysis:
ANN Versos SVM in Classification of Dysphonic Voices and Vocal Cords Paralysis

João Paulo Teixeira

ⓘD https://orcid.org/0000-0002-6679-5702

Research Centre in Digitalization and Intelligent Robotics (CEDRI) and Applied Management Research Unit (UNIAG), Instituto Politécnico de Bragança, Bragança, Portugal

Nuno Alves

Instituto Politécnico de Bragança, Bragança, Portugal

Paula Odete Fernandes

ⓘD https://orcid.org/0000-0001-8714-4901

Applied Management Research Unit (UNIAG), Instituto Politécnico de Bragança, Bragança, Portugal

ABSTRACT

Vocal acoustic analysis is becoming a useful tool for the classification and recognition of laryngological pathologies. This technique enables a non-invasive and low-cost assessment of voice disorders, allowing a more efficient, fast, and objective diagnosis. In this work, ANN and SVM were experimented on to classify between dysphonic/control and vocal cord paralysis/control. A vector was made up of 4 jitter parameters, 4 shimmer parameters, and a harmonic to noise ratio (HNR), determined from 3 different vowels at 3 different tones, with a total of 81 features. Variable selection and dimension reduction techniques such as hierarchical clustering, multilinear regression analysis and principal component analysis (PCA) was applied. The classification between dysphonic and control was made with an accuracy of 100% for female and male groups with ANN and SVM. For the classification between vocal cords paralysis and control an accuracy of 78,9% was achieved for female group with SVM, and 81,8% for the male group with ANN.

DOI: 10.4018/978-1-6684-2408-7.ch028

1. INTRODUCTION

Vocal Acoustic Analysis is often used for voice disorders assessment and diagnose (Bielamowicz et al., 1996; Brockmann-Bauser, 2011; Pylypowich, & Duff, 2016; Salhi, Mourad, & Cherif, 2010; Teixeira & Fernandes, 2015). The advantage of such techniques relies on the non-invasive character of the exam when compared with current practice in medicine, for example, laryngoscopy or stroboscopic exams (Brockmann-Bauser, 2011).

Both laryngoscopy and stroboscopic exam consist in inserting a thin tube into the throat or into the nostrils. Stroboscopy is painless, an office-based procedure done with topical anaesthesia. It is a special method used to visualize vocal fold vibration (Hirano, 1974). It uses a synchronized, flashing light passed through a flexible or rigid telescope. The flashes of light from the stroboscope are synchronised to the vocal fold vibration at a slightly slower speed, allowing the examiner to observe vocal fold vibration during sound production in what appears to be slow motion. The resulting video depicts video-stroboscopic examination of the vocal folds.

This incision technique will always be necessary to confirm or even support chirurgical operations on the vocal folds or in the larynx/pharynx.

Although voice disorders may be diagnosed by an auditory perceptual analysis made by the otolaryngologist, this may lead to different results depending on the practitioner experience (Teixeira & Fernandes, 2014).

It is common in daily life of primary care facilities the people complain about hoarseness in their voices. The dysphonia affects 30% of adults and 50% of older adults. This disease modifies voice quality and has a significant impact on life quality. This also represents a significant economic burden. In patients with a progressive pathology, it is important to do a diagnosis as fast as possible for the sake of having access to better treatment and prognosis (Pylypowich & Duff, 2016).

There are several acoustic parameters extracted from speech signal processing useful to identify the vocal pathology, yet no parameter alone is able to classify between healthy or pathologic voice.

Teixeira and Fernandes (2015) analysed the statistical significance of Jitter, Shimmer and HNR parameters for dysphonia detection. A statistical analysis was performed over the three parameters for the vowels /a/, /i/ and /u/ at three different tones, high, low and normal. In this work, Jitter and Shimmer are suggested as good parameters to be used in an intelligent diagnosis system of dysphonia pathologies.

To test this analysis, it is necessary to apply an intelligent tool and some reduction dimension and feature selection techniques. Feature selection is intended to select the best subset of predictors. The feature selection problem arises from large datasets who may contain redundant information and variables that have little or no predictive power (May, Dandy, & Maier, 2011). The correct choice of input features leads to a small subset that may boost/improve the performance when intelligent tools are used.

Henríquez et al. (2009) studied the usefulness of six nonlinear chaotic measures based on nonlinear dynamics theory in the discrimination between two levels of voice quality: healthy and pathological. The studied measures are first and second order Rényi entropies, the correlation entropy and the correlation dimension. The values of the first minimum of mutual information function and Shannon entropy were also studied. Two databases were used to assess the usefulness of the measures: a multi-quality and a commercial database (MEEI Voice Disorders). A classifier based on standard neural networks was implemented in order to evaluate the measures proposed. Global success rates of 82.5% (multi-quality database) and 99.7% (commercial database) were obtained. This difference in performance highlights the importance of having a controlled speech acquisition process.

In Forero et al. (2015), several parameters of glottal signal were used to identify nodule, unilateral paralysis or healthy voices. The database, obtained from a speech therapist, was composed by records of voices from 12 speakers with nodule, 8 speakers with vocal fold paralysis and 11 speakers with normal voices. Three different classifiers were used, an Artificial Neural Network, a Support Vector Machine (SVM) and Hidden Markov Model. The best accuracy, 97.2%, was reached using glottal signal parameters and MFCC's with SVM classifier.

Markaki and Stylianou (2011) explored the information provided by a joint acoustic and modulation frequency representation, referred to as modulation spectrum, for detection and discrimination of voice disorders. The initial representation is first transformed to a lower dimensional domain using higher-order singular value decomposition (HOSVD). For voice pathology detection an accuracy of 94.1% was achieved using one SVM as classifier.

In Panek et al. (2015) a vector made up of 28 acoustic parameters was evaluated using Principal Component Analysis (PCA), kernel principal component analysis (kPCA) and an auto-associative neural network (NLPCA) in four kinds of pathology detection (hyperfunctional dysphonia, functional dysphonia, laryngitis and vocal cord paralysis) using the /a/, /i/ and /u/ vowels, spoken at a high, low and normal tones. The results show best efficiency levels of around 100%.

Al-Nasheri et al. (2016) investigated different frequency bands using correlation functions. The authors extracted maximum peak values and their corresponding lag values from each frame of a voiced signal by using correlation functions as features to detect and classify pathologic samples. Three different databases were used, Arabic Voice Pathology Database (AVPD), Saarbrücken Voice Database (SVD) and Massachusetts Eye and Ear Infirmary (MEEI). A Support Vector Machine was used as classifier. For the detection of pathology, an accuracy of 99.8%, 90.9% and 91.1% was achieved for the three databases respectively. In the classification of the pathology task an accuracy of 99.2%, 98.9% and 95.1%, respectively, was achieved for the three databases.

In Sellam and Jagadeesan (2014), an attempt was made to analyse and to discriminate pathologic voice from normal voice in children using different classification methods. The classification of pathologic voice from normal voice was implemented using Support Vector Machine (SVM) and Radial Basis Functional Neural Network (RBFNN). Several acoustic parameters were extracted such as the signal energy, pitch, formant frequencies, mean square residual signal, reflection coefficients, Jitter and Shimmer. The best accuracy results were obtained by RBFNN with, 91%, and for the SVM 83%.

The artificial neural networks are among the most used classifiers for this kind of task although SVM is also used often (Al-Nasheri et al., 2016; Forero et al., 2015; Henríquez, et al., 2009; Markaki & Stylianou, 2011; Panek et al., 2015; Sellam & Jagadeesan, 2014).

Cordeiro (2017) presented a set of experiments to identify the best set of features from the vocal tract (MFCC, Line Spectral Frequencies (LSF), Mel-Line Spectral Frequencies (MLSF) and first peak of the spectral envelop) and the best classifiers amongst SVM and Gaussian Mixture Models (GMM) for the identification of pathologic voices. He achieved an accuracy of 84.4% for the identification between 3 groups (healthy subjects, subjects with physiological larynx pathologies - vocal fold nodules and edemas, and subjects with neurological larynx pathologies - unilateral vocal fold paralysis). He also used Regression Trees to the pathological voice recognition based on formant analysis and harmonic-to-noise ratio with 95% recognition rate.

In Teixeira and Gonçalves (2014) an algorithm was presented to automatically extract the jitter, shimmer and HNR features. The accuracy of measurements was compared with the ones extracted with

Praat software (Boersma & Weenink, 2009) and showed better accuracy for synthesized speech signals and similar values as the Praat software for real signals.

Teixeira, Fernandes and Alves (2017) published the classification of dysphonic voices. A set of Jitter, Shimmer, and HNR parameters extracted from 3 sustained vowels at different tone levels was analysed. Three methods were used to reduce the features dimension set to be used in an ANN to classify between control and dysphonic voices. In this present research, the same dataset and methodology were used, but an additional classification tool was experimented with. The SVMs were compared with the ANNs. In this work, besides the dysphonia pathology, also the vocal cords paralysis pathology is used.

Next section describes the methodology. In this section the database is presented, as well as the set of features, a brief description of the used pathologies and the ANN and SVM architectures, the methods used to reduce the features dimension and the description of the used measures to evaluate the performance of the model. Section 3 presents the results obtained for the classification of each pathology by gender using ANN and SVM with selected features by the feature selection methods. Finally, section 4 presents the conclusions.

2. METHODS AND METHODOLOGY

The Saarbrücken Voice Database (SVD) (Barry & Pützer, 2007) was used in this study. For each subject, one segment of speech record was used for sustained vowels /a/, /i/ and /u/ for High, Low and Mid/Neutral tones in a total of 9 speech segments. Each segment of speech consists of a steady state sustainable pronunciation of the respective vowel. For each speech segment a set of jitter, shimmer and HNR parameters, detailed below, was determined using the algorithm developed by Teixeira and Gonçalves (2016). This algorithm extracts a set of Jitter parameters (jitta, jitter, rap and ppq5), Shimmer (ShdB, Shim, apq3 and apq5) and HNR (Harmonic to Noise Ratio). A subset of the control subjects was selected in order to have similar distribution between gender and age of each pathologic group.

Two voice pathologies were used separately in this study, dysphonia and vocal cords paralysis (VCP). Each pathology was compared to control subjects. The control subjects consist of voice segments of healthy persons.

The classification in healthy/pathological voice was carried out for women and men separately. The number of samples taken from control group was the same of the pathologic group under examination (Panek et al., 2015). More details of the number of samples and distribution of ages can be seen in Table 1. A similar set of databases for dysphonia pathologic group was used in (Teixeira et al., 2017).

Pathology sets (dysphonia and VCP) include all subjects available in the SVD, meanwhile the subjects of the respective control groups were selected in order to have the most similar possible age. Anyhow, the available control subjects are mostly younger than pathologic subjects turning difficult to have very similar age in control and pathologic groups. The standard deviation between pathologic and control groups is mainly similar except in the female control dysphonia/dysphonia. The effect of ageing on voice quality is recognised, anyhow, the authors believe that the small difference in the average and standard deviation age groups does not affect the study results.

Table 1. Gender and age distribution of the subjects in the chosen subset of SVD

	# Subjects		Margin of Years Old		Average (Standard Deviation) Years Old	
	Female	Male	Female	Male	Female	Male
Control Dysphonia	41	29	19-56	20-69	24.8 (7.32)	41.2 (18.7)
Dysphonia	41	29	18-73	11-77	45.6 (14.8)	48.7 (18.0)
Control VCP	126	69	18-84	18-69	31.0 (15.9)	34.8 (15.8)
VCP	126	69	21-79	23-81	55.8 (12.4)	59.1 (14.4)

2.1. Dysphonia

Dysphonia is a medical term meaning disorder (dys-) of voice (-phonia) (Teixeira & Fernandes, 2015). The airflow moving through the vocal cords originates the human voice. Voice is different from speech, which is modulated by the pharynx, tongue and oral cavity (Pylypowich & Duff, 2016). Although there are many causes of dysphonia, it can be characterised by a disturbance in the phonation mechanism causing alteration in voice pitch. Voice dysfunction is not a disease by itself but can be a symptom of an underlying pathology.

2.2. Vocal Cords Paralysis

Vocal cord paralysis is a voice disorder that occurs when one (unilateral) or both (bilateral) vocal folds do not open or close properly. Unilateral paralysis is a common disorder, while bilateral paralysis is rarer and life-threatening.

The vocal cords are two elastic bands present in the larynx just above the trachea. When they are breathing, they remain distant and in swallowing they are closed. However, in the production of voice, the air coming from the lungs causes them to vibrate oscillating between the open and closed position.

In cases of paralysis, the vocal chords may remain open leaving the airways and lungs unprotected. This type of pathology can either occur after trauma to the head, neck or chest as well as in people with neurological problems such as multiple sclerosis, Parkinson's disease or who have suffered a stroke.

Symptoms may manifest as hoarseness, breathiness, trouble breathing, wheezing and swallowing problems. There may also be changes in voice quality such as loss of volume or fundamental frequency.

Bilateral vocal cord paralysis refers to the neurologic causes of bilateral vocal fold immobility and specifically refers to the reduced or absent function of the vagus nerve or its distal branch, the recurrent laryngeal nerve. Vocal fold immobility may also result from mechanical derangement of the laryngeal structures, such as the cricoarytenoid joint (Netter, 2014).

2.3. Parameters

Jitter, shimmer and HNR parameters were extracted with the algorithm developed by Teixeira and Gonçalves (2015). Jitter is defined as the periodic variation from cycle to cycle, and shimmer relates to the magnitude variation of the glottal period. A perspective of jitter and shimmer can be seen in Figure 1. Patients with lack of control of the vibration of vocal folds have tendency to have higher values of jitter. Reduction of glottal resistance and mass lesions causes a variation in the magnitude of the glottal period correlated with breathiness and noise emission, causing higher shimmer. The jitter and shimmer can be measured usually by four different forms. Jitter can be measured as absolute (jitta), relative (jitter), Relative Average Perturbation (rap) and the Period Perturbation Quotient (ppq5), according to Equations 1 to 4. Shimmer can be measured as absolute value in dB (ShdB), as relative value (Shim), as Amplitude Perturbation Quotient in 3 cycles (apq3) and as Amplitude Perturbation Quotient in 5 cycles (apq5), as Equations 5 to 8:

$$jitta = \frac{1}{N-1}\sum_{i=1}^{N-1}|T_i - T_{i-1}| \tag{1}$$

$$jitter\,(relative) = \frac{\frac{1}{N-1}\sum_{i=1}^{N-1}|T_i - T_{i-1}|}{\frac{1}{N}\sum_{i=1}^{N}T_i} \times 100 \tag{2}$$

$$rap = \frac{\frac{1}{N-1}\sum_{i=1}^{N-1}\left|T_i - \frac{1}{3}\sum_{n=i-1}^{i+1}T_n\right|}{\frac{1}{N}\sum_{i=1}^{N}T_i} \times 100 \tag{3}$$

$$ppq5 = \frac{\frac{1}{N-1}\sum_{i=2}^{N-2}\left|T_i - \frac{1}{5}\sum_{n=i-2}^{i+2}T_n\right|}{\frac{1}{N}\sum_{i=1}^{N}T_i} \times 100 \tag{4}$$

where Ti is the i glottal period lengths and N is the number of glottal periods.

$$ShdB = \frac{1}{N-1}\sum_{i=1}^{N-1}\left|20 * \log\left(\frac{A_{i+1}}{A_i}\right)\right| \tag{5}$$

$$Shim = \frac{\frac{1}{N-1}\sum_{i=1}^{N-1}|A_{i+1} - A_i|}{\frac{1}{N}\sum_{i=1}^{N}A_i} \times 100 \tag{6}$$

$$apq3 = \frac{\frac{1}{N-1}\sum_{i=1}^{N-1}\left|A_i - \left(\frac{1}{3}\sum_{n=i-1}^{i+1}A_n\right)\right|}{\frac{1}{N}\sum_{i=1}^{N}A_i} \times 100 \tag{7}$$

$$apq5 = \frac{\frac{1}{N-1}\sum_{i=2}^{N-2}\left|A_i - \left(\frac{1}{5}\sum_{n=i-2}^{i+2}A_n\right)\right|}{\frac{1}{N}\sum_{i=1}^{N}A_i} \times 100 \qquad (8)$$

where A_i is the i peak-to-peak glottal magnitude and N the number of periods.

Figure 1. Jitter and Shimmer perturbation measures in speech signal of a sustained vowel /a/

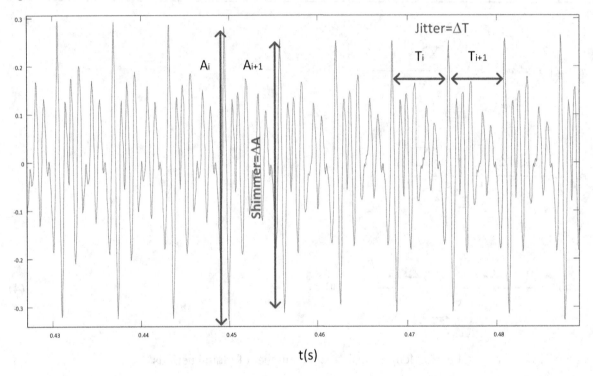

The Harmonic to Noise Ratio (HNR), Equation 9, provides an indication of the overall periodicity of the voice signal by quantifying the ratio between the periodic (harmonic part) and aperiodic (noise) components. This parameter is usually measured as an overall characteristic of the signal. The overall value of the HNR of the signal varies because different vocal tract configurations involve different amplitudes for the harmonics:

$$HNR = 10 * \log_{10}\frac{AC_V(T)}{AC_V(0) - AC_V(T)} \qquad (9)$$

where $AC_V(0)$ is the total energy of the signal and $AC_V(T)$ is the energy of the first harmonic.

2.4. Artificial Neural Network (ANN)

For the ANN classifier, a Multilayer Perceptron (MLP) structure, trained with the back-propagation algorithm was used. Different typologies were examined with a different number of neurons in the hidden layer to seek the best generalization performance. The dataset was divided into three subsets, train, validation and test sets. The quantity of each dataset was 70%, 15%, 15%, respectively.

The ANN is composed of weights and bias trying to adapt to the desired output. The model has one neuron in the output layer. The output target was composed of zeros and ones. The output given by the ANN is not always exactly zero or one and so it had to be post-processed to be zero or one. For this process, a threshold of 0.5 was experimentally established for the output. The number of input nodes and hidden nodes is different for each model.

2.5. Support Vector Machines

A support vector machine (SVM) is a type of intelligent tool based on minimizing structural risk. They can be used to solve classification and regression problems. The main idea of SVM is to construct hyperplanes as the optimal separation surface between positive and negative examples in a binary classification context (Almeida, 2010; Sellam & Jagadeesan, 2014).

Since problems are not always linear, it is necessary to transform the data so that it can be linearly separated. For this separation, the SVM use Kernel methods that make a non-linear transformation to the data for a multi-dimensional space where it will be an image of the data that allows a linear separation (Cruz, 2007).

Among the most used kernel methods are the linear, polynomial, radial basis function (RBF) and multi-layer perceptron (MLP). In the training of the SVM, the hyperplane parameters are adjusted so that the distance of the hyperplane to the data is maximum. The SVM also has another set of parameters called hyper-parameters of which the kernel function is dependent as the constant C of the boundary lines that border the hyperplane, the width of the Gaussian kernel and the degree of the polynomial kernel, among others (Ben-Hur & Weston, 2010). The choice of kernel can be important for the success of the SVM.

The implementation of the Support Vector Machine was done using two main functions to train the SVM and determine the predictive power of the classifier. The SVM requires the input matrix to be divided into two subsets, the training and the test. The percentage used for training was 85% and 15% for test.

All combinations of input parameters of the training function were experimented. The combinations refer to the different Kernel types, parameters associated with these Kernels, and different methods that allows to find the separation hyperplane. The precision, sensitivity and specificity under the test set were recorded for all experiments. The precision, sensitivity and specificity are in accordance with the next section.

2.6. Performance Evaluation

In order to evaluate the results, a confusion matrix was used and sensitivity, specificity and accuracy measures were calculated, as presented in Table 2 and Equation 10:

$$Accuracy = \frac{TP + TN}{TP + FN + TN + FP} \tag{10}$$

Table 2. Confusion matrix used in the analysis.

		Results From Classification	
		Healthy	**Pathology**
Diagnosed	Healthy	True Positive (TP)	False positive (FP)
	Pathology	False Negative (FN)	True Negative (TN)
		Sensitivity = TP/(TP+FN)	Specificity=TN/(TN+FP)

2.7. Feature Selection

The selection of input features is a fundamental consideration in identifying the optimal functional form of statistical models. The task of selecting input features is common to the development of all statistical models, and is largely dependent on the discovery of relationships within the available data to identify suitable predictors of the model output (May, Dandy & Maier, 2011). The process intends to explain the data in the simplest way eliminating redundant features. Applied to regression analysis, this implies that the smallest model that fits the data is the best. Unnecessary parameters will add noise to the estimation of other quantities. It is the attempt to avoid collinearity, caused by having too many variables giving the same information. Feature selection allows to save time and money reducing the problem dimension, turning the system more efficient from the computational point of view (Guyon & Elisseeff, 2003).

Three methods were used, the first two of feature selection and the last one of dimension reduction.

2.7.1. First Method - Hierarchical Clustering (HC)

Hierarchical clustering was used in the first method (Rokach & Maimon, 2005). The basic idea of this method is to create groups with variables most correlated. Then, only one parameter is selected from each group by its Euclidian distance. The parameter with the greater Euclidian distance is selected. The Euclidian distance is calculated for all parameters and between the classes being compared, healthy or pathologic.

2.7.2. Second Method - Multilinear Regression Analysis (MRA)

In the second method, a multilinear regression analysis was applied (Rokach & Maimon, 2005). It is a systematic method for adding and removing terms from a multilinear model based on their statistical significance in a regression. An initial model is created and the static significance is evaluated. At each step, one variable is added or removed based on this analysis. Resulting in an output model that will feed the neural network.

2.7.3. Third Method - Principal Components Analysis (PCA)

In the third method was applied a technique called Principal Components Analysis (PCA) (Smith, 2002). It is a statistical technique that uses the mathematical concepts like standard deviation, covariance, eigenvalues and eigenvectors. First, it is necessary to subtract the mean from each data dimensions. This produces a data set whose mean is zero, called data adjusted. Next, the eigenvectors and eigenvalues are calculated from covariance matrix. It is necessary to decide how many principal components to pick. The principal components are determined and in the output the eigenvalues are already ordered, it is just necessary to calculate the cumulative percentage of these values. Therefore, the first few eigenvectors corresponding to 90% or 95% of the cumulative percentage are selected. This means that the first few eigenvectors explain 90 or 95% of the data. Finally, the adjusted data is multiplied by the inverse of the eigenvectors matrix selected. To get results closer to the real the mean value is calculated only for the train set and subtracted to validation and test set. For the two pathologies, seven principal components were selected.

3. ANALYSIS OF RESULTS

The classification in healthy or pathological was carried out separately for each pathology and for women and men also separately. The number of samples taken from the control group is the same as the pathological group under examination. A vector of 9 parameters (4 of Jitter, 4 of Shimmer and HNR) times three tones (High, Low and Normal), times three vowels (/a/, /i/ and /u/) was created using the algorithm developed by Teixeira and Gonçalves (2016). Once the features vector was made up 81 variables, some dimension reduction and feature selection techniques were applied. This reduces the processing time and shows up the variables capable to distinguish between healthy and pathologic subject. An ANN and the SVM were used for the classification task. For the ANN, different typologies were experimented with a different number of neurons in the hidden layer to find the best generalization model. For the SVM different kernel and values of the hyper-parameters were tested. These alternatives of the ANN and the SVM were experimented with the selected features made with hierarchical clustering method, multilinear regression analyses methods and the components of the PCA method for each pathological group.

3.1. Feature Selection Analysis

Each pathologic group and its counterpart of controls was analysed by the feature selection methods HC and MRA to select the features along the initial set of 81 features. Table 3 presents the selected features resultant from the methods HC and MRA applied for the dysphonia and vocal cords paralysis pathologies, by gender. The top line presents the pathologic group, feature selection method and gender. The left column presents the features extracted from each speech file, the number of features selected for each method and the best accuracy in the test set given by the ANN and SVM classification models. Inside the table, the selected speech file for each feature is presented in the format VT (V- vowel, T- tone). For instance, the method MRA for dysphonia male group selected the jitter feature extracted from vowel /a/ low tone and Rap from vowel /a/ high tone and achieved an accuracy of 100% in the test set.

The feature selection method with the best accuracy achieved was clearly the MRA. This method, generally, selected a small number of features. The features selected more often are: jitta for the three vowels and three tones, shim also for the three vowels and tones, and HNR for the three vowels and tones except for /u/ at high tone. This can be justified because /u/ vowel has high frequency components that are more mixed with noise components, and at high tones, the harmonic components can be more difficult to separate from noisy components. The other features were used more rarely but with improved results by the MRA selection method.

Table 3. Set of selected features for HC and MRA feature selection methods by pathology and gender

Features	Dysph HC Female	Dysph HC Male	Dysph MRA Female	Dysph MRA Male	VCP HC Female	VCP HC Male	VCP MRA Female	VCP MRA Male
	Pathology/Method/Gender							
Jitta	ul, ih, an, un, in, ah, al	in, an, il, ih, al, uh			al, un, ah, an, ul, il	un, il, ul, ih, an, ah	an	ah
Jitter				al				
Rap				ah				in
Ppq5							un	
ShdB								
Shim	il, ul, in, ih, an	ah, al, an, in	in			un, ah, al	uh	
Apq3			an, ah, uh				ah	
Apq5			in					
HNR	ih, il, ul, al	al, ul, ah, un	al		al		al, in	an
# features	16	14	6	2	7	9	6	3
Best accuracy	83.3	70.0	100.0	100.0	73.7	72.7	78.9	81.8

3.2. Dysphonia/Control Classification

Although, the accuracy has been calculated for validation and training set, only the test set accuracy is analysed here. This means that the accuracy was measured in a set that was never seen during training stage. Anyhow, this test set complies only 15% of the subject in each case.

The dysphonia/control classification was made separately for female and male subjects with the ANN and SVM.

Table 4 presents the best results between several experiments with ANN. This table shows the number of input nodes, hidden and output layers [I,H,O], the transfer function in hidden and output layers (TF-H, TF-O), the training function (TR func), the correlation coefficient (R) and Accuracy determined for the test set. The columns of the table display for each case of the selected parameters method and for female and male groups the best architecture of the ANN concerning the number of nodes, transfer function and training function. The best architecture was selected using the performance along the training and validations sets together. The final performance is presented in the table for the test set. Concerning the number of features, 4 situations were considered: using the all set of features, features selected by HC and MRA, and a vector created by the PCA method.

The transfer function used in the ANN are the tangent sigmoidal (tansig), logarithmic sigmoidal (logsig) and linear (purelin). The experimented training functions were the Levenberg-Marquardt (trainlm) based on Marquardt (1963), Resilient back-propagation (trainrp) based on Reidmiller and Braun (1993), and scale conjugate gradient (trainscg) (Moller, 1993).

Concerning the female group, the best accuracy was 100% using the MRA feature selection method. This method reduced from 81 to 6 features and yet achieved an excellent accuracy. The other situations of input features used higher number of features but accuracy remained at 83%. For the male group, the best accuracy was 90%, achieved again by the MRA and PCA methods. Anyhow, the MRA used only 2 features against the 7 used by PCA.

Table 4. Dysphonia, ANN

Input	All features		HC		MRA		PCA	
	Female	Male	Female	Male	Female	Male	Female	Male
Arch. [I,H,O]	[81,20,1]	[81,10,1]	[16,10,1]	[14,20,1]	[6,15,1]	[2,15,1]	[7,15,1]	[7,10,1]
TF-H	tansig	logsig	tansig	logsig	tansig	logsig	tansig	tansig
TF-O	purelin	purelin	purelin	purelin	purelin	purelin	purelin	purelin
TR func.	trainlm	trainlm	trainlm	trainlm	trainscg	trainlm	trainlm	trainscg
R	0.67	0.50	0.71	0.41	1.00	0.82	0.67	0.82
Accuracy	83.3	70.0	83.3	70.0	**100.0**	**90.0**	83.3	**90.0**

Table 5 displays the performance of the SVM for female and male dysphonia groups. The table presents the sensitivity, specificity and accuracy determined under the test set for best kernel and parameters of SVM using all features, features selected by MRA and parameters determined by PCA. The performance achieved by HC features selection method was very poor compared with the other method and therefore it was excluded from the table.

For female and male groups, the best performance was achieved again by the MRA feature selection method and with different kernel and parameters of the SVM model for female and male groups. The accuracy was of 100% using only 6 and 2 features for female and male groups, respectively. For this model, the sensibility and specificity were also 100% for both genders.

Table 5. Dysphonia, SVM

Input	All Features		MRA		PCA	
	Female	Male	Female	Male	Female	Male
Kernel	linear	linear	linear	Gaussian	Gaussian	linear
Parameters	C = 0.1	C = 0.1	C = 0.1	S = 0.1, C = 0.2	S = 2, C = 10	C = 1
Sensitivity	100.0	100.0	100.0	100.0	83.3	100.0
Specificity	83.3	75.0	100.0	100.0	83.3	75.0
Accuracy	91.7	87.5	**100.0**	**100.0**	83.3	87.5

As a conclusion, for dysphonia/control classification the set of features selected for female and male groups achieve 100% accuracy using the best ANN and SVM, and for male group achieved 90% accuracy with the best ANN and 100% with the best SVM.

According to Table 3, the best set of features for the female group is:

- Shim: /i/ vowel at normal tone
- Apq3: /a/ vowel at normal and high tones; /u/ vowel at high tone
- Apq5: /i/ vowel at normal tone
- HNR: /a/ vowel at low tone

For the male group:

- Jitter: /a/ vowel at low tone
- Rap: /a/ vowel at high tone

3.3. Vocal Cords Paralysis/Control Classification

The same type of analysis is presented for vocal cords paralysis using ANN in Table 6 and using SVM in Table 7.

Considering the results presented in Table 6 with ANN for the female group the best accuracy was 76.3% using the all set of features. The feature selection method did not get any improvements in the performance of the ANN.

For the male group, the best accuracy was achieved using the MRA feature selection method and PCA. In both cases, the best accuracy was 81.8% for test set. The MRA selected only 3 features to use in the input layer of the ANN. The PCA changes the features dimension of 81 features to 7 new features.

Table 6. Vocal cords paralysis, ANN

Input	All Features		HC		MRA		PCA	
	Female	Male	Female	Male	Female	Male	Female	Male
Arch. [E,CE,S]	[81,10,1]	[81,15,1]	[7,15,1]	[10,15,1]	[6,20,1]	[3,25,1]	[7,10,1]	[7,15,1]
FTCE	tansig	logsig	tansig	logsig	tansig	tansig	tansig	logsig
FTS	purelin	purelin	purelin	purelin	purelin	purelin	purelin	purelin
FT	trainlm	trainlm	trainlm	trainlm	trainlm	trainscg	trainlm	trainlm
R	0.527	0.567	0.484	0.462	0.436	0.647	0.476	0.636
Accuracy	**76.3**	77.3	73.7	72.7	71.1	**81.8**	73.7	**81.8**

Table 7 presents the best results using the SVM for VCP/control classification. The data follows the same structure described for Table 5. Once more, the HC feature selection method resulted in poor results not presented here.

Concerning the results for the female group, the best accuracy was 78.9% achieved when it was used the all set of features and repeated with the feature selected by MRA method.

For the male group, the best accuracy was 80.0% achieved with the 7 parameters of PCA.

Considering both ANN and SVM models the best results for the female group was 78.9% accuracy achieved using SVM and 76.3% with the ANN. For the male group, the best accuracy was 81.8% attained by the ANN, and 80.0% achieved by SVM.

Table 7. Vocal cords paralysis, SVM

Input	All Features		MRA		PCA	
	Female	**Male**	**Female**	**Male**	**Female**	**Male**
Kernel	Polynomial	Gaussian	Polynomial	linear	Gaussian	Polynomial
Parameters	O=2, C=0.04	S=4, C=0.2	O=2, C=10	C=0.1	S=1, C=0.1	O=4, C=1
Sensitivity	84.2	80.0	89.5	90.0	84.2	80.0
Specificity	73.7	70.0	68.4	60.0	68.4	80.0
Accuracy	**78.9**	75.0	**78.9**	75.0	76.3	**80.0**

The best set of features for the female group is the all dataset or only the following features:

- Jitta: /a/ vowel at normal tone
- Ppq5: /u/ vowel at normal tone
- Shim: /u/ vowel at high tone
- Apq3: /a/ vowel at high tone
- HNR: /a/ vowel at low tone and /i/ vowel at normal tone

For the male group:

- Jitta: /a/ vowel at high tone
- Rap: /i/ vowel at normal tone
- HNR: /a/ vowel at normal tone

A final consideration about the accuracy should be made. The accuracy was measured in the test set that consists of 15% of all dataset. Therefore, the test set consists of 12 subjects for the Dysphonia/female, 9 subjects for Dysphonia/male, 38 subjects for VCP/female and 21 subjects for VCP/male. An accuracy of 100% means that all the subjects of the test set of the pathology/gender get a correct diagnosis. However, since the number of subjects is not too high this result must be seen carefully.

4. CONCLUSION

Vocal acoustic analysis technique was applied to classify between dysphonic and healthy voices and between vocal cords paralysis and healthy voices. The classification was made for female and male with different models and architectures. The ANN and SVM were used as classifier tools. Different architectures of the ANN and SVM were experimented. The ANN and the SVM made the classification using a subset of features selected by hierarchical cluster method, multilinear regression analysis, or a set of new features obtained with the PCA method. These methods select a subset of features from the 4 measures of jitter, 4 measures of shimmer and HNR extracted from speech sound files with 3 vowels pronounced at three tones, in a total of 81 features.

The accuracy of the classification between pathologic/control measured in the test set was used to compare the models.

The best results for the classification between dysphonic/control female subjects was 100% of accuracy, achieved using ANN and SVM with the set of features selected by RMA method. For the male group, the best result was also 100% of accuracy, obtained by the SVM with the MRA features.

The MRA method reduced from 81 to 6 features for female and 2 features for male groups. The SVM showed to be very powerful to classify dysphonic voices of both genders.

The vocal cords paralysis showed to be more difficult to classify. The same methodology achieved an accuracy of 78.9% for the female group with SVM, and 81.8% for the male group with ANN.

The MRA method reduced the 81 features to 6 features for the female group with the same accuracy, and to only 3 features for the male group.

Comparing the ANN and SVM models both proved to be adequate tools to classify between control and pathologic voices with high accuracy.

Some future challenges in this work consists in extend the development of the diagnosis system to including other pathologies and then classify the pathology. The major limitation concerns with the short length of the speech database with clinical labelled pathologies.

ACKNOWLEDGMENT

The authors thank the HCIST 2017 conference for the invitation to publish this article.

REFERENCES

Al-nasheri, A., Muhammad, G., Alsulaiman, M., & Ali, Z. (2016). Investigation of Voice Pathology Detection and Classification on Different Frequency Regions Using Correlation Functions. *Journal of Voice*, *31*(1), 3–15. doi:10.1016/j.jvoice.2016.01.014 PMID:26992554

Almeida, N. C. (2010). Sistema inteligente para diagnóstico de patologias na laringeutilizando máquinas de vetor de suporte. Universidade Federal do Rio Grande do Norte. Retrieved from https://repositorio.ufrn.br/jspui/handle/123456789/15149

Barry, W. J., & Pützer, M. (2007). Saarbruecken Voice Database. *Stimmdaten Bank*. Retrieved from http://www.stimmdatenbank.coli.uni-saarland.de/help_en.php4

Ben-Hur, A., & Weston, J. (2010). A User's Guide to Support Vector Machines. *SourceForge*. Retrieved from http://pyml.sourceforge.net/doc/howto.pdf

Bielamowicz, S., Kreiman, J., Gerratt, B., Dauer, M., & Berke, G. (1996). Comparison of Voice Analysis Systems for Perturbation Measurement. *Journal of Speech and Hearing Research*, *39*(1), 126–134. doi:10.1044/jshr.3901.126 PMID:8820704

Boersma, P., & Weenink, D. (2009). Praat Manual: doing phonetics by computer. 5.1.18. [Computer program]. Retrieved from http://www.fon.hum.uva.nl/praat/download_win.html

Brockmann-Bauser, M. (2011). Improving jitter and shimmer measurements in normal voices [PhD Thesis]. Newcastle University.

Cordeiro, H. T. (2017). Reconhecimento de patologias da voz usando técnicas de processamento da fala. Retrieved from https://run.unl.pt/handle/10362/19915

Cruz, A. (2007). Data Mining via Redes Neuronais Artificiais e Máquinas de Vectores de Suporte.

Forero, L. A., Kohler, M., Vellasco, M., & Cataldo, E. (2015). Analysis and Classification of Voice Pathologies Using Glottal Signal Parameters. *Journal of Voice*, *30*(5), 549–556. doi:10.1016/j.jvoice.2015.06.010 PMID:26474715

Guyon, I., & Elisseeff, A. (2003). An Introduction to Variable and Feature Selection. *Journal of Machine Learning Research*, *3*, 1157–1182. Retrieved from http://www.jmlr.org/papers/volume3/guyon03a/guyon03a.pdf

Henríquez, P., Alonso, J. B., Ferrer, M. A., Travieso, C. M., Godino-Llorente, J. I., & Díaz-di-María, F. (2009). Characterization of Healthy and Pathological Voice Through Measures Based on Nonlinear Dynamics. *IEEE Transactions on Audio, Speech, and Language Processing*, *17*(6), 1186–1195. doi:10.1109/TASL.2009.2016734

Hirano, M. (1974). Morphological structure of the vocal cord as a vibrator and its variations. *Folia Phoniatrica*, *26*(2), 89–94. doi:10.1159/000263771 PMID:4845615

Markaki, M., & Stylianou, Y. (2011). Voice Pathology Detection and Discrimination Based on Modulation Spectral Features. *IEEE Transactions on Audio, Speech, and Language Processing*, *19*(7), 1938–1948. doi:10.1109/TASL.2010.2104141

Marquardt, D. W. (1963). An Algorithm for Least-Squares Estimation of Nonlinear Parameters. *Journal of the Society for Industrial and Applied Mathematics*, *11*(2), 431–441. doi:10.1137/0111030

May, R., Dandy, G., & Maier, H. (2011). *Review of Input Variable Selection Methods for Artificial Neural Networks*. In Methodological Advances and Biomedical Applications. doi:10.5772/16004

Moller, M. F. (1993). A Scaled Conjugate Gradient Algorithm for Fast Supervised Learning. *Neural Networks*, *6*(4), 525–533. doi:10.1016/S0893-6080(05)80056-5

Netter, F. (2014). *Atlas of Human Anatomy* (6th ed.). Philadelphia, PA: Saunders Elsevier.

Panek, D., Skalski, A., Gajda, J., & Tadeusiewicz, R. (2015). Acoustic Analysis Assessment in Speech Pathology Detection. *International Journal of Applied Mathematics and Computer Science*, *25*(3), 631–643. doi:10.1515/amcs-2015-0046

Pylypowich, A., & Duff, E. (2016). Differentiating the Symptom of Dysphonia. *The Journal for Nurse Practitioners*, *12*(7), 459–466. doi:10.1016/j.nurpra.2016.04.025

Reidmiller, M., & Braun, H. (1993). A direct adaptive method for faster backpropagation learning: The RPRO algorithm. In *Proceedings of the IEEE International Conference on Neural Networks*. 10.1109/ICNN.1993.298623

Rokach, L., & Maimon, O. (2005). Clustering Methods. In *Data Mining and Knowledge Discovery Handbook* (pp. 321–352). New York: Springer-Verlag; doi:10.1007/0-387-25465-X_15

Salhi, L., Mourad, T., & Cherif, A. (2010). Voice Disorders Identification Using Multilayer Neural Network. *The International Arab Journal of Information Technology*, 177–185.

Sellam, V., & Jagadeesan, J. (2014). Classification of Normal and Pathological Voice Using SVM and RBFNN. *Journal of Signal and Information Processing*, 5(1), 1–7. doi:10.4236/jsip.2014.51001 PMID:24513981

Smith, L. I. (2002). A tutorial on Principal Components Analysis. Retrieved from http://www.iro.umontreal.ca/~pift6080/H09/documents/papers/pca_tutorial.pdf

Teixeira, J. P., & Fernandes, P. O. (2014). Jitter, Shimmer and HNR classification within gender, tones and vowels in healthy voices. *Procedia Technology*, 16, 1228–1237. doi:10.1016/j.protcy.2014.10.138

Teixeira, J. P., & Fernandes, P. O. (2015). Acoustic Analysis of Vocal Dysphonia. *Procedia Computer Science*, 64, 466–473. doi:10.1016/j.procs.2015.08.544

Teixeira, J. P., Fernandes, P. O., & Alves, N. (2017). Vocal Acoustic Analysis - Classification of Dysphonic Voices with Artificial Neural Networks. *Procedia Computer Science*, 121, 19–26. doi:10.1016/j.procs.2017.11.004

Teixeira, J. P., & Gonçalves, A. (2014). Accuracy of Jitter and Shimmer Measurements. *Procedia Technology*, 16, 1190–1199. doi:10.1016/j.protcy.2014.10.134

Teixeira, J. P., & Gonçalves, A. (2016). Algorithm for jitter and shimmer measurement in pathologic voices. *Procedia Computer Science*, 100, 271–279. doi:10.1016/j.procs.2016.09.155

This research was previously published in the International Journal of E-Health and Medical Communications (IJEHMC), 11(1); pages 37-51, copyright year 2020 by IGI Publishing (an imprint of IGI Global).

Chapter 29

Infant Cry Recognition System:
A Comparison of System Performance based on CDHMM and ANN

Yosra Abdulaziz Mohammed
University of Fallujah, Baghdad, Iraq

ABSTRACT

Cries of infants can be seen as an indicator of pain. It has been proven that crying caused by pain, hunger, fear, stress, etc., show different cry patterns. The work presented here introduces a comparative study between the performance of two different classification techniques implemented in an automatic classification system for identifying two types of infants' cries, pain, and non-pain. The techniques are namely, Continuous Hidden Markov Models (CHMM) and Artificial Neural Networks (ANN). Two different sets of acoustic features were extracted from the cry samples, those are MFCC and LPCC, the feature vectors generated by each were eventually fed into the classification module for the purpose of training and testing. The results of this work showed that the system based on CDHMM have better performance than that based on ANN. CDHMM gives the best identification rate at 96.1%, which is much higher than 79% of ANN whereby in general the system based on MFCC features performed better than the one that utilizes LPCC features.

INTRODUCTION

For infants, crying is a communication tool, a very limited one, but similar to the way an adult communicates. They use cries to express their physical, emotional and psychological states and needs (Drummond & McBride, 1993). An infant may cry for a variety of reasons, and many scientists believe that there are different types of cries which reflects different states and needs of infants, thus it is possible to analyze and classify infant cries for clinical diagnosis purposes.

Based on the information carried by the crying wave, the infant's physical state can be determined, and thus it can be detected if the infant is suffering a physical pain or just hunger or anger. Given that

DOI: 10.4018/978-1-6684-2408-7.ch029

the processing of the information in the infant cry is basically a kind of pattern recognition, the task was approached by using the same techniques used for automatic speech recognition.

Hidden Markov Model is based on double stochastic processes, whereby the first process produces a set of observations which in turns can be used indirectly to reveal another hidden process that describes the states evolution (Rabiner,1989). This technique has been used extensively to analyze audio signals such as for biomedical signal processing (Lederman, Cohen, & Zmora, 2002) and speech recognition (Al-Alaoui, Al-Kanj, Azar, & Yaacoub, 2008). Neural Networks are defined as systems which have the capability to model highly complex nonlinear problems and composed of many simple processing elements, that operate in parallel and whose function is determined by the network's structure, the strength of its connections, and the processing carried out by the processing elements or nodes.

In this work, a series of an observable feature vector is used to reveal the cry model hence assists in its classification. First, the paper describes the overall architecture of an automatic recognition system which main task is to differentiate between an infant 'pain' cries from 'non-pain' cries. The performance of both systems is compared in terms of recognition accuracy, classification error rate and F-measure under the use of two different acoustic features, namely Mel Frequency Cepstral Coefficient (MFCC) and Linear Prediction Cepstral Coefficients (LPCC). Separate phases of system training and system testing are carried out on two different sample sets of infant cries recorded from a group of babies which ranges from newborns up to 12 months old.

The prime objective of this paper is to compare the performance of an automatic infant's cry classification system applying two different classification techniques, Artificial Neural Networks and continuous Hidden Markov Model.

Background

A number of research work related to this line have been reported, whereby many of which are based on Artificial Neural Network (ANN) classification techniques. (Petroni, Malowany, Johnston, & Stevens,1995) for example, have used three different varieties of supervised ANN technique which include a simple feed-forward, a recurrent neural network (RNN) and a time-delay neural network (TDNN) in their infant cry classification system. In their study, they have attempted to recognize and classify three categories of cry, namely 'pain', 'fear' and 'hunger' and the results demonstrated that the highest classification rate was achieved by using feed-forward neural network. Another research work carried out by (Cano & Escobedo, 1999) used the Kohonen's self-organizing maps (SOM) which is basically a variety of unsupervised ANN technique to classify different infant cries. (Rosales-Pérez, Reyes-Garcia, Gonzalez, & Arch-Tirado, 2012) used Genetic Selection of a Fuzzy Model (GSFM) for classification of infant cry where GSFM selects a combination of feature selection methods, type of fuzzy processing, learning algorithm, and its associated parameters that best fit to the data and have obtained up to 99.42% in recognition accuracy. (Al-Azzawi, 2014) designed an automatic infant cry recognition system based on the fuzzy transform (F-transform) that classifies two different kinds of cries, which come from physiological status and medical disease, a supervised MLP scaled conjugate ANN was used and the classification accuracy obtained was 96%.

Apart from the traditional ANN approach, another infant cry classification technique studied is Support Vector Machine (SVM) which has been reported by (Barajas & Reyes, 2005). Here, a set of Mel Frequency Cepstral Coefficients (MFCC) was extracted from the audio samples as the input features.

On the other hand, (Orozco & Reyes, 2003a), use the linear prediction technique to extract the acoustic features from the cry samples of which are then fed into a feed-forward neural network recognition module. Recently (CY. Chang, CW. Chang, Kathiravan, & Chen, 2017) have proposed an infant cry classification system to categorize the types of infant crying into hunger; pain; and feeling sleepy. Fifteen features were extracted from each crying frame and the sequential forward floating selection was adopted to pick out high discriminative features. The directed acyclic graph support vector machine was used to classify infant crying. The proposed system showed a classification accuracy of 92.17%.

(Orlandi, Reyes-Garcia, Bandini, Donzelli, & Manfredi, 2016) studied the differences between full-term and preterm infant cry comparing four classifiers: Logistic Curve, Multilayer Perceptron, Support Vector Machine, and Random Forest. They managed to assess differences between preterm and full-term newborns with about 87% of accuracy. Best results were obtained with the Random Forest method (receiver operating characteristic area, 0.94).

MATERIALS AND METHODS

Experimental Data Sets

The infant cry corpus collected is a set of 150 pain samples and 30 non-pain samples recorded from a random time interval. The babies selected for recording varies from newborns up to 12-month-old, a mixture of both healthy males and females. The records are then sampled at 16000 Hertz. It is important to highlight here that the pain cry episodes are the result of the pain stimulus carried out during routine immunization at a local pediatric clinic, in Darnah, Libya. Recordings resulting from anger, or hunger were considered as non-pain utterances were recorded at quiet rooms at various infants' home. Recordings were made on a digital player at a sample rate of 8000 Hertz and 4-bit resolution with a microphone placed between 10 to 30 centimeters away from the infant's mouth. The audio signals were then transferred for analysis to a sound editor and then re-sampled at 16000 with 16-bit resolution (Petroni et al.,1995; Baeck & Souza, 2001). The final digital recordings were stored as WAV files.

Here, a series of an observable feature vector is used to reveal the cry model hence assists in its classification. First, the paper describes the overall architecture of an automatic recognition system which main task is to differentiate between an infant 'pain' cries from 'non-pain' cries. The performance of both systems is compared in terms of recognition accuracy, classification error rate and F-measure under the use of two different acoustic features, namely Mel Frequency Cepstral Coefficient (MFCC) and Linear Prediction Cepstral Coefficients (LPCC). Separate phases of system training and system testing are carried out on two different sample sets of infant cries recorded from a group of babies which ranges from newborns up to 12 months old.

System Description

In this paper, we consider two recognition engines for infant's cry classification system. The first is an artificial neural network (ANN) which is a very popular pattern matching in the field of speech recognition. Feedforward multilayer perceptron (MLP) network with a backpropagation learning algorithm is the most well-known of ANN. The other technique is a continuous density hidden Markov model (CDHMM). The overall system is as depicted in Figure1 below:

Figure 1. Infant cry recognition system architecture

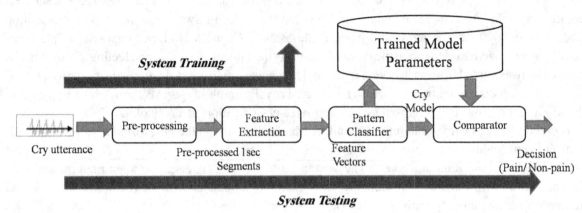

From Figure 1, we can say that infant cry recognition system implies three main tasks,

- Signal Preprocessing
- Feature Extraction
- Pattern Matching

Pre-Processing

The first step in the proposed system is the pre-processing step which requires the removal of the 'silent' periods from the recorded sample. Recordings with cry units lasting at least 1 second from the moment of stimulus event were used for the study (Petroni et al.,1995; Orozco & Reyes, 2003a). The cry units are defined as "the duration of the vocalization only during expiration" (Baeck & Souza, 2001, p. 2174).

The audio recordings were then divided further into segments of exactly 1 second length, where each represents a pre-processed cry segments as recommended by (Barajas & Reyes, 2005; Petroni et al., 1995; Orozco & Reyes, 2003a; Suaste, Reyes, Diaz, & Reyes,2004). Before these one second segments can be used for feature extraction, a process called pre-emphasis is applied. Pre-emphasis aims at reducing the high spectral dynamic range, and is accomplished by passing the signal through a FIR filter whose transfer function is given by,

$$F(z) = 1 - kz^{-1}, (0<k<1) \tag{1}$$

A typical value for the pre-emphasis parameter 'k' is usually 0.97. Consequently, the output is formed as follow:

$$y(n) = s(n)k.s(n-1) \tag{2}$$

where $s(n)$ is the input signal and $y(n)$ is the output signal from the first order FIR filter.

Every segment of 1 second is divided thereafter in frames of 50-milliseconds with successive frames overlapping by 50% from each other. The next step is to use a window function on each individual frame in order to minimize discontinuities at the beginning and end of each frame. Typically, the window function used is the Hamming window shown in Figure 2 and has the following form:

$$w(n) = 0.54 - 0.46 \cos\left(\frac{2\pi n}{N-1}\right), \ 0 \leq n \leq N-1 \tag{3}$$

Given the above window function and assuming that there are N samples in each frame, we will obtain the following signal after windowing.

$$y(n) = x(n)w(n), \ 0 \leq n \leq (N-1) \tag{4}$$

Figure 2. Hamming window

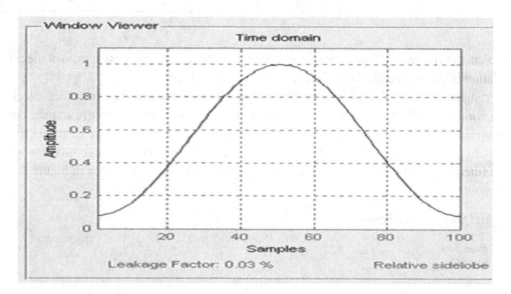

Off the 150 pain and 30 non-pain recording samples, 625 and 256 one second cry segments were obtained respectively. Off these 881 cry segments, 700 were used for system training and 181 were used for system testing. In order to ensure that the trained model is not biased by this dataset, the 1-second segments used for the training phase were coming from t cry episodes different than those used in testing phase. It is important to use a separate set of cry segments for training and testing purposes in order to avoid obtaining biased testing results.

Feature Extraction

Mel-Frequency Cepstral Coefficients (MFCC)

MFCCs are one of the more popular parameter used by researchers in the acoustic research domain. It has the benefit that it is capable of capturing the important characteristics of audio signals. Cepstral

Figure 3. Extraction of MFCC from audio signals

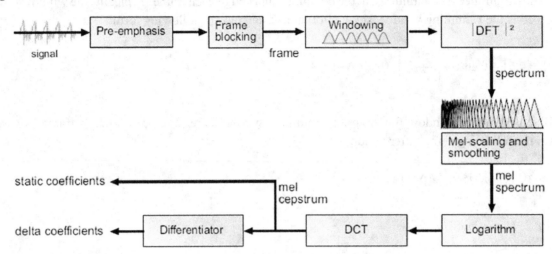

analysis calculates the inverse Fourier transform of the logarithm of the power spectrum of the cry signal, the calculation of the mel cepstral coefficients is illustrated in Figure 3.

The cry signal must be divided into overlapping blocks first, (in our experiment the blocks are in Hamming windows) which is then transformed into its power spectrum. Because human perception of the frequency contents of sounds does not follow a linear scale, they are approximately linear with logarithmic frequency beyond about 1000 Hz. The mel frequency warping is most conveniently done by utilizing a filter bank with filters centered according to mel frequencies as shown in Figure 4.

Figure 4. Mel spaced filter banks

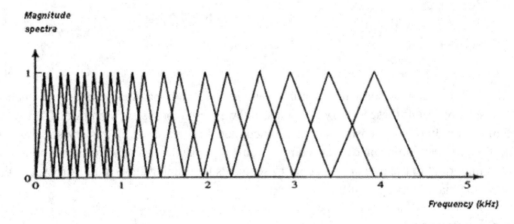

The mapping is usually done using an approximation (where *fmel* is the perceived frequency in mels),

$$f_{mel}(f) = 2595 \times \log\left(1 + \frac{f}{700}\right) \qquad (5)$$

These vectors were normalized so that all the values within a given 1 second sample would lie between ±1 in order to decrease their dynamic range (Petroni et al., 1995).

Linear Prediction Cepstral Coefficients (LPCC)

LPCC is Linear Predicted Coefficients (LPC) in the cepstrum domain. The basis of linear prediction analysis is that a given speech sample can be approximated with a linear combination of the past p speech samples (Orozco & Reyes, 2003b). This can be calculated either by the autocorrelation or covariance methods directly from the windowed portion of audio signal (Wong & Sridharan, 2001). This method of linear prediction is known as an appropriate technique to process speech and some works also have been performed based on this technique (Saraswathy, Hariharan, Yaacob, & Khairunizam, 2012). In this study the LPC coefficients were calculated using the autocorrelation method that uses Levinson-Durbin recursion algorithm. Hence, LPCC can be derived from LPC using the recursion as follows:

$$c_0 = r(0) \tag{6}$$

where $c_0 = r(0)$, r is derived from the LPC autocorrelation matrix

$$c_m = a_m + \sum_{k=1}^{m-1} (\frac{k}{n}) c_k a_{m-k} \text{ for } 1<m<P \tag{7}$$

$$c_m = \sum_{k=m-p}^{m-1} (\frac{k}{n}) c_k a_{m-k} \text{ for } m>P \tag{8}$$

where p is the so called prediction order, a_m represents the mth LPC coefficient and m is the number of LPCC's needed to be calculated. Whereas c_m is the mth LPCC. The calculation of LPCC is depicted in Figure 5

Figure 5. Extraction of LPCC from audio signals

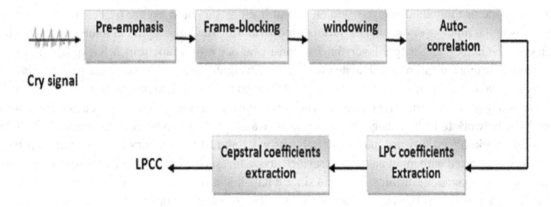

Dynamic Features

The cepstral coefficients are usually referred to as static features, since they only contain information from a given frame. It has been proved that system performance may be enhanced by adding time derivatives to the static parameters (Wong & Sridharan, 2001). The extra information about the temporal dynamics of the signal is obtained by computing first and second derivatives of cepstral coefficients (Rao, Sreenivasa, Reddy, Ramu, Maity, Sudhamay, 2015). The first order derivative is called delta coefficients, and the second order derivative is called delta-delta coefficients. Delta coefficients tell about the signal rate, and delta-delta coefficients provide information similar to acceleration of signal.

The first order derivatives can be calculated as shown in formula 9,

$$d_t = \frac{\sum_{\theta=1}^{\Theta} \theta \left(c_{t+\theta} - c_{t-\theta} \right)}{2\sum_{\theta=1}^{\Theta} \theta^2} \tag{9}$$

where d, is the delta coefficient at time t, computed in terms of the corresponding static coefficients $c_{t-\theta}$, to $c_{t+\theta}$, and Θ is the size of delta window.

The delta-delta coefficients are computed by taking the first order derivative of the delta coefficients.

Patter Matching

Artificial Neural Network (ANN) Approach

Neural network is a technology which tries to mimic human brain functions. With the improvement of neural network these past few decades, using neural network in speech and speaker recognition has become very popular and successful (Barr, Hopkins, & Green, 2000). ANN are defined as systems which has the capability to model highly complex nonlinear problems and composed of many simple processing elements, that operate in parallel and whose function is determined by the network's structure, the strength of its connections, and the processing carried out by the processing elements or nodes.

The feedforward multilayer perceptron (MLP) network architecture using a backpropagation learning algorithm is one of the most popular neural networks. It consists of at least three layers of neurons: an input layer, one or more hidden layers and an output layer as shown in Figure 6 . Processing elements or neurons in the input layer only act as buffers for distributing the input signal xi to neurons in the hidden layer. The hidden and output layers have a non-linear activation function. A backpropagation is a supervised learning algorithm to calculate the change of weights in the network. In the forward pass, the weights are fixed, and the input vector is propagated through the network to produce an output. An output error is calculated from the difference between actual output and the target. This is propagated backwards through the network to make changes to the weights (Kasuriya, Wutiwiwatchai, & Tanprasert, 2001).

For this work, a feed-forward multilayer perceptron using full connections between adjacent layers was trained and tested with input patterns described above in a supervised manner with scaled conjugate gradient back-propagation learning algorithm since it has shown good results in classifying infant's cries than other NN algorithms (Orozco & Reyes, 2003c). The number of computations in each iteration is significantly reduced mainly because no line search is required. Different feature sets were used in order to determine the set that results in optimum recognition rate. Sets of 12 MFCC, 12MFCC+1ST derivative, 12 MFCC+1st & 2nd derivative, 20 MFCC, 16 LPCC and 16 LPCC+ 1st derivative was used. Two frame length was used, 50ms and 100 ms in order to determine the right choice that gives the best results. Two architectures were investigated in this study. First, with one hidden layer then with two hidden layers. The number of hidden neurons was varied to obtain optimum performance. The number of neurons in the input layer is decided by the number of elements in the feature vector. Output layer has two neurons each for one cry class the activation function used in all layers in this work is hyperbolic tangent sigmoid transfer function 'TANSIG'. Training stops when any of these conditions occur:

- The maximum number of epochs (repetitions) is reached. we established 500 epochs at maximum because above this value, the convergence line do not have any significant change.
- The networks were trained until the performance is minimized to the goal i.e. mean squared error is less than 0.00001.

Figure 6. MLP neural network

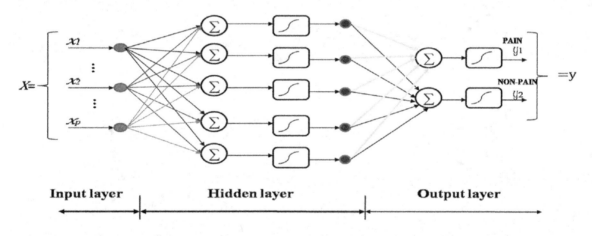

Input layer   Hidden layer   Output layer

Hidden Markov Model (HMM) Approach

Gaussian mixture continuous density HMM (CDHMM) is the most popular and successful model for pattern recognition. It has been successfully implemented in handwritten character recognition, speech recognition, speaker identification, signature verification and many other applications. The continuous HMM is chosen over the discrete counterparts since it avoids losing of critical signal information during discrete symbol quantization process and that it provides for better modeling of continuous signal representation such as the audio cry signal (Picone, 1991). However, computational complexity when using the CHMMs is more than the computational complexity when using DHMMs. It normally takes more time in the training phase (Tolba, 2009).

An HMM is specified by the following:

- N, the number of states in the HMM;

- $\pi i\_P(x1\_si_j$, the prior probability of state si being the first state of a state sequence. The collection of $\pi 1$ forms the vector $\pi = \{\ \pi 1,\ ...,\ \pi N_j\}$;
- $a_{ij} = P\left(x_{t+1} = s_j | x_t = s_i\right)$, the transition coefficients gives the probability of going from state s_i immediately to state s_j. The collection of a_{ij} forms the transition matrix A.
- Emission probability of a certain observation o, when the model is in state s_i. The observation o can be either discrete or continuous (Tolba, 2009). However, in this study a continuous HMM is applied whereby continuous observations $o \in \mathfrak{R}^D . b_i = P\left(o_t \mid x_t = s_i\right)$ indicates the probability density function (pdf) over the observation space for the model being in state s_i.

In this study, a five states ergodic model was used as shown in Figure 7.

Figure 7. Ergodic model structure of HMM

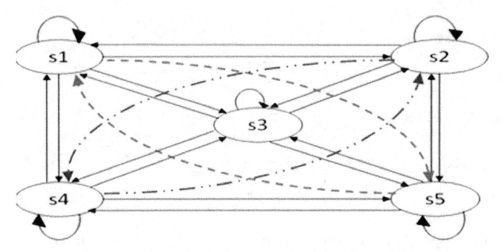

For the continuous HMM, the observations are continuous and the output likelihood of an HMM for a given observation vector, can be expressed as a weighted sum of M multivariate Gaussian probability densities (Cai, Bouselmi, Laprie, & Haton, 2009) as given by the equation

$$b_j\left(o_t\right) = \sum_{m=1}^{M} C_{jm} \aleph\left(o_t; \mu_{jm}, \Sigma_{jm}\right), \text{ for } 1 \leq j \leq N \tag{10}$$

where o_t is a d-dimensional feature vector, M is the number of Gaussian mixture components m is the mixture index ($1 \leq m \leq M$), C_{jm} is the mixture weight for the mth component, which satisfies the constraint

- $C_{jm} > 0$
- $\sum_{m=1}^{M} C_{jm} = 1$, $1 \leq j \leq N$, $1 \leq m \leq M$

where N is the number of states, j is the state index, μ_{jm} is the mean vectors of the mth Gaussian probability densities function, and $\aleph$ is the most efficient density functions widely used without loss of generality (Tolba, 2009 ; Cai et al., 2009)which is defined as,

$$\aleph\left(o_t;\mu_{jm},\sum_{jm}\right) = \frac{1}{\sqrt{(2\pi)^d |\Sigma|}} \exp\left\{-\frac{1}{2}\left(o_t - \mu_{jm}\right)^{\tau} \sum_{jm}^{-1}(o_t - \mu_{jm})\right\} \tag{11}$$

In the training phase, and in order to derive the models for both 'pain' and'non-pain' cries (i.e. to derive λ_{pain} and $\lambda_{non\text{-}pain}$ models respectively) we first have to make a rough guess about the parameters of an HMM, and based on these initial parameters more accurate parameters can be found by applying the Baum-Welch algorithm. This mainly requires for the learning problem of HMM as highlighted by (Rabiner, 1989) in his HMM tutorial. The re-estimation procedure is sensitive to the selection of initial parameters. The model topology is specified by an initial transition matrix. The state means and variances can be initialized by clustering the training data into as many clusters as there are states in the model with the K-means clustering algorithm and estimating the initial parameters from these clusters (Resch, n.d.).

The basic idea behind the Baum-Welch algorithm (also known as Forward-Backward algorithm) is to iteratively re-estimate the parameters of a model, and to obtain a new model with a better set of parameters, which satisfies the following criterion for the observation sequence $O=(o_1,o_2,\ldots,o_t)$,

$$P\left(O|\bar{\lambda}\right) \geq P\left(O|\lambda\right) \tag{12}$$

where the given parameters are, $\lambda = \left(\pi, A, \mu_j, \sum_j\right)$. By setting, $\lambda=\bar{\lambda}$, at the end of every iteration and re-estimating a better parameter set, the probability of $P(O|\lambda)$ can be improved until some threshold is reached. The re-estimation procedure is guaranteed to find in a local optimum. The flow chart of the training procedure is shown in Figure 8

Once the system training is completed, system testing is carried out to investigate the accuracy of the recognition system. The classification is done with a maximum-likelihood classifier, that is the model with the highest probability with respect to the observations sequence, i.e., the one that maximizes $P(Model \mid Observations)$ will be the natural choice,

$$\hat{\lambda}_{ML} = \arg\max_{1\leq k\leq K} P\left(O|\lambda_k\right) \tag{13}$$

This is called the maximum likelihood (ML) estimate. The best model in maximum likelihood sense is therefore the one that is most probable to generate the given observations.

Separate untrained samples from each class where fed into the HMM classifier and were compared against the trained 'pain' and 'non-pain' model. This testing process mainly requires for evaluation problem of HMM as highlighted by (Rabiner, 1989). The classification follows the following algorithm:

If P(test_sample$|\lambda_{pain}$) > P(test_sample$|\lambda_{non\text{-}pain}$)

Then test_sample is classified *'pain'*

Else

test_sample is classified *'non_pain'*   (14)

Figure 8. Training flow chart

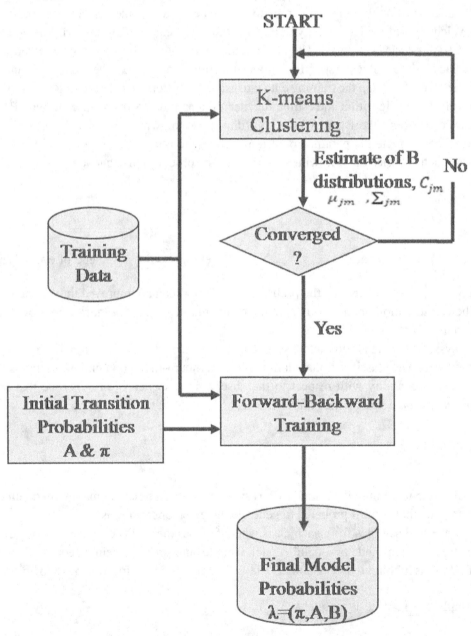

EXPERIMENTAL RESULTS

A total of 700 cry segments of 1 second duration is used during system testing. Each feature vector is extracted at 50ms windows with 75% overlap between adjacent frames. The size of the input data frame used was 50ms and 100ms in order to determine which would yield the best results for this application. These settings were used in all experiments reported in this paper which compare between the performance of both types of infant cry recognition systems described above utilizing 12 MFCCs (with 26 filter banks) and 16LPCCs (with 12th order LPC) acoustic features. The effect of the dynamic coefficients for both used features was also investigated.

After optimizing system's parameters by performing some preliminary experiments, it was found that a fully connected (an ergodic) HMM topology shown in Figure 7 with five states and eight Gaussian mixture per state is the best choice to model the cry utterances because it scored the best identification rate. On the other hand, a fully connected feedforward MLP NN trained with backpropagation with Scaled Conjugate Gradient algorithm, with one hidden layer and five hidden neurons as shown in Figure 6 has given the best recognition rates. The best results for both systems were obtained using 50 ms frame length.

The results of training and testing datasets are evaluated using standard performance measures defined as follows:

- The classification accuracy which is calculated by taking the percentage number of correctly classified test samples.

$$\text{System Accuracy (\%)} = \frac{x_{correct}}{T} \times 100\% \qquad (15)$$

where $x_{correct}$ is the total number of correctly classified test samples and T is the overall total number of test samples.

- The classification error rate (CER) which is defined as follows (Liu & Shriberg, 2007):

$$CER = \frac{fn + fp}{tp + fn + fp + tn} \qquad (16)$$

- F- measure which is defined as follows [14] (Liu & Shriberg, 2007),

$$precision = \frac{tp}{tp + fp} \qquad (17)$$

$$\left(sensitivity\right) = \frac{tp}{tp + fn} \qquad (18)$$

$$F - measure = \frac{2 \times precision \times sensitivity}{precision + sensitivity} \qquad (19)$$

F-measure varies from 0 to 1, with a higher *F*-measure indicating better performance (Liu, & Shriberg, 2007). where tp is the number of pain test samples successfully classified, fp is the number of misclassified non-pain test samples, fn is the number of misclassified pain test samples, and finally tn the number of correctly classified non-pain test samples.

Table 1 and Table 2 show the results obtained from both systems for different feature sets. Figure 9 summarizes a comparison between the performance of both systems for different feature sets used.

Whereas Table 3, Figure 10, and Figure 11 summarizes a comparison between performance of both systems using different performance metrics for the optimum results obtained with both MFCC and LPCC features.

Table 1. Performance of HMM system

Feature Set	Accuracy	HMM Topology &Window size
20 MFCC	96.1%	8Gaussians 5 states, 50 ms
12 MFCC	82.3%	10Gaussians, 5 states, 100 ms
12MFCC+ energy+DEL,	92.3%	8Gaussians, 5 states, 50 ms
12 MFCC+ energy + DEL+ DEL DEL	91.2%	8Gaussians, 5 states, 50 ms
16 LPCC	72.4%	14 Gaussians, 5 states, 50 ms
16 LPCC + DEL	78.5%	10 Gaussians 5 states,, 50 ms

Table 2. Performance of ANN system

Feature Set	Accuracy	NN Structure & window size
20MFCC	79%	1 hidden layer, 5 nodes, 50ms
12 MFCC	73%	1 hidden layer, 5 nodes, 100ms
12MFCC+ energy+DEL	76.2%	2 hidden layers, 5 nodes each, 50ms
12 MFCC+ energy + DEL+ DEL DEL	72.4%	1 hidden layer, 5 nodes, 100ms
16 LPCC	70.2%	1 hidden layer, 5 nodes,50ms
16 LPCC+DEL	66.3%	2 hidden layers, 10 nodes, 50ms

DISCUSSION

Both systems performed optimally with 20 MFCC's 50 ms window. For the NN based system the hierarchy of one hidden layer having 5 hidden nodes showed to be the best, while an ergodic HMM with 5 states and 8 Gaussians per state has resulted in the best recognition rates. The optimum recognition rates obtained were 96.1% for HMM trained with 20 MFCC, whereas for ANN the highest recognition rate was 79% using 20 MFCC also. For both systems trained with LPCC's, the best recognition rate obtained for HMM was 78.5% using 16 LPCC+DEL, 10 Gaussians, 5 states and 50 ms whereas for ANN was 70.2% using 16 LPCC, 5 states, 8 Gaussians per state and 50 ms window.

For HMM system, the combination of the static coefficients and their first derivative yielded better classification rates for LPCC than the static coefficients alone. Addition of the second derivative MFCC coefficients has not improved the system performance, it has reduced the rate by 1%. It is obvious that MFCC's performed better than LPCC's, though the addition of the DEL LPCC has improved its performance.

Table 3. Overall system accuracy

Performance Measures	Features			
	MFCC		LPCC	
	ANN	HMM	ANN	HMM
F-measure	0.83	0.97	0.75	0.84
CER%	20.99	3.87	29.83	21.55
Accuracy%	79	96.1	70.2	78.5

Figure 9. Identification rate of ANN and CDHMM

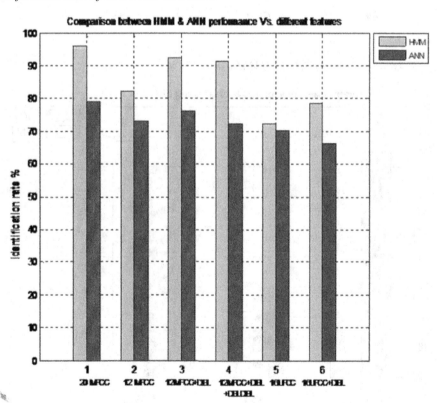

Figure 10. Comparison between ANN and using MFCC

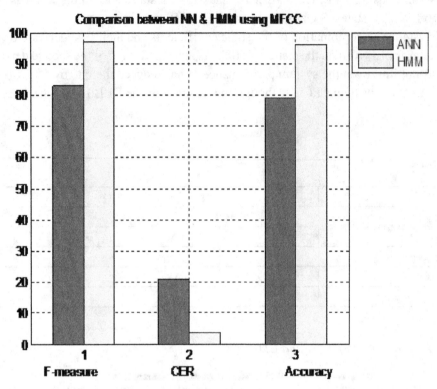

Figure 11. Comparison between ANN and HMM using LPCC

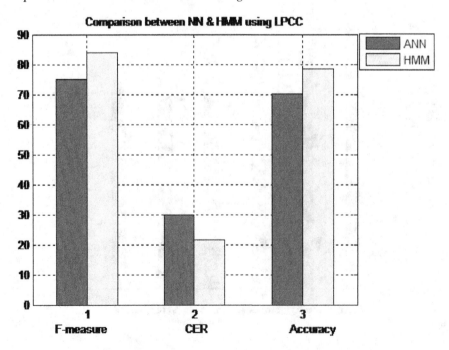

CONCLUSION

Two artificial intelligence techniques were applied to identify infant pain and non-pain cries. From the obtained results, it is clear that HMM has been proved to be the superior classification technique in the task of recognition and discrimination between infants' pain and non-pain cries with 96.1% classification rate with 20 MFCC's extracted at 50ms. From our experiments, the optimal parameters of CDHMM developed for this work were 5 states, 8 Gaussians per state, whereas the ANN architecture that yielded the highest recognition rate of 79% was with one hidden layer and 5 hidden nodes. In general, both systems performed better with 50 ms frame length than with 100 ms. The results also show that the system accuracy performs better with MFCC's rather than with LPCC's features. For future work in this project, we suggest testing new neural networks, new kinds of hybrid models, or combining neural networks with fuzzy logic and genetic algorithms, or other complementary models.

The proposed method can assist pediatricians in preliminary diagnosis of the infant from the cry signals.

REFERENCES

Al-Alaoui, M. A., Al-Kanj, L., Azar, J., & Yaacoub, E. (2008). Speech recognition using artificial neural networks and hidden Markov models. In *The 3rd International Conference on Mobile and Computer Aided Learning, IMCL Conference*. Amman, Jordan.

Al-Azzawi, N. A. (2014). Automatic Recognition System of Infant Cry based on F-Transform. *International Journal of Computers and Applications*, *102*(12), 28–32. doi:10.5120/17869-8800

Baeck, H. E., & Souza, M. N. (2001). Study of Acoustic Features of Newborn Cries that Correlate with the context, In *Proceedings of the IEEE 23rd Annual Conference in Engineering in Medicine and Biology*. Turkey: IEEE. 10.1109/IEMBS.2001.1017201

Barajas-Montiel, E. S., & Reyes-Garcia, C. A. (2005). Identifying Pain and Hunger in Infant Cry with Classifiers Ensembles. In *Proceedings of the 2005 International Conference on Computational Intelligence for Modeling, Control and Automation, and International Conference on Intelligent Agents, Web Technologies and Internet Commerce*. Vienna, Austria: IEEE 10.1109/CIMCA.2005.1631561

Barr, R. G., Hopkins, B., & Green, J. A. (2000). *Crying as a sign, a symptom, & a signal: clinical, emotional, and developmental aspects of infant and toddler crying*. London, UK: Mac Keith Press.

Cai, J., Bouselmi, G., Laprie, Y., & Haton, J. P. (2009). Efficient likelihood evaluation and dynamic Gaussian selection for HMM-based speech recognition. *Computer Speech & Language*, *23*(2), 147–164. doi:10.1016/j.csl.2008.05.002

Cano-Ortiz, S. D., & Escobedo-Becerro, D. I. (1999). *Classificacion de Unidades de Llanto Infantil Mediante el Mapa Auto- Organizado de Koheen. In I Taller (Ed.), AIRENE sobre Reconocimiento de Patrones con Redes Neuronales* (pp. 24–29). Chile: Universidad Católica del Norte.

Chang, C. Y., Chang, C. W., Kathiravan, S., & Chen, S. T. (2017). DAG-SVM based infant cry classification system using sequential forward floating feature selection. *Multidimensional Systems and Signal Processing*, *28*(3), 961–976. doi:10.100711045-016-0404-5

Drummond, J. E., McBride, M. L., & Wiebe, C. F. (1993). The Development of Mother's Understanding of Infant Crying. *Clinical Nursing Research*, 2(4), 396–441. doi:10.1177/105477389300200403 PMID:8220195

Kasuriya, S., Wutiwiwatchai, C., & Tanprasert, C. (2001). Comparative Study of Continuous Hidden Markov Models (CHMM) and Artificial Neural Network (ANN) on Speaker Identification System. *International Journal of Uncertainty, Fuzziness and Knowledge-based Systems*, 9(6), 673–683. doi:10.1142/S0218488501001149

Lederman, D., Cohen, A., & Zmora, E. (2002). On the use of Hidden Markov Models in Infants' Cry Classification. In *22nd IEEE Convention*, Israel. IEEE. 10.1109/EEEI.2002.1178499

Liu, Y., & Shriberg, E. (2007). Comparing Evaluation Metrics For Sentence Boundary Detection. In *Proceedings of IEEE International Conference on Acoustics, Speech and Signal Processing - ICASSP '07*, Honolulu, HI. IEEE. 10.1109/ICASSP.2007.367194

Orlandi, S., Reyes-Garcia, C. A., Bandini, A., Donzelli, G., & Manfredi, C. (2016). Application of pattern recognition techniques to the classification of full-term and preterm infant cry. *Journal of Voice*, 30(6), 656–663. doi:10.1016/j.jvoice.2015.08.007 PMID:26474712

Orozco, J., & Reyes-Garcia, C. A. (2003a). *Mel-Frequency Cepstrum Coefficients Extraction from Infant Cry for Classification of Normal and pathological cry with Feed- forward Neural Networks. In Proceedings of international joint conference on neural Networks*. Portland, OR: IEEE.

Orozco, J., & Reyes-Garcia, C. A. (2003b). Implementation and Analysis of Training Algorithms for the Classification of Infant Cry with Feed-forward Neural Networks. In *IEEE International Symp. Intelligent Signal Processing*, Puebla, Mexico. IEEE. 10.1109/ISP.2003.1275851

Orozco, J., & Reyes-Garcia, C. A. (2003c). Detecting Pathologies From Infant Cry Applying Scaled Conjugate Gradient Neural Networks. In *Proceedings Of European Symposium On Artificial Neural Networks, Computational Intelligence And Machine Learning*, Bruges, Belgium

Petroni, M., Malowany, A. S., Johnston, C. C., & Stevens, B. J. (1995). A Comparison of Neural Network Architectures for the Classification of Three Types of Infant Cry Vocalizations. In *Proceedings of the IEEE 17th Annual Conference in Engineering in Medicine and Biology Society*, Montreal, Quebec, Canada. IEEE. 10.1109/IEMBS.1995.575380

Picone, J. (1990, July). Continuous Speech Recognition Using Hidden Markov Models. *IEEE ASSP Magazine*, 7(3), 26–41. doi:10.1109/53.54527

Rabiner, L. R. (1989). A tutorial on hidden Markov models and selected applications in speech recognition. *Proceedings of the IEEE*, 77(2), 257–286. doi:10.1109/5.18626

Rao, K. S., Reddy, V. R., & Maity, S. (2015). *Language Identification Using Spectral and Prosodic Features*. Retrieved from https://www.springer.com/gp/book/9783319171623

Resch, B., (n.d.). Hidden Markov Models, A tutorial of the course computational intelligence, *Signal Processing and Speech Communication Laboratory*. doi:10.1.1.145.3877

Rosales-Pérez, A., Reyes-García, C. A., Gonzalez, J. A., & Arch-Tirado, E. (2012). Infant Cry Classification Using Genetic Selection of a Fuzzy Model. In L. Alvarez, M. Mejail, L. Gomez, et al. (Eds.), *Progress in Pattern Recognition, Image Analysis, Computer Vision, and Applications: proceedings of 17th Iberoamerican Congress* (pp. 212-219). Buenos Aires, Argentina: Springer. 10.1007/978-3-642-33275-3_26

Saraswathy, J., Hariharan, M., Yaacob, S., & Khairunizam, W. (2012). Automatic classification of infant cry: A review. In *International Conference on Biomedical Engineering*, Penang Malaysia. IEEE.

Suaste, I., Reyes, O.F., Diaz, A., & Reyes, C.A. (2004). Implementation of a linguistic fuzzy relational neural network for detecting pathologies by infant cry recognition. In *Advances of Artificial Intelligence-IBERAMIA* (pp. 953-962).

Tolba, H. (2009). Comparative Experiments to Evaluate the Use of a CHMM-Based Speaker Identification Engine for Arabic Spontaneous Speech, In *2nd IEEE International Conference on Computer Science and Information Technology*. Beijing: IEEE. 10.1109/ICCSIT.2009.5234955

Wong, E., & Sridharan, S. (2001). Comparison of linear prediction cepstrum coefficients and mel-frequency cepstrum coefficients for language identification. In *Proc. Int. Symp. Intelligent Multimedia, Video and Speech Processing*. Hong Kong: IEEE. 10.1109/ISIMP.2001.925340

This research was previously published in the International Journal of Advanced Pervasive and Ubiquitous Computing (IJA-PUC), 11(1); pages 15-32, copyright year 2019 by IGI Publishing (an imprint of IGI Global).

Chapter 30

A Novel Prediction Perspective to the Bending Over Sheave Fatigue Lifetime of Steel Wire Ropes by Means of Artificial Neural Networks

Tuğba Özge Onur
Zonguldak Bulent Ecevit University, Turkey

Yusuf Aytaç Onur
Zonguldak Bulent Ecevit University, Turkey

ABSTRACT

Steel wire ropes are frequently subjected to dynamic reciprocal bending movement over sheaves or drums in cranes, elevators, mine hoists, and aerial ropeways. This kind of movement initiates fatigue damage on the ropes. It is a quite significant case to know bending cycles to failure of rope in service, which is also known as bending over sheave fatigue lifetime. It helps to take precautions in the plant in advance and eliminate catastrophic accidents due to the usage of rope when allowable bending cycles are exceeded. To determine the bending fatigue lifetime of ropes, experimental studies are conducted. However, bending over sheave fatigue testing in laboratory environments require high initial preparation cost and a long time to finalize the experiments. Due to those reasons, this chapter focuses on a novel prediction perspective to the bending over sheave fatigue lifetime of steel wire ropes by means of artificial neural networks.

DOI: 10.4018/978-1-6684-2408-7.ch030

INTRODUCTION

Wire ropes are frequently used in elevators, cranes, bridges, aerial ropeways, mine hoisting, and so on. Personnel, materials, cargo, etc. are lifted by steel wire ropes in a vast variety of material handling systems. Carbon steel rods are drawn to make steel wires with different shapes and sizes. The very high strength of the rope wires allows wire ropes to endure large tensile loads and to run over sheaves with relative small diameters. One or several layers of steel wires laid helically around a center wire form a strand. Traditional stranded steel wire ropes have six or eight strands wound around a core. Rotation resistant ropes have higher number of strands in order to resist rotation (Feyrer, 2015). Cars and counterweights are suspended by steel wire ropes in traction elevators. That is, steel wire ropes are used to lift personnel and freight in the car of the elevator (Janovsky, 1999). In cranes, ropes are used to lift, convey, and discharge heavy goods from one location to another location within a specific area. Crane ropes are selected to maintain a certain lifetime period in service (Suner, 1988). A Koepe (friction) system is often used in mine hoisting to lift heavy loads from deep shafts by means of steel wire ropes with large diameters (Onur, 2012). Wire ropes deteriorate gradually as a result of normal running or misuse while operating. Those deteriorations exhibit themselves in different ways after a certain period of time. Mostly, degradations that occur on steel wire ropes are due to fatigue. Furthermore, under almost all operational conditions, wire ropes are subjected to fatigue due to alternate bending and longitudinal movements. The fatigue in ropes can be divided into two main categories in general. One of the dominant fatigue types in rope applications is tension-tension fatigue in which ropes are subjected to alternate tensile load with time, such as with suspension bridges. Another type is known as bending over sheave (BoS) fatigue in which ropes are subjected to dynamic repetitive bending and straightening travel due to the winding of wire rope on a drum or sheaves, such as with cranes.

Fatigue causes degradation on the rope and reduces the lifetime of steel wire ropes. Knowing the lifetime of the rope is an important issue in terms of occupational safety. Rope manufacturers are also eager to extend their rope's lifetime. Therefore, it is an important research topic to investigate the fatigue lifetime of steel wire ropes.

This study addresses the BoS fatigue of steel wire ropes. Numerous studies have been conducted to shed light on the effect of BoS fatigue on the lifetime of the steel wire ropes.

Gibson et al. (Gibson et al., 1974) performed bending fatigue tests by using 6x36 Warrington Seale rope with a steel core, 6x24 Warrington Seale rope with a fiber core, and 6x26 Warrington Seale rope with a steel core. Each rope has right regular lay. The 6x24 Warrington Seale rope is made of galvanized high carbon steel, and the other two ropes are made of bright high carbon steel. Samples with diameters of 12.7 millimeters (1/2 inch) and 19.05 millimeters (3/4 inch) were used for bending fatigue tests. According to the results, the 6x36 Warrington Seale rope and 6x26 Warrington Seale rope had almost the same fatigue performance, while the 6x24 Warrington Seale rope had lower values. The authors explained that this rope may be used in applications where a low modulus of elasticity is desired. Therefore, it should not be used in applications where better fatigue performance is expected. The authors also measured temperature fluctuations at 45.72 m/min (150 feet/min) and declared that a low diameter ratio and high tensile load would lead to a rapid increase in temperatures occuring on the rope (Onur, 2010).

Bartels et al. (Bartels, McKewan, &Miscoe, 1992) examined the factors that affect the life of wire rope. Two 50.8 mm (2 inch) diameter 6x25 Filler ropes with fiber cores were degraded on a bending fatigue machine. The authors determined the number of wire breaks, residual breaking loads, and percent elongations at break due to the number of bending cycles. The test results indicated that once a wire rope nears the end of its service life, both deterioration and the consequent loss of rope strength begin to increase at an accelerated rate (Onur, 2010). Verreet (Verreet, 1998) used Feyrer's theoretical rope breaking lifetime and discarding lifetime formulas and prepared a computer program by taking into consideration the parameters such as rope type, rope diameter, sheave diameter, tensile load, wire strength, and the length of the most stressed rope section in his research report. He found generalized rope breaking lifetime and discarding lifetime results related to drive group and load collective. Suh and Chang (Suh & Chang, 2000) conducted experimental studies to investigate the effects of the stress variation, mean stress, and rope lay length on the lifetime of wire ropes subjected to tensile-tensile fatigue. Authors observed that outstanding temperature variation was in the range of 2.5–4 Hz frequency. Other authors (Chaplin, Ridge, &Zheng, 1999; Ridge, Chaplin, &Zheng, 2001) assessed effects of wire breaks, abrasive wear, corrosion, plastic wear, torsional imbalance, and slack wires and strands on the BoS fatigue lifetime. Therefore, the similar types of damages that are specified were created on the rope samples, which were 6x25 Filler rope and rotation resistant rope with 34 compacted strands before the test. Furthermore, the Feyrer's theoretical rope fatigue lifetime equations were used to compare experimental results gathered. In Gibson's handbook (Gibson, 2001), an attempt was made to correlate rope contact length on sheave with the rope fatigue lifetime. It is found that there was a reduction in the rope fatigue lifetime until contact length is equal to the pitch length and there is no change in larger contact lengths. Torkar and Arzensek (Torkar & Arzensek, 2002) performed a failure analysis of a 6x19 Seale steel rope broken while running on a crane. The authors concluded that the main reasons for the failure of the wire rope were fatigue and poor inspection. Feyrer's book (Feyrer, 2015) presented recent developments in instrumentations and experimental measurements in order to exhibit static and dynamic behaviors of rope structures. The author revealed the effects of tensile load and diameter ratio, rope wire strength, rope diameter, rope bending length on the sheave or drum, rope core type, zinc coating, lubrication, groove geometry and its material, and reverse bending on the BoS fatigue lifetime. A regression analysis was performed by using the obtained experimental results. Gorbatov et al. (Gorbatov et al., 2007) investigated the variation of the rope BoS fatigue lifetime with the type of rope core and type of rope core lubricant. A 6x36 Warrington-Seale rope with 16 mm in diameter was used. The authors revealed that the steel wire rope, which has jute core and is lubricated by ASKM-1A, has a superior BoS fatigue lifetime than a steel wire rope, which has a hemp core and is lubricated by E-1. In the technical bulletin published by Wire Rope Works Inc. (Wirerope Works Inc., 2008), the rope lifetime curve developed by the wire rope industry was explained in order to extract the effect of sheave diameter accurately to the performance of wire ropes subjected to the BoS fatigue by using rope samples that were 12.7 mm (1/2 inch) in diameter. The report revealed that increasing the diameter ratio provides longer BoS fatigue lifetime. In the case of the diameter ratio becoming 55 instead of 40, the BoS fatigue lifetime increased 91%. Pal et al. (Pal, Mukhopadhyay, Sharma, & Bhattacharya, 2018) investigated why a 6x36 steel wire rope failed after nine months of service and tried to estimate bending fatigue life as per the Niemann equation. The authors recommended changing the schedule of the investigated wire rope from nine to six months. Zhang et al. (Zhang, Feng, Chen, Wang, &Ni, 2017) used a custom-made bending fatigue test machine to judge the bending fatigue behavior of a 6x19 steel wire rope that had pre-broken wires before the test. The effect of different distributions of pre-broken wires on bending fatigue behavior was determined. The authors concluded that the broken wires changed the stress state of the inner wire strands and this led to a concentration of severe wear, which accelerated the density of broken wires. Kim et al. (Sung-Ho, Sung-Hoon, & Jae-Do, 2014) studied an 8x19 Seale elevator rope. Rope samples were corroded by a salt-water test chamber and a bending fatigue test apparatus was used to evaluate the effect of corrosion fatigue on life expectancy. The authors concluded that a greater amount of corrosion, an increase in the tensile load, and repeated bending cycles produced a rapid increase in the number of broken wires.

However, in addition to the investigations summarized above, although the usage of optimization methods like artificial neural networks (ANN) and a genetic algorithm (GA) for the prediction of bending fatigue lifetime of steel wire ropes is not sufficiently discussed in the present literature, Dou and Wang (Dou & Wang, 2012) used ANN to analyze the characteristics of wire ropes. According to their idea, because of the recent advances in computer technology, the use of ANN become more feasible. Also, ANN has the potential to solve certain types of complex problems that have not been satisfactorily handled by more traditional methods.

BoS fatigue testing of steel wire ropes requires high initial preparation cost and significant time to finalize the experiments and performance experienced by investigating numerous parameters in order to determine the rope lifetime in the related literature. In addition, mathematical equations must be found in order to evaluate the results obtained from the performed tests. Furthermore, it is impossible to handle all kinds of parameters and conditions in the tests performed in order to determine the rope lifetime. For example, there are limited studies on how the rope BoS fatigue lifetime will change as the rotation speed increases and that determine the effects of parameters such as insufficient lubrication and twisting on the rope on BoS fatigue lifetime. Due to those reasons, the use of computer systems is accepted as an alternative method to minimize the high cost and performance performed during the tests. For this purpose, techniques such as artificial neural networks (ANN), fuzzy logic, and a genetic algorithm can be used as an alternative to traditional methods in determining rope life with developing computer technology. ANN also have the ability to generate solutions quickly by creating an algorithm. ANN, which are basically an algorithm based on the human nervous system, are used more frequently than genetic algorithms because of their faster solutions for the problems that are large scaled, nonlinear, and discontinuous/missing.

In this chapter, authors focus on a novel prediction perspective to the bending over sheave fatigue lifetime of steel wire ropes by means of artificial neural networks. On the other hand, in order to research the robustness and accuracy of the designed ANN model, theoretical calculations are done by using Feyrer equations (Feyrer, 2015). Furthermore, the results obtained from ANN are compared with the data presented in the literature (Onur & İmrak, 2012).

ROPES

The ropes generally consist of several strands laid helically in one or more layers around a core of fiber or steel. A strand has two or more wires wrapped in a peculiar sequence around its core. Ropes are used extensively as traction component of systems for lifting and transporting due to their flexible structure and convenient use (Cürgül, 1995). Ropes can be thought as a machine that has many moving parts and should be manufactured properly. It should be selected according to the place it is to be used. Furthermore, ropes are manufactured in various compositions, like machines, when their application areas are taken into consideration. An identical rope may be suitable in one system, while it may not suitable for another system (Cookes Limited, 2007). Ropes are divided into two groups, fiber ropes and wire ropes, according to the material they are made of. The ropes made by steel wires are the highest stressed and the most important component of transport machines. Different operating conditions are necessary to manufacture various types of ropes. The characteristic properties of wire ropes are little known in practice.

If the operating personnel lack the necessary information about the maintenance, control, and the use of wire ropes, a proper and safe operation cannot be carried out. Apart from the designer, the user must also have the necessary information about wire ropes (Demirsoy, 1991). As a result of the improvements in wire ropes, chains, which were used previously in cranes, are not used in crane manufacturing today. The superiorities of wire ropes over the chains can be listed as follows:

- Due to their light weight, there is little mass effect on the lifting machines working at elevated speeds.
- Their operating safety is high and operation controls are easy.
- They resist light impacts since they are more flexible than chains.
- They operate silently at high speeds.
- The unit prices are cheaper than the chains, conditionally.

Wire ropes don't break suddenly like chains and, with taking care of initiation of broken wires, safety precautions can be taken. The above qualities outline the reasons to choose wire ropes over chains. Furthermore, wire ropes have a high lifting capacity. They don't lose much of their strength due to fatigue and moisture effects while operating. Operation safety is quite high due to the fact that the load is distributed over a large number of wires in the rope. Wire ropes can be operated at high operation speeds. There is a convenient rate between their weights and lifting capacity, and they have a large amount of elastic elongation. It is possible to visually control them easily during operation. The lifting capacity and operation properties of wire ropes don't change with low temperatures. However, ropes with fiber cores should not be operated at temperatures above 100°C, and ropes with steel cores should not be operated at temperatures above 250°C. The rope end connection should be checked very carefully at low and high temperatures (Demirsoy, 1991). A wire rope structure is depicted in Figure 1.

Figure 1. Wire rope structure

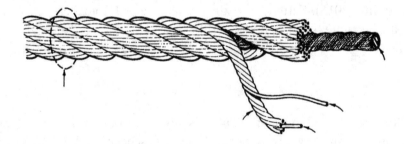

Wire ropes can also be classified considering core material. Core material is either steel or fiber; wire ropes can also be classified as parallel lay rope and cross lay rope, according to their strand arrangements (Adıvar çelik halat, 2010) and can also be classified as special ropes (Çelik Halat ve Tel Sanayi A.Ş., 1999; Cürgül, 1995; Demirsoy, 1991; Türk Standartları Enstitüsü, 2005). Wire ropes are widely used in mining, oil wells, the transportation of heavy loads, elevators, trams, naval applications, fishery, forestry, ships and yachts, aerial ropeways, and in general engineering applications (Çelik Halat ve Tel Sanayi A.Ş., 1999).

ARTIFICIAL NEURAL NETWORKS

The nervous system consists of nerves and specialized cells known as neurons. There are approximately 10^{11} neurons in the human body (Kohonen, 1988). The brain is composed of the combination of the neurons, which exist not only in the brain, but also in the whole body in the nervous system. Neurons can be called a network since they work in groups. Each neuron in this network has input (dendrite), output (axon), connections (synapse), and a cell nucleus. A neuron structure is depicted in Figure 2.

Figure 2. Structure of a neuron
(Şen, 2004)

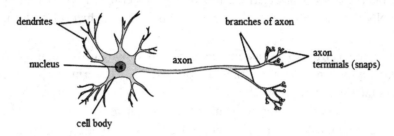

Connections provide the communication between the cells. A neuron takes the signals incoming from other neurons to the inlet part via the connections. Incoming signals are weakened or amplified by the connections, then these signals are transmitted to the cell nucleus. If the signals incoming to the cell nucleus exceed a certain threshold value as a result of their interaction with each other, a signal is sent to the outlet and the nerve becomes active. If threshold value is not be exceeded, the signal cannot be sent. In view of this situation, artificial neural networks models have been developed. The first study on artificial neural networks was made in 1943 by a neurophysicist, McCulloch, and a mathematician, Pitts. In this study, a cell model was developed according to a definition of an artificial nerve (McCulloch & Pitts, 1943). In 1949, a study was conducted giving an idea about how a neural network can perform the learning, and the "Hebbian Rule," which is the basis of most of the learning rules used today, has emerged from this study (Hebb, 1949). A model that reacts to the stimuli and is able to be adaptable was created for the first time in 1954 (Farley & Clark, 1954). The perceptron was developed by Rosenblatt and was the most important step after the emergence of the Hebbian Rule in 1958. This development also forms the basis for the learning algorithms of today's machines (Şen, 2004). The ADALINE (Adaptive Linear Combiner) learning rule was developed in 1960. This learning rule has passed the literature as Widrow-Hoff learning rule. Its most important feature is to aim to minimize the error that occurred during the training of the model (Office of Naval Research Contract, 1960). In 1969, the book entitled "Perceptron" was published and indicated that single-layer perceptrons could not solve complex problems, with the example of an XOR problem. After the beginning of the more effective use of computers in the 1980s, remarkable improvements emerged about ANN. It can be said that the modern era started in ANN with the study of "Neural Networks and Physical Properties" in 1982. Nonlinear networks were developed in this study (Hopfield, 1982). In the same years, the studies about ANN have accelerated with the development of non-instructional learning systems in the studies performed by Kohonen (Kohonen, 1982) and Anderson (Anderson, 1983). In 1986, the back propagation algorithm was developed for multi-layer perceptrons. Since this developed algorithm has a strong structure, it provided resolutions for the previously encountered problems (Rumelhart, Hinton, & Williams, 1986). The back propagation algorithm is one of the most widely used algorithms. Today, the use of ANN has gained a great intensity in parallel with the developments in computer systems. New learning algorithms are being developed daily, and new studies about the network architectures are being done.

Artificial neural networks can be used in almost every discipline and science. There are many problems solved with ANN, in many areas, such as science, mathematics, medicine, business, and finance. ANN is used in many fields, such as classification, clustering, prediction, pattern recognition, function approach, and optimization. Brief explanations of these fields are stated in the following.

- Classification is the process of determining that one object belongs to which class in more than one class. ANN provides to detect the next data belong to which class by using an existing classification.
- Clustering is different from classification, and it is done notwithstanding a certain limit. There is no need for any information about the data processing. Clustering is performed by including similar data in the same group.
- The most popular application area of artificial neural networks is the prediction. Prediction is producing an idea about the future data with regard to data in the past. Market volatility, sales amount, and weather forecast can be given as examples. ANN gains an important advantage for the estimation of variables, especially in a linear structure (Li, Mehrotra, Mohan, &Ranka, 1990).
- The accurate one of the distorted patterns can be obtained by defining distorted or missing patterns to ANN and comparing the patterns. This method can be used for processes such as face recognition or retina recognition, which are similar. Authentication is possible with those processes.
- There are many calculation methods for which the mathematical expressions are unknown. In other words, although its inputs and outputs are certain, there are situations in which the intermediate function is unknown. The function approach is to define the function that will produce approximately the same output data in response to the same output data. Function and prediction approaches are similar models.
- Optimization is the action of finding the best or most effective performance under the given constraints by maximizing desired factors and minimizing undesired ones for many commercial and scientific events. In engineering, optimization is widely used, especially in the design phase. Optimization can be basically divided into two groups. The first one is the traditional optimization, which is done by creating a function based on the mathematical data. The second one is the optimization technique done by using artificial intelligence. This method is used for the optimization of complex structures that are cannot be expressed as a function. Artificial neural networks also use this method (Civalek & Çatal, 2004).

Structure of ANN

Artificial neural networks consist of many artificial nerve cells. It is desired to combine this structure resembling the biologic nervous system with the process elements on the same direction. The basic architecture consists of three types of neuron layers: input, hidden, and output layers, as shown in Figure 3.

The input layer is the layer where incoming data are received and transferred to the hidden layer. No transaction is performed when transferring data in some network structures (Svozil, Kvasnicka, &

Pospichal, 1997). The intermediate layer, also known as the hidden layer, processes the data incoming from the input layer and sends them to the output layer. There can be multiple hidden layers in ANN. The output layer processes the information incoming from the hidden layer and produces the output that must be generated for the data presented to the input layer.

Figure 3. Basic structure of artificial neural network

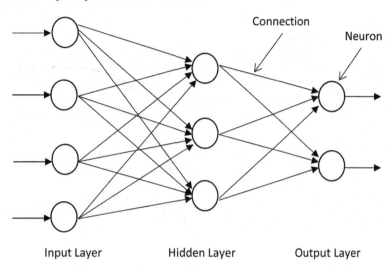

The information that comes to the cell from the external environment in the structure of ANN is input. It forms an input layer by combining with the cell. The data formed in the input layer go to the processing element with the weights on the connections. The weights indicate the mathematical coefficient of an input acted on a process in the hidden layer. Weights are randomly assigned when the calculation starts. Depending on the procedure, it can continue to change the weights until the error is minimum. The input data combined with the weights are added by the joint function. The joint function can be the maximum or minimum field or multiplication function according to the network structure. The output is defined by processing the input obtained from the joint function with the activation function. There are several types of activation functions. The most appropriate activation function is determined by the trials of the designer. There are several activation functions used in ANN architectures as linear, sigmoid, and tangent hyperbolic activation functions (Ozkan & Sunar, 2003). Since sigmoid activation function is preferred as an activation function for the designed artificial neural network model in order to estimate BoS fatigue lifetimes of 6×36 WS rope, it will be briefly explained with a subhead below.

Sigmoid Activation Function

Sigmoid activation function is differentiable and it is the most used function due to the continuity of both itself and its derivative. The sigmoid function curve looks like a S-shape as depicted in Figure 4. The sigmoid activation function produces only positive values and is defined by the following formula in Equation (1):

$$f(x) = \frac{1}{1 + e^{-x}} \tag{1}$$

After a brief definition of the sigmoid activation function, Figure 5 is the simple representation of ANN process elements. In Figure 5, x is the input, W is the weight, *Net* is the adding function, $F(x)$ is the activation function, and Y is the output value.

Figure 4. Sigmoid activation function

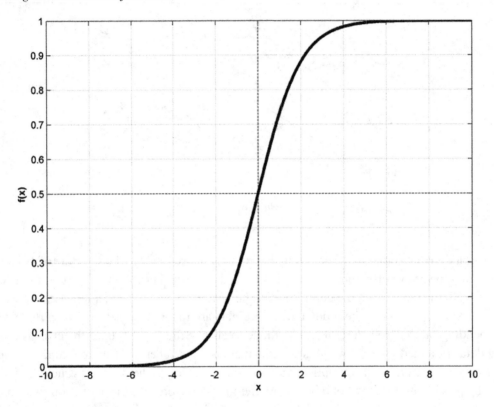

Figure 5. Architecture of ANN

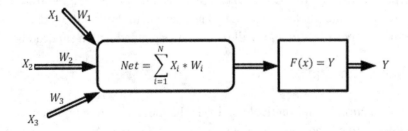

Learning Types and Rules in ANN

The most widely used learning rules in artificial neural networks are the Hebb rule, Hopfield rule, Kohonen rule, delta rule, and backpropagation algorithm (Hebb, 1949). Since backpropagation and Levenberg-Marquardt (LM) algorithms are preferred for the designed artificial neural network model in order to estimate BoS fatigue lifetimes of 6×36 WS rope, they will be briefly explained with subheads below.

LM Algorithm

Also known as the damped least squares algorithm, the *LM algorithm* is an approach to Newton's method. The LM algorithm is the method to research the minimum. A parabolic approach is used to approach the error surface in each iteration and the solution of the parabola for that step is created. The LM learning rule uses the Hessian matrix given by Equation (2).

$$H = J^T J \tag{2}$$

where J represents the Jacobian matrix. The Jacobian matrix as indicated in Equation (3) is the first derivative of the network errors by weights.

$$J(n) = \frac{\delta e(n)}{\delta w(n-1)} \tag{3}$$

In Equation (3), n is the iteration number; δ is the derivative symbol; e is the network errors vector; w is the connection weights. In this case, the gradient is found by using Equation (4),

$$g = J^T e \tag{4}$$

and the connection weight between the neurons is obtained by using Equation (5),

$$w_{k+1} = w_k \left[J^T J + \mu I \right]^{-1} J^T e \tag{5}$$

where w_k, is the weight at iteration k; I is the unit matrix; μ is the Marquardt parameter. The Marquardt parameter is a scalar value. The LM method is named as a Newton algorithm when the Marquardt parameter is zero. The Levenberg-Marquardt learning algorithm produces very fast results when compared with other algorithms (Rojas, 1996).

Back Propagation Algorithm

The back propagation algorithm, or the generalized delta rule, is the most commonly used learning rule. The algorithm produced by Rumelhart, Hinton, and Williams (Rumelhart, Hinton, & Williams, 1986) has given an important acceleration for artificial neural networks. Error is propagated backwards in the back propagation algorithm. The weights are changed by back propagation of the error between the actual outputs and calculated ones. As with all learning algorithms, the goal is to determine the weights to ensure the best fit between the input and output data. The back propagation algorithm is the version of the delta algorithm where momentum term is appended. The momentum term helps to find the point where the error is minimum and to adjust the direction (Caudill, 1988).

ANN by Network Structures

Cells and connections may come together in many different ways. Considering their structures, ANN differ from each other according to the directions of the connections between the neurons and the direction of flow within the network. Artificial neural networks are divided into two groups adhering to their structures, which are feedforward artificial neural networks and feedback artificial neural networks.

Figure 6. Feedforward ANN

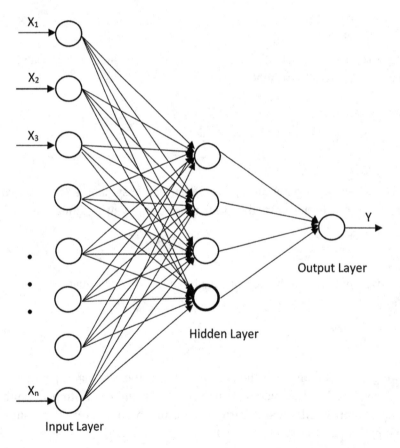

The processes are transmitted from input layer to output layer in feedforward artificial neural networks, as shown in Figure 6. The input layer transfers the information received from outside to the cells in the hidden layer without any modification. Data are processed in these layers and transmitted to the output layer. Every output value in the hidden layers is used as an input value for the next layer (Wang, 2007). In Figure 6, X_i and Y are the inputs and output of the network, respectively.

In feedback artificial neural networks, the output of at least one cell is given to itself or to another neuron as input. The information exchange in the feedback network can be not only between cells located at same layer, but also between cells located at an interlayer. The feedback network can be used effectively for the solution of nonlinear problems by exhibiting a dynamic behavior with this structure. Feedback ANN are often used in digital filter designs. The feedback ANN operate more slowly than feedforward ANN (Uçan, Danacı, & Bayrak, 2003). The well-known feedback network types are Hopfield network, cellular artificial neural network, Grossberg network, Adaptive Resonance Theory-1 (ART1), and ART2 networks (Hakimpoor, Arshad, Tat, Khani, & Rahmandoust, 2011).

APPLICATION OF ANN TO DETERMINE ROPE LIFETIME

The Properties of Used Rope

In order to demonstrate the application of ANN to estimate steel wire rope lifetime, steel wire rope presented in Onur and İmrak's work (Onur & İmrak, 2012) is used. The investigated rope construction in (Onur & İmrak, 2012) their study is 6×36 Warrington-Seale (WS) steel wire rope. It has Independent Wire Rope Core (IWRC) and 10 mm diameter (*d*). In addition, it has six strands around a steel core, which is a wire rope itself. The 6×36 Warrington-Seale rope offers optimum resistance in fatigue and crushing; thereby, it can be used in mine hoisting, oil industry, cranes, etc. A cross-section of a 6×36 Warrington-Seale rope with IWRC is depicted in Figure 7.

Onur and İmrak (2012) employed eight different tensile loads and two sheaves with 250 mm and 100 mm diameters for BoS fatigue tests to determine the effects of tensile load and sheave diameter to the BoS fatigue lifetimes of 6×36 WS rope with 10 mm diameter in their work. Tensile loads that are 15 kN, 20 kN, 25 kN, and 30 kN have been employed when a sheave with a 250 mm diameter is used,

Figure 7. Cross section of 6 x 36 Warrington-Seale rope with IWRC
(Onur & İmrak, 2011)

and tensile loads that are 10 kN, 15 kN, 20 kN, and 25 kN have been employed when sheave with a 100 mm diameter is used.

Theoretical Calculation of the Investigated Rope

Theoretical BoS fatigue life estimations have been performed by using the Feyrer equation that is given in Equation (6).

$$
\log(N) = b_0 + \left(b_1 + b_3 \log\left(\frac{D}{d}\right)\right) \cdot \left(\log\left(\frac{S}{d^2}\right) - (0.4) \cdot \log\left(\frac{R_0}{1770}\right)\right)
$$

$$
+ b_2 \cdot \log\left(\frac{D}{d}\right) + \log\left(\frac{0.52}{-0.48 + \left(\dfrac{d}{16}\right)^{0.3}}\right) + \log\left(\frac{1.49}{2.49 - \left(\dfrac{l/d - 2.5}{57.5}\right)^{-0.14}}\right) + \log(f_c)
$$

(6)

where D/d is the diameter ratio; S/d^2 is the specific tensile load; R_o is the wire grade; d is the rope diameter; l is the bending length; f_c is the rope core and number of strands factor. The constants b_i's in Equation (6) are given in Feyrer's book (Feyrer, 2015). Table 1 includes the constants and parameters for 6×36 WS rope.

Feyrer proposes that the numbers of bending cycles calculated by means of constants in Table 1 are valid for up to a few million bending cycles if some conditions are provided. The conditions proposed by Feyrer are: well lubricated with viscous oil or Vaseline for the wire rope samples, having steel grooves for sheaves, groove radius-rope diameter ratio r/d is 0.53, there is no side deflection, and it is in a dry environment. In the case of different conditions in operation, in order to determine the final BoS fatigue life calculation, correction factors must be taken into consideration.

Table 1. Constants and parameters used for 6x36 Warrington-Seale rope

	Constants and Parameters	Values
Parameters	d (mm)	10
	R_o (N/mm²)	1960
	l (mm)	600
	f_c	0.81
Constants	b_0	1.278
	b_1	0.029
	b_2	6.241
	b_3	-1.613

ANN Application

For devising an artificial neural network model in order to estimate the BoS fatigue lifetimes of 6×36 WS rope, experimental test data given in Onur and İmrak's study (Onur & İmrak, 2012) have been used and the back propagation learning algorithm is utilized to predict the data obtained from the data set. In this ANN model, specific tensile load S/d^2 and diameter ratio D/d parameters have been chosen as the input parameters, and the number of bending cycles (N) has been regarded as the output parameter (Onur, İmrak, & Onur, 2016). In order to decide the optimum structure of the neural network, the rate of error convergence was checked by changing the number of hidden neurons. The networks were trained up to cycles where the level of the mean square error (MSE) is satisfactory and further cycles had no significant effect on error reduction. MSE is calculated by using Equation (7),

$$MSE = \frac{1}{m} \sum_{k=1}^{m} \left(de_i - O_i \right)^2 \qquad (7)$$

where de_i is the desired or actual value, O_i is the predicted output value, and m is the number of data. For simulating an automated neural network model, MATLAB software has been used. A structure with 18 neurons in the hidden layer is formed and a logistic sigmoid function is preferred as the activation function. During training, the automated neural network is presented by the data thousands of times, which is referred to as cycles. After each cycle, the error between the automated neural network output and desired values are propagated backward to adjust the weight in a manner to mathematically guarantee to converge (Haykin, 1998). MSE is used to stop training automatically. Furthermore, 45% of the data set given in Onur and İmrak's study (Onur & İmrak, 2012) are used for training the network, and 30% are selected randomly to test the performance of the trained network. A final check on the performance of the trained network is made using a validation set (Vadood, Semnani, & Morshed, 2011).

Table 2 includes the results obtained by experimental data given in Onur and İmrak's study (Onur & İmrak, 2012), theoretical results obtained by using Feyrer's equation given in Equation (6), and results acquired by means of simulating designed ANN.

Table 2. Results obtained by Feyrer's theoretical estimation, experimental results (N_{test}) in [47,] and ANN results (N_{ANN}) for 6×36 Warrington-Seale rope

S/d² (N/mm²)	D/d	l/d	N$_{ANN}$(cycles)	N$_{feyrer}$(cycles)	N$_{test}$(cycles)
150	25	60	174693.96	171146	163456
200	25	60	86791.95	90213	86792
250	25	60	70295.48	54898	69619
300	25	60	35504.97	36585	38505
100	10	60	32515.07	25951	32516
150	10	60	28832.41	13653	27774
200	10	60	15469.40	8656	13170
250	10	60	4683.89	6078	4684

For running ANN simulation, either MATLAB ANN toolbox or commands can be utilized. In order to intervene in the simulation performance and conditions, MATLAB commands can be used in the command window instead of an ANN toolbox. The following command lines are utilized to simulate the designed ANN model in order to predict the BoS fatigue lifetimes of wire rope investigated.

```matlab
%Matlab scripts for calculating the BoS fatigue lifetimes.
%%Input data
p1 = input('Please input input1 data:','s') ; % data of s/d²
p2 = input('Please input input2 data:','s'); %data of D/d
p=[p1; p2]; %input vector includes p1 and p2
%%Output data
t = input('Please input output data:','s'); % Output data N_test
%%Normalization
[pn,minp,maxp,tn,mint,maxt] = premnmx(p,t);
%%Designing, training and simulation of ANN
net=newff(minmax(pn), [N 1], {'logsig' 'purelin'},'trainlm'); % N %is the num-
ber of hidden layers
net.performFcn = 'mse';
net.trainFcn = 'trainlm';
net.layers{1}.transferFcn = 'logsig';
net.layers{1}.initFcn = 'initnw';
net.layers{2}.transferFcn = 'logsig';
[net1, tr] = train(net,pn,tn);
an = sim(net1,pn);
[a] = postmnmx(an,mint,maxt); %Inverse of normalization
y= sim(net1,pn);
e=t-y;
%%Plotting training data and output of ANN
figure(1),plot3(p1(1,:),p2(1,:),t,'o');
hold on,plot3(p(1,:),p2(1,:),a,'r*'),grid on;
legend('Exact value','Output of ANN'),xlabel('p1'),ylabel('p2'),zlabel('t')
view(net)
%%Preparing test data
ptest=[p(1,1:3);p(2,1:3)]
ttest = [t(1,1:3)]
[ptn,minpt,maxpt,ttn,mintt,maxtt] = premnmx(ptest,ttest);
atn = sim(net,ptn); %Simulasyon
[at] = postmnmx(atn,mintt,maxtt);
%%Plotting test data and output of ANN
figure(2),plot3(ptest(1,:),ptest(2,:),ttest,'o');
hold on,plot3(ptest(1,:),ptest(2,:),at,'r*'),grid on;
legend('Exact value','Output of ANN'),xlabel('p1'),ylabel('p2'),zlabel('t'),ti
tle('Test data')
plotregression(t,y,'Regression')
```

```
plotfit(net1,p,t);
plottrainstate(tr);
plotperform(tr);
```

In order to provide convenience for comparing the results given in Table 2, a graphic has been plotted and shown in Figure 8.

Results obtained by experimental tests given in Onur and İmrak's study (Onur & İmrak, 2012) and the designed ANN model results are very close to each other, with 0.0036577, 0.0029135, and 0.0001987 minimum square errors for testing, training, and validation, respectively, as shown in Figure 8. Although theoretical estimations of BoS fatigue lifetime can be performed by using Feyrer's equations given in Equation (6), as it can be seen, it requires substantial expertise in the mathematical definitions. Therefore, artificial neural networks can be considered as a useful tool in order to predict the BoS fatigue lifetime of 6×36 Warrington-Seale steel wire ropes.

Figure 8. BoS fatigue lifetime results given in Table 2

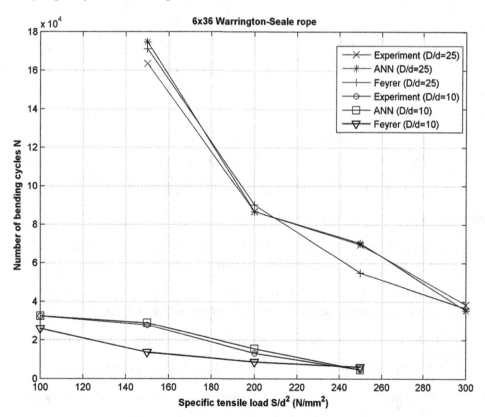

CONCLUSION

This chapter aimed to evaluate the artificial neural network in predicting Bos fatigue lifetime. Although there are some more theoretical estimations and analysis for BoS fatigue lifetime predictions, they require substantial expertise in the mathematical definitions of equations. As an alternative to the existing references, it is evident from the present study that the ANN model has good prediction capability to predict the BoS fatigue lifetimes of 6×36 Warrington-Seale steel wire ropes with input parameters like specific tensile load S/d^2 and diameter ratio D/d. Based on the study, it is established that the ANN approach seems to be a better option for the appropriate prediction of BoS fatigue lifetimes of 6×36 Warrington-Seale steel wire ropes. The results predicted with this designed ANN model are compared to calculations with Feyrer's equations and with the experimental data presented in Onur and İmrak's study (Onur & İmrak, 2012). Errors obtained are within acceptable limits. It has been concluded that the ANN model can be effectively utilized as a prediction tool for such a purpose. Furthermore, the developed ANN model can be used to estimate the BoS fatigue lifetimes of different types of wire ropes for a wide range of parameters for future research.

REFERENCES

Adıvar çelik halat. (2010). *Adıvar çelik halat kataloğu*. Retrieved from http://www.adivarcelikhalat.com

Anderson, J. A. (1983). Cognitive and psychological computation with neural models. *IEEE Transactions on Systems, Man, and Cybernetics*, *SMC-13*(5), 799–814. doi:10.1109/TSMC.1983.6313074

Bartels, J. R., McKewan, W. M., & Miscoe, A. J. (1992). *Bending fatigue tests 2 and 3 on 2-Inch 6 x 25 fiber core wire rope*. Retrieved from https://www.cdc.gov/niosh/mining/UserFiles/works/pdfs/ri9429.pdf

Caudill, M. (1988). Neural networks primer, part III. *AI Expert*, *3*(6), 53–59.

Çelik Halat ve Tel Sanayi A.Ş. (1999). *Çelik halat ürün kataloğu*. İzmit, Turkey.

Chaplin, C. R., Ridge, I. M. L., & Zheng, J. (1999, July). *Rope degradation and damage*. Retrieved from http://www.hse.gov.uk/research/otopdf/1999/oto99033.pdf

Civalek, Ö., & Çatal, H. H. (2004). Geriye yayılma yapay sinir ağları kullanılarak elastik kirişlerin statik ve dinamik analizi. *DEÜ Mühendislik Fakültesi Fen ve Mühendislik Dergisi*, *1*, 1–16.

Cookes Limited. (2007). *Wire rope handbook*. Auckland, New Zealand: Cookes Limited.

Cürgül. İ. (1995). Materials handling. İzmit, Turkey, Kocaeli University Publications.

Demirsoy, M. (1991). *Materials Handling* (Vol. I). İstanbul, Turkey: Birsen Publishing House.

Dou, Z., & Wang, M. (2012). *Proceedings of the International Conference on Automatic Control and Artificial Intelligence*, 1614-1616.

Farley, B. G., & Clark, W. A. (1954). Simulation of self-organizing systems by digital computer. *Transactions of the IRE Professional Group on Information Theory*, *4*(4), 76-84. 10.1109/TIT.1954.1057468

Feyrer, K. (2015). *Wire ropes: tension, endurance, reliability.* New York, NY: Springer.

Gibson, P. T. (2001). Operational characteristics of ropes and cables. In J. F. Bash (Ed.), *Handbook of oceanographic winch, wire and cable technology* (pp. 8-3–8-50). USA.

Gibson, P. T., White, F. G., Schalit, L. A., Thomas, R. E., Cote, R. W., & Cress, H. A. (1974, Oct. 31). *A study of parameters that influence wire rope fatigue life.* Retrieved from https://apps.dtic.mil/dtic/tr/fulltext/u2/a001673.pdf

Gorbatov, E. K., Klekovkina, N. A., Saltuk, V. N., Fogel, V., Barsukov, V. K., Barsukov, E. V., ... Kurashov, D. A. (2007). Steel rope with longer service life and improved quality. *Journal of Metallurgist, 51*(5-6), 279–283. doi:10.100711015-007-0052-y

Hakimpoor, H., Arshad, K. A. B., Tat, H. H., Khani, N., & Rahmandoust, M. (2011). Artificial neural networks applications in management. *World Applied Sciences Journal, 14*(7), 1008–1019.

Haykin, S. (1998). *Neural networks: a comprehensive foundation.* New York, NY: Prentice Hall.

Hebb, D. (1949). *The organization of behavior: a neuropsychological theory.* New York, NY: Wiley.

Hopfield, J. J. (1982). Neural networks and physical systems with emergent collective computational abilities. *Proceedings of the National Academy of Sciences of the United States of America, 79*(8), 2554–2558. doi:10.1073/pnas.79.8.2554 PMID:6953413

Janovsky, L. (1999). *Elevator mechanical design.* USA: Elevator World Inc.

Kohonen, T. (1982). Self-organized formation of topologically correct feature maps. *Biological Cybernetics, 43*(1), 59–69. doi:10.1007/BF00337288

Kohonen, T. (1988). An introduction to neural computing. *Neural Networks, 1*(1), 3–16. doi:10.1016/0893-6080(88)90020-2

Li, M., Mehrotra, K., Mohan, C. K., & Ranka, S. (1990). Forecasting sunspot numbers using neural networks. *Electrical Engineering and Computer Science Technical Reports, 67.*

McCulloch, W. S., & Pitts, W. (1943). A logical calculus of the ideas immanent in nervous activity. *The Bulletin of Mathematical Biophysics, 5*(4), 1–19. doi:10.1007/BF02478259

Office of Naval Research Contract. (1960). *Adaptive switching circuits.* Stanford, CA: B. Widrow and M. E. Hoff.

Onur, Y. A. (2010). *Theoretical and experimental investigation of parameters affecting to the rope lifetime* (Unpublished doctoral dissertation). Istanbul Technical University Institute of Science, Turkey.

Onur, Y. A. (2012). Condition monitoring of Koepe winder ropes by electromagnetic non-destructive inspection. *Insight (American Society of Ophthalmic Registered Nurses), 54*(3), 144–148.

Onur, Y. A., & İmrak, C. E. (2011). The influence of rotation speed on the bending fatigue lifetime of steel wire ropes. *Proceedings of the Institution of Mechanical Engineers. Part C, Journal of Mechanical Engineering Science, 225*(3), 520–525. doi:10.1243/09544062JMES2275

Onur, Y. A., & İmrak, C. E. (2012). Experimental and theoretical investigation of bending over sheave fatigue life of stranded steel wire rope. *Indian Journal of Engineering and Materials Sciences, 19,* 189–195.

Onur, Y. A., İmrak, C. E., & Onur, T. Ö. (2016). Investigation of bending over sheave fatigue life of stranded steel wire rope by artificial neural networks. *International Journal of Mechanical And Production Engineering, 4*(9), 47–49.

Ozkan, C., & Sunar Erbek, F. (2003). The comparison of activation functions for multispectral landsat TM image classification. *Photogrammetric Engineering and Remote Sensing, 69*(11), 1225–1234. doi:10.14358/PERS.69.11.1225

Pal, U., Mukhopadhyay, G., Sharma, A., & Bhattacharya, S. (2018). Failure analysis of wire rope of ladle crane in steel making shop. *International Journal of Fatigue, 116,* 149–155. doi:10.1016/j.ijfatigue.2018.06.019

Ridge, I. M. L., Chaplin, C. R., & Zheng, J. (2001). Effect of degradation and impaired quality on wire rope bending over sheave fatigue endurance. *Journal of Engineering Failure Analysis, 8*(2), 173–187. doi:10.1016/S1350-6307(99)00051-5

Rojas, R. (1996). *Neural networks: a systematic introduction.* Berlin, Germany: Springer-Verlag. doi:10.1007/978-3-642-61068-4

Rumelhart, D. E., Hinton, G. E., & Williams, R. J. (1986). Learning representations by back propagation error. *Nature, 32*(6088), 533–536. doi:10.1038/323533a0

Şen, Z. (2004). *Yapay sinir ağları ilkeleri.* Su Vakfı Yayınları.

Suh, J. I., & Chang, S. P. (2000). Experimental study on fatigue behaviour of wire ropes. *International Journal of Fatigue, 22*(4), 339–347. doi:10.1016/S0142-1123(00)00003-7

Suner, F. (1988). *Crane bridges.* Istanbul, Turkey: Egitim Publications.

Sung-Ho, K., Sung-Hoon, H., & Jae-Do, K. (2014). Bending fatigue characteristics of corroded wire ropes. *Journal of Mechanical Science and Technology, 28*(7), 2853–2859. doi:10.100712206-014-0639-8

Svozil, D., Kvasnicka, V., & Pospichal, J. (1997). Introduction to multi-layer feed-forward neural networks. *Chemometrics and Intelligent Laboratory Systems, 39*(1), 43–62. doi:10.1016/S0169-7439(97)00061-0

Torkar, M., & Arzensek, B. (2002). Failure of crane wire rope. *Journal of Engineering Failure Analysis, 9*(2), 227–233. doi:10.1016/S1350-6307(00)00047-9

Türk Standardları Enstitüsü. (2005). Çelik tel halatlar-güvenlik-bölüm 2: tarifler, kısa gösteriliş ve sınıflandırma. Ankara, Turkey.

Uçan, O. N., Danacı, E., & Bayrak, M. (2003). *İşaret ve görüntü işlemede yeni yaklaşımlar:yapay sinir ağları.* İstanbul Üniversitesi Mühendislik Fakültesi Yayınları.

Vadood, M., Semnani, D., & Morshed, M. (2011). Optimization of acrylic dry spinning production line by using artificial neural network and genetic algorithm. *Journal of Applied Polymer Science, 120*(2), 735–744. doi:10.1002/app.33252

Verreet, R. (1998). *Calculating the service life of running steel wire ropes*. Retrieved from http://fast-lift.co.za/pdf/CASAR%20%20Calculating%20the%20service%20life%20of%20running%20steel%20wire%20ropes.pdf

Wang, Q. (2007). Artificial neural networks as cost engineering methods in a collaborative manufacturing environment. *International Journal of Production Economics*, *109*(1), 53–64. doi:10.1016/j.ijpe.2006.11.006

Wirerope Works Inc. (2008). *Bethlehem elevator rope technical bulletin 9*. Williamsport, PA.

Zhang, D., Feng, C., Chen, K., Wang, D., & Ni, X. (2017). Effect of broken wire on bending fatigue characteristics of wire ropes. *International Journal of Fatigue*, *103*, 456–465.

KEY TERMS AND DEFINITIONS

Architecture: The structure of a neural network consists of the number and connectivity of neurons. An input layer, one or more hidden layers, and an output layer are the layers that generally form the network.

Back Propagation Learning Algorithm: The algorithm for multi-layer perceptron networks to adjust the connection weights until the optimum network is obtained. In the back propagation algorithm, errors are propagated back through the network and weights are adjusted in the opposite direction to the largest local gradient.

Computer Simulation: It is a simulation that runs on a computer to model the behavior of a system.

Fatigue Testing: It is a type of test performed to determine the behavior of materials under fluctuating loads. In fatigue testing, a specified mean load and an alternating load are applied to a specimen and the number of cycles that are required to produce fatigue life is determined.

Lifetime Prediction: It is the prediction of lifetime by using some methods.

Multi-Layer Perceptron: It is one of the most widely used networks, which consists of multiple layers interconnected in a feedforward way.

Neuron: The basic building block of a neural network. A neuron sums the weighted inputs, processes the weighted inputs by means of an activation function, and produces an output at the last stage.

Rope Lifetime: It is the time for using the rope effectively. In other words, the time until the rope is considered unusable.

This research was previously published in Artificial Intelligence and Machine Learning Applications in Civil, Mechanical, and Industrial Engineering; pages 39-58, copyright year 2020 by Engineering Science Reference (an imprint of IGI Global).

Section 4
Utilization and Applications

Chapter 31
Literature Survey for Applications of Artificial Neural Networks

Pooja Deepakbhai Pancholi
Ganpat University, India

Sonal Jayantilal Patel
Ganpat University, India

ABSTRACT

The artificial neural network could probably be the complete solution in recent decades, widely used in many applications. This chapter is devoted to the major applications of artificial neural networks and the importance of the e-learning application. It is necessary to adapt to the new intelligent e-learning system to personalize each learner. The result focused on the importance of using neural networks in possible applications and its influence on the learner's progress with the personalization system. The number of ANN applications has considerably increased in recent years, fueled by theoretical and applied successes in various disciplines. This chapter presents an investigation into the explosive developments of many artificial neural network related applications. The ANN is gaining importance in various applications such as pattern recognition, weather forecasting, handwriting recognition, facial recognition, autopilot, etc. Artificial neural network belongs to the family of artificial intelligence with fuzzy logic, expert systems, vector support machines.

CHARACTER RECOGNITION APPLICATION

Now a day, character recognition has become important because portable devices like Palm Pilot are becoming more and more famous. NN can be used to identify the latter.

Given the ability of ANN to receive a large amount of information and process them to derive hidden, complex and non-linear relationships, ANNs play an significant role in character recognition.

The classification of character recognition is as shown in Figure 1.

DOI: 10.4018/978-1-6684-2408-7.ch031

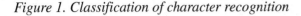

Figure 1. Classification of character recognition

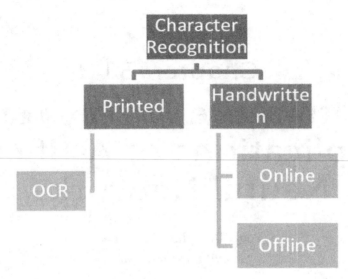

OPTICAL CHARACTER RECOGNITION (OCR)

OCR is a procedure that converts a printed document or a page scanned into ASCII characters that a computer can identify. Computer systems prepared with such an OCR system improve the input speed, reduce certain person error and allow solid storage space, speedy recovery and additional file manipulations. Accurateness, elasticity and velocity are the major characteristics of a excellent OCR system. Some character recognition algorithms based on feature selection have been developed. The performance of the systems was limited by police dependence, size and orientation. The recovery rate in these algorithms depends on the choice of features. Most existing algorithms involve complete image processing before feature extraction, which increases the calculation time. In this topic, discuss a method of character recognition based on a neural network that would efficiently shrink picture processing time though maintaining effectiveness and flexibility. The parallel computing efficiency of NN ensure big identify rate, which is essential for a mercantile domain. The neural network access has been recycled for character identify, although entire system that beset totally the characteristics of a pragmatic OCR system has not still been developed. The main elements besmeared in the execution are: an optimum collecting of characteristics that indeed define the expansion of the alphabets, the count of characteristics and a reduced image processing time (Mani 1997).

HANDWRITTEN CHARACTER RECOGNITION

Character recognition is an art of detecting, segmenting and identifying characters in an image. One of the main purposes of recognizing handwritten characters is to imitate human reading abilities therefore that the computer can read, perceive and performance in the same way as text. The identity of handwriting has been different majorities like charming and difficult analysis domain in the scope of picture processing and pattern indentify in nearly season. It greatly devotes to progress of the automatism procedure and rectified the interface among person and device in huge applications. Some analysis studies have focused on recent technology and schemes to decrease processing period and provide superior identity accuracy. Letter identity is mostly dual types: one is online and other is offline. At the time of online letter identity, data is cached at the time of writing procedures using a particular pen on an electronic level. At the time of offline identity, the prewritten content commonly written on a page of document is scanned. In usual, everything printed or written letters are sorted as offline. Offline manuscript identity refers to as process of character recognition in scanned document from a surface like paper sheet and stored digitally in grayscale formation. The repository of scanned documents must be huge and major processing applications, such as content search, modifying, preservation are difficult or not possible. The online identification style is generally use for identify simply handwritten letters. Here in case, the writing is caught and preserved in digital appearance through various ways. Generally, a special pen through computerized surface is used. When pen moves on the apparent, the 2dimensional coordinate of the succeeding points are appear as a task of time and preserved in sequence. In recent times, because major utilization of handheld devices, handwritten online identification has involved the awareness of researchers around the world. The handwritten online identification is intended to present a natural interface for persons to type on the display instead of typing on the keyboard. Handwriting recognition online has considerable possible to get better communication between the person and the computer (Pradeep 2011).

Figure 2. Optical character recognition example

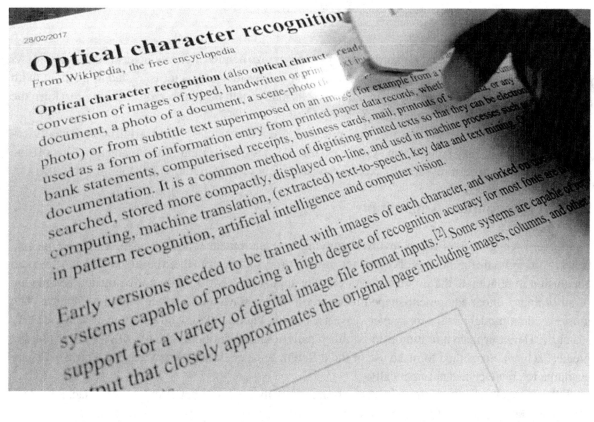

Feed-Forward Networks - Character Recognition

Figure 3. A feed-forward network for character recognition.

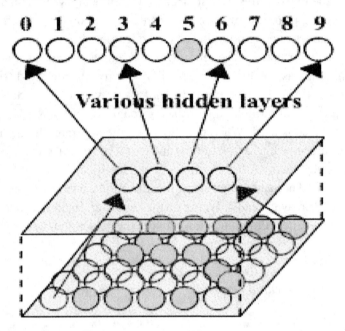

Another one idea of using feed forward networks to recognize handwritten characters is quite simple. As in most supervised exercise, the bitmap pattern of the handwritten character is treated as an input, with the correct letter or number as the desired output. Normally, such programs require the user to form the network by providing handwritten design.

Many applications like mail sorting, bank processing, document reading and postal address identification require handwriting recognition systems offline. As a result, recognition of manual writing offline remains an active area of research to explore new techniques that can improve recognition accuracy.

Pattern Recognition Application

The Pattern recognition of forms involves studying how equipment can monitor the surroundings and study to differentiate the motives of concern from their origins. And from them build sensible and practical conclusion in relation to the group of form. Despite approximately 50 years of investigate, the drawing of an ordinary-intent equipment-shaped recognition device stays a difficult ambition to achieve. The most excellent model identifiers in every case are human, but don't know how as human being identify structure. Here our main ambition is to establish pattern identification by the use of ANN. For that the greatest achievable method to make use of the different sensors, domain knowledge and processors are available to create choice automatically.

Till now discussion, the pattern identification are mainly use for direct calculation by machines. This direct calculation is depending on mathematical methods. After that topic will introduce idea related to bionics in pattern identification. The meaning of bionics is the application of biological concept to electronic equipment. The neural methods implement biological idea to equipment to identify the structure. So the achievement after this processes the innovation of the network of artificial neurons.

A neural network is known as an information processing system. These are simple and massive working element with a high level of interlinking among every element. The working element work in cooperation with altogether and allow corresponding cluster distributed processing. The drawing and purpose of NN imitate several functionality of biological brain power and neuronal structure. NNs have the different benefits like self –organization, error acceptance and their adaptive learning skill. Because of these different exceptional abilities, NNs are used for pattern identification purpose. Several most excellent neuronal models are backscatter, high order networks, moment delay NNs and recurring networks.

Generally, pattern identification is done by only progress networks. The meaning of feed-forward is no comments on the post. Just like humans taught from fault, NNs can also learn from their fault by giving response to input models. So this kind of return would be utilized to rebuild participation models and eliminate them from any errors; as a result increasing the work of NNs. Clearly, it is extremely difficult to construct this kind of NNs. These types of networks are called self-associating NNs.

Figure 4. Pattern recognition example

Face Recognition Application

Face recognition is a problem of recognition of visual forms. In detail, a facial recognition system with the entry of an arbitrary image will search the database to produce the identification of the people in the input image. A facial recognition system generally comprises four modules: detection, alignment, feature extraction and matching, with location and normalization (face detection and alignment) that are processing steps before facial recognition (removal and matching of facial features).

Face detection segments the areas of the background face. In the case of a video, it may be necessary to follow the detected faces using a face tracking component. Face alignment aims to achieve a more precise location and normalization of faces, while face detection provides approximate estimates of the location and scale of each face detected. The components of the face are located, such as the eyes, the nose, the mouth and the contour of the face; Depending on the location points, the image of the participation face is normalized by value to geometric properties, like size and pose, through geometric alteration. The features are generally more standardized through esteem to picture metric effects like lighting and grayscale. Once a face is geometrically and picture metrically normalized, characteristic taking out is executed to give useful information to distinguish faces of people who are different and constant from geometric and photometric variations. For face matching, the characteristic vector extracted from the participation face is compared with those faces which registered in the record; returns the identity of the face when a equal is establish through enough confidence or indicates an unidentified face (Le 2011).

Figure 5. Face recognition

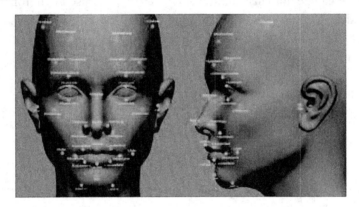

Spelling Check Application

ANN are a hopeful technology for natural language process because one of ANN's strengths is its "sensible" ability to make reasonable decisions even in the face of new information, even as the limitation of natural language process applications is weakness in the problem of ambiguous situations. Word is a part where ambiguity is excellent, words can be spell wrongly, they can have different legal spelling and can be homologous. Strong term identification functions may get better applications that involve text comprehension and form core component of applications, like spell examination and given name search. For artificial neural networks to identify variation and homologous word style, words have to be changed into a style that makes sense to artificial neural networks. The edge with the ANN consists of enter and production layers, each one consisting of unchanging number of nodes. Every node is linked through a number assessment, generally among 0 and 1. Therefore, words, variable length of strings, symbols, must be transformed into tables of preset length statistics so that ANNs can process them. The resulting verbal illustration should preferably: I) In the form, that allows an ANN to recognize likeness and spelling variation; 2) characterize every letters of the words; 3) Brief sufficient to permit the dealing out of a big digit of terms in a sensible moment. To date, ANN investigate has unseen these lowstage enter problems, still they have a critical impact on "superior stage processing. A general opinion have that various methods of representation don't have a significant effect on the presentation of ANN. However, this topic presents word representations that considerably improve artificial NN performance in NL words (Lewellen 1998).

Figure 6. Spelling check

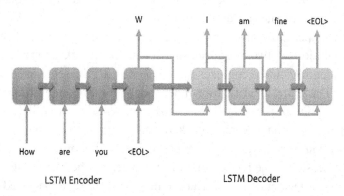

Autopilot Application

The main obligation of the autopilot is to keep the ship heading in a predefined direction using mainly the rudder. Transport safety and efficiency depend directly on the performance of the autopilots. For this, many techniques such as proportional-integral-derivative controller, optimal control theory, adaptive control and non-linear control are used to improve the performance of the autopilot. The main feature of these approaches is that they require accurate knowledge of the dynamics of controlled objects, which is difficult to obtain in practice due to the complexity of the hydrodynamics of ships. For adaptive and nonlinear control, there are some disadvantages, such as difficult design and stability analysis. The above mentioned drawbacks can be overcome through the use of an artificial neural network (ANN) due to its ability to approximate arbitrary smooth functions with the required precision. The first way of application of ANN to ship steering is to use a conventional controller for training the neural network (NN) controller. Another way to develop an NN controller is to integrate NN with other control techniques for adaptive control. The structure of this article is organized as shown in Figure 7 (Unar 1999).

Voice Recognition Application

Lecture and vocal identification is the upcoming defense and verification field for the future. Wording and picture password nowadays are subject to assault. In majority case common wording passwords applied, person must handle various passwords for email, Internet banking, etc. Therefore, they pick secret code those are simple to keep in mind. However they are sensitive in region of privacy. In case of illustrated secret code, they are sensitive to shoulder navigation and additional hacking methods. Moving forward in vocal technology has aroused great attention in the realistic appliance of voice detection. So, this structure provides person by way of the suitable and valuable technique of verification system based on volume identification. The vocal is as well a physiological characteristic for the reason that each human has a various voice, although the vocal identification is based primarily on the learning of how a human speaks, usually categorized as behavioral. The lecturer verification focuses on the vocal features that the speech produces and not on the vocal or pronunciation of the speech itself. The sound features rely on the measurement of the sound zone, the mouth, the nasal cavities and the additional verbal communication processing method of the human body. Biometric voice systems can be classified into two category one is voice processing and other one is biometric security. This double affiliation has powerfully influenced the function of biometric voice tools in the real world. Speech therapy, like other speech therapies, tools, voice biometrics extracts information from the voice flow to perform its work. They can be configured to operate on many of the same acoustic parameters as their closest relative voice recognition. Voice recognition has two categories that depend on the text and are independent of the text. Text-dependent sound identification recognizes the speaker facing the sentence that was specified at the moment of registration. The sound identification independent of the text identifies the speaker regardless of what person say. This technique is extremely repeatedly used in sound identification because it requires incredibly few calculations, although it requires additional support from speakers. In this matter, the content in the authentication stage is variant from that in the training or registration stage. An important application of audio processing is the recognition of the voice and the speaker used in the investigation of voice texts, human-machine interactions and autonomous robots. Several related research studies have been published, each of which differs in the applied algorithms. These include dynamic neural networks based on Synapse for the classification of temporal patterns found in speech to perform verification and recognition of the speaker at normal noise levels, as well as the genetic algorithm (GA) (Mansour 2015).

Figure 7. Autopilot

Figure 8. Voice recognition

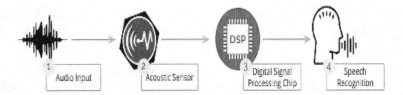

Weather Forecasting Application

Climate prediction is a procedure of recognizing and forecasting weather conditions with some precision using various technologies. Many living systems depend on weather conditions to make the essential adjustments to the systems. Quantitative forecasts such as temperature, moisture and rainfall are important in the agricultural area and for traders in the commodity market. Today, we use many approaches for climate prediction. Mathematical modeling, statistical modeling and AI methods are among them. The mathematical models of the climate to forecast future climate conditions based on present climate situation are digit climate prediction. It requires information of dynamics atmosphere and include calculations with a huge number of variables and data sets. With advances in modern computer hardware, many improvements have been made in the prediction of the digital climate. We use ANN, which is based on an intelligent analysis of the trend based on past records. The additional models are precise in the calculations although not in the prediction, they cannot adapt the irregular data structures that cannot be written as a function or deduced in the form of a formula. Climate prediction report need ingenious computing that can read nonlinear information and make regulation and models to practice from inspect record to forecast future climate conditions. The utilization of artificial NN will provide a additional perfect outcome. At this point, the mistake may or may not be absolutely reduced. However, accurateness will get better compared to earlier prediction. The forecast and weather forecast (WRF) models, common forecast model, seasonal weather forecast, global data prediction model, are at present admissible models for climate forecasting. In addition, the calculation of all these forecasting models is extremely costly due to the intensive nature of the calculation. In contrast, data mining models operate with past records, probability models and / or similarity. For every forecast categories, the model workings similarly and expects moderate accuracy. In weather forecasts, model output may be needed for a on a daily basis climate guide or weekly basis or monthly basis climate scheduling. Therefore, the accurateness of the outcome is extremely essential feature of the forecast in order to provide the most excellent outcome amongst the entire additional climate forecast models (Bashir 2009).

The Traveling Saleman's Problem Application

There are two methods to solve the Sales Passenger (TSP) problem. First of all the ant system (Ant colony system (ACS)). Second, Neural Network (Hopfield Neural Network).At ACS a number of cooperating agents, called ants, work together to find good solutions for TSPs. Ants work together using an indirect form of pheromone-mediated communication that they deposit on the edges of the TSP chart while building solutions. A proposed algorithm and a standard algorithm are derived that are applied to the sales traveler problem (TSP). ACS study represented by conducting experiments to understand how it works. Many algorithm that uses a continuous neural network from Hopfield to resolve the TSP. To enable N neurons in the TSP network to calculate a solution to the problem, the network must be described by an energy function in which the lowest energy state (the most stable state of the network) corresponds to the best path.

Figure 9. Weather forecasting

5-day forecast
8/23 - 8/27

Today 8/23	Tomorrow 8/24	Sat 8/25	Sun 8/26	Mon 8/27
Rain	Rain	Rain	Cloudy	Rain
29°C	29°C	29°C	29°C	27°C
25°C	25°C	24°C	25°C	24°C
Cloudy	Rain	Cloudy	Cloudy	Cloudy
Southwest Force 4	Southwest Force 3	Southwest Force 4	Southwest Force 3	Southwest Force 3

Figure 10. Weather forecasting

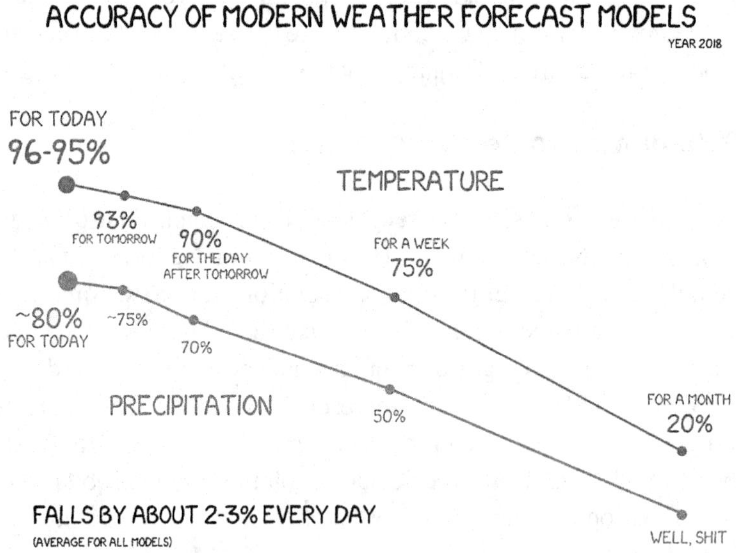

ACCURACY OF MODERN WEATHER FORECAST MODELS
YEAR 2018

FOR TODAY
96-95%

TEMPERATURE

93%
FOR TOMORROW

90%
FOR THE DAY
AFTER TOMORROW

FOR A WEEK
75%

~80%
FOR TODAY

~75%

70%

PRECIPITATION

50%

FOR A MONTH
20%

FALLS BY ABOUT 2-3% EVERY DAY
(AVERAGE FOR ALL MODELS)

WELL, SHIT

Figure 11. The traveling saleman's problem

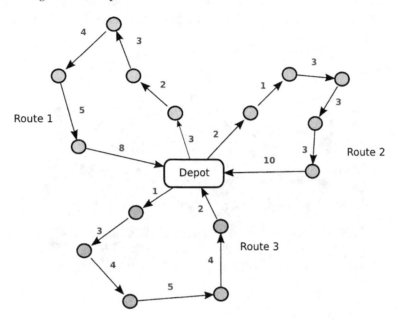

Image Processing Application

ANN are supporting tools for image processing. The pre-processing of images with neural networks generally falls into one of two categories: image reconstruction and restoration. The Hopfield neural network is one of the most widely used neural works for image reconstruction. Artificial neural networks retain their role as non-parametric classifiers, non-linear regression operators or extractors of monitored functions.

The purpose of image recovery is noise removal (sensor noise, movement shadow, and so on.) on or after the pictures. The easiest probable way used for noise elimination is different kinds of filters, like low-pass filters or median filters. Many advanced techniques take a representation of how local picture formation seems to be distinguished from noise. By initial examine the image records in terms of local picture construction, like lines or edges, and then controlling the filtering based on local information from the investigation phase, we usually get a better level of noise removal than most approaches. Simple an example in this area is painting.

Medical Diagnosis Application

ANN have clear benefits above statistical categorization methods. The ANNs are appropriate in cases where traditional categorization methods unsuccessful due to noisy or unfinished data. Neural networks also advantage from multivariable categorization troubles with a high degree of correlation. The analysis of diseases is excellent example of such difficult classification troubles. Through correctly applying artificial neural networks in this region to achieve symptom interdependence and correct diagnosis, this dependence can be generalized, depend on this generalized model. So after that categorize the input models that represent different symptoms of diseases. In the application procedure, however, it is not required to specify the algorithm or otherwise recognize the disease. The application just requires input schedules. The entire diagnostic procedure of diseases in medical exercises is exposed in Figure 13.

Figure 12. Image processing

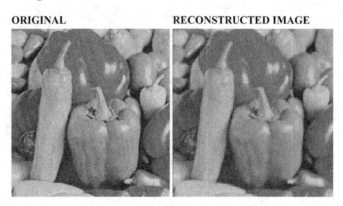

Figure 13. Medical diagnosis

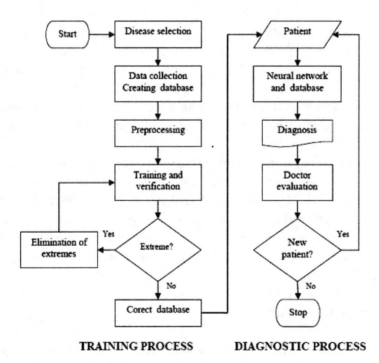

The entire diagnostic procedure of diseases can be separated into training and diagnostic part. Mostly the training procedure starts through the selection of target diseases to which the classification trouble will be correlated. After an adequate selection of the disease, it is essential to determine the exact parameters, symptoms and laboratory outcome that explain the nature of this disease in detail. In the next step, a database is created based on this data that must be validated and the extreme values removed outside the range. The neural network is trained via this database and then the outcome obtained in this practice are verified. If the outcome of the trained neural network are true, the neural model can be applied in medical practice. The diagnostic procedure starts with this step. Patient data is processed via the neural network, which determines the likely diagnosis. This outcome is then validated with the treating physician. The concluded diagnosis is the outcome of the doctor's decision, who evaluates every facts of the disease and the outcome of the neural network categorization based on his own experiences.

Object Recognition Application

Object recognition is one of the most fascinating skills that people have easily possessed since childhood. With a simple glance at an object, people can tell their identity or category, despite the changes in appearance due to the change in posture, enlightenment, consistency, distortion and occlusion. Moreover, people can easily generalize from observing a series of objects to recognizing objects that have never been seen before. Considerable efforts have been made to develop representation schemes and algorithms aimed at recognizing generic objects in images created under different imaging conditions (for example, viewpoint, illumination, and occlusion).

The approach based on the artificial neural network for the recognition of different objects is investigated via various functions. The aim is to configure and teach an ANN to recognize an object using a set of functions consisting of Principal Component Analysis (PCA), Frequency Domain and Discrete Cosine Transform (DCT) components. The proposal is to use these different components to create a unique hybrid function set to catch up the related information of the objects for recognition using an ANN that is a Perceptron Multi Layer (MLP) trained for work in learn (error) from the Back Propagation.

Game Playing Application

Video games are not only fun. They offer a platform for neural networks to learn to deal with dynamic environments and to solve complex problems, just like in real life. Video games have been used for decades to evaluate the performance of artificial intelligence.

Unlike the traditional game, the general game involves the agents who can play game classes. Given the rules of an unidentified game, the agent must play well without human involvement. In favor of this reason, agent systems that use deterministic searching in the game tree must automatically build a grade value function to cicerone the search. Successful systems of this kind use assessment functions that are derived solely from the regulations of the game, whereby further improvements are neglected by experience. Moreover, these functions are preset in their outline and do not essentially have to capture the function of the true value of the game. In this topic, current perspective to obtain assessment functions based on neural networks that overcome the above troubles. An initialization of the network extracted from the game regulations guarantees proper behavior without prior training. However, the subsequent training can lead to important improvements in the excellence of the assessment, as our results point out.

Signature Verification Application

Signatures are one of the mainly convenient traditions to authorize and authenticate a person in lawful communication. The signature proof procedure is a non-vision based method. In support of this application, the first approach is to take out the function, or somewhat, the set of geometric features that represent the signature. By way of these function sets, we must train neural networks with an efficient neural network algorithm. This educated neural network classifies the signature as authentic or fake in the confirmation phase.

REFERENCES

Bashir, Z. A., & El-Hawary, M. E. (2009). Applying wavelets to short-term load forecasting using PSO-based neural networks. *IEEE Transactions on Power Systems, 24*(1), 20–27. doi:10.1109/TP-WRS.2008.2008606

Basu, J. K., Bhattacharyya, D., & Kim, T. H. (2010). Use of artificial neural network in pattern recognition. *International Journal of Software Engineering and Its Applications, 4*(2).

Burns, R. S. (1995). The use of artificial neural networks for the intelligent optimal control of surface ships. *IEEE Journal of Oceanic Engineering, 20*(1), 65–72. doi:10.1109/48.380245

Chow, T. W. S., & Leung, C. T. (1996). Neural network based short-term load forecasting using weather compensation. *IEEE Transactions on Power Systems, 11*(4), 1736–1742. doi:10.1109/59.544636

Le, T. H. (2011). Applying artificial neural networks for face recognition. *Advances in Artificial Neural Systems, 2011*, 15. doi:10.1155/2011/673016

Lewellen, M. (1998, August). Neural network recognition of spelling errors. In *Proceedings of the 36th Annual Meeting of the Association for Computational Linguistics and 17th International Conference on Computational Linguistics-Volume 2* (pp. 1490-1492). Association for Computational Linguistics.

Mani, N., & Srinivasan, B. (1997, October). Application of artificial neural network model for optical character recognition. In *1997 IEEE International Conference on Systems, Man, and Cybernetics. Computational Cybernetics and Simulation* (Vol. 3, pp. 2517-2520). IEEE. 10.1109/ICSMC.1997.635312

Mansour, A. H., Zen, G., Salh, A., Hayder, H., & Alabdeen, Z. (2015). *Voice recognition Using back propagation algorithm in neural networks*. Academic Press.

Pao, Y. (1989). *Adaptive pattern recognition and neural networks*. Academic Press.

Pradeep, J., Srinivasan, E., & Himavathi, S. (2011, March). Neural network based handwritten character recognition system without feature extraction. In 2011 international conference on computer, communication and electrical technology (ICCCET) (pp. 40-44). IEEE. doi:10.1109/ICCCET.2011.5762513

Schürmann, J. (1996). *Pattern classification: a unified view of statistical and neural approaches*. Wiley.

Unar, M. A., & Murray-Smith, D. J. (1999). Automatic steering of ships using neural networks. *International Journal of Adaptive Control and Signal Processing, 13*(4), 203–218. doi:10.1002/(SICI)1099-1115(199906)13:4<203::AID-ACS544>3.0.CO;2-T

This research was previously published in Applications of Artificial Neural Networks for Nonlinear Data; pages 1-17, copyright year 2021 by Engineering Science Reference (an imprint of IGI Global).

Chapter 32

An Assessment of Imbalanced Control Chart Pattern Recognition by Artificial Neural Networks

Ramazan Ünlü

https://orcid.org/0000-0002-1201-195X

Gumushane University, Turkey

ABSTRACT

Manual detection of abnormality in control data is an annoying work which requires a specialized person. Automatic detection might be simpler and effective. Various methodologies such as ANN, SVM, Fuzzy Logic, etc. have been implemented into the control chart patterns to detect abnormal patterns in real time. In general, control chart data is imbalanced, meaning the rate of minority class (abnormal pattern) is much lower than the rate of normal class (normal pattern). To take this fact into consideration, authors implemented a weighting strategy in conjunction with ANN and investigated the performance of weighted ANN for several abnormal patterns, then compared its performance with regular ANN. This comparison is also made under different conditions, for example, abnormal and normal patterns are separable, partially separable, inseparable and the length of data is fixed as being 10,20, and 30 for each. Based on numerical results, weighting policy can better predict in some of the cases in terms of classifying samples belonging to minority class to the correct class.

INTRODUCTION

Quality control engineering provides some strategies to ensure a product is satisfied with some predetermined quality standards before market release. It provides the necessary mathematical and statistical tools to improve a process, to assure safety, and to analyze reliability (Montgomery, 2007). Quality control process can also help to detect a failure in the production systems such as machine failure. Sequential production of an item that does not satisfy the quality standards can be a sign of a machine

DOI: 10.4018/978-1-6684-2408-7.ch032

failure (Panagiotidou & Tagaras, 2012; Paté-Cornell, Lee, & Tagaras, 1987). Early detection of a machine failure can help to avoid expensive equipment and reducing repair cost. Over the years, various rules are implemented such as zone tests or run tests (Jill A Swift & Mize, 1995). Manual quality control process can be a tedious task and highly relies on human skills and experience. For this reason, automated systems to detect abnormal behavior in a control chart is developed by researchers (Hachicha & Ghorbel, 2012). Automated methods provide sophisticated techniques to distinguish abnormal and normal pattern during the production process. Over the years, various normal and abnormal patterns reported in real production systems. In an early study of Western Electric Company, seven abnormal patterns are identified and formulized which are named as uptrend (UT), downtrend (DT), upshift (US), downshift (DS), cyclic (C), systematic (S), stratification (F) patterns are shown in Figure 1, also the mathematical formulations of all these abnormal patterns are given in APPENDIX-A.

Figure 1. Example of six abnormal patterns vs normal pattern

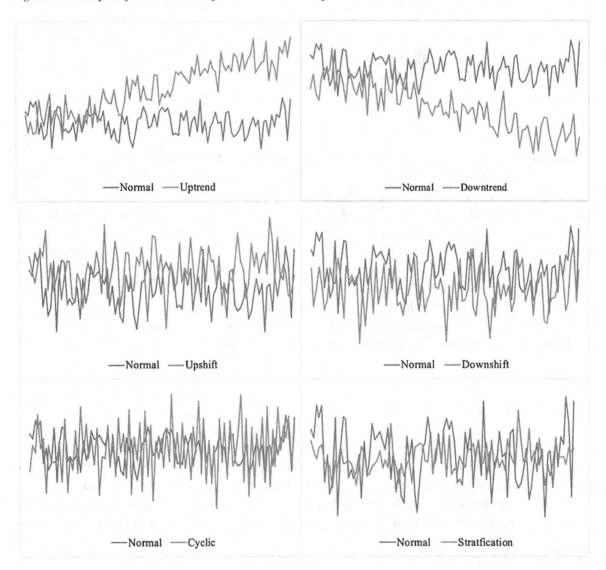

Each pattern is associated with a particular failure type. In the crankcase manufacturing operations, tool wear and malfunction problems yield Uptrend and downtrend abnormality (Hachicha & Ghorbel, 2012). They are also observed in stamping tonnage and paper making and viscosity process (Chinnam, 2002; Cook & Chiu, 1998; Jin & Shi, 2001). Upshift and downshift patterns might be related to the variation of operator, material or machine instrument (Davy, Desobry, Gretton, & Doncarli, 2006; El-Midany, El-Baz, & Abd-Elwahed, 2010). Variability of the power supply voltage is usually pinpointed by cyclic abnormal patterns (Kawamura, Chuarayapratip, & Haneyoshi, 1988). Uptrend, downtrend, cyclic, and systematic patterns are also observed in the automotive industry (Jang, Yang, & Kang, 2003). Since each pattern is associated with some certain type of malfunctions, the best possible method has to be implemented with the purpose of efficient identification of abnormal patterns. By doing this, system sustainability can be provided, an extensive cost can be avoided, and maintenance can be lowered. Early control chart pattern recognition studies focused on basic statistical approaches to identify changes in mean and variance with regards to normal pattern (Jill Anne Swift, 1987). Knowledge-based expert systems and artificial intelligence-based methods are employed in several studies. (H Brian Hwarng & Hubele, 1992) implemented Boltzmann machines (BM), a special type of neural network, to detect cyclical and stratification pattern. Based on their numerical results, BM is a quite powerful control chart pattern recognition tool. In another study of (H. B. Hwarng, 1995), multilayer perceptron is used to detect a cyclic pattern in which each perceptron deals with the cycles of a certain period. The proposed methodology performs superiorly in detecting higher noise and cycles of higher amplitudes. Backpropagation approach is also used for control chart pattern recognition. (H. B. Hwarng & Hubele, 1993) implemented backpropagation algorithm, suitable for real-time statistical process control, to recognize cyclic or trend patterns and they have evaluated the results based on Type 1 and Type 2 errors. Artificial neural networks is used in various control chart pattern recognition studies. (Pugh, 1989) used ANN with backpropagation algorithm and they alleged that ANN performs reasonably well under most conditions. (Cheng & Cheng, 2008) implemented ANN and SVM which are used to detect shift pattern and classify them. In addition to regular SVM, weighted SVM (WSVM) is used by (Xanthopoulos & Razzaghi, 2014) in which they compared SVM and WSVM in terms of detecting seven abnormal patterns and comparison is made based on data mining-based evaluation metrics and ARDLIX. One can see some other control chart pattern recognition methods in the literature such as principal component analysis (PCA) (Aparisi, 1996), time series analyzing (Alwan & Roberts, 1988), regression(Mandel, 1969), and correlation analysis technique (Al-Ghanimai, Amjed M Ludeman, 1997; Yang & Yang, 2005). Soft computing and data mining approaches are also utilized to detect abnormality during the production process. (Ghazanfari, Alaeddini, Niaki, & Aryanezhad, 2008) proposed a clustering methodology to estimate Shewhart control chart change points. As different from classical methods, the proposed methodology does not depend on known values of parameters and even the distribution of the process variables. Despite the capability in monitoring the variability of the process, control charts can fail to identify a real-time of changes in a process. In order to handle this, (Zarandi & Alaeddini, 2010) proposed a fuzzy clustering approach for estimating real-time change in a variable. Another data mining-based approach called decision trees used by (C.-H. Wang, Guo, Chiang, & Wong, 2008). They have used decision trees approach to identify six anomaly types including systematic pattern, cyclic pattern, upshift pattern, downshift pattern, uptrend pattern, and downtrend pattern. In terms of classification accuracy and computational cost, decision trees produce reasonably good results based on given numerical results. In addition to these methods, Support Vector Machines is another one of the commonly used data mining based methods. It has some advantages over other methods such as its performance is not affected when control chart data does not fit to a normal distribution (Sun & Tsung, 2003). Rather than other statistical as well as machine learning methods, SVM might give a better result especially is the control chart data from facilities are often autocorrelated (Chinnam, 2002).

Since control chart pattern recognition can be considered as a classification problem, Artificial neural networks (ANNs) might be a powerful tool to detect an abnormal pattern. Over the last decades, with the advancement of computational power, deep ANNs architectures have been started to use to reveal hidden patterns from an extremely complex dataset. To date, to the best of author knowledge, despite ANNs is used in control chart pattern recognition, size of normal and abnormal classes are not taking into consideration. If we consider a production dataset, we can expect that the rate of abnormal pattern will be much lower than the rate of normal class. Thus, the equal contribution of samples from normal class and abnormal class has no bases and might get misguiding classification accuracy. In order to handle with this problem, different weights can be assigned to each class based on their size. Thanks to the simplicity of high-level ANNs libraries, assigning different weights to each class is a straightforward process but can yield much better results. Thus, in this study, our core objective is explaining how class weighting strategy can be utilized in conjunction with ANNs and show how the algorithm's performance differ from no weighted case. For this objective, we have used simulated abnormal and normal patterns with fixed size and different parameters. The remainder of the study is organized as follows. In the Materials and Methods section, we have described the dataset, gave the details of the design of the experiment, algorithms evaluation metrics. In section Computational Results, we have given the detailed numerical results, the graphical illustration of the study and discussed the performance of the methods. Finally, we have completed the study with the Conclusion section.

MATERIALS AND METHODS

Dataset

In this section we have described the dataset and mathematical background of used strategies through the experiment. As we mentioned above, there available seven basic abnormal pattern, namely (1) normal (N) (2) uptrend (Ut) (3) downtrend (Dt) (4) upshifts (Us) (5) downshift (Ds) (6) cyclic (C) (7) systematic (S) (8) stratification (F).

As we can see in Figure 1, each abnormal pattern has deviated from the normal pattern based on its own parameters. Based on the literature, these parameters lie within the range of the certain values. The magnitude of these parameters (see Table 1) play the main role in how well an abnormal pattern distinguished from the normal pattern.

Among given six abnormal patterns we have chosen four of them UT, DT, US, and DS. The mathematical formulation of all abnormal patterns is given in APPENDIX-A. Because the rate of samples from abnormal class is much lower than the normal pattern during the entire process, we have focused on weighting policies and convert them balanced in the context of the classification problem. To do this we have implemented two main strategies as follows 1) Simple Artificial Neural Network 2) Weighted Artificial Neural network.

Table 1. Summary of parameters for abnormal patterns

Name	Symbol	Range
Mean of process (all pattern)	μ	0
Standard deviation of normal process	σ	1
Slope (UT and DT)	λ	[0.005 σ, 0.605 σ]
Shift (US and DS)	ω	[0.005 σ, 1.805 σ]
Standard deviation (F)	ε_t	[0.005 σ, 0.8 σ]
Cyclic parameter (C)	α	[0.005 σ, 1.805 σ]
Systematic parameter (S)	k	[0.005 σ, 1.805 σ]

Based on abnormal parameters, it might very difficult to distinguish the normal pattern from an abnormal pattern while its parameter value is too low, and it might be a very easy task while its parameter value is high. In real-world application, it is possible to see any kind of difficulty level. That's why we have set parameter values as being inseparable, partial separable, and separable.

Artificial Neural Network (ANNs)

The main idea of ANNs comes from the neural structure of the brain (Anderson & McNeill, 1992). Since long, it has been widely used to reveal hidden nonlinear relationship in many different problems such as image processing (N. Wang & Yeung, 2013), text mining (Berry & Castellanos, 2004), natural language processing (Manning, Manning, & Schütze, 1999), clustering (Jain, Murty, & Flynn, 1999; Ünlü & Xanthopoulos, 2017, 2019) etc.. A simple ANN architecture consists of some connected layers formed by neurons. The first layer in an ANN architecture is called the input layer in which the number of neurons is equal to the number of data features plus one (bias value). The next layer is named as the hidden layer which plays the main role to uncover the nonlinearity (Onur, İmrak, & Onur, 2017). There is no explicit rule of determining the number of neurons in this layer. However, some heuristics and statistical approaches are proposed in different studies (Fujita, 1998; Hagiwara, 1994; Islam & Murase, 2001; Keeni, Nakayama, & Shimodaira, 1999; Onoda, 1995; Tamura & Tateishi, 1997). The last layer of the ANNs architecture is called as the output layer in which the number of neurons is equal to the number of class size (i.e. the number of neurons in the last layer is two for a binary classification problem). And, each layer is connected by some weights $W \in \mathbb{R}^{m+n}$.

The most well-known systematic of an ANNs is known as a feed-forward neural network. The main idea of the feed-forward system is that each layer (or neurons) is fed by the previous layers' outcomes until the output layer. Then, the overall cost of the system is minimized by an algorithm which is called backpropagation algorithm. To make it more concrete assume we have a given dataset $X \in \mathbb{R}^{n+1}$, where n is the number of features and ground true outputs $y \in \mathbb{R}^m$ where m is the number of samples. In this case, the input layer is formed by n+1 neurons. The output of each neuron is equal to the value of each feature and the output of the bias neuron is equal to a constant bias term. Every single neuron except the bias one in the first hidden layers will be fed by the output of each neuron in input layer in a way that the input of the neurons will be calculated as in Equation 1.

$$h_w(x) = w^T X \tag{1}$$

The next layer, which can be another hidden layer or the output layer, is fed by the outcome of an activation function which is a function of $h_w(x)$. There are numerous activation functions in the literature and we have used the rectified linear unit (ReLU). So, inputs of each neuron in the next layer will be calculated based on the following rule shown in Equation 2 . The function of ReLu is shown in Figure 2

$$R(h_w(x)) = Max(0, h_w(x)) \tag{2}$$

Figure 2. The function of rectified linear unit (ReLU)

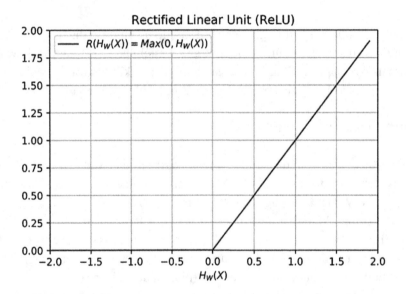

The outcome of the activation function will be the input of each neuron in the next layer including the output layer. The outcome of the activation function in the output layer is the prediction of the systems $\hat{y} \in \mathbb{R}^m$. Finally, one can easily calculate the average error of the system based on Equation 3.

$$J\left(W\right) = -\frac{1}{m}\left[\sum_{i=1}^{m}\sum_{k=1}^{K}y_k^{(i)}\log\left(h_W\left(x^{(i)}\right)\right)_k + \left(1 - y_k^{(i)}\right)\log(1 - \left(h_W\left(x^{(i)}\right)\right)_k\right] + \frac{\lambda}{2m}\sum_{l=1}^{L-1}\sum_{i=1}^{s_l}\sum_{j=1}^{s_{l+1}}\left(W_{ji}^{(l)}\right)^2 \tag{3}$$

where $h_w(x) \in R^K$, L is the total number of layers in the network, is the number of non-bias neurons in layer , K is the total number of classes (in other words number of neurons in output layer), is the regularization term. After completing the first iteration, the system produces the initial cost of . The next step is being to utilize the back-propagation algorithm to optimize every single with the purpose of minimizing overall error. In other words, ANNs will learn through the iterations what each weight should be to get the minimum average error. The detailed representation of the ANNs for a binary classification problem (i.e. the number of neurons in the output layer is equal to 2) is shown in Figure 3.

Figure 3. A) Representation of the ANN model B) The process of a single neuron

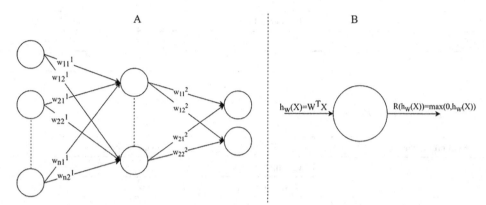

Described ANN model is not a cost-sensitive model. So, it assigns equal weights to each sample regardless of their class size. In order to handle with this problem, it can be easily assigned different weights to each class based on their class size. By doing this, we can force samples to equally contributes to the training process.

Weighting the Samples

In real-world applications, having an imbalanced data (i.e. machine failure) is a commonly seen fact and it is not as easy as analyzing a balanced dataset. In order to solve this problem, we can transform the learning strategy by giving different weights to each class depend on their class size. These weights are simply calculated as shown in Equation 4.

$$classweights = \frac{n}{K * n^{K_i}} \tag{4}$$

where n is the total number of samples, K is the number of classes, n^{K_i} is the number of samples in the ith class.

Performance Measures: Various performance measures can be used to appraise the performance of a machine learning method for an imbalanced dataset. Some of the evaluation measurements can be calculated directly or indirectly based on confusion matrix which is a square matrix $C \in R^{KxK}$ with each entry of the matrix represent the number of samples assigned to the class K_i while belongs to the class K_j. For binary classification problem, for example, the confusion matrix is structured as shown in Table 2 in which TP, TF, FP, and FN stand for True positive, True False, False Positive, and False Negative. Obviously, the higher values of the diagonal refer a better classification result. A commonly used performance measure is so-called accuracy which can be calculated as TP+TN/(TP+TN+FP+FN). For an imbalanced problem, the accuracy can be a valid performance measure. However, it can possibly be a misleading measurement for the imbalanced problem because majority class dominates the behavior of this metric. For example, assigning all data samples to the class of y=1 will yield 98% accuracy in an imbalanced data where 98% of the data belongs to the class of y=1 and 2% of the class of y=0. To avoid this problem, some other metrics can be used based on the given formulations in Table 3.

Table 2. Confusion matrix for a binary classification problem

	Predicted Positive Class	**Predicted Negative Class**
Actual Positive Class	TP	FP
Actual Negative Class	FN	TN

Table 3. The formulations of the evaluation metrics

Evaluation Metrics	**Formulations**
Sensitivity/Recall	TP/Actual Positive
Specificity	TN/Actual Negative
Precision	TP/Predicted Positive
Prevalence	Actual Positive/Total number of samples
F1 score	2 x (Precision x Recall)/(Precision + Recall)
G-Mean	$\sqrt{Sensitivity \times Specificity}$

COMPUTATIONAL RESULTS AND DISCUSSIONS

In this section, we present the experimental results of applied ANNs strategies. The model is created in Python version of 3.5 by using Keras version of 2.2.1 and run on an Intel Core i5, 2.6 GHz with 16gb Ram. It is because we have focused on detecting tool wear and malfunction and some kind of variations (i.e. variation of a machine instrument), we have used associated patterns called Uptrend (UT) and Downtrend (DT). The synthetic data is created based on Equation 4 and Equation 5 for UT and DT patterns, respectively.

$$\zeta(i) = \mu - \varepsilon_i - \lambda_i \tag{4}$$

$$\zeta(i) = \mu - \varepsilon_i - \omega \tag{5}$$

where $\zeta(i)$ represents the simulated control chart pattern, μ is a constant term process mean, εi is a random and normally distributed term, λ is the trend slope in terms of $\sigma\varepsilon$, and i is the time unit. One needs to note that the parameter $\lambda>0$ should be chosen for UT and $\lambda<0$ for DT, ω is the shift magnitude. $\Omega>0$ for US pattern and $\omega<0$ for DS pattern. Without loss of generality, we use $\mu=0$ and $\varepsilon_i \sim N(0,1)$. All parameters are given in Table 4.

Through the experiment, we have determined sample size as 1000, window lengths are 10,20, and 30 for both trend and shift pattern. UT and DT patterns categorized as separable, partially separable, and inseparable by choosing the value of λ as 0.6, 0.06, 0.006 respectively. In the same way, US and DS are categorized as separable, partially separable, and inseparable by choosing the value of ω as 1.8, 1, 0.006 respectively. Each pattern versus the normal pattern is illustrated in Figure 4 and Figure 5.

Table 4. Summary of parameters for chosen abnormal patterns

Name	Symbol	Range
Length of the data	w	[10,30]
Mean of the process	μ	0
Standard deviation of normal process	σ	1
Slope (UT and DT)	λ	0.006 σ, 0.06 σ, 0.6 σ
Shift (US and DS)	ω	0.006 σ, 1 σ, 1.8 σ

Figure 4. Downtrend and uptrend patterns vs. normal pattern along with different parameters

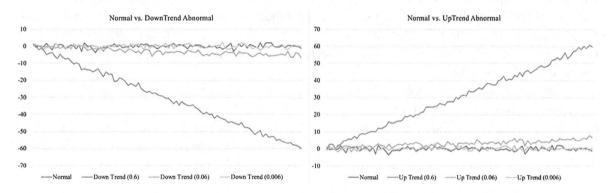

Figure 5. Downshift and upshift patterns vs. normal pattern along with different parameters

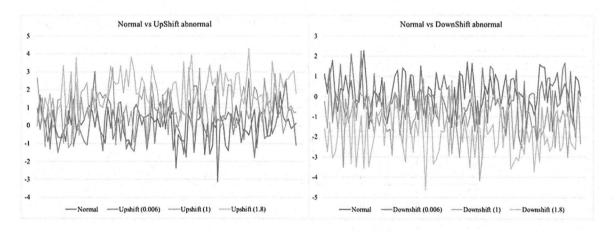

At first glance, we can see that inseparable patterns are not distinguishable from normal patterns. So that it is not an easy task to classify them correctly especially with having limited data (i.e w=10). On the other hand, separable cases are rather different from the normal pattern. In this case, important point is to detect failure earlier such as while w<=10. The critical case is partially separable cases. It might be expected to get different performance measures from WANN and ANN in this case since it can be said neither partially separable cases are very similar to normal pattern nor totally different.

Through experiment the rate of abnormal samples is determined as 5% and all data samples are normalized with z-score before training phase. After completing mentioned data preprocessing, we have compared regular ANN and weighted ANN (WANN) for the separable problem ($\lambda=0.6$, $\omega=1.8$) for both trend and shift patterns for which window lengths are assigned as 10, 20, and 30. The following Table 5 shows the assignment results of ANN and WANN for the separable problem. Regardless of the window length, ANN and WANN are a powerful prediction model for the separable problem. They successfully assign all points to the correct class for both trend and shift patterns. Obviously, both methodologies give the best possible results in terms of the evaluation metrics as shown in Table 6. As we pointed out before, this is an expected outcome from both method due to the high difference between normal patterns and separable uptrend, downtrend, upshift, and downshift patterns. It can be visually seen in that there is no difference between the performance of both methodologies in Figure 6. Although both approaches perform well for separable problems, they might not be practical in real-world application. Separable problems can be defined as abnormality becomes a serious problem and it detected just before the machine failure. That's why the purpose of protecting overall systems by detecting might be unsuccessful due to late detection.

For the separable problem, it can be expected to get similar results because of the simplicity of the problem. However, solving the classification problem for partially separable or inseparable cases might be more difficult. To compare the performance of the chosen methodology, we set the value of λ as 0.06 and $\omega=1$ to create a partially separable dataset for downtrend, uptrend, downshift and upshift patterns. Same training and test set is used for both ANN and WANN. The following Table 7 shows the classification performance of the methods and Table 8 illustrated the comparison of both methods in terms of evaluation metrics.

Table 5. Confusion matrices for the separable problem ($\lambda=0.6$, $\omega=1.8$) with different window lengths

			w=10		w=20		w=30	
			PC	NC	PC	NC	PC	NC
Uptrend	WANN	PC	285	0	283	0	283	0
		NC	0	15	0	17	0	17
	ANN	PC	285	0	283	0	283	0
		NC	0	15	0	17	0	17
Downtrend	WANN	PC	283	0	283	0	283	0
		NC	0	17	0	17	0	17
	ANN	PC	283	0	283	0	283	0
		NC	0	17	0	17	0	17
Upshift	WANN	PC	285	0	283	0	283	0
		NC	0	15	0	17	0	17
	ANN	PC	285	0	283	0	283	0
		NC	0	15	0	17	0	17
Downshift	WANN	PC	283	0	283	0	283	0
		NC	0	17	0	17	0	17
	ANN	PC	283	0	283	0	283	0
		NC	0	17	0	17	0	17

Table 6. Performance of ANN and WANN for the separable UT, DT, DS, and US patterns

		w=10		w=20		w=30	
		WANN	ANN	WANN	ANN	WANN	ANN
Uptrend	Sensitivity/Recall	1.00	1.00	1.00	1.00	1.00	1.00
	Specificity	1.00	1.00	1.00	1.00	1.00	1.00
	Precision	1.00	1.00	1.00	1.00	1.00	1.00
	Prevalence	0.95	0.95	0.94	0.94	0.94	0.94
	F1 score	1.00	1.00	1.00	1.00	1.00	1.00
	G-Mean	1.00	1.00	1.00	1.00	1.00	1.00
Downtrend	Sensitivity/Recall	1.00	1.00	1.00	1.00	1.00	1.00
	Specificity	1.00	1.00	1.00	1.00	1.00	1.00
	Precision	1.00	1.00	1.00	1.00	1.00	1.00
	Prevalence	0.94	0.94	0.94	0.94	0.94	0.94
	F1 score	1.00	1.00	1.00	1.00	1.00	1.00
	G-Mean	1.00	1.00	1.00	1.00	1.00	1.00
Upshift	Sensitivity/Recall	1.00	1.00	1.00	1.00	1.00	1.00
	Specificity	1.00	1.00	1.00	1.00	1.00	1.00
	Precision	1.00	1.00	1.00	1.00	1.00	1.00
	Prevalence	0.95	0.95	0.94	0.94	0.94	0.94
	F1 score	1.00	1.00	1.00	1.00	1.00	1.00
	G-Mean	1.00	1.00	1.00	1.00	1.00	1.00
Downshift	Sensitivity/Recall	1.00	1.00	1.00	1.00	1.00	1.00
	Specificity	1.00	1.00	1.00	1.00	1.00	1.00
	Precision	1.00	1.00	1.00	1.00	1.00	1.00
	Prevalence	0.94	0.94	0.94	0.94	0.94	0.94
	F1 score	1.00	1.00	1.00	1.00	1.00	1.00
	G-Mean	1.00	1.00	1.00	1.00	1.00	1.00

Figure 6. Representation of the performance of methods for separable problem

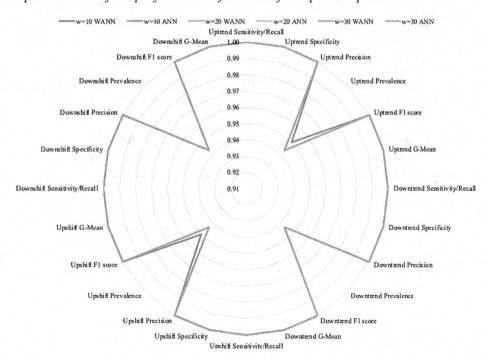

Table 7. Confusion matrices for the separable problem ($\lambda=0.6$, $\omega=1$) with different window lengths

			w=10		w=20		w=30	
			PC	NC	PC	NC	PC	NC
Uptrend	WANN	PC	288	0	280	4	281	0
		NC	12	0	6	10	0	19
	ANN	PC	288	0	280	3	281	0
		NC	12	0	12	5	0	19
Downtrend	WANN	PC	281	0	285	5	290	0
		NC	19	0	2	8	0	10
	ANN	PC	281	0	285	5	289	1
		NC	19	0	4	6	0	10
Upshift	WANN	PC	285	0	281	2	283	0
		NC	15	0	2	15	0	17
	ANN	PC	285	0	279	4	283	0
		NC	15	0	7	10	0	17
Downshift	WANN	PC	283	0	280	3	283	0
		NC	17	0	3	14	0	17
	ANN	PC	283	0	280	3	283	0
		NC	17	0	4	13	0	17

Table 8. Performance of ANN and WANN in terms of the evaluation metrics

		w=10		w=20		w=30	
		WANN	ANN	WANN	ANN	WANN	ANN
Uptrend	Sensitivity/Recall	1.00	1.00	0.99	0.99	1.00	1.00
	Specificity	0.00	0.00	0.63	0.29	1.00	1.00
	Precision	0.96	0.96	0.98	0.96	1.00	1.00
	Prevalence	0.96	0.96	0.95	0.94	0.94	0.94
	F1 score	0.98	0.98	0.98	0.97	1.00	1.00
	G-Mean	0.00	0.00	0.78	0.54	1.00	1.00
Downtrend	Sensitivity/Recall	1.00	1.00	0.98	0.98	1.00	1.00
	Specificity	0.00	0.00	0.80	0.60	1.00	1.00
	Precision	0.94	0.94	0.99	0.99	1.00	1.00
	Prevalence	0.94	0.94	0.97	0.97	0.97	0.97
	F1 score	0.97	0.97	0.99	0.98	1.00	1.00
	G-Mean	0.00	0.00	0.89	0.77	1.00	1.00
Upshift	Sensitivity/Recall	1.00	1.00	0.99	0.99	1.00	1.00
	Specificity	0.00	0.00	0.88	0.59	1.00	1.00
	Precision	0.95	0.95	0.99	0.98	1.00	1.00
	Prevalence	0.95	0.95	0.94	0.94	0.94	0.94
	F1 score	0.97	0.97	0.99	0.98	1.00	1.00
	G-Mean	0.00	0.00	0.94	0.76	1.00	1.00
Downshift	Sensitivity/Recall	1.00	1.00	0.99	0.99	1.00	1.00
	Specificity	0.00	0.00	0.82	0.76	1.00	1.00
	Precision	0.94	0.94	0.99	0.99	1.00	1.00
	Prevalence	0.94	0.94	0.94	0.94	0.94	0.94
	F1 score	0.97	0.97	0.99	0.99	1.00	1.00
	G-Mean	0.00	0.00	0.90	0.87	1.00	1.00

As we pointed out above, the performance of ANN and WANN differs to solve the partially separable problem. In the case of feeding neural network with enough historical data (in other words having enough attributes) (i.e. w=30), ANN and WANN can produce similar results. This fact can be seen in the values of evaluation metrics for w=30 and in Table 8. In this case, regardless of the class size, both ANN and WANN behaves similarly. On the other hand, if limited information is given (i.e. w=20), WANN outperforms ANN much better with higher G-mean for downtrend, uptrend, downshift, and upshift patterns. However, the biggest problem for the partially separable cases is that both methods fail to classify samples if there available very limited information such as w=10. This can be commented as that neural networks might likely yields poor performance in terms of early detection of the abnormal patterns no matter what weighting strategy used. But in general, WANN can be preferred rather than regular ANN based on especially G-mean score. In Figure 7, we can also visually see how ANN and WANN differ based on given parameters and set window lengths in terms of given performance measures.

Figure 7. Representation of the performance of methods for partially separable problem

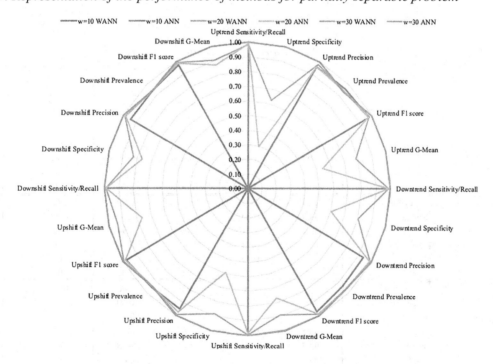

For the cases from the real-world production dataset, it is possible to have an inseparable normal and abnormal pattern. For this reason, we have compared the chosen methods for inseparable control chart patterns with the value of λ=0.006, ω=0.006. The following Table 9 and Table 10 shows the comparison of the ANN and WANN for the inseparable problem for downtrend, uptrend, downshift and upshift abnormal patterns.

As shown in Table 10, ANN or WANN cannot classify samples in the minority class if given data is very limited (w=10). In other words, it cannot differentiate the abnormal patterns from the normal patterns. On the other hand, WANN gives better results if there available limited or enough information before the abnormal pattern occurred.

Table 9. Confusion matrices for the inseparable problem ($\lambda=0.006$, $\omega=0.006$) with different window lengths

			w=10		w=20		w=30	
			PC	NC	PC	NC	PC	NC
Uptrend	WANN	PC	280	0	288	0	288	0
		NC	20	0	9	3	0	12
	ANN	PC	280	0	288	0	288	0
		NC	20	0	12	0	0	12
Downtrend	WANN	PC	283	0	283	0	283	0
		NC	17	0	13	4	0	17
	ANN	PC	283	0	283	0	283	0
		NC	17	0	17	0	0	17
Upshift	WANN	PC	285	0	286	1	283	0
		NC	15	0	8	5	0	17
	ANN	PC	285	0	287	0	283	0
		NC	15	0	13	0	0	17
Downshift	WANN	PC	283	0	287	0	283	0
		NC	17	0	8	5	0	17
	ANN	PC	283	0	287	0	283	0
		NC	17	0	13	0	0	17

Table 10. Performance of ANN and WANN in terms of the evaluation metrics

		w=10		w=20		w=30	
		WANN	ANN	WANN	ANN	WANN	ANN
Uptrend	Sensitivity/Recall	1.00	1.00	1.00	1.00	1.00	1.00
	Specificity	0.00	0.00	0.25	0.00	1.00	1.00
	Precision	0.93	0.93	0.97	0.96	1.00	1.00
	Prevalence	0.93	0.93	0.96	0.96	0.96	0.96
	F1 score	0.97	0.97	0.98	0.98	1.00	1.00
	G-Mean	0.00	0.00	0.50	0.00	1.00	1.00
Downtrend	Sensitivity/Recall	1.00	1.00	1.00	1.00	1.00	1.00
	Specificity	0.00	0.00	0.24	0.00	1.00	1.00
	Precision	0.94	0.94	0.96	0.94	1.00	1.00
	Prevalence	0.94	0.94	0.94	0.94	0.94	0.94
	F1 score	0.97	0.97	0.98	0.97	1.00	1.00
	G-Mean	0.00	0.00	0.49	0.00	1.00	1.00
Upshift	Sensitivity/Recall	1.00	1.00	1.00	1.00	1.00	1.00
	Specificity	0.00	0.00	0.38	0.00	1.00	1.00
	Precision	0.95	0.95	0.97	0.96	1.00	1.00
	Prevalence	0.95	0.95	0.96	0.96	0.94	0.94
	F1 score	0.97	0.97	0.98	0.98	1.00	1.00
	G-Mean	0.00	0.00	0.62	0.00	1.00	1.00
Downshift	Sensitivity/Recall	1.00	1.00	1.00	1.00	1.00	1.00
	Specificity	0.00	0.00	0.38	0.00	1.00	1.00
	Precision	0.94	0.94	0.97	0.96	1.00	1.00
	Prevalence	0.94	0.94	0.96	0.96	0.94	0.94
	F1 score	0.97	0.97	0.99	0.98	1.00	1.00
	G-Mean	0.00	0.00	0.62	0.00	1.00	1.00

If we take the hardness of the problem into the consideration, performance of the WANN is respectively good even though it correctly classifies a few samples from minority class for both trends and shift abnormal patterns. In the case of feeding neural network with enough information (i.e. w=30), both ANN and WANN gives good results in terms of evaluation metrics. The overall poor performance of the methods can be visually seen in Figure 8.

Figure 8. Representation of the performance of methods for partially inseparable problem

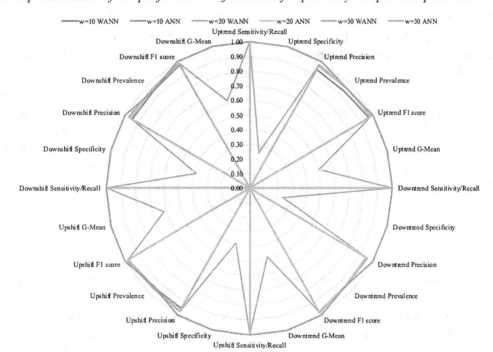

Based on the result for 3 different scenarios, there are some main facts should be taken into consideration.

- ANN framework can be used with the purpose of early detection of the abnormal patterns during a control chart pattern process. However, the success of the methods highly depends on the parameter of the abnormality. Although giving extra weight to the abnormal pattern increase the performance of the ANN, it might fail in the case of having very limited information before an abnormal pattern occurs. This can cause late failure detection in a system.
- By having limited information such as w=20 WANN can predict better than regular ANN if the pattern is partially separable even though its performance is not perfect. Thus, we can say that weighting policy can help to earlier detection.
- In the case of the inseparable problem, feeding neural networks with enough data (i.e. w=100) might help to detect an abnormal pattern. However, this can cause late detection of the tool wear and malfunctions (uptrend and downtrend patterns) and variation of material, operator, or machine (downshift and upshift pattern), so serious problem can occur.

- In general, no matter which methods are used a classical evaluation metrics (i.e. accuracy) can misguide the users in terms of detecting abnormal control chart patterns. Instead, some other metrics given in Table 3 should be used to get the realistic measurements regarding the performance of methods.

CONCLUSION

In this study, we have investigated a weighting strategy in conjunction with artificial neural networks to detect abnormal patterns during a production system. Because the rate of abnormal sample size is much lower than the rate of normal sample size, giving different weights to each class based on their sizes might help to create a more powerful classification model. With the purpose of explaining how to apply weighting strategy for control chart pattern recognition, we have chosen four different abnormal patterns namely uptrend, downtrend, upshift, and downshift. For each pattern, we have created a synthetic dataset with different parameters in order to create separable, partial separable, and inseparable problems. And, each problem is analyzed with different window length (different size of input data). Based on numerical results, both methodologies fail if input data is very limited (w=10) regardless of how well separable data is.

On the other hand, if there exist limited data, WANN outperforms ANN for each inseparable, partially separable, and separable problems in terms of all evaluation metrics. In the case of having enough data, both methodologies perform reasonably well.

One of the weaknesses of giving different weights to each class is that can reduce the sensitivity.

Because our main objective is giving a detailed explanation of how to use weighting strategy we have used limited window lengths and just three different parameters. For the extension of the study, more different parameter values and window lengths should be examined. Another comparison can be made in computational time. In real-world applications, this is a crucial metric since data will be in the online form and algorithm have to deal with the ongoing data in real time. Another approach can be analyzing online data in which multiple abnormal patterns can occur. In this case, multiclassification problem needs to be solved by adjusting weights in the same way.

To sum up, we have investigated how different weights can be given to abnormal class based on class size and how the performance of the artificial neural network can be affected. It can be said that with enough input data artificial neural networks gives better results when classes are weighted.

REFERENCES

Al-Ghanim, A. M. & Ludeman, L. C. (1997). Automated unnatural pattern recognition on control charts using correlation analysis techniques. *Computers & Industrial Engineering, 32*(3), 679-690.

Alwan, L. C., & Roberts, H. V. (1988). Time-series modeling for statistical process control. *Journal of Business & Economic Statistics*, 6(1), 87–95.

Anderson, D., & McNeill, G. (1992). Artificial neural networks technology. *Kaman Sciences Corporation*, 258(6), 1–83.

Aparisi, F. (1996). Hotelling's T2 control chart with adaptive sample sizes. *International Journal of Production Research*, *34*(10), 2853–2862.

Berry, M. W., & Castellanos, M. (2004). Survey of text mining. *Computer Review*, *45*(9), 548.

Cheng, C.-S., & Cheng, H.-P. (2008). Identifying the source of variance shifts in the multivariate process using neural networks and support vector machines. *Expert Systems with Applications*, *35*(1–2), 198–206. doi:10.1016/j.eswa.2007.06.002

Chinnam, R. B. (2002). Support vector machines for recognizing shifts in correlated and other manufacturing processes. *International Journal of Production Research*, *40*(17), 4449–4466. doi:10.1080/00207540210152920

Cook, D. F., & Chiu, C.-C. (1998). Using radial basis function neural networks to recognize shifts in correlated manufacturing process parameters. *IIE Transactions*, *30*(3), 227–234. doi:10.1080/07408179808966453

Davy, M., Desobry, F., Gretton, A., & Doncarli, C. (2006). An online support vector machine for abnormal events detection. *Signal Processing*, *86*(8), 2009–2025. doi:10.1016/j.sigpro.2005.09.027

El-Midany, T. T., El-Baz, M. A., & Abd-Elwahed, M. S. (2010). A proposed framework for control chart pattern recognition in multivariate process using artificial neural networks. *Expert Systems with Applications*, *37*(2), 1035–1042. doi:10.1016/j.eswa.2009.05.092

Fujita, O. (1998). Statistical estimation of the number of hidden units for feedforward neural networks. *Neural Networks*, *11*(5), 851–859. doi:10.1016/S0893-6080(98)00043-4 PMID:12662787

Ghazanfari, M., Alaeddini, A., Niaki, S. T. A., & Aryanezhad, M.-B. (2008). A clustering approach to identify the time of a step change in Shewhart control charts. *Quality and Reliability Engineering International*, *24*(7), 765–778. doi:10.1002/qre.925

Hachicha, W., & Ghorbel, A. (2012). A survey of control-chart pattern-recognition literature (1991–2010) based on a new conceptual classification scheme. *Computers & Industrial Engineering*, *63*(1), 204–222. doi:10.1016/j.cie.2012.03.002

Hagiwara, M. (1994). A simple and effective method for removal of hidden units and weights. *Neurocomputing*, *6*(2), 207–218. doi:10.1016/0925-2312(94)90055-8

Hwarng, H. B. (1995). Multilayer perceptions for detecting cyclic data on control charts. *International Journal of Production Research*, *33*(11), 3101–3117. doi:10.1080/00207549508904863

Hwarng, H. B., & Hubele, N. F. (1992). Boltzmann machines that learn to recognize patterns on control charts. *Statistics and Computing*, *2*(4), 191–202. doi:10.1007/BF01889679

Hwarng, H. B., & Hubele, N. F. (1993). Back-propagation pattern recognizers for X control charts: Methodology and performance. *Computers & Industrial Engineering*, *24*(2), 219–235.

Islam, M. M., & Murase, K. (2001). A new algorithm to design compact two-hidden-layer artificial neural networks. *Neural Networks*, *14*(9), 1265–1278. doi:10.1016/S0893-6080(01)00075-2 PMID:11718425

Jain, A. K., Murty, M. N., & Flynn, P. J. (1999). Data clustering: A review. [CSUR]. *ACM Computing Surveys*, *31*(3), 264–323. doi:10.1145/331499.331504

Jang, K.-Y., Yang, K., & Kang, C. (2003). Application of artificial neural network to identify non-random variation patterns on the run chart in automotive assembly process. *International Journal of Production Research*, *41*(6), 1239–1254. doi:10.1080/00207540210000442409

Jin, J., & Shi, J. (2001). Automatic feature extraction of waveform signals for in-process diagnostic performance improvement. *Journal of Intelligent Manufacturing*, *12*(3), 257–268. doi:10.1023/A:1011248925750

Kawamura, A., Chuarayapratip, R., & Haneyoshi, T. (1988). Deadbeat control of PWM inverter with modified pulse patterns for uninterruptible power supply. *IEEE Transactions on Industrial Electronics*, *35*(2), 295–300.

Keeni, K., Nakayama, K., & Shimodaira, H. (1999). Estimation of initial weights and hidden units for fast learning of multilayer neural networks for pattern classification. In *Proceedings IJCNN'99-International Joint Conference on Neural Networks*. (Vol. 3, pp. 1652–1656). IEEE. 10.1109/IJCNN.1999.832621

Mandel, B. J. (1969). The regression control chart. *Journal of Quality Technology*, *1*(1), 1–9. doi:10.1080/00224065.1969.11980341

Manning, C. D., Manning, C. D., & Schütze, H. (1999). *Foundations of statistical natural language processing*. Cambridge, MA: MIT Press.

Montgomery, D. C. (2007). *Introduction to statistical quality control*. Hoboken, NJ: John Wiley & Sons.

Onoda, T. (1995). Neural network information criterion for the optimal number of hidden units. In *Proceedings of ICNN'95-International Conference on Neural Networks* (Vol. 1, pp. 275–280). IEEE. 10.1109/ICNN.1995.488108

Onur, Y. A., İmrak, C. E., & Onur, T. Ö. (2017). Investigation on bending over sheave fatigue life determination of rotation resistant steel wire rope. *Experimental Techniques*, *41*(5), 475–482. doi:10.100740799-017-0188-z

Panagiotidou, S., & Tagaras, G. (2012). Optimal integrated process control and maintenance under general deterioration. *Reliability Engineering & System Safety*, *104*, 58–70. doi:10.1016/j.ress.2012.03.019

Paté-Cornell, M. E., Lee, H. L., & Tagaras, G. (1987). Warnings of malfunction: The decision to inspect and maintain production processes on schedule or on demand. *Management Science*, *33*(10), 1277–1290. doi:10.1287/mnsc.33.10.1277

Pugh, G. A. (1989). Synthetic neural networks for process control. *Computers & Industrial Engineering*, *17*(1–4), 24–26. doi:10.1016/0360-8352(89)90030-2

Sun, R., & Tsung, F. (2003). A kernel-distance-based multivariate control chart using support vector methods. *International Journal of Production Research*, *41*(13), 2975–2989. doi:10.1080/1352816031000075224

Swift, J. A. (1987). *Development of a knowledge based expert system for control chart pattern recognition and analysis*. Oklahoma State University.

Swift, J. A., & Mize, J. H. (1995). Out-of-control pattern recognition and analysis for quality control charts using LISP-based systems. *Computers & Industrial Engineering*, *28*(1), 81–91. doi:10.1016/0360-8352(94)00028-L

Tamura, S., & Tateishi, M. (1997). Capabilities of a four-layered feedforward neural network: Four layers versus three. *IEEE Transactions on Neural Networks, 8*(2), 251–255. PMID:18255629

Ünlü, R., & Xanthopoulos, P. (2017). A weighted framework for unsupervised ensemble learning based on internal quality measures. *Annals of Operations Research*, 1–19.

Ünlü, R., & Xanthopoulos, P. (2019). Estimating the number of clusters in a dataset via consensus clustering. *Expert Systems with Applications*.

Wang, C.-H., Guo, R.-S., Chiang, M.-H., & Wong, J.-Y. (2008). Decision tree-based control chart pattern recognition. *International Journal of Production Research, 46*(17), 4889–4901. doi:10.1080/00207540701294619

Wang, N. & Yeung, D.-Y. (2013). Learning a deep compact image representation for visual tracking. In Advances in neural information processing systems (pp. 809–817).

Xanthopoulos, P., & Razzaghi, T. (2014). A weighted support vector machine method for control chart pattern recognition. *Computers & Industrial Engineering, 70*, 134–149. doi:10.1016/j.cie.2014.01.014

Yang, J.-H., & Yang, M.-S. (2005). A control chart pattern recognition system using a statistical correlation coefficient method. *Computers & Industrial Engineering, 48*(2), 205–221. doi:10.1016/j.cie.2005.01.008

Zarandi, M. H. F., & Alaeddini, A. (2010). A general fuzzy-statistical clustering approach for estimating the time of change in variable sampling control charts. *Information Sciences, 180*(16), 3033–3044. doi:10.1016/j.ins.2010.04.017

This research was previously published in Artificial Intelligence and Machine Learning Applications in Civil, Mechanical, and Industrial Engineering; pages 240-258, copyright year 2020 by Engineering Science Reference (an imprint of IGI Global).

APPENDIX

The western electric company first proposed several abnormal patterns and those abnormal patterns are used in different studies over the years. The synthetically created control charts data $\zeta(i)$ have three main parameters 1) mean of the process μ 2) a random and normally distributed term ε_i 3) $\Delta(i)$ that is the function of abnormal patterns. Thus, the general formulation of the abnormal patterns can be written as:

$$\zeta(i) = \mu - \varepsilon_i + \Delta(i) \tag{6}$$

The formulation of each abnormal patterns can be written as follows:

1.   Up/Downtrends

$$\zeta(i) = \mu - \varepsilon_i + \lambda_t \tag{7}$$

where λ is the trend slope in terms of σ_ε. The parameter $\lambda > 0$ for uptrend pattern and $\lambda < 0$ for the downtrend pattern.

2.   Up and Downshift

$$\zeta(i) = \mu - \varepsilon_i + \omega \tag{8}$$

where ω is the shift magnitude. $\omega > 0$ for upshift pattern and $\omega < 0$ for downshift pattern.

3.   Cyclic pattern

$$\zeta(i) = \mu - \varepsilon_i + \alpha\sin\left(\frac{2\pi t}{©}\right) \tag{9}$$

where α is the amplitude of the cyclic pattern, and Ω is the cyclic pattern period.

4.   Systematic pattern

$$\zeta(i) = \mu - \varepsilon_i + k(-1)^t \tag{10}$$

where k is the magnitude of the systematic pattern.

5.   Stratification trend

$$\zeta(i) = \mu - \varepsilon_i + \dot{\varepsilon}_t \tag{10}$$

where $\dot{\varepsilon}_t$ is a fraction of normal process standard deviation

Chapter 33
Gene Expression Dataset Classification Using Artificial Neural Network and Clustering–Based Feature Selection

Audu Musa Mabu
SHUATS, Uttar Pradesh, India

Rajesh Prasad
ⓘ https://orcid.org/0000-0002-3456-6980
African University of Science and Technology, Abuja, Nigeria

Raghav Yadav
SHUATS, Uttar Pradesh, India

ABSTRACT

With the progression of bioinformatics, applications of GE profiles on cancer diagnosis along with classification have become an intriguing subject in the bioinformatics field. It holds numerous genes with few samples that make it arduous to examine and process. A novel strategy aimed at the classification of GE dataset as well as clustering-centered feature selection is proposed in the paper. The proposed technique first preprocesses the dataset using normalization, and later, feature selection was accomplished with the assistance of feature clustering support vector machine (FCSVM). It has two phases, gene clustering and gene representation. To make the chose top-positioned features worthy for classification, feature reduction is performed by utilizing SVM-recursive feature elimination (SVM-RFE) algorithm. Finally, the feature-reduced data set was classified using artificial neural network (ANN) classifier. When compared with some recent swarm intelligence feature reduction approach, FCSVM-ANN showed an elegant performance.

DOI: 10.4018/978-1-6684-2408-7.ch033

1. INTRODUCTION

A huge quantity of data generation driven the progression of numerous complex strategies and tools aimed at visualization and scrutiny of information. These tremendous measures of data, especially aimed at the biological examination along with explanations, are made accessible by microarray technology Kohbalan, *et al.,* (2013). The microarray technology advent has profited research workers in directing extensive experiments on chiliads of genes via scrutinizing the difference of communications amongst genes Muhammad, (2017). Actually, just few genes are exceptionally connected to a similar example classes. Those genes are alluded to as the information gene. These enclose the samples' classification information Jiang, Xie, *et al.,* (2013). Numerous cases have been established that extensive observing of GE through microarrays is the utmost propitious strategies to enhance medicinal diagnostics in addition to functional genomics studies Muhammad, (2017). In the uprightness of gene microarray examination, precise categorization of tumor subtypes might progress toward becoming reality, taking into consideration particular treatment that amplifies efficacy, further, limits toxicity Liu, *et al.,* (2007).

Microarray technologies as of late have initiated numerous chances to explore cancer utilizing gene expressions. The essential onus of a microarray data analysis stands to decide a computational model as of specified microarray data which foresee the type of the specified unidentified examples. The accuracy, value, and also strength are imperative components of microarray analysis Hala, *et al.,* (2014). The tumor diagnosis along with classification of GE data stands as a two interesting topics recently. As it may be, GE data contains a chiliads of genes with few samples that makes it tough to examine and process. In addition, it is linearly indivisible, noisy besides being imbalanced Huijuan, *et al.,* (2017). In the preceding decade, a few endeavors are dutiful to the improvement of classification techniques for higher-dimensional GE data started by means of microarray experiments Carlotta and Carlo, (2013). It is obvious that K-means is the most popular clustering algorithm, but can only generate local optimal solution. Swarm optimization clustering algorithms are more advantageous as they perform a globalized search over entire search space. A PSO+K-means algorithm has the ability to search globally, thereby enhancing fast convergence than using conventional K-means algorithm alone. It is promising to generate multi-objective PSO based K-means clustering algorithm that has the ability to cluster both genes and samples simultaneously for GE data Cui and Potok, (2005). The categorization of diverse tumor sorts in GE data is of extraordinary significance in cancer analysis besides drug discovery. Nevertheless, it is intricate attributable to its enormous size. There are many of techniques attainable to assess gene expression profiles. A general trait for these means is picking a subset of genes which is extremely instructive aimed at classification process furthermore to decrease the dimensionality issue of profiles Udhaya, *et al.,* (2014). Dimensionality reduction is especially applicable in bio-informatics research, especially with regards to microarray data, described by moderately little samples in a high-dimensional gene (feature) spaces. Unrelated genes (features) prompt deficient classification accuracy and furthermore include additional troubles in discovering possibly valuable information Amit, *et al.,* (2014).

Microarray technology, designed to screen a chiliads of GE patterns concurrently intended for recognition of ailment development. Managing highly-dimensional data in feature spaces which debases classification proficiency is the troublesome task in examining microarray data Jacophine, *et al.,* (2016). The primary cause is that DNA microarray dataset encloses 10,000 genes together with few experimental samples or remarks concerning cancer. This implies chiliads of genes are insignificant or noisy or else redundant aimed at specific gene assortment along with classification algorithms Hernández-Montiel, *et al.,* (2014). This bane of dimensionality, a noteworthy impediment in machine learning in addition to data mining henceforth feature selection in addition to dimensionality reduction dependably is a dynamic research subject in bioinformatics Jun, *et al.,* (2015). As the commencement of higher throughput systems, as microarrays, the heap of genomic data expanded geometrically, alongside that the requirement aimed at computational techniques that will comprehend those data George, *et al.,* (2016). Discoveries in gene analyses accounts for various symptoms thereby results in discoveries of molecular mechanisms with which proper understanding of genes and gene expressions Sreeja and Vinayan, (2017).

DNA microarray technology that gauges the expression stages in numerous genes concurrently of biological tissues area then creates cancer databases in light of GE data has astonishing potentiality on the research of cancer. Since the customary diagnosis technique aimed at malignancy is imprecise, GE data is generally utilized to recognize cancer biomarkers intently connected with cancer Shuaiqun, *et al.,* (2016). Likewise, an ever rising number of statistical strategies was produced and implement to the malady classification utilizing microarray GE data Pingzhao, *et al.,* (2011). The microarray data technology utilization permits observing simultaneously chiliads of GE levels over numerous cases. GE data assumes a crucial part as a biomarker aiding in an assortment of work, for example, cancer diagnosis, categorization of various kinds of tumors, or viable medication devise on a molecular point Alarcón-Paredes, *et al.,* (2017). Since, an extensive quantity of GE data was amassing rapid, so a fresh method ought to be investigated to separate its biological functions which are obscure and to accumulate data from tissue samples in regards with gene expression contrasts which will be valuable in diagnosing ailment Shulin, (2006). Recently, cancer biomarker analyses and discovery is among the most valuable research discussion. The conventional methods usually focus on genes that are differently expressed in various cancer stages Myungjin and Kenta, (2018).

The arrangement of the given paper is systematized like this: The Sec. 2 assessed the associated works pertaining to the proposed technique. In Sec. 3, a short discourse about the proposed technique is exhibited, Sec. 4 examines the investigational outcome and Sec. 5 finishes up the paper.

2. LITERATURE REVIEW

Classification using gene datasets is normally based on a trivial number of samples in which tens of thousands of GE dimensions have been obtained. Usually the most significant aspect of GE classification problem is the challenging issue of high dimensional data analysis and interpretation. To justify this context the literatures above have various degrees of drawbacks alternating from higher computational time, unnecessary overheads and lesser classification accuracies. Yousef, *et al.,* (2007), suggested a classification method known as SVM-RCE (Recursive Cluster Elimination) centered on groups of interconnected genes which at times reveals better performance compared to classification by means of single genes.

Khare, *et al.,* (2012), presented a hybrid method using Rank Correlation, Principal Component Analysis (PCA) and SVM. The system is used for the diagnosis of detecting the existence and/or non-existence of cardiac Arrhythmia from Electrocardiogram (ECG) data. The techniques of Feature Selection, Feature Extraction and Binary Classification are also applied on the UCI Cardiac Arrhythmia data set to detect arrhythmia automatically to aid the process; the researchers used spearman Rank Correlation for dimension reduction to increase the accuracy of the classifier. The result revealed that the accuracy rate in percentages and the performance of the SVM classifier is subjected to the cost and kernel parameter sigma classification frequency based on the count of features selected by Rank Correlation. The hybrid approach showed superior performance than the individual methods.

Kun-Huang, *et al.*, (2014), applied PSO based decision tree classifier for cancer classification with GE data. Decision tree and PSO was used for selection of the most informative genes. Classification result showed outstanding results when compared with traditional classifiers.

Alshamlan, *et al.*, (2015) proposed a swarm intelligence based feature selection technique based on minimum Redundancy Maximum Relevance and Artificial Bee colony (mRMR-ABC) to select the most informative gene. The method used SVM to measure classification accuracy for the concerned genes. Performance of the proposed method was measured then compared on six binary and multiclass GE data sets with previously known methods then with mRMR-Genetic Algorithm and mRMR-PSO. The results indicated that mRMR-ABC achieved outstanding accuracy and hence it is a good approach for gene feature selection and classification.

Ramyachitra, *et al.*, (2015) classified resultant data sets using existing techniques then Improvised Internal Value Classification with PSO (IVPSO) for feature selection. The outcome of the result of IVPSO outperformed other algorithms under some performance evaluation functions tested on eighteen sample data sets.

Yuan, *et al.,* (2016) presented a measure termed relative simplicity (RS). It assessed the gene pairs as per mixing vertical with the horizontal contrast, at last constructed RS-based direct classifier (RS-based DC) in view of an assortment of descriptive genes equipped for binary discrimination with a paired vote technique. To approve the new technique's performance, nine multiple class GE datasets including cancers in human were utilized. It got the 91.40 percent mean independent test's accuracy, 20.56 of descriptive mean gene quantity, and finest generalization test performance when contrasted with the 9 reference models. Contrasted with the 4 reference feature selection strategies, RS likewise got the uppermost average test accuracy of 3 classifiers (Naïve Bayes, KNN along with SVM), additionally the merely RS enhanced the SVM performance. Diverse gene pairs patterns could be accentuate all the more completely whilst integrating vertical with horizontal contrast procedure. Over-fitting was successfully controlled by the core DC classifier. The presented classifier prompts the more vigorous assortment of informative genes along with classification accuracy.

Narumol, *et al.,* (2016) built up an approach by actualizing the Gene Network based Feature Set (GNFS) system with the presented gene-set-centered (GS) search in addition to parent-node-centered (PN) search algorithms, to distinguish sub-networks, labeled Gene Sub-Network-centered Feature Selection (GSNFS). To approve the outcomes, the researchers utilized an extra dataset. The two presented searching algorithms aimed at the sub-network development were worried about the connectivity level together with the scoring plan aimed at constructing the sub-networks along with their topology. Aimed at every cycle of the extension, the neighbor genes of a present sub-network, whose expression data enhanced the general sub-network score, was enrolled. Whilst the GS search figured the sub-network score utilizing an action score of a present sub network in addition the GE values of its neighbors, the PN seek utilized the matching parent's expression value of every neighbor gene. Aimed at sub-network identification, four cancer expression dataset were utilized. Additionally, utilizing pathway data besides protein with protein communication as network data with the intention of regarding the interaction amongst important genes were discuss. The classification was done to contrast the distinguished gene sub networks performance with the 3 sub-network recognition algorithms.

Hala, *et al.*, (2016), analyzed microarray datasets with the aid of ABC algorithm and proposed a classification model with the aid of SVM termed (ABC-SVM). Experimentation of result of the proposed method on six binary and multiclass microarray data sets showed a promising way for selecting gene features and cancer classification with good classification accuracy accompanied by lowest average gene selected after comparison with other normal swarm intelligence techniques.

Maolong, *et al.*, (2016), applied basic binary quantum behaved PSO (BQPSO) for feature selection of cancer data. It was a discretized version of the conventional QPSO used as binary 1-0 optimization problem. BQPSO is combined with SVM and Leave One-Out Cross Validation (LOOCV) and achieved high classification accuracy. The technique was tested for feature selection with five microarray data sets that showed significant results.

Shunmugapriya, & Kanmani, (2017) posited a Swarm based hybrid algorithm AC-ABC Hybrid that consolidated traits of Ant Colony (AC) furthermore Artificial Bee Colony (ABC) to advance the feature selection. It furthermore consolidates the exploitation demeanor of Ant Colony Optimization (ACO) along with ABC algorithms, in addition, had indicated propitious demeanor in enhancement selecting the feature's subset. Through hybridizing, they attempt to dispose the stagnation conduct of the ant, in addition tedious global search meant for primary elucidations through the engaged bees. Here, Ants utilized exploitation via the Bees to pick out the supreme Ant along with the feature's subset; Bees adapted the feature subsets created through the Ants to be their sustenance origins. Thirteen University of California, Irvine (UCI) standard datasets was utilized for the estimation of the presented algorithm. Experimental results come about demonstrated the propitious conduct of presented technique for expanding the classification accuracy with selecting optimum features.

Rabia *et al.*, *(2017)* suggested a blend of feature selection/extraction approach aimed at Artificial Neural Network (ANN) classification of highly dimensional micro arrayed data that utilized an Independent Component Analysis (ICA) as a mining method and Artificial Bee Colony (ABC) as an optimization technique. The investigation evaluated the proffered ABC+ICA algorithm's performance by directing broad experiments on 5 binary and also 1 multi-class GE microarray data set, furthermore, contrasted the presented algorithm and ABC+ICA. The presented technique indicated predominant performance as it accomplished the most astounding classification accuracy alongside the least average number of chosen genes. Furthermore, the existing work analyzed the presented ABC+ICA algorithm with prominent filter techniques and also with other comparative bio-inspired algorithms with ICA. The experimental comes about exhibited that the offered algorithm gave more precise classification rate for ANN classifier. Consequently, ABC+ICA were a promising methodology for elucidating gene selection along with cancer classification issues utilizing microarray data.

Sankhadeep, *et al.*, (2017) concentrated on distinguishing two unique varieties, specifically dengue fever (DF) and dengue hemorrhagic fever (DHF). A revised bag of features technique was posited to choose the utmost encouraging differentiation process of genes. A short time later, an advanced cuckoo search optimization algorithm was employed to assist the ANN- Modified Cuckoo Search optimization (ANN-MCS) to categorize the obscure elements into 3 distinct classes to be specific, Dengue Fever and Dengue Hemorrhagic Fever (DF- DHF), in addition a further class holding recuperate besides ordinary cases. This technique had been contrasted with other 3 famous classifiers, in particular, Multilayer perceptron feed-forward network (MLP-FFN), ANN-MCS, besides ANN-Particle Swarm Optimization (ANN-PSO). Experiments were taken place with an alternative of clusters aimed at the preliminary bag-of-features-centered feature's selection stage. Subsequent to getting the diminished datasets, the ANN-MCS model was utilized for the differentiation process. The outcomes were analyzed as far as the confusion matrix-centered performance estimating measurements. The experimental outcomes showed a very statistically important enhancement with the presented classifier against the conventional ANN-Cuckoo Search optimization (ANN-CS) model.

Chang, *et al.*, (2017), recommended an effectual gene selection technique to opt the finest subdivisions of genes aimed at micro arrayed data with the insignificant as well as redundant genes expelled. Contrasted to the actual data, chose gene subset profit the classification undertaking. They detailed the selection undertaking of the gene as an abundant standardized subdivision learning issue. In depth, projection matrix was utilized to extend the first high dimensional micro arrayed data to small dimensional subdivision, additionally the limitation that the original genes are extensively detailed by the preferred genes. In the interim, the local abundant structure of actual data was protected by means of Laplacian graph regularization in the small dimensional data partitions. The projection matrix filled in as an imperative pointer of various genes. A repetitive update algorithm was created aimed at taking care of the issue. Experimental outcomes about in 6 freely accessible microarray datasets along with 1 clinical dataset exhibited that this technique acted superior when contrasted with other cutting edge strategies regarding microarray data classification.

Salem, *et al.*, (2017), maintained that regular limitations of DNA microarray data analysis, even though the standard machine learning (ML) approaches can efficiently be important in classifying significant genes to identify new cases, handling small samples and high dimensional feature of gene expressions limits its investigative, medical and logical uses. Believing that interpretability of prospect and forecast methodologies in addition to precision handling, would aid the analysis of GE profiles data in DNA microarray dataset proficiently. On this background they proposed new methodology that combines both Information Gain (IG) and Standard Genetic Algorithm (SGA). Initially IG was used for feature selection, and then Genetic Algorithm (GA) served as feature reduction tool to end the process Genetic Programming (GP), used for cancer types' classification. GA improves the classification efficiency of other classifiers and thereby the techniques outperformed other machine learning methodologies.

Lu, *et al.*, (2017), proposed a hybrid feature selection procedure which chains the mutual information maximization (MIM) and adaptive genetic algorithm (AGA) to tackle the effect of the increasing sample size and dimensional feature of GE data to develop an efficient and robust feature selection algorithm for GE data classification in the field of DNA microarray research to aid in diagnosing cancer. The experimental result of the research showed that, the proposed MIMAGA-Selection method significantly decreases the dimension of gene expression data and hence removed the redundancies for better gene classification. The reduced GE dataset offers highest classification accuracy in relation to conventional feature selection algorithms.

Previous study with huge gene features exhibits numerous gene interaction networks which offer an important resource for classification studies using interacting genes. We now propose an algorithm which integrates network information with recursive feature reduction to be executed with the assist of Feature Clustering-SVM (FC-SVM) which exhibits virtuous performance and increases the biological interpretability of the outcomes. K-means clustering algorithm is utilized to group genes into different gene clutches, ANN finally classify the gene accurately.

3. GENE EXPRESSION DATA CLASSIFICATION AND CLUSTERING BASED FEATURE SELECTION

Aimed at the proficient and viable classification of malignancies, GE profile might be exploited. On account of the immense amount of genes besides generally little measure of samples in GE data, this is a computationally difficult assignment. The given paper proposes a system aimed at the classification of GE dataset and clustering based feature selection. Pre-processing of the GE dataset is vital to do at first, to get great classification performance. In the wake of preprocessing stage, feature selection to be executed with the assist of Feature Clustering Support Vector Machine (FCSVM). To start with, the k-means clustering algorithm is utilized to group genes into different gene groups, wherein every gene has comparative expression profile. At that point, a representative gene was found to signify gene collections. Thusly, a representative gene set is gotten. At that point, SVM-RFE is implemented to rank these representative genes and from the best positioned features, a desirable number of highest informative genes can be selected as the features. FCSVM can lessen the computational intricacy and the redundancy amongst genes. At last, classification is performed utilizing ANN classifier. Figure 1 is the proposed framework is displayed in the.

Figure 1. The Proposed Framework

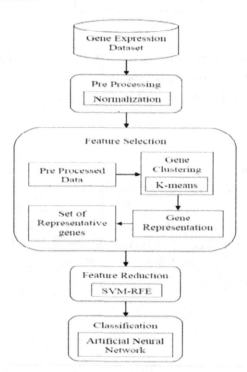

Let $G = \begin{bmatrix} g_1, g_2, \ldots, g_n \end{bmatrix} \varepsilon R^{d \times n}$ be an original dataset, among which every column is the d-dimensional feature vector of the tester and n is the aggregate number of the samples. The proposed strategy initially acknowledges GE dataset as input patterns and continues the further advances as represented.

3.1. Pre-Processing

To form the GE data to be appropriate aimed at feature selection / classification furthermore to help the algorithm run faster, the preprocessing step is incorporated. In pre-processing, normalization of the dataset is performed.

3.1.1. Normalization

The data preprocessing basic step is exchanging every single symbolic characteristic into numerical values which are said as normalization. Data normalization is a procedure of scaling the value of every attribute into a well-balanced range so the inclination for features with better values is disposed as of the dataset.

Normalizing the data guarantees the allotment of equivalent weight to every variable. Each feature inside each record is normalized by the relevant maximum value and falls into a same scope of [0-1]. Consequently, normalization decreases the training error, by this means demonstrating the classification issue's accuracy. The expression level aimed at every gene are normalized at this progression to [0, 1] utilizing the standard strategy which is appeared in Equation 1:

$$g = lower + \left[upper - lower \times \frac{val - val\_min}{val\_\max - val\_min} \right] \tag{1}$$

Here, among all the expression levels of the gene in consideration, *val_max* is the maximum original value, *val_min* is the least original value, upper (lower) is 1 (0) and *g* is the normalized expression level. So for all genes after normalization, *val_max* will be 1 and *val_min* will be 0.

3.2. Feature Selection

It is used for the selection of useful information as of huge datasets, and the meta-heuristic algorithms can explore for the optimal solution via scrutinizing in the propitious sections of search space. It is considered as the optimization issue with the principle goal to augment the classification accuracy rate with the littler size of features. It stands as a preprocessing system hoping to choose the utmost informative genes that can isolate groups, i.e., cancer types. In the proposed work, an alternate perspective in the choice of features is presented. The features were chosen utilizing FCSVM procedure. FCSVM incorporates two stages, specifically:

- Gene Clustering
- Gene Representation

3.2.1. Gene Clustering

Here, genes which have comparable expression profiles will be grouped into a gene set. Genes that encompass a place with a same gene set might hold partly redundant information aimed at the classification task, while the information kept through various gene sets is unique. It stands vital to think about a decent clustering algorithm. Aimed at Gene Clustering, the k-means clustering algorithm that supports its easiness along with the efficiency is employed.

3.2.1.1. K-Means Clustering Algorithm

Here, each gene has a place only with one cluster or collection. Basically, K-means circulates K centers all over the data (Pirim, Eksioglu, Perkins, & Yuceer, 2012). The gene is allotted to a group for which the center stands closest to them. Meanwhile, the center is evacuated to curb the separation amongst themselves together with their allotted genes. This procedure is reiterated till the point that the center is stable. Various distance measures be able to be employed so as to determine the distance betwixt genes and the center. The Euclidean distance stands as the utmost ordinarily utilized in addition to least complex measures. The value of *k* is the optimal count of cluster and it is obtained using direct technique known as elbow method in that way the overall intra-cluster disparity is minimized so that the appropriate number of clusters can be obtained. The pseudocode aimed at K-means clustering algorithm appears in Figure 2.

Figure 2. Pseudocode for k-means algorithm

Input: $g_{i,}$ Training genes
K, Number of cluster centers
T, Iteration times

Output: K Gene Groups

Arbitrarily choose K genes from g_i as the initial centers;
Initialize $t = 1$;
Repeat
    (a) Assign each gene to a cluster to the center nearest to the cluster.
    (b) Calculate the new center for each of the clusters
    (c) $t = t+1$
Until $t \geq T$

K-Means algorithm incorporates the accompanying steps:

Step 1: Define several desired clusters.
Step 2: Select primary cluster centroid arbitrarily. These signify the "temporary" methods for the clusters.
Step 3: Calculate the squared Euclidean distance (sum of square error) as of every gene to every cluster furthermore every gene is allotted to the adjacent cluster as takes after:

$$SumofSquareErrorSSE = \sum_{i=1}^{t}\sum_{g \in K_i} dist^2\left(m_i, g\right) \qquad (2)$$

where *g* stands as a data point in the cluster, m_i stands as the centroid of the cluster *K*.

Step 4: Aimed at every cluster, the new centroid is figured, and every centroid value is currently supplanted by the individual cluster centroid.

Step 5: Recur Step 3 along with 4 till the point when no point vary its cluster.

3.2.2. Gene Representation

Though the genes are compressed and get K gene collections utilizing gene clustering, gene selection activity isn't done. Every gene set comprises few genes encompassing a comparative profile along with a conceivably comparable function. Therefore, a gene is utilized to signify the gene cluster. It is important to choose the representative gene that ought to convey most helpful information contrasted with all the genes in the cluster. By doing as such, the numerous genes from G to K is diminished. Predominantly, the core of the cluster might be utilized to be a representative point. Nevertheless, the midpoint might not be the genuine gene, only a faux gene. Albeit midpoint can't be viewed as the representative genes specifically, the gene is able to be chosen as of a gene cluster that has the least distance as of the relating focus.

Let G_m stand for the mth gene cluster. The representative gene $\bar{g}_m$ aimed at the mth gene group is driven using the Equation 3.

$$\bar{g}_m = \arg \min_{g_n \in G_m} g_n - c_{m2}^2, m = 1, 2, \ldots, K \tag{3}$$

Here, $g_n - c_{m2}^2$ signifies the Euclidean Distances, c_m is the mth cluster's core. By doing in this way, the original information conveyed by GEs can be held that is more persuading aimed at gene classification.

3.3. Feature Reduction

As K representative genes generally are chosen, there can be any guarantee that the entire K genes are helpful. A set of key features can be obtained to condense the number of random variables of utmost concern in an effort to select important features and discard the immaterial ones. Subsequently, these genes should be positioned by their significance concerning the classification jobs. SVM-RFE (Support Vector Machine Recursive feature elimination technique) is utilized so as to grade the K representative genes. Every gene is identified with a score that decides the gene importance is the fundamental thought following SVM-RFE.

Subsequent to gene clustering together with gene representative, acquired a new training sample set $(u_n, v_n)_{n=1}^{N}$, in which, $u_i \in R^K$ and $v_n \in (+1, -1)$. On every one of the repetition, a linear SVM is trained based on the chosen feature subset to produce weight vector, $w = [w_1, w_2, \ldots, w_K]$.

3.3.1. Support Vector Machine

It stands as a supervised learning framework that finds a partition hyper-plane which fulfills the class prerequisite. The training dataset comprises of n points in $(u_1, v_1), \ldots, (u_n, v_n)$, the fundamental thought of SVM is specified in the accompanying advances (Vanitha, Devaraj, & Venkatesulu, 2015):

1. Look for an optimal hyperplane which fulfills the request of classification.

The partition hyperplane is characterized via the Equation (4):

$$z.u + a = 0 \tag{4}$$

wherein, the normal vector of the partition hyper plane is z and the offset of the hyperplane is a.

2.   Make the separation border next to the optimal hyper-plane maximum that guarantees the accuracy of right classification.

A partition hyper-plane makes the bilateral blank area maximum have to be established to make the partition hyper-plane as a long way as of the point in training dataset possibly. This is stated via the Equation (5):

$$Minimize \theta \left(w \right) = \frac{1}{2} w^2 \tag{5}$$

3.   Finally, the corresponding genes are classified into their relevant classes viably.

The classification is centered upon the Equations (6) and (7):

$$z.u_i + a \geq 1, \text{ if } v_i{=}1 \tag{6}$$

$$z.u_i + a \leq \text{-}1, \text{ if } v_i{=} \text{-}1 \tag{7}$$

Presently, SVM-RFE figures the score for every gene utilizing the weights acquired in SVM.

3.4. SVM-RFE

Recursive feature elimination technique clarifies the matching gene into their appropriate classes/clusters. This is attained by a new process of gene selection that exploits SVM method based on RFE. It chooses a small subclass of gene from the comprehensive gene expression data and chooses either the best or exceptionally bad performing feature is abandoned. After that the technique continues by rehashing the procedure with features available recursively until the entire features in the data set are depleted. Gene features are then positioned. This is a greedy optimization envisioned to find the optimum performing subset of the features. The score aimed at the gene m is defined in Equation (8):

$$s_i = w_i^2 \tag{8}$$

The higher the score s_m is, the superior is the significance of the feature. The detailed algorithm intended for SVM-RFE appears in Figure 3.

Subsequent to grade the genes as signified by its significance, a desirable number of best positioned genes can well be selected as the features. This is to maintain a minimum subgroup of features that produce the finest classification performance by means of estimating various sets of the original input features.

Figure 3. Pseudocode for gene ranking

Input: Training Samples $(u_i, v_i)_{i=1}^N$
Output: Ranked List of Features K

Begin

Initialize Selected Feature Subset $S = \{1,2,....,K\}$
Initialize Ranked List of Features $R = \phi$
Repeat Until $S = \phi$
(a) Restrict training samples to the designated feature subset
(b) Train a linear SVM to obtain w .
(c) Compute Ranking conditions $s_i = w_i^2$
(d) Find the feature with smallest ranking criterion $p = \arg \min s_i$
(e) Update Ranked list of features $R = \{f\} \cup R$ by adding feature f into R .
(f) Update designated feature subset $S = S - p$ by removing feature p from S .
End

3.5. Classification Using Ann

ANN is trainable algorithms which can train to cope with intricate issues from training data that encompasses a set of pairs of inputs and desired outputs (targets). It is formed out of neurons set (indicated by functions) associated with others sorted out in various layers where each layer is made out of neurons (Satya, & Neha, 2016). The issue to be solved is represented by input designs, which is sent via the layers. The information is mapped by methods for the comparing synaptic weights.

In ANN, the weights are progressively adjusted centered upon an input set and relating set of anticipated output goals. The synaptic weight adaptation comprises in changing its value until the point when it achieves the desired behavior. Each of the iteration comprises two sweeps: advancing activation to create solution together with a backward propagation of the computed error to alter weights in the layer. The forward along with backward sweeps are performed repetitively until the ANN solution concurs with the anticipated value inside a pre-determined resilience. The ANN structure is exhibited in Figure 4.

ANN contains of three layers specifically; Input, hidden and Output layers, every layer influence the subsequent layer. In Figure 4 above, $(f_1, f_2, \dots f_k)$ are the input to the ANN and $(z_1, z_2, \dots z_N)$ are the predictive values of the network. A relation function map occurs between k independent variables and N dependent variables. Back propagation algorithm was employed to train the neural network, which is portrayed in the accompanying advances.

Step 1: Generate random weights within the interim [0, 1] and relegate it to the hidden layer neurons together with the production layer neurons. Keep up a unity value weight for the input layer's entire neurons.

Step 2: the training dataset G is inputted to the classifier, furthermore, decide the BP error as takes after:

Figure 4. Structure of artificial neural network

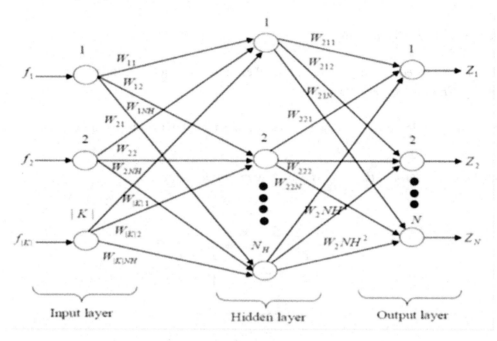

$$BP_{err} = Z_{tar} - Z_{out} \tag{9}$$

In Equation (9), Z_{tar} is the target output and Z_{out} is the network output that is resolved as $Z_{out} = \left[X_2^{(1)} \quad X_2^{(2)} ... X_2^{(N)} \right]$, $X_2^{(1)}$, $X_2^{(2)},...,X_2^{(N)}$ are the network outputs. The network outputs is driven as:

$$X_2^{(l)} = \sum_{r=1}^{N_H} w_{2r1} X_1 \left(r \right) \tag{10}$$

where:

$$X_1 \left(r \right) = \frac{1}{1 + \exp(-w_{11r} \cdot Z_{in})} \tag{11}$$

Equations (10) and (11) represents the initiation function performed in the output layer along with hidden layer correspondingly.

Step 3: Adjust all neurons' weights as $w=w+\Delta w$, where, Δw is the variation in weight that can well be driven as:

$$\Delta w = \gamma.X2\,BPe_{rr} \tag{12}$$

In Equation (12), γ is the learning rate, generally, it covers from 0.2 to 0.5.

Step 4: Recur the procedure from step 2, until BP error gets restricted to the minimum value. Fundamentally, BP_{err}<0.1 is the criterion to be met.

The Flowchart in Figure 5 shows the entire process depicted in the proposed FCSVM_ANN.

Figure 5. Flowchart showing the process depicting proposed method

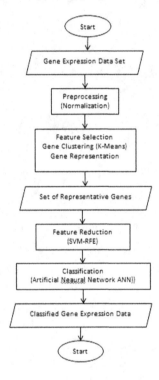

4. RESULT AND DISCUSSION

This area exhibits the proposed ANN classification of GE dataset with clustering based feature selection's performance assessment. The proposed work uses the databases from the National Center for Biotechnology Information (NCBI), which gives access to biomedical and also genomic information.

The outcomes are estimated counter to the diagnostic performance measures, for example, Positive instances along with Negative instances. That is True Positive (TP), True Negative (TN), False Positive (FP) besides False Negative (FN). TP stances as the quantity of instances which are positive analyzed accurately. TN stands as the quantity of instances which are negative analyzed effectively. FP stands as the quantity of instances which are negative distinguished as positive.

FN stands as the quantity of instances which are positive distinguished as negative. These are computed first and after that utilized to compute Recall, Accuracy, Precision, specificity together with F-measure:

$$Accuracy = \frac{\left(TP + TN\right)}{\left(TP + FP + TN + FN\right)} \tag{13}$$

$$Specificity = \frac{TN}{FP + TN} \tag{14}$$

$$\Pr ecision = \frac{TP}{TP + FP} \tag{15}$$

$$\mathrm{Re}\,call = \frac{TP}{TP + FN} \tag{16}$$

$$FMeasure = 2\frac{precision \times recall}{precision + recall} \tag{17}$$

4.1. Performance Evaluation

Proposed FCSVM based ANN (FCSVM_ANN) classification's performance is contrasted with other conventional classifiers, for example, Naïve Bayes, SVM and also K Nearest Neighbor (KNN) concerning Accuracy, Sensitivity, Precision, Recall, computation time, besides F-Measure. The sample number, the gene number and the labeled classes for the Central Nervous System (CNS) tumor and the Colon tumor dataset are abridged in Table 1.

Table 1. Gene expression profile

Data Set	Sample Number	Gene Number	Sample	
			Positive	Negative
CNS Tumor	60	7129	21	39
Colon Tumor	62	6500	22	40

As appeared in Table 1, on the GE profile, every sample comprises of two labeled classes in particular, positive and also negative for the dataset of both the CNS tumor and Colon tumor. CNS tumor dataset has sixty samples along with Colon tumor data set has 62 samples.

4.1.1. CNS Tumor Dataset

Performance metrics, for example, Accuracy, Sensitivity, Precision, Recall, computation Time besides F-Measure are figured for the CNS tumor dataset. The FCSVM_ANN system is contrasted with the existing classifiers, for example, Naïve Bayes, SVM, besides KNN based these metrics.

Figure 6. Comparison of precision, recall and F-measure for CNS_Dataset

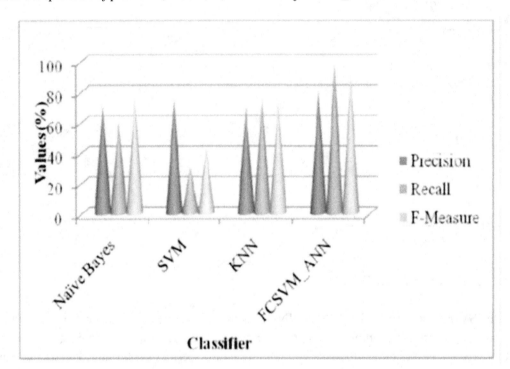

Figure 6 represents the performance metrics, for example, precision, recall along with F-measure of the FCSVM_ANN classifier with the prevailing classifiers. The precision of FCSVM_ANN supersedes, next to it is SVM algorithm, then Naïve Bayes and KNN. For recall, the proposed method of FCSVM_ANN outperformed, SVM follows then KNN and Naïve Bayes has the lowest recall. Coming to the F-measure, FCSVM_ANN has the highest value compared to Naïve Bayes, KNN and SVM has the lowest value. Nevertheless, the proposed FCSVM_ANN demonstrate the uppermost performance for the entire metrics in contrast to the existing classifiers.

Figure 7 exhibits the correlation of performance metrics, for example, accuracy together with specificity intended for the proposed FCSVM_ANN classifier together with the prevailing classifiers, say, Naïve Bayes, SVM together with KNN. Here the classifiers Naïve Bayes along with KNN demonstrate relatively comparative performance. Though the accuracy along with specificity of the SVM is vastly improved, the proposed FCSVM_ANN has the uppermost performance than the SVM and furthermore other compared classifiers.

Figure 7. Comparison of accuracy and specificity for CNS_Dataset

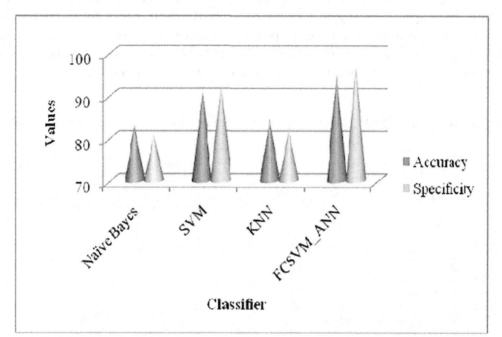

Figure 8. Comparison of computation time for the existing and the proposed classifiers for CNS_Dataset

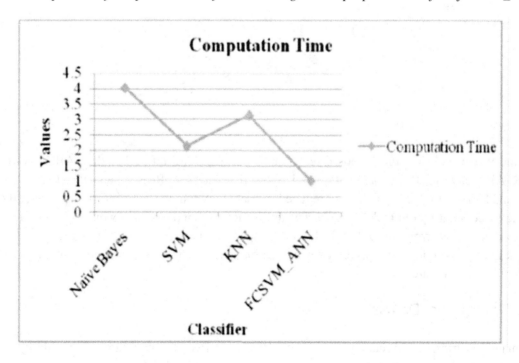

Figure 8 matches the computation time aimed at the FCSVM_ANN classifier together with the existing classifiers, for example, Naïve Bayes, SVM together with KNN. On contrasting the entire classifiers, Naïve Bayes together with KNN demonstrate poor performance, while the SVM and FCSVM_ANN performance is great. On considering SVM and FCSVM_ANN, the proposed FCSVM_ANN demonstrates the minimum time taken for calculation, which indicates the finest classifier.

Figure 9. Comparison of FCSVM_ANN with some recent swarm intelligence technique for CNS_Dataset

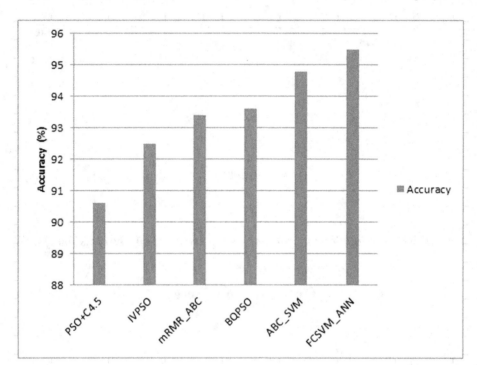

Figure 9 depicted that, the proposed technique's accuracy is a bit higher than ABC_SVM, then mRMR_ABC, BQPSO, IVPSO and PSO+C4.5 followed respectively. Reason being that data set normalization and SVM_RFE feature reduction reduced the data to obtain the most informative gene, thereby resulting to the accuracy of FCSVM_ANN. The result showed that the accuracy of the proposed method outperformed the swarm optimization techniques discussed in the literature of this piece of research. Nevertheless, Swarm approaches are better in accuracy when compared with conventional methods considered in this research.

4.1.2. Colon Tumor Dataset

Performance metrics, say, Accuracy, Sensitivity, Precision, Recall, computation Time along with F-Measure are processed for the Colon tumor dataset. The proposed FCSVM_ANN system is contrasted with the prevailing classifiers, for example, Naïve Bayes, SVM and also KNN based these metrics.

Figure 10. Comparison of precision, recall and F-measure for Colon_Dataset

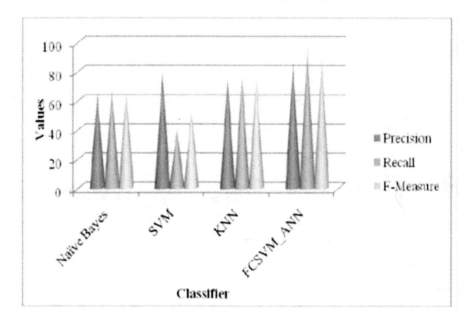

Figure 10 portrays the proposed FCSVM_ANN performance and that of the existing Naïve Bayes, SVM and also KNN classifiers regarding precision, review and also F-measure. On considering precision, Naïve Bayes has the slightest value. On considering the recall, SVM demonstrates poor performance than every other classifier. On considering F-measure, Naïve Bayes has the poor performance. Be that as it may, regarding the entire measurements, the proposed strategy demonstrates the best performance.

Figure 11 exhibits the contrast of performance metrics, say; accuracy and also specificity aimed at the FCSVM_ANN classifier together with the prevailing classifiers, for example, Naïve Bayes, SVM and also KNN intended for the colon tumor dataset. Here, the classifiers Naïve Bayes together with KNN demonstrate closer values for both the metrics. The classifiers SVM besides the proposed FCSVM_ANN have about equivalent values, yet the proposed classifier has the uppermost value and along these lines good performance.

Figure 12 compares the computation time meant for the proposed FCSVM_ANN classifier together with the prevailing classifiers, for example, Naïve Bayes, SVM and also KNN intended for the Colon tumor dataset. Amongst the entire compared classifiers, KNN demonstrate minimal performance, wherein the time taken for computation is too high than every single other classifier. The proposed FCSVM_ANN shows the highest performance, wherein the time in use for computation is too low.

Figure 13 compared the result of the accuracy level of the proposed technique with some swarm intelligence optimization techniques which are discussed in the literatures. The proposed FCSVM_ANN showed an encouraging accuracy level among the techniques of ABC_SVM, mRMR_ABC, BQPSO, IVPSO and PSO+C4.5. This due to an effective preprocessing technique used to obtain highly effective most informative genes that feeds the FCSVM_RFE classifier. The result showed that the accuracy of ABC_SVM followed the proposed method, then mRMR_PSO the least being PSO+C4.5. Comparison of the results for colon data sets showed that swarm intelligence approaches outperformed the traditional methods that are discussed in this research work.

Figure 11. Comparison of accuracy and specificity for Colon_Dataset

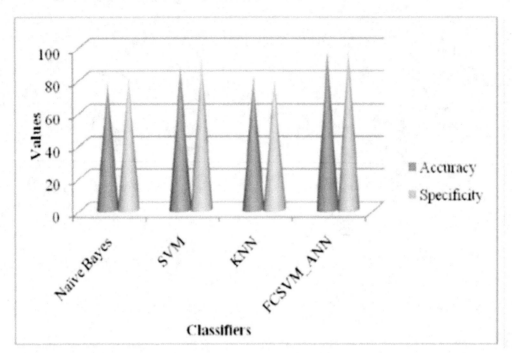

Figure 12. Comparison of computation time for the existing and the proposed classifiers for Colon_Dataset

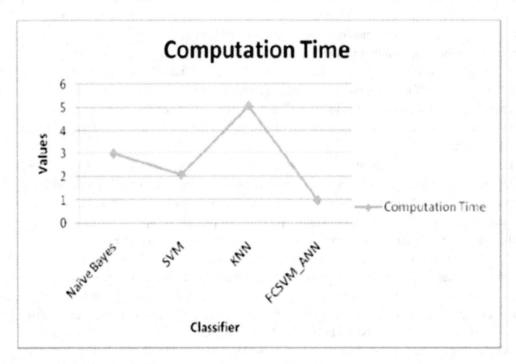

Figure 13. Comparison of FCSVM_ANN with some recent swarm intelligence technique for Colon_Dataset

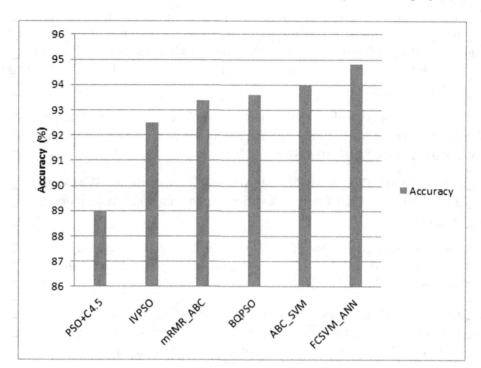

5. CONCLUSION AND FUTURE WORK

Classifying cancer microarray GE data is difficult mission on the grounds that microarray consists of high dimensional along with low sample dataset. It is additionally critical to decide the informative genes that are the root cancer to enhance cancer classification and premature cancer diagnosis. To become familiarized to such conditions, proposed system aimed at the GE dataset classification with clustering based feature selection. The given paper utilizes FCSVM aimed at feature selection by joining K-means clustering algorithm furthermore applied it to ANN classification. The wide experimentation permitted to decide the proposed strategies behavior in the GE dataset classification. Broad experiments were accomplished with the two gene expression datasets, say, Colon tumor and CNS tumor dataset. The FCSVM_ANN performance is examined and also contrasted with the prevailing classifiers, say, Naïve Bayes, SVM along with KNN centered upon the metrics, for example, Accuracy, Sensitivity, Precision, Recall, computation time accompanied by F-Measure. Experimental outcomes exhibited that the proposed work beats the various regular procedures. FCSVM_ANN used SVM-RFE for feature reduction and was also compared with some recent swarm intelligence approaches of PSO+C4.5, IVPSO, mRMR-ABC BQPSO and ABC-SVM nevertheless FCSVM_ANN outperformed in accuracy.

Swarm Optimization techniques such as PSO, ABC, Ant Colony Optimization (ACO) or Bacterial Foraging Optimization (BFO) can be used in combination with FCSVM_ANN as ideal pre-processing technique to speed up and improve upon SVM-RFE feature reduction process and minimize the needed computational resources. For this reason, swarm intelligence techniques follows very simple rule, the behavior of agent is mostly local, hence interaction of the gene gives an intelligent global behavior.

REFERENCES

Alarcón-Paredes, A., Gustavo, A. A., Eduardo, C., & Cuevas-Valencia, R. (2017). Simultaneous Gene Selection and Weighting in Nearest Neighbor Classifier for Gene Expression Data. In *International Conference on Bioinformatics and Biomedical Engineering*, (pp. 372-381). Springer. 10.1007/978-3-319-56154-7_34

Alshamlan, H., Badr, G., & Alohali, Y. (2015). mRMR-ABC: A Hybrid Gene Selection Algorithm for Cancer Classification Using Microarray Gene Expression Profiling. *BioMed Research International, 2015*, 1–15. doi:10.1155/2015/604910 PMID:25961028

Alshamlan, Badr, & Alohali. (2016). ABC-SVM: Artificial Bee Colony and SVM Method for Microarray Gene Selection and Multi Class Cancer Classification. *International Journal of Machine Learning and Computing, 6*(3).

Amit, P., Jaya, S., & Chitrangada, D. M. (2014). *Dimension Reduction of Gene Expression Data for Designing Optimized Rule Base Classifier. In Recent Advances in Information Technology* (pp. 133–140). New Delhi: Springer.

Carlotta, O., & Carlo, V. (2013). Dimensionality reduction via isomap with lock-step and elastic measures for time series gene expression classification. In *European Conference on Evolutionary Computation, Machine Learning and Data Mining in Bioinformatics* (pp. 92-103). Springer.

Chang, T., Lijuan, C., Xiao, Z., & Minhui, W. (2017). Gene selection for microarray data classification via subspace learning and manifold regularization. *Medical & Biological Engineering & Computing*, 1–14. PMID:29256006

Cui, X., & Potok, T. E. (2005). Document Clustering using Particle Swarm Optimization. *IEEE Swarm Intelligence Symposium*, 185-191.

George, I. L., Maria, B., Panagiotis, K., Ioannis, K., Dimitra, I., Tzortzia, K., ... Dimitrios-Dionysios, K. (2016). Complex Dynamics in Tumor Gene Regulatory Networks: Oncogenesis Dynamics Driven by "Genes Gone Crazy". In *XIV Mediterranean Conference on Medical and Biological Engineering and Computing* (pp. 507-511). Springer.

Hala, A., Ghada, B., & Yousef, A. (2014). A comparative study of cancer classification methods using microarray gene expression profile. In *Proceedings of the First International Conference on Advanced Data and Information Engineering* (pp. 389-398). Springer.

Hernández-Montiel, A. L., Bonilla-H, E., Morales-Caporal, R., & Guevara-García, A. J. (2014). Selection and classification of gene expression data using a MF-GA-TS-SVM approach. In *International Conference on Intelligent Computing*, (pp. 300-308). Springer.

Huijuan, L., Yaqiong, M., Ke, Y., Yu, X., & Zhigang, G. (2017). Classifying Non-linear Gene Expression Data Using a Novel Hybrid Rotation Forest Method. In *International Conference on Intelligent Computing* (pp. 732-743). Springer.

Jacophine, S. S., Khanna, N. H., Kannan, A., & Jabez, C. (2016). *Relevant Gene Selection and Classification of Leukemia Gene Expression Data. In Emerging Research in Computing, Information, Communication and Applications* (pp. 503–510). Singapore: Springer.

Jiang, Y., Xie, G., Chen, N., & Chen, S. (2013). A New gene expression profiles classifying approach based on neighborhood rough set and probabilistic neural networks Ensemble. In *International Conference on Neural Information Processing* (pp. 484-489). Springer.

Jun, C. A., Habibollah, H., & Haza, N. A. (2015). Semi-supervised SVM-based feature selection for cancer classification using microarray gene expression data. In *International Conference on Industrial, Engineering and Other Applications of Applied Intelligent Systems* (pp. 468-477). Springer.

Khare, S., Bhandari, A., Singh, S., & Arora, A. (2012). ECG arrhythmia classification using spearman rank correlation and support vector machine. In *Proceedings of the International Conference on Soft Computing for Problem Solving (SocProS 2011)* (pp. 591-598). Springer. 10.1007/978-81-322-0491-6_54

Kohbalan, M., Mohd, S., Bin, M., & Safaai, D. (2013). Multiple gene sets for cancer classification using gene range selection based on random forest. In *Asian Conference on Intelligent Information and Database Systems* (pp. 385-93). Springer.

Kun-Huang, C., Kung-Jeng, W., Kung-Min, W., & Melani-Adrian, A. (2014). Applying particle swarm optimization-based decision tree classifier for cancer classification on gene expression data. *Applied Soft Computing, 24*, 773–780. doi:10.1016/j.asoc.2014.08.032

Liu, J., Luo, F., & Zhu, Y. (2007). *An Improved FMM Neural Network for Classification of Gene Expression Data. In Fuzzy Information and Engineering* (pp. 65–74). Berlin: Springer.

Lu, H., Chen, J., Yan, K., Jin, Q., Xue, Y., & Gao, Z. (2017). A hybrid feature selection algorithm for gene expression data classification. *Neurocomputing, 256*, 56–62. doi:10.1016/j.neucom.2016.07.080

Maolong, X., Jun, S., Li, L., Fangyun, F., & Xiaojun, W. (2016). Cancer Feature Selection and Classification Using a Binary Quantum-Behaved Particle Swarm Optimization and Support Vector Machine. *Computational and Mathematical Methods in Medicine*. doi:10.1155/2016/3572705 PMID:27642363

Muhammad, A. R., Kauthar, M. D., Hui, W. N., Mohd, S. M., Safaai, D., Sigeru, O., ... Ghazali, S. (2017). K-Means Clustering with Infinite Feature Selection for Classification Tasks in Gene Expression Data. In *International Conference on Practical Applications of Computational Biology & Bioinformatics* (pp. 50-57). Springer.

Myungjin, M., & Kenta, N. (2018). Integrative analysis of gene expression and DNA methylation using unsupervised feature extraction for detecting candidate cancer biomarkers. *Journal of Bioinformatics and Computational Biology, 16*(2), 1850006. doi:10.1142/S0219720018500063 PMID:29566639

Narumol, D., Worrawat, E., Jonathan, H. C., & Asawin, M. (2016). GSNFS: Gene subnetwork biomarker identification of lung cancer expression data. *BMC Medical Genomics, 9*(3), 70. PMID:28117655

Pingzhao, H., Shelley, B., & Hui, J. (2011). Gene network modules-based liner discriminant analysis of microarray gene expression data. In *International Symposium on Bioinformatics Research and Applications* (pp. 286-296). Springer.

Pirim, H., Eksioglu, B., Perkins, A. D., & Yuceer, C. (2012). Clustering of high Throughput Gene Expression Data. *Computers & Operations Research*, *39*(12), 3046–3061. doi:10.1016/j.cor.2012.03.008 PMID:23144527

Rabia, A., Verma, C. K., Manoj, J., & Namita, S. (2017). Artificial neural network classification of microarray data using new hybrid gene selection method. *International Journal of Data Mining and Bioinformatics*, *17*(1), 42–65. doi:10.1504/IJDMB.2017.084026

Ramyachitra, D., Sofia, M., & Manikandan, P. (2015). Interval-value Based Particle Swarm Optimization algorithm for cancer-type specific gene selection and sample classification. *Genomics Data*, *5*, 46–50. doi:10.1016/j.gdata.2015.04.027 PMID:26484222

Salem, H., Attiya, G., & El-Fishawy, N. (2017). Classification of human cancer diseases by gene expression profiles. *Applied Soft Computing*, *50*, 124–134. doi:10.1016/j.asoc.2016.11.026

Sankhadeep, C., Nilanjan, D., Fuqian, S., Amira, S. A., Simon, J. F., & Soumya, S. (2017). Clinical application of modified bag-of-features coupled with hybrid neural-based classifier in dengue fever classification using gene expression data. *Medical & Biological Engineering & Computing*, 1–12. PMID:28891000

Satya, E. J., & Neha, C. (2016). Artificial neural networks as classification and diagnostic tools for lymph node-negative breast cancers. *Korean Journal of Chemical Engineering*, *33*(4), 1318–1324. doi:10.100711814-015-0255-z

Shuaiqun, W., Zheng, T., Shangce, G., & Yuki, T. (2016). Improved Binary Imperialist Competition Algorithm for Feature Selection from Gene Expression Data. In *International Conference on Intelligent Computing* (pp. 67-78). Springer.

Shulin, W., Ji, W., Huowang, C., & Boyun, Z. (2006). SVM-based tumor classification with gene expression data. In *International conference on advanced data mining and applications* (pp. 864-870). Springer.

Shunmugapriya, P., & Kanmani, S. (2017). A hybrid algorithm using ant and bee colony optimization for feature selection and classification (AC-ABC Hybrid). *Swarm and Evolutionary Computation*, *36*, 27–36. doi:10.1016/j.swevo.2017.04.002

Sreeja, A., & Vinayan, K. P. (2017). Multidimensional knowledge-based framework is an essential step in the categorization of gene sets in complex disorders. *Journal of Bioinformatics and Computational Biology*, *15*(06), 1750022. doi:10.1142/S0219720017500226 PMID:29113563

Udhaya, K. S., Hannah, I. H., & Senthil, K. S. (2014). *Improved bijective-soft-set-based classification for gene expression data. In Computational Intelligence, Cyber Security and Computational Models* (pp. 127–132). New Delhi: Springer.

Vanitha, D. A., Devaraj, D., & Venkatesulu, M. (2015). Gene Expression Data Classification using Support Vector Machine and Mutual Information-based Gene Selection. *Procedia Computer Science*, *47*, 13–21. doi:10.1016/j.procs.2015.03.178

Yuan, C., Lifeng, W., Lanzhi, L., Hongyan, Z., & Zheming, Y. (2016). Informative gene selection and the direct classification of tumors based on relative simplicity. *BMC Bioinformatics*, *17*(1), 17–44. PMID:26729273

This research was previously published in the International Journal of Swarm Intelligence Research (IJSIR), 11(1); pages 65-86, copyright year 2020 by IGI Publishing (an imprint of IGI Global).

Chapter 34
Enrichment of Distribution System Stability Through Artificial Bee Colony Algorithm and Artificial Neural Network

Gummadi Srinivasa Rao
V. R. Siddhartha Engineering College (Autonomous), India

Y. P. Obulesh
VIT University, India

B. Venkateswara Rao
ⓘ https://orcid.org/0000-0003-4281-8831
V. R. Siddhartha Engineering College (Autonomous), India

ABSTRACT

In this chapter, an amalgamation of artificial bee colony (ABC) algorithm and artificial neural network (ANN) approach is recommended for optimizing the location and capacity of distribution generations (DGs) in distribution network. The best doable place in the network has been approximated using ABC algorithm by means of the voltage deviation, power loss, and real power deviation of load buses and the DG capacity is approximated by using ANN. In this, single DG and two DGs have been considered for calculation of doable place in the network and capacity of the DGs to progress the voltage stability and reduce the power loss of the system. The power flow of the system is analyzed using iterative method (The Newton-Raphson load flow study) from which the bus voltages, active power, reactive power, power loss, and voltage deviations of the system have been achieved. The proposed method is tested in MATLAB, and the results are compared with particle swarm optimization (PSO) algorithm, ANN, and hybrid PSO and ANN methods for effectiveness of the proposed system.

DOI: 10.4018/978-1-6684-2408-7.ch034

INTRODUCTION

Losses are a very key role when constructing and arrangement of the power system. Losses are predictable in every set of links; however, the quantity can fluctuate considerably depending on the planning of the power system. The power flows in the system decide the loss. One of the largest consumer markets in the world is the electric power industry. The cost of electricity is estimated at around 50% for fuel, 20% for generation, 5% for transmission and 25% for distribution. Distribution systems must deliver electricity to each customer's service entrance at an appropriate voltage rating. The X/R ratio for distribution levels is low as compared to transmission levels, causing high power losses and a drop in voltage magnitude along radial distribution lines. Studies have indicated that just about 13% of the total power generated is consumed as real power losses at the distribution level. Such non-negligible losses have a direct impact on the financial issues and overall efficiency of distribution utilities. The installation of Distributed Generation (DG) units is becoming more famous in distribution systems due to their overall positive impacts on power networks such as energy competence, deregulation, diversification of energy sources, ease of finding sites for smaller generators, shorter erection times and lesser investment costs of smaller plants, and the nearness of the generation plant to heavy loads, which decreases transmit costs. (K. Varesi, 2011) Hence the allotment of DG units gives a possibility to decrease power loss (S. A. Hosseini, M. Karami and S. S. KarimiMadahi, 2011 &NareshAcharya, PukarMahat and N. Mithulananthan, 2006& Nadweh et al,2018).

The addition of Distributed Generation (DG) units changes the load features of the distribution system, which slowly becomes an active load network and involves changes in the power flows. The performance of the network by addition of each DG can be determined by performing the load flow solution. For that reason, it is required to build up mathematical optimization that can be implemented in the network to decrease the power loss and to maintain the voltage magnitudes at each bus within the acceptable limits. Hence the author is interested in the area of optimization methods in the domain of Smart Micro-Grid and power system operation and control. The different optimization methods for improvement of performance of the network are already developed such as Genetic Algorithm (GA), Particle swarm optimization (PSO), Artificial Neural Network (ANN) and Artificial Bee Colony (ABC) etc. are supportive for optimizing the DG size and location in decreasing the power loss and for enhancement of voltage profile (F. S. Abu-Mouti, El-Hawary, 2011 &H. Nasiraghdam and S. Jadid, 2012& Madisie et al, 2018).A hybrid technique which is the amalgamation of Particle Swarm Optimization (PSO) and Artificial Neural Network (ANN) has been implemented to find out the optimal location and rating of DG to diminish the power loss in the network and voltage profile enhancement at all buses (F. S. Abu-Mouti and M. E. El-Hawary, 2009 & Gummadi SrinivasaRao and Y.P.Obulesh, 2013).In 2016 (Hassan Haes Alhelouand M. E. H. Golshan, 2016) A high penetration level of RERs causes some problems to the grid operator, e.g., lack in primary reserve. This paper proposes a new scheme to provide necessary primary reserve from electric vehicles by using hierarchical control of each individual vehicle. The proposed aggregation scheme determines the primary reserve and contracts it with system operator based on electricity market negotiation.

A comprehensive literature reviews and state of arts in nature inspired optimization algorithm could be found in (Mehdi Khosrow-Pour, 2018). In this Incorporating Nature-Inspired Paradigms in Computational Applications is a critical scholarly resource that examines the application of nature-inspired paradigms on system identification.In this year (H. HaesAlhelou,M.E. HamedaniGolshan and J. Askari-Marnani, 2018), propose the use of unknown input observer for detection of faults in interconnected smart power systems in presence of renewable energy resources and electric vehicles. In this fault detection and isolation scheme has been proposed for smart grids. Due to proper isolation of faults the stability of the system has been improved.In 2018 (Carlo Makdisie, BadiaHaidar and Hassan HaesAlhelou, 2018) authors propose the optimal photovoltaic system based on neuro fuzzy control for future smart grids. The proposed PV conditioner with the neuro-fuzzy control compensates the nonlinear and unbalanced loads of the electrical power systems then improve the system performance.

In the last decade, there are several major directions for optimization technology development (ÖmürTosun, 2014, Alhelou et al, 2018), use Artificial Bee Colony Algorithm for solving single and multi-objective ptimization problems. (MasoudHajiakbariFini, Gholam Reza Yousefi, and Hassan HaesAlhelou, 2016) present the various optimization techniques for tuning and load frequency control for multi area power system by considering single and multi objective functions.(Hassan S. Haes Alhelou ; M.E.H. Golshan ; Masoud HajiakbariFini, 2015) proposes a new scheme to provide necessary primary reserve from electric vehicles by using multi-agent control of each individual vehicle. The proposed scheme determines the primary reserve based on vehicle's information such as initial state of charge (SOC), the required SOC for the next trip, and the vehicle's departure time. Which is useful for improve the performance the system consists of more number of distribution generation sources.

In this book chapter it is extended to optimize rating and position of two DGs using a novel hybrid technique which is the combination of Artificial Bee Colony (ABC) and Artificial Neural Network (ANN) to improve the voltage profile and to decrease the system loss. The performance of this method has been compared with other optimization methodologies such as PSO, ANN and hybrid PSO & ANN to reveal the effectiveness of the proposed method.

PROBLEM FORMULATION

The DG unit is positioned in an optimal approach, the power loss and instability troubles have been reduced in the distribution system. For this reason, a combined approach is anticipated for optimizing the placement and size of DGs for improvement of voltage profile and lessening in the power loss of the system. Thus the considered problem is nonlinear optimization problem.

The problem is loss minimization is taken as an objective function and stated as follows,

$$O = \sum_{q=1}^{N} P_L \tag{1}$$

where, 'O' represents the objective function of the system, P_L = Active Power loss of the system

The objective function is subjected to equality and inequality constrictions such as the real & reactive power balance and the bus voltage limits.By the placement of DGs, the active power loss in the network is premeditated using the subsequent equation.

$$P_L = \sum_{m=1}^{N} \sum_{n=1}^{N} [\alpha_{mn}(P_m P_n + Q_m Q_n) + \beta_{mn}(Q_m P_n + P_m Q_n)] \tag{2}$$

where,

$$\alpha_{mn} = \frac{r_{mn}}{v_m v_n} \cos(\delta_1 - \delta_m) \tag{3}$$

$$\beta_{mn} = \frac{r_{mn}}{v_m v_n} \sin(\delta_m - \delta_n) \tag{4}$$

$$Z_{mn} = r_{mn} + jx_{mn} \tag{5}$$

P_m, Q_m = m[th] bus real and reactive power injection
N = number of buses.

Voltage Boundary Limitation

The magnitudes of the bus voltages should be within functional limits can be represented as,

$$V_{min} \leq V_m \leq V_{max} \tag{6}$$

Here, V_{min} = Lower bound bus voltage, V_{max} = upper bound bus voltage, and V_m = root mean square value of the mth bus voltage.

The difference between the reference voltage and the voltage of the particular bus is called voltage deviation V_m on can be calculated as follows,

$$V_{dev} = 1 - V_m \tag{7}$$

Here, V_{dev} = voltage deviation, V_m = m[th] node voltage and $m=1,2,3...N$

Active and Reactive Power Constraint

The active and reactive power for insertion at buses are calculated using,

Real power injection = Real power generation$_m$ – Real power demand$_m$ (8)

$$P_m = P_{DGm} - P_{Dm} \tag{9}$$

$$Q_m = Q_{DGm} - Q_{Dm} \tag{10}$$

Here, P_{DGm}, Q_{DGm}, P_{Dm} and Q_{Dm} are indicated as the active power injection, reactive power injection, real & reactive power demands at m[th] bus subject to the lower & upper limits of power generation constraints of DGs at bus m,

$$P_{Gm,min} \leq P_{Gm} \leq P_{Gm,max} \tag{10}$$

$$Q_{Gm,min} \leq Q_{Gm} \leq Q_{Gm,max} \tag{11}$$

HYBRID ABC-ANN APPROACH

In proposed hybrid approach, ABC computes an optimal position of the DG systems and ANN is sized the DGs rating. The best possible position is estimated by means of the voltage deviation, power loss and real power deviation of load buses. Then, by using ANN, the exact ratings of DGs are calculated to progress the voltage stability and reduce the power loss of the system.

Artificial Bee Colony (ABC)

The ABC algorithm is used to optimize the location of the DGs. The bus voltages, line data and voltage limits have been considered the input. It consists of a set of possible solutions (V_i) that are represented by the location of the food sources. This algorithm consists of four stages, such as initialization stage, employed bee stage, onlooker bee stage and scout bee stage (Gummadi Srinivasa Rao and Y. P. Obulesh, 2015). In a multi dimensional search, the employed bees choose food sources depending on the experience of themselves. The onlooker bees choose food resources based on their nest mates experience and adjust their positions. Scout bees fly and choose the food sources randomly without using experience (Cheng-Jian Lin and Shih-ChiehSu, 2012 & Alshahrestani et al, 2018 & Njenda et al, 2018 & Alhelou et al, 2018). The nectar amount of the food source stands for the fitness of the solution.

Description of ABC Algorithm

Step 1: Initialization

Generate the input values such as, bus voltage, line data and voltage limits in the population.

$$V_m = \{V_0^j, V_1^j, ...V_P^j\}, 0 \leq j \leq d-1 \tag{12}$$

Here, V_m = m^{th} node bus voltage of the population in p^{th} position, d = 1, 2, 3...., n., d is the dimensional space and the inputs are specified by the minimum and maximum values.

Step 2: Fitness Function

Evaluate the fitness value of each bus and then calculate the best voltage values.

$$\text{Fitness function F(m)} = \begin{cases} if\ f_m \leq 0, select\ the\ particular\ bus; \\ otherwise, update\ the\ bus\ positions \end{cases} \tag{13}$$

Here, $f_m = 1 - V_m$, $V_m = $ mth node bus voltage.
The bus voltage is calculated Based on fitness function.

Step 3: Employed Bee Phase

The bus positions are revised using the equation,

$$Y_{m,n} = V_{m,n} + \varphi m_{,n}(Vm_{,n} - Vk_{,n}) \tag{14}$$

Here, $Y_{m,n}$ = new value of the nth position and φ = randomly produced number in the range [-1, 1].
Then evaluate the fitness values and apply the greedy selection between them $Y_{m,n}$ and $V_{m,n}$.
The probability values for the solutions $V_{m,n}$ can be determined by means of their fitness values using the equation,

$$\text{Pr}_m = \frac{F_m}{\sum_{m=1}^{d} F_m} \tag{15}$$

Pr_m = probability of the mth bus value.

Step 4: Onlooker Bee Phase

Generate the new positions Y_m for the onlookers from the solutions V_m, selected depending upon the probability value P_m and calculate them. Then, the fitness function (maximum voltage deviation) is determined for the new position. In order to select the best bus, apply greedy selection for the onlooker bee between V_m and Y_m

Step 5: Scout Bee Phase

The abandoned solution, if exist, and replace it with a new randomly produced solution V_m. Memorize the best food source position achieved. The particular bus has been selected for an optimal location finding process. This practice is continual until the maximum iteration is reached otherwise the practice is terminated. When the procedure is done the optimum locations are determined. The flowchart for the suggested ABC algorithm is illustrated in Figure 1.

Artificial Neural Network (ANN)

ANN has only one input, and three outputs, contains two stages. (Training stage and testing stage) (Partha, Kayal and Chandan Kumar Chanda, 2013).The training of the neural network is done with back propagation algorithm. The testing is done by giving bus number as input to the neural network and the ratings of DGs are obtained as outputs. The structure of ANN is given in Figure 2

Figure 1. Flow chart for finding an optimal location using ABC algorithm

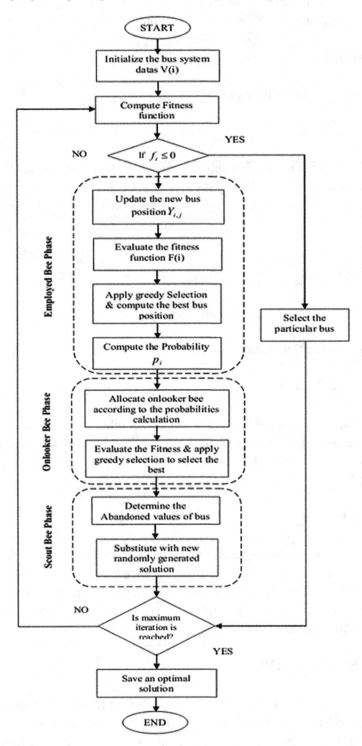

Figure 2. Structure of ANN for training

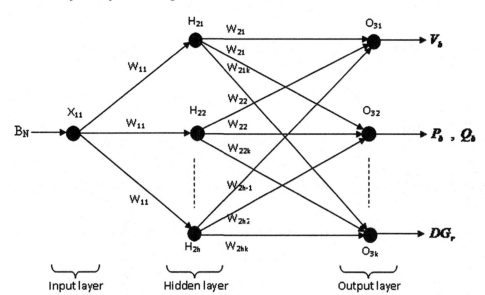

Training Algorithm (Back Propagation)

Initialize the weights of all the neurons of the network. The neuron weights of the hidden layer and the output layer are initiated in the particular interval [w_{min}, w_{max}]. The outputs of the network are stated as shown,

$$V_b = \sum_{d=1}^{h} [W_{2d1} * V_b(d)] \tag{16}$$

here

$$V_b(d) = \frac{1}{1 + \exp(-w_{11d} * c)} \tag{17}$$

$$P_b = \sum_{d=1}^{h} [W_{2d1} * P_b(d)] \tag{18}$$

here

$$P_b(d) = \frac{1}{1 + \exp(-w_{11d} * c)} \tag{19}$$

$$Q_b = \sum_{d=1}^{h} [W_{2d2} * Q_b(d)] \qquad (20)$$

here

$$Q_b(d) = \frac{1}{1 + \exp(-w_{11d} * c)} \qquad (21)$$

$$DG_r = \sum_{d=1}^{h} [W_{2d3} * DG_r(d)] \qquad (22)$$

here

$$DG_r(d) = \frac{1}{1 + \exp(-w_{11d} * c)} \qquad (23)$$

From the above equations, 'c' is corresponded to an input variable, and $(w_{211}, w_{212}, ...w_{2hk})=$ The hidden layer to the output layer weights.

Here, $B_N =$ Input data (bus number) is applied to the ANN and h = number of hidden layers.

The weights are adjusted to all the neurons by giving the input and outputs to the network in the training process.

RESULTS AND DISCUSSION

The effectiveness of the anticipated amalgam optimization methodology is tested on IEEE 30 bus system and realized in MATLAB software package. Later fitting only DG and earlier fitting only DG, the voltage profile at various buses are given in Table1. The single week bus is recognized from this with the support of voltage deviation which is bus number 19 using hybrid ABC - ANN method. The voltage of the weak bus earlier fitting DG is 1.019p.u and it is improved to 1.0018p.u later fitting DG at bus number 19.

The bus voltage shape earlier and later fitting DG is revealed in the Figure 3. It is observed that the voltages at various optimal buses are approximately nearer to 1p.u. after placing the DG.

The optimal rating of DG and power loss in the system earlier fitting to the only DG later fitting to the only DG for all the expected optimization methodologies are given in Table 2 and Table 3 respectively. From Table 2, it is observed that the optimal rating of DG is 5.986MW using the anticipated hybrid ABC - ANN method and from Table 3, it is observed that the power loss of the test system is reduced to 7.904MW from the normal power loss of the system is 10.714MW by fitting of DG with a capacity of 5.986MW at bus 19.Similarly, after fitting only DG at bus number 19 with an optimal rating of 7.754MW, at bus number 26 with an optimal rating of 25.0213MW, and at bus 19 with an optimal rating of 7.086MW, the loss are reduced to 10.214 MW, 9.501MW, 8.057MW by means of PSO, ANN and hybrid PSO - ANN respectively.

Figure 3. Comparison of bus voltages when earlier and later fitting of DG using ABC-ANN methodology

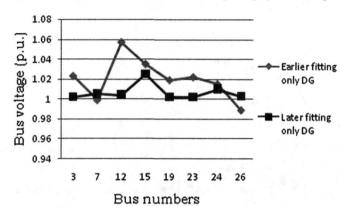

Table 1. Bus voltage profile of optimally positioned buses earlier to and later fitting of only DG for a variety of methodologies

Most Favorable Bus Number	Voltage Profile					Voltage Deviation			
	Earlier to Fitting DG	Later to Fitting DG							
		ANN	PSO	Hybrid PSO-ANN Scheme	Hybrid ABC - ANN Scheme	ANN	PSO	Hybrid PSO-ANN Scheme	Hybrid ABC - ANN Scheme
3	1.023	1.026	1.024	1.027	1.002	0.040	0.066	0.062	0.040
7	0.999	1.005	1.005	1.005	1.005	0.022	0.062	0.121	.0001
12	1.057	1.060	1.060	1.041	1.004	0.058	0.201	0.047	0.025
15	1.035	1.041	1.041	1.038	1.025	0.040	0.094	0.141	0.017
19	1.019	1.027	1.025	1.024	1.002	0.024	0.079	0.097	0.091
23	1.022	1.031	1.032	1.012	1.002	0.005	0.068	0.141	0.022
24	1.015	1.025	1.026	1.010	1.010	0.008	0.071	0.024	0.015
26	0.989	1.002	1.004	1.005	1.003	0.012	0.023	0.058	0.011

Reduction of power loss for methodologies is revealed in the Figure 4 and it is perceived that the hybrid ABC - ANN methodology decreases the power loss from 10.714MW to 7.904MW. Table 4, Table 5 and Table 6 gives the bus voltages before and after installing DGs, DG capacity and power loss of the system before and after installing two DGs by using ANN method, PSO method and hybrid PSO - ANN methods respectively. From Table 4, it is noticed that the feeble buses are 21 and 30 and after fitting the two DGs at those buses, the loss is condensed to 9.144MW, from Table 5, it is noticed that the feeble buses are 19 and 12 and fitting the two DGs at those buses, the loss is condensed to 9.914MW and from Table 6, it is noticed that the feeble buses are 4 and 23 and after fitting the two DGs at those buses, the loss is condensed to 4.435MW.Bus voltages of the test system earlier to and later fitting of DGs at two bus locations for joint ABC -ANN approach is demonstrated in Figure 5. It can be observed that the voltage profile at the buses is enriched after fixing two DGs and the power loss is reduced to 2.168MW.

Figure 4. Assessment of loss reduction in only DG for various methodologies

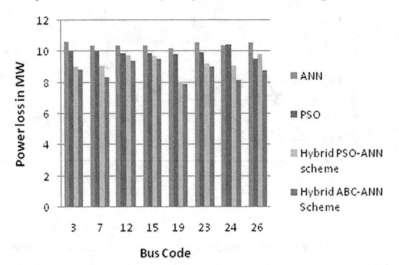

Table 2. Best possible sizes of DG units by different methodologies

Most Favorable Bus Number	Load Power (MW)	DG Capacity (MW)			
		ANN	PSO	Hybrid PSO & ANN Scheme	Hybrid ABC & ANN Scheme
3	2.4	3.002	5.986	5.127	2.037
7	22.8	13.273	3.027	3.020	2.064
12	11.2	7.924	8.011	7.935	5.999
15	8.2	5.999	5.127	20.069	4.036
19	9.5	7.754	8.029	7.086	5.986
23	3.2	8.926	14.031	7.764	3.036
24	8.7	8.030	15.037	7.024	6.010
26	3.5	4.001	25.021	20.069	3.036

Table 3. Power loss earlier and later fitting of only DG for a variety of methodologies

Most Favorable Bus Number	Power Loss (MW)				
	Earlier to Placing of DG	Later Fitting Single DG			
		ANN	PSO	Hybrid PSO-ANN Scheme	Hybrid ABC - ANN Scheme
3		10.630	10.014	9.015	8.836
7		10.392	10.030	9.077	8.381
12		10.418	9.883	9.784	9.381
15	10.714	10.404	9.866	9.738	9.526
19		10.214	9.865	8.057	7.904
23		10.577	9.941	9.241	9.028
24		10.414	10.430	9.063	8.156
26		10.581	9.501	9.828	8.783

Figure 5. Bus voltages earlier to and later fitting of DGs at two bus locations for joint ABC - ANN approach

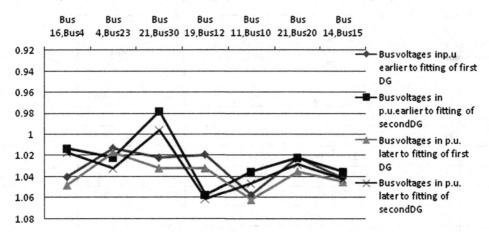

The bus voltages earlier and later fitting of two DGs, power loss and an most favourable capacity of DG units are revealed in Table 7. It is noticed that the feeble buses by using united ABC-ANN methodology are (16,4), (4,23), (21,30), (19,12), (12,10), (21,20), and (14,15). From which combinations, it is observed that the optimal bus combinations for placement of two DGs is bus number 14 and bus number 15. The power loss of the test system after placing two DG sat these locations is reduced to 2.168MW from the normal power loss of 10.714 MW before installing the DGs. The voltage profile at these weak buses has been improved to (0.989, 0.100), (1.010, 0.990), (1.019, 0.979), (1.015, 0.990), (0.989, 0.999), (1.004, 0.999), and (1.009, 1.002) respectively after installing the two DGs. As shown in Table 7.

Figure 6. Total power losses for all recommended methodologies

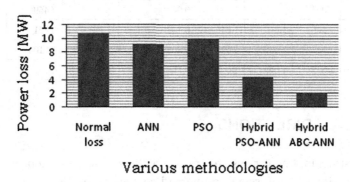

The drop of power loss for all recommended methodologies is shown in Figure 6. From Figure 6, it is observed that the suggested ABC-ANN method is very useful in dipping the power loss as compared to the previous ANN, PSO and hybrid PSO-ANN methodologies.

Table 4. Power loss and bus voltages earlier to and later fitting of two DG units by ANN methodology

Most Favorable Bus Numbers		Bus Voltages Earlier to Fitting of DGs		Bus Voltages Later Fitting of DGs		DG Rating		Power Loss Earlier to Fitting of DGs	Power Loss Later Fitting of DGs
B1	B2	p.u.	p.u.	p.u.	p.u.	MW	MW	MW	MW
16	4	1.040	1.014	1.047	1.017	2.528	4.164		10.305
4	23	1.013	1.022	1.017	1.031	3.873	1.952		10.295
21	30	1.022	0.978	1.031	0.996	9.271	4.995		9.144
19	12	1.019	1.057	1.028	1.060	6.017	7.814	10.714	10.019
12	10	1.057	1.035	1.060	1.046	9.864	4.326		10.446
21	20	1.022	1.022	1.031	1.031	7.019	1.026		9.531
14	15	1.041	1.035	1.039	1.041	13.687	5.018		10.154

Table 5. Power loss and bus voltages earlier to and later fitting of two DG units by PSO methodology

Most Favorable Bus Numbers		Bus Voltages Earlier to Fitting of DGs		Bus Voltages Later to Fitting of DGs		Max PSO Voltage Deviation	DG Rating		Power Loss Earlier to Fitting of DGs	Power Loss Later to Fitting of DGs
B1	B2	p.u.	p.u.	p.u.	p.u.	p.u.	MW	MW	MW	MW
16	4	1.040	1.013	1.048	1.017	0.080	2.539	6.148		10.534
4	23	1.013	1.022	1.017	1.032	0.153	13	2.367		10.616
21	30	1.022	0.978	1.032	0.996	0.038	30.012	7.683		10.059
19	12	1.019	1.057	1.032	1.061	0.043	5.150	7.469	10.714	9.914
12	10	1.057	1.035	1.062	1.046	0.147	5.150	6.821		10.126
21	20	1.022	1.022	1.035	1.028	0.068	1.582	14.104		10.289
14	15	1.041	1.035	1.045	1.042	0.186	7.268	6.183		10.573

FUTURE RESEARCH DIRECTIONS

Placing of DGs in restructured power system creates challenges to the Independent System Operator (ISO) in finding the optimal transmission pricing and congestion management in each transaction of DG. Hence, this work may expand to new methodologies for conduction lines pricing and overcrowding organization.

Table 6. Power loss and bus voltages earlier to and later fitting of two DG units by hybrid PSO - ANN methodology

Most Favorable Bus Numbers		Bus Voltages Earlier to Fitting of DGs		Bus Voltages Later Fitting of DGs		Max PSO Voltage Deviation	DG Capacity		Power Loss Earlier to Fitting of DGs	Power Loss Later Fitting of DGs
B1	B2	p.u.	p.u.	p.u.	p.u.	p.u.	MW	MW	MW	MW
16	4	1.049	1.019	1.040	1.013	0.101	12.807	2.000		8.702
4	23	1.019	1.033	1.013	1.022	0.052	1.820	12.807		4.435
21	30	1.032	0.996	1.022	0.978	0.092	7.764	6.024		9.389
19	12	1.031	1.062	1.019	1.057	0.083	6.019	5.310	10.714	8.841
12	10	1.061	1.051	1.057	1.035	0.061	32.106	21.950		7.353
21	20	1.032	1.0318	1.022	1.022	0.152	2.184	1.024		8.860
14	15	1.029	1.043	1.019	1.035	0.120	4.974	5.310		4.801

Table 7. Power Loss and bus voltages earlier to and later fitting of two DG units by hybrid ABC - ANN methodology

Most Favorable Bus Numbers		Bus Voltages Earlier Fitting of DGs		Bus Voltages Later Fitting of DGs		DG Ratings		Load Power at the Buses		Power Loss Earlier Fitting of DGs	Power Loss Later Fitting of DGs
B1	B2	p.u.	p.u.	pu	pu	MW (B1)	MW (B2)	MW	MW	MW	MW
16	4	1.040	1.013	0.989	1.000	2.060	1.901	3.500	7.600		8.112
4	23	1.013	1.022	1.010	0.990	1.104	2.177	7.600	3.200		4.274
21	30	1.022	0.978	1.019	0.978	7.000	5.141	17.500	10.600		8.478
19	12	1.019	1.057	1.016	0.989	5.002	0.173	9.500	11.200	10.714	8.375
12	10	1.057	1.035	0.989	0.999	3.020	6.019	11.200	5.800		6.242
21	20	1.022	1.022	1.004	0.999	1.088	0.999	17.500	2.200		2.410
14	15	1.041	1.035	1.009	1.002	2.000	3.000	6.200	8.200		2.168

CONCLUSION

In this chapter, the performance of IEEE 30 bus test system for a hybrid ABC-ANN optimization methodology has been verified for demonstrating the effectiveness of proposed methodology as compared to other methodologies like ANN, PSO and hybrid PSO-ANN. Optimal locations of DGs have been determined with the support of voltage deviation by applying the ABC algorithm and optimal ratings of the DGs have been found by using ANN approach.

The power loss in the system is reduced to 7.904MW from 10.214MW when only DG is placed at bus number 19 with an optimal capacity of 5.986MW using ABC-ANN approach. It is noticed that, this power loss is less as compared to other methodologies implementation such as ANN, PSO and PSO-ANN and also voltage profile has been improved and also proves that the proposed methodology increases the system voltage profile and power loss of the system is decreased from 10.714MW to 2.1681MW when two DGs are placed at optimal locations such as at bus numbers 14 & 15 with an optimal capacities of 2MW and 3MW respectively

Comparison has been made among PSO, ANN, hybrid PSO-ANN with the hybrid ABC-ANN optimization methodologies. It can be concluded that the hybrid ABC-ANN is more professional in dropping the loss as compared to the other methodologies.

REFERENCES

Abu-Mouti, F. S., & El-Hawary, M. E. (2011). Optimal Distributed Generation Allocation and Sizing in Distribution Systems via Artificial Bee Colony Algorithm. *IEEE Transactions on Power Delivery*, *26*(4), 2090–2101. doi:10.1109/TPWRD.2011.2158246

Abu-Mouti, F. S., & El-Hawary, M. E. (2009). Modified artificial bee colony algorithm for optimal distributed generation sizing and allocation in distribution systems. Proceedings of IEEE Conference on Electrical Power & Energy, 1-9. doi:10.1109/EPEC.2009.5420915

Acharya, N., Mahat, P., & Mithulananthan, N. (2006). An analytical approach for DG allocation in primary distribution network. *Electrical Power and Energy Systems*, *28*(10), 669–678. doi:10.1016/j.ijepes.2006.02.013

Alhelou, H., Hamedani-Golshan, M. E., Zamani, R., Heydarian-Forushani, E., & Siano, P. (2018). Challenges and Opportunities of Load Frequency Control in Conventional, Modern and Future Smart Power Systems: A Comprehensive Review. *Energies*, *11*(10), 2497. doi:10.3390/en11102497

Alhelou, H. H. (2018). *Fault Detection and Isolation in Power Systems Using Unknown Input Observer. In Advanced Condition Monitoring and Fault Diagnosis of Electric Machines* (p. 38). Hershey, PA: IGI Global.

Alhelou, H. H., Golshan, M., & Fini, M. (2018). Wind Driven Optimization Algorithm Application to Load Frequency Control in Interconnected Power Systems Considering GRC and GDB Nonlinearities. *Electric Power Components and Syst.*

Alhelou, H. H., & Golshan, M. E. H. (2016, May). Hierarchical plug-in EV control based on primary frequency response in interconnected smart grid. In *Electrical Engineering (ICEE), 2016 24th Iranian Conference on* (pp. 561-566). IEEE. 10.1109/IranianCEE.2016.7585585

Alhelou, H. H., Golshan, M. H., & Askari-Marnani, J. (2018). Robust sensor fault detection and isolation scheme for interconnected smart power systems in presence of RER and EVs using unknown input observer. *International Journal of Electrical Power & Energy Systems*, *99*, 682–694. doi:10.1016/j.ijepes.2018.02.013

Alhelou, H. H., Hamedani-Golshan, M. E., Heydarian-Forushani, E., Al-Sumaiti, A. S., & Siano, P. (2018, September). Decentralized Fractional Order Control Scheme for LFC of Deregulated Nonlinear Power Systems in Presence of EVs and RER. In *2018 International Conference on Smart Energy Systems and Technologies (SEST)* (pp. 1-6). IEEE. 10.1109/SEST.2018.8495858

Alhelou, H. S. H., Golshan, M. E. H., & Fini, M. H. (2015, December). Multi agent electric vehicle control based primary frequency support for future smart micro-grid. In *Smart Grid Conference (SGC)* (pp. 22-27). Academic Press.

Alshahrestani, A., Golshan, M. E. H., & Alhelou, H. H. (2018, November). WAMS Based Online Estimation of Total Inertia Constant and Damping Coefficient for Future Smart Grid Systems. In *Smart Grid Conference (SGC)* (pp. 1-5). Academic Press.

Fini, M. H., Yousefi, G. R., & Alhelou, H. H. (2016). Comparative study on the performance of many-objective and single-objective optimisation algorithms in tuning load frequency controllers of multi-area power systems. *IET Generation, Transmission & Distribution*, *10*(12), 2915–2923. doi:10.1049/iet-gtd.2015.1334

Hosseini, & Karami, & KarimiMadahi. (2011). Optimal capacity, location and number of distributed generation at 20 kv substations. *Australian Journal of Basic and Applied Sciences*, *5* (10), 1051-1061.

Khosrow-Pour. (2018). *Incorporating Nature-Inspired Paradigms in Computational Applications*. IGI Global.

Lin & Su. (2012). Using an Efficient Artificial Bee Colony Algorithm for Protein Structure Prediction on Lattice Models. *International Journal of Innovative Computing, Information and Control*, *8*(3B), 2049-2064.

Makdisie, C., Haidar, B., & Alhelou, H. H. (2018). An Optimal Photovoltaic Conversion System for Future Smart Grids. In *Handbook of Research on Power and Energy System Optimization* (pp. 601–657). IGI Global. doi:10.4018/978-1-5225-3935-3.ch018

Nadweh, S., Hayek, G., Atieh, B., & Haes Alhelou, H. (2018). Using Four – Quadrant Chopper with Variable Speed Drive System Dc-Link to Improve the Quality of Supplied Power for Industrial Facilities. Majlesi Journal of Electrical Engineering.

Nasiraghdam & Jadid. (2012). Optimal hybrid PV/WT/FC sizing and distribution system reconfiguration using multi-objective artificial bee colony (MOABC) algorithm. *International Journal of Solar Energy*, *86*(10), 3057–3071.

Njenda, T. C., Golshan, M. E. H., & Alhelou, H. H. (2018, November). WAMS Based Intelligent Under Frequency Load Shedding Considering Online Disturbance Estimation. In *Smart Grid Conference (SGC)* (pp. 1-5). Academic Press.

Njenda, T. C., Golshan, M. E. H., & Alhelou, H. H. (2018, November). WAMS based Under Frequency Load Shedding Considering Minimum Frequency Prediction and Extrapolated Disturbance Magnitude. In *Smart Grid Conference (SGC)* (pp. 1-5). Academic Press.

Partha, K., & Chanda, C. K. (2013). A simple and fast approach for allocation and size evaluation of distributed generation. *International Journal of Energy and Environmental Engineering*, *4*(1), 1–9.

Rao, G. S., & Obulesh, Y. P. (2013). Optimal Location of DG for Maintaining Distribution System Stability: A Hybrid Technique. *International Journal of Power and Energy Conversion*, *4*(4), 387–403. doi:10.1504/IJPEC.2013.057036

Rao & Obulesh. (2015). ABC and ANN based minimization of power loss for distribution system stability. *Proceedings of 10th IEEE conference on Industrial Electronics and Applications (ICIEA)*, 772-777.

Tosun. (2014). *Artificial Bee Colony Algorithm. In Encyclopedia of Business Analytics and Optimization* (pp. 1–14). IGI Global.

Varesi, K. (2011). Optimal allocation of dg units for power loss reduction and voltage profile improvement of distribution networks using PSO algorithm. *World Academy of Science, Engineering and Technology*, *60*, 1938–1942.

KEY TERMS AND DEFINITIONS

Artificial Bee Colony (ABC) Algorithm: Artificial bee colony (ABC) algorithm is an optimization technique that simulates the foraging manners of honey bees, and has been effectively applied to a variety of practical problems. ABC belongs to the assembly of swarm intelligence algorithms.

Artificial Neural Network (ANN): Artificial neural networks (ANN) are the pieces of a computing system designed to simulate the way the human brain analyzes and processes information. ANN has self-learning capabilities that enable them to produce better results.

Distribution Generations (DG): It is an approach that makes use of small-scale technologies to generate electricity nearer to the end users. In many cases, distributed generators can provide lower-cost electricity and higher power consistency.

Optimization: It is the action of making the finest or most successful use of a situation or resource.

Particle Swarm Optimization (PSO) Algorithm: It is a computational method that optimizes a problem by iteratively trying to improve a candidate solution with regard to a given measure of quality. PSO is a metaheuristic as it makes few or no assumptions about the problem being optimized and can search very large spaces of candidate solutions.

Voltage Stability: It refer to the ability of power system to maintain steady state voltages at all buses in the power system after subjected to a faults from a given initial operating point.

This research was previously published in the Handbook of Research on Smart Power System Operation and Control; pages 35-55, copyright year 2019 by Engineering Science Reference (an imprint of IGI Global).

APPENDIX A: IEEE 30 BUS TEST SYSTEM SINGLE LINE DIAGRAM

Figure 7. Single line diagram of IEEEE 30 bus system

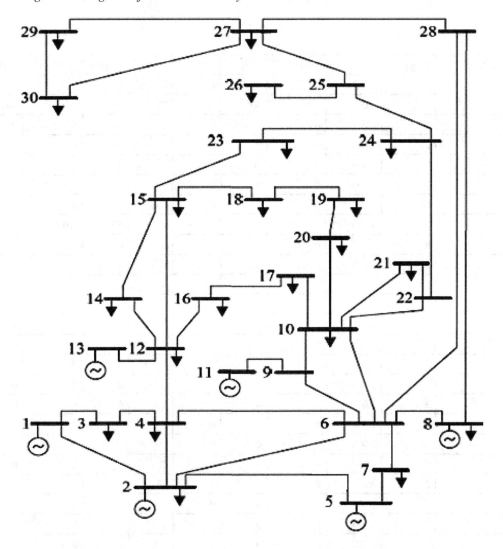

APPENDIX B: BUS DATA OF IEEE 30 BUS SYSTEM

Table 8 provides the bus data of 30 bus system.

Table 8. Bus data

Bus No	Type	Vsp	Theta	Pgi	Qgi	Pli	Qli	QMin	Qmax
1	1	1.060	0	0	0	0	0	0	0
2	2	1.043	0	40	50	22	13	-40	50
3	3	1.000	0	0	0	2	1	0	0
4	3	1.060	0	0	0	8	2	0	0
5	2	1.010	0	20	37	94	19	-40	40
6	3	1.000	0	0	0	0	0	0	0
7	3	1.000	0	0	0	23	11	0	0
8	2	1.010	0	12	37	30	30	-10	40
9	3	1.000	0	0	0	0	0	0	0
10	3	1.000	0	0	19	6	2	0	0
11	2	1.082	0	12	12	0	0	-6	24
12	3	1.000	0	0	0	11	8	0	0
13	2	1.071	0	15	11	0	0	-6	24
14	3	1.000	0	0	0	6	2	0	0
15	3	1.000	0	0	0	8	3	0	0
16	3	1.000	0	0	0	4	2	0	0
17	3	1.000	0	0	0	9	6	0	0
18	3	1.000	0	0	0	3	1	0	0
19	3	1.000	0	0	0	10	3	0	0
20	3	1.000	0	0	0	2	1	0	0
21	3	1.000	0	0	0	18	11	0	0
22	3	1.000	0	0	0	0	0	0	0
23	3	1.000	0	0	0	3	2	0	0
24	3	1.000	0	0	4	9	7	0	0
25	3	1.000	0	0	0	0	0	0	0
26	3	1.000	0	0	0	4	2	0	0
27	3	1.000	0	0	0	0	0	0	0
28	3	1.000	0	0	0	0	0	0	0
29	3	1.000	0	0	0	2	1	0	0
30	3	1.000	0	0	0	11	2	0	0

APPENDIX C: LINE DATA OF IEEE 30 BUS SYSTEM

Table 9 provides the line data of 30 bus system.

Table 9. Line data

Line No.	From Bus	To Bus	Series Impedance		Half Line Charging Susceptance (p.u)	Tap Setting	MVA Rating
			R	X			
1	1	2	0.01920	0.05750	0.02640	--	130
2	1	3	0.04520	0.18520	0.02040	--	130
3	2	4	0.05700	0.17370	0.01840	--	65
4	3	4	0.01320	0.03790	0.00420	--	130
5	2	5	0.04720	0.19830	0.02090	--	130
6	2	6	0.05810	0.17630	0.01870	--	65
7	4	6	0.01190	0.04140	0.00450	--	90
8	5	7	0.04600	0.11600	0.01020	--	70
9	6	7	0.02670	0.08200	0.00850	--	130
10	6	8	0.01200	0.04200	0.00450	--	32
11	6	9	0.00000	0.20800	0.00000	1.01550	65
12	6	10	0.00000	0.55600	0.00000	0.96290	32
13	9	11	0.00000	0.20800	0.00000	--	65
14	9	10	0.00000	0.11000	0.00000	--	65
15	4	12	0.00000	0.25600	0.00000	1.01290	65
16	12	13	0.00000	0.14000	0.00000	--	65
17	12	14	0.12310	0.25590	0.00000	--	32
18	12	15	0.06620	0.13040	0.00000	--	32
19	12	16	0.09450	0.19870	0.00000	--	32
0	14	15	0.22100	0.19970	0.00000	--	16
21	15	17	0.08240	0.19320	0.00000	--	16
22	15	18	0.10700	0.21850	0.00000	--	16
23	18	19	0.06390	0.12920	0.00000	--	16
24	19	20	0.03400	0.06800	0.00000	--	32
25	10	20	0.09360	0.20900	0.00000	--	32
26	10	17	0.03240	0.08450	0.00000	--	32
27	10	21	0.03480	0.67490	0.00000	--	32
28	10	22	0.07270	0.14990	0.00000	--	32
29	21	22	0.01160	0.02360	0.00000	--	32
30	15	23	0.10000	0.20200	0.00000	--	16
31	22	24	0.11500	0.17900	0.00000	--	16

Line No.	From Bus	To Bus	Series Impedance		Half Line Charging Susceptance (p.u)	Tap Setting	MVA Rating
			R	X			
32	23	24	0.13200	0.27000	0.00000	--	16
33	24	25	0.18850	0.32920	0.00000	--	16
34	25	26	0.25440	0.38000	0.00000	--	16
35	25	27	0.10930	0.20870	0.00000	--	16
36	28	27	0.00000	0.36900	0.00000	0.95810	65
37	27	29	0.21980	0.41530	0.00000	--	16
38	27	30	0.32020	0.60270	0.00000	--	16
39	29	30	0.23990	0.45330	0.00000	--	16
40	8	28	0.06360	0.20000	0.02140	--	32
41	6	28	0.01690	0.05990	0.00650	--	32

Chapter 35
A Proposal for Parameter-Free Surrogate Building Algorithm Using Artificial Neural Networks

Srinivas Soumitri Miriyala
Indian Institute of Technology Hyderabad, India

Kishalay Mitra
Indian Institute of Technology Hyderabad, India

ABSTRACT

Surrogate models, capable of emulating the robust first principle based models, facilitate the online implementation of computationally expensive industrial process optimization. However, the heuristic estimation of parameters governing the surrogate building often renders them erroneous or undertrained. Current work aims at presenting a novel parameter free surrogate building approach, specifically focusing on Artificial Neural Networks. The proposed algorithm implements Sobol sampling plan and intelligently designs the configuration of network with simultaneous estimation of optimal transfer function and training sample size to prevent overfitting and enabling maximum prediction accuracy. A novel Sample Size Determination algorithm based on a potential concept of hypercube sampling technique adds to the speed of surrogate building algorithm, thereby assuring faster convergence. Surrogates models for a highly nonlinear industrial sintering process constructed using the novel algorithm resulted in 7 times faster optimization.

INTRODUCTION

Optimization techniques are frequently applied in chemical process and manufacturing industries, business, economics, health-care, finance and energy management (Ries, Beullens & Wang, 2012; Vasant, 2014; Dostal, 2014; Yuce & Mastrocinque, 2016; Lechuga, Martinez & Ramirez, 2016; Vasant, 2011; Pombo, Garcia, Bousson, & Felizardo 2017). Although the advent of high performance computers has empowered the industries by tremendously increasing the speed of processing, control and optimization

DOI: 10.4018/978-1-6684-2408-7.ch035

of industrial problems still remain to be computationally intensive (Mitra, Majumdar & Raha, 2004). The genesis of large computational times lies with the simulation of complex first principle based model for generating the candidates for optimization (Miriyala, Mittal, Majumdar & Mitra, 2016). The first principle based models, such as, those trying to capture the dynamics of reaction networks in a polymer industry or a model handling the wake effects or turbulence in fluid flow, etc. usually involve several highly nonlinear coupled Ordinary and Partial Differential Equations (ODEs & PDEs) (Khan, Hussain, Mansourpour, Mostoufi, Ghasem & Abdullah, 2014; Yousefi & Karimi, 2013; Mogilicharla, Chugh, Majumdar, & Mitra, 2014). This necessitates the involvement of robust simulation packages, such as, ASPEN, Computational Fluid Dynamics (CFD), or Differential Algebraic solvers etc., to solve the system of ODEs and PDEs to facilitate their implementation at industrial scale (Azargoshasb, Mousavi, Amani, Jafari, & Nosrati, 2015; Douguet 2010; Espinet, Shoemaker & Doughty, 2013; Jin & Sendhoff, 2009). The intrinsic complexity of these models forms the genesis for the large computational time consumed by the optimizer, compelling the entire process to run over several weeks or even months (Mogilicharla, Mittal, Majumdar, & Mitra, 2014). The problem grows by multiple folds when the considered system is multi-dimensional in nature (say m dimensions) with optimization formulation involving multiple conflicting objective functions instead of one (Miriyala et al., 2016). The conflicting nature of the objective functions results in a set of non-dominating solutions called Pareto Optimal (PO) solutions (Deb, Sindhya & Hakanen, 2016). The selection of single solution from the PO set is through some higher order information, often provided by the decision maker (Deb, 2001). The solution obtained in this way aims at enabling a decision support system to program and simulate the given process in an optimum fashion. This concept of online optimization is practically imbibed in industry when the combined functioning of optimizer and controller is realized in real time of the live process.

The tremendous industrial growth and ever-expanding demand over the last decade have created strong need for the solutions, which could cater multiple objectives at the same time. This requires solving the underlying multi-objective optimization problem (MOOP) (Deb, Agrawal, Pratap & Meyarivan, 2000). Until date, owing to the advent of fast computing machines, the ability of modern evolutionary methods for solving the MOOP has remained unparalleled (Deb, 2002). On the other hand, due to the predominant condition, wherein absence or expensive computation of gradient information of the complex models has become a common scenario, the modern evolutionary optimization techniques have gained enormous prominence over their classical counterparts, which provide every future course of movements depending on the current gradient information (Deb, 2001). The procedure of solving the MOOP by the robust evolutionary techniques, which primarily work with population of candidate solutions, necessitates multiple function evaluations in order to generate those solutions required in optimization process (Nain & Deb, 2002). These aspects together make the concept of online optimization a far-fetched impractical concept confined to theory, which cannot be realized practically unless the optimization happens in real time (Miriyala et al. 2016). The key to this problem lies with fast and accurate surrogate models, which essentially are data based models trying to emulate the given complex first principle or physics based models (Jin 2011; Tabatabaei, Hakanen, Hartikainen, Miettinen, & Sindhya, 2015; Assefi, Ghaedi, Ansari, Habibi, & Momeni, 2014). These surrogates then replace the original physics based models in the optimization algorithm thereby shielding them from the optimizer while generating the candidate solutions. With surrogates in place, the entire optimization algorithm may proceed in a fast manner thus enabling a step towards online optimization (Miriyala, Pantula, Majumdar & Mitra, 2016).

However, the surrogate building approaches in general contain certain parameters such as the optimal number of training sample points, which needs to be estimated a priori. The existing methodologies (as discussed in the subsequent sections of this chapter) provide only heuristic values to such parameters thus leading to either under-fitting or over-fitting of the surrogate model. This prevents the data based models to qualify as potential surrogates capable of replacing the physics based model during the process optimization. The objective of this chapter is two folded – a) to identify significant parameters associated with construction of Artificial Neural Networks (ANNs) and present a methodology for their intelligent estimation. This, the authors believe, might eliminate the problems of over-fitting and data greedy nature of ANNs, thereby allowing them as efficient surrogate models and b) to implement ANNs in surrogate based optimization of a complex industrial process for testing the feasibility of its online implementation.

Literature Survey

Artificial Neural Networks (ANNs) are one of the prominent candidates for surrogate models by virtue of their immense potential to recognize complex patterns (Esfandian, Samadi-Maybodi, Parvini & Khoshandam, 2016; Fattahi, Kazemeini, Khorasheh, & Rashidi, 2014; Asl Ahmadi, Ghiasvand, Tardast, & Katal 2013; Hafizi, Ahmadpour, Koolivand-Salooki, Heravi & Bamoharram, 2013; Shojaeimehr, Rahimpour, Khadivi, & Sadeghi, 2014). ANNs are mathematical models in form of network of nodes, whose functioning is motivated by the impeccable parallel networking of neurons in the human brain. They are widely acknowledged across all engineering and scientific disciplines for their immense applications in various fields such as computer science and electrical engineering (Bevrani, Habibi & Shokoohi, 2012; Yegnanarayana, 1994), nanoscience (Esmaeili & Dashtbayazi, 2014), geosciences (Badel, Angorani, & Panahi, 2011), chemical engineering (Karimi & Ghaedi, 2014; Himmelblau, 2000) and biological sciences (Betiku & Taiwo, 2015) and so on. In this article, an elaborate study is conducted on the perceptron networks, which without any loss of generality can be extended to the specific class of recurrent networks. The parameters, in terms of weights and biases of the network, enable several degrees of freedom to capture the overall nonlinear behavior in the given complex system. This unique ability of the ANN to capture the global trend of the complex model with maximum accuracy, not only assures it a status of an efficient surrogate for optimization but also allows for its wide applicability as a highly efficient interpolator which then finds an edge in several numerical techniques (Haykin, 1994). Several other notable surrogate models listed in literature are Kriging Interpolation (KI) (Jones, 2001), Support Vector Machines (SVM) and Response Surface Methodologies (RSM) (Kleijnen, 2008). Kriging Interpolators are one state of art data modelling method which is based on statistical estimation of an error function at every iteration of training. This error function is further used for infill of a sample point such that the resulting error is reduced in subsequent iterations.

Other prominent statistical regression based methods belong to the class of Generalized Linear models (GLM). Among these, the Generalized Partial Linear models (GPLM) and Multivariate Adaptive Regression Splines (MARS) are known in literature for their data modelling and classification abilities. MARS (Friedman, 1991) can cope with nonlinearities and handles the multivariate interactions between variables efficiently. MARS model constitutes the product of spline basis functions which are also flexible in high dimensions. Tikhonov Regularization (TR), is used to penalize the complexity of MARS, which can be expressed and studied as a Conic Quadratic Problem leading to the method CMARS. CMARS is more model-based and employs continuous and well-structured convex optimization which enables the use of Interior Point Methods. In GPLMs, a semiparametric model, the usual parametric terms (which arise from the GLM models) are augmented with a single non-parametric component. The parameters of GPLM are estimated using methods such as the Penalized Maximum Likelihood. (Özmen, Weber,

Çavuşoğlu & Defterli, 2011; Özmen & Weber, 2012; Weber, Çavuşoğlu, & Özmen, 2012; Taylan, Weber, Liu & Yerlikaya-Özkurt, 2010) The contribution of a continuous regression model such as CMARS and a discrete regression model such as Logistic Regression is combined to construct the Conic Generalized Partial Linear Models (CGPLM). CGPLM essentially reduces the complexity of CMARS by decreasing the number of parameters used in CMARS algorithm. RCMARS (Robust CMARS) and RCGPLM (Robust CGPLM) are efficient versions of CMARS and CGPLM, respectively which have the capability to handle the noisy data which introduce the uncertainties into the model. The parameters of these models are estimated by optimization methods under uncertainty (Özmen & Weber, 2012).

One of the flaws with implementation of the ANNs is the inability to optimally design the architecture of the network (Asl et al. 2013). The architecture of the network is obtained based on the method of hit and trial, which often leads to an impasse. One rule of thumb in this heuristic based design, applied widely in order to reduce the complexity of aforementioned hit and trial procedure, is the assumption that for any given data, a single hidden layer with some arbitrary number of nodes would be sufficient to predict any model with reasonable accuracy (Hagan & Demuth, 2002). The potential of ANNs lies within their ability to segregate the data into exclusive regions. This can be visualized geometrically by considering one layer as an m-dimensional hyper-plane trying to separate out the existing data into two sub spaces, where m is the number of inputs feeding to that layer. A multi-layer perceptron network may, therefore, provide more accuracy for an unseen data, which might be linearly inseparable (Haykin, 1994). This rationale justifies for the fact that the aforementioned assumption may not be true in all cases. Apart from this, the sample size required for training also effects the predictability of the network significantly in accordance with the network architecture (Haykin, 1994; Fattahi et al., 2014). Thus, there is strong obligation to device a logical approach to design the architecture of a given network, simultaneously, along with sample size determination.

Some of the prominent contributions in the literature are mixed integer nonlinear programing (MINLP) approach (Dua, 2010), the Akaike Information Criteria (AIC) (Giri, Petterson, Saxen, & Chakraborti, 2013), etc. to come up with the optimal design of ANN architecture. However, apart from being computationally expensive, none of them addressed the problem of simultaneous design of architecture and sample size determination. With this backdrop, the authors present a schematic for the current scenario of a primal surrogate building algorithm for ANN as surrogate model in Figure. 1. The simple layout in Figure. 1 clearly shows that the surrogate building algorithm is governed by several parameters whose values are usually fixed based on some heuristic, thus inviting potential errors and credible variations in the predictability of the surrogates. Also, any extrapolation out of the m-dimensional input space, calls for re-construction of the surrogate model, which would require a significant amount of computational time. Thus, the surrogate building algorithm should be fast enough, apart from being parameter free to make the surrogate models universal and process of optimization online.

MAIN FOCUS OF THE CHAPTER

In this work, the authors have presented a novel parameter free surrogate building algorithm especially focusing on the automated design of configuration of ANNs along with the simultaneous determination of the sample size required for maximizing the prediction accuracy, without over-fitting the network. The authors have then investigated for the slowest step in the proposed algorithm and presented three different novel approaches to make it fast enough to ensure online surrogate based optimization. An industrially validated model for sintering process, used in steel plants, is considered next for the optimization case study. A comprehensive comparative study between the results of optimization using the ANN surrogates obtained from the proposed novel parameter free surrogate building algorithm, incorporating the three different approaches, is presented in details.

Figure 1. Schematic showing the generic surrogate building algorithm

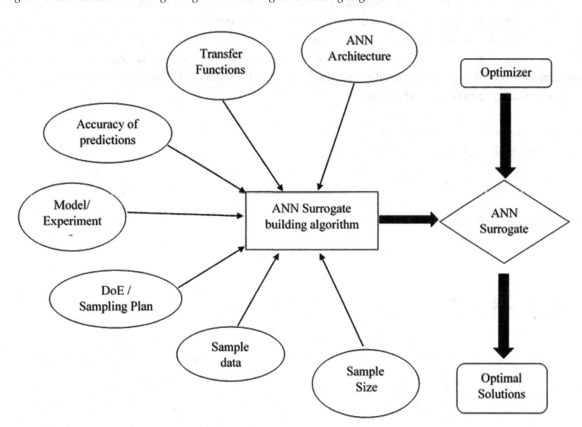

Parameters in Surrogate Building Algorithm

With reference to Figure 1, the parameters involved in surrogate building algorithm are listed down before describing them further in details.

1. Accuracy of prediction
2. Sampling plan or design of experiments (DoE)
3. Sample size
4. Architecture of the network
5. Activation function

Accuracy of Prediction

The accuracy of the surrogate model is a necessary parameter, which needs to be specified prior to the modelling by the decision maker. It is obvious that any decision maker would like to have a maximum value of accuracy for the surrogate model but, it may come at the cost of large computational time and large number of sample points for training. With such dubious nature of this issue, the decision maker without any prior experience would hesitate to provide a particular value of accuracy. This may not allow the algorithm to build a surrogate model capable of maximum predictability. Thus, there is a need to ensure that without providing a specific value of accuracy as an input to the algorithm, it must be able to build a surrogate model having maximum predictability without overfitting. The authors have considered two well-known statistical measures (Forrester, Sóbester, & Keane, 2008) for estimating the accuracy of the predictions by the network:

1. Root mean square error: RMSE
2. Correlation coefficient r^2:

$$r^2 = \left(\frac{\mathrm{cov}\left(y, \hat{y}\right)}{\sqrt{\mathrm{var}\left(y\right)\mathrm{var}\left(\hat{y}\right)}} \right)^2$$

$$\mathrm{cov}\left(y, \hat{y}\right) = n_t \sum_{i=0}^{n_t} y^{(i)} \hat{y}^{(i)} - \sum_{i=0}^{n_t} \hat{y}^{(i)} \sum_{i=0}^{n_t} y^{(i)}$$

$$\mathrm{var}\left(y\right) = n_t \sum_{i=0}^{n_t} y^{(i)2} - \left(\sum_{i=0}^{n_t} y^{(i)} \right)^2$$

where y is the original output coming from physics driven model or data and $\hat{y}$ is the predicted output from the surrogate model.

Sampling Plan or DoE

The sampling plan is at the heart of the surrogate building algorithm as it directly influences the number of sample points and thereby the number of function evaluations, apart from accuracy of prediction and architecture of the network. The sampling plan can be easily interpreted as a scheme of placing some arbitrary probes in an m-dimensional space to capture the behaviour of the model (m being the number of inputs). An ideal case would be to divide the entire space into grids and place a probe at every junction which leads to the full factorial sampling plan (Morris, 1991). This will ensure maximum accuracy based on the precision of the grid size, but the number of probes required will be extremely large making it an impractical proposition. However, the ability to capture the dynamics of the system at every cross joint would certainly make the sampling plan uniform and such a sampling plan is said to have the feature of space-filling (Forrester et al., 2008). The characteristic trait of any efficient sampling plan should be able to probe the dynamics of the entire m-dimensional input space with least possible function evaluations or in other terms least possible sample points. Several sampling plans exist in literature displaying the feature of space filling, but none of them reports of performing the task in least possible number of function evaluations. One such example is Latin hyper cube sampling technique (LHS) (Forrester et al., 2008; Tang, 1993), which would ensure the space filling nature of the system but when prompted for an additional sample point, would generate a set of points, completely different from previous set constituting the sampling plan. This essentially abandons the previously collected sample points and calls for several new function evaluations. Sobol sampling plan (Sobol, 1967), based on highly convergent Sobol sequence, is one sampling plan, which ensures both space filling attribute and maintains the sequence even if prompted for a new sample point. The projection of the distribution of 200 sample points in 3-dimensional space obtained using the Sobol sampling plan is compared with the distribution of those obtained using LHS sampling plan and is presented in Figure. 2. One can easily decipher qualitatively the enhanced uniformity and space filling nature of Sobol points over the LHS points. A metric, called the φ (PHI) metric, proposed in literature (Morris & Mitchel, 1995) of sampling techniques (explained later in the paper), measures the space filling attribute of any given sampling plan. Lower the value of this φ metric, better the space filling ability of the sampling plan. The space filling nature of both LHS and Sobol sampling plans are measured using this PHI metric for the distribution of 200 points as given in Figure. 2 and the results along with the computational times required for obtaining the points are presented in Table 1. It is evident from Table 1 that Sobol sampling plan emerges out to be one of the best alternatives among the existing options. Thus, Sobol sampling plan is selected by the authors for implementation in the surrogate building algorithm.

Figure 2. The distribution of 200 sample points using the a) Sobol sampling plan and b) LHS sampling plan

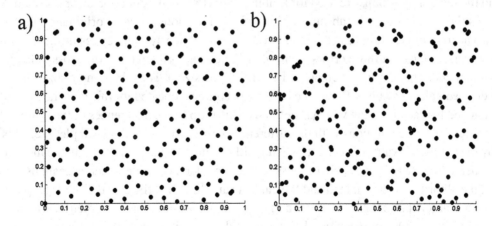

Table 1. Comparison of different sampling plans in terms of PHI metric and computational time for 200 sample points

Sampling Plan	The Measure of PHI Metric	Computational Time
LHS-200	205.367	588.69 seconds
Sobol-200	201.939	0.0251 seconds

Sample Size

ANNs are infamous for their data greedy nature. The scarce amount of literature available on realizing the ANNs as potential surrogates reveals that no proper rationale is devised to decide the number of data points required for training (Roy, Potter, & Landau, 2006). In most of the cases, the general rule of thumb of considering 70% of the available data for training is applied. Such kind of heuristic based assumption may cause the network to be either over-fitted or under trained because of the unavailability of any exact measure of the number of sample points required for training. One significant contribution in literature (Nuchitprasittichai & Cremaschi, 2012) showcases a novel algorithm for Sample Size Determination of the given network. Their approach is based on the fact that, the training error of the network is minimized by increasing the sample size. Although this is true, but the fact that the network might get over-fitted as the sample size is increased cannot be ruled out. Thus, in order to ensure the parsimonious nature of the network, they incorporated the K-fold model evaluation technique (Kohavi, 1995; Rao, Fung, & Rosales, 2008) (with K = 10) along with a variant of LHS called the incremental-LHS (i-LHS) sampling plan for sample size determination. Their algorithm starts with an initial guess value of the sample size, for a given architecture, which they proposed to consider 10 times the number of dimensions in the model. The sample size is given to the i-LHS sampling algorithm, which then generates the training set and it is then divided equally into K-groups or folds. Out of the K available folds, one group is selected for validation and the remaining groups are used for training the network. A validation error is obtained, which is defined as the maximum of the absolute values of the deviations between original output and fitted quantities. The fold for validation can be considered in K different ways thereby resulting in K number of validation errors. A mean of those errors is thus considered and is denoted as the cross-validation error of the current model (models are differentiated by the sample sizes). Then the sample size is incremented by a user defined value (say plus 10) and the entire procedure is repeated for this new model. A quantity is then evaluated for each iteration which is defined as the ratio of the differences of the cross-validation errors of two consecutive iterations with the difference in their corresponding sample size. This ratio is divided by the maximum value of such ratios found till the current iteration to obtain the measure called slope ratio percentage (SRP). If this SRP is less than some tolerance value which is again user specified (say 0.01), the algorithm is terminated and the current sample size is fixed as the final sample size. The essence of their algorithm in brief is to find a minima of cross validation error metric, which is a function of the sample size. One of the major drawbacks of this algorithm is the large computational time of K-fold based validation method. Another disadvantage is the extensive number of function evaluations deliberately called by the i-LHS sampling plan, as described previously. The current work proposes a variant of this method for Sample Size Determination and demonstrates the problem of computational time involved in this approach. A novel hypercube sampling technique is proposed as an alternative in the subsequent section on sampling plan to avoid this problem.

Architecture of the Network

The architecture of the network is perhaps the most important input, which influences the ANN surrogate building algorithm to maximum extent than any other parameter. The design of architecture has popularly been determined through a heuristic assumption of considering a single hidden layer and varying the nodes in that layer until some desired accuracy is found. The authors in this current work propose a novel algorithm to design the architecture of the network along with simultaneous determination of the sample size, sampling plan and transfer function, which would enable the network to predict results with maximum accuracy. The central theme upon which this algorithm is built is fairly simple. The increase in number of parameters in the network (weights and biases) would certainly allow more handles to capture the dynamics of the complex systems thereby enabling it to predict with more accuracy with less sample points. On the other hand, an increase in number of parameters may also lead to the over-fitting of the network. Thus, a delicate balance is essential between these two conflicting objectives, which would allow for maximum accuracy and minimal sample size requirement without over-fitting the surrogate model. This idea motivated the authors to derive a multi-objective unconstrained optimization problem, the functioning of which is explained in details in the subsequent section.

Transfer Function

This parameter specific to the ANNs describes the necessity of considering various possible alternatives to ensure proper activation of the inputs, which would lead to an efficient training of the ANN. The authors have considered to analyse the effect of two prominent activation functions listed in literature (Hagan et al., 2002):

1.   The continuous log-sigmoid transfer function:

$$y\left(x\right) = \frac{1}{1+e^{-x}} \ and \ \frac{dy}{dx} = y\left(1-y\right)$$

2.   The continuous tan-sigmoid transfer function:

$$y\left(x\right) = \frac{e^{x}-e^{-x}}{e^{x}+e^{-x}} \ and \ \frac{dy}{dx} = \left(1-y^{2}\right)$$

These activation functions are enabled into the architecture as the decision variables of the optimization formulation mentioned in the previous section. The authors in this paper have limited the variability of the activation function to the level of entire network instead of variation at the level of each node. Although this can be implemented with slight modification, the authors intentionally avoided it to honour the computational time constraint on the algorithm. The output layers in any given networks are always activated by pure linear activation function (Hagan et al., 2002).

Industrial Sintering Model and Optimization Problem Formulation

The industrial process considered in this article is the iron ore sintering process that produces raw material for the blast furnace operation in steel plants. High quality sinter is essential for better chances of running the blast furnace. Optimum melting achieved during the sintering operation determines the quality of the sinter. Therefore, it is one important parameter supervising the performance of the sintering process. If the melting is less than the optimum, the blast furnace witnesses the granule breakage, while if the melting is more than optimal point, the reducing ability of the sinter drastically decreases leading to operational problems in the blast furnace. The consumption of coke is one another important metric of sintering operation. In order to ensure better sintering process, consumption of coke should be minimal due to the direct correlation of coke consumption with carbon footprint of the plant. The lesser the coke consumption, higher the efficiency of the plant in terms of energy, which leads to lower carbon footprint value of the operation and thus lower the cost of operation. The conventional sintering process starts with the raw materials being charged on a moving strand (30–60 cm thick) proceeding for sintering. The combustion of the coke, to attain the desired temperature during sintering process, begins in the top where the charge is ignited. This is the region where cold air is forced inside by the vacuum created by suction pressure. The cold air cools the corresponding zone resulting in melting lower than the desired. On the other hand, the preheated air, making its way from the top zone where coke is burnt, creates a broad melting zone in the bottom region, which is way higher than the optimum. Thus, the melting of the charge is not uniform because of different temperatures owing to the different conditions of combustions at both upper and lower regions of the charge. In order to avoid this, the charging process is split into two layers, where the combustion of coke is different but uniform in each of the layers, and this ensures uniform melting of the sinter mix.

A dynamic sintering process model has been developed considering a two-dimensional Cartesian coordinate system. The variations in the lateral direction are assumed to be negligible. The temperatures and compositions of both solids and gas at any position of the sinter bed can be calculated using this model. For predicting the gas velocity, the well-known Ergun's equation is used:

$$\frac{\Delta P}{L} = \frac{150\mu \cdot V \left(1 - \varepsilon^2\right)}{d_p^2 \varepsilon^3} + \frac{1.75\rho_g \cdot V^2 \left(1 - \varepsilon\right)}{d_p \varepsilon^3}$$

The following equation is used in general for predicting the transport variables, temperature, and concentration of gas and solid state species:

$$\frac{d\phi}{dt} + \left(V_x \frac{d\phi}{dx} + V_y \frac{d\phi}{dy}\right) = \alpha \left(\frac{d^2\phi}{dx^2} + \frac{d^2\phi}{dy^2}\right) + S_c + S_p \phi$$

where ϕ is transport variable, and S_c and S_p are the source terms. The initial conditions for solving this ODE are provided at the inlet boundary while zero gradient condition is used at the outlet. The convective terms in the rate expression (given below) are used to calculate the velocities of the solids.

$$\frac{dX}{dt} + V_s \frac{dX}{dx} = \sum \frac{R_i}{\rho_{s,i}}$$

All the prominent reactions and phase transformations considered for developing the sintering model are listed in Table 2. The details of the kinetic models and the parameters involved in reaction mechanisms can be obtained from the literature (Mitra, 2013; Nath & Mitra, 2005).

Optimization Problem Formulation

Extensive simulation studies reveal that the twin objectives of

1. Achieving good quality sinter by maximization of melting with
2. Minimum coke consumption are conflicting in nature. This kind of optimization problem with conflicting objective functions is ideal for a multi-objective optimization framework where the trade-off between the objectives can be captured. For the current sintering problem considered, it is observed that 30% melting is the optimal value for the sinter quality for melting (SQM). The first objective is, therefore, defined as to achieve a maximum of 100% when the SQM equals 30%. The combined weighted average of the coke consumed in both the layers (C_w) is considered as the second objective. The height (B) of any one of the two layers in sintering process and the percentages of coke present in each of the two layers (C_A, C_B) can be considered as the decision variables of this optimization problem. The lower and upper bounds for the decision variables are represented by superscripts L and U, respectively. The Non-linear programing problem for Sintering process is presented in Table 3. The well-known NSGA II was chosen to solve the aforementioned optimization problem.

Table 2. Kinetic model of the Sintering system

Sl. No.	Reaction Name	Equation
1.	Iron oxides reduction	$Fe_2O_3 \xrightarrow{CO/H_2} FeO \xrightarrow{CO/H_2} Fe$
2.	Limestone decomposition	$CaCO_3 \rightleftarrows CaO + CO_2$
3.	Combustion of coke	$C + O_2 \rightleftarrows CO_2; 2C + O_2 \rightleftarrows 2CO$
4.	Solution loss reaction	$C + CO_2 \rightleftarrows 2CO$
5.	Water gas reaction	$C + H_2O \rightleftarrows CO + H_2$
6.	Water gas shift reaction	$H_2O + CO \rightleftarrows CO_2 + H_2$
7.	Water vapour formation	$H_2 + 0.5O_2 \rightleftarrows H_2O$
8.	Condensation and drying	$H_2O \rightleftarrows (H_2O)$
9.	Solidification and melting	[Solid Sinter] Û Liquid Sinter

Table 3. Multi objective optimization formulation of the Sintering model

Objective Functions	Decision Variables
$\max\limits_{C_A, C_B, B} SQM$	$C_A^L \leq C_A \leq C_A^U$
$\min\limits_{C_A, C_B, B} C_W$	$C_B^L \leq C_B \leq C_B^U$
	$B^L \leq B \leq B^U$

Figure 3. Novel parameter free ANN surrogate building algorithm

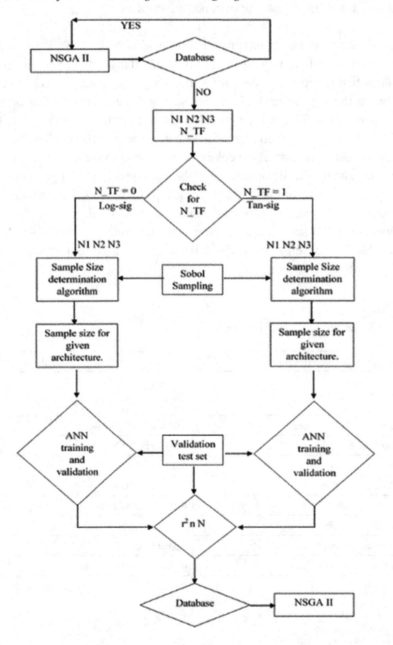

SOLUTIONS AND RECOMMENDATIONS

Novel Parameter Free Surrogate Building Algorithm

The multi-objective optimization formulation, on which the novel parameter free surrogate building algorithm is based upon, is described in Table 4 and the same is solved using the efficient real and binary coded non-dominated sorting genetic algorithm (NSGA II) (Deb, 2001). The proposed algorithm is described schematically in Figure 3. The maximum number of layers considered for estimating the architecture by this algorithm is limited to 3 and maximum number of nodes per layer is limited to 8. The main reason for this bound over the maximum values of layers and nodes is to avoid large number of parameters in terms of weights and biases, which then automatically prohibits one possible route to over-fitting. This maximum limit can easily be changed in the algorithm, if needed. The decision variables of the algorithm N1, N2 and N3 corresponding to the number of nodes in the hidden layers 1, 2, and 3, respectively, and N_TF which is a variable for representing the transfer function are all whole numbers.

Table 4. The multi objective optimization framework, which drives the proposed parameter free surrogate building algorithm

Objective Function	Decision Variables (Only Integral Values)
Maximize the accuracy (r^2) Minimize total number of nodes (**N**) Minimize the sample size required (**n**)	$1 \leq \mathbf{N1} \leq 8$ $0 \leq \mathbf{N2} \leq 8$ $0 \leq \mathbf{N3} \leq 8$ $0 \leq \mathbf{N\_TF} \leq 1$

For instance, if the decision variable set is [3 2 0 1] (N1-N2-N3-N_TF), it means that the architecture consists of two hidden layers (N3 = 0 indicating no third hidden layer) with three nodes in the first hidden layer and two nodes in the second hidden layer. The value of N_TF = 1 describes tan sigmoidal activation function while its counterpart, the log sigmoidal activation is described by the value 0 of N_TF. The lower and upper bounds of the decision variables are designed in such a way that, there exists a bare minimum of one hidden layer in the network. A decision variable set [3 0 2 1] would allot zero number of nodes to the second hidden layer and in such case, irrespective of the value of N3, the network is truncated at one hidden layer itself in order to maintain the sense of connectivity in the network. Once the NSGA II framework provides the architecture of the network along with the activation function, the sample size required for ensuring maximum predictability of the network is determined using a Sample Size Determination algorithm, which is described in the following section. The Sobol sampling plan generates the same number of m-dimensional sample points as that obtained from the Sample Size Determination algorithm. The network training is performed by a code developed indigenously by the authors' group, which takes any multiple layered architecture and N_TF as an input along with validation and training set to provide the RMSE and r^2 values of the network prediction. The validation set used for validating various networks is always kept same but is ensured to be completely different from the training set. The validation set comprises of 200 sample points obtained using the LHS sampling technique. The number of weight and biases, collectively called as the parameters present in the network, are directly related to the total number of nodes present in the network. Therefore, only for the sake of simplicity, the algorithm calculates the total number of nodes (N) present in the network instead of all the parameters involved. Thus, the outputs of the algorithm are the final sample size (n), which is obtained from Sample Size Determination algorithm, total nodes (N) and r^2 value. These values are stored in a database before being sent back to NSGA II in order to check the redundancy over the generations of genetic algorithm. This database management system saves credible amount of computational time, which adds to the speed of the surrogate building algorithm. The credentials of the real and binary coded NSGA II are reported in Table 5. The surrogate building algorithm, which is essentially the multi objective optimization framework, therefore, finally provides with the best surrogate model which ensures maximum prediction accuracy along with optimal configuration of ANN and sample size required for attaining the corresponding accuracy. The Sample Size Determination algorithm is described in the following section.

Sample Size Determination Algorithm

Approach 1: K-Fold-Based Approach

The Sample Size Determination algorithm considered in this paper draws its inspiration from the work of Nuchitprasittichai & Cremaschi (2012). However, the major distinction in the algorithm proposed by the authors in the current work lies in the way the points are sampled using the given sampling plan. The authors here have used the Sobol sampling plan, which provides continuous samples in the range of 0 to 1 within no time. The Sobol sampling ensures two striking differences from the algorithm mentioned before in Nuchitprasittichai & Cremaschi (2012).

1. The computational time of the algorithm proposed earlier for obtaining the sample points is drastically reduced by considering the Sobol sampling plan in place of i-LHS sampling plan.
2. The characteristic of Sobol to maintain the same sequence upon generating any new sample point ensures that no function call is ever wasted. This was not the case with i-LHS, where at every iteration all the points were supposed to be obtained by new function evaluations.

The algorithm for Sample Size Determination is depicted in Figure 4. The central theme of this paper was to identify a fast and parameter free surrogate building algorithm to ensure online optimization of complex processes. A section-wise analysis of the entire algorithm revealed that the NSGA II framework including the ANN training and validation collectively required a very small percentage of the total computational time of the surrogate-building algorithm. Whereas, the Sample Size Determination algorithm that hosts the computationally expensive K-fold based technique consumed the maximum time. Unfortunately, the feature, which is the prime reason for the computational expense of K-fold, is the same reason, which makes it one of the robust model evaluation techniques i.e. the extensive selection of validation set in all possible ways that ensures that every part of the training set is considered for validation as well as training without any bias. This is the feature, which is responsible for preventing the over-fitting of the ANN model. Instead of approaching the problem of over-fitting with the extensive method of K-fold, if a validation set is found which ensures maximum space filling attribute in the corresponding m-dimensional input space at each iteration of the sample determination algorithm, the need to perform multiple training (as in K-fold method) of the network can be safely avoided.

Figure 4. Sample size determination algorithm

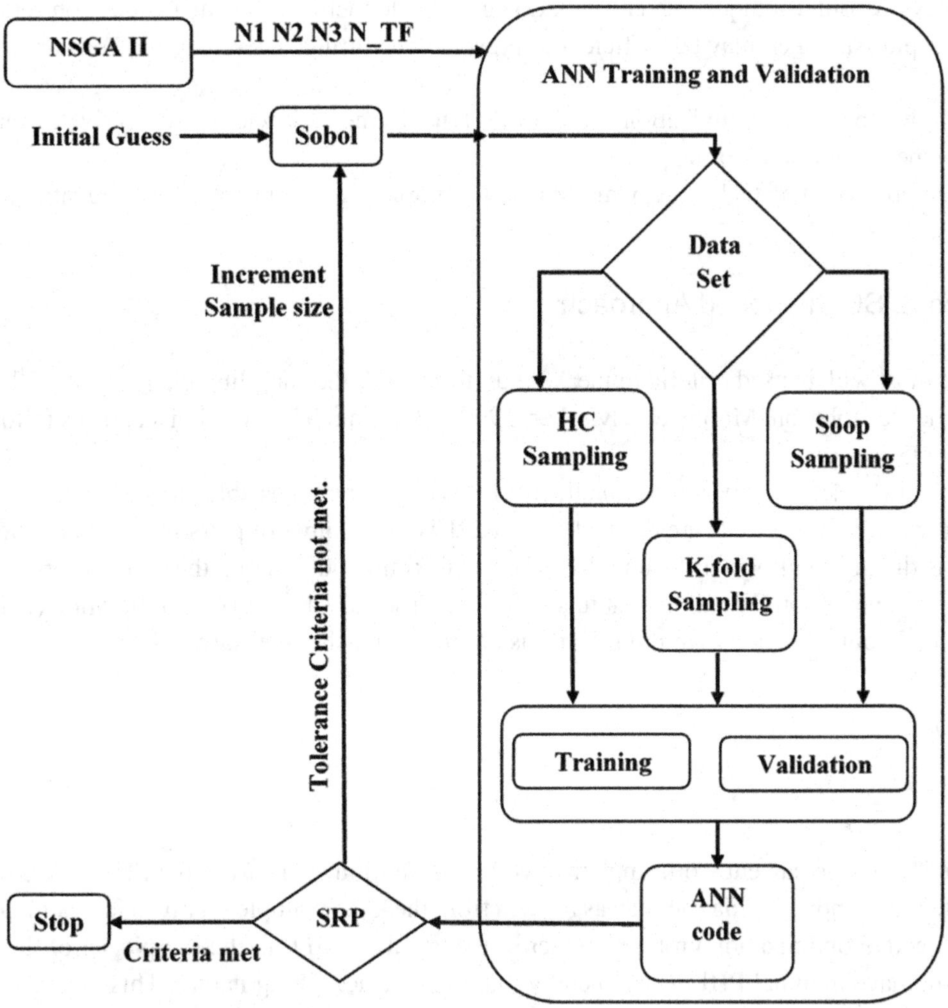

Table 5. Parameters of non-dominated sorting genetic algorithm used in proposed algorithm

No.	Parameter Name	Value
1	Maximum generation size	100
2	Population size	100
3	Crossover probability	0.9
4	Mutation probability	0.01
5	Number of objectives	3
6	Number of Decision variables	4 (all binary)
7	Number of constraints	0

Without the loss of generality, the authors present two new approaches for replacing the computationally expensive K-fold technique, which chalk down a simple method to form a validation set out of the existing sample set, which may be sufficient to prevent over-fitting. These two methods are:

1. A Single Objective Optimization Problem (SOOP) framework with the objective of minimizing the φ metric of the sampling plans.
2. Hypercube sampling technique, which ensures a simple yet elegant approach to identify the validation set.

Approach 2: SOOP-Based Approach

One of the most widely used criteria to measure uniformity of the sampling plans (space-filling) is the max-min metric (Johnson, Moore, & Ylvisaker, 1990) whose modified version stands as follows (Morris et al., 1995).

When $d_1, d_2, d_3, \ldots d_i$ represent the unique distances between all possible pairs of points in sampling plan X and when $J_1, J_2, J_3, \ldots J_i$, are defined such that J_i is the number of pairs separated by the distance d_i, then X is the most uniform max-min plan when it maximizes d_1, among the plans where this is true, it minimizes J_1, and so on. To implement this definition, a scalar valued criterion function (PHI, φ) was devised, which ranked various sampling plans as per the increasing measure of φ.

$$\varphi = \left(\sum_{k=1}^{m} \frac{J_k}{d_k^2} \right)^2$$

The authors in the current work implemented this definition to measure the PHI metric of a given sample set. There upon a validation set was formed from the larger sample set given for training by using a single objective optimization problem, which was formulated to find the sample set of desired size, which would have minimal PHI metric thereby maximum space filling nature. This validation set was then used to find the validation error for the current model. The complete Sample Size Determination algorithm using the SOOP sampling based approach can be listed in steps as follows:

Step 1: Given an architecture by the NSGA II algorithm, start with some initial sample size (n). An intelligent guess would be to start with 10 times the number of dimensions.

Step 2: Find the number of sample points required for validation ~ 30% of sample size. Call it as n_v.

Step 3: The objective is to find a set of points of size n_v from the given sample set which would minimize the PHI metric. This forms an unconstrained SOOP formulation, which can be solved using any credible optimization algorithm. The authors used elitist genetic algorithm to identify the n_v number of sample points, which formed the validation set.

Step 4: The remaining points formed the training set and were used to train the network which was then validated with the sample set found in step 3. The validation error is denoted by V.

Step 5: If iteration = 1, increment the sample size by a credible measure (say plus 10) and repeat all the above steps to find the validation error V_i for each iteration i.

Step 6: Find the slope defined as:

$$\frac{1}{100} * \frac{abs\left(V_{i+1} - V_i\right)}{\left(n_{i+1} - n_i\right)}$$

Step 7: The slope ratio percentage is obtained by dividing this value for the current iteration with the maximum value of the slopes obtained till the current iteration.

Step 8: If this SRP < tolerance, terminate the algorithm and return the current sample size.

This approach based on optimization framework although ensures the best space filling validation set, suffers from the intrinsic disadvantage of the evolutionary optimization techniques, which is the problem of convergence in given time frame. To avoid any ambiguity in this regard, the authors have come up with a much simpler method, which despite of being able to come up with a similar space filling validation set, completely eliminates the underlying optimization framework and the concept of φ metric. This method is called the Hypercube sampling method and is described next. Although the hypercube sampling method is extremely fast, the SOOP sampling method can always serve as a benchmark method for testing the hypercube sampling method.

Approach 3: Hypercube Sampling

Figure 5. Left hand side figure represents the sample space containing sample points (dots) and right hand side figure represents hypercube sampling. Once the bins (represented by rectangles) are formed a single data point can be sampled from each bin

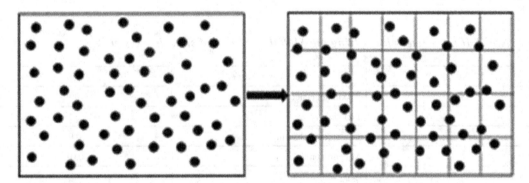

The central theme of hypercube sampling is to divide the given m-dimensional input space into bins of equal volume and then sample single point from each of the bins to form the validation set. This kind of sampling ensures the validation set to retain a flavour of every region of the given sample data. The rest of the points will be used for network training. In this way, the entire m-dimensional space is sampled without going either for the concept of multiple validation sets as was the case with K-fold based algorithm or for the SOOP concept. This central theme is depicted in the schematic of Figure. 5 for a 2 dimensional space. Similar to the SOOP sampling method, in the HC sampling algorithm, the number of points for validation is determined by the general rule of thumb i.e. 30% of entire data set comprises the validation set. The algorithm for Sample Size Determination is described below:

Step 1: For the given architecture, initiate the algorithm with some trivial sample size (n). An intelligent guess would be to start with 10 times the number of dimensions.

Step 2: Find the number of sample points required for validation ~ 30% of sample size. Say it as n_v.

Step 3: With the given sample set, form the n-dimensional sample space and divide it into n_v hyper-cubes of equal volume. Distribute the given sample points into these bins.

Step 4: Sample a single point from each bin. If any bins are empty, go to Step 5. If the number of points sampled from the bins ~ 30% of sample size then go to Step 6.

Step 5: Increment n_v and repeat Step 3 to Step 4.

Step 6: Train the ANN algorithm with given architecture and find the validation error (V) by validating with the sample set obtained in Step 4.

Step 7: Increment the sample size and repeat from Step 2 to 6.

Step 8: Find the slope at the current iteration defined as:

$$\frac{1}{100} * \frac{abs\left(V_{i+1} - V_i\right)}{\left(n_{i+1} - n_i\right)}$$

Step 9: The slope ratio percentage is obtained by dividing the current slope with maximum value of the slopes recorded till the current iteration.

Step 10: If this SRP < tolerance, terminate the algorithm and return the current sample size.

RESULTS AND DISCUSSIONS

Table 6. NSGA II parameters for solving the MOOP problem of sintering system

No.	Parameter Name	Value
1	Maximum generation size	30
2	Population size	50
3	Crossover probability	0.9
4	Mutation probability	0.01
5	$C_A^L, C_A^U \left(in\%\right)$	3,10
6	$C_B^L, C_B^U \left(in\%\right)$	3,10
7	$B^L, B^U(in\ cm)$	1,16

The robust industrially validated model considered in the current study is a 3 input 2 output Sintering model whose validation results can be obtained from literature (Mitra, 2013). The MOOP formulation presented in Table 3 is solved using the real and binary coded NSGA II algorithm (whose parameters are listed in Table 6) and the original expensive physics driven model (Mitra, 2013; Nath & Mitra, 2005). Although the NSGA II algorithm was run for 30 generations, it was observed that the PO front was saturated at generation number 25 with each generation containing 50 populations. Thus, the total function evaluations required to perform the optimization run with original model in place, were nearly 1300 (= 50*26, including the 0th generation). The results of the current work are reported in the sequence of the simulations conducted:

Step 1

The first step in this study is the construction of ANN surrogate models using the novel parameter free surrogate building algorithm.

The ANN code is formulated to handle one output at a time thereby making it a multiple input single output (MISO) code. This in fact simplifies the surrogate building approach in view of the fact that multiple MISO codes can be run simultaneously to build the surrogate models for all outputs in the same time. The Sample Size Determination algorithm is started with initial sample size of 30 and the tolerance for SRP is kept at 0.01. A very low value of the tolerance check would lead to a near infinite time for the algorithm to converge while a very high value would lead to dubious results. The authors have converged at the value of 0.01 but any change in this tolerance value is always encouraged. Although the authors do not impose any constraint in the way the sample size is incremented, but over a period of thorough study, it was observed that the optimal increment in the sample size for the considered model might be plus ten per iteration. These parameters were kept same for all three approaches implemented to obtain the final sample size using the Sample Size Determination algorithm. The NSGA II technique which forms the basis for the proposed novel surrogate building algorithm was run for 100 generations with 100 populations in each of the generation. The cross over probability was set at 0.9 and mutation probability at 0.01 as depicted in Table 5. Although the NSGA II runs were allowed to proceed till 100 generations, the saturation of the PO front was observed at around 30th generation for all the three approaches. A three-dimensional Pareto front was obtained for the objectives of maximizing r^2, minimizing total nodes and minimizing the total sample size. The Pareto front obtained for the output 1, using the three approaches of HC based sampling, K-fold based sampling and SOOP sampling methods are shown in Figures 6, 7 and 8, respectively. Similar PO fronts were obtained for output 2, which are not shown here for the sake of brevity.

The computational time required for each iteration with respect to the sample size is plotted in Figure 9 for an arbitrarily chosen architecture for output 1. One can clearly observe the rapid increase in complexity of K-fold based method in terms of computational time as the sample size increases. The SOOP sampling method serves as the best possible alternative to K-fold based method, with a sound basis for preventing the over-fitting aspect by implementing an optimization framework for selecting the best set for validation. While the HC sampling based method inspired from SOOP sampling, provides altogether a different route designed on pure logic, although there does not exist a theoretical proof for it to be the best possible alternative (as is the case with SOOP sampling).

Figure 6. The 3-D PO front distribution for output -1 using HC method

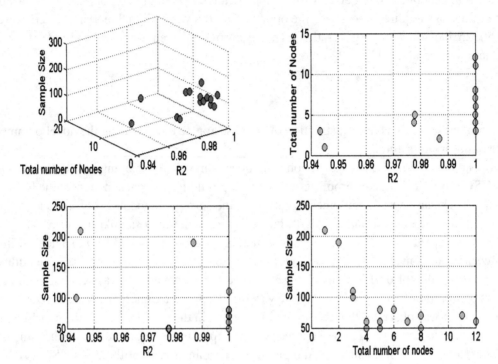

Figure 7. The 3-D PO front distribution for output -1 using K-fold method

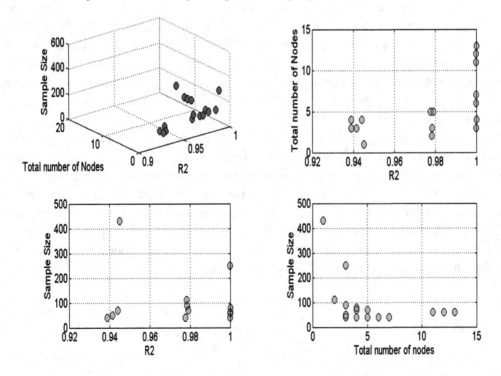

Figure 8. The 3-D PO front distribution for output -1 using SOOP method

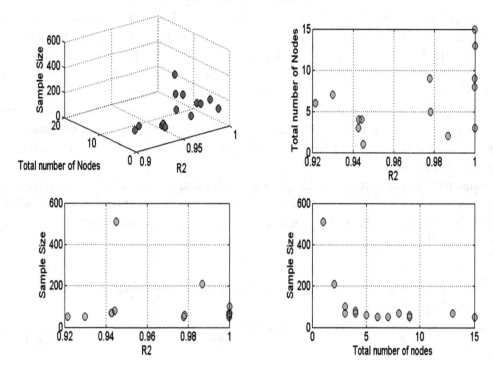

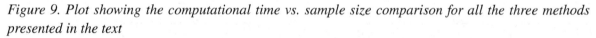

Figure 9. Plot showing the computational time vs. sample size comparison for all the three methods presented in the text

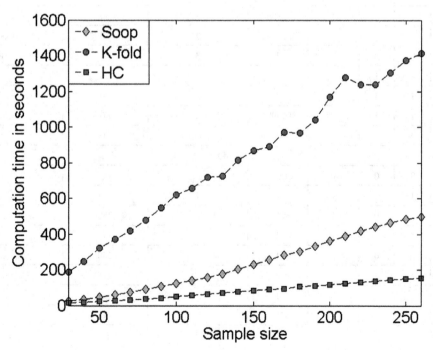

However, it can be observed from Figure 9 that, HC sampling based technique is nearly 10 times faster than the K-fold based technique in terms of computational time. Thus, the proposal for replacing the K-fold based Sample Size Determination algorithm with HC sampling based Sample Size Determination algorithm is justified without any dispute. As mentioned previously, selection of one architecture with corresponding sample size from the list of optimal solutions is based on some higher order information provided by the decision maker. However, the authors have selected the point in the PO front, which, apart from being accurate enough, was found to be closest to the nadir point (Deb, 2002). The accuracy of the selected architectures was ensured to be more than r^2 value of 0.98. The nadir point for the current optimization formulation is (1, 0, 0) corresponding to maximum accuracy 1, minimum nodes 0 and minimum sample size 0.

The results of the novel surrogate building algorithm for output 1 along with the results of selection procedure based on the higher order information are shown in Table 7 while the corresponding results for output 2 are shown in Table 8. The selected architectures, corresponding sample sizes, and their predictions accuracies are listed in Table 9.

Table 7. Higher order analysis to select 1 architecture from PO front obtained for Output-1 using HC and K-fold sampling approach

N1	N2	N3	N_TF	r^2	Total Nodes (N)	Data Size (n)	Dist. from Nadir Point
HC Results							
6	0	0	0	1	6	80	80.22
6	2	0	1	0.99993	8	50	50.63
5	0	0	1	0.99999	5	80	80.15
3	1	0	1	0.99993	4	60	60.13
6	1	0	1	0.99993	7	60	60.40
3	0	0	1	1	3	110	110.04
5	2	1	1	1	8	70	70.45
7	1	4	1	0.99993	12	60	61.18
3	1	1	0	0.99993	5	60	60.20
5	2	4	1	1	11	70	70.85
K-Fold Results							
3	3	0	0	0.99	6	40	40.44
3	1	0	1	1	4	80	80.09
3	0	0	1	1	3	250	250.0
6	4	1	1	1	11	60	61
3	0	0	0	1	3	250	250.0
5	6	1	1	1	12	60	61.18
4	7	2	1	1	13	60	61.39
6	1	0	1	0.99	7	40	40.6

The following inferences can be drawn from these results:

1. The complete replacement of the original model with ANN surrogate in the optimization algorithm resulted in saving an enormous 70% of the function evaluations {[(1300 − 390)/1300] * 100} thereby resulting in nearly 4 times {1300/390} faster optimization.

2. Although for a safer side, the validation set is considered here to be of 200 points, the optimization run can be made much faster by considering lower number of validation points. With respect to training set alone, the proposed algorithm resulted in multilayered architectures which emulate the original model with an average accuracy of 99% and performed the optimization run nearly 7 (~ 1300/190) times faster.

3. The emergence of multi layered networks as results of the surrogate building algorithm, justifies the need for exploring the potential of multi layered perceptron networks. This result justifies the elimination of the assumption based on heuristic to consider only single hidden layered architectures.

4. The time comparison between the three approaches presented in Figure 12, reveals that the hyper-cube sampling technique is nearly 10 times faster when compared with the K-fold based approach. This clearly displays the HC sampling based technique is a clear winner out of the three approaches suggested.

5. Although the architectures are bound to be different due to the intrinsic algorithmic differences, the similarities in the results of the HC based and K-fold based approaches in terms of final sample size, accuracy of predictions, multi-layered architectures, etc. clearly display the robustness of HC sampling based approach when compared with K-fold based method.

The parity plot for the results of output 1 and 2 obtained using the proposed algorithm implementing HC sampling and K-fold based sampling methods for Sample Size Determination (for architectures as listed in the Table 7) are shown in Figure 10 and 11, respectively. In order to assess the amount of nonlinearity present in the considered sintering model, the contour plots in the form of tile plots for two inputs taken at a time are represented in Figure 12 for output 1 and output 2. The nonlinear curves and the drastic intensity variations in these tile plots clearly indicate the complicated behavior of the sintering model.

Table 8. Higher order analysis to select 1 architecture from PO front obtained for Output-2 using HC and K-fold sampling approach

N1	N2	N3	N_TF	r²	Total Nodes (N)	Data Size (n)	Dist. from Nadir Point
HC Results							
6	2	5	1	0.995	13	220	220.38
6	3	1	0	0.994	10	300	300.16
6	1	0	0	0.984	7	490	490.05
5	4	1	1	0.99	10	190	190.26
7	1	1	1	0.98	9	280	280.14
K-Fold Results							
7	3	1	0	0.99	11	220	220.2

Table 9. ANN surrogates obtained using the parameter free surrogate building algorithm for the outputs of industrially validated sintering model

	Architect (Inputs-N1-N2-N3-Outputs)	N_TF	N	r2	Data Size	Total Function Calls (Training + Validation)
Approach 1: HC						
Output1	3-6-2-0-1	1	8	0.99	50	190 + 200 = 390
Output 2	3-5-4-1-1	1	10	0.99	190	
Approach 2: K-Fold						
Output 1	3-3-3-0-1	1	6	0.99	40	220 + 200 = 420
Output 2	3-7-3-1-1	0	11	0.99	220	

Figure 10. Parity plot for Output 1 using the architecture = 3-3 -3-1 with R2 = 0.999 obtained using (a) HC sampling technique (b) K-fold based technique

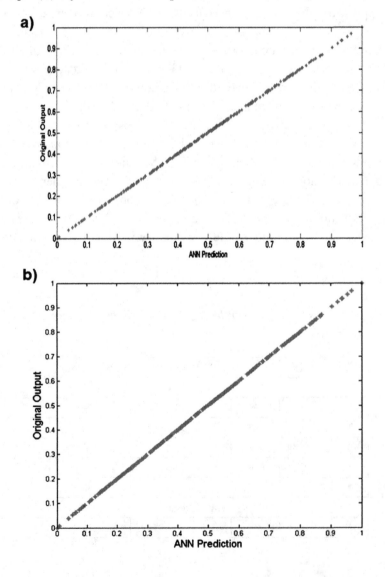

Figure 11. Parity plot for Output 2 using the architecture = 3-7-3-1-1 with R2 = 0.995 obtained using (a) HC sampling technique (b) K-fold based technique

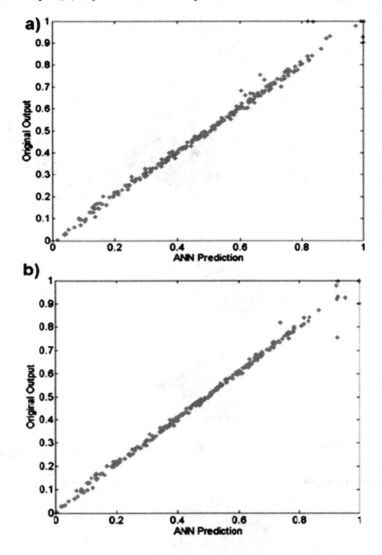

Figure 12. Contour plots of Output-1(left) and 2 (right) with respect to two inputs at a time

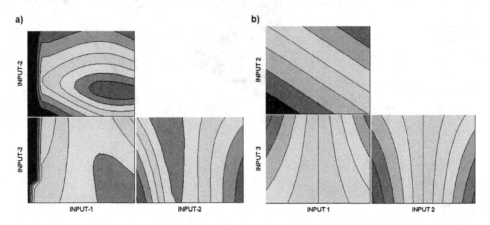

Figure 13. Evolution of ANN surface for Output 1 with sample size for HC based method

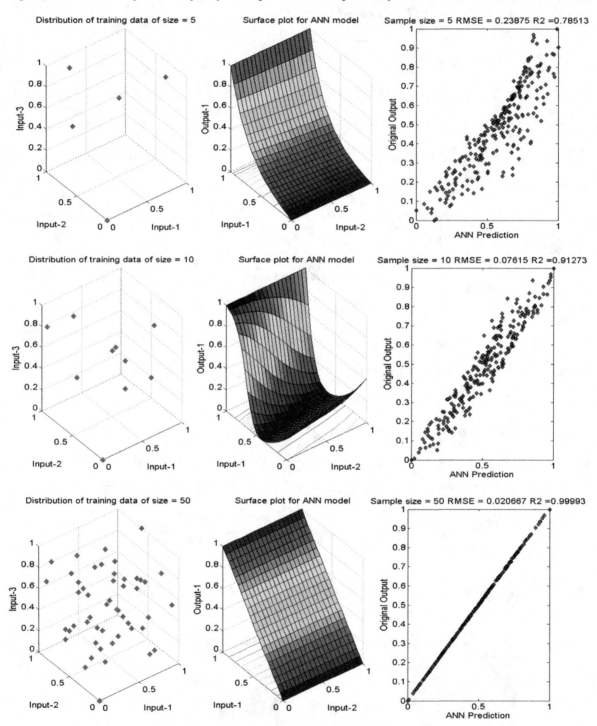

The evolution of the ANN surrogates with increment in sample size for output 1 is shown in Figure 13 for HC sampling method. This figure shows the distribution of the sample points in the three dimensional space in the left subfigure, the surface plot of the formed ANN surrogate model in center while the parity plot of the corresponding ANN surrogate is depicted in the right subfigure.

Step 2

The second step is to replace the sintering model with ANN surrogate models in conventional optimization algorithm and compare the obtained PO fronts

The ANN surrogate models obtained using the Sample Size Determination approach based on HC sampling and K-fold based methods for both the outputs are then allowed to replace the original sintering model in the conventional optimization algorithm. The NSGA II simulation runs were completed in no time and the final Pareto Optimal front comparisons are shown in Figure 14.

Figure 14. PO front comparison of optimization using ANN surrogate built by HC based sampling method, K-Fold based sampling method and original first principle Sintering model

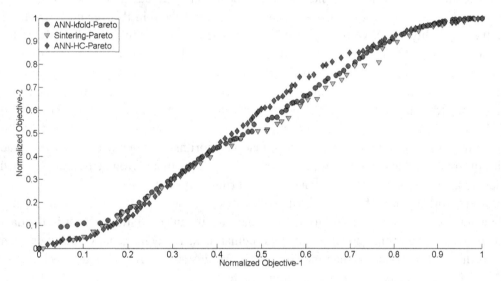

For the sake of obtaining a clear cut qualitative estimation of the result observed in Figure 14, the inputs of the PO points obtained using the ANN surrogate based optimization using both HC based sampling and K-fold based sampling are sent to the original sintering model and the corresponding outputs are compared to measure the RMSE values. An average RMSE (averaged over output 1 and 2) of 0.05 and 0.01 were obtained for HC and K-fold based methods, respectively. A significant work reported previously in the literature by one of authors (Mitra, 2013) suggested using the combination of ANN surrogates along with the original model in NSGA II algorithm while optimizing the sintering model. This hybrid based optimization resulted in nearly 45-60% savings in computational time. Since the ANN surrogates were built only during the optimization runs, the resultant ANN surrogates, despite predicting with higher accuracies, emulate the original model in only a specified zone guided by the optimizer in the feasible search space. However, the proposed surrogate building algorithm in this work, builds the

ANN surrogate models which emulate the first principle model over the entire domain specified by the training set. Thus, the ANN models in the current paper are generic enough as opposed to the simpler models built in the works of Mitra (2018) which are highly specific to only optimization algorithm. The work which essentially used the hybrid ANN – GA based optimization resulted in 700 function calls thereby concurring to the fact that the surrogate models obtained in the current work, despite being superior in terms of parsimonious predictions, are nearly 2 times faster than the former ones. All these results speak out the capability of the proposed novel parameter free surrogate building algorithm and the ANN surrogate based optimization of complex methods. Although all the simulations were carried out in Intel(R) Xeon(R) CPU E5-2690 0 @ 2.90GHz (2 processors) 128 GB RAM machine, the algorithm presented in this work displays a huge scope of parallelization which would increase the speed of the algorithm by several folds, thereby enabling the optimization process online

FUTURE RESEARCH DIRECTIONS

Surrogate assisted optimization is one of the emerging trends and serves as a potential tool in cases of complex optimization. Lack of physics based models in many practical situations is quite common scenario in industries. The data based models are thus of great help in this regard. The authors have explored the possibility of ANNs, one of the efficient classification methods, for their ability to qualify as potential surrogates. The proposed algorithm could build intelligent and efficient feed forward neural networks, which allowed for the online implementation of complex industrial process optimization. This successful implementation of Multi layered Perceptron networks as surrogates provides immense boost to the vision of parameter free surrogate building and optimization. Although the methods presented in this article are confined to steady state data, surrogate building can easily be extended to dynamic case studies. The development of Sample Size Determination algorithm without disturbing the characteristic properties of time series data along with the parameter free dynamic surrogate building algorithm can be considered as the subsequent future work for the current proposal.

The current work assumes the data to be noise-less which is far from practical situation. Thus a considerable extension of this work could to be to account for the uncertainties present in the data which might arise mainly due to the model parameters, human centric phenomena, or other environmental aspects. Further a comparison of such method with existing state of art techniques such as RCGPLM and RCMARS would justify the scope of its applicability.

CONCLUSION

A systematic approach for enabling the online optimization of complex industrial processes by making use of surrogate based optimization methods has been proposed. ANNs have been specifically chosen due to their robustness and inherent potential to capture the behaviour of any complicated nonlinear system. Since ANNs have a large number of parameters exposed to tuning ability of an expert user for its success, there was a necessity for developing a parameter free surrogate building algorithm, which would minimize the human intervention thereby reducing potential errors and making the tuning process universal. In the proposed approach, authors made use of only the data generator, could either be a simulation model or an experimental setup as input, and estimated all other parameters viz. (a) architecture of

ANN, (b) sample size required by the ANN, (c) maximum possible accuracy of prediction, (d) a robust sampling plan and (e) transfer function choice for node activation etc., automatically using an intelligent multi-objective optimization based framework. The prime objective of this novel algorithm apart from being parameter free was to be fast enough to ensure online optimization. To achieve this, three different approaches of Sample Size Determination have been proposed, which would speed up the process of this rate determining step. Finally, all these three different versions of Sample Size Determination have been utilized to find the surrogate models for a complicated nonlinear sintering process, utilized for successful operation of the blast furnace in the steel plants. The results of the surrogate based optimization revealed that all three surrogate based optimization methods were 4 to 7 times faster than the conventional method. The hyper cube sampling based parameter free ANN-surrogate algorithm reduced the function evaluations by a dramatic 70% clearly making way for online optimization of the considered industrial sintering model. It makes way for an intelligent design of ANN surrogates eliminating the heuristic based assumptions, thus enables the practical implementation of online optimization of the complex industrial processes.

ACKNOWLEDGMENT

The authors would like to acknowledge the Indian Institute of Technology for continuous support and Ministry of Human Resources and Development for funding the project.

REFERENCES

Asl, S. H., Ahmadi, M., Ghiasvand, M., Tardast, A., & Katal, R. (2013). Artificial neural network (ANN) approach for modeling of Cr (VI) adsorption from aqueous solution by zeolite prepared from raw fly ash (ZFA). *Journal of Industrial and Engineering Chemistry, 19*(3), 1044–1055. doi:10.1016/j.jiec.2012.12.001

Assefi, P., Ghaedi, M., Ansari, A., Habibi, M. H., & Momeni, M. S. (2014). Artificial neural network optimization for removal of hazardous dye Eosin Y from aqueous solution using Co 2 O 3-NP-AC: Isotherm and kinetics study. *Journal of Industrial and Engineering Chemistry, 20*(5), 2905–2913. doi:10.1016/j.jiec.2013.11.027

Azargoshasb, H., Mousavi, S. M., Amani, T., Jafari, A., & Nosrati, M. (2015). Three-phase CFD simulation coupled with population balance equations of anaerobic syntrophic acidogenesis and methanogenesis reactions in a continuous stirred bioreactor. *Journal of Industrial and Engineering Chemistry, 27*, 207–217. doi:10.1016/j.jiec.2014.12.037

Badel, M., Angorani, S., & Panahi, M. S. (2011). The application of median indicator kriging and neural network in modeling mixed population in an iron ore deposit. *Computers & Geosciences, 37*(4), 530–540. doi:10.1016/j.cageo.2010.07.009

Betiku, E., & Taiwo, A. E. (2015). Modeling and optimization of bioethanol production from breadfruit starch hydrolyzate vis-à-vis response surface methodology and artificial neural network. *Renewable Energy, 74*, 87–94. doi:10.1016/j.renene.2014.07.054

Bevrani, H., Habibi, F., & Shokoohi, S. (2012). ANN-based self-tuning frequency control design for an isolated microgrid. In *Meta-Heuristics Optimization Algorithms in Engineering, Business, Economics, and Finance* (p. 357).

Deb, K. (2001). Nonlinear goal programming using multi-objective genetic algorithms. *The Journal of the Operational Research Society*, *52*(3), 291–302. doi:10.1057/palgrave.jors.2601089

Deb, K. (2002). A fast elitist non-dominated sorting genetic algorithm for multi-objective optimization: NSGA-2. *IEEE Transactions on Evolutionary Computation*, *6*(2), 182–197. doi:10.1109/4235.996017

Deb, K., Agrawal, S., Pratap, A., & Meyarivan, T. (2000, September). A fast elitist non-dominated sorting genetic algorithm for multi-objective optimization: NSGA-II. In *Proceedings of the International Conference on Parallel Problem Solving From Nature* (pp. 849-858). Springer Berlin Heidelberg. 10.1007/3-540-45356-3_83

Deb, K., Sindhya, K., & Hakanen, J. (2016). Multi-objective optimization. In Decision Sciences: Theory and Practice (pp. 145-184). CRC Press. doi:10.1201/9781315183176-4

Dostál, P. (2014). The use of soft computing in management. In Handbook of research on novel soft computing intelligent algorithms: Theory and practical applications (pp. 294-326).

Douguet, D. (2010). e-LEA3D: A computational-aided drug design web server. In *Nucleic Acids Research*. PMID:20444867

Dua, V. (2010). A mixed-integer programming approach for optimal configuration of artificial neural networks. *Chemical Engineering Research & Design*, *88*(1), 55–60. doi:10.1016/j.cherd.2009.06.007

Esfandian, H., Samadi-Maybodi, A., Parvini, M., & Khoshandam, B. (2016). Development of a novel method for the removal of diazinon pesticide from aqueous solution and modeling by artificial neural networks (ANN). *Journal of Industrial and Engineering Chemistry*, *35*, 295–308. doi:10.1016/j.jiec.2016.01.011

Esmaeili, R., & Dashtbayazi, M. R. (2014). Modeling and optimization for microstructural properties of Al/SiC nanocomposite by artificial neural network and genetic algorithm. *Expert Systems with Applications*, *41*(13), 5817–5831. doi:10.1016/j.eswa.2014.03.038

Espinet, A., Shoemaker, C., & Doughty, C. (2013). Estimation of plume distribution for carbon sequestration using parameter estimation with limited monitoring data. *Water Resources Research*, *49*(7), 4442–4464. doi:10.1002/wrcr.20326

Fattahi, M., Kazemeini, M., Khorasheh, F., & Rashidi, A. (2014). Kinetic modeling of oxidative dehydrogenation of propane (ODHP) over a vanadium–graphene catalyst: Application of the DOE and ANN methodologies. *Journal of Industrial and Engineering Chemistry*, *20*(4), 2236–2247. doi:10.1016/j.jiec.2013.09.056

Forrester, A., Sobester, A., & Keane, A. (2008). *Engineering design via surrogate modelling: a practical guide*. John Wiley & Sons. doi:10.1002/9780470770801

Friedman, J. H. (1991). Multivariate adaptive regression splines. *Annals of Statistics*, *19*(1), 1–67. doi:10.1214/aos/1176347963

Giri, B. K., Pettersson, F., Saxén, H., & Chakraborti, N. (2013). Genetic programming evolved through bi-objective genetic algorithms applied to a blast furnace. *Materials and Manufacturing Processes*, *28*(7), 776–782. doi:10.1080/10426914.2013.763953

Hafizi, A., Ahmadpour, A., Koolivand-Salooki, M., Heravi, M. M., & Bamoharram, F. F. (2013). Comparison of RSM and ANN for the investigation of linear alkylbenzene synthesis over H 14 [NaP 5 W 30 O 110]/SiO 2 catalyst. *Journal of Industrial and Engineering Chemistry*, *19*(6), 1981–1989. doi:10.1016/j.jiec.2013.03.007

Hagan, M. T., & Demuth, H. B. (2002). Mark Beale. In *Neural network design* (pp. 19-22).

Haykin, S. (1994). *Neural Networks: A Comprehensive Foundation*. New York: Macmillan College Publishing Company.

Himmelblau, D. M. (2000). Applications of artificial neural networks in chemical engineering. *Korean Journal of Chemical Engineering*, *17*(4), 373–392. doi:10.1007/BF02706848

Jin, Y. (2011). Surrogate-assisted evolutionary computation: Recent advances and future challenges. *Swarm and Evolutionary Computation*, *1*(2), 61–70. doi:10.1016/j.swevo.2011.05.001

Jin, Y., & Sendhoff, B. (2009). A systems approach to evolutionary multiobjective structural optimization and beyond. *IEEE Computational Intelligence Magazine*, *4*(3), 62–76. doi:10.1109/MCI.2009.933094

Johnson, M. E., Moore, L. M., & Ylvisaker, D. (1990). Minimax and maximin distance designs. *Journal of Statistical Planning and Inference*, *26*(2), 131–148. doi:10.1016/0378-3758(90)90122-B

Jones, D. R. (2001). A taxonomy of global optimization methods based on response surfaces. *Journal of Global Optimization*, *21*(4), 345–383. doi:10.1023/A:1012771025575

Karimi, H., & Ghaedi, M. (2014). Application of artificial neural network and genetic algorithm to modelling and optimization of removal of methylene blue using activated carbon. *Journal of Industrial and Engineering Chemistry*, *20*(4), 2471–2476. doi:10.1016/j.jiec.2013.10.028

Khan, M. J. H., Hussain, M. A., Mansourpour, Z., Mostoufi, N., Ghasem, N. M., & Abdullah, E. C. (2014). CFD simulation of fluidized bed reactors for polyolefin production–A review. *Journal of Industrial and Engineering Chemistry*, *20*(6), 3919–3946. doi:10.1016/j.jiec.2014.01.044

Kleijnen, J. P. (2008). Response surface methodology for constrained simulation optimization: An overview. *Simulation Modelling Practice and Theory*, *16*(1), 50–64. doi:10.1016/j.simpat.2007.10.001

Kohavi, R. (1995, August). A study of cross-validation and bootstrap for accuracy estimation and model selection. Ijcai, 14(2), 1137-1145.

Lechuga, G. P., Martínez, F. V., & Ramírez, E. P. (2016). Stochastic Optimization of Manufacture Systems by Using Markov Decision Processes. In Handbook of Research on Modern Optimization Algorithms and Applications in Engineering and Economics (pp. 185–208). Hershey, PA: IGI Global. doi:10.4018/978-1-4666-9644-0.ch007

Miriyala, S. S., Mittal, P., Majumdar, S., & Mitra, K. (2016). Comparative study of surrogate approaches while optimizing computationally expensive reaction networks. *Chemical Engineering Science*, *140*, 44–61. doi:10.1016/j.ces.2015.09.030

Miriyala, S. S., Pantula, P. D., Majumdar, S., & Mitra, K. (2016, January). Enabling online optimization and control of complex models through smart surrogates based on ANNs. In *Proceedings of the 2016 Indian Control Conference (ICC)* (pp. 214-221). IEEE. 10.1109/INDIANCC.2016.7441131

Mitra, K. (2013). Evolutionary surrogate optimization of an industrial sintering process. *Materials and Manufacturing Processes*, *28*(7), 768–775. doi:10.1080/10426914.2012.736668

Mitra, K., Majumdar, S., & Raha, S. (2004). Multiobjective optimization of a semibatch epoxy polymerization process using the elitist genetic algorithm. *Industrial & Engineering Chemistry Research*, *43*(19), 6055–6063. doi:10.1021/ie034153h

Mogilicharla, A., Chugh, T., Majumdar, S., & Mitra, K. (2014). Multi-objective optimization of bulk vinyl acetate polymerization with branching. *Materials and Manufacturing Processes*, *29*(2), 210–217. doi:10.1080/10426914.2013.872271

Mogilicharla, A., Mittal, P., Majumdar, S., & Mitra, K. (2015). Kriging surrogate based multi-objective optimization of bulk vinyl acetate polymerization with branching. *Materials and Manufacturing Processes*, *30*(4), 394–402. doi:10.1080/10426914.2014.921709

Morris, M. D. (1991). Factorial sampling plans for preliminary computational experiments. *Technometrics*, *33*(2), 161–174. doi:10.1080/00401706.1991.10484804

Morris, M. D., & Mitchell, T. J. (1995). Exploratory designs for computational experiments. *Journal of Statistical Planning and Inference*, *43*(3), 381–402. doi:10.1016/0378-3758(94)00035-T

Nain, P. K., & Deb, K. (2002). A computationally effective multi-objective search and optimization technique using coarse-to-fine grain modeling. In Proceedings of the 2002 ppsn workshop on evolutionary multiobjective optimization comprehensive survey of fitness approximation in evolutionary computation.

Nath, N. K., & Mitra, K. (2005). Mathematical modeling and optimization of two-layer sintering process for sinter quality and fuel efficiency using genetic algorithm. *Materials and Manufacturing Processes*, *20*(3), 335–349. doi:10.1081/AMP-200053418

Nuchitprasittichai, A., & Cremaschi, S. (2013). An algorithm to determine sample sizes for optimization with artificial neural networks. *AIChE Journal. American Institute of Chemical Engineers*, *59*(3), 805–812. doi:10.1002/aic.13871

Özmen, A., & Weber, G. W. (2012, November). Robust conic generalized partial linear models using RCMARS method-A robustification of CGPLM. In N. Barsoum, D. Faiman, & P. Vasant (Eds.), AIP Conference Proceedings (Vol. 1499, pp. 337–343). AIP. doi:10.1063/1.4769011

Özmen, A., Weber, G. W., Çavuşoğlu, Z., & Defterli, Ö. (2013). The new robust conic GPLM method with an application to finance: Prediction of credit default. *Journal of Global Optimization*, *56*(2), 233–249. doi:10.100710898-012-9902-7

Pombo, N., Garcia, N., Bousson, K., & Felizardo, V. (2017). Machine Learning Approaches to Automated Medical Decision Support Systems. In Artificial Intelligence: Concepts, Methodologies, Tools, and Applications (pp. 1653-1673). Hershey, PA: IGI Global. doi:10.4018/978-1-5225-1759-7.ch066

Rao, R. B., Fung, G., & Rosales, R. (2008, April). On the dangers of cross-validation. An experimental evaluation. In *Proceedings of the 2008 SIAM International Conference on Data Mining* (pp. 588-596). Society for Industrial and Applied Mathematics. 10.1137/1.9781611972788.54

Ries, J., Beullens, P., & Wang, Y. (2012). Instance-specific parameter tuning for meta-heuristics. In *Meta-Heuristics Optimization Algorithms in Engineering, Business, Economics, and Finance* (p. 136).

Roy, N. K., Potter, W. D., & Landau, D. P. (2006). Polymer property prediction and optimization using neural networks. *IEEE Transactions on Neural Networks*, *17*(4), 1001–1014. doi:10.1109/TNN.2006.875981 PMID:16856662

Shojaeimehr, T., Rahimpour, F., Khadivi, M. A., & Sadeghi, M. (2014). A modeling study by response surface methodology (RSM) and artificial neural network (ANN) on Cu 2+ adsorption optimization using light expended clay aggregate (LECA). *Journal of Industrial and Engineering Chemistry*, *20*(3), 870–880. doi:10.1016/j.jiec.2013.06.017

Sobol', I. Y. M. (1967). On the distribution of points in a cube and the approximate evaluation of integrals. *Zhurnal Vychislitel'noi Matematiki i Matematicheskoi Fiziki*, *7*(4), 784–802.

Tabatabaei, M., Hakanen, J., Hartikainen, M., Miettinen, K., & Sindhya, K. (2015). A survey on handling computationally expensive multiobjective optimization problems using surrogates: Non-nature inspired methods. *Structural and Multidisciplinary Optimization*, *52*(1), 1–25. doi:10.100700158-015-1226-z

Tang, B. (1993). Orthogonal array-based Latin hypercubes. *Journal of the American Statistical Association*, *88*(424), 1392–1397. doi:10.1080/01621459.1993.10476423

Taylan, P., Weber, G. W., Liu, L., & Yerlikaya-Özkurt, F. (2010). On the foundations of parameter estimation for generalized partial linear models with B-splines and continuous optimization. *Computers & Mathematics with Applications (Oxford, England)*, *60*(1), 134–143. doi:10.1016/j.camwa.2010.04.040

Vasant, P. (Ed.). (2011). *Innovation in Power, Control, and Optimization: Emerging Energy Technologies: Emerging Energy Technologies*. IGI Global.

Vasant, P. (2014). Hybrid Optimization Techniques for Industrial Production Planning: A Review. In Handbook of Research on Novel Soft Computing Intelligent Algorithms: Theory and Practical Applications (Vol. 2, pp. 41-68).

Weber, G. W., Çavuşoğlu, Z., & Özmen, A. (2012). Predicting default probabilities in emerging markets by new conic generalized partial linear models and their optimization. *Optimization*, *61*(4), 443–457. doi:10.1080/02331934.2011.654343

Yegnanarayana, B. (1994). Artificial neural networks for pattern recognition. *Sadhana*, *19*(2), 189–238. doi:10.1007/BF02811896

Yousefi, F., & Karimi, H. (2013). Application of equation of state and artificial neural network to prediction of volumetric properties of polymer melts. *Journal of Industrial and Engineering Chemistry, 19*(2), 498–507. doi:10.1016/j.jiec.2012.09.001

Yuce, B., & Mastrocinque, E. (2016). Supply Chain Network Design Using an Enhanced Hybrid Swarm-Based Optimization Algorithm. In Handbook of Research on Modern Optimization Algorithms and Applications in Engineering and Economics (pp. 95–112). Hershey, PA: IGI Global. doi:10.4018/978-1-4666-9644-0.ch003

Chapter 36
Applications of Big Data and AI in Electric Power Systems Engineering

Tahir Cetin Akinci
Istanbul Technical University, Turkey

ABSTRACT

The production, transmission, and distribution of energy can only be made stable and continuous by detailed analysis of the data. The energy demand needs to be met by a number of optimization algorithms during the distribution of the generated energy. The pricing of the energy supplied to the users and the change for investments according to the demand hours led to the formation of energy exchanges. This use costs varies for active or reactive powers. All of these supply-demand and pricing plans can only be achieved by collecting and analyzing data at each stage. In the study, an electrical power line with real parameters was modeled and fault scenarios were created, and faults were determined by artificial intelligence methods. In this study, both the power flow of electrical power systems and the methods of meeting the demands were investigated with big data, machine learning, and artificial neural network approaches.

INTRODUCTION

In today's modern societies, electric energy is an inevitable concept. Electrical energy is a social and economic requirement for the development of society. For the last thirty years, a great deal of research has been undertaken to analyze and solve the problems of electrical power systems. Most of the research is on control theory, power electronics drivers and economic analysis. In recent years, the development of artificial intelligence and its methods has made this technology applicable in many areas. In this study, some methods have been proposed in order to provide supply balance by investigating the methods of using electric power systems with artificial intelligence techniques. Research on electrical power system can be examined in two groups as modeling and analysis. In this study, fault scenarios were created by using the energy transmission line model: these defects were then determined by artificial intelligence methods.

DOI: 10.4018/978-1-6684-2408-7.ch036

BACKGROUND

Literature Review

Recent developments in energy system energy systems seek solutions for the ongoing liberalization of energy markets, optimization of power system efficiency and power quality, emergency energy demands and challenges in dispersed energy transmission lines (Hidayatullah et al., 2011; Kadar, 2013). As a solution, the connection of renewable energy systems to the power system necessitates the control of electrical power systems by artificial intelligence techniques (Fikri et al., 2018). Artificial Intelligence techniques, along with traditional analytical techniques, can significantly contribute to the solution of related problems. Recent scientific studies emphasize that an intelligent energy transmission and distribution system should be used with evolutionary programming and other artificial intelligence methods (Akinci, 2011; Jiang et al., 2016; Bogdan et al., 2009; Paracha, 2009; Russel & Norvig, 2016).

Nowadays identified as the information age, all activities performed during the day are getting recorded with several technologies. The most valid reason for this logging is to establish-confidence for the benefit of people and society, such as security and public service. However, the smart phones and watches that people carry unconsciously are continuously recording their activities in their daily life and converting them into data (Bryant, 2014; Zimmer & Kurlanda, 2017). During a regular home-based work trip, individuals who have been able to adapt to the information age allow the system to collect data as they open the security alarm of their house when they leave for work, pass by security cameras on their route to work and use their ID card to enter the workplace. During the day, all the performance at the workplace, photos taken and shared on social network by colleagues with their smart phone and data of heart rate monitoring by smart watches are constantly being recorded. Here, copious information and copious data, from the rotational speed of the industrial machine to its temperature, the profit-loss statements of the wage paid to the workers by the company and even the company's stock exchange, are recorded. In this human-machine interactive interface world, all information has the potential to be turned into data. This data eventually becomes so large that is defined as big data. Storing and analyzing processed and unprocessed data now requires special methods and tools. The recording of all these data in daily life has led to the creation of storages in massive sizes. These storages have become centers that provide specific information called cloud. The processing of this gigantic information as well as its storage enabled an important software branch to emerge that has revealed a new profession called data analytics (Begoli & Horey, 2012; Papageorgiou, 2019; Grover et al., 2018).

Data analysts undertake critical tasks such as making companies profitable by producing meaningful results from the data presented or extracting disease information from biological data. They also undertake vital tasks such as optimizing the continuity of the system by ensuring that the bearings of an industrial machine are integrally disengaged or optimizing and making plans to ensure the availability of continuous and reliable electrical energy. These tasks find their field of application in social sciences and engineering (Dong et al., 2009; Chen et al., 2014; Grover et al., 2018).

Electrical engineering has been the most affected by the development of information and communication technologies. The first input of artificial intelligence technology to electrical power engineering was with smart meters. In the first studies, smart meter and sensor technologies and data collection systems were installed on energy users (Ongsakul & Vo, 2013; Alahakoon & Yu, 2015). Thus, the data collection from the traditional data distribution systems can be performed instantaneously. Information layers were added to traditional transmission and distribution lines for the immediately analysis of the data collected. The concept of intelligent networks is expanding: this essentially concerns data collection of the sensors and the evaluation of this collected data. In order to be smarter this requires initial energy transmission lines to be traceable at every point. As a result of monitoring and data collection, it is necessary to analyze the data collected including the characterization of the data to contribute to the healthy operation of the network. Although typical data analysis can produce meaningful results for general problems, detailed analysis of multi-point information in the system may be possible by using advanced algorithms. Geographical information requests and the addition of data from meteorological information systems to the analysis data in the energy transmission lines will make a significant contribution to the energy continuity of the existing power system. These contributions will improve customer satisfaction and social welfare by offering better quality, uninterrupted energy to users (Ongsakul & Vo, 2013; Klaimi et al., 2016).

This study focuses on the approaches of artificial intelligence and big data to electrical power systems engineering.

Artificial Intelligence (AI)

Artificial Intelligence (AI) can be defined as a technology that allows machines to produce, like humans, solutions to complex problems. Today this discipline, which was first proposed by John McCarthy in 1956 at the Dartmouth Conference, is a term used in every field of technology (McCarthy, 1992; Rajarman, 2014). In general, Artificial intelligence can be examined in two categories: software that addresses a narrower area designed for a specific task and more powerful software having human cognitive abilities. The latter has the ability to recommend the best solutions to problems. It is safe to say that the advanced artificial intelligence approach started with the Turing Test developed by Alan Turing in 1950 (Turing, 1950; Li et. al., 2018).

Initially, artificial intelligence software was developed so that experiences could not be used in future activities. With the development of Artificial Neural Network (ANN) models AI has become software, which can learn, make predictions, and analyze. This method is now widely used in smart car technology and autopilot systems. Artificial intelligence technology, which can understand the decisions and reactions of people and socially connect, will be possible in the future. Automatic machines, which have been developing since the Industrial Revolution, have evolved into robots that have artificial intelligence systems and can be programmed to perform high volume tasks. Today in the health sector, artificial intelligence is used to analyze the data obtained from the patients and to determine the most economical treatments methods to reduce costs. The AI in finance applications provides financial advice by collecting personal data. It also contributes to faster decision making and more accurate document matching in the practice of law (Turing, 1950; Mijwel, 2015; Bohanec, 2009).

Artificial intelligence (AI) is now used as a common name for many intelligent computer-based techniques. AI imitates the human brain with software techniques by investigating human behavior and rules and can make decisions and control operations very quickly. AI is inspired by the human brain. Artificial intelligence techniques comprise brain science; based on neurology, software and statistics sciences. AI is a system that simulates the behavior of the human brain and solves the problems in the fastest manner. Consequently, AI can make logical, reasoning theorems and proof that can execute fast programming, natural language processing problems can solve. However, the ability of self-development is increasing day-by-day (Li & Du, 2018).

Figure 1. The relationship between artificial intelligence and other disciplines

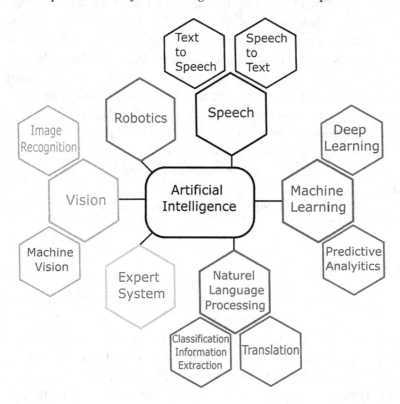

In the light of all these definitions and applications, with an ideal approach, artificial intelligence is an artificial operating system that is expected to exhibit high cognitive functions or autonomous behaviors, such as perception, learning, thinking, reasoning, problem solving, communicating, deducing and decision-making, all of which are specific to human intelligence. Figure 1 shows the relationship of artificial intelligence with other algorithms (Uliyar, 2017; Amazonaws, 2019; Brain, 2019; Ertel, 2017). Here, it is seen that AI bears a general meaning that involves machine learning and other learning algorithms.

The statistics of the artificial intelligence terms via Google are given in Figure 2 (Upwork, 2019). In-these statistics, AI, Deep Learning, ANN and Big Data were examined with data between 2004 and 2019. When data is analyzed, it is possible to understand the popularity of these terms by period. Artificial Neural Networks (ANN) was the most popular research subject in 2004 (it was known since the beginning of 1990's. In the early 2000's, Big Data and Deep Learning were limited, so the frequency of these terms is also limited. After 2012, Big Data and Deep Learning terminology-was popular in the Google search engine as well as in scientific studies. Nowadays, AI is less investigated because all these methods are grouped under the AI method (Google, 2019).

All artificial intelligence methods are closely related to the science of statistics. Moreover, the basis of these methods; machines learn from experience, adapt to new inputs, predict next steps, and perform many tasks as would human beings. Autonomous vehicles, chess-playing computers, and mobile phones can instantly translate into many examples. The real application of-artificial intelligence techniques that can make the right decisions on our behalf is industry. Artificial intelligence techniques are very practical and economical in heavy working conditions, which require intensive calculation as a result of decision-

Figure 2. Google statistics for investigating Artificial Intelligence methods (Google, 2019)

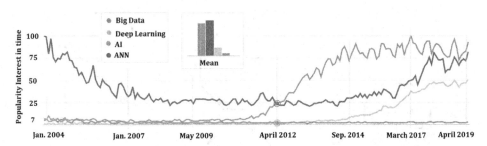

making mechanisms (Min, 2010; Witten et al., 2017). In areas where heavy industrial machines are used, industrial robots go beyond their software and apply the information they learned from previous experiences in different situations. AI can enable existing products to behave intelligently through software. Usually, these products are not sold as an individual application but they are being developed with the software that will provide AI capabilities to the product. Today, mobile phones are the best example for this definition. Perform programming of collected data using AI progressive learning algorithms. The algorithm here learns the structure of the data as a classifier or determinant. These learning algorithms reveal the ability of the AI structure to teach and teach. When it meets new data, it can adjust the model and make adjustments and adjustments in the model (Witten et al., 2017).

With its multi-layer or multi-layered structure (with a network of neural networks), AI provides more detailed analysis of data. Deep learning algorithms provide these. In an environment where massive amounts of data are received, learning systems can be created with direct data. The fact is that data that is applied to deep learning algorithms is more accurate. AI can analyze the data and bring them into intellectual property while making conclusions. With AI, the role of data is increasing, and it is the basis for the formation of new sectors and markets to increase competition in the sector.

Nowadays, the optimization and decision-making problems that arise in the stages of generation, delivery and marketing of energy in electric power systems are solved by artificial intelligence approaches (Zhang et al., 2018). These approaches and algorithms ensure that the system is more reliable, economical and efficient, and provide more comfortable facilities to users. Most of the smart grid approaches are artificial intelligence-oriented systems.

Machine Learning (ML)

Safety is the most important element in the electrical power systems and their functions. The need for deregulation of the power system and the increased need to operate systems closer to the operating limits require the use of more systematic approaches to safety to keep reliability at an acceptable level. It has been proven that a multiple control security application and evaluation can only be made with ML applications (Uliyar, 2017).

ML, a sub-branch of Artificial Intelligence, was developed from digital learning and model recognition studies. ML investigates the working systems of algorithms that can learn and make estimations using the data. These in contrast to static algorithms, have the ability to take decisions by making database estimates from model-based sample inputs. ML uses supervised learning and unsupervised learning methods to make inferences (Figure 3) (Mathworks, 2019; Sahu, 2018).

Figure 3. ML Learning Algorithm

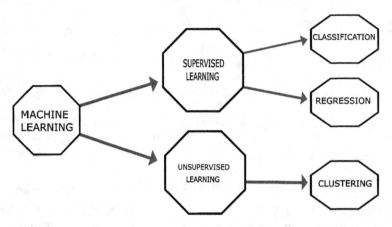

When scientific research revealed that the machines had to learn the data after a certain stage, the problems started to be solved by various symbolic approaches. In particular, this method has found use in automated medical diagnostic systems. These developments have allowed ML to be considered as a separate area and have been redeveloped since 1990. The aim of accepting ML as a separate field was to find solutions to practical problems with a new perspective. In this sense, the methods used by data mining are significantly overlapping. However, here; machine learning focuses on estimates made from data learned based on known features. Data mining focuses on revealing unknown (historical) features in the data. It can be described as feature extraction from these databases. In fact, data mining uses the general ML methods to extract information (Alpaydin, 2010).

Figure 4. Machine Learning and other related areas

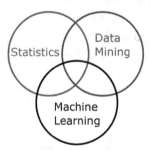

The general relationship graph given in Figure 4 shows the association between the science of machine learning, data mining and statistics (Papageorgiou, 2019). In fact, when artificial intelligence and other learning algorithms are involved in this relationship analysis, a much more sociable and complex structure will emerge. ML in the near future is expected to develop by focusing on cyber physical systems, online learning, sensor integration methods, smart electricity networks, data acquisition, data integration and state imaging. Optimizing transmission and distribution networks in electrical power systems is a versatile field for ML applications. ML offers very practical approaches to solving optimization problems.

Artificial Neural Networks (ANN)

Artificial neural networks (ANN) are parallel computing devices that emerged with the idea of making a computer model of the brain. The goal of artificial neural networks is to develop a system for making complex computer operations faster than traditional systems: in other words, artificial neural networks. Inspired by the human brain, mathematical modeling of the learning process emerged. Therefore, the mathematical model of a neuron in artificial neural networks is an important step for artificial intelligence applications. Each element in the biological nerve cell is shown in Figure 6. However, the simplified version of biological systems is used for the mathematical model. In fact, a biological nerve cell is known to perform more complex biological and chemical processes. In the mathematical model structure, there are three sections in general terms. These are input, network structure and output. The network structure and hidden layers of the system can be composed of many layers depending on the type of problem (Figure 5.) (Haykin, 2009).

Figure 5. Block Diagram of Nervous System

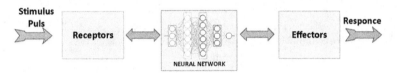

Effector transforms the electrical impulses produced by the brain into appropriate responses as organisms. Information in the central neural network is evaluated in the direction of forward and backward feeding between the receptor and response nerves to produce appropriate responses. In this respect, the biological nervous system is similar to the closed loop control system. The general usage area of artificial neural networks is decision making, classification and optimization but it is also used in pattern recognition and optimization problems. (Brain, 2019).

In the 1980s, the idea of a machine thinking like a person demonstrated a great improvement in the artificial neural networks technology in the 1990's. ANN is a subset of artificial intelligence. It generalizes the data and when introduced to unknown data and is capable of making a decision based on what it has previously learned. Today, because of its learning and generalization features, ANN has the ability to successfully solve complex problems in every field. The first computational model on which ANN is based was Pitts' and McCulloch's work (Pitts & McCulloch, 1947; Hertz et al., 2018; Shanmuganathan, & Samarasinghe, 2016). In 1954, Farley and Clark developed a model that can react and adapt to warnings within a network (Farley & Clark, 1954; Clark & Farley, 1955). The first programmable computer in the literature is Z3 developed by Zuse. Zuse also developed a first high-level programming language. (Giloi, 1997). Although the first digital computer was developed in 1941, the first neural computer was completed in 1950 (Paluszek & Thomas, 2017). While the work on the ANN models until the 1980s was very inefficient, in 1985 ANN finally obtained its well-known structure. Artificial neural networks have been applied in all fields, from economy to health and engineering, with high success rate in researches such as forecasting, estimation, failure analysis (Akinci et al., 2012; Nogay, 2016; Shahid et al., 2019; Yuce & Avci, 2017; Nogay et al., 2012). ANN is the approach that reflects the nervous system model in living organisms to the electronic environment with a programming discipline. In this sense, it has the skills of learning, remembering and updating the knowledge learned. In order to model the behaviors of the nervous system, the model should be built in compliance with its structure. Accordingly, scientists have used the structure of the nervous system to model the ANN. The biological structure of a simple nerve cell is shown in Figure 6 (Brain, 2019) and the mathematical structure of a neuron is given in Figure 7. (Richard, 2018).

Figure 6. Biological Representation of a Nerve Cell

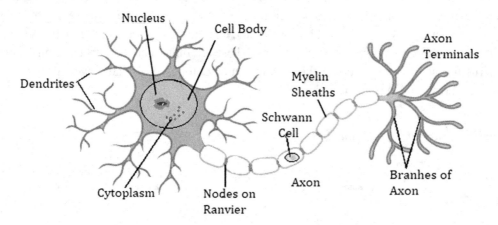

Dendrites are electrically passive arms that collect the signals from other cells and are the entrance to the system. Here, the axon is an electrically active body in which output pulses are generated and also the output of the system that provides one-way transmission. The synapse provides the connection of the axons of the cells with other dendrites. The myelin sheath acts as an insulating material that affects the spreading speed. The nucleus allows the periodic reproduction of the signals along the axon (Haykin, 2009; Richard, 2018; Akbal, 2018). The mathematical model of a human nerve cell is given in Figure 7.

Figure 7. Mathematical Representation of a Nerve Cell

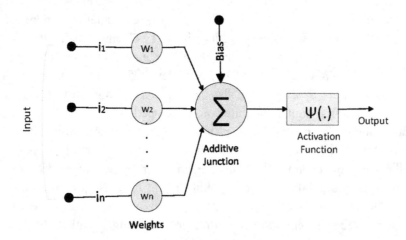

$$S = w1.i1 + w2.i2 + \ldots\ldots + wn. \in -\theta = \sum_{i=1}^{n} wi.ii - \theta \tag{1}$$

ANN is composed of various forms of artificial nerve cells connected to each other and is usually arranged in layers. As hardware, it can be implemented as software in electronic circuits or computers. In accordance with the brain's information processing method, ANN is a parallel-scattered processor capable of collecting information after a learning process, linking weights between cells, and storing and generalizing this information. The learning process involves learning algorithms that allow ANN's weights to be regenerated to achieve the desired goal. Figure 6. shows an artificial neural network model (Brain, 2019; Haykin, 2009; Richard, 2018). It can be understood that ANN is derived from its parallel scattered structure as well as its ability to learn and generalize. Generalization implies that ANN also produces appropriate responses for entries that are not encountered during learning.

In accordance with its structure, ANN can use many different algorithms such as Back-propagation Algorithm, Flexible Propagation Algorithm, Delta Algorithm, Rapid Propagation Algorithm and the Levenberg-Marquardt Method (Haykin, 2009; Richard, 2018). These algorithms are successful approaches that can predict the demands in the electrical power systems in advance.

In electrical power systems, load flow planning, anticipation of energy demands and taking the necessary action are very important issues. The current load on the energy transmission lines, which are fed by either hydroelectric power plants or by renewable power plants, needs to be transferred safely to needy users. In determining the immediate and the short-term need of this load, the artificial neural networks approach performs very well compared to traditional methods.

Deep Learning (DL)

Although there are solutions to a number of power control and decision-making problems in electrical power systems with different algorithm approaches, the studies on searching for the algorithm with the fastest and highest performance ratio are still in progress. While the ANN method has a high success rate, it has been observed that in terms of decision-making speed it has a very low performance when introduced to excessive visual data (Brownlee, 2013; Schmidhuber, 2015; Suk, 2017).

Although there are solutions to power control and decision-making problems in electrical power systems with different approach algorithms, the studies on seeking the algorithm with the fastest and highest performance ratio are still in progress. Although the ANN method has a high success rate, it has been observed that it has very low performance when faced with high visual data in terms of decision-making speed (Papageorgiou, 2019; Brownlee, 2013).

Nowadays as artificial intelligence, machine learning and deep learning are being compared with human intelligence, these terms are often confused with each other. Although artificial intelligence and machine learning are usually perceived as synonyms, they are quite different from each other (Magesh & Swarnalatha, 2017; Mocanu et al., 2016). In 1950, Alan Turing performed a study on whether machines could think or not. With the Turing Test he assembled, it was possible to determine if a machine was intelligent. If a person could not distinguish whether the interaction encountered was from a machine or a human, then that machine was considered as being intelligent. In 1956, John McCarthy premised a more in-depth study of artificial intelligence (McCarthy, 1992; Rajarman, 2014).

While ML is capable of processing on a single layer, DL has the ability to operate on several layers at the same time. Thus, DL can use a group of machine learning algorithms simultaneously and achieve a result in a single operation. DL algorithms are very rapid and successful in language processing and image recognition by adopting large output layers and using decision trees. The relationship between AI, ML and DL is given in Figure 8. (Brain, 2019).

Common faults in electrical power systems are load flow problems, energy supply problem, malfunctions occurring in transmission lines, faults occurring in generator and production plants. These faults can also be caused by a combination of several different faults. In other words, faults that have occurred it may also contain a lot of different failure. These are classified as difficult to understand and difficult to solve. The detection time of the fault and the repair of the fault is very important. Detection of a fault in a power grid consisting of long transmission lines is a very difficult task. Detection of the fault can only be made by analyzing a number of numerical signals and image data. If there are images between the data for the analysis of the fault, deep learning is mandatory.

In case such visual data processing takes time, the approaches made with deep learning algorithms offer much faster and more reliable solutions. This method provides brand-new approaches to the analysis of future needs in electrical power systems.

Figure 8. Relationship between Artificial Intelligence and Deep Learning

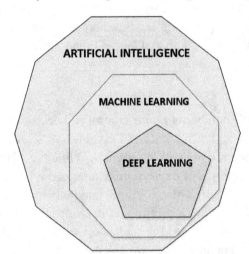

Big Data (BD)

The data produced during the transmission, distribution and marketing of electricity includes details that cannot be calculated by conventional methods. Storage and analysis of produced information are among the most important research topics (Begoli, & Horey, 2012; Zhang, et al., 2018). The amount of information produced and stored at the global level is too large to calculate. BD focuses on what can be done with the data rather than the data size. In this sense, BD provides the best decision by time and money optimization while using data from any source. With big data analysis, manufacturers can improve quality, reduce losses and obtain key roles in the financial market. It is also used in government institutions to extract information from many databases such as tax transactions, legal procedures, traffic congestion and medical applications (Chen et al., 2014; Samuel et al., 2015; Magesh & Swarnalatha 2017; Zhou et al., 2016).

Currently, as data is constantly produced by our mobile devices, software records, cameras, microphones, social media and all of our movements on the internet, it is transformed into stored data (Begoli & Honey, 2012). The continuous growth of data in terms of size, diversity and complexity has made it possible for the big data produced to become a focus of solutions with cloud computing. In addition, the internet of objects, big data and cloud computing provide rapid solutions to users. All these approaches are applied in other engineering fields as well as in the field of electrical power systems to analyze the data collected from consumers, meet the energy demands and solve the dynamic problems during the production of electrical energy. All data on the system is collected by Supervisory Control and Data Acquisition (SCADA) in electrical power systems. These data are collected in two groups. The first group is electrical data such as active power, reactive power, current, voltage, capacity changes. The second group consists of the mechanical and material data of all components on the energy transmission and distribution system. The size of these data is quite large. For this reason, the data collection time and the sampling time in the analysis are limited so that the collected data can be analyzed. These analyzes can only be done using big data methods. The method has limitations in terms of real-time processing of data and engineering operations in today's technology. In addition to all these electrical and mechanical variables, the data produced by renewable energy plants in energy systems are affected by meteorological factors. This complex situation allows too many parameters to be generated. This complexity is made possible by big data methods with the topology of the data and the strategy of processing the collected data with artificial intelligence methods.

METHODOLOGY

Today, due to non-linear loads, electrical networks are very complex. Faults on the network must be solved immediately. In this study's methodology it was found necessary to determine all the difficulties in the application of different electrical power systems of energy transmission lines. In the system center, a systematic combination of modern power electronic drivers for system theory, control engineering and optimization was prepared. Thus, advanced network integration was provided for interface elements for power electronics circuits. Modulation methods for medium and high-power lines in the network were developed and control and artificial intelligence algorithms formulated and implemented. In addition, flexible distributed operational strategies were created for next generation power systems. These strategies were based on artificial intelligence. Advanced software techniques were elaborated for power system analysis safety assessment, and preventive control. Finally, software-was designed to provide the economic supply demand balance for the network. In addition, a real energy transmission line model was created by the artificial intelligence methods to identify failure.

FINDINGS AND ANALYSIS

Applications of Electrical Power Systems Engineering

In recent years, data has become a very important criterion in electrical power systems engineering. Due to the variable (dynamic) load on the consumer side, generation, transmission and distribution of electrical energy requires instant planning and control. Currently, in addition to the classical energy generation methods, renewable energy sources feed the network. Large power plants, renewable energy sources and micro plants supply the power grid. The system also has storage units. The flow of energy in the network is monitored at every stage up until the end user. In energy distribution stations, SCADA systems are widely used to monitor the flow of energy (Manimuthu & Ramadoss, 2019). SCADA systems are uniquely used for observation. In the last ten years, many SCADA systems have been computer controlled. However, optimization and control cannot be done with the SCADA system. In order to control a system, it must have a data collection system. Collected data should be processed for analysis, control and planning. Data collected from the electricity network (production, transmission and distribution) are evaluated by various statistical analyses. The data collected here is considered as big data. Collecting and processing this data is done using special methods rather than classical methods (Wang et al., 2016). Mobile power stations are added or removed according to the demand. The development of renewable energy resources also increases investment incentives in this area. Many energy companies want to add a renewable energy source to the grid. Consumption also tends to increase on the user side. This dynamic change can only be controlled by artificial intelligence-based systems. Data management and real time monitoring systems for gas turbines are now being used in power plants (Frantz & Hunt, 2003). In most of these plants, real-time data analysis, data model results, optimization and dependency-analysis are performed.

The artificial neural networks method is widely-utilized to determine the location of the wind, power plant and planning, the production in concordance with energy markets as well as estimating the wind energy power source.

Figure 9. The real electric power network systems

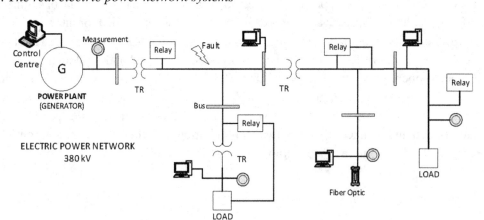

Figure 9 shows a real electric transmission line model. All operations on the power transmission line are controlled by the central control system which is also seen on the model. There are also sub-stations for communication in certain centers.-Fiber-optic transmission lines are utilized for communication and measurement at many points. The simulations can be simulated on-line. Short circuit failures for faults are investigated. In addition, the types of faults that occur can be classified by artificial intelligence methods.

Figure 10 shows the voltage fluctuation in the measuring stations of the three-phase normal system. This system has a voltage amplitude value of 380kV. However, the high amplitude region in the first second's results from the initial conditions. As it is known, in the initial conditions, the electrical machines can reach the amplitude values which are 3 to 5 times more than their nominal values. Figure 11 shows the analysis graphs for the normal voltage fluctuation given in Figure 10.

Figure 10. Normal voltage condition for measurement station 1

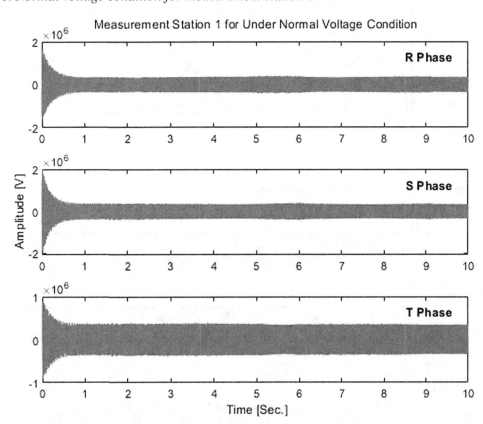

Figure 12. shows the voltage fluctuation of the three phase-ground short circuit faults of the three-phase system. Figure 13. shows the analysis graphs of the faulty voltage fluctuation given in Figure 12.

Data versus graphics normal and defective condition can be clearly identified. The control center opens the circuit to protect the system as soon as this graph reaches the data. The type and location of the fault can also be detected.

Figure 11. Normal voltage condition for measurement station 1

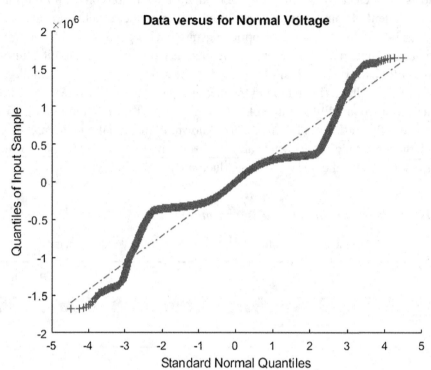

Figure 12. Fault voltage condition for measurement station 1

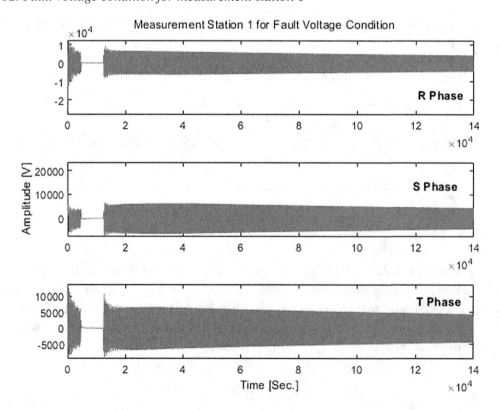

Figure 13. Data versus for normal voltage condition

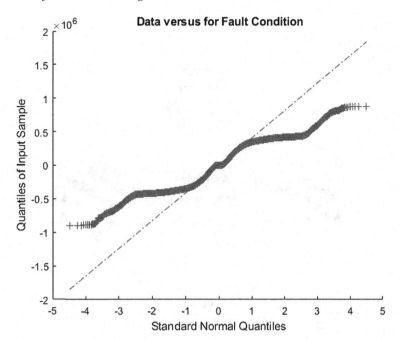

Optimization in Electric Power System

Electrical power engineering has the most comprehensive historical background in the basic electrical engineering science. Here, it is the main area of interest to deliver the energy from the production to the end-user. Therefore, it must use many different numerical optimization methods for the transmission and distribution of energy. By optimizing the system, the energy-generating plant reduces costs and provides enormous economic benefits. In optimization, the cost of fuel, energy security, continuity, quality criteria are calculated. Its main purpose is to minimize the various limitations of the enterprise and to minimize the cost of production in energy systems. It is also to increase the efficiency and efficiency of renewable energy sources in energy production. Figure 14 illustrates the relationship between artificial intelligence and management systems in electrical power systems (Zhao & Zhang, 2016).

Recently, artificial intelligence-based methods are widely used to solve optimization problems in electrical power systems (Paracha, 2009; Ongsakul & Vo, 2013). These methods have great advantages compared to the solution of problems that cannot be solved by the classical method. Advances in software and hardware technology have led to the development of artificial intelligence-based methods. The solution of problems such as control, planning, estimation, timing in electrical power systems is-facilitated by AI. This concerns especially the problem of optimization which is considered the most fundamental problem of electric power systems. The continuous change in the number of users and the energy consumed in the electrical system requires instant programming for optimal distribution of energy. AI methods provide excellent opportunities to system engineers in planning and analysis and even in predictive fault detection (Banu & Suja, 2012; Hessine & Saber, 2014; Zhang et al., 2018).

Figure 14. The relationship between artificial intelligence and management systems in electric power systems

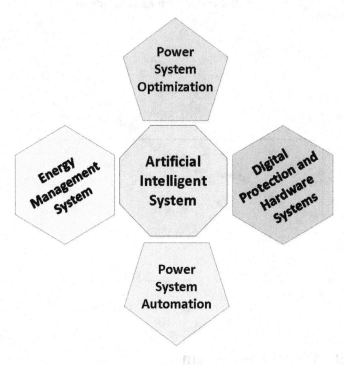

In the structure of a typical electrical power system, there are generators, AC and DC transmission systems, distribution systems load and Flexible AC Transmission Systems (FACTS) devices. The main purpose is to plan the low-cost expansion of the electrical power system. Therefore, supply and demand must be met at minimum cost. In order to achieve a variable supply-demand balance, components need to be continuously optimized by controlling artificial intelligence. In this planning, all parameters such as demand, energy transmission line, FACTS layout, environmental effects should be considered.

FUTURE RESEARCH DIRECTIONS

In the future, electric power systems will gain many different dimensions in both transmission and distribution stages. In this sense, it is thought that the components used in the transmission and distribution side in electric power systems will change greatly. The fiber-optics and components of the transmission lines provide the following benefits:

- Losses in energy transmission line is reduced.
- Collect quality data online.
- Reduces the danger of high voltage on power transmission lines.

However, fiber-optic technology has a high cost and requires large investment. Fiber-optics and technology imply the meaning of the integration of power systems engineering with communications engineering applications. In addition, research on superconductivity is not possible to apply the super-conductivity technology to power transmission lines in the short and medium term. All these researches show that the transmission and distribution technology of electric energy will change dramatically in the future. The use of renewable energy sources will be used in the production of electricity. Renewable energy-based power plants will be installed in places where thermal based power plants will be reduced. Renewable power plants will be installed in smart micro-grid systems by establishing them close to local areas. All these electrical networks will be equipped with artificial intelligence methods and energy users will be provided with high quality and cheap electric energy. All electrical energy systems will be equipped with traceable and controllable systems over the cloud (Akinci et al., 2019).

CONCLUSION

In recent years artificial intelligence techniques and big data have found a field of application in every field. Electrical engineering and technologies are at the top of these fields. Many scholars consent that transmission, distribution, planning and economics of electrical energy require enormous expenses and involve very important engineering problems. The production, transmission and distribution of electrical energy, which together are called electrical power engineering are subjects that separately demand optimization and analysis. Estimation of the energy demands in electric power systems and estimation of future predictions are possible with artificial intelligence methods. Since the data produced by the electricity users are massive, processing and evaluation can only be analyzed with the big data approach. In this study, the ANN method and DL algorithms approach were investigated in order to meet the power flow and demands in the electric power systems. Also, the types of short circuit faults on electrical power network were determined by artificial intelligence methods.

REFERENCES

Akbal, B. (2018). Hybrid GSA-ANN methods to forecast sheath current of high voltage underground cable lines. *Journal of Computers*, *13*(4), 417–425.

Akinci, T. C. (2011). Short term speed forecasting with ANN in Batman, Turkey. *Elektronika ir Elektrotechnika*, *107*(1), 41–45.

Akinci, T. C., Korkmaz, U., Turkpence, D., & Seker, S. (2019). Big Data Base Energy Management System. *3rd International Symposium on Innovative Approaches in Scientific Studies-Engineering and Natural Sciences, (ISAS 2019)*, 48.

Akinci, T. C., Nogay, H. S., & Yilmaz, O. (2012). Application of artificial neural networks for defect detection in ceramic materials. *Archives of Acoustics*, *37*(3), 279–286. doi:10.2478/v10168-012-0036-1

Alahakoon, D., & Yu, X. (2015). Smart electricity meter data intelligence for future energy systems: A survey. *IEEE Transactions on Industrial Informatics*, *12*(1), 1–12.

Alpaydin, E. (2010). *Introduction to machine learning*. Cambridge, MA: The MIT Press.

Amazonaws. (2019). *Machine Learning*. Retrieved from https://wordstream-files-prod.s3.amazonaws.com/s3fs-public/machine-learning.png

Banu, G., & Suja, S. (2012). ANN based fault location technique using one end data for UHV lines. *European Journal of Scientific Research, 77*(4), 549–559.

Begoli, E., & Horey, J. (2012). Design Principles for effective knowledge discovery from big data. In *Joint working conference on Software Architecture & 6ᵗʰ European Conference on Software Architecture*, (pp. 215-218). Helsinki, Finland: IEEE. 10.1109/WICSA-ECSA.212.32

Bogdan, Ž., Cehil, M., & Kopjar, D. (2009). Power system optimization. *Energy, 32*(6), 955–960. doi:10.1016/j.energy.2007.01.004

Bohanec, M. (2009). Decising Making: A computer-science and information- technology viewpoint. *Interdisciplinary Description of Complex Systems, 7*(2), 22–37.

Brain, C. (2019). *The artificial intelligence ecosystem*. Retrieved from https://medium.com/@b.james-curry/the-artificial-intelligence-ecosystem-f11107f7b306

Brownlee, J. (2013). *A tour of machine learning algorithms*. Retrieved from https://machinelearning-mastery.com/a-tour-of-machine-learning-algorithms/

Bryant, A. (2014). Thinking about the information age. *Informatics, 1*(3), 190–195. doi:10.3390/informatics1030190

Chen, M., Mao, S., & Liu, Y. (2014). Big data: A survey. *Mobile Networks and Applications, 19*(2), 171–209. doi:10.100711036-013-0489-0

Clark, W. A., & Farley, B. G. (1955). Generalization of Pattern Recognition in a Self-Organizing System. *Western Joint Computer Conference*, 86-91. 10.1145/1455292.1455309

Dong, Z., Zhang, P., Ma, J., Zhao, J., Ali, M., Meng, K., & Yin, X. (2009). *Emerging techniques in power system analysis*. Beijing: Springer, Higher Education Press.

Ertel, W. (2017). *Introduction to artificial intelligence*. Springer International Publishing. doi:10.1007/978-3-319-58487-4

Farley, B. G., & Clark, W. A. (1954). Simulation of self-organizing systems by digital computer. *Transaction of the IRE*, 76-84. 10.1109/TIT.1954.1057468

Fikri, M., Cheddadi, B., Sabri, O., Haidi, T., Abdelaziz, B., & Majdoub, M. (2018). *Power Flow Analysis by Numerical Techniques and Artificial Neural Networks. IEEE, Renewable Energies, Power Systems & Green Inclusive Economy*. Casablanca, Morocco: REPS-GIE.

Frantz, R. J., & Hunt, S. R. (2003). *System and method for monitoring gas turbine plants*. General Electric Company. Retrieved from https://patents.google.com/patent/US6542856B2/en

Giloi, W. K. (1997). Konrad Zuse's Plankalkül: The first high-level, "non von Neumann" programming language. *IEEE Annals of the History of Computing, 19*(2), 17–24. doi:10.1109/85.586068

Google. (2019). Retrieved from https://ai.google/research

Grover, V., Chiang, R. H. L., Liang, T. P., & Zhang, D. (2018). Creating strategic business value from big data analytics: A research framework. *Journal of Management Information Systems*, *35*(2), 388–423. doi:10.1080/07421222.2018.1451951

Haykin, S. (2009). *Neural Networks and Learning Machines*. Pearson-Prentice Hall Publish.

Hertz, J., Krogh, A., & Palmer, R. G. (2018). *Introduction to the theory of neural computation*. CRC Press. doi:10.1201/9780429499661

Hessine, M. B., & Saber, S. B. (2014). Accurate fault classifier and locator for EHV transmission lines based on artificial neural networks. *Mathematical Problems in Engineering*, *2*, 1–19. doi:10.1155/2014/240565

Hidayatullah, N. A., Stojcevski, B., & Kalam, A. (2011). Analysis of distributed generation systems, smart grid technologies and future motivators influencing change in the electricity sector. *Smart Grid and Renewable Energy*, *2*(03), 216–229. doi:10.4236gre.2011.23025

Jiang, Y., Liu, C. C., & Xu, Y. (2016). Smart distribution systems. *Energies*, *9*(4), 297–317. doi:10.3390/en9040297

Kadar, P. (2013). Application of optimization techniques in the power system control. *Acta Polytechnica Hungarica*, *10*(5), 221–236.

Khan, N., Yaqoob, I., Haskem, I. A. T., Inayat, Z., Ali, W. K. M., Alam, M., ... Gani, A. (2014). Big data: Survey, technologies, opportunities, and challenges. *The Scientific World Journal*, 1–18. PMID:25136682

Klaimi, J., Rahim-Amoud, R., Merghem-Boulahia, L., & Jrad, A. (2016). Energy Management Algorithms in Smart Grids: State of the Art and Emerging Trends. *International Journal of Artificial Intelligence and Applications*, *7*(4), 25–45. doi:10.5121/ijaia.2016.7403

Li, D., & Du, Y. (2018). *Artificial Intelligence with uncertainty*. CRC Press, Taylor & Francis.

Li, L., Zheng, N. N., & Wang, F. Y. (2018). On the crossroad of artificial intelligence: A revisit to Alan Turing and Norbert Wiener. *IEEE Transactions on Cybernetics. Early Access*, 1-9.

Magesh, G., & Swarnalatha, P. (2017). Big data and its applications: A survey. *Research Journal of Pharmaceutical, Biological and Chemical Sciences*, *8*(2), 2346–2358.

Manimuthu, A., & Ramadoss, R. (2019). Absolute Energy Routing and Real-Time Power Monitoring for Grid-Connected Distribution Networks. *IEEE Design & Test, 36*(2). Retrieved from https://ieeexplore.ieee.org/abstract/document/8636507

Mathworks. (2019). *Machine learnin with Matlab*. Retrieved from https://www.mathworks.com/campaigns/offers/machine-learning-with-matlab.html

McCarthy, J. (1992). Reminiscences on the history of time sharing. *IEEE Annals of the History of Computing*, *14*(1), 19–24.

Mijwel, M. M. (2015). *History of artificial intelligence*. Retrieved from https://www.researchgate.net/publication/322234922_History_of_Artificial_Intelligence

Min, H. (2010). Artificial intelligence in supply chain management: Theory and applications. *International Journal of Logistics: Research and Applications*, *13*(1), 13–39. doi:10.1080/13675560902736537

Mocanu, E., Nguyen, P. H., Gibescu, M., & Kling, W. L. (2016). Deep learning for estimating building energy consumption. *Sustainable Energy. Grids and Networks*, *6*, 91–99.

Nogay, H. S. (2016). Determination of leakage reactance in monophase transformers using by cascaded neural network. *Balkan Journal of Electrical & Computer Engineering*, *4*(2), 89–96.

Nogay, H. S., Akinci, T. C., & Eidukeviciute, M. (2012). Application of artificial neural networks for short term wind speed forecasting in Mardin, Turkey. *Journal of Energy in Southern Africa*, *23*(4), 2–7. doi:10.17159/2413-3051/2012/v23i4a3173

Ongsakul, W., & Vo, D. N. (2013). *Artificial Intelligence in Power System Optimization*. CRC Press.

Paluszek, M., & Tomas, S. (2017). *MATLAB machine learning*. Apress Pub. doi:10.1007/978-1-4842-2250-8

Papageorgiou, A. (2019). *Exploring the meaning of AI, data science and Machine Learning with the latest Wikipedia Clickstream*. Retrieved from https://towardsdatascience.com/exploring-the-meaning-of-ai-data-science-and-machine-learning-with-the-latest-wikipedia-5fea5f0a2d46

Paracha, Z. J., Kalam, A., & Ali, R. (2009). A novel approach of harmonic analysis in power distribution networks using artificial intelligence. In *International Conference on Information and Communication Technologies*, (157-160). Karachi, Pakistan: Academic Press. 10.1109/ICICT.2009.5267198

Pitts, W., & McCulloch, W. S. (1947). How we know universals, the perception of auditory and visual forms. *The Bulletin of Mathematical Biophysics*, *9*(3), 127–147. doi:10.1007/BF02478291 PMID:20262674

Rajarman, V. (2014). John McCarthy-father of artificial intelligence. *Asia Pacific Mathematics Newsletter.*, *4*(3), 15–20.

Richard, N. (2018). *The differences between Artificial and Biological Neural Networks*. Retrieved from https://towardsdatascience.com/the-differences-between-artificial-and-biological-neural-networks-a8b46db828b7

Russell, S. J., & Norvig, P. (2016). *Artificial intelligence a modern approach*. Pearson Education Limited.

Sahu, D. K. (2018). *Supervised and unsupervised learning in data mining*. Retrieved from https://www.digitalvidya.com/blog/supervised-and-unsupervised-learning-in-data-mining/

Samuel, S. J., Koundinya, P. V. P., Sashidhar, K., & Bharathi, C. R. (2015). A Survey on big data and its research challenges. *Journal of Engineering and Applied Sciences (Asian Research Publishing Network)*, *10*(8), 3343–3347.

Schmidhuber, J. (2015). Deep Learning in Neural Networks: An Overview. *Neural Networks*, *61*, 85–117. doi:10.1016/j.neunet.2014.09.003 PMID:25462637

Shahid, N., Rappon, T., & Berta, W. (2019). Applications of artificial neural networks in health care organizational decision-making: A scoping review. *PLoS One*, *14*(2), 1–22. doi:10.1371/journal.pone.0212356 PMID:30779785

Shanmuganathan, S., & Samarasinghe, S. (2016). *Artificial neural network modelling*. Springer International Publishing. doi:10.1007/978-3-319-28495-8

Suk, H. I. (2017). An introduction to neural networks and deep learning. In *Deep Learning for Medical Image Analysis*. Academic Press.

Turing, A. M. (1950). Computing machinery and intelligence. *Mind*, *4*(256), 433–460. doi:10.1093/mind/LIX.236.433

Uliyar, S. (2017). *A Primer: oracle intelligent bots - powered by artificial intelligence*. Oracle. Retrieved from http://www.oracle.com/us/technologies/mobile/chatbots-primer-3899595.pdf

Upwork. (2019). *Overview of artificial intelligence and natural language processing*. Retrieved from https://www.upwork.com/hiring/for-clients/artificial-intelligence-and-natural-language-processing-in-big-data/

Wang, P., Liu, B., & Hong, T. (2016). Electric load forecasting with recency effect: A big data approach. *International Journal of Forecasting*, *32*(3), 585–597. doi:10.1016/j.ijforecast.2015.09.006

Witten, I. H., Frank, E., Hall, M. A., & Christopher, J. P. (2017). *Data mining: Practical machine learning tools and techniques*. Cambridge, MA: Morgan Kaufman-Elsevier.

Yuce, H., & Avci, K. (2017). Establishment of diagnosing faults and monitoring system with neural networks in air conditioning systems. *The Journal of Cognitive Systems*, *2*(1), 63–69.

Zhang, Y. Z., Huang, T., & Bompard, E. F. (2018). Big data analytics in smart grids: A review. *Energy Informatics*, *1*(8), 1–24.

Zhao, Z., & Zhang, X. (2016). Artificial intelligence applications in power system. Advances in intelligent systems research. In *2ⁿᵈ International Conference on Artificial Intelligence and Industrial Engineering*, (133, 158-161). Atlantis Press.

Zhou, K., Fu, C., & Yang, S. (2016). Big data driven smart energy management: From big data to big insights. *Renewable & Sustainable Energy Reviews*, *56*, 215–225. doi:10.1016/j.rser.2015.11.050

Zimmer, M., & Kurlanda, K. K. (2017). *Internet research ethics for the social age: New challenges, cases, and contexts*. Peter Lang International Academic Publishers. doi:10.3726/b11077

This research was previously published in AI and Big Data's Potential for Disruptive Innovation; pages 240-260, copyright year 2020 by Engineering Science Reference (an imprint of IGI Global).

Chapter 37
Application of ANN and PSO Swarm Optimization for Optimization in Advanced Manufacturing:
A Case With CNC Lathe

Nehal Dash
Birla Institute of Technology, India

Sanghamitra Debta
Birla Institute of Technology, India

Kaushik Kumar
Birla Institute of Technology, India

ABSTRACT

CNC lathe is one of the best machining techniques which provides us with better accuracy and precision. Considering speed, feed and depth of cut as inputs and among all possible outputs, in the present work Material Removal Rate and Surface Roughness would be considered as the factors those affect the quality, machining time and cost of machining. Design of experiments (DOE) would be carried out in order to minimize the number of experiments. In the later stages application of Artificial Neural Network (ANN) and Particle Swarm Optimization (PSO) would be used for the Optimization in the advanced manufacturing considering CNC lathe. The obtained output would be minimized (for surface roughness) and maximized (for MRR) using Artificial Neural Network (ANN) and Particle Swarm Optimization (PSO). The combination of various input parameters for the same would be identified and a comparison would be drawn with the various above methods.

DOI: 10.4018/978-1-6684-2408-7.ch037

INTRODUCTION

Computer Aided Numerical Controlled (CNC) machining has become an essential piece of machining industry in the present scenario. By applying various conventional machining techniques the exactness, precision and accuracy could not be obtained as accomplished through CNC. Yet at the same time there is a space for blunders in a CNC machine and essentially the expertise and experience of the labourer matters to get the measurements right. Also the machine execution and item attributes obtained by CNC machining are not ensured to be adequate in all cases. From different parameters which could be considered as the output of the machining operations, the material removal rate (MRR) and Surface roughness (SR) were considered for this work as the factors specifically influences the quality, machining cost and the machining hour rate.

Conventionally in all cases for any machining techniques an operator decides the input parameters like speed, feed and depth of cut, depending upon type of job and the sliding controls are controlled by hand. In a CNC machine the controls and sliding movements are controlled by motors using computer programs. CNC machine consists of machine control unit (MCU) which decides the various factors like speed, feed, depth of cut, coolant on and off, selection of tools etc. In the form of numerical data commands are issued by MCU to the motors that position the slides and tool according to the input provided.

CNC machining no doubt is one of the finest machining techniques still there are room of errors in this. These errors can be avoided by using skilled and experienced workers. In the present work Material Removal Rate (MRR) and Surface Roughness (SR) are considered as the most influencing factors for the quality of machining, cost of machining and the rate of machining.

Finding the optimized set of inputs for obtaining the relevant outputs has always been a challenge for researchers since years. Aggarwal et al. (2008); Asilturk et al. (2016); Liu et al. (2010); Dutta and Majumdar (2010) and Singh and Kumar (2006) are some of the researchers who have tried to optimize the machining parameters incorporating various methods like Genetic Algorithm, Simulated Annealing method, Multi objective Evolutionary Algorithm etc. Cayda (2010) evaluated the machining of AISI 4340 steel by varying cutting tool and Negrete et al. (2013) tried to optimize the cutting parameters minimizing the cutting power.

Machining is broadly classified as Conventional and Non Conventional machining. Conventional machining has a direct contact of tool and the work piece. It involves physical contact between the cutting tool and the material to be processed. Non Conventional Machining uses modern and advanced technology for processing of materials. Tools such as laser beams, electric beams, electric arc, infrared beam, plasma cutting etc are used in Non conventional machining processes. Non conventional tool are more accurate than the conventional machining tools, with a better tool life and also doesn't lead to any noise pollution. Although they are having a complex setup and spare machining parts are difficult to avail in case of breakdown.

In this work the authors have performed the multi-objective optimization of Material Removal Rate and Surface Roughness using Artificial Neural Network and Particle Swarm Optimization, where in the fundamental objective functions (Regression Equations) of MRR and SR are used in for minimizing and maximizing SR and MRR respectively. On application of these Optimization techniques it was very suitable for the mass production of components of machines where there is a fast movement of consumer goods. In some cases these optimal values developed using PSO in this work can be adopted or the regression equation can be used for the cases that are having some variation in the levels of input parameters for prediction of output parameters.

OPERATIONS OF CNC LATHE

CNC lathe is a machine that rotates the work piece on an axis in order to carry on various operations like facing, turning, knurling etc. Some of the other common applications of lathe are metal spinning, metal working, turning, grooving etc. The most common input parameters those are considered before performing any operations on lathe are the speed, feed and depth of cut. Each lathe operation has got some factors those are needed to be considered before performing the work. In order to avoid the mishandlings and mishaps these factors are needed to be kept in mind. For achieving the precision with every cut desired speed, depth and feed of lathe machine were changed. Types of lathe operations are Facing, Tapering, Parallel turning, Parting etc.

NECESSITY OF OPTIMIZATION

In the present scenario technologies are developing for application of advanced manufacturing methods into industrial field. In order to achieve these advanced manufacturing criteria industries always need to optimize the various process parameters so that both money and time are saved. Many researchers like Asilturk et al. (2016); Korkut et al. (2004); Mahapatra et al. (2006); Suhail et al. (2010); Vasant et al. (2016); Vasant et al. (2011) have performed optimization considering various process parameters in order to obtain best set of process parameters those can be used for advance manufacturing techniques. Keeping in mind the operations of CNC lathe, MRR and Surface Roughness always are considered as the important parameters where the main aim was to get the minimum Surface Roughness and maximum MRR. For getting these desired machining characteristics process parameters like depth of cut, feed rate and cutting speed are to be finalized in advance.

BACKGROUND OF WORK AND RELATED WORKS

The two parameters those are most effective for the manufacturing methodologies in CNC Lathe are Surface Roughness and Material Removal Rate. Researchers like Asilturk et al. (2016); Korkut et al. (2004); Mahapatra et al. (2006); Suhail et al. (2010); have identified the Design of Experiments and performed optimization for obtaining the optimum values of the machining parameters where they have applied several optimization techniques like Taguchi, Grey Taguchi, Genetic Algorithm etc. Other machining applications like Plasma Arc Cutting, Electrical Discharge Machining, Electro-Chemical Machining etc. where some of these optimization algorithms are applied by researchers. In this present work the authors have applied the concept of Design of Experiments to minimize the number of experiments to be carried out and hence further the ANN and PSO can be carried out like Vo and Schegner (2012) had carried out the PSO in Optical power flow phenomenon, for obtaining the optimum values of Surface Roughness and Material Removal Rate.

OPTIMIZATION METHODS

In this work authors have tried to provide solution to the problems using Artificial Neural Network (ANN) and Particle Swarm optimization (PSO).

Articial Neural Network (ANN)

In machine learning, artificial neural networks (ANNs) are a cluster of models enlivened by biological neural networks and are utilized to surmised functions that can rely on upon a substantial number of sources of info called as inputs and are for the most part obscure or not known. ANNs are introduced as frameworks of interconnected "neurons" which trade messages between each other. The associations or connections have weights that can be tuned, making neural nets versatile and adaptive to inputs and equipped for learning. The capacity of the ANNs to precisely estimated obscure capacities to know the unknown function. Neural systems have been utilized to unravel a wide assortment of assignments that are difficult to understand utilizing standard manage based programming. Some of the applications of ANN are for solving the Travelling Saleman's problems, Security and loan applications, Market predictions etc.

Various applications of ANN are inspired biologically from the computer programs in order to stimulate in a way exactly the human brain does. It gathers or accumulates the knowledge by detecting the pattern and relationship. From numerous single units, an ANN was formed and these are connected with weights, which are consisting of the neural structure those are organized in form of layers. Each processing element has weighted inputs, transfer function and output. These weights are the parameters those can be adjusted hence this allows us to say that a neural network is parameterized system.

Among all the Neural network configurations Rosenblatt (1958) perceptron is the most used artificial neuron. It is based on the models those are proposed by McCulloch and Pitts (1943) which are nonlinear in nature. Here the neurons are considered as the set of input units or weights, for summing of the input parameters an added is required and a function for activation which can either be linear or non linear. The input parameters or signals are generally defined as x_i, where $i = 0, 1, 2,..., N_i$ and its results correspond to the level; of internal activity of a neuron net_j where $x_0 = +1$ is considered as the polarization potential of neurons. y_j is the output parameter or signal and the activation function response $\phi(.)$ to the activation net_j. Equations (1) and (2) are the characteristic equations for ANN.

$$net_j = \sum_{i=0}^{N_i} w_{ji} \cdot x_i \qquad (1)$$

$$y_j = \Phi(net_j) \qquad (2)$$

Modular ANN is purely based on the principle of divided to rule/conquer. Here a large number of tasks are divided into sub tasks so that they can be solved in easier way. Modular ANN can be defined as set of experts, whose decisions are combined in order to obtain better solutions than the solutions those are obtained individually. Hence it leads to a machine with better performance.

Some of the reasons for adopting ANN for this work are the advantages those were obtained from this technique. Some of the advantages are the classification of unknown samples is very easy in ANN.

It is also useful for finding the inner structure of measurement space to which the samples belong and making direct and inverse models for prediction of behaviour or effects of the unknown samples.

Particle Swarm Optimization (PSO)

Particle Swarm Optimization (PSO) is a computational technique that optimizes an issue by iteratively attempting to enhance an applicant arrangement with respect to a given measure of value. It takes care of an issue by having a populace of candidate solutions, here named particles, and moving these particles around in the inquiry space as indicated by basic numerical formulae over the particle's position and velocity. Every particle's development is affected by its neighbourhood best known position, but on the other hand is guided toward the best known positions in the search space, which are upgraded as better positions are found by other particles. This is relied upon to move the swarm toward the best arrangements or solutions. Particle swarm optimization is considered as an efficient, robust and one of the simplest optimization techniques. In many cases it is found that PSO studies are empirical and it generally concentrates on the understanding of particle trajectories.

Particle Swarm Optimization method was first introduced by Kennedy and Eberhart (1955). It was found to be robust in complex systems and was derived from social and psychological theory. Here each particle is considered as valueless particle in the search space and keeps the tract of the coordinates in the problem space for obtaining the best possible solution, instead of using the evolutionary operators for manipulating individual particle.

Some of the advantages of applying PSO are it can be applied into both scientific research and engineering use. Secondly, since it lacks any overlapping and calculations related to mutation the search that has to be carried out is smooth and is related to speed of the particle. This also indicates that the speed of the particle is very fast. Also the calculation in PSO is very simple as compared to the other developing algorithms and hence it occupies bigger optimization ability and can be completed easily. PSO adopts the real number code and is directly decided by the solution.

Some of the disadvantages of PSO are this method often leads to partial optimization which causes less exactness in the speed and direction. Secondly, Non coordinate system problems like providing solution to energy field and moving rules of particles in energy field etc. cannot be solved by PSO.

EXPERIMENTATION

Input Process Parameters to Be Considered

In the present work cutting speed, feed rate and depth of cut would be taken into consideration as the input machining parameters. Table 1 shows the process parameters Depth of Cut, Feed Rate and Cutting Speed with their levels for turning.

Table 1. Process parameters and their levels for turning

Process Parameters	Unit	Level 1	Level 2	Level 3
Depth of Cut	mm	1	1.5	2
Feed Rate	mm/rev	0.15	0.2	0.25
Cutting Speed	m/min	50	100	150

Output Considered

MRR

It is the rate at which the material is removed from the work-piece. The weight of the work-piece material is recorded before carrying out the machining process and is compared with the weight after machining (using Equation 3).

$$\text{MRR (gm/min)} = \frac{Wi - Wf}{t} \tag{3}$$

where,

W_i = Initial weight of work piece material (gms)
W_f = Final weight of work piece material (gms)
t = Time taken for machining in minutes

For various industrial applications MRR is most important parameter. These applications desires larger MRR, hence it was optimized based on larger for better condition.

Surface Roughness

Surface roughness is usually defined as the deviation of a surface from an ideal level and is defined according to international standard (ISO 4287:1997). Surface roughness regularly abbreviated to roughness, is a part of surface texture. It is evaluated by the deviations I the direction of vector of a real surface from its optimal frame. If deviations are vast, the surface is rough; if they are found to be small, the surface is smooth. Roughness is regularly thought to be the high-frequency, short-wavelength part of a deliberately measured surface. Practically speaking it is frequently important to know both the amplitude and frequency to guarantee that a surface is fit for a purpose.

Always smaller SR is desired for most of the machining operations. Hence it is optimized on basis of smaller for better condition. The Arithmetic Mean Surface Roughness Ra is depicted in Figure 1.

Figure 1. Arithmetic Mean Surface Roughness Ra

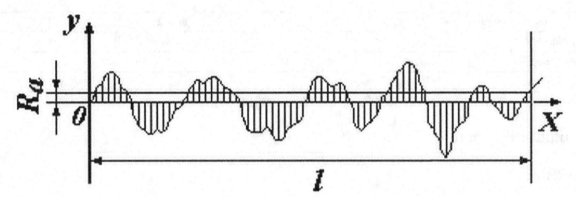

Material

Tungsten Carbide and mild steel (SAE 1020) are identified as tool and material respectively. It can be seen that turning operation is carried out in steps. Considering a constant time period of 1 min. Calculation was performed for MRR. The length gets varied with change in feed and speed. To save the material machining is carried out in a single sample machining with more than one set of parameters. Some of the machined samples are as sown in Figure 2.

Figure 2. Machined samples

Machine and Instrument

CNC lathe utilized for the experimentation was EMCO concept Turn 105 (Figure 3). Although there are different methods of measurement of surface roughness (Correia and Davim (2011); in this work a concept of Mitutoyo SJ201 instrument (Figure 4) was used to measure surface roughness (R_a) and weight measurement was done using a Talysurf (Make – Taylor Hobson, UK) and Mettle Toddler electronic balance (Figure 5).

Figure 3. EMCO concept turn 105

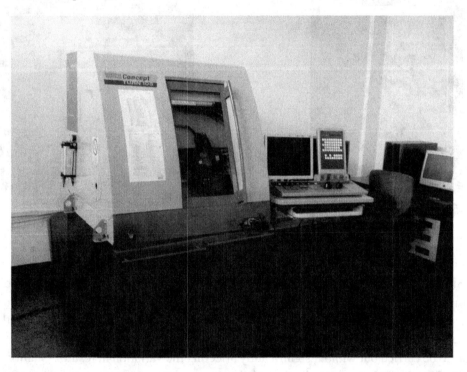

DESIGN OF EXPERIMENTS

In order to find out the relationship between the factors those affect the process and output of the process, Design of Experiments (DOE) is considered as the best systematic process. It helps us in processing the inputs in order to optimize the output. Some of the terms those are used in the DOE process are controllable and non controllable input factors, responses, blocking, replication, hypothesis testing, interaction etc. Input parameters/factors that can be changed over time complexity are called Controllable factors, where as the factors those cannot be modified in an experiment are called as Uncontrollable factors. In order to understand how these factors are going to affect the response, they are needed to be recognized in advance. In order to reduce the cost of design by speeding up the process of design, and avoiding the late changes in design methodology, reducing the material for product development and labour complexity experimental design methods are adopted. DOE also helps in reducing the manufacturing cost by minimizing the variation in the process and reducing rework, scrap and needs for inspections.

Figure 4. Mitutoyo SJ201

Figure 5. Mettle toddler electronic balance

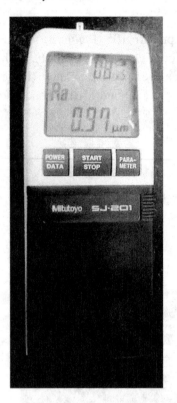

This work always required a correct Design of Experiments. For this Taguchi method of DOE was followed. Since it was considered as a methodology for formulating the engineering problems using statistical models, this methodology specified the methods or procedures particularly in case of hypothesis testing. For acquiring the best process parameters it was always necessary to perform the required number of experiments. But this statistical method allowed the researchers to minimize the number of experiments to be carried out without significantly affecting the variation in results. Quality control and process control methods also used statistics as tool for managing conformance to various specifications of manufacturing processes and products. The main aim of this DOE is to examine the data and suggest and help in planning of future experiments. In various real-time engineering applications the goal is more often to optimize a process or product, hence incorporating this no doubt reduced the time of experimentation and also cost of experimentation. Some other fields of applications of DOE are Time and methods engineering which uses statistics for studying repetitive operations in manufacturing systems, Reliability engineering for checking the reliability of the system or product by performance of its intended functions, Probabilistic design which involves use of probability in product development process, System identification methods also uses statistical methods for building mathematical models which includes the optimal design of experiments for efficiently generating the informative data for fitting of these mathematical models.

The three input process parameters are Depth of Cut (A), Feed Rate (B) and Cutting Speed (C) were considered in the study with three equally spaced variables in an operating range. In this present work, research work experimentation was planned following the Taguchi's design of Experiments method.

Taguchi (1990) suggested that total degrees of freedom (DOF) of selected orthogonal array must be greater than or equal to total DOF of standard orthogonal array (OA). Here total DOF for four factor and their interactions in 20 (4x2+3x4) and standard OA for four factors with three levels are L9 with 8 DOF and L27 with 26 DOF. Thus L27 OA has been selected for experimental work and tabulated in Table 2.

Table 2. DOE using L27 orthogonal array

Exp. No.	Depth of Cut (A) Mm	Feed Rate (B) mm/rev	Cutting Speed (C) m/min	SR	MRR	Exp. No.	Depth of Cut (A) mm	Feed Rate (B) mm/rev	Cutting Speed (C) m/min	SR	MRR
1	1.0	0.15	50	0.000190	0.2820	15	2.0	0.20	100	0.001917	0.2625
2	1.5	0.15	50	0.000990	0.1539	16	1.0	0.25	100	0.001295	0.2505
3	2.0	0.15	50	0.000443	0.1813	17	1.5	0.25	100	0.002807	0.2398
4	1.0	0.20	50	0.000456	0.1172	18	2.0	0.25	100	0.001420	0.2066
5	1.5	0.20	50	0.000503	0.1556	19	1.0	0.15	150	0.001920	0.3835
6	2.0	0.20	50	0.000532	0.1504	20	1.5	0.15	150	0.002339	0.4520
7	1.0	0.25	50	0.000408	0.1298	21	2.0	0.15	150	0.002722	0.3416
8	1.5	0.25	50	0.000522	0.1587	22	1.0	0.20	150	0.001903	0.3353
9	2.0	0.25	50	0.000597	0.1491	23	1.5	0.20	150	0.003088	0.2654
10	1.0	0.15	100	0.002400	0.3299	24	2.0	0.20	150	0.001633	0.2297
11	1.5	0.15	100	0.004129	0.3548	25	1.0	0.25	150	0.001610	0.2141
12	2.0	0.15	100	0.003195	0.2946	26	1.5	0.25	150	0.001690	0.2287
13	1.0	0.20	100	0.003521	0.2661	27	2.0	0.25	150	0.001024	0.1680
14	1.5	0.20	100	0.002178	0.2545						

OPTIMIZATION OF MRR AND SR USING ARTIFICIAL NEURAL NETWORK (ANN)

Considering the Depth of cut (A), Feed Rate (B) and Cutting Speed (C) as the inputs Surface roughness and Material Removal Rate are determined as output. L27 orthogonal array (OA) design is utilized and the data obtained from respective experiments are utilized for analysing the SR and MRR, where SR and MRR were considered as the responses. Since for various practical applications MRR has to be maximum whereas SR has to be minimum hence for analysis the maximization and minimization equations are applied.

The following flow diagram (Figure 12) describes the sequential procedure of the optimization using ANN technique. This sequence was followed for obtaining the optimized values for MRR and SR that is the maximized value of MRR and minimized value of SR.

As depicted in the flowchart (Figure 6), initially the input and the output data are noted in the workspace of Matlab R2015b and these data were imported into the network window. A new network was created using these input and output data thus listed in the workspace. The following ANN (Figure 7) was obtained as the desired network.

Now the values which are already imported are trained. The training state plot (Figure 8), performance plot (Figure 9), regression plot (Figure 10), MRR plot (Figure 11) and SR (Figure12) plot are as shown below.

Figure 6. Step by step procedure followed in ANN optimization technique

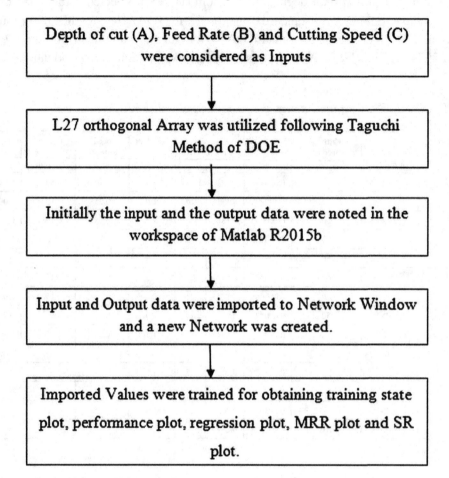

Figure 7. Artificial Neural Network

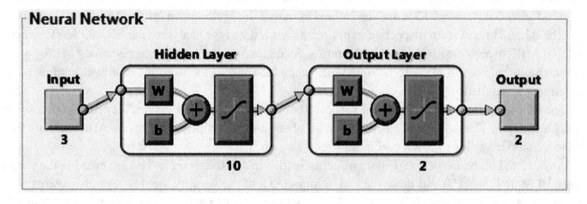

The mode of operation for that of SR and MRR are the same but the difference was the selection of response. The best validation performance was found to be 0.00072442 at 3 epoch 3.

Figure 8. Training state plot (from ANN)

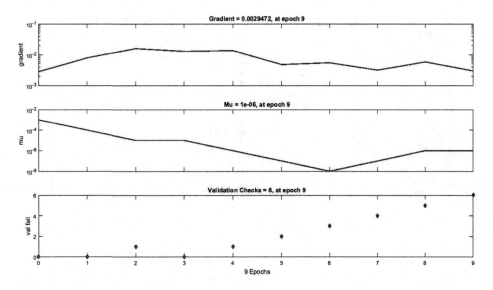

Figure 9. Performance plot (from ANN)

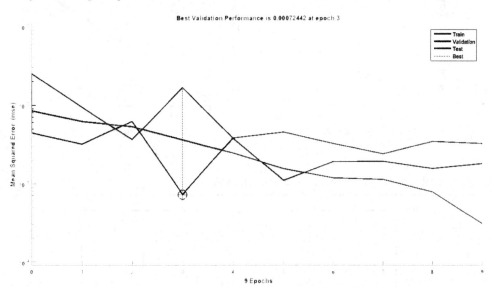

Figure 10. Regression plot (from ANN)

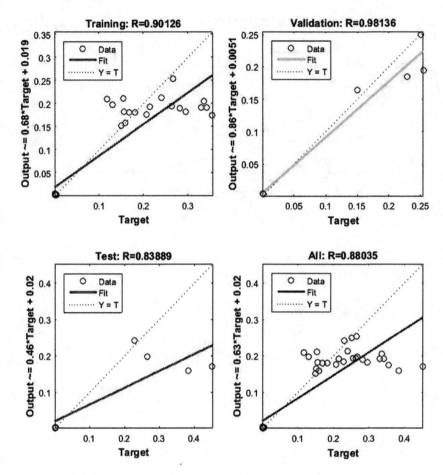

Figure 11. Plot for Material Removal Rate (MRR) from ANN

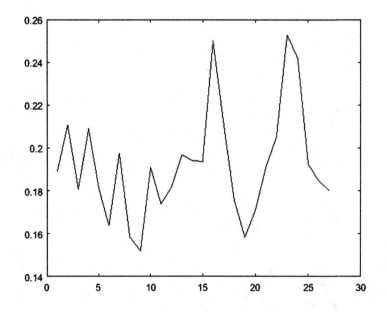

Figure 12. Plot for Surface Roughness (SR) from ANN

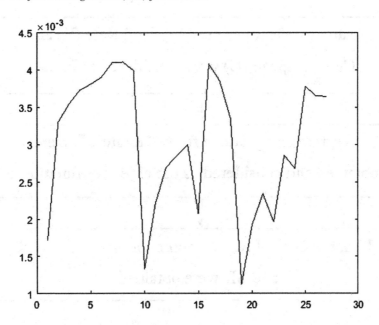

MULTI-OBJECTIVE OPTIMIZATION OF MRR AND SR USING PARTICLE SWARM OPTIMIZATION (PSO)

For the obtained values using MiniTab16 for 27 experimental readings of Depth of Cut, Feed Rate, Cutting Speed, MRR and SR, optimization is carried out using PSO coding for obtaining the optimum values of all the parameters listed above. The following Regression Equations (3) and (4) were obtained for MRR and SR in terms of Depth of Cut (A in mm), Feed Rate (B in mm/rev) and Cutting Speed (C in m/min).

$$MRR = 0.124789 + 0.152033A - 0.010544B - 0.0116667C - 0.032225A * B + 0.00893333B * C - 0.0121167C * A \tag{3}$$

$$SR = -0.000748222 + 0.00126039A + 0.000394111B + 0.000436778C - 0.000213417A * B - 4.76667e - 005A * C - 0.000176833B * C \tag{4}$$

The flow diagram in Figure 13 shows the steps followed in optimization of method MRR and SR by PSO. Initially the inputs were considered and regression equations of MRR and SR were utilized for simulation of PSO code for obtaining the optimum values of MRR and SR.

As indicated in Flow Chart (Figure 13), the optimum values for MRR and SR are obtained utilising Matlab R2015b. Code for multivariable optimization using PSO (Vasant (2012), Vo and Schegner (2012), Vasant (2014)) was simulated which provided the following plots which showed that the optimal values for Depth of cut (A), Feed Rate (B) and Cutting Speed (C) are approximately found to be 1.2 mm, 0.15 mm/rev and 100 m/min respectively. For these values of Depth of cut (A), Feed Rate (B) and Cutting Speed (C) the respective optimal values for MRR and SR are determined approximately as 0.3548 and 0.004129. Figure 14 and Figure 15 shows the Maximization Plot for Material Removal Rate (MRR) and Minimization Plot for Surface Roughness (SR) respectively.

Figure 13. Steps followed in PSO technique

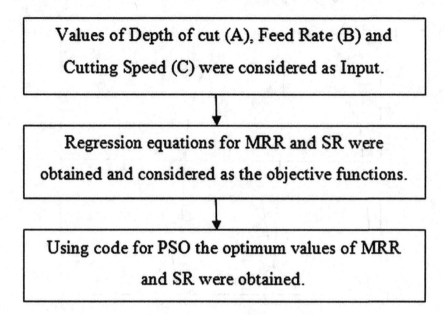

Figure 14. Maximization plot for Material Removal Rate (MRR)

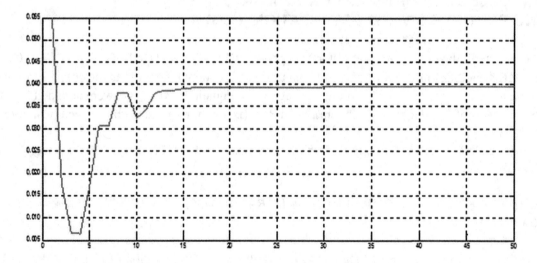

RESULTS AND DISCUSSION

Experiments were performed according to the sequence of L27 OA and the experimental results of MRR and SR are calculated. These analysis of experimental results were carried out using Minitab 16 statistical software. In this case the interaction between the particles is also taken into consideration before analysing these experimental data using software. As per ANN method the experimental data are imported into the workspace of Matlab R2015b and then the neural Network as depicted above was obtained. Further by training the input and the target values the plots for Training State, Performance, Regression, MRR and SR are obtained.

Figure 15. Minimization plot for Surface Roughness (SR)

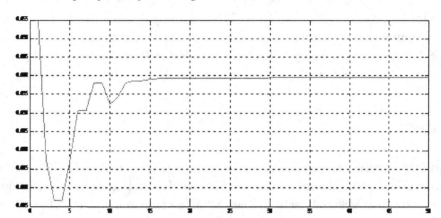

It can be noted that for Training case: R is 0.90126 with an output of 0.68*Target + 0.019; whereas for case of Testing R is determined as 0.83889 with an output of 0.46*Target + 0.02. For validation case R is found to be 0.98136 with output of 0.86*Target + 0.0051 and the miscellaneous results case R is determined as 0.88035 and output is found to be 0.63*Target +0.02. The results for MRR and SR and the DOE are tabulated below in Table 3.

Table 3. DOE and results for MRR and SR

Exp. No.	Depth of Cut (A) mm	Feed Rate (B) mm/rev	Cutting Speed (C) m/min	SR	MRR	Exp. No.	Depth of Cut (A) mm	Feed Rate (B) mm/rev	Cutting Speed (C) m/min	SR	MRR
1	1.0	0.15	50	0.000190	0.2820	15	2.0	0.20	100	0.001917	0.2625
2	1.5	0.15	50	0.000990	0.1539	16	1.0	0.25	100	0.001295	0.2505
3	2.0	0.15	50	0.000443	0.1813	17	1.5	0.25	100	0.002807	0.2398
4	1.0	0.20	50	0.000456	0.1172	18	2.0	0.25	100	0.001420	0.2066
5	1.5	0.20	50	0.000503	0.1556	19	1.0	0.15	150	0.001920	0.3835
6	2.0	0.20	50	0.000532	0.1504	20	1.5	0.15	150	0.002339	0.4520
7	1.0	0.25	50	0.000408	0.1298	21	2.0	0.15	150	0.002722	0.3416
8	1.5	0.25	50	0.000522	0.1587	22	1.0	0.20	150	0.001903	0.3353
9	2.0	0.25	50	0.000597	0.1491	23	1.5	0.20	150	0.003088	0.2654
10	1.0	0.15	100	0.002400	0.3299	24	2.0	0.20	150	0.001633	0.2297
11	1.5	0.15	100	0.004129	0.3548	25	1.0	0.25	150	0.001610	0.2141
12	2.0	0.15	100	0.003195	0.2946	26	1.5	0.25	150	0.001690	0.2287
13	1.0	0.20	100	0.003521	0.2661	27	2.0	0.25	150	0.001024	0.1680
14	1.5	0.20	100	0.002178	0.2545						

Further after obtaining the above results from ANN, PSO was used for finding the optimum values of for MRR and SR in terms of Depth of Cut (A in mm), Feed Rate (B in mm/rev) and Cutting Speed (C in m/min). Using the Multi variable code in Matlab R2015b for the regression equations for MRR and SR mentioned above in equation 3 and 4 as objective function respectively it was found that the optimal values for Depth of cut (A), Feed Rate (B) and Cutting Speed (C) are approximately found to be 1.2 mm, 0.15 mm/rev and 100 m/min respectively from the minimization and maximization plots as depicted above. For these values of Depth of cut (A), Feed Rate (B) and Cutting Speed (C) the respective optimal values for MRR and SR are determined approximately as 0.3548 and 0.004129.

CONCLUSION

The main aim of this experimentation was to optimize the work piece on CNC lathe undergoing straight turning operation using Artificial Neural Network (ANN) and Particle Swarm Optimization (PSO) techniques for maximization of Material Removal Rate (MRR) and minimizing the surface Roughness (SR). Here in this present work Depth of Cut (A), Feed Rate (B) and Cutting Speed (C) were considered with equally spaced three levels within the operating range for each of the process parameters as the input parameters. From the results and discussions as stated above it can be concluded that:

For mass production of components of machines where there is a fast movement of consumer goods it is highly necessary for the Industrialists or the Manufacturers to use the optimized values of the parameters obtained from MRR. For the cases where levels are not matching enough to their desired characteristics of input parameters, using the regression equations is always an option for them for prediction of proper output.

In some cases there are products where MRR plays least role in the product development where as SR is significant enough for the manufacturing of the product. Then the optimal values thus developed using PSO in this work can be adopted or the regression equation can be used for the cases that are having some variation in the levels of input parameters for prediction of output parameters.

For the products where both MRR and SR are to given equal amount of importance, optimized values for both MRR and SR are to be considered for predicting the output.

SCOPES OF FUTURE RESEARCH

This present work can also be used or applied to several other directions. This same work can also be enriched by incorporating or considering several other input parameters like that of cooling medium, tool-wear etc. and several other responses can be obtained like modality, stress developed etc. In order to obtain the solutions other solution platform can also be utilized like Simulated annealing, Synchronization or Hybridization of two parallel methods can also be done like Simulated annealing in Genetic Algorithm (SAGA) etc. for obtaining optimized results.

ACKNOWLEDGMENT

The authors sincerely acknowledge the comments and suggestions of the reviewers that have been instrumental for improving and upgrading the paper in its final form.

REFERENCES

Aggarwal, A., Singh, H., Kumar, P., & Singh, M. (2008). Optimizing power consumption for CNC turned parts using response surface methodology, A comparative analysis. *Journal of Materials Processing Technology*, *200*, 373–384. doi:10.1016/j.jmatprotec.2007.09.041

Arvindan, S. (2008). A machinability study of GFRP pipes using statistical techniques. *International Journal Advance Manufacturing Technology*, *37*, 1069-1081.

Asilturk, I., Neseli, S., & Ince, M. A. (2016). Optimization of Parameters affecting surface roughness of Co28Cr6Mo medical material during CNC lathe machining by using Taguchi and RSM Methods. *Measurement*, *78*, 120–128. doi:10.1016/j.measurement.2015.09.052

Cayda, U. (2010). Machinability evaluation in hard turning of AISI 4340 steel with different cutting tools using statistical techniques. *Proc Inst Mech Eng B-J Eng Ma*, *224*(7), 1043-1055. DOI: doi:10.1243/09544054JEM1822

Chen, M. C., & Su, C.-T. (1998). Optimization of machining conditions for turning cylindrical stocks into continuous finished profiles. *International Journal of Production Research*, *36*(8), 2115–2130. doi:10.1080/002075498192805

Correia, A. E., & Davim, J. P. (2011). Surface roughness measurement in turning carbon steel AISI 1045 using wiper inserts. *Measurement*, *44*(5), 1000–1005. doi:10.1016/j.measurement.2011.01.018

Dhiman, S. (2008). Machining behavior of AISI 1018 steel during turning. *Journal of Scientific & Industrial Research*, *67*, 355-360.

Dutta, R., & Majumdar, A. (2010). *Optimization of Turning Process parameters Using Multi-Objective Evolutionary Algorithm*. IEEE. doi:10.1109/CEC.2010.5586296

Fraley, S., Oom, M., Terrien, B., & Date, J. Z. (2006). *Design of Experiments via Taguchi Methods: Orthogonal Arrays*. The Michigan Chemical Process Dynamic and Controls Open Text Book.

Groover, M. P. (2012). Automation, Production Systems & Computer-Integrated Manufacturing. PHI Learning Private Limited.

Kennedy, J., & Eberhart, R. C. (1995). Particle Swarm Optimization. *Proceedings of IEEE International Joint Conference on Neural Networks*, 1942-1948. 10.1109/ICNN.1995.488968

Korkut, I., Kasap, M., & Seker, U. (2004). Determination of optimum cutting parameters during machining of AISI 304 austenitic stainless steel. *Materials & Design*, *25*(4), 303–305. doi:10.1016/j.matdes.2003.10.011

Latha, B., & Senthilkumar, V. S. (2010). Modeling and analysis of surface roughness parameters in drilling GFRP composites using fuzzy logic. *Materials and Manufacturing Processes*, *25*(8), 817–827. doi:10.1080/10426910903447261

Liu, Y. T., Chang, W. C., & Yamagata, Y. (2010). A study on optimal compensation cutting for an aspheric surface using Taguchi Method. *Journal of Manufacturing Science and Technology.*, *3*(1), 40–48. doi:10.1016/j.cirpj.2010.03.001

Mahapatra, S. S., Patnaik, A., & Patnaik, P. (2006). Parametric analysis and optimization of cutting parameters for turning operations. *Proceedings of the Int. Conference on Global Manufacturing and Innovation*, 1–6.

Manna, A. & Bhattacharyya, B. (2004). Investigation for optimal combination for achieving Better surface finish during turning of Al/ Sic-MMC. *International Journal Advance Manufacturing Technology, 23*, 658-665.

Minitab User Manual Release 16. (2010). MINITAB Inc.

Montgomery, D. C. (2001). *Design and analysis of experiments*. New York: John Wiley.

Munawar, M. (2009). Optimization of surface finish in turning operation by considering the machine tool vibration. *Mehran University Research Journal of Engineering and Technology, 31*, 51–58.

Negrete, C., Calderón-Nájera, J., & Miranda, J. C. V. (2013). *Optimization of Cutting Parameters in Turning of AISI 1018 Steel With Constant Material Removal Rate Using Robust Design for Minimizing Cutting Power*. Paper No. IMECE 2013-62520.

Palanikumar, K. (2010). Modeling and analysis of delamination factor and surface roughness in drilling GFRP composites. *Materials and Manufacturing Processes, 25*(10), 105 1067.

Park, S. H. (1998). *Robust Design and Analysis for Quality Engineering*. London: Chapman & Hall.

Phadke, M. S. (2012). *Quality Engineering using Robust Design*. New Delhi: Pearson.

Rosenblatt, F. (1958). The Perceptron: A probabilistic model for information storage and organization in the brain. *Psychological Review, 65*(6), 386–408. doi:10.1037/h0042519 PMID:13602029

Ross, J. (n.d.). *Fuzzy Logic with Engineering Application* (3rd ed.). Wiley Publication.

Ross, P. G. (1996). *Techniques for Quality Engineering* (2nd ed.). New York: McGrawhill.

Saini, S. K., & Pradhan, S. K. (2014). Soft Computing Techniques for the Optimization of Machining Parameter in CNC Turning Operation. *International Journal of Emerging Technology and Advanced Engineering, 4*, 117–124.

Suhail, A. H., Ismail, N., Wong, S. V., & Abdul Jali, N. A. (2010). Optimization of cutting parameters based on surface roughness and assistance of workpiece surface temperature in turning process. *American Journal of Engineering and Applied Sciences, 3*(1), 102–108. doi:10.3844/ajeassp.2010.102.108

Sun, H., & Lee, S. (2005). Response surface approach to aerodynamic optimization design of helicopter rotor blade. *International Journal for Numerical Methods in Engineering, 64*(1), 125–142. doi:10.1002/nme.1391

Taguchi, G. (1990). *Introduction to Quality Engineering*. Tokyo: Asian Productiviy Organization.

Tian-Syung, L. (2010). Fuzzy Deduction Material Removal Rate Optimization for Computer Numerical Control Turning. *American Journal of Applied Sciences, 7*(7), 1026-1031. DOI: doi:10.3844/ajassp.2010.1026.1031

Unitek Miyachi Group. (1999). Welding Material Control. *Technical Application Brief, 2*, 1–5.

Vasant, P. M. (Ed.). (2014). *Handbook of Research on Artificial Intelligence Techniques and Algorithms.* IGI Global.

Vasant, P. M., Weber, G., & Diew, V. N. (Ed.). (2016). Handbook of Research on Modern Optimization Algorithms and Applications in Engineering and Economics. IGI Global.

Vasant, P. M., Barsoum, N., & Webb, J. (Eds.). (2011). *Innovation in Power, Control, and Optimization: Emerging Energy Technologies.* IGI Global.

Vo, D. N., & Schegner, P. (2012). An Improved Particle Swarm Optimization for Optimal Power Flow. In P. M. Vasant (Ed.), *Meta-Heuristics Optimization Algorithms in Engineering, Business, Economics, and Finance* (pp. 1–40). IGI Global.

Wang, Z., Meng, H., & Fu, J. (2010). Novel method for evaluating surface roughness by grey dynamic filtering. *Measurement, 43*(1), 78–82. doi:10.1016/j.measurement.2009.06.008

Chapter 38
Identification of Optimal Process Parameters in Electro–Discharge Machining Using ANN and PSO

Kaushik Kumar
Birla Institute of Technology, India

J. Paulo Davim
University of Aveiro, Portugal

ABSTRACT

Electrical Discharge Machining (EDM) process is a widely used machining process in several fabrication, construction and repair work applications. Considering Pulse-On Time, Pulse OFF time, Peak-Current and Gap voltage as the inputs and among all possible outputs, in the present work Material Removal Rate and Surface Roughness are considered as outputs. In order to reduce the number of experiments Design of Experiments (DOE) was undertaken using Orthogonal Array and later on the outputs were optimized using ANN and PSO. It was found that the results obtained from both the techniques were tallying with each other.

INTRODUCTION

Electrical Discharge Machining (EDM), in line with a book composed by Elman C. Jameson (Jameson 2001), happens to be non-conventional machining technique used for making the machined surface with the aid of electrical energy. The foremost vital advantage of victimising this system is that the absence of surface contact between the tool and the work piece that takes place within the presence of a dielectric medium (Paraffin oil). The Die Sinking EDM method was developed simultaneously in USA and USSR in the period of 2nd World War. During then a technique was required to process very hard materials used in military vehicles, equipment and ammunitions. Later on the method of Die Sinking EDM

DOI: 10.4018/978-1-6684-2408-7.ch038

was developed in various countries and was utilised in numerous Defences, Automotive, Aeronautics and many other industrial areas worldwide. The method is endlessly used for years to carry out varied very important experiments connected with the method of optimization. The process is used continuously from time to time to analyze the various machine parameters like Over-cut, Material removal rate, surface roughness, etc. Since multiple inputs are being used, hence optimizing these becomes essential for obtaining desired output. Out of the various parameters that may be thought of as the output of the machining operations, the material removal rate (MRR) and Surface roughness (SR) would be thought of for the current work as the factors specifically influences the standard, price of machining and therefore the machining hour rate.EDM is an essential machining process in many industries that give importance to precision and accuracy. Several researchers have studied EDM process considering different machining characteristics. Koshy et al. (1993) have studied EDM process for MRR, tool wear rate, relative electrode wear, corner reproduction accuracy and surface finish aspects using a rotating disk electrode and compared the results with a stationary electrode. It is seen that the effective flushing of the working gap improves MRR and surface finish. Zhang et al. (1997) have investigated MRR, surface roughness and diameter of discharge points in EDM on ceramics. From the experimental results, they have shown that MRR, surface roughness and also the diameter of discharge point directly varies with pulse-on time and discharge current. Lee and Li (2001) have investigated the result of machining parameters like the tool materials, tool polarity, gap voltage, peak current, pulse length, pulse interval and flushing on the machining characteristics, like MRR, surface end and relative tool wear in EDM of WC. It's ascertained that MRR usually decreases with the rise of gap voltage and surface roughness will increase with increasing peak current. Ramaswamy and Blunt (2002, 2004) have shown that the electrical energy is that the most dominant factor in modifying the surface texture, particularly the root mean square of peaks, the material volume in EDM of M300 tool steel. Puertas and Luis (2003) have shaped centre line average roughness value (Ra) and root mean sq. roughness price (Rq) in terms of current, pulse on time and Off time in EDM on soft steel (F-1110). It's seen that this intensity has the foremost influence on surface roughness and there's a strong interaction between this current intensity and also on the spark on time. Guu et al. (2003) have studied the results of different machining parameters on surface roughness in EDM of AISI D2 steel and being brought to a conclusion that surface roughness is inversely proportional to power input. Petropoulos et al. (2004) have stressed the relation between surface texture parameters and methodology parameters in EDM of Ck60 steel plates. They have thought of amplitude, spacing, hybrid, nonetheless as random methodology and type parameters that's perennial at each scale. Amorim and Weingaertner (2005) have targeting the terms of constant quantity influence of machining parameters on volumetric relative wear, MRR and surface roughness (Ra) in EDM of AISIP20 using copper tool electrodes. Puertas et al. (2005) have done a study on the influence of EDM processing parameter quality (current intensity, pulse time, duty cycle, gap voltage and dielectric flushing pressure) across 2 spacing parameters- mean spacing between peaks and therefore the range of peaks per cm in machining of siliconised or reaction-bonded carbide (SiSiC). From the results, it's seen that intensity, pulse time and duty cycle are most potent factors arousing result on the chosen responses. Guu (2005) has terminated that a lot of outstanding discharge energy leads to a lot of poor surface structure in EDM of AISI D2 steel. Yan et al. (2005) have examined scientifically the influences of the tactic parameters (dielectric sort, peak current and pulse duration) on MRR, conductor wear rate and surface roughness parameter in EDM of pure Ti metals. Keskin et al. (2006) have represented that surface roughness enhances with rise within the discharge length. Routara et al. (2007) have depicted the roughness models of EDM method for 3 dissimilar roughness parameters employing a methodology called response surface methodology (RSM) and shown that the machining parameters like pulse current and pulse on time have the best influence on the roughness parameters whereas pulse off time has no substantial result on roughness parameters. Kiyak and Cakir (2007) have studied the influences of method parameters (pulse current, pulse time and pulse pause time) on surface roughness in EDM of 40CrMnNiMo864 alloy steel and discovered that surface roughness of sample and tool are determined by factors like pulse current and pulse time. Pradhan and Biswas (2008) have developed MRR model for 3 numerous input parameters specifically pulse current, discharge time and pulse time for EDM method of AISI D2 steel using RSM. Jaharah et al. (2008) have studied the results of input parameters (peak current, pulse on-time, and pulse Off time) on surface roughness (Ra), tool wear rate (EWR) and MRR in EDM of AISI H13 alloy steel and discovered that the peak current is of bigger importance influencing MRR and surface roughness. Chiang (2008) has analysed the implications of input parameters like discharge current, pulse on time, duty cycle and gap voltage on MRR, tool wear ratio, and surface roughness employing RSM in EDM of Al2O3+TiC mixed ceramic materials and delineated that the discharge current and duty factor are most substantial factor of MRR and the discharge current and spark – on – time have significance related to statistics on both the value of the tool wear ratio and surface finish. Kuppan et al. (2008) have studied the results of input parameters (peak current, pulse on-time, duty cycle and tool speed) on MRR and depth averaged surface roughness in EDM (small deep hole drilling) of alloy 718 materials employing RSM. Habib (2009) has developed a mathematical model utilizing RSM for association of the varied machining parameters (pulse on time, peak current, average gap voltage and therefore the volume fraction percentage of SiC within the Al matrix) on MRR, EWR, gap size and therefore the surface properties. Amin et al. (2009) have studied the influences of input parameters (peak current, voltage, pulse duration and interval time) in EDM of WC employing Taguchi methodology and shown that the peak current considerably affects the EWR and surface roughness, while, the spark duration primarily impresses MRR. Sahoo et al. (2009) have inquired concerning the influence of machining input parameters (pulse current, pulse on time and pulse Off time) on the quality of surface created in EDM victimising three completely different work-piece materials viz. mild steel, brass and Tungsten Carbide. Rahman et al. (2010) studied the influences of input parameters on MRR employing RSM in EDM of Ti6Al4V and created clear that peak current and pulse on time are the substantial machining parameters influencing MRR. They also showed that MRR is directly proportional to peak current and pulse on time. Pradhan and Biswas (2010) have investigated the results of machining parameters in EDM of AISI D2 steel and indicated that the pulse current, pulse time, voltage and pulse on time have substantial consequences in dominant MRR. Effects of tool materials on the responses are studied by altogether completely different researchers. Haron et al. (2008) have studied the results of copper and carbon tool on EWR and MRR. Jahan et al. (2009) have investigated the results of tool materials (tungsten, copper metallic element and silver metallic element) and came to a conclusion that silver tungsten tool produces sander (with minimum Ra and Rmax) among the 3 electrodes in EDM of XW42 alloy steel. Choudhury et al. (2010) have used copper, brass and carbon electrodes and depicts that copper electrode offers greater MRR and brass electrode offers greater surface finish in EDM of EN 31 die steel.

NECESSITY OF OPTIMIZATION

For the applications of advanced manufacturing methodologies, technologies are developing in rapid pace. In order to achieve these advanced manufacturing criteria the industries, companies and manufacturing units need to optimize the process parameters to save money and time. Many researchers have carried out the optimization of the process parameters using many machining techniques like EDM, ECM, Wire EDM, PAC, etc. by applying various optimizations techniques like Artificial Neural Network, Particle Swarm Optimization, Genetic Algorithm, Fuzzy Logic Algorithm etc. Researchers like Asilturk et al. (2016); Korkut et al. (2004); Mahapatra et al. (2006); Vasant et al. (2016); Vasant et al. (2011) have performed optimization considering various process parameters in order to obtain best set of process parameters those can be used for advance manufacturing techniques. Considering EDM in this present work, MRR and Surface Roughness are believed as the parametric quantity where the primary aim was to obtain the optimized minimized values of Surface Roughness and optimized Maximized values of Material Removal Rate. For getting these desired machining characteristics the machining parameters like Pulse on Time (T_{On}), Pulse Off time (T_{off}), Peak-Current (I_p), Gap voltage (V_g) has been considered as the input.

OPTIMIZATION METHODS

In this work authors have tried to provide solution to the problems using Particle Swarm optimization (PSO) and Artificial Neural Network (ANN).

ARTICIAL NEURAL NETWORK (ANN)

In machine learning, artificial neural networks (ANNs) are a group of models enlivened by biological neural networks and are utilized to surmised functions that can rely on upon a substantial number of sources of info called as inputs and are for the most part obscure or not known. Artificial Neural Network has derived its origin from the human nervous system that consists of large number of neurons inter-connected to it and performs various analyzing tasks in no time. They are introduced as frameworks of interconnected "neurons" which trade messages between each other. The simulated neurons take inputs and give outputs through their non-linear connections (Sitton et al., 2017). The associations or connections have weights that can be tuned, making neural nets versatile and adaptive to inputs and equipped for learning. It provides several reconciling and perceptual solutions and re-appraisal of parametric model quality in comparatively less complicated configurations when examined to different approaches of modelling. It is an optimization technique in which less number of errors is encountered and high accuracy can be achieved (Pappu and Gummadi, 2017). Artificial Neural Network modelling technique is one of the most practical, authentic and precise modelling proficiency which is able to demonstrate non-linear relations in case of machining processes (Patra et al., 2017). ANN has the potential to show better results in the fatigue loading conditions and range of spectral type and properties of the material (Durodola et al., 2017). The capacity of the ANNs to precisely estimated obscure capacities to know the unknown function. Neural systems have been utilized to unravel a wide assortment of assignments that are difficult to understand utilizing standard manage based programming. Some of the applications of ANN are for solving the Travelling Salesman's problems, Security and loan applications, Market predictions etc.

PARTICLE SWARM OPTIMIZATION (PSO)

Particle Swarm Optimization (PSO) involves computation technique that optimizes a consequence by using a series of iterations attempting to heighten an applicant arrangement with respect to a given measure of value. It is a random optimization technique which was brought forth by Kennedy and Eberhart to provide various advantages such as fast occurrence of two or more things coming together, easy principle and simple execution (Rafiraeed et al., 2017). PSO provides accurate and authentic modelling results. As a hybrid type of algorithm, it has got outstanding feature of mixing the abilities of worldwide scope or applicability and local analyzing (El-Wakeel, 2014). PSO is mostly recommended and used algorithm due to its uncomplicated concept and simple coding implementation, it takes lesser time in optimizing results when compared to other techniques (Yu-Zhen et al., 2012). One of the main reason to work with PSO is its appealing characteristics that is lesser number of parameters are to be adjusted to use it and it covers wide range of application (Katherasan et al., 2012). It takes care of a problem by having a people of candidate solutions, here named particles, and moving these particles within the inquiry space as indicated by basic numerical formulae over the particle's position and rate. Every particle's growth is influenced by its neighbourhood best known position, but on the other way it is guided toward the best-known positions in the search space, which are upgraded as comparatively better positions are found by other particles.

EXPERIMENTATION

The choice of applicable input machining conditions for EDM characteristics like material removal rate and surface finish are having a base on the analysis associated with the varied input parameters for material removal and roughness. Attempting frequent or large number of experimental runs also is not economically viable. Expertise disclosed that the sort of material yields extra influence on the EDM performance. On the opposite hand when new and advanced materials seem within the field, it's unimaginable to use available models and thus experimental investigations are continually needed.

Input Parameters Considered

Pulse-On Time (T_{On}), Pulse Off time (T_{off}), Peak-Current (I_p), Gap voltage (V_g)

Output Parameters Considered

Material Removal Rate (MRR) and Surface Roughness (SR)

Material Used

EN 19 Tool Steel as work-piece and electrolytic copper as a tool electrode (positive polarity).

Machine Used

The entire experiment was carried out on a Die sinking EDM machine (Electronica EMT-43 Machine) (Figure 1).

Figure 1. EDM Machine

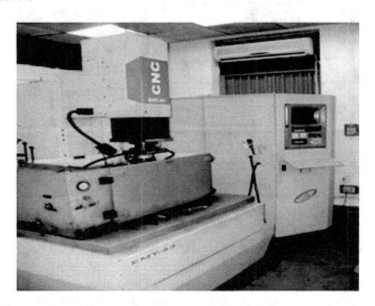

The work-piece on that the EDM method was disbursed was an EN19 material whereas the tool for EDM operation was Copper. Paraffin oil was hand-picked as insulator medium. After machining operation, surface roughness (Ra) was determined employing a stylus type profilometer, known as Talysurf (Taylor Hobson, 3+) (Figure 2). A traverse speed of 1 mm/sec, cut off length of 0.8 mm and an analysis length of 8 mm were set for the stylus to work. A group of three totally different readings were evaluated for varied values of surface roughness and arithmetic mean of those values was used.

DESIGN OF EXPERIMENTS (DOE)

Industrial physicists will now not afford to conduct experiment in a very trial-and-error manner, dynamically one issue at a time, the manner early scientists like Edison, Madam Curie, J.C.Bose did whereas inventing and developing things. A way more effective methodology is to use a computer-enhanced, systematic approach to experimentation, one that considers all factors at the same time. That approach is named design of experiments (DOE), and firms worldwide are assuming it as a cost-effective way to solve serious issues affecting their operations. The design of experiments technique may be a terribly very potent tool, that permits holding out the modelling and analysis of the influence of technique variables on the response variables. The response variable is associate degrees unknown perform of the method variables, which are referred to as design factors. The aim of running experiments is to characterize unknown relations and dependencies that exist inside the determined design or method, i.e. to seek out

Figure 2. Stylus type profilometer(Talysurf)

the affecting design variables and therefore the response to variations within the design variable values. A methodical scientific approach to being after the experiment must be utilized if the results are to be figured out performing minimum number of experiments. The statistical design of experiments refers to the process of planning the experiment so that relevant data that can be analyzed by statistical methods will be brought together in one place, leading in valid and objective conclusions in a logical way. Statistical methodology becomes the only logical approach for analysis when the problem involves data that may contain experimental errors. Sometimes, experiments are recurrent with a specific set of levels for all the factors to visualize the statistical technique validation and repeatability by the replicate data. This is often known as replication. to eradicate any biasness, allocation of experimental material and therefore the order of experimental runs are chosen in a random manner. This is often known as randomisation. To rearrange the experimental material into lots, or blocks, that ought to have higher homogeneity than the complete set of data is named block. So, once experiments are being undertaken this part is ought to be kept in mind. There are many totally different methodologies for style of experiments. During this work Orthogonal Array (OA) technique was used for performing the experiments.

ORTHOGONAL ARRAY

Orthogonal Arrays (OA) are special matrices used as the design matrices in the fractional factorial design for the estimation of the effect of several factors in a highly efficient way. These designs are applicable even when the factors have more than two levels and for mixed level experiments where that components do not have same number of levels. In general, when the number of process parameter enhances, large number of experiments has to be carried out for factorial design. But using orthogonal array smaller number of experiments can be performed in the specified range and the effects of process parameters can be observed quite effectively. For a two level factors 8 (L8) experiments are needed for the experimentation whereas for a three-level orthogonal arrays can be based on 9 (L9), 27 (L27) or 81(L81) experimental points. For any pair of columns in the design matrix, all combinations of the factor levels appear equal number of times.

Table 1. Different variables used in the experiment and their levels

Variable	Coding	Level		
		1	2	3
Pulse On (Ton) in µs	A	200	300	400
Pulse Off (Toff) in µs	B	1800	1700	1600
Discharge Current (Ip) in A	C	8	12	16
Voltage (V) in V	D	40	60	80

In the present study four factors are taken with three levels, (Shown in Table 1) which have 20 degrees of freedom (4*2 + 3*2*2). Hence, L27 OA is used in the study. The three-level Orthogonal arrays (L27) for four factors viz. A, B, C and D are presented in Table 2.

Table 2. DOE using L27 Orthogonal Array

Exp. No.	A (Ton)	B (TOff)	C (Ip)	D (V)	Exp. No.	A (Ton)	B (TOff)	C (Ip)	D (V)
1	1	1	1	1	15	2	2	3	2
2	1	1	2	2	16	2	3	1	1
3	1	1	3	3	17	2	3	2	2
4	1	2	1	2	18	2	3	3	3
5	1	2	2	3	19	3	1	1	3
6	1	2	3	1	20	3	1	2	1
7	1	3	1	3	21	3	1	3	2
8	1	3	2	1	22	3	2	1	1
9	1	3	3	2	23	3	2	2	2
10	2	1	1	2	24	3	2	3	3
11	2	1	2	3	25	3	3	1	2
12	2	1	3	1	26	3	3	2	3
13	2	2	1	3	27	3	1	3	2
14	2	2	2	1					

EXPERIMENTATION AND MEASUREMENT OF MRR

The experiment was performed on the basis of design of experiments using L27 orthogonal array. Measuring the weight of each sample before and after each experiment, MRR was calculated experimentally. The obtained value of the MRR was employed to obtain the corresponding S/N ratio values using the Minitab 16 software. As higher MRR is a desired condition hence Larger the Better condition was used and results are tabulated in Table 3.

Table 3. Experimental Results for MRR

Exp. No.	A (Ton)	B (T_{off})	C (Ip)	D (V)	MRR	S/N Ratio	Exp. No.	A (Ton)	B (T_{off})	C (Ip)	D (V)	MRR	S/N ratio
1	1	1	1	1	7.22	17.17	15	2	2	3	2	27.82	28.88
2	1	1	2	2	12.16	21.62	16	2	3	1	1	11.30	21.06
3	1	1	3	3	16.53	24.36	17	2	3	2	2	21.06	26.47
4	1	2	1	2	7.38	17.36	18	2	3	3	3	28.87	29.25
5	1	2	2	3	14.1	22.98	19	3	1	1	3	4.699	13.43
6	1	2	3	1	31	29.83	20	3	1	2	1	15.93	24.04
7	1	3	1	3	7.83	17.87	21	3	1	3	2	4.65	27.32
8	1	3	2	1	24.9	27.92	22	3	2	1	1	9.143	19.22
9	1	3	3	2	31.96	30.09	23	3	2	2	2	5.517	24.74
10	2	1	1	2	5.57	14.91	24	3	2	3	3	23.73	27.50
11	2	1	2	3	11.18	20.97	25	3	3	1	2	8.95	19.03
12	2	1	3	1	24.63	27.83	26	3	3	2	3	17.43	24.82
13	2	2	1	3	6.09	15.69	27	3	1	3	2	41.73	32.11
14	2	2	2	1	20.27	26.14							

The regression equation for MRR based on the input parameters and their levels was also generated (Eqn. 1)

$$MRR = 0.222579 + 0.000681 * Ton + 0.053207 * Toff + 0.096158 * Ip - 0.043101 * V + 0.013372 * Ton^2 + 0.018285 * V^2 + 0.021314 * Ip * Toff - 0.012999 * Toff * V - 0.018288\ V * Ip \qquad (1)$$

EXPERIMENTATION AND MEASUREMENT OF SURFACE ROUGHNESS (RA)

The machined surfaces of the work-pieces were introduced to the profilometer and surface roughness (Ra) was measured. The obtained value of the Ra was employed to obtain the corresponding S/N ratio values using the Minitab 16 software. As lower Ra is always desired hence Smaller the Better condition was used and results are tabulated in Table 4

Table 4. Experimental Results of Surface Roughness (R$_a$)

Exp. No.	A (Ton)	B (TOff)	C (Ip)	D (V)	Ra	S/N Ratio	Exp. No.	A (Ton)	B (TOff)	C (Ip)	D (V)	Ra	S/N ratio
1	1	1	1	1	9.41	-19.47	15	2	2	3	2	13.27	-22.45
2	1	1	2	2	11.6	-21.28	16	2	3	1	1	9.46	-19.51
3	1	1	3	3	11.65	-21.32	17	2	3	2	2	16.27	-24.22
4	1	2	1	2	8.49	-18.57	18	2	3	3	3	15.9	-24.02
5	1	2	2	3	14.43	-23.18	19	3	1	1	3	10.23	-20.19
6	1	2	3	1	11.41	-21.14	20	3	1	2	1	15.23	-23.65
7	1	3	1	3	10.53	-20.44	21	3	1	3	2	14.97	-23.50
8	1	3	2	1	10.71	-20.59	22	3	2	1	1	11.17	-20.96
9	1	3	3	2	13.77	-22.77	23	3	2	2	2	19.6	-25.84
10	2	1	1	2	10.67	-20.56	24	3	2	3	3	13.3	-22.47
11	2	1	2	3	14.63	-23.30	25	3	3	1	2	11.07	-20.88
12	2	1	3	1	15.8	-23.97	26	3	3	2	3	16.2	-24.19
13	2	2	1	3	9.87	-19.88	27	3	1	3	2	12.8	-21.56
14	2	2	2	1	14.57	-23.26							

The regression equation for Surface Roughness based on the input parameters and their levels was also generated (Eqn. 2)

$$SR = 11.0648 + 0.496 * Ton - 0.1428 * Toff + 1.1833 * Ip - 0.0392 * V - 0.2807 * Ip^2 + 0.2433 * V^2$$

(2)

OPTIMIZATION OF MRR AND SR USING PARTICLE SWARM OPTIMIZATION (PSO)

For the obtained values using MiniTab16 for 27 experimental readings of Pulse-On Time (T$_{On}$), Pulse OFF time (T$_{off}$), Peak-Current (I$_p$), Gap voltage (V$_g$), MRR and SR, optimization is carried out using PSO coding for obtaining the optimum values of all the parameters listed above. The Regression Equations (1) and (2) obtained for MRR and SR in terms of Pulse-On Time (μs), Pulse Off time (μs), Peak-Current (A), Gap voltage (V).

In order to obtain the optimum values for MRR and SR, Matlab R2015b was used. Code for multivariable optimization using PSO was simulated which provided the plots which showed the optimal values for Pulse-On Time (A), Pulse Off time (B), Peak-Current (C), Gap voltage (D). For these values of Pulse-On Time (A), Pulse OFF time (B), Peak-Current (C), Gap voltage (D) the respective optimal values for MRR and SR were determined. Figure 3 and 4 shows the Maximization Plot for Material Removal Rate (MRR) and Minimization Plot for Surface Roughness (SR) respectively.

Figure 3. Maximization Plot for Material Removal Rate (MRR)

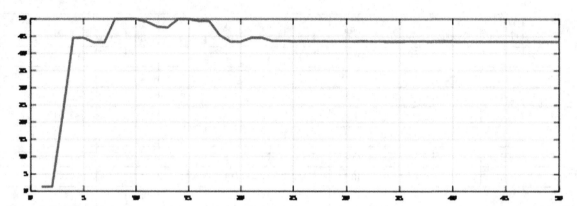

Figure 4. Minimization Plot for Surface Roughness (SR)

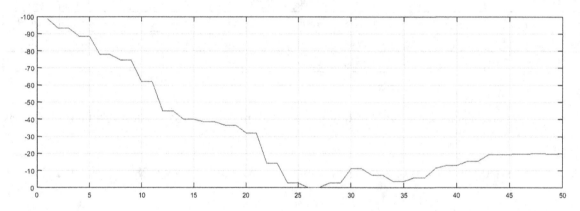

OPTIMIZATION OF MRR AND SR USING ARTIFICIAL NEURAL NETWORK

The confront study addresses with the development of artificial neural network to depict the suitable machining process parameters in order to receive optimum MRR and surface roughness characteristics in EDM process. Artificial neural network with Error Back Propagation Training Algorithms (EBPTA) has been used for the training and testing purpose of the experimental data. Initially a data set is required to train the ANN model. Then developed experimental database was used to train and simulated the ANN model to determine the predicted value. The EBPTA is based on universal delta-rule that involves dynamic weight updates system so as to reduce the mean squared error (MSE).

In this part, ANN model was used for prediction of MRR and SR. The experimental study illustrated the error for the MRR and SR properties. So, with reference to the mid-level quality characteristics supported by Artificial Neural Network the degree of non-linearity that exists in nature between the output and input variable was identified.

Figure 5. Multi-layer feed forward artificial neural network

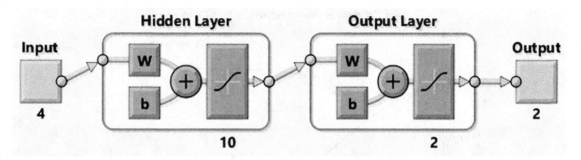

The multi-layer ANN network shown in Figure 5 comprises of input, output and hidden neurons layer. Multi-layer ANN architecture consists of 4-30-2 network model is used for simulation. Four neurons in the input layer corresponding to 4 inputs variable, two neurons in the output layer. One hidden layer with 30 neurons was found suitable employed in the present study. For training and testing 'nntool' is used which is available in optimization tool box in 'MATLAB' software. When maximum number of epoch and minimum MSE is achieved, training of ANN model is stopped. The mean square error (MSE) is computed using equation3

$$MSE = \frac{1}{NP} \sum_{P=1}^{NP} \sum_{k=1}^{k} \left(d_{kp} - o_{kp} \right)^2 \qquad (3)$$

where

NP = number of training patterns,
dk, p = desired output for the pth pattern and O_{kp} is predicted output for the pth pattern.

ARTIFICIAL NEURAL NETWORK TRAINING AND TESTING

The training of ANN has been carried out for 27 input–output patterns with the help of 'nntool' available in *MATLAB* software (2012a). The factors are used for training purpose are:

- Learning rate = 0.05
- Momentum factor = 0.85
- Maximum number of epochs = 1000
- Tolerance for MSE= 0.0001

The ANN training and simulation was carried out with the help of "*training dx*" function. The variation of MSE with number of epoch is shown in Figure 6.

The training state and output regression plots (depicted in Figures 7 and 8) are generated providing the final optimal solutions and also ensures the efficacy of the system chosen.

Figure 6. The variation of mean squared error (MSE)

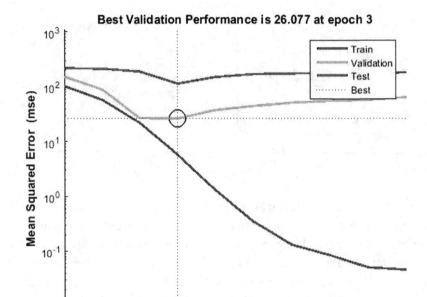

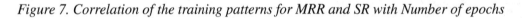

Figure 7. Correlation of the training patterns for MRR and SR with Number of epochs

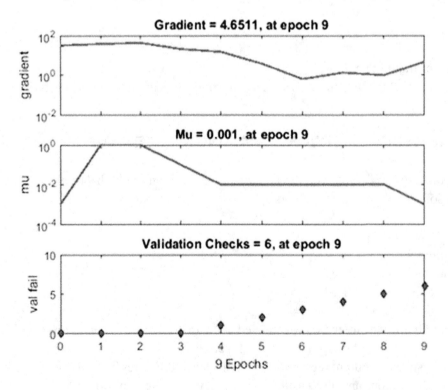

Figure 8. Regression plot for MRR and SR using ANN

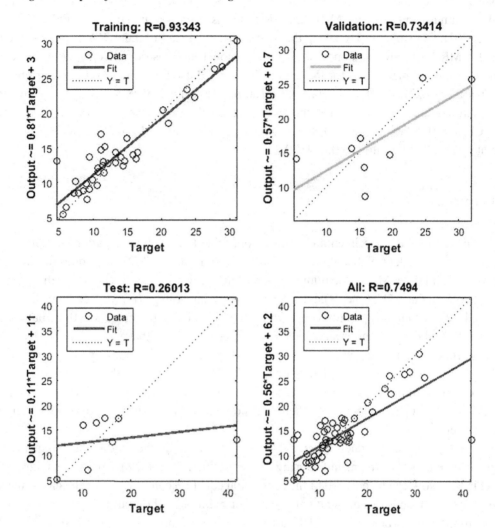

RESULTS AND DISCUSSION

Experiments were performed according to the sequence of L27 OA and the experimental results of MRR and SR are calculated. These analyses of experimental results were carried out using Minitab 16 statistical software. In this case the interaction between the particles is also taken into consideration before analysing these experimental data using software. As per ANN method the experimental data are imported into the workspace of Matlab R2015b and then the neural Network as depicted above was obtained. Further by training the input and the target values the plots for Training State, Performance, Regression, MRR and SR are obtained.

It can be noted that for Training case: R is 0.93343 with an output of 0.81*Target + 3; whereas for case of Testing R is determined as 0.26013 with an output of 0.11*Target + 11. For validation case R is found to be 0.73414 with output of 0.57*Target + 0.6.7 and the miscellaneous results case R is determined as 0.7494 and output is found to be 0.56*Target +0.02.

Further after obtaining the experimental and regression equations, ANN and PSO was used for finding the optimum values of for MRR and SR in terms of Pulse-On Time (A), Pulse Off time (B), Peak-Current (C), Gap voltage (D). Using the Multi variable code in Matlab R2015b for the regression equations for MRR and SR mentioned above in equation 1 and 2as objective function respectively it was found that the optimal values for Pulse-On Time (A), Pulse Off time (B), Peak-Current (C), Gap voltage (D) are approximately found to be400μs, 1600μs, 16A and 40V respectively from the minimization and maximization plots as depicted above. For these values of Pulse-On Time (A), Pulse Off time (B), Peak-Current (C), Gap voltage (D) the respective optimal values for MRR and SR are determined approximately as 0.3548 g/min and 0.004129μm.

CONCLUSION

The main purpose of this experimentation was to optimize the machining parameters of EDM using Artificial Neural Network (ANN) and Particle Swarm Optimization (PSO) techniques for maximization of Material Removal Rate (MRR) and minimizing the surface Roughness (SR). Here in this present work Pulse-On Time (A), Pulse Off time (B), Peak-Current (C), Gap voltage (D) were conceived with equally spaced three levels within the operating range for each of the process parameters as the input parameters. From the results and discussions as stated above it can be concluded that:

For mass production of components of machines where there is a fast movement of consumer goods it is highly necessary for the Industrialists or the Manufacturers to use the optimized values of the parameters obtained from MRR. For the cases where levels are not matching enough to their desired characteristics of input parameters, using the regression equations is always an option for them for prediction of proper output.

In some cases, there are products where MRR plays least role in the product development where as SR is significant enough for the manufacturing of the product. Then the optimal values thus developed using PSO in this work can be adopted or the regression equation can be used for the cases that are having some variation in the levels of input parameters for prediction of output parameters.

For the products where both MRR and SR are to given equal amount of importance, optimized values for both MRR and SR are to be considered for predicting the output.

The results derived from the optimization techniques used here are quite agreeing to the results obtained by other researchers considering the same input, output parameters and identical levels using other techniques like Taguchi, GA, ABC etc. But it varies considerably in case some other parameters and levels are considered.

SCOPE OF FUTURE RESEARCH

This present work can also be used or applied to several other directions. This work can also be enriched by incorporating or considering several other input parameters like tool rotation, different dielectric medium, flushing pressure etc. and several other responses like tool wear, thermal stress developed etc. In order to obtain the optimized parameters other recent techniques like Hill Climbing, Grey Wolf, Stochastic Optimization, Fuzzy Optimization, Grey Optimization, Uncertain Preference, Fuzzy Multiobjective Optimization, Grey Multiobjective Optimization, Stochastic Multiobjective Optimization,

Fuzzy Multilevel Programming, Grey Multilevel Programming, Stochastic Multilevel Programming, etc. can also be utilized or Hybridization of two parallel methods like Simulated annealing in Genetic Algorithm (SAGA) etc. can be employed.

ACKNOWLEDGMENT

The authors sincerely acknowledge the comments and suggestions of the reviewers that have been instrumental for improving and upgrading the paper in its final form.

REFERENCES

Amin, A. K. M. N., Lajis, M. A., & Radzi, H. C. D. M. (2009). The implementation of Taguchi method on EDM process of tungsten carbide. *European Journal of Scientific Research, 26*, 609–617.

Amorima, F. L., & Weingaertner, W. L. (2005). The influence of generator actuation mode and process parameters on the performance of finish EDM of a tool steel. *Journal of Materials Processing Technology, 166*(3), 411–416. doi:10.1016/j.jmatprotec.2004.08.026

Asilturk, I., Neseli, S., & Ince, M. A. (2016). Optimization of Parameters affecting surface roughness of Co28Cr6Mo medical material during CNC lathe machining by using Taguchi and RSM Methods. *Measurement, 78*, 120–128. doi:10.1016/j.measurement.2015.09.052

Chiang, K. T. (2008). Modeling and analysis of the effects of machining parameters on the performance characteristics in the EDM process of Al2O3+TiC mixed ceramic. *International Journal of Advanced Manufacturing Technology, 37*(5-6), 523–533. doi:10.100700170-007-1002-3

Choudhary, R., Kumar, H., & Grag, R. K. (2010). Analysis and evaluation of heat affected zones in electric discharge machining of EN-31 die steel. *Indian Journal of Engineering Materials Sciences, 17*, 91–98.

Durodola, J. F., Ramachandra, S., Li, N., & Thite, A. N. (2017). A pattern Recognition artificial neural network method for random fatigue loading life prediction. *International Journal of Fatigue, 99*, 55–67. doi:10.1016/j.ijfatigue.2017.02.003

El-Wakeel, A. S. (2014). Design optimization of PM couplings using hybrid Particle Swarm Optimization-Simplex Method (PSO-SM) Algorithm. *Electric Power Systems Research, 116*, 29–35. doi:10.1016/j.epsr.2014.05.003

Guu, Y. H. (2005). AFM surface imaging of AISI D2 tool steel machined by the EDM process. *Applied Surface Science, 242*(3-4), 245–250. doi:10.1016/j.apsusc.2004.08.028

Guu, Y. H., Hocheng, H., Chou, C. Y., & Deng, C. S. (2003). Effect of electrical discharge machining on surface characteristics and machining damage of AISI D2 tool steel. *Materials Science and Engineering, 358*(1-2), 37–43. doi:10.1016/S0921-5093(03)00272-7

Habib, S. S. (2009). Study of the parameters in electrical discharge machining through response surface methodology approach. *Applied Mathematical Modelling*, *33*(12), 4397–4407. doi:10.1016/j.apm.2009.03.021

Haron, C. H. C., Ghani, J. A., Burhanuddin, Y., Seong, Y. K., & Swee, C. Y. (2008). Copper and graphite electrodes performance in electrical-discharge machining of XW42 tool steel. *Journal of Materials Processing Technology*, *201*(1-3), 570–573. doi:10.1016/j.jmatprotec.2007.11.285

Jahan, M. P., Wong, Y. S., & Rahman, M. (2009). A study on the fine-finish die-sinking micro-EDM of tungsten carbide using different electrode materials. *Journal of Materials Processing Technology*, *209*(8), 3956–3967. doi:10.1016/j.jmatprotec.2008.09.015

Jaharah, A. G., Liang, C. G., Wahid, S. Z. M. N., Rahman, A., & Hassan, C. H. C. (2008). Performance of copper electrode in electrical discharge machining (EDM) of AISI H13 harden steel. *International Journal of Mechanical and Materials Engineering*, *3*, 25–29.

Jameson, E. C. (2001). *Electrical discharge machining*. Society of Manufacturing Engineers.

Katherasan, D., Elias, J. V., Sathiya, P., & Haq, A. N. (2012). Flux Cored Arc Welding Parameter Optimization Using Swarm Optimization Algorithm. *Procedia Engineering*, *38*, 3913–3296. doi:10.1016/j.proeng.2012.06.449

Keskin, Y., Halka, H., & Kizil, S. M. (2006). An experimental study for determination of the effects of machining parameters on surface roughness in electrical discharge machining (EDM). *International Journal of Advanced Manufacturing Technology*, *28*(11-12), 1118–1121. doi:10.100700170-004-2478-8

Kiyak, M., & Cakir, O. (2007). Examination of machining parameters on surface roughness in EDM of tool steel. *Journal of Materials Processing Technology*, *191*(1-3), 141–144. doi:10.1016/j.jmatprotec.2007.03.008

Korkut, I., Kasap, M., & Seker, U. (2004). Determination of optimum cutting parameters during machining of AISI 304 austenitic stainless steel. *Materials & Design*, *25*(4), 303–305. doi:10.1016/j.matdes.2003.10.011

Koshy, P., Jain, V. K., & Lal, G. K. (1993). Experimental investigations into electrical discharge machining with a rotating disk electrode. *Precision Engineering*, *15*(1), 6–15. doi:10.1016/0141-6359(93)90273-D

Kuppan, P., Rajadurai, A., & Narayanan, S. (2008). Influence of EDM process parameters in deep hole drilling of Inconel 718. *International Journal of Advanced Manufacturing Technology*, *38*(1-2), 74–84. doi:10.100700170-007-1084-y

Lee, S. H., & Li, X. P. (2001). Study of the effect of machining parameters on the machining characteristics in electrical discharge machining of tungsten carbide. *Journal of Materials Processing Technology*, *115*(3), 344–358. doi:10.1016/S0924-0136(01)00992-X

Mahapatra, S. S., Patnaik, A., & Patnaik, P. (2006). Parametric analysis and optimization of cutting parameters for turning operations. *Proceedings of the Int. Conference on Global Manufacturing and Innovation*, 1–6.

Pappu, J. S. M., & Gummadi, N. (2017). Artificial Neural Network and regression coupled genetic algorithm to optimize parameters for enhanced xylitol production by Debaryomycesnepalensis in bioreactor. *Biochemical Engineering Journal, 120*, 136–145. doi:10.1016/j.bej.2017.01.010

Patra, K., Jha, A. K., Szalay, T., Ranjan, J., & Monostori, L. (2017). Artificial Neural Network Based tool condition monitoring in micro mechanical peck drilling used thrust force signals. *Precision Engineering, 48*, 279–291. doi:10.1016/j.precisioneng.2016.12.011

Petropoulos, G., Vaxevanidis, N. M., & Pandazaras, C. (2004). Modeling of surface finish in electro-discharge machining based upon statistical multi-parameter analysis. *Journal of Materials Processing Technology, 155-156*, 1247–1251. doi:10.1016/j.jmatprotec.2004.04.189

Pradhan, M. K., & Biswas, C. K. (2008). Neuro-fuzzy model on material removal rate in electrical discharge machining in AISI D2 steel. *Proceedings of the 2nd International and 23rd All India Manufacturing Technology, Design and Research Conference, 1*, 469-474

Pradhan, M. K., & Biswas, C. K. (2010). Investigating the effect of machining parameters on EDMed components a RSM approach. *Journal of Mechanical Engineering, 7*, 47–64.

Puertas, I., & Luis, C. J. (2003). A study on the machining parameters optimization of electrical discharge machining. *Journal of Materials Processing Technology, 143-144*, 521–526. doi:10.1016/S0924-0136(03)00392-3

Puertas, I., Luis, C. J., & Villa, G. (2005). Spacing roughness parameters study on the EDM of silicon carbide. *Journal of Materials Processing Technology, 164-165*, 1590–1596. doi:10.1016/j.jmatprotec.2005.01.004

Rahman, M.M., Khan, K., A.R., K., Maleque, M.A., & Bakar, R.A. (2010). Parametric optimization in EDM of Ti-6Al-4V using copper tungsten electrode and positive polarity: A Statistical Approach. *Mathematical Methods and Techniques in Engineering and Environmental Science, 6*, 23–29.

Ramaswamy, H., & Blunt, L. (2002). 3D surface characterisation of elctropolished EDMed surface and quantitative assessment of process variables using Taguchi Methodology. *International Journal of Machine Tools & Manufacture, 42*(10), 1129–1133. doi:10.1016/S0890-6955(02)00057-3

Ramaswamy, H., & Blunt, L. (2004). Effect of EDM process parameters on 3D surface topography. *Journal of Materials Processing Technology, 148*(2), 155–164. doi:10.1016/S0924-0136(03)00652-6

Routara, B. C., Bandyopadhyay, A., & Sahoo, P. (2007). Use of desirability function approach for optimization of multiple performance characteristics of the surface roughness parameters in CNC turning. *Proceedings of the International Conference on Mechanical Engineering.*

Sahoo, P., Routara, B. C., & Bandyopadhyay, A. (2009). Roughness modelling and optimization in EDM using response surface method for different work piece materials. *International Journal of Machining and Machinability of Materials, 5*(2/3), 321–346. doi:10.1504/IJMMM.2009.023398

Sitton, D. J., Zeinali, Y., & Story, A. (2017). Rapid soil classification using artificial neural network for use in constructing compressed earth blocks. *Construction & Building Materials, 138*, 214–221. doi:10.1016/j.conbuildmat.2017.02.006

Vasant, P. M., Weber, G., & Diew, V. N. (Eds.). (2016). Handbook of Research on Modern Optimization Algorithms and Applications in Engineering and Economics. IGI Global.

Vasant, P. M., Barsoum, N., & Webb, J. (Eds.). (2011). *Innovation in Power, Control, and Optimization: Emerging Energy Technologies*. IGI Global.

Yan, B. H., Tsai, H. C., & Huang, F. Y. (2005). The effect in EDM of a dielectric of a urea solution in water on modifying the surface of titanium. *International Journal of Machine Tools & Manufacture*, *45*(2), 194–200. doi:10.1016/j.ijmachtools.2004.07.006

Yu-Zhen, Y. U., Xin-yi, R., Feng-Shan, D., & Jun-jie, S. (2012). Application of Improved PSO Algorithm in Hydraulic Pressing System Identification. *Journal of Iron and Steel Research International*, *19*(9), 29–35. doi:10.1016/S1006-706X(13)60005-9

Zhang, J. H., Lee, T. C., & Lau, W. S. (1997). Study on the electro-discharge machining of a hot pressed aluminium oxide based ceramic. *Journal of Materials Processing Technology*, *63*(1-3), 908–912. doi:10.1016/S0924-0136(96)00012-X

Chapter 39
Optimizing Material Removal Rate Using Artificial Neural Network for Micro–EDM

Ananya Upadhyay
Birla Institute of Technology Mesra, India

Ved Prakash
Central Mechanical Engineering Research Institute (CSIR), India

Vinay Sharma
Birla Institute of Technology Mesra, India

ABSTRACT

Machining can be classified into conventional and unconventional processes. Unconventional Machining Process attracts researchers as it has many processes whose physics is still not that clear and they are highly in market-demand. To predict and understand the physics behind these processes soft computing is being used. Soft computing is an approach of computing which is based on the way a human brain learns and get trained to deal with different situations. Scope of this chapter is limited to one of the soft computing optimizing techniques that is artificial neural network (ANN) and to one of the unconventional machining processes, electrical discharge machining process. This chapter discusses about micromachining on Electric Discharge Machining, its working principle and problems associated with it. Solution to those problems is suggested with the addition of powder in dielectric fluid. The optimization of Material Removal Rate (MRR) is done with the help of ANN toolbox in MATLAB.

MANUFACTURING AND MACHINING

Manufacturing is the process of value addition to raw material. It is broadly classified into four processes which are casting, forming, machining and joining. Machining is one of the four basic manufacturing processes in which material removal takes place in the form of chips. Machining is used almost in

DOI: 10.4018/978-1-6684-2408-7.ch039

manufacturing of all the products. (Rao, 2009) It is one of the most expensive and energy consuming manufacturing process as material is removed from workpiece to complete the process. Machining process has a machine tool and a workpiece. Machining processes can be classified as traditional and non-traditional processes. The traditional or conventional machining processes include a machine tool and workpiece which are in direct contact during the machining. Some of the traditional processes are drilling, milling, grinding, polishing etc. The nontraditional methods came into picture to fix some of the drawbacks that conventional methods had which were the high cutting force due to which the material of tool should always be harder than that of the workpiece. With this constraint, it is difficult to machine materials like titanium alloy, tungsten carbide, and many others. Nonconventional processes can machine hard materials too. Most of them are contactless processes which remove the constraint of high cutting force impact on workpiece due to tool. Some of nontraditional processes are electro discharge machining, electrochemical machining, abrasive water jet machining, ultrasonic machining etc.

Micromachining

The rapidly developing technology aims at development of miniaturized products with multiple functions embedded in them. In the last few years, CIRP (College International Pour La Researche En Productique) has contributed significantly towards spreading awareness of micromachining and its different methods (Dornfeld et.al.,2006). The continuous demand to follow the trend of miniaturization requires advancement in micro manufacturing techniques.It has wide applications in the field of aerospace, automobile, biomedical, electronics and many others where miniaturization of parts is on high demand. Micro-holes on turbine blades, MEMS, Micro- gears, are few examples of applications of micro-manufacturing processes. Micro-EDM is a nontraditional process which can be an alternative to fulfill these demands of miniaturization of parts to an extent (Hong et. al., 2016).

The basic principle of EDM (Electro Discharge Machining) and Micro-EDM for metal removal is melting and vaporization. The basic difference between EDM and Micro- EDM is the size of tool, the limits of movements of the X, Y and Z axes and the amount of discharge energy supplied.

Electro- Discharge Machining (EDM)

In 1770, English chemist Joseph Prisetly found the effect of erosion from electrical spark (S.Webzell, 2001). Later in 1943 at Moscow University, Dr. B.R. Lazarenko and Dr. N.I. Lazarenko invented the resistance-capacitance (RC) circuit which is also known as Lazarenko circuit for EDM. This was for the first time when the erosion effect was used for machining difficult to cut material. At around same time, three American employees came up with this application of electrical spark for removal of broken tapes and drill in hydraulic valve. This became the basis for electrically controlled servo system for automatically maintaining the gap between tool and electrode (Jameson, 2001). In 1980, with the development of Computer Numerical Control (CNC) in EDM that most of the things became automatic and the process got many more modifications and still the researchers are contributing towards development of this process through modifications (Houman, 1983).

One of the latest and most popular developments of EDM is micro-EDM. It is gaining popularity and attention of researchers because of its diverse application in machining. Some of its application is manufacturing of micro-holes and shafts of 5μm diameter, intricate shapes and complex features of 3D cavities (Ho, 2003). Micro-EDM process has a wide range of applications in aerospace, electronics and automotive industries as it is capable of producing intricate shapes.

It is one of the unconventional processes which have a wide range of application due to its ease and accurate machining performance. The contactless nature of this process avoids vibrations, chatter and mechanical stresses. This process can be used to machine materials with high hardness, high strength and brittleness. The principle of working that EDM follows is the conversion of electrical energy to thermal energy and material removal takes place due to melting and vaporization. The basic requirement of the process is an electrode and workpiece with opposite polarities, a dielectric fluid and power source. The power source is a DC generator that supplies electrical energy to the system. There is a gap between workpiece and electrode which creates a potential difference due to which an electric field is developed. During discharge the electrical energy is converted into thermal energy and plasma is generated between the electrode and workpiece. The temperature of plasma can shoot up to 20,000°C (McGeough, 1988), normally temperature is in the range of 8000°C to 12000°C (Boothroyd and Winston, 1989). Due to the high temperature of plasma the portion where spark strikes the workpiece and electrode gets melted and when the dielectric passes through gap between them evaporates the removed material.

Micro-EDM

(Jahan, 2013) Micro-EDM came into picture in 1968 when Kurafuji and Masuzawa came up with its first application by drilling a minute hole in a 50 μm thick carbide plate (Masuzawa, 2000). Micro Electro Discharge Machining is an advanced manufacturing process which gives freedom to machine any conducting and semi-conducting material irrespective of its hardness with respect to tool. Micro-EDM process has a wide range of applications in industries as it is capable of producing intricate shapes. It is a non-contact process and so the problems related to impact forces of the tool on workpiece are absent. (Baraskar et.al., 2013) Also this process has a very slow MRR and the tool wear is high.

It follows the same working principle as that of the EDM. The basic difference between EDM and micro-EDM is of the amount of energy, temperature of plasma and dimension of electrode and workpiece. Macro EDM requires a DC source which can provide a pulse energy of 1μJ whereas Micro EDM requires few nJ energy and most of micro EDM work on RC circuit so the energy is stored in the capacitors. The temperature of plasma can shoot up to a maximum of 50,000°C while the minimum temperature being 4000°C. In the case of micro-EDM, polarity of the electrode is kept as negative to reduce tool wear whereas in the case of Macro-EDM the polarity of the electrode is kept as positive.

There are different approaches to perform micro-EDM processes. Only two of them are discussed in details, as these two approaches are used in the experiment that is discussed later in this chapter.

Die-sinking micro-EDM is one of the most frequently used approaches as it reduces the machining time when compared to other EDM approaches. The die sinking micro-EDM has a tank in which workpiece and electrode set up is there. This tank is completely filled with the dielectric fluid during the process. This approach is preferred for complex and intricate shapes.

Micro-Drilling on Micro-EDM is preferred over conventional drilling when the precise hole is required on a hard workpiece. Drilling on Micro-EDM is also preferred when high aspect ratio is requirement of the job. A cylindrical electrode is used for machining in micro-EDM. One of the important differences between micro drilling through EDM and conventional drilling is the tapering effect. Although this defect cannot be totally eliminated but Micro-drilling on EDM has less tapering effect compared to conventional drilling. (Modica et.al., 2017)

Many other approaches are micro-EDM milling; micro-turning, wire electro discharge grinding and wire cut EDM.

Powder Mixed Micro-EDM

To increase and enhance the machining efficiency of the Micro-EDM process, many new modifications were tried by researchers. Powder mixed micro-EDM is one of them. So far it has been concluded that if at the right concentration, particles of a particular size are mixed with the dielectric, it can be helpful in increasing MRR, decreasing TWR and increasing the surface quality.

LITERATURE SURVEY

Powder mixed micro-EDM is used for good surface finish and high MRR. Due to presence of particles in the dielectric fluid bridging effect occurs which increases the gap between workpiece and electrode. This helps the dielectric to flush away debris. The effect on surface quality due to deposition of debris, short circuiting and arcing gets lowered down due to its proper flushing.

Chaudhary et.al., 2017 has investigated the powder mixed EDM process on EN-19 steel with copper tungsten electrode. Tungsten powder was added in the dielectric fluid. The process parameters decided by authors were powder concentration, peak current and pulse on time. The performance parameters were MRR, Surface quality and TWR. They concluded from the paper that by regression analysis that the most significant process parameter is powder concentration.

Tripathy and Tripathy, 2017 have investigated the powder mixed EDM process on H-11 die steel with SiC powder mixed in dielectric fluid and copper as electrode. A separate tank of 20 litres capacity was installed with a pump and stirrer to maintain the circulation of the dielectric fluid and not letting the powder to settle down. It was reported by the authors that MRR and surface finish gets improved with addition of powder in dielectric fluid.

Toshimitsu et. al., 2016 have studied the effect of chromium powder on surface quality enhancement of EDM process. Alloy Tool steel SKD 11 was machined with a cylindrical copper electrode having diameter of 25 mm. Chromium layer is deposited on the workpiece surface and it enhances the surface finish, water repellency and corrosion resistance of the workpiece.

Talla et. al., 2016, investigated the powder mixed EDM process with an Inconel 625 machined with a copper electrode. Graphite powder was mixed in the kerosene dielectric fluid and an arrangement for continuous stirring is done to not let the powder particles settle down. The effect of the powder concentration is that the surface roughness decreases, crater size increases and the thickness of recast layer get reduced.

Kuriachen and Mathew, 2015 have studied the powder mixed micro-EDM process to enhance the surface quality and machining parameters. Silicon Crabide (SiC) micro particles was mixed in EDM-3 oil dielectric to enhance the performance efficiency when working on a titanium alloy Ti-6Al-4V workpiece with a tungsten carbide electrode. It is observed by the authors that powder concentration is one of the significant factors for influencing the performance parameters.

Zain et.al., 2014 have discussed the effect of tantalum carbide powder in kerosene dielectric fluid on EDM of stainless steel with copper electrode. It has been observed by the authors that Tantalum Carbide(TaC) powder gets deposited on the surface of workpiece and increases the micro hardness and corrosion resistance of the machined surface. The corrosion resistance enhancement was achieved due to addition of powder in the dielectric fluid because in conventional EDM process the corrosion resistance decreases.

Adepu and Kolli, 2014, have studied the PMMEDM titanium alloy. For aerospace industry Titanium alloy is important as it has high strength, excellent thermal properties, is light in weight, has low modulus of elasticity, corrosion resistance and fracture resistance. The powder that is added in this case was sorbitan (4g/lt.) and graphite (14g/lt.). The addition of powder was done with continuous stirring to check the uniform mixing. Surfactant was added in order to reduce the surface tension of sediments particles, to distribute uniformly graphite particles and during discharge they get oxidized and will increase the explosion. According to author, powder suspension is found to increase MRR and decrease TWR.

Prihandana et. al., 2012, suggested that if the flushing of debris is not proper it will lead to short circuiting which will result in increase of machining time. It is reported that the introduction of nano-graphite powder in the dielectric fluid was found to be helpful to fix this issue. It is also found that this has resulted in speeding up the process to five times faster. The workpiece is vibrated with the help of PZT actuator in Y- axis direction. Stirrer is used to mix the powder in the dielectric fluid, formation of chain by these nano-particles leads to bridging effect between the electrode and workpiece, which results in increasing the gap between them and removing debris through effective flushing.

Kung et.al., 2009 investigated the process of PMEDM with a conductive aluminum powder on a cobalt-bonded tungsten carbide workpiece with a copper electrode. The aluminum powder was added in different grain size and concentration in the commercially available dielectric fluid mineral oil EDM44. A circulation system is provided with dielectric system to not let the powder settle down. With the increase in grain size MRR and TWR increases. With increase in powder concentration till a certain value MRR increases and TWR decreases after that if further concentration is increased MRR decreases and TWR increases.

Lee and Tzeng, 2001, studied effect of different additives which includes copper, aluminum, silicon carbide and chromium on EDM process. The author has done selection of additives keeping in mind the thermo-physical properties. They concluded that chromium is most effective as the MRR is highest and TWR is lowest and copper should not be used as additive because it had no effect on the process.

The conclusion that can be drawn from the literature review of 10 papers is addition of powder to dielectric is effective for EDM as well as micro-EDM processes. If powder is added in right concentration, the performance parameters will be enhanced and the process will become more efficient. Table 1 shows the different types of powder used in PMEDM process and the research findings associated with covered papers.

The conclusion that can be drawn from the literature review is addition of powder to dielectric is effective for EDM as well as micro-EDM processes. If powder is added in right concentration, the performance parameters will be enhanced and the process will become more efficient.

Table 1. Different types of powder used in PMEDM process and the research findings associated with covered papers

S. No.	Authors	Powder Mixed in Dielectric Fluid	Research Findings
1.	Chaudhary et. al., 2017	Tungsten powder	According to Regression analysis powder concentration is most influencing factor for performance parameters.
2.	Tripathy and Tripathy, 2017	SiC Powder	Surface roughness decreases and MRR increases
3.	Toshimitsu et. al., 2016	Chromium powder	Surface Roughness decreases, water repellency and corrosion resistance increases.
4.	Talla et. al., 2016	Graphite powder	Surface roughness decreases, crater size gets enlarged with increase in the concentration of powder, surface cracks are less and a thin recast layer is formed
5.	Kuriachen and Mathew, 2015	SiC micro Particles	High MRR and low TWR are achieved at a fixed powder concentration increasing this can contribute in deceasing MRR and increasing TWR
6.	Zain et.al., 2014	Tantalum Carbide	Increases micro-hardness and corrosion resistance of the machined surface.
7.	Adepu and Kolli, 2014	Graphite and sorbitan	Powder suspension increases MRR and decreases TWR.
8.	Prihandana et.al., 2012	Nano- graphite powder	Machining time can be reduced.
9.	Kung et. al., 2009	Aluminum Powder	MRR and TWR increases with increase in grain size. MRR increases and TWR decreases to o a certain value of powder concentration. If the powder concentration is increased further MRR decreases and TWR increases.
10.	Lee and Tzeng, 2001	Copper, aluminum, silicon carbide and chromium.	Chromium is the most effective powder. Copper should not be used as additive in PMEDM. The concentration of powder is important factor. Too high or low concentration can lead to decrease in the efficiency of the process.

INTRODUCTION TO ARTIFICIAL NEURAL NETWORK

Neural network is one of the soft computing tools that are basically used for stochastic processes. Artificial Neural Network is a network architecture that can learn from a set of experimental data to describe a non-linear and interaction effect with great success (Chandrashekar et. al., 2010).The advantage of using ANN for making a model is that the model can be easily constructed by giving a set of input and output data and then it can be trained with a set of data to accurately predict process dynamics (Somashekhar et.al., 2010). ANN is useful whenever complete understanding of a physical process is not there. Whenever it is difficult to obtain an analytical model based on the physics of the process, ANN can be used to build a model.

ANN structure is based on the human nervous system. The architecture of ANN is inspired from the neurons of human brain. The network of any ANN model has at least three layers; first is the input layer, second layer is the hidden layer and third is the output layer. The main elements of the network are activation function and the weight factors. The weight factors are adjusted to minimize the error. Error is the difference between the output of network and targeted output of the process. In this work, the error is reduced by using the back-propagation method and the network is constructed by using feed forward network. (Porwal and Yadav, 2012).

ARTIFICIAL NEURAL NETWORK BACKGROUND

ANN acquires knowledge through a learning process. (McCulloch and Pitts, 1943) In this research the first mathematical model of the neuron was outlined. (Hebb, 1949) In this work for the first time the concept of learning of networks was introduced through synaptic weights. (Rumelhart et.al., 1986) researched and found the back propagation algorithm which resulted into a powerful tool to minimize error. Since then, researchers have been found exploring the wide range of applications of ANN in different fields. These fields include pattern recognition, industrial processes, manufacturing processes like welding, machining, molding and many others. Many authors (Coit et.al., 1998, Haykin, 2008, Al-Ahmari, 2007) have chosen ANN to solve problems due to two reasons; the first is that it learns through examples and the second, it can generalize the network for unseen data also. Learning happens with a set of data which is collected through experimental runs. The more the number of runs the better will be the accuracy of network. The generalizing feature of ANN is unique as it can produce results with a data set which was not used for training the network.

Tsai and Wang, 2001, have done estimation of surface finish for EDM process when electrode polarity is varying. The author has done this through six different neural network models and one neural fuzzy model. The network architecture is based on previous semi empirical models developed. The number of input parameters is taken as 5 and output parameter as 1, the number of hidden layer is taken as 1 by the author to start the analysis. The six different neural network models were logistic sigmoid multilayered perceptron (LOGMLP), hyperbolic tangent sigmoid multi-layered perceptron (TANMLP), Radial Basis function network (RBFN), fast error back propagation multi layered network with hyperbolic tangent function (error TANMLP), TANMLP with adaptive learning rate (adaptive TANMLP), Radial Basis function network with adaptive learning rate(adaptive RBFN) and Neuro-fuzzy model was Adaptive network based fuzzy inference system. It has been concluded on the basis of result showed that TAN-MLP, RBFN, adaptive RBFN and ANFIS models have smaller error compared to other models and experimental verifications agree with the obtained results. Tsai and Wang, 2001, followed the research work by estimation of Material Removal Rate for the EDM process keeping all the process parameters same as in the previous work. The estimation is done following the same six neural network models and one neuro-fuzzy model. In the work it is mentioned that for the adaptive network based fuzzy inference system (ANFIS) the input parameters should be less than 7 with one output parameter. It is found that the previous semi empirical models satisfy the conditions for constructing an architecture of ANFIS model. The results show that ANFIS is most accurate amongst all the 7 models considered for estimation of MRR. These models were found to be applicable for industrial applications. Panda and Bhoi, 2005, have used the Multilayer perceptron feed forward network with Back propagation algorithm to predict the MRR for EDM process. The number of neurons and hidden layers is obtained with the help of trial and error method. Three network architectures were selected based on the R- square coefficients which are 3-4-3-1, 3-7-1 and 3-10-1.It is found that 3-7-1 network results has closest R-efficiency and so it is selected for further investigation of this work. The author has mentioned that increase in the number of epochs increases the efficiency of the model but after a certain limit when the epochs are increased it results in decrease of the efficiency of model which indicates the saturation of training program. The model developed has not much sensitivity to noise. Cus and Zuperl, 2006, developed a neural optimization algorithm to develop a model which is helpful to determine optimum cutting parameters for turning operation. The architecture of neural network model is 3-3-6-1. Two neural networks models are used, feed forward and radial basis neural network. It is found that feed forward network results are more accurate but time taken by algorithm to do computation is more when compared to RBNN. Mandal et.al., 2007, has discussed about a feed forward neural network with back propagation learning algorithm which uses gradient search technique to minimize the mean square error of the output of the network. The optimization of the process is done through non-dominating sorting genetic algorithm-II. The authors have also mentioned that ANN is selected for this process as the physics of the process is not clear. The architecture of the network was 3-10-10-2 with learning coefficient of 0.5. It is found that the model is suitable to predict the output responses. Rao et. al., 2008, discusses a multi layered perceptron neural network which is used to build a relationship between process parameters and performance parameters in die-sinking EDM process. The input parameters that were selected are peak current, machining time, type of material and voltage and the output parameter is MRR. Sensitivity analysis is used to estimate the relative influence of process parameters on performance measures. Genetic algorithm is used to adjust the weights as well as for the optimization of process parameters. It is found that type of material has the highest influence on the performance measures.

Joshi and Pande, 2009, In their research work discuss about the thermal modeling of the EDM using Finite Element Method (FEM) and the relationship is being established between process parameters and performance parameters using artificial neural network (ANN). The network architecture used for the analysis is 4-8-12-4. Two ANN models are tried, Radial basis neural network (RBNN) and Back propagation neural network (BPNN). It is found that BPNN produces more accurate results when compared to RBNN. Pradhan and Chandan, 2010, discussed three models namely; artificial neural network and two neuro-fuzzy models to estimate the MRR, TWR and radial overcut in a die sinking EDM process. The artificial neural network used for this work is feed forward neural network with back propagation learning algorithm with architecture of 4-1-1. The learning rate was 0.05 and momentum parameter is 1.05 for back propagation leaning algorithm. The analysis of variance suggests that discharge current is the most influencing factor for MRR than any other parameter. It is found that ANN and two neuro-fuzzy models predict results under acceptable limits. Gaitonde and Karnik, 2012, have optimized the process parameter for burr size during drilling operation with the help of Artificial Neural Network (ANN) and particle swarm optimization (PSO). A multi- layered feed forward network with error back propagation learning algorithm with architecture of 3-13-2is constructed to estimate the burr size of the drilling operation. The input parameters decided by the authors are feed, drill diameter and point angle and the response parameters are burr height and burr thickness. The neural network and PSO combination produce results in an acceptable range. Hence this combination can be used for building relationship and optimizing the process parameters to produce response.

Suganthi et. al., 2013, in this paper, two approaches of soft computing are used for prediction of quality responses of the micro-EDM process. The two approaches, ANFIS- adaptive neuro- fuzzy inference system and Artificial Neural network with back propagation training algorithm. The architecture for ANN model is 4-6-6-6-3, which is decided using trial and error method. Both the models produce results within acceptable limit and are used to build relationship between input and output parameters. According to the authors, ANFIS model is faster and more accurate when compared to BP- based ANN.

Majumder, 2014, In this paper, ANN is used to establish relationship between input parameters and output parameters and three different algorithms, simulated annealing, genetic algorithm and particle swarm optimization are used to optimize the process parameters so as to result in maximum MRR and minimum wear ratio. For training the neural network back propagation algorithm is used. BPNN model acts as the fitness function to optimize the process parameters. It is concluded that Particle Swarm Optimization is better than simulated annealing algorithm and Genetic Algorithm optimization for modeling and optimization of EDM process.

The training of network is done by two ways: supervised and unsupervised training. The supervised training of network is done with a set of input data and a set of targeted output data. Now, the network tries to train itself and produce output close to or equal to targeted output data. Whereas, the unsupervised training technique does not require targeted output data, which means only a set of input data is provided to the network and it learns by its own discovering and adapting to structural features in the input pattern. (Pattanaik, 2017)

Table 2. Different combination of neural networks used for micro-EDM

S. No.	Authors	Neural Network Used	Research Findings
1.	Prabhu and Vinayagam, 2015	Adaptive Neuro Fuzzy Inference System (ANFIS)	Used for predicting Surface Roughness. This approach can be used for on line control and optimization.
2.	Majumder, 2014	ANN with BP training algorithm	Relationship between input and output parameters can be built through ANN.
3.	Suganthi et. al., 2013	ANFIS and BP based ANN	Relation between process and performance parameters is built. ANFIS is faster than BP based ANN.
4.	Gaitonde and Karnik, 2012	BP based ANN with PSO	Optimization of process parameter for burr size of drilled micro holes.
5.	Pradhan and Chandan, 2010	BP based ANN and Neuro Fuzzy Network	It is able to predict optimal values of performance parameters for die-sinking EDM.
6.	Joshi and Pande, 2009	BPNN and RBNN	BPNN is faster than RBNN. Relationship between input and output parameters can be built through neural networks for calculations of optimal performance parameters.
7.	Rao et. al., 2008	MLP-ANN with GA	Optimization of process parameters for die-sinking EDM. Most influencing factor can be predicted.
8.	Mandal et.al., 2007	ANN with BP algorithm	ANN should be used were nature of process is stochastic.
9.	Cus and Zuperl, 2006	Feed Forward Neural Network and RBNN	Optimum cutting parameters for turning operation is predicted. Feed forward neural network is accurate but slow than RBNN.
10.	Panda and Bhoi, 2005	ANN with BP learning algorithm	MRR can be predicted with ANN models for EDM process. Epochs can result in increasing the efficiency of network to a certain limit after that if epochs are increased it can lead to lowering down the efficiency.

ARCHITECTURE OF ARTIFICIAL NEURAL NETWORK

(Fabricio et.al., 2010) In this paper, the network architecture and its working has been explained. The working is each neuron in the input layer is assigned to a parameter from the input data set. In the input layer, the neuron is responsible to produce an output which is a scaled value of each input parameter data. The hidden layer, in case of multilayer feed forward network is present between the input and the output layer. The job allotted to the neurons of the hidden layer is the computation of an output which is a scalar product of neuron's input vector and the vector of weights associated to its input. The result produced is compared with a threshold limit. If the value exceeds the threshold limit then the scalar product is used as an independent variable of an activation function whose output will be neuron's output.

Any neural network can be represented with the help of directed graph (see Figures 1-3).

Figure 1. Representation using directed graph

Figure 2. This symbol indicates the neuron

Figure 3. This symbol indicates the direction of flow of network computation

The ANN architecture can be basically two types:

- Single layer feed forward ANN
- Multilayer feed forward ANN

Single Layer Feed Forward ANN

As the name suggests single layer feed forward will have single layer for input to be fed in the network. The structure of the network is shown in Figure 4.

It has two layers, input layer and output layer. All signals move in one direction. It is not reverted back. Although it has two layers the input layer and output layer but since all computation is alone done with output layer so its name is single feed forward network. The input layer has m number of neurons and output layer has n number of neurons. The $x_1, x_2, .., x_m$ are the input parameters and $y_1, y_2, ..., y_n$ are the output parameters. The $w_{11}, w_{12}, ..., w_{mn}$ are the weights of synaptic link in the format w_{ij} which is the weights of synaptic link between i^{th} and j^{th} neuron where i and j are the index for input and output neurons.

Figure 4. The network architecture of single layer feed forward network

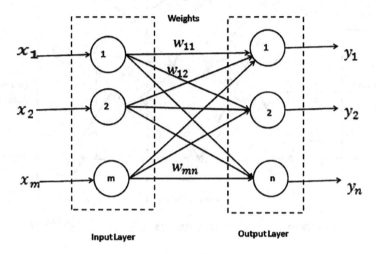

Multilayer Feed Forward ANN

It has a minimum of three layers. The two layers, input and output layers are common to a single feed forward network and one additional layer named as hidden layer is added to increase the calculation accuracy. Now the hidden layer and output layer neurons will be involved in computational concerns. Again, the input layer will not be involved in any computation. The network structure of a Multilayer feed forward network is shown in Figure 5.

The nomenclature of this network is done (l-m-n) where l, m, n indicate the number of neurons in the input layer, hidden layer and output layer respectively.

Neural Network on MATLAB

MATLAB – MATrixLABoratory is a software for numerical computation and visualization. It is a versatile and a multi-dimensional software. One of its tools is Neural Network.

Neural Network design steps:

Step 1: Choose the area in which the problem falls. It has four application areas:
- Function fitting
- Pattern recognition
- Clustering
- Time series analysis

Step 2: Collect data. For ANN it is suggested to collect more data. The accuracy of network increases with the increase in the amount of data.

Figure 5. The architecture of multilayer feed forward network

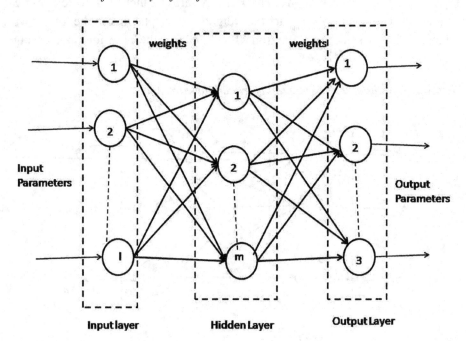

Step 3: Creating a network. Choose the number of input parameters and output parameters. In this step the target output is also decided for which the network will be trained.

Step 4: Configuring the network which includes trying and finding the number of hidden layers and number of neurons that will provide an optimized result for the network.

Step 5: Initialize the weights and biases. In MATLAB this can be done automatically by use of the software i.e. selecting the weights randomly. The weights that each input parameter should be given can be decided manually also and then it can be fed to the network.

Step 6: Training the network. A part of the total data is used to train the network. Training the network makes the network adapt to the working condition with given input parameters and target output.

Step 7: Validating the network. This step is done to check the status of training of the network. If training of network is done properly the network can produce output for any randomly selected parameter. Validation of network is done by randomly selecting data from the set of data provided for training. If the result is close to targeted output then the network is trained properly.

Step 8: When the validation step is over and the regression value (a graph is obtained with a black continuous line which indicates the targeted output and a scattered output produced through network. regression value is the value of deviation from targeted slope of line.) is equal to or above 0.93, the network is ready to be used for a generalized data set of that particular working condition.

In this chapter the problem falls under fitting. To solve a problem there are two ways:

- Graphical User Interface (GUI)
- Command line function

In this chapter command line technique is used for optimizing the Material Removal Rate. The GUI can also be used and then automatically command line script can be generated.

Objective

Model Development with the help of Neural Network:

A model is being developed using Artificial Neural Network (ANN) to determine the Material Removal Rate (MRR) for Micro-EDM.

Effect of different types of additives on Micro-EDM process:

Determine the effect of conductive (Aluminum) as well as semi conductive (Silicon Carbide) additives on the Micro-EDM process.

Case Study

In the EDM process the gap between tool & workpiece is more than 10 μm, so during the process of material removal, the gap is enough to let the dielectric flush away debris easily. In contrast to this, in micro-EDM the gap between tool and workpiece is very small, in the range of 1 to 5μm which makes the flushing away of debris difficult.

If the debris is not flushed away properly, it will have the following effects on the process:

- The debris will get accumulated in this gap and deteriorate the surface finish of workpiece.
- The MRR will also get reduced as debris will obstruct the flow of dielectric.
- The tool wear will increase due to the clogging of debris instead of sparking, arcing results.
- The surface finish is also affected as the clogging results in short circuit which eventually leads to arcing.
- All these problems will further increase as the depth of cut will increase.

The solution to these problems is to increase the gap between tool and workpiece which can provide this process with proper flushing away of debris with the help of dielectric.

In this research, additives are added in the dielectric fluid and then it is passed from the gap. It is found that this slight modification in the process solves these problems to some extent.

Process Parameters

Selection of process parameter depends on the following factors, the material of electrode and workpiece, the feature and final dimension required on the product, the surface quality of the finished product, the amount of energy required for the erosion process to occur.

There are many other factors which can be considered other than these for selection of process parameters.

The main process parameters that are used as input parameters for micro-EDM process can be:

- Voltage
- Capacitance
- Current

- Electrode polarity
- Delay time
- Frequency
- Dielectric fluid
- Tool rotation speed
- Tool feed rate

Mostly, current is calculated after measuring other parameters. Frequency is the reciprocal of total time interval within which spark takes place. Electrode polarity can be negative or positive depending upon the work requirement. Choice of dielectric fluid is important as it responsible for the flushing the debris. If the debris are not flushed away properly the efficiency of the process drops as short circuit occurs frequently which increases machining time. The dielectric fluid should be eco-friendly and safe. The tool rotation speed is responsible for uniform tool wear and it can also assist removal of debris. If the removed material gets deposited it lowers down the efficiency of process as well as the dimensions of final product is also disturbed.

In order to understand the effect of different process parameters on MRR following parameters are being investigated:

- Voltage
- Capacitance
- Additives

Performance Parameters

There are some parameters to check the efficiency of the electro discharge machining process. These parameters which help us define the quality of work done are known as performance parameters. Some of the performance parameters for micro-EDM process are Material Removal Rate (MRR), Tool Wear Rate (TWR), surface roughness and dimensional accuracy. (Rahman,2012)

These parameters are checked by different equipment and instruments. The MRR can be checked with the help of a weighing balance. Atomic Force Microscope (AFM), scanning tunnel microscope(STM) can also be helpful to define the profile. Tool Wear Rate can be checked with Laser micrometer or image processing. The surface quality and dimensional accuracy can be checked with the help of profilometer, Scanning Electron Microscope (SEM) and Energy Dispersive Spectroscopy (EDS).

The input parameters were voltage, capacitance, electrode cross section area and additives. The output parameter is Material Removal Rate (MRR).

SELECTION OF RANGE OF PROCESS PARAMETERS

Literature Survey

Mahendran et.al., 2010, has done the review of micro-EDM process. The author has found that the working principle of EDM and Micro-EDM is similar only with difference in the amount of discharge energy. The process and performance parameters has been found to be similar. Some of the process parameters that were discussed are discharge voltage, peak current, pulse duration, pulse interval, pulse waveform, polarity and electrode gap. The performance parameters were MRR, surface finish and tool wear ratio. Banu et.al., 2014, discussed the investigation of micro-EDM process for a ceramic workpiece using assisting electrodes. The electrode used to machine it is tungsten with an assisting electrode. The die-sinking approach of micro EDM is been investigated with focusing the analysis on MRR and hardness of recast layer. It is found that copper adhesive as assisting electrode gives better results as compared to other considered assisting electrodes. The process parameters considered were gap voltage 80-110V, feed rate 1-6 µm/s, and rotational speed of 100-700 rpm. Jahan et. al., 2015, has discussed about micro-EDM drilling process on aluminum alloy (AA 2024) with tungsten electrode of 0.3 µm.. The optimum process parameters found to maximize MRR and minimize the tool wear ratio were voltage, capacitance, resistance and spindle speed. Saxsena et. al., 2016, has investigated machining of ceramic on Micro-EDM. The optimization of the process parameters is done using ANOVA. It has been concluded that the process performance depends on all the three process parameters gap voltage, capacitance and threshold value. The performance parameters considered were MRR, tool wear ratio, surface finish and radial over cut. Voltage was taken in the range of 110-150 V, capacitance 10nF- 0.4µF and threshold as 40 -80%. It is found that the discharge energy depends on the product of capacitance and square of voltage. Any variation in discharge energy is proportional to capacitance and voltage.

From the literature review it is concluded that voltage and capacitance are two process parameters that have major influence on the micro-EDM process performance. So for this study voltage and capacitance are taken as two process parameters and to check the effect of additives on the performance one more factor is considered as additives.

- **Voltage:** The values of voltage can range between 80 – 130 V for the µ- EDM machine considered but for milling and drilling operations, the voltage is taken between 105- 115 V because below 105 V the MRR is very less and above 115 V the deposition of debris on workpiece and electrode is predominant.
- **Capacitance:** The range of capacitance available on this machine is 0- 6 pF. It is observed that below 4 pF the MRR is very low so the optimal range for capacitance is 4-6 pF.
- **Additives:** To understand the effect of additives on the process the following three cases are considered for investigation; without additive, with conductive additive and with semi-conductive additive. The conductive additive used is aluminum powder and the semi-conductive additive used is silicon carbide powder. The semi-conductive SiC powder is chosen as it is used as abrasive in machining processes so in this process also with the addition of this powder the material removal can be enhanced and also the surface finish is expected to improve.

Preparation of Electrode

The electrode is prepared on the hybrid Micro-EDM machine (DT-110 Model) MIKROTOOL using turning process. A 4*mm* brass rod is mounted on the spindle and the turning process occurs. The turning process occurs between the carbide tool present on the machine and the rotating brass rod. The tool preparation is done on the same machine because if not, while mounting on the spindle problems like deflection and centering are likely to occur.

Experimental Set-Up

In this experiment the circulation of powder and flushing is a problem. In this machine, the dielectric flushing has to pass through a filter channel. This filter channel will filter additives also. So to maintain the additives in dielectric an auxiliary arrangement was done. In the whole set-up one extra jar is attached. This jar will collect used dielectric mixed with additive from the dielectric tank. For the circulation two submersible pumps are fixed. One of the pumps is in the dielectric tank and the other in the jar. These pumps regulate the flow of dielectric mixed with additives from tank to jar and jar to tank. (Upadhyay, et. al., 2016)

The input parameters for the process are capacitance and voltage and the output parameter is Material Removal Rate (MRR). Theoretical MRR is calculated with the formula:

$$MRR = (Volume\ of\ Machining) / (Total\ time\ of\ machining) \tag{1}$$

Time is recorded with the help of a stopwatch. The operation that is considered for this study is drilling. The dimensions of the machined part are diameter of 0.5mm and depth of 0.1mmand the diameter of the tool is 0.5 mm. The volume of machining is calculated with the formula:

$$Volume\ of\ Machining = depth \times \frac{\pi}{4} \times diameter\ of\ electrode^2 \tag{2}$$

Table 3. Process parameters and their range considered for this experiment

Parameters	Units	Values
Voltage	Volts (V)	105, 110, 115
Capacitance	pF	4,5,6
Additives	-	No additive, conductive, semi-conductive

Table 4. Different additives used and their properties

Name of Additive	Type of Additive	Concentration (gram/Litre)	Conductivity (S/m)
Al Powder	Conductive	4	3.50×10^7
SiC powder	Semi Conductive	2	310

Table 5. The conditions under which experiment was performed and the equipment used

Machine	Micro-EDM Machine, Model- DT110, MIKROTOOL
Workpiece (Anode)	20×20*mm*, brass sheet
Electrode (Cathode)	0.5*mm* diameter, brass rod
Dielectric Fluid	EDM oil
Thickness of Workpiece	0.1*mm*
Cross Sectional Area of Electrode	0.19625*mm*²

Table 6. The input parameters, experimental and theoretical MRR

RUN	Voltage	Capacitance	MRR (Experimental)	MRR (Theoretical)
1	110	6	0.00677	0.0062
2	110	6	0.00643	0.0062
3	110	6	0.00735	0.0062
4	110	5	0.00878	0.00889
5	110	5	0.00934	0.00889
6	110	5	0.00835	0.00889
7	105	4	0.0022	0.002
8	105	4	0.00242	0.002
9	105	4	0.00238	0.002
10	110	4	0.00291	0.003
11	110	4	0.003911	0.003
12	110	4	0.00256	0.003
13	115	5	0.00919	0.0093
14	115	5	0.00892	0.0093
15	115	5	0.00878	0.0093

The result shows that the experimental and theoretical values of MRR are not the same. The experimental MRR is obtained with an error of 2.405% when compared to the theoretical MRR.

Implementation of ANN for Calculation of MRR

The approach for solving the problem statement isfirst with the help of MATLAB codes number of neurons is selected which can give minimum root mean square error (RMSE) and then a network is created with the optimum number of neurons and number of hidden layers.

The network which has two input parameters (Voltage and Capacitance), four neurons in the hidden layer and one output parameter (MRR). The result is shown in Table 9.

The result shows that the network has 3.52% error. Therefore, the output produced is 96.48% accurate.

RESULTS AND DISCUSSION

In this work, an attempt has been made to find the significant factors that influence the MRR of Micro-EDM process with additives in the dielectric fluid. The ANN result predicts that the network constructed has 96.48% accuracy. The error that is obtained in the network is within acceptable limits. The input parameters for the processes were capacitance and voltage. The output parameter for this network was MRR. Optimum result is obtained with a network structure of 2-4-1 which means 2 neurons in the input layer, 4 neurons in the hidden layer and 1 neuron in the output layer. The network is limited to 4 to 6 pF capacitances and 105 to 115 V voltages. Additionally, the effect of a conductive additive is more than a semi-conductive one. When the material removal rate was compared it was found for conductive additive it is more whereas for semi-conducting it is less.

Table 7. The Root Mean Square Error corresponding to number of neurons

S. No.	Number of Neurons	Root Mean Square Error
1	1	0.011
2	2	3.77E-04
3	3	6.28E-04
4	4	3.42E-04
5	5	3.59E-04
6	6	3.99E-04
7	7	6.08E-04
8	8	0.0022
9	9	3.65E-04
10	10	5.83E-04
11	11	3.50E-04
12	12	3.75E-04
13	13	3.56E-04
14	14	3.64E-04
15	15	3.43E-04

Table 9. MRR targeted and MRR through ANN

S.No.	MRR (Tagret)	MRR (ANN)
1	0.0062	0.0062
2	0.0062	0.0062
3	0.0062	0.0062
4	0.00889	0.0091
5	0.00889	0.0091
6	0.00889	0.0091
7	0.002	0.0025
8	0.002	0.0025
9	0.002	0.0025
10	0.003	0.0025
11	0.003	0.0025
12	0.003	0.0025
13	0.0093	0.0091
14	0.0093	0.0091
15	0.0093	0.0091

Table 8. Number of hidden layers with 4 neurons and corresponding RSM error

S. No.	No. of Layers	Root Mean Square Error
1	1	3.42E-04
2	2	0.0017
3	3	3.45E-04
4	4	3.44E-04
5	5	3.50E-04
6	6	0.0069
7	7	3.79E-04
8	8	3.64E-04
9	9	0.0032
10	10	3.10E-03

The graph shows that the targeted output and the actual output obtained from ANN has close proximity. On the y-axis is MRR and on the x-axis, the number of experimental runs. Since the results are in close proximity it can be used to calculate the MRR for Micro-EDM process when a brass sheet is machined with an electrode of brass with input parameters as voltage and capacitance.

Figure 6. The plot between MRR and no. of experimental runs; the target output and ANN output comparison

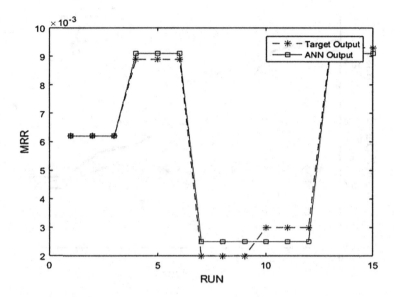

Figure 7. Error histogram for network 2-4-1

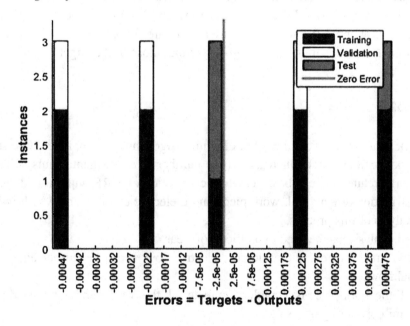

Error histogram shows the spread of error. The yellow vertical line indicates zero error and it is called zero error line. The bars indicate the data having that error. The bar has three colors, blue, red and green. Blue color indicates training data, red indicates test data and green indicates validation data.

The bar which is closest to the histogram indicates that has the least error. The network 2-4-1 has least error of -2.5e-05 with training data for 1 instance and testing data till 3 instances starting from 1.

Figure 8. Plot between the mean square error and epochs for network 2-4-1

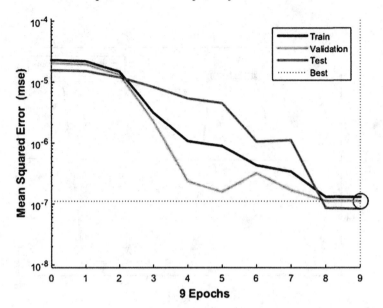

The lines indicate the variation of mean square data with epochs. The colors blue, red and green indicate the training, testing and validation data respectively. The plot above shows that validation and training data are close at epoch 9. Close to epoch 8 all the three data lines come close to each other and hence show that the network is trained and is giving output close to the target output.

FUTURE SCOPE

- Use of Back Propagation Neural Network learning algorithm can improve the result.
- The network accuracy can be increased if the number of experimental runs is increased. So,the same network architecture can be checked for calculation of MRR with more data.
- Energy distribution among tool, work-piece and dielectric can be done which will be helpful in thermal analysis of this process.
- The thermal analysis can be used to predict tool wear.
- This work is limited to one-dimensional dielectric flow, it can be further analyzed with multi-dimensional flow.
- In this work the work piece is a conductive material, this work can be extended to a work piece which is semi-conducting or insulating.
- The machining of ceramics and glass on micro-EDM can be thought of, as machining of hard and brittle materials with conventional machining techniques is extremely difficult.

REFERENCES

Adepu, K., & Kolli, M. (2014). Effect of Additives Added in Dielectric Fluid on Electrical Discharge Machining of Titanium Alloy. *International Conference onAdvanced Research & innovations in Mechanical, Material science, Industrial Engineering & Management*, 247-250.

Al-Ahmari, A. M. A. (2007). Predictive machinability models for a selected hard material in turning operations. *Journal of Materials procesing. Technology (Elmsford, N.Y.)*, *190*, 305–311.

Banu, A., Ali, M. Y., & Rahman, M. A. (2014). Micro-Electro Discharge Machining of non-conductive zirconia ceramic: Investigation of MRR & recast layer hardness. *International Journal of Advanced Manufacturing Technology*, *75*(1-4), 257–267. doi:10.100700170-014-6124-9

Baraskar, S. S., Banwait, S. S., & Laroiya, S. C. (2013). Multiobjective Optimization of Electrical Discharge Machining Process Using a Hybrid Method. *Materials and Manufacturing Processes*, *28*(4), 348–354. doi:10.1080/10426914.2012.700152

Bembde, M. S., & Sawale, J. K. (2014). Review of Powder Mixed Dielectric on Material Removal Rate in EDM. *International Journal of Science and Research*, *12*(4), 821–824.

Boothroyd, G., & Winston, A. K. (1989). *Non-Conventional Machining Processes. In Fundamentals of Machining & Machine Tools* (p. 491). New York: Marcel Dekker Inc.

Chandrashekar, M., Muralidhar, M., Murali Krishna, C., & Dixit, U. S. (2010). Application of soft computing techniques in machining performance prediction & optimization: A literature review. *International Journal of Advanced Manufacturing Technology*, *46*(5-8), 445–464. doi:10.100700170-009-2104-x

Chaudhury, P., Samantaray, S., & Sahu, S. (2017). Multi Response Optimization of Powder Additive Mixed Electrical Discharge Machining by Taguchi Analysis. *Materials Today: Proceedings*, *4*(2), 2231–2241. doi:10.1016/j.matpr.2017.02.070

Coit, D. W., Jackson, B. T., & Smith, A. E. (1998). Static Neural Network process models: Considerations and case studies. *International Journal of Production Research*, *36*(11), 2953–2967. doi:10.1080/002075498192229

Cus, F., & Zuperl, U. (2006). Approach to optimization of cutting conditions by using Artificial Neural network. *Journal of Materials Processing Technology*, *173*(3), 281–290. doi:10.1016/j.jmatprotec.2005.04.123

Dornfeld, D., Min, S., & Takeuchi, Y. (2006). Recent Advances in Mechanical Micromachining. *Annals of the CIRP*, *55*(2), 1–25. doi:10.1016/j.cirp.2006.10.006

Fabricio, J. P., Joao, R. F., Messias, B. S., Anderson, P. P., & Pedro, P. B. (2010). Artificial neural networks for machining processes surface roughness modeling. *International Journal of Advanced Manufacturing Technology*, *49*(9-12), 879–902. doi:10.100700170-009-2456-2

Gaitonde, V. N., & Karnik, S. R. (2012). Minimizing burr size in drilling using Artificial Neural Network-Particle Swarm optimization approach (PSO). *Journal of Intelligent Manufacturing*, *23*(5), 1783–1793. doi:10.100710845-010-0481-5

Gunawan, S. P., Tutik, S., & Muslim, M. (2012). Improvement of Machining time through workpiece vibration and graphite powder mixed in dielectric fluid. *Indian Journal of Engineering and Materials Sciences, 19*, 375–378.

Haykin, S. (1999). *Introduction. In Neural networks and learning machines* (3rd ed.). Pearson Prentice Hall, New Jersy.

Hebb, D. O. (1949). *The organization of behavior A Neuropsychological theory*. New York: John Wiley & Sons,Inc.

Ho, K. H., & Newman, S. T. (2003). State of the art electrical discharge machining (EDM). *International Journal of Machine Tools & Manufacture, 43*(13), 1287–1300. doi:10.1016/S0890-6955(03)00162-7

Hong, Y., Chunmei, W., Wujun, F., & Xuyang, C. (2017). Analysis of mechanism based on two types of pulse generators in micro-EDM using single pulse discharge. *International Journal of Advanced Manufacturing Technology, 89*(9), 3217–3230.

Houman, L. (1983). Total EDM. In E. C. Jameson (Ed.), *Electrical Discharge Machining: Tooling, Methods and Applications* (pp. 5–19). Dearborn, MI: Society of Manufacturing Engineers.

Jahan, M. P. (2013). Micro-Electrical Discharge Machining. In J.P. Davim (Ed.), Non traditional Machining Processes. Springer-Verlag.

Jahan, M. P., Kakavand, P., Kwang, E. L. M., Rahman, M., & Wong, Y. S. (2015). An experimental investigation into the micro-electro-discharge machining behavior of aluminium alloy (AA 2024). *International Journal of Advanced Manufacturing Technology, 78*(5-8), 1127–1139. doi:10.100700170-014-6712-8

Jameson, E. C. (2001). Description and development of electrical discharge machining (EDM). In *Electrical Discharge Machining* (Vol. 12). Dearborn, MI: Society of Manufacturing Engineers.

Joshi, S. N., & Pande, S. S. (2009). Development of an intelligent process model for Electro-Discharge Machining. *International Journal of Advanced Manufacturing Technology, 45*, 300–317. doi:10.100700170-009-1972-4

Kung, K. Y., Horng, J. T., & Chiang, K. T. (2009). Material removal rate and electrode wear ratio study on the powder mixed electrical discharge machining of cobalt-bonded tungsten carbide. *International Journal of Advanced Manufacturing Technology, 40*(1-2), 95–104. doi:10.100700170-007-1307-2

Kuriachen, B., & Mathew, J. (2015). Effect of Powder Mixed Dielectric on Material Removal and Surface Modification in Micro Electric Discharge Machining of Ti-6Al-4V. *Materials and Manufacturing Processes*, 1–30.

Mahendra, S., Devarajan, R., Nagarajan, T., & Majdi, A. (2010). A review of Micro-EDM. *Proceedings of International Multiconference of Engineers & computer scientists, 2*.

Majumder, A. (2014). Comparative study of three evolutionary algorithms coupled with neural network model for optimization of electric discharge machining process parameters. *Proceedings of the Institution of Mechanical Engineers, Part B: Journal of Engineering Manufacture*, 1-13.

Mandal, D., Pal, S. K., & Saha, M. (2007). Modelling of EDM process using back propagation neural network and multi-objective optimization using non-dominating sorting genetic algorithm-II. *Journal of Materials Processing Technology, 186*, 154–162. doi:10.1016/j.jmatprotec.2006.12.030

Masuzawa, T. (2000). State of the art micromachining. *Annual CIRP, 49*(2), 473–488. doi:10.1016/S0007-8506(07)63451-9

McCulloch, W. S., & Pitts, W. (1943). A logical calculus of the ideas immanent in nervous activity. *Bulletin of Mathematical Biology, 52*(1/2), 99–115. PMID:2185863

McGeough, J. A. (1988). *Electro Discharge Machining. In Advanced Methods Machine* (p. 130). London: Chapman & Hall.

Modica, F., Morrocco, V., & Fassi, I. (2017). *Micro-Electrodischarge Machining. In Micro-Manufacturing Technologies & their Applications*. Springer International Publishing.

Panda, D. K., & Bhoi, R. K. (2005). Artificial Neural Network Prediction of Material Removal Rate in Electro Discharge Machining. *Materials and Manufacturing Processes, 20*(4), 645–672. doi:10.1081/AMP-200055033

Pattanaik, L. N. (2017). Artificial Neural Network(MATLAB). In Analytical Tools in Research (pp. 250-261). Dwarka, India: Educreation Publishing.

Porwal, R.K., & Yadava, V. (2012). ANN Modelling For The Prediction Of Material Removal Rate And Machined Hole Overcut In Hole Drilling Electro Discharge Micro Machining. *International Journal of Mechanical Engineering and Robotics Research, 1*(2), 1-16.

Prabhu, S., & Vinayagam, B. K. (2015). Adaptive neuro fuzzy inference system modelling of multi-objective optimisation of electrical discharge machining process using single-wall carbon nanotubes. *Australian Journal of Mechanical Engineering, 13*(2), 97–117. doi:10.7158/M13-074.2015.13.2

Pradhan, M. K., & Chandan, B. K. (2010). Neuro- fuzzy and Neural Network Based prediction of various responses in EDM of AISI D2 steel. *International Journal of Advanced Manufacturing Technology, 50*, 591–610. doi:10.100700170-010-2531-8

Prihandana, G. S., Sriani, T., & Mahardika, M. (2012). Improvement of machining time in micro-EDM with workpiece vibration and graphite powder mixed in dielectric fluid. *Indian Journal of Engineering and Materials Sciences, 19*, 375–378.

Rahman, M. M. (2012). Modeling of Machining Parameters of Ti-6Al-4V for EDM: A neural network approach. *Scientific Research and Essays, 7*(8), 881–890. doi:10.5897/SRE10.1116

Rao, G. K. M., Janardhana, G. R., Rao, D. H., & Rao, M. S. (2008). Development of hybrid model & optimization of Material Removal Rate in EDM using Artificial neural Network and Genetic Algorithm. *Journal of Engineering and Applied Sciences (Asian Research Publishing Network), 3*(1), 19–30.

Rao, P. N. (2009). Introduction. In Manufacturing Technology (vol. 2, pp. 1-5). New Delhi: Tata McGraw-Hill.

Rumelhart, D. E., Hinton, G. E., & Williams, R. J. (1986). Learning representations by back-propagating errors. *Nature*, *323*(6088), 533–536. doi:10.1038/323533a0

Saxsena, K. K., Srivastava, A. S., & Agarwal, S. (2016). Experimental Investigation into micro- EDM characteristics of conductive SiC. *Ceramics International*, *42*(1), 1597–1610. doi:10.1016/j.ceramint.2015.09.111

Somashekhar, K. P., Ramchandran, N., & Mathew, J. (2010). Optimization of Material Removal Rate in Micro-EDM Using Artificial Neural Network and Genetic Algorithms. *Materials and Manufacturing Processes*, *25*(6), 467–475. doi:10.1080/10426910903365760

Suganthi, X. H., Natarajan, U., Sathiyamurthy, S., & Chidambaram, K. (2013). Prediction of quality responses in micro-EDM process using adaptive neuro- fuzzy inference system (ANFIS) model. *International Journal of Advanced Manufacturing Technology*, *68*(1-4), 339–347. doi:10.100700170-013-4731-5

Talla, G., Gangopadhyay, S., & Biswas, C. K. (2016). Influence of Graphite Powder Mixed EDM on the Surface Integrity Characteristics of Inconel 625. *Particulate Science and Technology*, 1–26.

Toshimitsu, R., Okada, A., Kitada, R., & Okamoto, Y. (2016). Improvement in Surface Characteristics by EDM with Chromium Powder Mixed Fluid. *Procedia CIRP*, *42*, 231–235. doi:10.1016/j.procir.2016.02.277

Tripathy, S., & Tripathy, D. K. (2017). Surface Characterization and Multi-response optimization of EDM process parameters using powder mixed dielectric. *Materials Today: Proceedings*, *4*(2), 2058–2067. doi:10.1016/j.matpr.2017.02.051

Tsai, K. M., & Wang, P. J. (2001). Predictions on surface finish in EDM based upon Neural Network Models. *International Journal of Machine Tools & Manufacture*, *41*, 1385–1403. doi:10.1016/S0890-6955(01)00028-1

Tsai, K. M., & Wang, P. J. (2001). Comparisons of neural network models on Material Removal Rate in EDM. *Journal of Materials Processing Technology*, *117*, 111–124. doi:10.1016/S0924-0136(01)01146-3

Tzeng, Y. F., & Lee, C. Y. (2001). Effects of Powder Characteristics on EDMing Efficiency. *International Journal of Advanced Manufacturing Technology*, *17*, 586–592. doi:10.1007001700170142

Upadhyay, A., Prakash, V., Pandey, V., & Sharma, V. (2016, November). *Effect of different types of Additives Added in Dielectric Fluid on Micro-EDM of Brass sheet.* Paper presented at International Conference on Evolutions in Manufacturing: Technologies and Business strategies for Global Competitiveness, Mesra, India.

Webzell, S. (2002). That first step into EDM. Machinery, (4040), 41.

Zain, Z. M., Ndaliman, M. B., Khan, A. A., & Ali, M. Y. (2014). Improving micro-hardness of stainless steel through powder-mixed electrical discharge machining. *Proceedings of the Institution of Mechanical Engineers, Part C: Journal of Mechanical Engineering Science*, 1-8. 10.1177/0954406214530872

This research was previously published in Design and Optimization of Mechanical Engineering Products; pages 209-233, copyright year 2018 by Engineering Science Reference (an imprint of IGI Global).

Chapter 40
Analyzing Intraductal Papillary Mucinous Neoplasms Using Artificial Neural Network Methodologic Triangulation

Steven Walczak

https://orcid.org/0000-0002-0449-6272

School of Information, University of South Florida, Tampa, USA

Jennifer B. Permuth

Departments of Cancer Epidemiology and Gastrointestinal Oncology, H. Lee Moffitt Cancer Center and R, Tampa, USA

Vic Velanovich

Department of Surgery, College of Medicine, University of South Florida, Tampa, USA

ABSTRACT

Intraductal papillary mucinous neoplasms (IPMN) are a type of mucinous pancreatic cyst. IPMN have been shown to be pre-malignant precursors to pancreatic cancer, which has an extremely high mortality rate with average survival less than 1 year. The purpose of this analysis is to utilize methodological triangulation using artificial neural networks and regression to examine the impact and effectiveness of a collection of variables believed to be predictive of malignant IPMN pathology. Results indicate that the triangulation is effective in both finding a new predictive variable and possibly reducing the number of variables needed for predicting if an IPMN is malignant or benign.

DOI: 10.4018/978-1-6684-2408-7.ch040

INTRODUCTION

Pancreatic cancer is a disease with very high mortality rates (Maitra et al., 2005; Walczak & Velanovich, 2018). Unfortunately, most pancreatic cancers present as an advanced disease with survival generally less than one year (Fesinmeyer et al., 2005). Fewer patients present with early stage disease that is amenable to surgical therapy or other adjuvant therapies that can lead to longer term survival. Survival can be improved with early detection and surgery, but how can earlier detection be achieved?

Intraductal papillary mucinous neoplasms (IPMN) are a type of pancreatic tumor or cyst (D'Angelica et al., 2004). IPMN were first discovered in the early 1980's (Ohashi, 1982) and named in the 1990's (Adsay et al., 2002; Furukawa et al., 2005). Since then, IPMN have become recognized as a cystic precursor to pancreatic cystadenocarcinomas (Date et al., 2018; Lüttges et al., 2001; Maitra et al., 2005; Permuth et al., 2016). Definitive preoperative diagnosis techniques still remain elusive (Liao & Velanovich, 2007).

The research reported in this article uses methodologic triangulation using artificial neural networks (ANNs) to examine the 14 radiomic variables used by Permuth et al. (2016) to determine which variables are contributing to the estimated 77% prediction accuracy of their logistic regression model and to determine if a smaller set of variables or different variables can achieve the same or better prediction accuracy.

The next section, Background, provides an extensive background on IPMN including prevalence and consequent impact on survival for pancreatic cystadenocarcinomas. The Method section presents the methodological triangulation methodology and describes how various combinations of potential predictor variables are selected and the ANN architectures and learning methods utilized. The Results sections presents the IPMN prediction performance for all of the various triangulated ANN models developed and compares the performance of the ANN models to decision tree and regression models. The paper then concludes with a summary of the results, implications for research and practice, and recommendations for future research.

BACKGROUND

"The category of IPMN was created originally to embrace all mass-forming pre-invasive neoplasia comprising mucinous ductal cells, arising from the native pancreatic ducts" (Fernández–del Castillo & Adsay, 2010, pg. 709). The chief symptoms of individuals with IPMN are: abdominal pain, weight loss, jaundice, nausea, and fatigue and may also be concomitant with diabetes or pancreatitis (Adsay et al., 2002; Fernández–del Castillo & Adsay, 2010; Sohn et al. 2001, 2004). However, the vast majority of patients are asymptomatic and IPMN are discovered incidentally when abdominal imaging is performed for other unrelated problems (Fernández–del Castillo & Adsay, 2010; Sahora & Fernández-del Castillo, 2015). The prevalence of asymptomatic IPMN in patients has been estimated using CT and/or MRI to be from 2.6% to 27% for MD-IPMN or 83% for BD-IPMN (Laffan et al., 2008; D'Angelica et al., 2004; de Pretis et al., 2017; (Pergolini et al., 2017; Salvia et al., 2004).

IPMN are typically detected using CT (computed tomography) or MR (magnetic resonance) imaging (Adsay et al., 2002; Fernández–del Castillo & Adsay, 2010; Sahora & Fernández-del Castillo, 2015). A recent research study in the USA found that IPMN occur in 2.5% of the total population over age 40, with prevalence increasing with age to over 7% and 8% in 70 year olds and 80 year olds respectively (Gardner et al., 2013). Other research, based on autopsies, estimates the prevalence of IPMN at 3.4% of the total population (Tanaka et al., 2006).

IPMN may be classified into three types dependent on interaction of the cyst with the pancreatic ductal system: main duct (MD-IPMN), branch duct (BD-IPMN), and mixed (Furukawa et al., 2005). Research that did not distinguish between IPMN types indicated IPMN development into a malignancy rate of 27% of patients (Morales-Oyarvide et al., 2018). A higher risk of progression of IPMN into pancreatic cancer is associated with MD-IPMN and mixed IPMN than BD-IPMN (Sahora & Fernández-del Castillo, 2015; Vanella et al., 2018). Rates of malignancy developing from MD-IPMN range from 31% to 34% (Adsay et al., 2002; Furukawa et al., 2005; Tanaka et al., 2017) up to 60-70% (Salvia et al., 2004; Tanaka et al., 2006, 2012). Reported BD-IPMN malignancy development rates range from 2.4% to 5.5% with a median of 3.8% (Han et al., 2018; Imbe et al., 2018; Khannoussi et al., 2012; Pergolini et al., 2017) up to 16-25% (Ridtitid et al., 2016; Tanaka et al., 2006, 2012).

Pancreatic cancers associated with IPMN (pancreatic cystadenocarcinoma) have more favorable outcomes than pancreatic cancers without IPMN (pancreatic ductal adenocarcinoma) (Adsay et al., 2002). Therefore, it is important to be able to identify the presence of an IPMN and determine whether there is main duct involvement. Importantly, there is an unmet need to develop accurate and reliable predictors to preoperatively distinguish between IPMNs that are lower-risk/indolent and can undergo surveillance from higher-risk/aggressive IPMNs that warrant surgical resection prior to the development of an invasive cancer (Shi & Hruban, 2012) and could lead to a surgical cure for pancreatic cystadenocarcinoma (Lan et al., 2018). Furthermore, distinguishing between benign and malignant IPMN would further improve the quality of medical care for patients with benign IPMN by drastically reducing unnecessary surgeries and the associated inconvenience, morbidity, and cost for patients (de Pretis et al., 2017; Permuth et al., 2016).

Tanaka et al. (2006) claim that imaging can distinguish between BD-IPMN and MD-IPMN. Research by Permuth et al. (2016) demonstrate that triangulating data sources to combine demographic, clinical, standard imaging, and genomic data improves prediction accuracy between low risk and high risk IPMN and further show that quantitative imaging or 'radiomic' features may have helped prevent overtreatment. Walczak (2012) and others (Kumar, Kumar, & Ali, 2012) use methodologic triangulation to combine ANNs with other machine learning or statistical methods to identify important variables and improve prediction performance. "Discovery of the contribution of variables to the medical decision-making process in clinical medicine is an important and ongoing research endeavor" (Walczak & Velanovich, 2018, pg. 113).

The treatment of IPMN is evolving as new evidence-based results are obtained (Imbe et al., 2018; Tanaka et al., 2006, 2012, 2017; Tsukagoshi et al., 2018). As indicated earlier, differences exist between the risk for pancreatic cancer associated with MD-IPMN versus BD-IPMN, with 5-year survival for BD-IPMN at approximately 90% (Han et al., 2018; Imbe et al., 2018) while MD-IPMN 5 year survival can be as high as 60% (Salvia et al., 2004). Research by Tsukagoshi et al. (2018) indicates that MD-IPMN and BD-IPMN occur at similar rates, with a smaller rate for mixed type IPMN.

Due to their much higher risk for progression to malignancy, MD-IPMN are always treated surgically, assuming the patient is fit to undergo surgery (Han et al., 2018). The progression of IPMN into malignancy is estimated to take from 3 to 5 years (Salvia et al., 2004; Shi & Hruban, 2012; Sohn et al., 2004). Therefore, low risk BP-IPMN are typically observed using ongoing CT or other imaging techniques for a period of 5 years. Several researchers have indicated that IPMN may progress to cancer after 5 years (Date et al., 2018; Imbe et al., 2018; Pergolini et al., 2017), indicating the need for ongoing monitoring of IPMN. Research has shown that 72% of IPMN patients show little to no increase in IPMN size after 5 years and less than 4% of IPMN patients developing pancreatic cancer after 7 years (Khanoussi et al., 2012).

BD-IPMN are treated surgically if they are considered high risk. Initially the definition of risk was primarily related to IPMN cyst size, with cysts over 3 cm (centimeters) considered high risk (Shi & Hruban, 2012; Sugiyama et al., 2003). Newer treatment guidelines have de-emphasized the size of the cyst (Tanaka et al., 2012, 2017) and now focus on other factors such as presence of a mural node (Han et al., 2018; Sugiyama et al., 2003), main pancreatic duct dilation (Tanaka et al., 2012; Tsukagoshi et al., 2018), or rapid growth of cysts (Sahora & Fernández-del Castillo, 2015). Research has indicated that almost 43% of IPMN cysts grow over a 5-year span with just over 5% of these cysts reaching a 3cm size (Yoen et al., 2017), with cysts growing at an average rate of 8 mm (millimeters) per year (Han et al., 2018). If cysts remain less than 1.5 cm for a period of 5 years, then less than 1% of these IPMN patients develop pancreatic cancer (Pergolini et al., 2017).

METHOD

The determination of predictive variables in medical diagnosis is extremely important (Walczak & Velanovich, 2018). Numerous researchers have shown that diagnostic and clinical predictive models can be improved by appropriate variable identification and reduction of non-discriminatory variables (Dag et al., 2016; Hunink et al., 2014). Reducing the overall number of variables in a predictive diagnostic model serves to clarify explanations of results (Liu & Chen, 2009) and may also serve to uncover diagnostic knowledge hidden when too many variables are present (Boudreau, Monteys, & Davidson, 2008). Most research disciplines outside of medicine also recognize the value and potential for model performance improvement through proper selection and minimization of independent variables (Chandrashekar & Sahin, 2014; Cheng, Zhou, & Cheng, 2011) and this is especially true for ANN-based modeling (May, Dandy, & Maier, 2011; Tahai, Walczak, & Rigsby, 1998). Using methodological triangulation with ANNs can assist in identification of contributing variables and variable reduction (Kumar, Kumar, & Ali, 2012; Walczak 2012).

Clinical decision making often relies on medical imaging (Shi & Hruban, 2012). Research in the domain of lung cancer has identified 329 radiologic features of tumors, including both texture and non-texture features (Balagurunathan et al., 2014). Radiologic data from CT and MR images may be transformed into radiomic data, which is the high throughput extraction of quantitative imaging features that may reveal predictive associations between image data and clinical outcomes (Kumar et al., 2012). Permuth et al. (2016) utilize logistic regression to determine a set of 14 radiomic variables, from a possible 112 radiomic variables, and use these 14 radiomic variables to predict the risk of IPMN malignancy for 37 IPMN cases (18 malignant, 19 benign).

ANN triangulation with multiple linear regression is used to determine the contribution of the 14 radiomic variables, along with a variation of one variable, to the prediction performance of the Permuth et al. (2016) IPMN prediction model. The flowchart of the various triangulated methods and consequent data selection is shown in Figure 1. The new variable, the difference or delta between the smallest and largest enclosing ellipse of the cyst, replaced one of the existing radiomic variables, the radius of the largest enclosing ellipse. The original radiomic data contained both the largest enclosing ellipse and the smallest enclosing ellipse, though only the largest enclosing ellipse values were used (Permuth et al., 2016). The reason for developing the delta between these two ellipses variable was that it might provide additional insight into cyst progression for the ANN IPMN malignancy prediction models.

Standard backpropagation was used to develop the ANN models that are evaluated using 3-fold cross validation. Single and two hidden layer architectures were developed following ANN best design practices (Medsker & Liebowitz, 1993; Walczak & Cerpa, 1999; Zhang 2007). The output of all ANNs was a single variable indicating malignant or benign pathology of the IPMN.

Figure 1. Flowchart of methodological triangulation analyzing IPMN variables

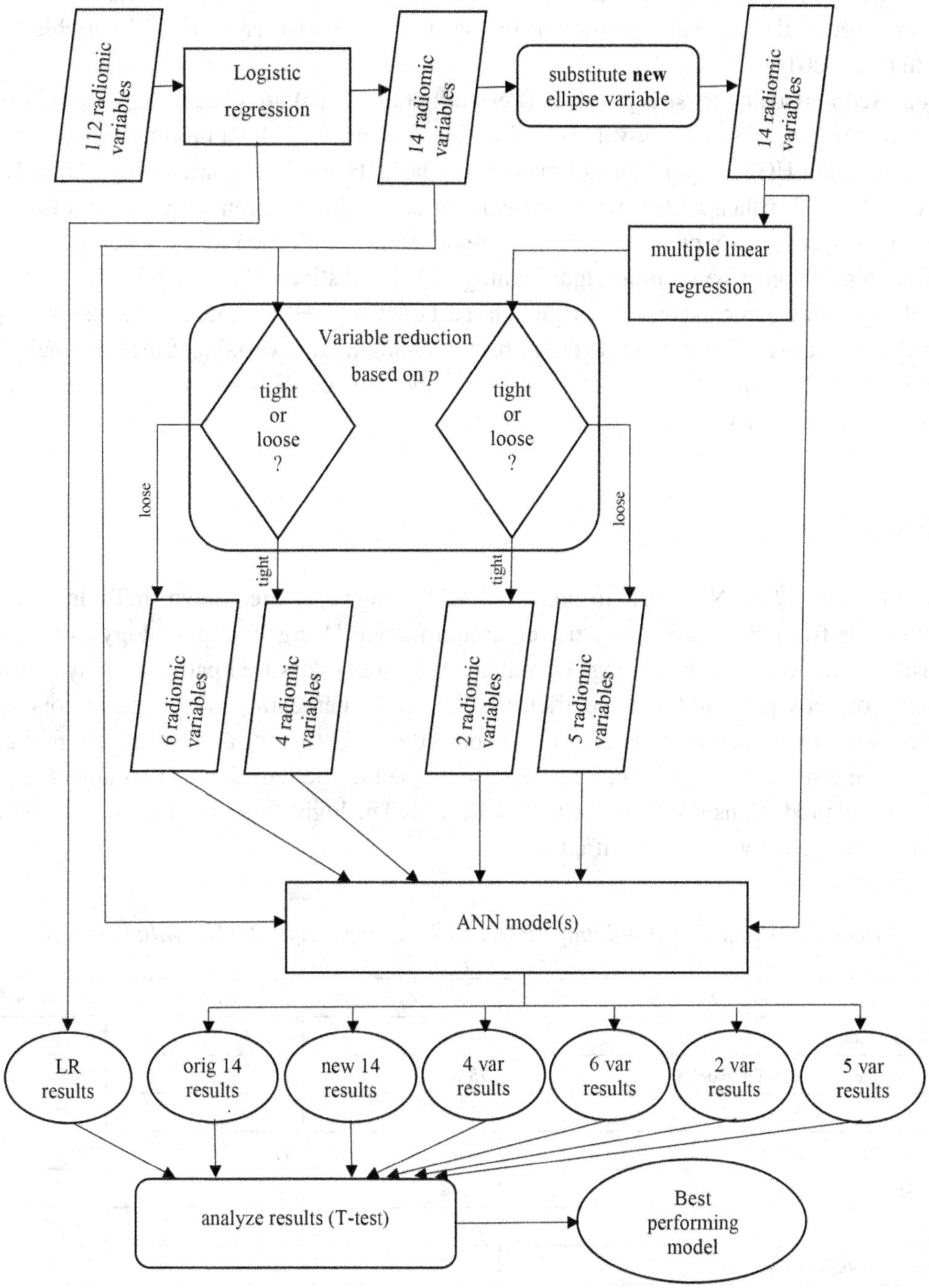

The single hidden layer backpropagation models outperformed the two hidden layer models except in one case.

Regression models are concurrently used on the 14 radiomic variables to identify possible reductions in the current set of variables. Two variables that had a $p < 0.1$, the enclosing ellipse delta and border length in pixels, form one alternate data set. Three additional variables: the co-occurrence matrix, the width in pixels, and the Fourier descriptor layer 1; that had a $p < 0.2$ were added to the first two to form a second input data set. The larger p-value cutoff for the second set of independent variables, although not indicating any significance, is used to examine the interplay of these variables since only 14 radiomic variables are used in the current regression as opposed to a much larger set of 112 variables examined in Permuth et al. (2016).

The reported logistic regression p-values (Permuth et al., 2016) are used to develop two additional limited input variables sets, using p-value cutoffs of less than 0.02, which produced 4 variables: width in pixels, run length HGRE layer 1, histogram energy layer 1, and histogram entropy layer 1; and less than or equal to 0.02, which added two additional variables: co-occurrence matrix and Laws features E5 E5 Energy Layer 1. ANN prediction models are developed with each of the 4 new sets of variables identified by regression as being most significant, yielding 6 distinct ANN models.

Parallel regression models using the original largest enclosing ellipse and the enclosing ellipse delta variables were built to further determine the impact of changing this variable. Since the logistic regression equation from Permuth et al. (2016) was not published, the prediction results were estimated based on the reported values for sensitivity and specificity.

RESULTS

The results for the six ANN models to predict IPMN malignancy are shown in Table 1, along with estimated results from the original logistic regression model. Using final pathology as the gold standard, sensitivity indicates the percentage of malignant tumors (classified pathologically as high-grade or invasive) correctly predicted and specificity indicates the percentage of benign tumors (classified pathologically as low-grade or moderate-grade) correctly predicted, for an N of 37 (18 malignant and 19 benign). The last row is for reference and represents the logistic regression (Permuth et al., 2016) as opposed to ANN predictions shown in the rest of Table 1. The logistic regression accuracy is estimated based on reported sensitivity and specificity.

Table 1. Results for ANN models predicting IPMN malignancy (highest ANN values in bold)

Variables	Accuracy	Sensitivity	Specificity
Original 14 variables	64.9%	**88.9%**	42.1%
13 original variables and new ellipse delta	**75.7%**	72.2%	**78.9%**
2 variables derived from regression	**75.7%**	72.2%	**78.9%**
5 variables derived from regression	73.0%	77.8%	68.4%
4 variables derived from Permuth et al. (2016)	64.9%	66.7%	63.2%
6 variables derived from Permuth et al. (2016)	64.9%	66.7%	63.2%
Estimated original logistic regression	78.4%	83.3%	73.7%

From Table 1, it can be seen that the new ellipse delta variable improves overall accuracy from the original set of variables, though the original set had higher sensitivity. An interesting phenomenon occurs when the 2 variable ANN data set is used in a backpropagation trained ANN with two hidden layers. While the accuracy remains the same, the sensitivity increases to 83.3% and the specificity drops to 68.4%. The fact that the two variables: the enclosing ellipse delta and border length in pixels, are able to produce the same results as the full 14 variable model indicates that a smaller data set using the new enclosing ellipse delta variable, has the same predictive power and therefore the remaining 12 variables are really not significant for predicting IPMN malignancy risk.

The linear regression model used to select two of the smaller variable sets showed that the enclosing ellipse delta variable was the only variable in that model with a significance of $p < 0.05$. Two multiple regression models, one with the original 14 variables and one with the 14 variables using the ellipse delta value instead of the largest enclosing ellipse, showed a net 10% improvement in prediction accuracy with the new ellipse delta variable, indicating that the ellipse delta is a strong candidate as a predictor variable for IPMN malignancy.

Various automated variable selection methods exist (Chandrashekar & Sahin, 2014), including decision trees and random forests (Genuer, Poggi, & Tuleau-Malot, 2010), genetic algorithms (Leardi, Seasholtz, & Pell, 2002), SVMs (support vector machines) (Rakotomamonjy, 2003), and others (Cheng, Zhou, & Cheng, 2011). However, prior research has shown that automated variable selection can produce suboptimal and unstable models in biomedical domains (Austin & Tu, 2004).

A full-scale analysis of automated selection is beyond the scope of this article, but an automated decision tree method based on the C4.5 method of Quinlan's (1986) ID3 algorithm was used to examine automated variable selection when using just the 14 variables from Permuth et al. (2016). The decision tree was able to determine a single variable that maximized the decision plane segmentation: run-length features: G1 D0 HGRE Layer 1. The decision tree had a classification accuracy of 81.1%, with a sensitivity of 72.2% and a specificity of 89.5%, which equals or is better than the ANN models. A more straightforward comparison was enabled by developing an ANN with just the decision tree identified variable. This ANN produced an overall accuracy of 67.6%, with sensitivity of 72.2% and specificity of 63.2%. The overall accuracy and specificity of the ANN using the decision tree selected variable was less than the two ANN models highlighted in Table 1 and identical with regard to sensitivity. The lower specificity causes unnecessary risk to patients with benign cysts.

Of course, methodological triangulation is about combining different methods to gain the benefits of each method while limiting the drawbacks. Since the decision tree and the multiple regression models each identified or selected different sets of variables, these three variables are combined into one final ANN model. The ANN with this combined set of variables from a decision tree and regression model increases its accuracy to 70.3% and sensitivity to 77.8%, but the specificity remained the same. Because this new model improved its accuracy and sensitivity, this further demonstrates the need to use either the ellipse delta, the border length, or both as meaningful variables in an IPMN risk prediction model.

CONCLUSION AND FUTURE RESEARCH

The research presented in this article has shown that ANN-based methodological triangulation (Walczak, 2012), specifically triangulated with linear and logistic regression in this case, may be used to reduce current model variable set size. In addition to the potential for improved prediction performance, these results also reduce the costs of data acquisition for model development and utilization. Furthermore, the triangulated use of ANNs with statistical algorithms enabled the rapid evaluation of a new prediction variable and could lead to new IPMN prediction heuristics.

The selection of an ANN to work as part of a combined ANN and statistical modeling IPMN malignancy prediction methodology is dependent upon the goals of the users. Higher sensitivity values indicate that patients at risk for having malignant tumors are identified and can undergo life-saving surgery, while selecting models with higher specificity would reduce the morbidity and costs associated with surgery for those patients who could safely be treated with observation.

Limitations

The primary limitation of the study reported in this article is the very small sample size of 37 patients with full data available. Another limitation is that the patient sample is from a single hospital, which may produce results influenced by the study population demographics and also the specific set of surgeons working at this facility. Both of these limitations can be addressed by future research using a much larger data sample of IPMN patients from across multiple hospitals from different geographic areas. These larger and more diverse population future research studies are needed to validate the current research and further demonstrate generalizability of the results.

Using this small sample size, a decision tree model was able to identify a single variable that outperformed the ANN models and the logistic regression model. Further research is needed to evaluate the predictive capability of the identified variable across a much larger and diverse population of IPMN patients. Other new research should examine combining other machine learning methods, such as decision trees and random forests, and statistical methods with ANNs to create hybrid triangulated ensemble models that can take advantage of the strengths of each of the individual methods while overcoming any disadvantages.

Implications for Research

The research reported in this article demonstrates that combining ANNs with statistical and other machine learning methods can identify smaller sets of variables. This indicates that methodological triangulation using ANNs (Walczak, 2012) is a reliable mechanism for determining variable influence. Researchers need to incorporate ANNs into their methods toolbox for examining healthcare and medical problems, especially if the shape of the solution surface is either unknown or nonlinear.

The field of medical research and particularly artificial intelligence applications in medicine is growing rapidly. Future research is needed to evaluate nonlinear predictive models with ANNs in other areas of oncology and medicine. Some of this new research expanding the current findings into other areas of medicine should examine using variable sets identified by the ANN triangulation methods to improve model performance and simultaneously reduce variable costs.

Implications for Practice

Identification of a reliable precursor to predict pancreatic cancer will significantly improve the quality of life for IPMN and pancreatic cystadenocarcinoma patients. Accurate prediction of these carcinomas will facilitate treatment decision making and may help reduce treatment decision regret for both physicians and patients (Walczak & Velanovich, 2018).

Out of the extremely large quantity of data collected for most oncology patients and those at risk, the ANN triangulation methods demonstrated in this article indicate that a much smaller variable set can reliably be used to obtain the same or better diagnostic results. The smaller variable sets will serve to reduce medical costs and potentially may reduce risk to patients, due to eliminating the need to collect all of these values with potentially risky pathology procedures.

While ANN methodological triangulation has been shown to be effective for evaluation of new independent variables and selecting smaller variable sets, future research is still needed to examine how to combine ANN and statistical model predictions that differ for individual patients to enable optimal combined sensitivity and specificity, versus the apparent tradeoff between sensitivity and specificity, as occurred in the current research. Triangulation facilitates the combination of multiple prediction models and would enable the maximization of the benefits from each of the employed methodologies and consequently improve the overall quality of care for IPMN patients.

As indicated above for research implications, future research is needed in practice to continue to develop ANN and triangulated predictive models in other fields of oncology and medicine. Future research will also be needed to develop these predictive systems into practical tools integrated into electronic medical records (EMRs) and with user interfaces that will be adopted and utilized by physicians.

CONCLUSION

Once pancreatic cancer becomes invasive it is usually fatal (Maitra et al., 2005). The development of triangulated prediction models may enable improved clinical decision making and ultimately lead to significantly better outcomes for patients with IPMNs (de Pretis et al., 2017; Lan et al., 2018; Shi & Hruban, 2012). Outcomes would be improved by longer life expectancy in patients with malignant cystadenocarcinomas from IPMN that are resected and avoidance of potentially life-threatening complication of surgery in patients with benign cysts (Liao & Velanovich, 2007).

REFERENCES

Adsay, N. V., Conlon, K. C., Zee, S. Y., Brennan, M. F., & Klimstra, D. S. (2002). Intraductal Papillary-Mucinous Neoplasms of the Pancreas. *Cancer*, *94*(1), 62–77. doi:10.1002/cncr.10203 PMID:11815961

Austin, P. C., & Tu, J. V. (2004). Automated variable selection methods for logistic regression produced unstable models for predicting acute myocardial infarction mortality. *Journal of Clinical Epidemiology*, *57*(11), 1138–1146. doi:10.1016/j.jclinepi.2004.04.003 PMID:15567629

Balagurunathan, Y., Gu, Y., Wang, H., Kumar, V., Grove, O., Hawkins, S., ... Gillies, R. J. (2014). Reproducibility and Prognosis of Quantitative Features Extracted from CT Images. *Translational Oncology*, *7*(1), 72–87. doi:10.1593/tlo.13844 PMID:24772210

Boudreau, R. L., Monteys, A. M., & Davidson, B. L. (2008). Minimizing variables among hairpin-based RNAi vectors reveals the potency of shRNAs. *RNA (New York, N.Y.)*, *14*(9), 1834–1844. doi:10.1261/rna.1062908 PMID:18697922

Chandrashekar, G., & Sahin, F. (2014). A survey on feature selection methods. *Computers & Electrical Engineering*, *40*(1), 16–28. doi:10.1016/j.compeleceng.2013.11.024

Cheng, Q., Zhou, H., & Cheng, J. (2011). The Fisher-Markov Selector: Fast Selecting Maximally Separable Feature Subset for Multiclass Classification with Applications to High-Dimensional Data. *IEEE Transactions on Pattern Analysis and Machine Intelligence*, *33*(6), 1217–1233. doi:10.1109/TPAMI.2010.195 PMID:21493968

D'Angelica, M., Brennan, M. F., Suriawinata, A. A., Klimstra, D., & Conlon, K. C. (2004). Intraductal Papillary Mucinous Neoplasms of the Pancreas: An Analysis of Clinicopathologic Features and Outcome. *Annals of Surgery*, *239*(3), 400–408. doi:10.1097/01.sla.0000114132.47816.dd PMID:15075659

Dag, A., Topuz, K., Oztekin, A., Bulur, S., & Megahed, F. M. (2016). A probabilistic data-driven framework for scoring the preoperative recipient-donor heart transplant survival. *Decision Support Systems*, *86*, 1–12. doi:10.1016/j.dss.2016.02.007

Date, K., Ohtsuka, T., Nakamura, S., Mochidome, N., Mori, Y., Miyasaka, Y., ... Nakamura, M. (2018). Surveillance of patients with intraductal papillary mucinous neoplasm with and without pancreatectomy with special reference to the incidence of concomitant pancreatic ductal adenocarcinoma. *Surgery*, *163*(2), 291–299. doi:10.1016/j.surg.2017.09.040 PMID:29221879

de Pretis, N., Mukewar, S., Aryal-Khanal, A., Bi, Y., Takahashi, N., & Chari, S. (2017). Pancreatic cysts: Diagnostic accuracy and risk of inappropriate resections. *Pancreatology*, *17*(2), 267–272. doi:10.1016/j.pan.2017.01.002 PMID:28117220

Fernández–del Castillo, C., & Adsay, N. V. (2010). Intraductal papillary mucinous neoplasms of the pancreas. *Gastroenterology*, *139*(3), 708–713. doi:10.1053/j.gastro.2010.07.025 PMID:20650278

Fesinmeyer, M. D., Austin, M. A., Li, C. I., De Roos, A. J., & Bowen, D. J. (2005). Differences in survival by histologic type of pancreatic cancer. *Cancer Epidemiology and Prevention Biomarkers*, *14*(7), 1766–1773. doi:10.1158/1055-9965.EPI-05-0120 PMID:16030115

Furukawa, T., Klöppel, G., Adsay, N. V., Albores-Saavedra, J., Fukushima, N., Horii, A., ... Lüttges, J. (2005). Classification of types of intraductal papillary-mucinous neoplasm of the pancreas: A consensus study. *Virchows Archiv*, *447*(5), 794–799. doi:10.100700428-005-0039-7 PMID:16088402

Gardner, T. B., Glass, L. M., Smith, K. D., Ripple, G. H., Barth, R. J., Klibansky, D. A., ... Pipas, J. M. (2013). Pancreatic Cyst Prevalence and the Risk of Mucin-Producing Adenocarcinoma in US Adults. *The American Journal of Gastroenterology*, *108*(10), 1546–1550. doi:10.1038/ajg.2013.103 PMID:24091499

Genuer, R., Poggi, J. M., & Tuleau-Malot, C. (2010). Variable selection using random forests. *Pattern Recognition Letters*, *31*(14), 2225–2236. doi:10.1016/j.patrec.2010.03.014

Han, Y., Lee, H., Kang, J. S., Kim, J. R., Kim, H. S., Lee, J. M., ... Jang, J. Y. (2018). Progression of Pancreatic Branch Duct Intraductal Papillary Mucinous Neoplasm Associates With Cyst Size. *Gastroenterology, 154*(3), 576–584. doi:10.1053/j.gastro.2017.10.013 PMID:29074452

Hunink, M. M., Weinstein, M. C., Wittenberg, E., Drummond, M. F., Pliskin, J. S., Wong, J. B., & Glasziou, P. P. (2014). Decision Making. In *Health and Medicine: Integrating Evidence and Values.* Cambridge University Press.

Imbe, K., Nagata, N., Hisada, Y., Takasaki, Y., Sekine, K., Mishima, S., ... Akiyama, J. (2018). Validation of the American Gastroenterological Association guidelines on management of intraductal papillary mucinous neoplasms: More than 5 years of follow-up. *European Radiology, 28*(1), 170–178. doi:10.100700330-017-4966-x PMID:28770404

Khannoussi, W., Vullierme, M. P., Rebours, V., Maire, F., Hentic, O., Aubert, A., ... Ruszniewski, P. (2012). The long term risk of malignancy in patients with branch duct intraductal papillary mucinous neoplasms of the pancreas. *Pancreatology, 12*(3), 198–202. doi:10.1016/j.pan.2012.03.056 PMID:22687372

Kumar, S., Kumar, D., & Ali, R. (2012). Factor Analysis Using Two Stages Neural Network Architecture. *International Journal of Machine Learning and Computing, 2*(6), 860–863. doi:10.7763/IJMLC.2012.V2.253

Kumar, V., Gu, Y., Basu, S., Berglund, A., Eschrich, S. A., Schabath, M. B., ... Goldgof, D. B. (2012). Radiomics: The Process and the Challenges. *Magnetic Resonance Imaging, 30*(9), 1234–1248. doi:10.1016/j.mri.2012.06.010 PMID:22898692

Laffan, T. A., Horton, K. M., Klein, A. P., Berlanstein, B., Siegelman, S. S., Kawamoto, S., ... Hruban, R. H. (2008). Prevalence of unsuspected pancreatic cysts on MDCT. *AJR. American Journal of Roentgenology, 191*(3), 802–807. doi:10.2214/AJR.07.3340 PMID:18716113

Lan, C., Li, X., Wang, X., Hao, J., & Ren, H. (2018). A new combined criterion to better predict malignant lesions in patients with pancreatic cystic neoplasms. *Cancer Biology & Medicine, 15*(1), 70–78. doi:10.20892/j.issn.2095-3941.2017.0152 PMID:29545970

Leardi, R., Seasholtz, M. B., & Pell, R. J. (2002). Variable selection for multivariate calibration using a genetic algorithm: Prediction of additive concentrations in polymer films from Fourier transform-infrared spectral data. *Analytica Chimica Acta, 461*(2), 189–200. doi:10.1016/S0003-2670(02)00272-6

Liao, T., & Velanovich, V. (2007). Asymptomatic Pancreatic Cysts: A Decision Analysis Approach to Observation Versus Resection. *Pancreas, 35*(3), 243–248. doi:10.1097/MPA.0b013e318068fc94 PMID:17895845

Liu, S. S., & Chen, J. (2009). Using data mining to segment healthcare markets from patients' preference perspectives. *International Journal of Health Care Quality Assurance, 22*(2), 117–134. doi:10.1108/09526860910944610 PMID:19536963

Lüttges, J., Zamboni, G., Longnecker, D., & Klöppel, G. (2001). The Immunohistochemical Mucin Expression Pattern Distinguishes Different Types of Intraductal Papillary Mucinous Neoplasms of the Pancreas and Determines Their Relationship to Mucinous Noncystic Carcinoma and Ductal Adenocarcinoma. *The American Journal of Surgical Pathology*, *25*(7), 942–948. doi:10.1097/00000478-200107000-00014 PMID:11420467

Maitra, A., Fukushima, N., Takaori, K., & Hruban, R. H. (2005). Precursors to Invasive Pancreatic Cancer. *Advances in Anatomic Pathology*, *12*(2), 81–91. doi:10.1097/01.pap.0000155055.14238.25 PMID:15731576

May, R., Dandy, G., & Maier, H. (2011). Review of Input Variable Selection Methods for Artificial Neural Networks. In K. Suzuki (Ed.), *Artificial Neural Networks-Methodological Advances and Biomedical Applications* (pp. 19–44). London, UK: InTech Open. doi:10.5772/16004

Medsker, L. R., & Liebowitz, J. (1993). *Design and Development of Expert Systems and Neutral Networks*. Prentice Hall PTR.

Morales-Oyarvide, V., Mino-Kenudson, M., Ferrone, C. R., Warshaw, A. L., Lillemoe, K. D., Sahani, D. V., ... Hruban, R. H. (2018). Intraductal Papillary Mucinous Neoplasm of the Pancreas in Young Patients: Tumor Biology, Clinical Features, and Survival Outcomes. *Journal of Gastrointestinal Surgery*, *22*(2), 226–234. doi:10.100711605-017-3602-z PMID:29047068

Ohashi, K. (1982). Four cases of "mucin-producing" cancer of the pancreas on specific findings of the papilla of Vater. *Progress of Digestive Endoscopy*, *20*, 348–352.

Pergolini, I., Sahora, K., Ferrone, C. R., Morales-Oyarvide, V., Wolpin, B. M., Mucci, L. A., ... Warshaw, A. L. (2017). Long-term Risk of Pancreatic Malignancy in Patients With Branch Duct Intraductal Papillary Mucinous Neoplasm in a Referral Center. *Gastroenterology*, *153*(5), 1284–1294. doi:10.1053/j.gastro.2017.07.019 PMID:28739282

Permuth, J. B., Choi, J., Balarunathan, Y., Kim, J., Chen, D. T., Chen, L., ... Latifi, K. (2016). Combining radiomic features with a miRNA classifier may improve prediction of malignant pathology for pancreatic intraductal papillary mucinous neoplasms. *Oncotarget*, *7*(52), 85785–85797. doi:10.18632/oncotarget.11768 PMID:27589689

Quinlan, J. R. (1986). Induction of decision trees. *Machine Learning*, *1*(1), 81–106. doi:10.1007/BF00116251

Rakotomamonjy, A. (2003). Variable selection using SVM-based criteria. *Journal of Machine Learning Research*, *3*(Mar), 1357–1370.

Ridtitid, W., DeWitt, J. M., Schmidt, C. M., Roch, A., Stuart, J. S., Sherman, S., & Al-Haddad, M. A. (2016). Management of branch-duct intraductal papillary mucinous neoplasms: A large single-center study to assess predictors of malignancy and long-term outcomes. *Gastrointestinal Endoscopy*, *84*(3), 436–445. doi:10.1016/j.gie.2016.02.008 PMID:26905937

Sahora, K., & Fernández-del Castillo, C. (2015). Intraductal papillary mucinous neoplasms. *Current Opinion in Gastroenterology*, *31*(5), 424–429. doi:10.1097/MOG.0000000000000198 PMID:26125316

Salvia, R., Fernández-del Castillo, C., Bassi, C., Thayer, S. P., Falconi, M., Mantovani, W., ... Warshaw, A. L. (2004). Main-Duct Intraductal Papillary Mucinous Neoplasms of the Pancreas: Clinical Predictors of Malignancy and Long-Term Survival Following Resection. *Annals of Surgery*, *239*(5), 678–687. doi:10.1097/01.sla.0000124386.54496.15 PMID:15082972

Shi, C., & Hruban, R. H. (2012). Intraductal Papillary Mucinous Neoplasm. *Human Pathology*, *43*(1), 1–16. doi:10.1016/j.humpath.2011.04.003 PMID:21777948

Sohn, T. A., Yeo, C. J., Cameron, J. L., Hruban, R. H., Fukushima, N., Campbell, K. A., & Lillemoe, K. D. (2004). Intraductal Papillary Mucinous Neoplasms of the Pancreas: An Updated Experience. *Annals of Surgery*, *239*(6), 788–799. doi:10.1097/01.sla.0000128306.90650.aa PMID:15166958

Sohn, T. A., Yeo, C. J., Cameron, J. L., Iacobuzio-Donahue, C. A., Hruban, R. H., & Lillemoe, K. D. (2001). Intraductal Papillary Mucinous Neoplasms of the Pancreas: An Increasingly Recognized Clinicopathologic Entity. *Annals of Surgery*, *234*(3), 313–322. doi:10.1097/00000658-200109000-00005 PMID:11524584

Sugiyama, M., Izumisato, Y., Abe, N., Masaki, T., Mori, T., & Atomi, Y. (2003). Predictive factors for malignancy in intraductal papillary–mucinous tumours of the pancreas. *British Journal of Surgery*, *90*(10), 1244–1249. doi:10.1002/bjs.4265 PMID:14515294

Tahai, A., Walczak, S., & Rigsby, J. T. (1998). Improving artificial neural network performance through input variable selection. In P. Siegel, K. Omer, A. deKorvin, & A. Zebda (Eds.), *Applications of Fuzzy Sets and The Theory of Evidence to Accounting II* (pp. 293–310). Stamford, Connecticut: JAI Press.

Tanaka, M., Chari, S., Adsay, V., Castillo, F. D. C., Falconi, M., Shimizu, M., ... Matsuno, S. (2006). International Consensus Guidelines for Management of Intraductal Papillary Mucinous Neoplasms and Mucinous Cystic Neoplasms of the Pancreas. *Pancreatology*, *6*(1-2), 17–32. doi:10.1159/000090023 PMID:16327281

Tanaka, M., Fernández-del Castillo, C., Adsay, V., Chari, S., Falconi, M., Jang, J. Y., ... Shimizu, M. (2012). International Consensus Guidelines 2012 for the Management of IPMN and MCN of the Pancreas. *Pancreatology*, *12*(3), 183–197. doi:10.1016/j.pan.2012.04.004 PMID:22687371

Tanaka, M., Fernández-del Castillo, C., Kamisawa, T., Jang, J. Y., Levy, P., Ohtsuka, T., ... Wolfgang, C. L. (2017). Revisions of International Consensus Fukuoka Guidelines for the Management of IPMN of the Pancreas. *Pancreatology*, *17*(5), 738–753. doi:10.1016/j.pan.2017.07.007 PMID:28735806

Tsukagoshi, M., Araki, K., Saito, F., Kubo, N., Watanabe, A., Igarashi, T., ... Kuwano, H. (2018). Evaluation of the International Consensus Guidelines for the Surgical Resection of Intraductal Papillary Mucinous Neoplasms. *Digestive Diseases and Sciences*, *63*(4), 860–867. doi:10.100710620-017-4667-y PMID:28667432

Vanella, G., Crippa, S., Archibugi, L., Arcidiacono, P. G., Delle Fave, G., Falconi, M., & Capurso, G. (2018). Meta-analysis of mortality in patients with high-risk intraductal papillary mucinous neoplasms under observation. *British Journal of Surgery*, *105*(4), 328–338. doi:10.1002/bjs.10768 PMID:29405253

Walczak, S. (2012). Methodological triangulation using neural networks for business research. *Advances in Artificial Neural Systems*, *2012*, 1–13. doi:10.1155/2012/517234

Walczak, S., & Cerpa, N. (1999). Heuristic Principles for the Design of Artificial Neural Networks. *Information and Software Technology, 41*(2), 107–117. doi:10.1016/S0950-5849(98)00116-5

Walczak, S., & Velanovich, V. (2018). Improving prognosis and reducing decision regret for pancreatic cancer treatment using artificial neural networks. *Decision Support Systems, 106*, 110–118. doi:10.1016/j. dss.2017.12.007

Yoen, H., Kim, J. H., Lee, D. H., Ahn, S. J., Yoon, J. H., & Han, J. K. (2017). Fate of small pancreatic cysts (< 3 cm) after long-term follow-up: Analysis of significant radiologic characteristics and proposal of follow-up strategies. *European Radiology, 27*(6), 2591–2599. doi:10.100700330-016-4589-7 PMID:27651145

Zhang, G. P. (2007). Avoiding pitfalls in neural network research. *IEEE Transactions on Systems, Man and Cybernetics. Part C, Applications and Reviews, 37*(1), 3–16. doi:10.1109/TSMCC.2006.876059

This research was previously published in the International Journal of Healthcare Information Systems and Informatics (IJHISI), 14(4); pages 21-32, copyright year 2019 by IGI Publishing (an imprint of IGI Global).

Chapter 41
Conventional and Non-Conventional ANNs in Medical Diagnostics:
A Tutorial Survey of Architectures, Algorithms, and Application

Devika G.

ⓘ https://orcid.org/0000-0002-2509-2867

Government Engineering College, K. R. Pet, India

Asha G. Karegowda

Siddaganga Institute of Technology, India

ABSTRACT

Computer technology advancements in recent days have offered professionals in different fields the ability to gather data, process information, store, and retrieve at a faster rate and make effective decisions. The large collection of data among all various applications including medical diagnosis has paved the need to employ advanced artificial neural networks (ANN). This chapter provides a detailed working view of ANN, covering its various architectures and design techniques in brief. A detailed analysis and summary of medical diagnostics applications using various ANN techniques will be leveraged. Imbalanced data is the major problem with medical data. This chapter briefs on the various methods to handle imbalanced data. Finally, future directions and potential current challenges are suggested for additional applications in neural networks.

DOI: 10.4018/978-1-6684-2408-7.ch041

INTRODUCTION

In recent time's artificial neural networks (ANNs) has become a popular and helpful model for classification, clustering, pattern recognition and prediction in many disciplines including medical. ANNs are one category of the of machine learning (ML) and has become relatively competitive to conventional regression and statistical models regarding usefulness (Dave, 2014). Currently, artificial intelligence, information security, big data, cloud computing, internet, and forensic science are all hotspots and exciting topics of information and communication technology (ICT). ANNs full applications can be evaluated with respect to data analysis factors such as accuracy, processing speed, latency, performance, fault tolerance, volume, scalability and convergence (He, 2009; Muzoffair, 2018). The great potential of ANNs is the high-speed processing provided in a massive parallel implementation and this has heightened the need for research in this domain (Izebudien, 2014). ANNs can be developed and used for image recognition, natural language processing and so on. Nowadays, ANNs are mostly used for universal function approximation in numerical paradigms because of their excellent properties of self-learning, adaptivity, fault tolerance, nonlinearity, and advancement in input to an output mapping (Wang, 2018). In (Raval, 2016) usage of machine learning techniques for medical diagnosis analysis of disease considering reports of lab and symptoms for acute analysis is considered.

Scope of the Work

ANN for medical diagnosis is an active research area currently, and researcher's estimates to it to be more widely used in biomedical systems for next few decades as its result are restricted to linear form. ANN will identify disease by learning method without using details of how to recognize the disease, hence it doesn't require any algorithm to identify disease.

Figure 1. Number of research work on ANN year wise from 1996-2019
(Source Google)

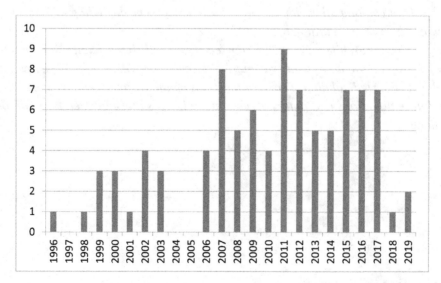

ANNs has significant advantages over statistical models, when both are relatively compared. In ANN models, there are no assumptions about data properties or data distribution. Therefore, ANNs are more useful in practical application. Also, unlike some statistical models that require certain hypothesis for testing, ANN models do not require any hypothesis. ANNs are very flexible, data reduction models, encompassing nonlinear regression models, discriminant models, and more fault tolerant. That is, they can handle incomplete and noisy data; and can solve non-linear problems, Also, trained ANNs, can generalize at high speed and make predictions. Furthermore, ANNs are scalable when relatively compared to support vector machine, extreme learning machine, and random forest. ANN processing is promising in several areas of medical analysis such as glucose monitoring (Catalogna, 2012), blood disorders (Raval,2018), diagnosis of various health related issues related to heart (Mihaela, 2019), eyes (Xiangyu Chen, 2015), kidney(Yafeng Ren, 2019), liver(Amitha, 2019), lung(Mehdi, 2018), brain(Ali, 2018) and many more. The number of research works on ANN carried out in period 1996-2019 indicated in figure 1.

ANN Overview

Artificial Neural Networks are the computational models that are inspired by the human brain. Many of the recent advancements have been made in the field of Artificial Intelligence, including Voice Recognition, Image Recognition, Robotics using Artificial Neural Networks. Artificial Neural Networks can be viewed as weighted directed graphs in which artificial neurons are nodes, and directed edges with weights are connections between neuron outputs and neuron inputs. The Artificial Neural Network receives information from the external world in the form of pattern and image in vector form. These inputs are mathematically designated by the notation x(n) for n number of inputs. Each input is multiplied by its corresponding weights. Typically weight represents the strength of the interconnection between neurons inside the Neural Network. Activation function decides, whether a neuron should be activated or not by calculating weighted sum and further adding bias to introduce non-linearity into the output of a neuron. The weighted inputs are all summed up inside the computing unit (artificial neuron). To limit the response to arrive at the desired value, the threshold value is set up. For this, the sum is passed through an activation function. The activation function is set to the transfer function used to get the desired output. There are linear as well as the nonlinear activation function. Some of the commonly used activation functions are: binary, sigmoidal (linear), tan hyperbolic sigmoidal functions (nonlinear), RELU(Rectified linear unit) and Softmax. The most common activation function's Plot and Equation are listed in Table 1.

- **Binary:** The output has only two values either 0 or 1. For this, the threshold value is set up. If the net weighted input is greater than 1, an output is assumed one otherwise zero.
- **Sigmoidal:** It is 'S' shape curve, specifically used for models where one need to predict the probability as an output since it's range is from (0 to 1).
- **Tan Hyperbolic:** This function has a 'S' shaped curve. It is considered to be stronger tan sigmoid function. The range of tanh function is from (-1 to 1). It is also called as scaled sigmoid function. It is mainly used for binary classification problems. Both tanh and logistic sigmoid activation functions are used in feed-forward nets.
- **ReLU(Rectified linear unit):** It signifies the pixel-wise function which is nonlinear in nature given by g(x) = max(0,x) i.e. it return x for all positive values, and zero for all negative values. . ReLU is the most commonly used activation function in neural networks, especially in CNNs

acting as a layer wise down-sampling nonlinear function. The advantage of ReLU is it t doesn't have the vanishing gradient problem as seen in activation functions like sigmoid or tanh. One of the matter of concern with ReLUs is that all the negative values become zero immediately which drops the ability of the model to fit or train from the data properly.

- **Softmax:** Softmax is often used in Convolutional neural networks, to map the non-normalized output of a network to a probability distribution over predicted output classes. It is used for multi-classification in logistic regression model. The range will 0 to 1, and the sum of all the probabilities will be equal to one; which not be the case for sigmoidal function. If the softmax function used for multi-classification model it returns the probabilities of each class; with the highest probability for the target class.

Table 1. Most common activation function's

Name	Plot	Equation	Output Value
Binary		$f(x) = \begin{cases} 0 \; for \, x < 0 \\ 1 \; for \, x > 0 \end{cases}$	0/1
Sigmoidal		$f(x) = \dfrac{1}{1 + e^{x}}$	0-1
Tanh		$f(x) = \tanh(x) = \dfrac{2}{1 + e^{-2x}} - 1$	-1 -1
Rectified Linear unit (ReLu)		$f(x) = \begin{cases} 0 \; for \, x < 0 \\ x \; for \, x > 0 \end{cases}$	Positive value with in x
Softmax		$f(x) = \log_e(1 + e^x)$	0-1

A neural network can be "shallow", in the sense it has an input layer, few number of hidden layer followed by an output layer. A Deep Neural Network (DNN) has many layers of neurons between the input and the output layer.

Contributions

Inspired by research focus of neural network in reshaping medical field, this work concentrates on its efforts in medical diagnostics. Neural network technique has reshaped the research landscape of medical field in almost all aspects such as algorithm designs, training/test data sets, application scenarios and even the evaluation protocols. Therefore, it is of great significance to review the breakthrough and rapid development process in recent years. Numerous survey work on medical diagnostics activates have been carried on (Litjens, 2017; Bolboca,2019), and also its subdomains. Most of these surveys summarize and compare adverse set of techniques related to specific technique (Razzak, 2017). Our paper distinguishes itself from earlier surveys from the following perspectives:

- We focus on ANN applications (in particular DNN) for medical diagnosis
- We discuss cutting-edge ANN techniques from the perspective of applications (focusing on their applicability to this area, whilst giving less attention to conventional models that may be out-of-date).
- Various method to handle imbalance data is addressed.
- A systematic review on the evolution of the network architectures and loss functions for deep FR.
- We analyze similarities between existing problems and those specific to medical diagnosis; based on this analysis we provide insights into both best ANN architecture selection strategies and adaptation approaches, so as to exploit the characteristics of ANN by conducting analysis and management tasks.
- Highlights will be provided with challenges and future directions for the successful and fruitful usage for various applications.

Artificial Neural Network Techniques

The artificial neural networks techniques can be broadly classified as follows:

Classification Neural Network

A Neural Network can be trained to classify given pattern or dataset into predefined class. The most common and state of art method is the one which uses Feed forward Networks. The ANN can be categorized based on learning strategies employed: supervised and unsupervised. In first learning method the network is trained in presence of input and output patterns. The input weights will be adjusted until desired output value reaches expected output value. The self-organizing map or other techniques will be devised in unsupervised learning method. The network has to calculate its own representation of input value by calculating acceptable connection weights. The values can be found by clustering input data and with features inherent problem.

Prediction Neural Network

A Neural Network can be trained to produce outputs that are expected from a given input for example: Stock market prediction. The usage of neural network for prediction will make it able to learn from examples only and that after their learning is finished, the algorithms are able to catch hidden and strongly non-linear dependencies. This can identify significant characters even in presence of noise in the training set. The neural network prediction can be classified based on criteria to predict as i) data that we have for teaching prediction and for prediction and ii) what we want to predict - value or trend. The first method is applicable for case when exact value or more values of a variable are needed for prediction and further is applicable for time series based.

Clustering Neural Network

The Neural network can be used to identify unique features of the data and classify them into different categories without any prior knowledge of the data. The commonly used clustering techniques in neural network are,

- Competitive networks
- Adaptive Resonance Theory Networks
- Kohonen Self-Organizing Maps.

Association Neural Network

A Neural Network can be trained to remember the particular pattern so that when the noise pattern is presented to the network, the network associates it with the closest one in the memory or discard it. E.g., Hopfield Networks which performs recognition, classification, and clustering, etc. the pattern based association support to store different patterns and at the time of giving an output, it will produce one of the stored patterns by matching them with the given input pattern,

Optimization Neural Network

The optimization problem will minimize or maximize certain objective function/s. The problem to be optimized are not linear or polynomial. ANN will resolve the problems of heuristic based and expects precise output. Neural networks approximate the objective function in optimization problems to make it possible to apply other techniques such as non-linear regression to resolve the problem to resolve an optimization problem. The derivate of the new objective function should be polynomial, so that the solution of the optimization problem can be calculated.

Pattern Recognition Neural Network

The neural network is trained to associate input and output patters for pattern recognition. The network is used to train; it identifies input pattern and tries to output for associated pattern. The networks comes to life when a pattern that has no output associated with it, is given as an input. In this case, the network gives the output that corresponds to a taught input pattern that is least different from the given pattern. During training, the network is trained to associate outputs within input patterns. When the network is used, it identifies the input pattern and tries to output the associated output pattern. The power of neural networks comes to life when a pattern that has no output associated with it, is given. In this case, the network gives the output that corresponds to a taught input pattern that is least different from the given pattern. Pattern recognition could be used for a design of proper learning algorithm, while learning algorithm could be used to enhance the result of pattern recognition.

Artificial Neural Network Architectures

A neural network can be "shallow", in the sense it has an input layer, few number of hidden layer followed by an output layer. A Deep Neural Network (DNN) has many layers of neurons between the input and the output layer.

Shallow Neural Network

This form of neural network as name suggests consist of less depth usually of only one or very few hidden layer as against many hidden layers in deep neural network. The number neurons in hidden layer may vary. The figure 2 indicates a shallow neural network of one input, hidden and output layer. The commonly used shallow neural networks such as feed forward, radial basis function, wavelet and time delay neural network are described below.

Figure 2. Shallow Neural Network

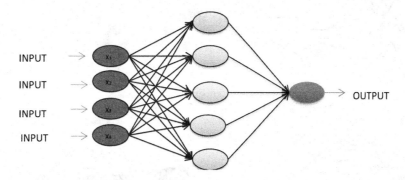

Feed-Forward Neural Networks

This type of neural network is common among practical applications. The architectural design includes one input, output and hidden layers which will compute series of transformations to change similarities between cases. The activation function for neurons a non-linear functioin will be applied.

Radial Basis Function Neural Networks

The model includes three-layer neural network one input, one hidden and one output layer. The hidden layer uses radial basis function as activation function. Radial basis function are real valued function gives outputs based on only Euclidean distance from origin or center to inputs and maximum frequently used function is Gaussian function. (Buliali, Hariadi, Saikhu, & Mamase, 2016). These networks are similar to the feed-forward Neural Network except radial basis function is used as the activation function of these neurons. The radial basis function is indicated in figure 3(a).

Wavelet Neural Networks

This model combines concept of wavelet theory and ANN. The wavelet neural network consists of only single input, hidden and output layer. The activation function in hidden layer is replaced with wavelet function. The structure of wavelet neural network is shown in figure 3(b). The wavelet model is applicable in time series prediction and signal processing (Yang & Hu, 2016).

Time Delay Neural Network

This model is defined as multilayer neural network with delayed input or states utilized through time shifting approach. A simple delayed neural network example is shown in figure 3(c). The neurons in hidden layer receive input value at time t as given from inputs t1 and t2. It is possible to use delay in other layers also.

Figure 3. (a) Radial Basis neural network (b) Wavelet Neural Network (c) Time delay based neural network

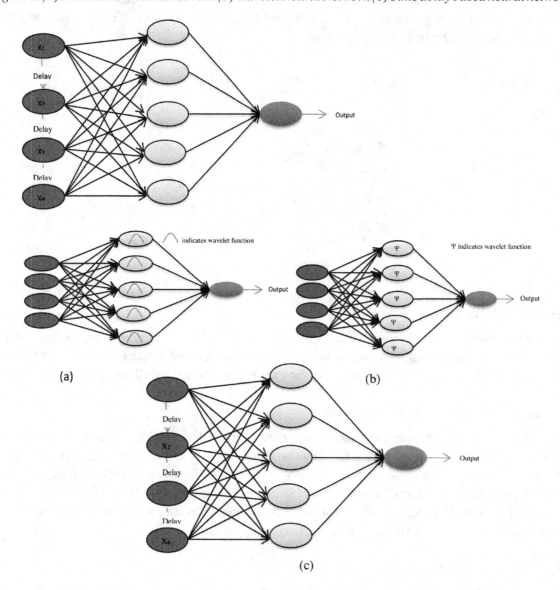

Deep Neural Network

The form of neural network usually consists of multiple hidden layers when compared against shallow neural network.

Recurrent NN (RNN)

RNN are well-made ML techniques for their quality in different fields of activity like signal processing, natural language processing and speech recognition. CNN considers only the current input while RNN considers the current input in addition to previously received inputs. The internal memory of RNN is used to store the previous input as shown in figure 4. CNN is apt for spatial data such as images, whereas RNN is apt for temporal data/sequential data. RNN use their internal memory to process arbitrary sequences of input temporal data. CNN contemplates only the present input while RNN considers both the present and recent past inputs. This is possible since RNN has its internal memory. The two variants of RNN long-short term memory (LSTM) and gated recurrent unit (GRU)(Kamilaris, 2018; Lecun, 1995;Tseng, 2018) are shown in figure 4(a).

Figure 4. Typical construction of (a) RNN (b) LSTM

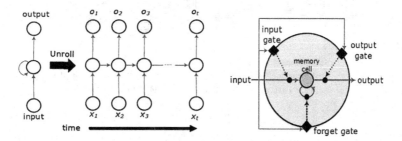

Long Short-Term Memory Neural Network (LSTM)

The type of Neural Network in which memory cell is incorporated into hidden layer neurons is called LSTM network. LSTM is extension of RNN. RNN has problem with vanishing and exploding gradients which is solved by LSTM. LSTM has three gates: forget gate, read /input gate and write/output gate. If forget gate is active the neuron writes its data to itself. If forget gate is turned off by sending a 0, then neuron forgets its last content. If write gate is set to 1, then connected neurons can write to that neuron. When read gate is set to 1, the connected neurons can reads the content of neuron. The figure 4(b) depicts the structure of LSTM. The main difference between RNN and LSTM units is that LSTM utilize forget gates to actively control the cell states and ensure not to degrade. The gates can use sigmoid or tanh as their activation function. Activation functions cause the problem of vanishing gradient during back propagation in the training phase of other models using them (Deng, 2014;Tseng, 2018).

Convolutional Neural Network

These networks have large number of hidden layers compared to conventional ANN and are primarily used for image, video, and audio processing. The typical CNN architecture includes exchange layer by connecting one or more fully connected layers at the end as next of convolution and pooling layers. For specific application, these fully connected layers will be replaced with global average pooling layer. In some cases, in order to optimize performance, the CNN will additionally include batch normalization and dropout in addition to learning stages as regulatory layers. The performance of CNN is totally based on the arrangement of different components in its new architecture. The CNN sequencing to classify handwritten digits is shown in figure 5 (a)(towardsdatascience.com). The CNN can be categorized based on features such as spatial exploitation, depth, multi-path, width, feature map exploitation, channel boosting, and attention as depicted in Figure 5(b) (khan, 2016).

Figure 5a. Typical CNN example for character identification

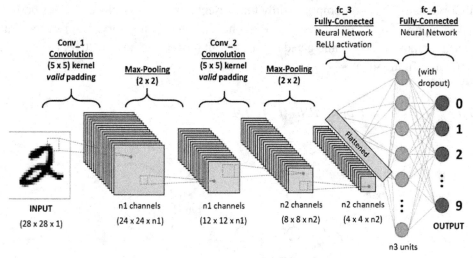

Figure 5b. Classification of CNN

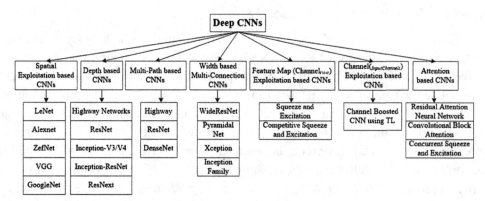

Figure 5c. Transfer learning method (left); Dropouts (right)
(Nitish, 2014)

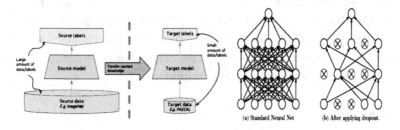

Figure 5d. Max pooling example (left); Batch Normalization (right)
(source: https://medium.com)

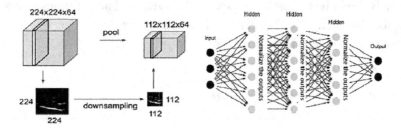

Transfer Learning method (TL) is used when pre-trained models require processing. In such case, the model will be reused as of starting point for an operations reused as the starting point. For example if CNN trained on one dataset, then according to training remove or retain on last layers. The training models are applied to recognize different higher level features. The training time will be reduced in transfer learning. It is helpful tool when enough data or training takes too much resource. The transfer learning is shown in figure 5(c)(Ruder, 2017).

In **Dropout address** (DA) problem of CNN where neurons are dropped or ignored randomly during training process. Larger the network it slows to use, making it difficult to deal with overfitting by combining predictions of many different large deep networks at training time. In dropout randomly dropped units from the neural network will prevents units from adapting much for training. This method normally improves performance of neural networks on supervised learning. The improved dropout method is presented in figure 5(d).

Max Pooling (MP) method involves discretization sample-based process. Its main objective is to down-sample input representation by minimizing its dimensionality and features contained in sub-regions case (**Sutskever, 2017**). This will provide an abstraction form of representation by reducing computational cost with reduction in number of parameters to learn and provide basic conversions invariance to its original representations. This method is suitable when applied with maximum filter without overlapping in subset regions of its original representations. A max pool example is shown in figure 5(e).

Batch Normalization (BN) is a process to routinely standardize (making mean as 0 and standard deviation as one) the activations and gradients proliferating through a network. In simple words the batch Normalization layer can be included in network model so as to standardize raw input variables or the outputs of a hidden layer with the objective of accelerating the training of deep learning neural networks and get improved results. The sample batch normalization process is given in figure 5(f).

Deep Auto Encoders

It is a method used to train input and output applying unsupervised neural network technique. It consists of one input, output and hidden layer. A hidden layer defines code to represent input. The two main operational parts of auto encoders are encode and decode functions. The encoding is done at input initially, and subsequently decoders construct code to rebuild the original input. Normally auto encoders produce an approximately same copy of input according to training data.

Deep Belief Network

This model is formed by multiple Restricted Boltzmann machines (RBM) layers. The probability distribution over the input are made with undirected connections layers. The first layer will be input layer, next layer is hidden layer and from there output will be forwarded to RBM to reconstruct the inputs. The output of one RBM will be forwarded to next RBM as input. The multiples layers of RBM can be grouped as stacks also. Normally deep belief network is used to construct supervised models. The figure 6 shows as example model of deep belief network.

Figure 6a. Example model of Deep Belief Network

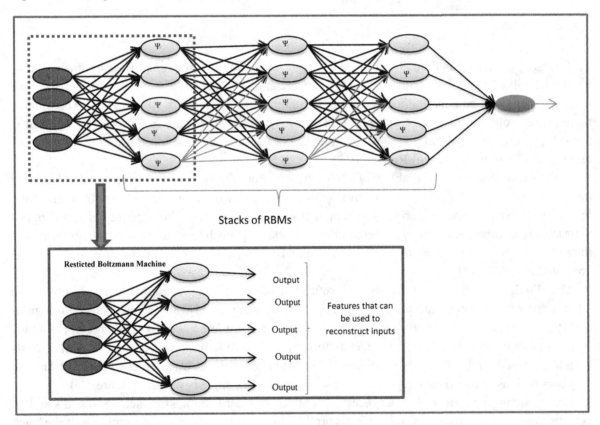

892

Multilayer Perceptron Neural Network

These networks use more than one hidden layer of neurons, unlike single layer perceptron. These are also known as Deep Feedforward Neural Networks.

Recurrent Neural Network

It is a type of Neural Network in which hidden layer neurons have self-connection. Recurrent Neural Networks possess memory. At any instance, hidden layer neuron receives activation from the lower layer as well as its previous activation value.

Gated Recurrent Unit (GRU)

In order to assist the computation and implementation of LSTM model, the neuron GRU was introduced. GRU uses update and reset gates the GRU to carry forward information over many time periods in order to influence a future time period. That value is stored in memory for a certain amount of time and at a critical point pulling that value out and using it with current state to update at next future data. GRU requires less number of parameters hence need less memory, less training time (hence fast) compared to LSTM. Figure 6 (b) depicts LSTM with i, f and o as input, forget and output. C and ~C denote memory and the new memory cell content. Figure 6 (c) shows r and z i.e. Reset and Update gate for GRU, h and ~ h are the activation and the candidate activation. Both LSTM and GRU are preferred for time series data for forecasting. GRU use less training parameters and therefore needs less memory, execute faster and train faster than LSTM's whereas LSTM is more accurate on dataset using longer sequence.

Figure 6b. Variants of RNN. LSTM (left); GRu (right)

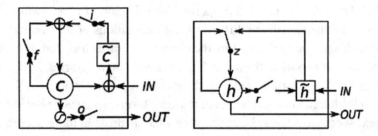

Other Neural Network

Hopfield Network

A fully interconnected network of neurons in each neuron is connected to every other neuron. The network is trained with input pattern by setting a value of neurons to the desired pattern. Then its weights are computed. The weights are not changed. Once trained for one or more patterns, the network will converge to the learned patterns. It is different from other Neural Networks.

Modular Neural Network

It is the combined structure of different types of the neural network like multilayer perceptron, Hopfield Network, Recurrent Neural Network, etc. which are incorporated as a single module into the network to perform independent subtask of whole complete Neural Networks.

Physical Neural Network

In this type of Artificial Neural Network, electrically adjustable resistance material is used to emulate the function of synapse instead of software simulations performed in the neural network.

Hardware Architecture for Neural Networks

Two types of methods are used for implementing hardware for Neural Networks.

- Software simulation in conventional computer
- Special hardware solution for decreasing execution time.

When Neural Networks are used with a fewer number of processing units and weights, software simulation is performed on the computer directly. E.g., voice recognition, etc.

APPLICATIONS OF DEEP LEARNING FOR MEDICAL DIAGNOSTICS

The design of the conventional ANN and steps involved for the purpose of medical diagnosis include: Initially patient's data to predict the diagnosis of a certain disease needs to be collected then target disease is predicted. The features are analyzed properly with selection of related attributes which provide the information needed to distinguish the different health conditions of the patient. This condition can be further analyzed with specific tools to allow the elimination of factors that provide redundant information or those that contribute only to the noise. The literature survey during 2015 and later reveal that researchers are adopting Deep learning medical diagnosis over conventional ANN methods. In deep learning models, data is filtered through a series of multiple layers, with each proceeding layer providing the output to the next successive layer. Deep learning models provide more accurate after processing huge amount of data and have the capability of learning from previous results to further enhance their ability to make correlations and connections between the unstructured data, identify the abnormalities in medical images with minimum involvement of human beings.

Compared to conventional ANN, the deep learning requires less preprocessing of data as it has self ahs the caliber to take care of many of the filtering and normalization tasks, feature extraction which was the tasks of the programmers in conventional ANN.

Deep learning has been applied for diagnosis of various health issues which include: Alzheimer's disease, diabetic retinopathy, lung cancer, liver cancer, heart related problem, fall event of elderly, benign and malignant detection in thyroid, and many more. This section covers few of the recent papers published pertaining to use of Deep learning for diagnosis of various health issues and compared its performance with conventional machine learning algorithms. The major steps of conventional method in diagnosis of medical images include image processing, segmentation followed by feature extraction; these steps are taken care by deep learning in automated fashion.

Alzheimer's disease (AD), is the most common form of dementia and is the major concern since it an irretrievable, progressive brain ailment marked by a deterioration in cognitive functioning with very poor disease modifying treatment. In this study(Siqu,2014), authors have designed a deep learning architecture, with stacked auto-encoders and a softmax regression layer as output layer, for diagnosis of AD and its prodromal stage, Mild Cognitive Impairment (MCI). The proposed method is semi-supervised which can be trained using unlabelled training samples, which are easy to obtain of less cost. Overall Results obtained are better with overall accuracy and the overall specificity of 47.42% and 83.75% respectively when compared with single-kernel SVM (SK-SVM) and multi-kernel SVM (MK-SVM) (using radial basis function (RBF) kernel) which used 'one against all' approach to classify four-class classification problem.

Most of the researchers have applied machine learning for predicting the current stage of Alzheimer's disease. Authors in (Xin Hong, 2019), have proposed Long short-term memory (LSTM) which is able to connect previous information to the present task using temporal relation between features and the next stage of Alzheimer's Disease. The work is carried out using (PET, CT and MRI)images from AD Neuroimaging Initiative (ADNI) database. The data pre-processing step includes reclassifying (eight categories are reclassified into three categories according to the stages of the disease: AD, NC, and MCI), data interpolation (for filling missing data), data normalization, data serialization, and time step preprocess. The proposed model, as depicted in figure 7 has 3 layers: the Pre-Fully Connected with fully connected layer and ReLU function; Cells Layer with one LSTM layer and a Dropout Wrapper; and the Post-Fully Connected Layer with one fully connected layer and a softmax layer. During the model training, the state of AD for next 6 months is predicted using pre-processed sequential data with time steps as input to the model. The proposed model outperform the performance of the following three work carried out by other researchers: (a) Discriminative Self-representation Sparse Regression for feature selection with SVM classifier (b) Random Forest (RF) for feature selection and Deep Neural Network (DNN) as classifier and (c) CNN along with PCA-LASSO for feature selection and SVM as classifier.

Figure 7. Alzheimer's disease prediction model with LSTM
(Xin Hong 2019)

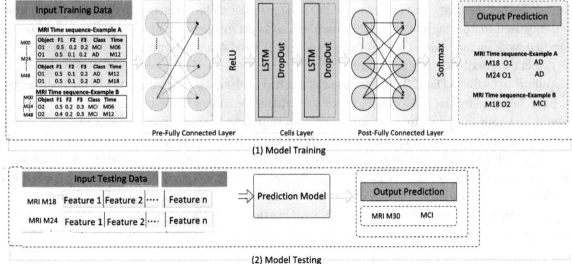

In, (Mehdi Fatan, 2018), authors have proposed CNN architecture with 3 convolution layers(to extract high order feature), 2 max-pooling layers, a full-connected layer, and a binary soft-max as depicted in figure 8 for Lung Cancer diagnostic. The fully-connected layer results in output of 10 dimensions which are passed to fully connected layer containing 2 softmax units, which indicates the probability of presence of lung cancer or not. Cross-entropy is used as the loss function of training model which is computed using multinomial logistic regression. The performance is measured using specificity, sensitivity, and F1 score on (Kaggle Data Science Bowl 2017) KDSB17 data set having CT scan images of non-cancer and cancer patients. The results obtained were better than those obtained by some of the high-ranked methods in Kaggle competition.

Figure 8. Proposed CNN architecture for lung cancer detection
(Mehdi Fatan 2018)

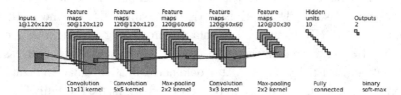

In (Goran,2019), authors have applied DNN for lung cancer detection. Two piles of images were done so as to create positives and negatives samples to train and test the network, but the groups in each pile were created so that Deep Neural Network would focus on recognizing same slice (angle) images of lung. The groups were created using K-means algorithm based on slice group. The Neural Network was adopted with additional layers to create the Deep Neural Network. The inner layers are composed of one convolution layer, max pooling layer, followed by double convolution layers (two convolutions) and an additional max pooling. The first convolution layer does the initial segmentation of the images and the interconnection of the nodes followed by max-pooling layer so as to avoid over-fitting. The second and the third convolution were used to make a more thorough search to obtain more precise information of where the cancer might be. They divided the images into small parts so that they can focus on (isolate) a certain part of the image and use that (smaller) image to search for a pattern. In the convolution function, they used sharpening and edge detection filters so as get images with sharp edges. They tested their proposed work on lung cancer images from Tx stages 2, 3 and 4 and determining at which Tx stage one can detect the possibility of lung cancer.

Authors in (Amitha Das, 2019), have used watershed Gaussian segmentation to CT image to extract the liver, followed by Gaussina mixure model to segment the cancer tissue in liver. Then the statistical, textural and geometrical feature are extracted from segmented cancer tissue in liver and provided as input to DNN to classify it as HEM, HCC and MET types of liver tumor. Work was carried out on 225 CT images with 75 cases each of hemangioma(HEM), hepatocellular carcinoma(HCC) and metastatic carcinoma(MET) types of cancer as shown in figure 11. Work is compared with other conventional classifiers like Naïve bayes, MLP, SVM, KNN, AdaBoost, J48, Random forest. The performance of proposed method is best with accuracy of 98.38%, sensitivity of 100%, specificity of 97.72%, Jaccard index of 95% and dice similarity coefficient (DSC) of 97.43%.

Figure 9. Deep learning model proposed by (Amitha Das, 2019) for liver cancer detection

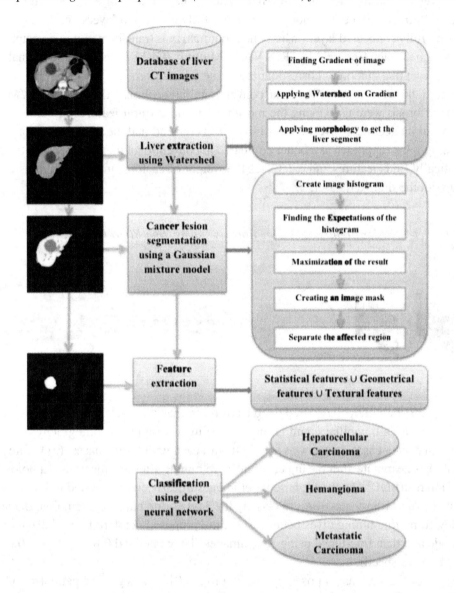

In (Tarek M, 2017), authors have applied deep network for diagnosing focal liver diseases. Firstly, level set method is used followed by Fuzzy -c-means clustering for segmentation of liver lesions. Then stacked sparse auto-encoder is used to extract the high-level features from the segmented images, which is input to the softmax layer for finally diagnosing the three focal liver diseases along with the normal liver. The Proposed work achieved accuracy, sensitivity and specificity of 97.2%, 98% and 95.7% respectively. The performance was better when compared with 3 traditional machine methods: multi-SVM, KNN, and Naïve Bayes.

(Yang Yu, 2018) have used 100 liver section of images of TAA-induced fibrotic rat using Second Harmonic Generation (SHG) microscopy with automatic feature extraction was carried out by deep learning-based algorithms using the convolution and max pooling layers. The input of AlexNet-CNN was replaced liver fibrosis assessment using SHG image. The 7 hidden layers was made up of 5 convolution layers (with intermediate max pool layer) and 2 fully connected layers i.e. the layer 6 and 7 are 4096-dimension fully connected layers where the input matrix is transformed into a vector for Softmax activation function through General MATRIX Vector Multiply (GEMV) approach. The final output layer has 5 nodes representing outcomes corresponding to the 5 liver fibrosis stages from F0 to F4 using the Metavir scoring (shown in figure 10) . Four conventional algorithms: ANN, MLR, SVM and RF for scoring of liver fibrosis were used using the morphology and textural features of collagen fibers. The proposed fully automated method results were similar to conventional methods. The authors appreciate the deep learning-based approach as a better compared to conventional methods because of two reasons: (a) it automatically finds features and calculates the weight of each feature and (b) transfer learning is helps to deal with the limited dataset.

Figure 10. AlexNet-CNN for predicting 5 liver fibrosis stages from F0 to F4
(Yang Yu, 2018)

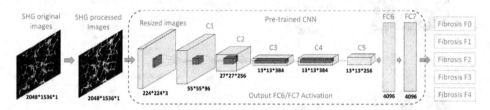

In (Seokmin, 2019), authors have used deep learning framework to differentiate 3 subtypes of renal cell carcinoma: clear cell, papillary, and chromophobe using computed tomography (CT) images. A total of 169 renal cancer cases dataset was acquired with each with three phases: (a) before injection of contrast agent; (b) one minute after the injection and (c) 5 minute after the injection. Radiologists marked the region of interest(ROI). The three-phase input images linearly combined and fed to the GoogLeNet after removal of two auxiliary classifiers to classify the 3 types of renal cell carcinoma. Because transfer learning followed by fine-tuning gives better results, the proposed network by initialized by ImageNet pertaining mode and then fine-tuned using RCC images. They obtained 0.85 accuracy, 0.64–0.98 sensitivity and 0.83-0.93 specificity.

The objective of the work as proposed by (Yafeng Ren, 2019), was given a patient who has been diagnosed with hypertension, predict the probability of the person to suffer from kidney disease. Authors have attempted to study kidney disease prediction in hypertension patients by using a hybrid neural network (shown in figure 12) which incorporates Bidirectional Long Short-Term Memory (BiLSTM) and Autoencoder networks to fully capture the information in Electronic Health Records (EHR). They worked on EHR dataset with 35,332 records from hypertension patients to achieve an accuracy of 89.7%. The textual features from EHR are learnt by BiLSTM and Autoencoder network capturing important numerical cues using numerical indicators from HER.

In (Ali, 2018), authors have used CNN (with convolution and maxpooling layers) for extracting hidden features which is fed as input to Extreme Learning Machines (ELM) with radial base function as a kernel function to classify three types of brain tumors including meningioma, glioma and pituitary tumors in T1-weighted contrast-enhanced MRI (CE-MRI) images. Results are compared with traditional

Figure 11. Bidirectional Long Short-Term Memory (BiLSTM) and Autoencoder networks Model for predicting the probability of person to suffer from kidney disease
(Yafeng Ren, 2019)

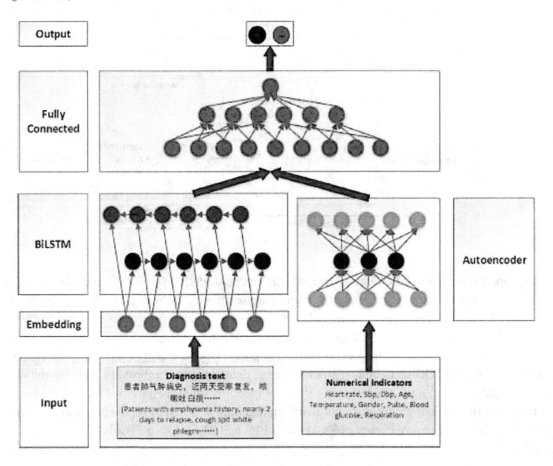

classifier which include Support Vector Machine, Radial Base Function, MLP, Stacking, and XGBoost classifiers. The proposes method resulted in an accuracy of 93.68%.

In, (Deepak, 2019), authors focus on a 3-class classification problem to differentiate among glioma, meningioma and pituitary tumors, which form three prominent types of brain tumor. The proposed classification system adopts the concept of deep transfer learning and uses a pre-trained GoogLeNet to extract features from brain MRI images. The fully connected (FC) layer in the original GoogLeNet was replaced by a new FC layer with an output size. The transfer learned model has a softmax classifier layer, which can classify image data from figshare into three tumor classes. The pretrained GoogLeNet provided the low level features and FC of the the modified GoogLeNet was used to study the high-level features specific to the target domain using fighshare dataset as shown in figure 12. The deep CNN features (provided by GoogLeNet) were tested using SVM and K-nearest neighbors classifiers in addition to softmax classifier within deep CNN. The classification accuracy of the deep transfer learned (standalone) was found to be 92.3±0.7% and that of SVM and KNN as 97.8±0.2% and 98.0±0.4%. respectively.

Figure 12. Deep learning architecture proposed by (Deepak, 2019) for tumor detection

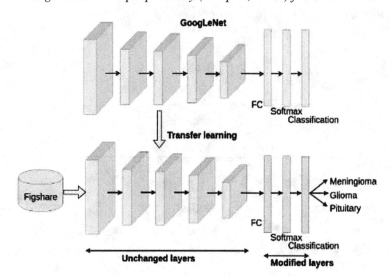

The proposed work for work multi-grade brain tumor classification system (Figure 14) is carried out in three steps: (a) the tumor regions from the dataset are segmented through a InputCascadeCNN CNN model (which contains two streams: one with 7 × 7 accessible fields for extracting local features and another with 13 × 13 accessible fields for extracting global features) (figure 15), (b) the segmented data is further augmented (using techniques: rotation, flipping, skewness, and shears for geometric transformations invariance, Gaussian blur, sharpening, edge detection, and emboss) to increase the number of data samples, and (c) a pre-trained VGG-19 CNN model is fine-tuned trained on MR brain images for final prediction of four grades of tumor (Muhammad Sajjad, 2019) . Proposed method achieved an Sensitivity, Specificity and Accuracy of 88.41%, 96.12% and 94.58% respectively.

Figure 13. InputCascadeCNN architecture for brain tumor segmentation through two way CNN (Muhammad Sajjad, 2019)

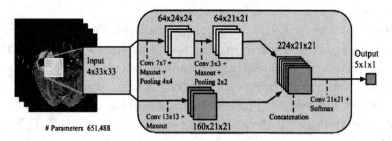

In (Mihaela, 2019), authors have presented CNN model for identifying Congestive Heart Failure(CHF) using raw electrocardiogram(ECG) heartbeat only. CHF is a pathophysiological ailment accountable for the let-down of the heart in pumping blood in the body. They used publicly available ECG BIDMC datasets (Beth Israel Deaconess Medical Center) which includes data related to 490,505 heart-beats. Each heartbeat was labeled with a binary value of 0 or 1 corresponding to healthy or suffering from

Figure 14. Proposed 1-D CNN architecture for beat classification and visualization of the class discriminative sequences in the input heartbeats
(Mihaela, 2019)

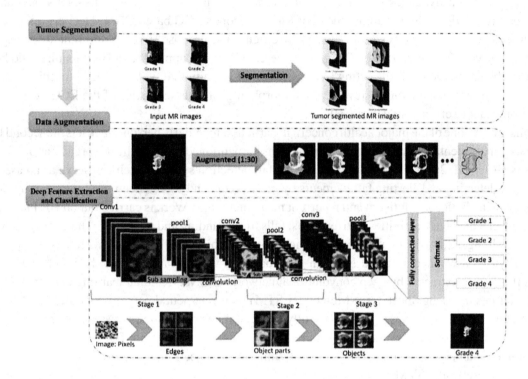

Figure 15. CNN assisted multi-grade tumor segmentation and classification framework
(Muhammad Sajjad, 2019)

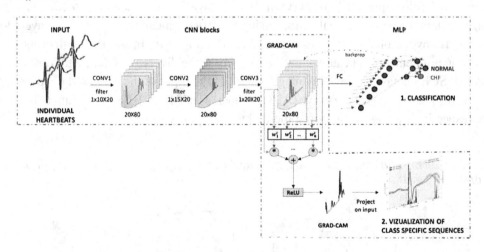

CHF, respectively. They obtained cent per cent accuracy in detection of CHF by identifying heart beat sequences and ECG's morphological characteristics. Proposed 1-D CNN classifier is depicted in figure 16 is used for feature extraction, and the MLP module for the classification of the raw ECG heartbeats. Work is compared with few of the conventional method on similar kind of dataset in literature study which include: CART based on HRV features; Linear discriminant analysis and Bayesian classifier based on HRV features; k-NN based on HRV features; Non-equilibrium decision-tree, support vector machine classifier based on dynamics of 5-minute short-term HRV measures, SVN and k-NNN on-standard HRV features; and one deep learning method: Raw, 2 seconds ECG based CNN. The performance was measured in terms of accuracy, sensitivity and specificity. The proposed work is different in two aspects: (a) previous work have used raw ECG signals, whereas CNN was applied with HRV features and hence results in better prediction of detecting CHF. (b) They also claim that with advanced machine learning approaches it was first attempt to reveal which morphological characteristics of the ECG beats are the most important to efficiently detect CHF.

Falls are also one of the major health concern in particular for elderly person, since it is the second leading cause of accidental or unintentional injury deaths as mentioned by world health organization(WHO). Authors (Ahemed, 2018), have proposed a robust fall detection system which can serve as an assistive device for detecting and alerting fall incidents by means of an end-to-end deep machine learning model designed using both convolutional and recurrent neural networks. Work is carried out on UR Fall Detection Dataset which has a activities distributed as: falls from standing and sitting on a chair, daily activities such as walking, sitting down, squatting and picking-up an object and sequences with fall-like activities such as lying on wooden sofa and lying on the floor. The visual features from the input sequence of depth frames are extracted by deep convolutional network: ResNet (residual learning network). On top of ResNet lies the Long Short-Term-Memory (LSTM) recurrent neural network module. The LSTM is to learn temporal dynamics which is fed to fully connected layer (logistic regression layer) for recognition of occurrence of a fall event as shown in figure 17. The proposed ConvLSTM is robust enough to focus on human body movements, and overlook static scene objects and outperforms to similar kind of work carried out using SVM.

Glaucoma is one of the common causes of blindness, which is caused by progressive damage of the the optic nerve. Authors (Xiangyu Chen, 2015) have used deep learning architecture with 4 convolutional layers and 2 fully connected layers (with dropout layers) for glaucoma detection. To reduce the over fitting problem, response-normalization (using Rectified Linear Units (ReLUs)) layers follow the first and second convolutional layers; followed by Max Pooling layer. In addition both dropout is used to avid over fitting problem and data augmentation to increase the diversity of data set. Work is carried out on SRIGA and SCES datasets. The ROI image is used as the input of the proposed deep Convolutional Neural Network. The area under the curve (AUC) values of 0:831 and 0:887 is obtained for ORIGA and SCES are, respectively using the proposed method for glaucoma detection.

Figure 16. Hybrid convolutional and recurrent neural networks for fall activity recognition (Ahemed, 2018)

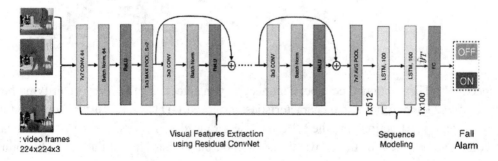

HANDLING IMBALANCED CLASS PROBLEM IN MEDICAL DATASETS

Imbalanced dataset has comparatively less number of observations belonging to one class than those belonging to the other classes. In medical domain, the major problem is imbalanced dataset since pathologic findings are by and large unusual. In addition the dataset may be very small or very large to fit in RAM, may have missing data which affects the performance of the classifier. The three common approaches to handle imbalanced data are:

- Over sampling: Replicate the dataset examples belonging to under- represented class. The drawback is, there is hike in the likelihood of overfitting because of replication of examples of under-represented class.
- Under sampling: Eliminate the percentage of dataset examples belonging to most represented class. The drawback is, discarding potentially useful information which could of importance for building the classifier model.
- Generate synthetic data: Generate new synthetic dataset examples from the under-represented class. The problem of over fitting which occurred in over sampling can be avoided, since a subset of data from the minority class is selected and not replicated but used to generated new synthetic dataset similar to data of minority class.

In addition to the above three methods other methods used for handling imbalanced data using ensemble methods; which modify the classification algorithms to make them apt for imbalanced data sets.

For deep learning, one of the major challenges is insufficient training data which usually leads to overfitting. Few of the techniques commonly adopted by deep learning to overcome the overfitting because of insufficient target data is to include techniques like dropout, transfer learning, and data augmentation.

Data Augmentation

Data augmentation techniques seek to expand the amount of training data automatically by applying automatic transformations to images using various traditional conventional techniques to list a few: horizontal image flips, cropping, translations, rotation, and advanced method which include elastic distortion, tilting, and theme adjustments. Most of the traditional data augmentation techniques usually produce highly correlated image training data. Few of the commonly used augmentation methods include:

- **Color augmentation**: Very simple color augmentations include isolating a single color channel such as R, G, or B followed by and adding 2 zero matrices from the other color channels. In addition, the RGB values can be easily modified by increasing or decreasing the brightness of the image. One more method under color augmentation involves deriving the color histogram followed by changing the intensity values in these histograms.
- **Translation**: In translation method, one can shift the images left, right, up, or down and henceforth to retain the spatial dimension after post augmentation, the remaining spaces are either padded with 0s or 255 or with random or Gaussian noise.
- **Rotation**: Rotation augmentations are carried out by rotating the image right or left on an axis Between 1° and 359°.

- **Noise injection**: It helps to construct CNN to learn more robust features by injecting a matrix of random values usually drawn from a Gaussian distribution.
- **Cropping**: Cropping images involves either cropping the central patch of each image or apply random cropping to provide effect of translation. The difference between cropping and translation is that the former reduces the size of input image whereas the special dimension is preserved in translation.
- **Flipping**: apply flipping either to horizontal or vertical axis and is most easy method to implement augmentation.
- **Mixing images**: Mixing images by averaging their pixel values is a very counterintuitive approach to Data Augmentation which may seem not useful to human observer; use of for used GANs to produce mixed images in the training data not only reduced training time but also enhanced the diversity of GAN samples(Daojun Liang et al.,2018)

In addition among the new upcoming methods GAN based data augmentation is becoming popular to generate synthetic images.

- **GAN based data augmentation**: GANs has two sub-models: the generator model which is trained to generated new (synthetic) instances and the discriminator model decides whether each instance is synthetic/fake/generated or real one from the domain. The two models are trained together in adversarial; awaiting the discriminator model accepts the plausible instances generated by generator model.

(Hoo et.al., 2018) have applied GAN to generate synthetic brain images with tumor using Alzheimer's Disease Neuroimaging Initiative (ADNI) and Multimodal Brain Tumor Image Segmentation Benchmark: (BRATS) datasets. Since the ADNI data set does not contain tumor information, authors trained the pix2pix model to segment normal brain anatomy from the T1-weighted images of the ADNI data set. The segmentation of neural anatomy, in combination with tumor segmentations provided by the BRATS data set, provide a complete segmentation of the brain with tumor. The GAN is trained to generate synthetic images by merging brain anatomy label (obtained from ADNI dataset) and tumor label separately (from BRATS dataset), by either altering the tumor characteristics such as size, location of the existing brain and tumor label set, or place tumor label on an otherwise tumor-free brain label. The process of generating synthetic brain images with tumor is illustrated in figure 18.

(Darius et al., 2019) adopted GAN trained on real human embryo cell images to generate a synthetic dataset of one-, two-, and four-cell embryo images. They have manipulated the size, position, and number of the artificially generated embryo cell images and used these images to train and validate other embryo image processing algorithms, to compensate when there is lack of availability or less number of real embryo images for training neural networks.

Dropout

Dropout is one the solution to avoid over fit a training data of small size by randomly dropping out nodes (i.e. ignoring few neurons chosen randomly) during training (Nitish Srivastava et al., 2014). The neurons may develop co-dependency amongst each other during training which limits the individual power of each neuron progressing to over-fitting of training data. (Xin Hong,2019), have proposed Long short-

Figure 17. GAN based synthetic brain image with tumor
(Hoo et.al., 2018)

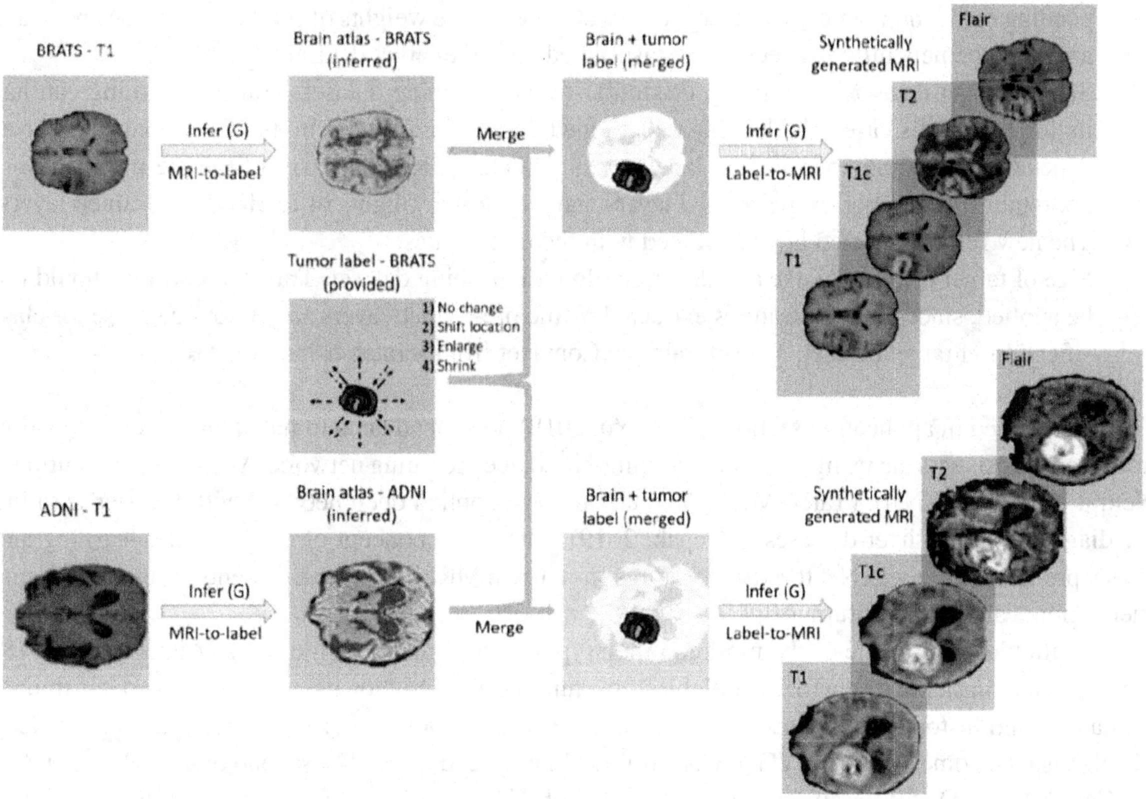

term memory (LSTM) to predict the next stage of Alzheimer's Disease using dropout concept. Dropout is used to avid over fitting problem for glaucoma detection (Xiangyu Chen, 2015).

Transfer Learning

When we have limited set of data which in not sufficient to train deep neural network then transfer learning is one of the solution. In transfer learning, training of neural network happens in two phases: (i) pre-training, where the network is generally trained on a large-scale benchmark dataset (to extract general features) representing a wide diversity of labels/categories (e.g., ImageNet); and (ii) fine-tuning, where the pre-trained network of first phase is further fine-tuned to extract more specific feature. In context to medical domain, the pre-trained weights of first phase are fine tuned in second phase for specific medical task for interpreting chest x-rays, diagnosing eye diseases, early detection of Alzheimer's disease and so on. The two main benefits of transfer learning are: fast training in second phase, since the model readily uses high level features obtained as part of pre-training phase; and one can manage model with less number of medical data for training in second phase.

Few of the rules of thumb to be followed for transfer learning, based on the size and similarity of the target data with trained dataset are as follows:

- Size of target dataset is small and similar to base training dataset. Transfer learning can has its impact in this case. The last layer of trained dataset is replaced by the fully connected layer depending on the number of class labels of target dataset. The weights of pre-trained phase are freeze and only the new fully connected layer is trained with the target dataset.
- Size of target dataset is small and dissimilar to base training dataset. Transfer learning can has its impact in this case. The last layer of trained dataset is replaced by the fully connected layer depending on the number of class labels of target dataset. Remove most of the pre-trained layers i.e. retain less number of pre-trained layers and freeze the weights of retained pre-trained layers. The new fully connected layer is trained with the target dataset.
- Size of target dataset is large and dissimilar to base training dataset. Transfer learning should not be applied, since the high features extracted by the pre-trained layers are of not much use for classification of target dataset; instead train the ConvNet from scratch using target dataset.

As explained in application section, (Yang Yu, 2018) developed an automated feature classification and liver fibrosis scoring using a transfer learning-based deep learning network, AlexNet-Convolutional Neural Networks (CNN). (Tarek M, 2017), authors have applied deep network with transfer learning for diagnosing focal liver diseases. (Deepak, 2019), adopts the concept of deep transfer learning and uses a pre-trained GoogLeNet to extract features from brain MRI images to differentiate among glioma, meningioma and pituitary tumors.

Medulloblastoma is one of the most common types of malignant brain tumors (Angel et al., 2018) have applied transfer learning for medulloblastoma tumor differentiation using two CNN models trained on natural and histopathology images for visual feature extraction. The first model is a 16 layer deep CNN: Visual Geometry Group (VGG) CNN trained ImageNet dataset. The second one is a 2-layer CNN (IBCa-CNN) trained for classifying breast cancer tumor. The new target dataset is medulloblastoma tumor diffrentiation with set of patches related to anaplastic and non-anaplastic class. Both CNNs are used as visual feature extractors of histopathology image are used separately for training softmax classifier to classify anaplastic and non-anaplastic medulloblastoma tumor (figure 19). IBCa-CNN feature resulted in enhanced accuracy of 89.8% compared to 76.6% accuracy of VGG-CNN. Thus transfer learning trained on histopathology images can be applied for classification task on different imbalanced target data.

Figure 18. IBCa-CNN and VGG-CNN based transfer learning for medulloblastoma tumor differentiation (Angel et al., 2018)

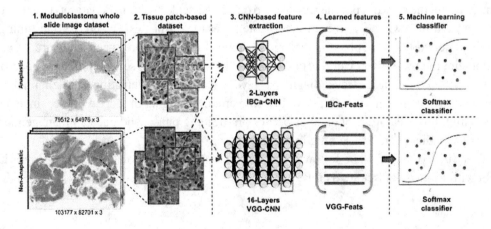

General Medical Diagnosis Scheme

From the literature reviewed, few of important steps to model neural network for diagnosis can be stated as follows:

- **Image data transformation:** The past and current studies indicate that it is unnecessary to transform or change data not normally or usually distributed that reveal non-regular periodic development or variant i.e. conventional data augmentation is not much use for medical field. Instead the modification of heteroscedasticity and trends in data are helpful in addition to, data normalization, GAN based transformation are of much use for medical domain for creating synthesized data to handle privacy issues in medical domain as well as for imbalanced data
- **Input model identification:** Input variables can be determined with the support of a priori knowledge, using a stepwise model-building method, transfer learning or analytical method like cross-correlation technique.
- **Network geometry choice**: One hidden layer may be enough as adequate in most network practical uses. However, mathematical expression could determine the upper bound of number of hidden nodes and hidden layer nodes required to approximate continuous function. Except, if non-convergent techniques, like cross-validation, the connection between the quantity of training and the quantity of hidden layer units likewise should be considered. The relationship can be investigated with the guide of the rules given in some literature.
- **Design of phased step for model development:** Researchers can focus on network characteristic at variable specification phase. Also, it is useful to conduct trials in determining required local minimum in the error surface, and oscillations in the R.
- **Training for different neural network operations:** Forecasting with continuous training, with different step sizes taken in weight space. These steps can be useful when selecting appropriate network parameters like (transfer function, momentum, epoch size, learning rate, and error) and how many training samples in the network for a case study.
- **Validation of model.** The validation of model is necessary for standardization and practical scenarios of ANNs for optimization of performance.

CHALLENGES AND FUTURE DIRECTION DISCUSSIONS

This section will provide details regarding known and unexposed problems of ANN in medical domain and suitable improvements that are to be included in future in order to develop better system design comparatively. The advanced ANN is powerful tool to help physicians for medical diagnosis as second opinion. The major advantages includes: ability to process large amount of data, reduce likelihood of overlooking relevant information, and reduce diagnosis time, automated feature identification for medical diagnosis.

Challenges

- **Lack of large training data sets:** the images used for medical diagnosis are developed or predicted, and for some diseases availability of dataset is more and rest absolute. Even for existing relevant annotations labeling for these images will not be included and in few cases turning reports into accurate annotations or structures labels in an automated manner requires sophisticated text-mining methods.

- **Classification and segmentation:** the medical data or images collected will be presented as binary task for either classification or segmentation. But this task is complex as both classes are normally with high heterogeneity.
- **Handling class imbalance:** Even this problem is currently found to be depending on task at hand. This issue can be solved with application of proper deep learning systems like transfer learning and data augmentation.
- **Standardization:** there is no standard policy and regulations in design of compatible devices or technologies for medical domain. In medical context, many vendors exist, they manufacture range of devices and new vendors join the race leading to interoperability issues. So, immediate actions are to be taken in this direction to provide knowledge to medical experts to handle diversity in medical domain.
- **Necessity to build medical care platforms:** A platform with a service oriented approach has to be taken so that service can be taken considering different application package interfaces together with platform, libraries and appropriate frameworks should be built. By this, effort medical care software developers and designers will be able to collaborated and construct documents, codes, classes, message templates, and other useful data in an effective and efficient manner. So, that further issues based on disease accessibility will be easier and useful.
- **Development of interactive app:** Regular updates on healthcare apps based on recent advances with inclusion of neural network like concepts with reach audience of interest at faster rate.
- **Require translation of technology:** still efforts are needed to move from legacy system to new medical diagnostic based approaches. Meanwhile there is a need to ensure backward compatibility and flexibility in the integration of existing devices.
- **New disease and disorders:** Continuous monitoring efforts are required from research and development activities to identify new type of diseases and disorders. The early detection will be bone for many individuals for long been an important task.
- **Data protection steps to be strengthened:** The data under analysis or being diagnosed requires protection from illicit access. Hence, stern polices and technical measures have to be devised at organization and Government level. The optimal security algorithms can also be developed between protection, detection, and reaction services to prevent various attacks, threats, and vulnerabilities.

Future Directions

This research essentially requires many areas in need of further investigation. Further research is required in the following areas:

- A greater focus on adaptive dynamic programming (ADP) could produce interesting findings that account more for significant contributions in the area of brain research and computational intelligence.
- Emerging topic in engineering and computer science include parameter adjustment technique in machine learning algorithms. The successful use of algorithms optimization in adjusting network variables should be well studied.

●● Further investigation into the applications of reinforcement-learning, unsupervised, semi-supervised methods to the deep neural network for complex and multi-complex systems.

● Future research should concentrate on the use of intelligent analysis such as neural network models, back propagation neural networks, probabilistic neural network, supervised associating networks, multi-layer perceptron neural network architectures, learning vector quantization, multi-layer neural network, and hybrid neural network models, since they promise better performance in the for diverse challenges of life-science applications.

● Since the use of inferential statistics and neural networks can be more predictive in data analysis. Hence, the predictive approach can also be another focus in the study of the subject in particular using recurrent networks (e.g. LSTM) because in many cases prediction of health related issues is more significant than just diagnosis.

● Research is required for implementation of DL algorithms interfacing with mobile gadgets. As recently, DL chips idea emerged that is attracting research interest.

● Public awareness training on artificial network neural models should continue regularly, especially on the need for providing useful information using empirical analysis and digital data.

● More investigation is required in the stability analysis of deep NN because, in recent times, the DNNs stability analysis has become a hot topic for research focus due to its advantages in many industrial sectors.

● With the new trend in big data technique, DL would be useful where large amounts of un-supervised data are applied. It would be interesting to construct DL models that can learn from fewer training data, particularly for visual and speech recognition systems.

● Further research should focus on the use of DNNs to nonlinear networked control systems. More understanding of complicated dynamics would help us establish how to obtain better performances in control, and filtering capability effectively and efficiently.

● The governments and institutions need to provide funds to carry out research in diverse application of neural networks for success, especially in this era of modern education, technology advancement, industrial growth, economic challenges, artificial intelligence development, and information and communication revolution.

CONCLUSION

This chapter reviews various techniques, architectures of both conventional and nonconventional ANN in general. Few of the conventional ANN have proved to be equally good with those of the nonconventional ANN in terms of accuracy. But the very fact that the nonconventional ANN are robust enough to handle noisy input and identify features autonomously, are few of key reasons for its popularity over conventional ANN methods. The chapter covers applications of Deep learning on various medical cases. One of the major drawbacks of CNN is that they need huge training data. In medical domain, the major problem is imbalanced dataset since pathologic findings are by and large unusual. Various methods to handle this imbalanced data are briefed with medical domain case studies. However, despite of wide application of ANN in modern diagnosis, they must be considered only as a tool to facilitate the final decision of a clinician, who is ultimately responsible for critical evaluation of the both conventional and nonconventional ANN diagnosis. Lastly the challenges and future scope of ANN for medical domain is discussed.

REFERENCES

Abobakr, Hossny, Abdelkader, & Nahavandi. (2018). *RGB-D Fall Detection via Deep Residual Convolutional LSTM Networks*. IEEE.

Altunay, Telatar, Erogul, & Aydur. (2009). A New Approach to urinary system dynamics problems: Evaluation and classification of uroflowmeter signals using artificial neural networks. *Expert Systems with Applications, 36*(3), 4891–4895.

Ameer. (2019). Brain tumor classification using deep CNN features via transfer learning. *Computers in Biology and Medicine, 111*, 103345. PMID:31279167

Angel, Arevalo, Judkins, Madabhushi, & Gonzalez. (n.d.). A method for Medulloblastoma Tumor Differentiation based on Convolutional Neural Networks and Transfer Learning. *Conference: Proc. SPIE 9681, 11th International Symposium on Medical Information Processing and Analysis*. DOI: 10.1117/12.2208825

Bakator & Radosav. (2018). Deep Learning and Medical Diagnosis: A Review of Literature. *Multimodal Technologies and Interact, 2*, 47. doi:10.3390/mti2030047

Bolboca. (2019). *Medical diagnosis tests: a test anatomy, phases and statistical treatment of data*. Hindawi.

Catalogna, Cohen, Fishman, Halpern, Nevo, & Ben-Jacob. (2012). ANN based controller for gloucose monitoring during, clamp test. *PLoS One, 7*, e44587.

Cetiner, Sari, & Aburas. (2009). Recognition of dengue disease patterns using artificial neural networks. *Proceedings of the 5th International Advanced Technologies Symposium (IATS'09)*, 359–362.

Chen, Xu, Wong, Wong, & Liu. (2015). Glaucoma Detection based on Deep Convolutional Neural Network. *2015 37th Annual International Conference of the IEEE Engineering in Medicine and Biology Society (EMBC)*. Doi:10.1109/EMBC.2015.7318462

Daojun, Feng, Tian, & Peter. (2018). Understanding mixup training methods. *IEEE Access, 6*, 58774-58783.

Das, Acharya, Panda, & Sabut. (2019). Deep learning based liver cancer detection using watershed transform and Gaussian mixture model techniques. *Cognitive Systems Research, 54*, 165–175.

Das, Turkoglu, & Sengur. (2009). Effective diagnosis of heart disease through neural networks ensembles. *Expert Systems with Applications, 36*(4), 7675–7680.

Dirvanauskas, Maskeli, Raudonis, Damaševičius, & Scherer. (2019). *HEMIGEN: Human Embryo Image Generator Based on Generative Adversarial Networks Sensors*. Academic Press.

Dutta. (2014). Neural network-based models for software effort estimation: a review. *Artif. Intell. Rev., 42*(2), 295-307.

Francisco, Manuel, Antonio, & Daniel. (2008). A robust model of the neuronal regulator of the lower urinary tract based on artificial neural networks. *Neurocomputing, 71*(4-6), 743–754.

Gil, Johnsson, Garicia Chemizo, Paya, & Fernandez. (2009). Application of Artificial Neural Networks in the Diagnosis of Urological Dysfunctions. *Expert Systems with Applications*, *36*(3), 5754–5760.

Han, Hwang, & Lee. (2019). The Classification of Renal Cancer in 3-Phase CT Images Using a Deep Learning Method. *Journal of Digital Imaging*, *32*, 638–643. doi:10.100710278-019-00230-2]

Hassan, Elmogy, & Sallam. (2017). Diagnosis of Focal Liver Diseases Based on Deep Learning Technique for Ultrasound Images. *Arabian Journal for Science and Engineering*. Advance online publication. doi:10.100713369-016-2387-9]

He & Garcia. (2009). Learning from imbalanced data. *IEEE Trans. Knowl. Data Eng., 21*(9), 1263-1284.

Heckerling, Canaris, Flach, Tape, Wigton, & Gerber. (2007). Predictors of urinary tract infection based on artificial neural networks and genetic algorithms. *International Journal of Medical Informatics*, *76*(4), 289–296. PMID:16469531

Hong, Lin, Yang, Zeng, Cai, Gou, & Yang. (2019). Predicting Alzheimer's Disease Using LSTM. *IEEE Access: Practical Innovations, Open Solutions*. Advance online publication. doi:10.1109/ACCESS.2019.2919385

Ibrahim, Taib, Abas, Guan, & Sulaiman. (2005). A novel dengue fever (DF) and dengue haemorrhagi fever (DHF) analysis using artificial neural network (ANN). *Computer Methods and Programs in Biomedicine*, *79*(3), 273–281. PMID:15925426

Izeboudjen, Larbes, & Farah. (2014). A new classification approach for neural networks hardware: from standards chips to embedded systems on chip. *Artif. Intell. Rev., 41*(4), 491-534.

Jakimovski & Davcev. (2019). Using Double Convolution Neural Network for Lung Cancer Stage Detection. *Applied Sciences (Basel, Switzerland)*, *9*, 427. doi:10.3390/app9030427]

Liu, Cai, Pujol, Kikinis, & Feng. (2014). *Early Diagnosis of Alzheimer's Disease with Deep Learning*. IEEE.

Moein, Monadjemi, & Moallem. (2009). A Novel Fuzzy-Neural Based Medical Diagnosis System. *International Journal of Biological & Medical Sciences*, *4*(3), 146–150.

Monadjemi & Moallem. (2008). Automatic Diagnosis of Particular Diseases Using a Fuzzy-Neural Approach. *International Review on Computers & Software*, *3*(4), 406–411.

Mozaffari, Emami, & Fathi. (2018). A comprehensive investigation into the performance, robustness, scalability and convergence of chaos-enhanced evolutionary algorithms with boundary constraints. *Artificial Intelligence Review*, 1–62.

Pashaei, S., & Jazayeri. (2018). Brain Tumor Classification via Convolutional Neural Network and Extreme Learning Machines. In *8th International Conference on Computer and Knowledge Engineering (ICCKE 2018)*. Ferdowsi University of Mashhad.

Pearce, Wong, Mirtskhulava, AlMajeed, Bakuria, & Gulua. (2016). Artificial Neural Network and Mobile Applications in Medical Diagnosis. *2015 17th UKSimAMSS International Conference on Modelling and Simulation*.

Porumb, Iadanza, Massarod, & Pecchia. (2020). A convolutional neural network approach to detect congestive heart failure. *Biomedical Signal Processing and Control, 55*, 101597. doi:10.1016/j.bspc.2019.101597

Rachata, Charoenkwan, Yooyativong, Chamnongthal, Lursinsap, & Higuchi. (2008). Automatic prediction system of dengue haemorrhagic-fever outbreak risk by using entropy and artificial neural network. In *Proceedings of the International Symposium on Communications and Information Technologies*. IEEE.

Raval, Bhatt, Kumhar, Parikh, & Vyas. (2016). Medical diagnosis system using machine learning. *International Journal of Computer Science & Communication, 7*(1), 177–182.

Razzak, Naz, & Zaib. (2017). *Deep Learning for Medical Image Processing: Overview, Challenges and Future.* arXiv:1704.06825v1

Razzak, Naz, & Zaib. (2017). *Deep Learning for Medical Image Processing: Overview, Challenges and Future, DL for medical imaging.* Cornell university.

Ren, Fei, Liang, Ji, & Cheng. (2019). A hybrid neural network model for predicting kidney disease in hypertension patients based on electronic health records. *BMC Medical Informatics and Decision Making, 19*(Suppl 2), 51. doi:10.118612911-019-0765-4

Sajjad, Khan, Muhammad, Wu, Ullah, & Baik. (2019). Multi-grade brain tumor classification using deep CNN with extensive data augmentation. *Journal of Computational Science, 30*, 174–182.

Serj, Lavi, Hoff, & Valls. (2018). *A Deep Convolutional Neural Network for Lung Cancer Diagnostic.* arXiv:1804.08170

Shin, Tenenholtz, Rogers, Schwarz, Senjem, Gunter, Andriole, & Michalski. (2018). *Medical Image Synthesis for Data Augmentation and Anonymization using Generative Adversarial Networks.* arXiv:1807.10225v2

Srivastava, Hinton, Krizhevsky, Salakhutdinov, & Sutskever. (2014). Dropout: a simple way to prevent neural networks from overfitting. *JMLR.*

van Ginneken & S´anchez. (2017). *A Survey on Deep Learning in Medical Image Analysis.* arXiv,1702.05747v2

Wang, He, & Liu. (2018). Intelligent optimal control with critic learning for a nonlinear overhead crane system. *IEEE Transact. Ind. Inf., 14*(7), 2932-2940.

Yu, Wang, Ng, Ma, Mo, Li, Fong, Xing, Song, Xie, Si, Wee, Welsch, So, & Yu. (2018). Deep learning enables automated scoring of liver fibrosis stages. *Scientific Reports, 8*(16016). Advance online publication. doi:10.103841598-018-34300-2

Chapter 42
New Artificial Neural Network Models for Bio Medical Image Compression:
Bio Medical Image Compression

G. Vimala Kumari
MVGR College of Engineering, Vizianagaram, India

G. Sasibhushana Rao
Andhra University College of Engineering, Visakhapatnam, India

B. Prabhakara Rao
Jawaharlal Nehru Technological University, Kakinada, Andhra Pradesh, India

ABSTRACT

This article presents an image compression method using feed-forward back-propagation neural networks (NNs). Marked progress has been made in the area of image compression in the last decade. Image compression removing redundant information in image data is a solution for storage and data transmission problems for huge amounts of data. NNs offer the potential for providing a novel solution to the problem of image compression by its ability to generate an internal data representation. A comparison among various feed-forward back-propagation training algorithms was presented with different compression ratios and different block sizes. The learning methods, the Levenberg Marquardt (LM) algorithm and the Gradient Descent (GD) have been used to perform the training of the network architecture and finally, the performance is evaluated in terms of MSE and PSNR using medical images. The decompressed results obtained using these two algorithms are computed in terms of PSNR and MSE along with performance plots and regression plots from which it can be observed that the LM algorithm gives more accurate results than the GD algorithm.

DOI: 10.4018/978-1-6684-2408-7.ch042

1. INTRODUCTION

Artificial neural networks (ANNs) are archetypes of the biological neuron system and thus have been drawn from the abilities of a human brain. The architecture of ANN being drawn from the concept of brain functioning, a neural network is a hugely reticulated network of a huge number of neurons which are processing elements. ANNs are employed to summarize and prototype some of the functional aspects of the human brain system in an effort so as to acquire some of its computational strengths. A NN consists of eight components: neurons, signal function, activation state vector, activity aggregation rule, pattern of connectivity, learning rule, activation rule, and environment. Recently, ANNs are applied in areas in which high rates of computation are essential and considered as probable solutions to problems of image compression. Generally, two different categories have been put forward for enhancing the performance of compression methods. Firstly, a method for compression by using ANN technology has to be developed to improve the design. Secondly, neural networks have to be applied to develop compression methods. Backpropagation algorithm is extensively used learning algorithms in ANNs. With generalization ability and high accuracy, the feedforward neural network architecture is capable of approximating most problems. This architecture is based on the learning rule of error-correction. Error propagation comprises of two passes, a forward pass and a backward pass through different layers of network. The effect, of input vector's application to the sensory nodes of the network, transmits through the network layer by layer in the forward pass. In the end, a set of outputs are produced as an actual response of this process. All the synaptic weights of the networks are fixed during the forward pass only and adjusted according to the need of error-correction during the back pass. The error signal is produced when the actual output of the network is subtracted from the expected output. This error signal is then propagated backward against the direction of synaptic conditions through the network. Until the actual output of the network so produced is nearer to the expected output, the synaptic weights are adjusted. To produce a complex output, the backpropagation neural network is essentially made of a network of simple processing elements working together. From the above knowledge of back propagation neural networks, image compression, and decompression can be achieved.

2. RELATED WORK

A new self-organization algorithm, which is based on the centroid learning rule and frequency-sensitive cost function in order to construct the codebooks. The results include a good adaptivity for varied statistics of source data (Chen, Sheu & Fang, 1994). A neural network data compression method which involves a new training method called as the Nested Training Algorithm (NTA), results in maintaining low distortion and high compression ratio (Chin & Arozullah, 1996). Image compression is achieved by appropriate image thresholding and these thresholds are obtained with a principle of moment preserving and was proposed by (Yang & Tsai, 1998). Block adaptive prediction based neural network scheme is used for lossless data compression. The results involve that the adaptations of the improvised method increases performance of the classical predictors evaluated (Logeswaran, 2002). Image compression can also be performed by a non-uniform thresholding and observed the effects of thresholding on reconstructed image quality (Sansgiry & Mihaila, 2003). The design of optimized codebooks by using the vector quantisation (VQ) that included the strategy of reinforced learning (RL). The results have shown that RL is insensitive to the selection of the initial codebook and an additional parameter known as learning rate parameter introduced by RL learning rate control parameter and was described by (Xu, Nandi, & Zhang, 2003). The method of Compression and encryption/decryption using neural networks was proposed and attained good quality decryption and reconstruction of 3D objects (Shortt, Naughton, & Javidi, 2006). A technique for noise removal and image compression in wavelet domain thresholding which is based on Partial Differential Equation (PDE) and it takes the advantage of variations in framework (Chan, & Zhou, 2007). Image compression method which consumes less time and follows a strategy where thresholds are optimized with optimization techniques for which objective function is distortion (Kaur, Gupta, Chauhan, & Saxena, 2007). An evolutional fuzzy particle swarm optimization (FPSO) learning algorithm to self-extract the nearest optimum codebook of vector quantization (VQ) to carry out image compression (Feng, Chen, & Ye, 2007). Image compression can also be performed with Multistage Lattice Vector Quantization (MLVQ) and by thresholding of DWT coefficients. Proposed combination tries to minimize the quantization error and its computational complexity is less compared to ordinary VQ (Salleh & Soraghan, 2007). Electrocardiography (ECG) signals are compressed by transforming the signal with the help of discrete wavelet transform (Mohammadpour & Mollaei, 2009). Another kind of image compression where image to be compressed is transformed to frequency domain with the help of bandlet and required bandlet coefficients are obtained with type II Fuzzy thresholding and results are compared with the ordinary thresholding (Rajeswari & Rajesh, 2012). Image compression is achieved by the neural network, the results are proved that the Training algorithm and the back propagation neural network can increase the performance and decrease the convergence time (Patel & Agrawal, 2013). In order to overcome the problem of haziness in decompressed image, various artificial neural networks are introduced and the results prove that gradient decent technology works better than the Genetic algorithm (Anusha, Madhura, & Lakshmikantha, 2014). Birge–Massart thresholding is inbuilt thresholding technique which is used for image compression and obtained results are compared with the uni-modal thresholding in terms of reconstructed image quality and compression ratio (Sidhik, 2015). Ship detection approach by using wavelet coefficients that is extracted from JPEG2000 compressed domain combined with extreme learning machine and deep neural network and was proposed by (Tang, Deng, Huang, & Zhao, 2015). VQ is an effective, logical, well-mannered source coding technique (Karri, Jena, & Harika, 2016). To account for the multimodal color distribution of objects, a deep tree-structured network that generates for every pixel multiple color hypotheses, was proposed by (Baig & Torresani, 2017). Different compression strategies based on data trend, and the linear regression in order to process that large sensing data along with the computational power of the cloud (Yang & Chen, 2017). Using computer aided diagnosis (CAD) systems, for classification of breast lesions achieved by integrating back propagation artificial neural network (BPANN), support vector machine (SVM) and radiologist feedback for better clinical efficiency (Singh, Verma, Panigrahi, & Thoke, 2017). An end-to-end one-two-one (OTO) network, was proposed to associate different deep models to solve the Compression artifacts reduction problem (Zhang et al., 2018).

3. IMAGE COMPRESSION

Image compression reduces the size of data that is needed to define an image by reducing redundancy in image pixels. The two basic types of image compression are lossless compression and lossy compression. The basic data redundancies are 1) interpixel 2) psychovisual 3) coding. The elimination of one or more of these data redundancies results in image compression. The process of image compression comprises two distinct blocks an encoder and a decoder. Figure 1 shows the block diagram of image compression.

Figure 1. Basic image compression block diagram

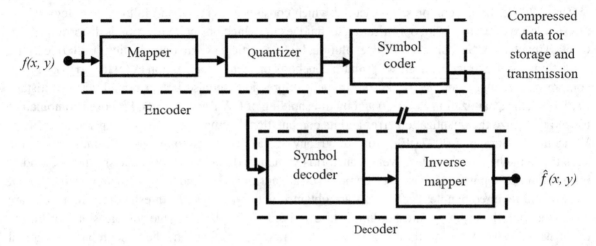

4. ARTIFICIAL NEURAL NETWORK

An Artificial Neural Network (ANN) is a data processing pattern. ANN is motivated by the human brain architecture. The original structure of the data processing system is the vital portion of this model. In order to resolve definite problems, numbers of exceedingly interconnected data processing elements (neurons) are used. Through a learning progression, an ANN is designed for a precise application, such as pattern recognition or data classification. Amendments to the synaptic connections that exist between the neurons lead to refinement of error in networks. ANN is a structure architected on the model of human brain structure and has many names in fields like neurocomputing. NNs may be utilized to excerpt patterns and identify trends which are very difficult to be perceived either by computers or humans as they have a significant capability to develop meaning from complex data. In the grouping of information, it has been set to evaluate, a trained neural network can be deemed as "proficient". The architecture of the neural network is shown in Figure 2.

5. LEARNING

Neural Networks being similar to brain are occasionally called machine-learning algorithms due to their acquisition of knowledge from experience. The network learns to solve a problem by varying its connection weights (training). The strength of nodes between the neurons is assigned as a synaptic weight-value for the particular node. The ANN acquires novel information by changing these weights of nodes. The learning skill of ANN is influenced by its architecture and the algorithmic method selected for the purpose of training. The learning method will be one of these three patterns: reinforcement learning, unsupervised learning, and supervised learning. The block diagram for training process is shown in Figure 3.

Figure 2. Neural network architecture

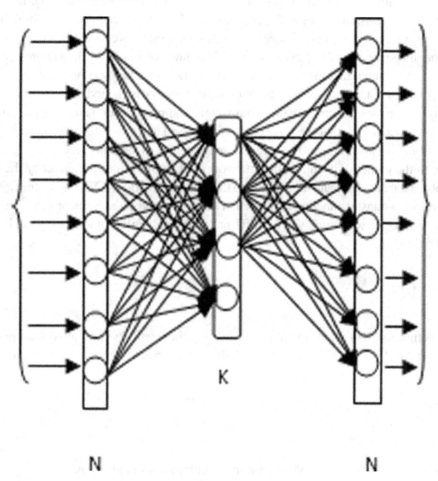

Figure 3. Block diagram for training process

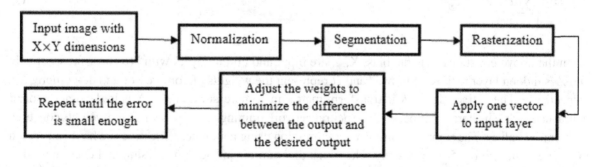

6. BACK PROPAGATION NEURAL NETWORK

For the data to be compressed to the desired level, the preliminary step to solve the problem is to determine the size of the network that will perform. To provide a reasonable data reduction factor, network architecture is to be selected which enables a recovery of close approximation of the original image from the encoded form. This network is a feed forward network comprising of three layers, one Input Layer (IL) with N neurons, one Output Layer (OL) with N neurons and one (or more) Hidden Layer (HL) with K neurons. In the network, connections are established between neurons from one layer to the other layer. The image is compressed because the hidden layer comprises of less neurons than the input layer. The size of the output and the input layer is the same and it helps in recovering the compressed image. The desired outputs being same as the inputs, the network is trained using a set of patterns with back propagation of error measures. The internal weight coding is developed by the network using the backpropagation process such that the image gets compressed to a ratio of number of input layer nodes to the number of hidden layer nodes. The original image can be reconstructed, by propagating the compressed image to the output units in identical networks, when the values produced by the hidden layer units in the network are read out and transmitted to the receiving station. ANN can be linear or non-linear network according to transfer function employed. The most common non-linear function was sigmoid activation function which was employed for different neural network problems as given in Equation 1.

$$g(z) = \frac{1}{1 + exp(-z)} \tag{1}$$

Where 'z' is linear sum of input signals after weighing them with the strengths of the respective connections. The output Z_K of the Kth neuron in the hidden layer in feedforward neural network is given as

$$Z_K = g\left(\sum_{i=1}^{N} J_{ki} X_i + b_k\right) \tag{2}$$

The output is given by Y_N of the Nth neuron in the output layer is given by

$$Y_N = g\left(\sum_{i=1}^{K} H_{Ni} Z_i + b_N\right) \tag{3}$$

In the above equations, b is the bias, X, Y are input and output layers with N neurons respectively and Z is hidden layer with K neurons. *J* and *H* represent the weights of compressor and de-compressor, respectively. The extracted $N \times K$ is transform matrix in compressor and $K \times N$ is in decompressor of neural network. The iterative process of the neural network training is stopped when the weights converge to their true values. The compression and decompression using neural network structure has been shown in Figure 4 and Figure 5, respectively. The block diagram for image compression and decompression using back propagation neural networks is shown in Figure 6.

Figure 4. Neural Network structure for compression

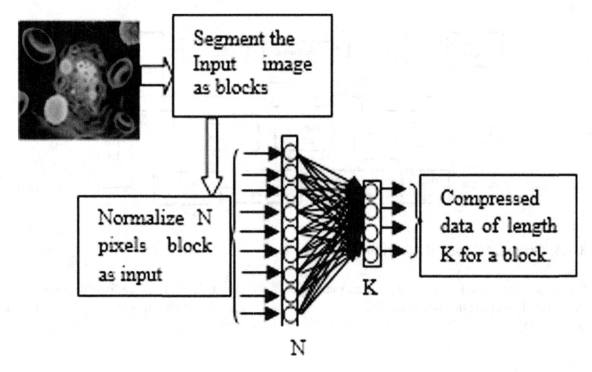

Figure 5. Neural Network structure for decompression

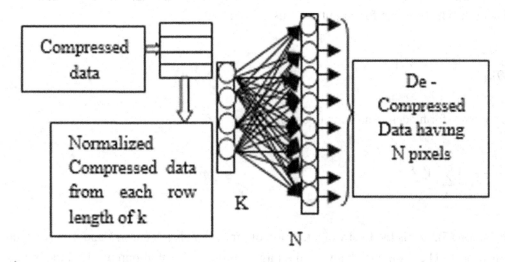

6.1. Training Algorithms

A procedure that modifies weights and biases a network is called training algorithm. Training rule has been applied to train network for image compression. In this section, a detailed description given about the algorithms of MRI image compression at high bit rate are explained.

Figure 6. Block diagram for image compression and decompression using Back Propagation Neural Network

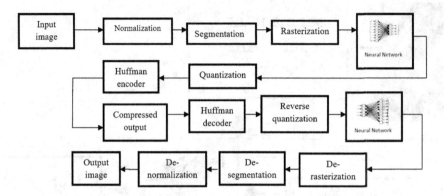

6.1.1. Gradient Descent Algorithm

The most widely used training algorithm, multilayer perception (MLP), is a Gradient Descent (GD) algorithm. It accords the difference ΔW_{nk}, the weight of a connection between neurons n and k, by the Equation (4).

$$\Delta W_{nk} = \eta \delta_k X_n \tag{4}$$

Where is the learning rate and the factor δ_k depending on whether neuron k is an output neuron or a hidden neuron. The equation for output neurons is Equation (5).

$$\delta_k = \frac{\partial g}{\partial net_k} \cdot \left(Y_k^{(t)} - Y_k \right) \tag{5}$$

The equation for hidden neurons is Equation (6).

$$\delta_k = \frac{\partial g}{\partial net_k} \cdot \left(\sum_q W_{kq} \delta_q \right) \tag{6}$$

In Equation (5), net_k is the total weighted sum of input signals to neuron k and $Y_k^{(t)}$ is the target output for neuron k. The difference between the target output and actual output of a hidden neuron k in Equation (6) is replaced by the weighted sum of the δ_q terms already obtained for neurons (q) connected to the output of k, as there are no target outputs for hidden neurons. The computation starts with the output layer and δ is computed for all neurons in every layer and the change in synaptic weight is arrived for all connections continuously till the epoch is completed. After the presentation of each learning pattern or whole set of learning patterns, the weight updating process occurs. A training epoch is deemed to be completed once all training patterns have been presented to MLP. The method usually adopted to expedite the modification of weights as given in Equation (7)

$$\Delta W_{nk}(t + 1) = \eta \delta_k X_n + \Delta W_{nk}(t) \tag{7}$$

Where $\Delta w_{nk}(t+1)$ is weight change in epoch $(t+1)$.

6.1.2. Levenberg Marquardt Algorithm

The Levenberg Marquardt Algorithm is the best adoptable to NN training where the performance index is the mean squared error. The performance index to be optimized for LM algorithm is defined in Equation (8)

$$G(W) = \Sigma[\Sigma(d_{kn} - a_{kn})^2] \tag{8}$$

Here, $W= [w_1 \ w_2 \ w_3 \dots w_M]^T$ consists of all weights of the network, d_{kn} is the desired value of the kth output and the nth pattern, a_{kn} is the actual value of kth output and n^{th} pattern, M is the number of weights, N is the number of patterns, and K is the number of network outputs. Equation (8) can also be expressed as Equation (9).

$$G(W) = E^T E \tag{9}$$

Here E is the Cumulative Error Vector (for all patterns)

$$E = [e_{11}, e_{k1}, e_{k2}, \dots e_{kn}]^T$$

$$e_{kn} = d_{kn} - a_{kn}, k = 1 \dots K, n = 1 \dots N$$

From Equation (9) the Jacobin matrix is defined as

$$R(W) = \begin{bmatrix} \dfrac{\partial e_{11}}{\partial w_1} & \dfrac{\partial e_{11}}{\partial w_2} & \cdots & \dfrac{\partial e_{11}}{\partial w_M} \\ \dfrac{\partial e_{21}}{\partial w_1} & \dfrac{\partial e_{21}}{\partial w_2} & \cdots & \dfrac{\partial e_{21}}{\partial w_M} \\ \vdots & \vdots & \vdots & \vdots \\ \dfrac{\partial e_{k1}}{\partial w_1} & \dfrac{\partial e_{k1}}{\partial w_2} & \cdots & \dfrac{\partial e_{k1}}{\partial w_M} \\ \dfrac{\partial e_{1n}}{\partial w_1} & \dfrac{\partial e_{1n}}{\partial w_2} & \cdots & \dfrac{\partial e_{1n}}{\partial w_M} \\ \vdots & \vdots & \vdots & \vdots \\ \dfrac{\partial e_{2n}}{\partial w_1} & \dfrac{\partial e_{2n}}{\partial w_2} & \cdots & \dfrac{\partial e_{2n}}{\partial w_M} \\ \dfrac{\partial e_{kn}}{\partial w_1} & \dfrac{\partial e_{kn}}{\partial w_2} & \cdots & \dfrac{\partial e_{kn}}{\partial w_M} \end{bmatrix}$$

The weights are calculated using Equation (10)

$$W_{t+1} = W_t - \left(R_t^T\left(W\right) R_t\left(W\right) + L_t I \right)^{-1} R_t^T\left(W\right)$$ (10)

Here "I" is identity unit matrix, "L" is a learning factor and "R" is Jacobin of k output errors with respect to M weights of the neural network. For L=0, it modifies as the Gauss-Newton method. If "L" is huge, then it modifies as the steepest decent algorithm. To secure convergence, the "L" parameter is automatically adjusted for all iterations. The LM algorithm needs computing Jacobin R matrix at each iteration and the inversion of R^{T}R square matrix.

7. RESULTS AND DISCUSSION

Various training algorithms of feedforward backpropagation neural networks are compared using two error metrics, the Peak Signal to Noise Ratio (PSNR) and Mean Square Error (MSE). The MSE is the cumulative squared error between the original and the decompressed image is given in Equation (11).

$$MSE = \frac{\sum_{i,j}\left(f\left(x,y\right) - \hat{f}\left(x,y\right)\right)^2}{M \times N}$$ (11)

Where $M{\times}N$ is the size of the image, M is the number of rows, N is the number of columns, f represents the original image and $\hat{f}$ represents the decompressed image. The quality of image coding is typically evaluated by the PSNR defined in Equation (12) as

$$PSNR\,in\,dB = 10\,\log_{10}\left(\frac{255^2}{MSE}\right)$$ (12)

Compression ratio (CR) is the ratio of number of input neurons to the number of hidden neurons and is given in Equation (13).

$$CR = \frac{n_i}{n_h}$$ (13)

Where n_i is the number of input neurons and n_h is the number of output neurons. The two backpropagation learning algorithms: GD and LM have been implemented on four standard medical test images, RBC, Angio, Lungs and Abdomen. The original images of RBC, Angio, Lungs and Abdomen have been shown in Figure 7. The code has been run for 500 epochs using MATLAB R2015a. Tables 1-4 gives the comparison of the performance metrics of two algorithms for 4 × 4, 8 × 8 block sizes with 4 and 9 hidden neurons on test images. From tables, it can be observed that for LM algorithm the PSNR is more when compared to that of GD algorithm and MSE is less than that of GD algorithm. The results of these experiments proved that by using the LM algorithm, the simulation and encoding times are almost similar when compared to that of GD algorithm. As it can be seen from tables, the training time is high for LM algorithm than GD. The change in PSNR values and MSE values with respect to 4×4 and 8×8 block sizes with 4 and 9 hidden neurons for test images RBC, Angio, Lungs and Abdomen have been shown in bar graphs in Figures 12-15 (a, b, c, and d). From bar graphs, it can be observed that the PSNR values when image is segmented in 4×4 blocks are greater than the values of PSNR when image is segmented into 8×8 blocks for two algorithms. For LM algorithm, as the number of hidden neurons increases, PSNR value increases and MSE value decreases and for GD algorithm, as the number of hidden neurons increases, PSNR value decreases and MSE value increases. Figures 8-11 shows the decompressed images of two training algorithms for test images RBC, Angio, Lungs and Abdomen before (a and b) and after (c and d) average filter respectively. Here average filter is used to enhance the quality of decompressed image. From the obtained decompressed images, it is observed that image quality is more for LM algorithm when compared to the other algorithm. The neural network training has been shown in Figure16 (a and b). The performance plot in the change in MSE has been plotted with respect to 500 epochs is shown in Figure 17 (a and b). The regression plot is shown in Figure 18 (a and b). From plots, it can be observed that regression plot is more linear for LM algorithm and almost reaches the ideal fitness graph when compared to the other algorithm. Also in the performance plots, the mean square error is less for LM algorithm.

Figure 7. Test images: (i) RBC (ii) Angio (iii) Lungs (iv) Abdomen

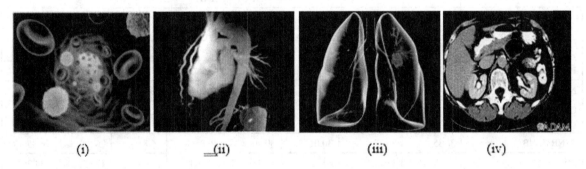

(i)   (ii)   (iii)   (iv)

Figure 8. Decompressed images of various training algorithms GD and LM for RBC image before (a and b) and after (c and d) filter respectively

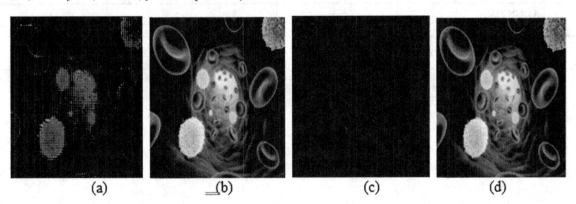

(a)   (b)   (c)   (d)

Table 1. Comparison of performance metrics of two algorithms for RBC image

TRAINING ALGORITHM	INPUT IMAGE							
	TRAIN LM				TRAIN GD			
BLOCK SIZE	4 × 4		8 × 8		4 × 4		8 × 8	
HIDDEN NEURONS	4	9	4	9	4	9	4	9
NETWORK SIZE	16-4-16	16-9-16	64-4-64	64-9-64	16-4-16	16-9-16	64-4-64	64-9-64
CR (COMPRESSION RATIO)	4	1.78	16	7.12	4	1.78	16	7.12
PSNR (in dB)	30.05	33.37	29.88	30.546	25.348	25.466	25.268	25.199
MSE	64.26	29.87	66.71	57.334	189.78	184.69	193.31	196.38
BPP	8	8	8	8	8	8	8	8
TRAINING TIME (in sec)	1348	3033	5405	17489	14.420	16.412	23.8	27.475
SIMULATION TIME (in sec)	0.038	0.022	0.021	0.2109	0.0158	0.0189	0.0147	0.0343
ENCODING TIME (in sec)	0.349	0.289	0.095	0.4888	0.1379	0.2154	0.0907	0.2189

Table 2. Comparison of performance metrics of two algorithms for Angio image

TRAINING ALGORITHM	INPUT IMAGE							
	TRAIN LM				TRAIN GD			
BLOCK SIZE	4 × 4		8 × 8		4 × 4		8 × 8	
HIDDEN NEURONS	4	9	4	9	4	9	4	9
NETWORK SIZE	16-4-16	16-9-16	64-4-64	64-9-64	16-4-16	16-9-16	64-4-64	64-9- 64
CR (COMPRESSION RATIO)	4	1.78	16	7.12	4	1.78	16	7.12
PSNR (in dB)	32.85	36.73	30.01	30.90	26.84	26.81	26.88	26.85
MSE	33.72	13.77	64.85	52.81	134.44	135.442	133.252	134.262
BPP	8	8	8	8	8	8	8	8
TRAINING TIME (in sec)	957.5	2503	5573	18721	16.06	16.57	38.91	35.33
SIMULATION TIME (in sec)	0.025	0.17	0.02	0.18	0.161	0.018	0.016	0.021
ENCODING TIME (in sec)	0.118	0.84	0.08	0.61	0.169	0.229	0.104	0.183

Table 3. Comparison of performance metrics of two algorithms for Lungs image

TRAINING ALGORITHM	INPUT IMAGE							
	TRAIN LM				TRAIN GD			
BLOCK SIZE	4 × 4		8 × 8		4 × 4		8 × 8	
HIDDEN NEURONS	4	9	4	9	4	9	4	9
NETWORK SIZE	16-4-16	16-9-16	64-4-64	64-9-64	16-4-16	16-9-16	64-4-64	64-9-64
CR (COMPRESSION RATIO)	4	1.78	16	7.12	4	1.78	16	7.12
PSNR (in dB)	31.77	32.37	31.79	31.1	27.57	27.5	27.69	27.65
MSE	43.24	37.63	43.02	49.7	113.6	115.5	110.48	111.4
BPP	8	8	8	8	8	8	8	8
TRAINING TIME (in sec)	1311	2693	5700	18162	14.85	16.25	39.71	36.14
SIMULATION TIME (in sec)	0.042	0.023	0.0215	0.017	0.014	0.017	0.0379	0.023
ENCODING TIME (in sec)	0.320	0.347	0.1146	0.119	0.132	0.214	0.2230	0.172

Table 4. Comparison of performance metrics of two algorithms for Abdomen image

TRAINING ALGORITHM	INPUT IMAGE							
	TRAIN LM				TRAIN GD			
BLOCK SIZE	4 × 4		8 × 8		4 × 4		8 × 8	
HIDDEN NEURONS	4	9	4	9	4	9	4	9
NETWORK SIZE	16-4-16	16-9-16	64-4-64	64-9-64	16-4-16	16-9-16	64-4-64	64-9- 64
CR(COMPRESSION RATIO)	4	1.78	16	7.12	4	1.78	16	7.12
PSNR (in dB)	27.86	28.4	27.9	27.62	25.63	25.86	25.73	25.69
MSE	106.3	92.5	105.39	112.2	177.81	168.5	173.61	175.1
BPP	8	8	8	8	8	8	8	8
TRAINING TIME (in sec)	1357	2687	5267.7	17678	10.6	16.69	31.63	36.05
SIMULATION TIME (in sec)	0.021	0.027	0.0157	0.022	0.0168	0.018	0.0382	0.016
ENCODING TIME (in sec)	0.205	0.378	0.0884	0.179	0.1747	0.248	0.2136	0.128

Figure 9. Decompressed images of various training algorithms GD and LM for Angio image before (a and b) and after (c and d) filter respectively

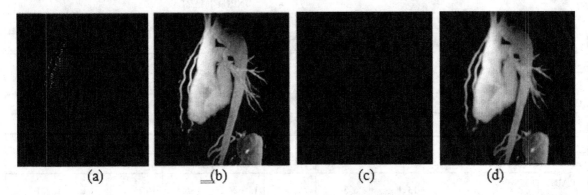

(a) (b) (c) (d)

Figure 10. Decompressed images of various training algorithms, GD and LM for Lungs image before (a and b) and after (c and d) filter, respectively

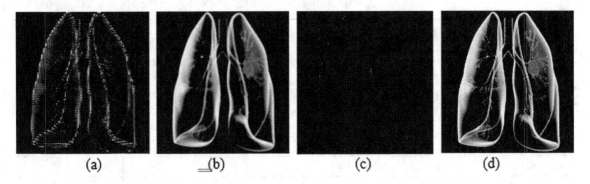

(a) (b) (c) (d)

Figure 11. Decompressed images of various training algorithms, GD and LM for Abdomen image before (a and b) and after (c and d) filter respectively

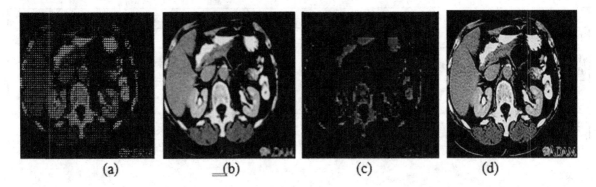

(a) (b) (c) (d)

Figure 12. Comparison of the PSNR values of various training algorithms for 4 hidden Neurons with 4 × 4 and 8 × 8 block size of Decompressed images of test Images (a) RBC (b) Angio (c) Lungs and (d) Abdomen

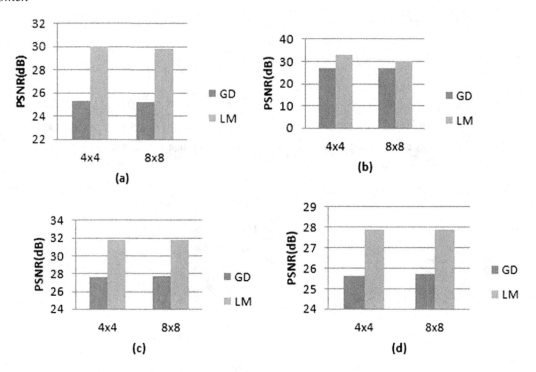

Figure 13. Comparison of the PSNR values of various training algorithms for 9 hidden Neurons with 4 × 4 and 8 × 8 block size of Decompressed images of test Images (a) RBC (b) Angio (c) Lungs and (d) Abdomen

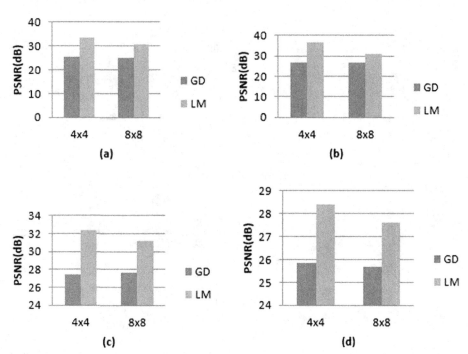

Figure 14. Comparison of the MSE values of various training algorithms for 4 hidden Neurons with 4 × 4 and 8 × 8 block size of Decompressed images of test Images (a) RBC (b) Angio (c) Lungs and (d) Abdomen

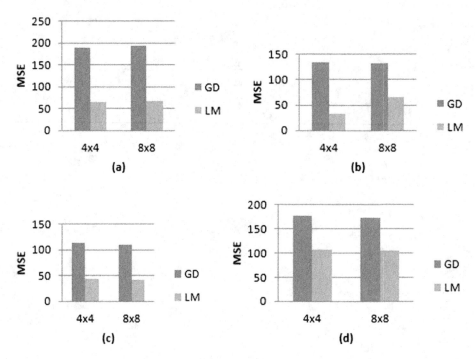

Figure 15. Comparison of the MSE values of various training algorithms for 9 hidden Neurons with 4 × 4 and 8 × 8 block size of Decompressed images of test Images (a) RBC (b) Angio (c) Lungs and (d) Abdomen

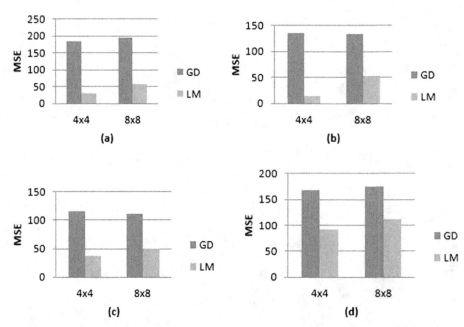

Figure 16. Neural network training for lungs image with 9 hidden neurons of 4 × 4 image block size: (a) GD (b) LM

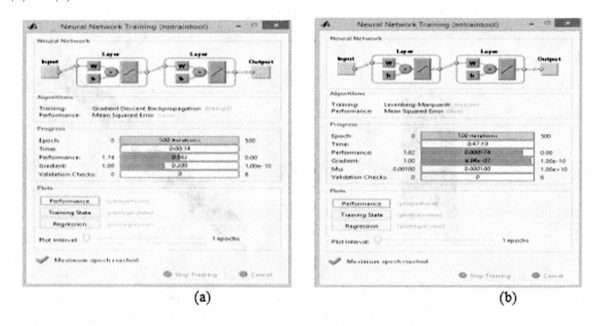

Figure 17. Performance plot with MSE vs epochs for lungs image with 9 hidden neurons of 4 × 4 image block size: (a) GD (b) LM

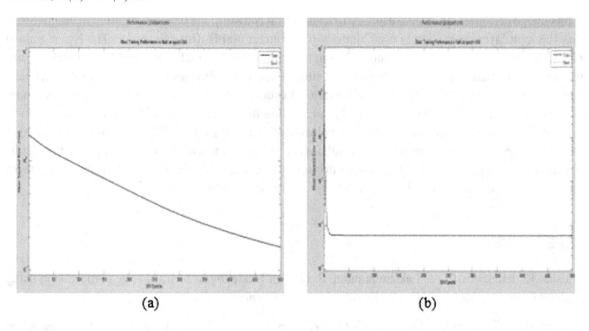

Figure 18. Regression plot for lungs image with 9 hidden neurons of 4 × 4 image block size: (a) GD (b) LM

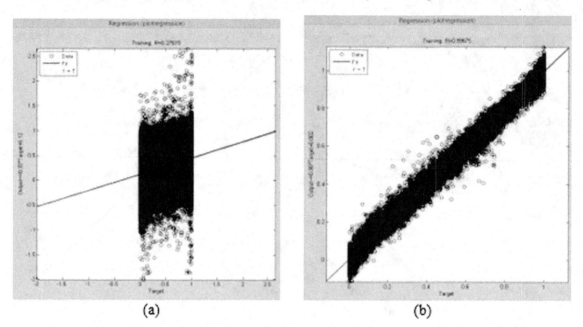

(a)   (b)

8. CONCLUSION

In this image compression system using Artificial Neural Network, the backpropagation neural network with the multilayer perception is used along with quantizer and Huffman encoder. The NN is trained with Levenberg Marquardt and Gradient Decent algorithms with a small 4 × 4 and 8 × 8 blocks of image. The performance of the two algorithms using MRI medical images of different resolutions have been studied and compared. Out of two algorithms, Levenberg Marquardt algorithm showed very good results for parameters like MSE and PSNR. The algorithms have been compared for performance metrics, performance plots and regression plots. From plots, it is found that Levenberg Marquardt backpropagation algorithm has shown more accurate results when compared to the other algorithm. All the results of experiments established that the LM algorithm will increase the fidelity of reconstructed images compared to other, so it would be very helpful in biomedical applications.

REFERENCES

Anusha, K., Madhura, G., & Lakshmikantha, S. (2014). Modeling of neural image compression using gradient decent technology. *IJES Of Engineering And Science*, *3*(12), 10–17.

Baig, M. H., & Torresani, L. (2017). Multiple hypothesis colorization and its application to image compression. *Computer Vision and Image Understanding*, *164*, 111–123. doi:10.1016/j.cviu.2017.01.010

Chan, T. F., & Zhou, H. M. (2007). Total variation wavelet thresholding. *Journal of Scientific Computing*, *32*(2), 315–341. doi:10.100710915-007-9133-0

Chen, O. C., Sheu, B. J., & Fang, W. C. (1994). Image compression using self-organization networks. *IEEE Transactions on Circuits and Systems for Video Technology, 4*(5), 480–489. doi:10.1109/76.322995

Chin, M. S., & Arozullah, M. (1996). Image compression with a hierarchical neural network. *IEEE Transactions on Aerospace and Electronic Systems, 32*(1), 326–338. doi:10.1109/7.481272

Feng, H. M., Chen, C. Y., & Ye, F. (2007). Evolutionary fuzzy particle swarm optimization vector quantization learning scheme in image compression. *Expert Systems with Applications, 32*(1), 213–222. doi:10.1016/j.eswa.2005.11.012

Karri, C., Jena, U. R., & Harika, A. (2016). Vector quantization using hybrid teaching learning and pattern search optimization for image compression. *Int. J. Computing Systems in Engineering, 2*(4), 209–221. doi:10.1504/IJCSYSE.2016.081382

Kaur, L., Gupta, S., Chauhan, R. C., & Saxena, S. C. (2007). Medical ultrasound image compression using joint optimization of thresholding quantization and best-basis selection of wavelet packets. *Digital Signal Processing, 17*(1), 189–198. doi:10.1016/j.dsp.2006.05.008

Logeswaran, R. (2002). A prediction-based neural network scheme for lossless data compression. *IEEE Transactions on Systems, Man and Cybernetics. Part C, Applications and Reviews, 32*(4), 358–365. doi:10.1109/TSMCC.2002.806744

Mohammadpour, T. I., & Mollaei, M. R. K. (2009). ECG compression with thresholding of 2-D wavelet transform coefficients and run length coding. *European Journal of Scientific Research, 27*(2), 248–257.

Patel, B., & Agrawal, S. (2013). Image compression techniques using artificial neural network. *International Journal of Advanced Research in Computer Engineering & Technology, 2*.

Rajeswari, R., & Rajesh, R. (2012). Type-2 fuzzy thresholded bandlet transform for image compression. *Procedia Engineering, 38*, 385–390. doi:10.1016/j.proeng.2012.06.048

Rajpurohit, J., Sharma, T. K., & Abraham, A., & V. (2017). Glossary of Metaheuristic Algorithms. *International Journal of Computer Information Systems and Industrial Management Applications, 9*, 181–205.

Salleh, M. F. M., & Soraghan, J. (2007). A new multistage lattice vector quantization with adaptive subband thresholding for image compression. *EURASIP Journal on Applied Signal Processing*, (1): 78–78.

Sansgiry, P., & Mihaila, I. (2003). Selective Thresholding in Wavelet Image Compression. In *Wavelets and Signal Processing* (pp. 377–381). Boston, MA: Birkhäuser. doi:10.1007/978-1-4612-0025-3_12

Sharma, T. K. (2017). Performance Optimization of the Paper Mill using Opposition based Shuffled frog-leaping algorithm. *International Journal of Computer Information Systems and Industrial Management Applications, 9*, 173–180.

Sharma, T. K., & Pant, M. (2017). Opposition-Based Learning Embedded Shuffled Frog-Leaping Algorithm. In *Proceedings of First International Conference on Soft Computing: Theories and Applications* (pp. 853-861).

Sharma, T. K., & Pant, M. (2017). Distribution in the placement of food in artificial bee colony based on changing factor. *International Journal of System Assurance Engineering and Management*, *8*(1), 159–172. doi:10.100713198-016-0495-2

Sharma, T. K., & Pant, M. (2017). Shuffled artificial bee colony algorithm. *Soft Computing*, *21*(20), 6085–6104. doi:10.100700500-016-2166-2

Shortt, A. E., Naughton, T. J., & Javidi, B. (2006). Compression of optically encrypted digital holograms using artificial neural networks. *Journal of Display Technology*, *2*(4), 401–410. doi:10.1109/JDT.2006.884693

Sidhik, S. (2015). Comparative study of Birge-Massart strategy and unimodal thresholding for image compression using wavelet transform. *Optik-International Journal for Light and Electron Optics*, *126*(24), 5952–5955. doi:10.1016/j.ijleo.2015.08.127

Singh, B. K., Verma, K., Panigrahi, L., & Thoke, A. S. (2017). Integrating radiologist feedback with computer aided diagnostic systems for breast cancer risk prediction in ultrasonic images: An experimental investigation in machine learning paradigm. *Expert Systems with Applications*, *90*, 209–223. doi:10.1016/j.eswa.2017.08.020

Tang, J., Deng, C., Huang, G. B., & Zhao, B. (2015). Compressed-domain ship detection on spaceborne optical image using deep neural network and extreme learning machine. *IEEE Transactions on Geoscience and Remote Sensing*, *53*(3), 1174–1185. doi:10.1109/TGRS.2014.2335751

Xu, W., Nandi, A. K., & Zhang, J. (2003). Novel fuzzy reinforced learning vector quantisation algorithm and its application in image compression. *IEEE Proceedings Vision, Image and Signal Processing*, *150*(5), 292-298.

Yang, C., & Chen, J. (2017). Efficient Nonlinear Regression-Based Compression of Big Sensing Data on Cloud. In Big Data Analytics for Sensor-Network Collected Intelligence (pp. 83-98).

Yang, C. K., & Tsai, W. H. (1998). Color image compression using quantization, thresholding, and edge detection techniques all based on the moment-preserving principle. *Pattern Recognition Letters*, *19*(2), 205–215. doi:10.1016/S0167-8655(97)00166-9

Zhang, B., Gu, J., Chen, C., Han, J., Su, X., Cao, X., & Liu, J. (2018). One-two-one networks for compression artifacts reduction in remote sensing. *ISPRS Journal of Photogrammetry and Remote Sensing*.

This research was previously published in the International Journal of Applied Metaheuristic Computing (IJAMC), 10(4); pages 91-111, copyright year 2019 by IGI Publishing (an imprint of IGI Global).

Chapter 43
Disease Classification Using ECG Signals Based on R–Peak Analysis With ABC and ANN

Suman Lata

(iD) https://orcid.org/0000-0002-8739-924X

National Institute of Technical Teachers Training and Research, Chandigarh, India

Rakesh Kumar

National Institute of Technical Teachers Training and Research, Chandigarh, India

ABSTRACT

ECG feature extraction has an important role in identifying a number of cardiac diseases. Lots of work has been done in this field but the most important challenges faced in previous work are the selection of proper R-peaks and R-R intervals due to the lack of appropriate pre-processing steps like decomposition, smoothing, filtering, etc., and the optimization of the features for proper classification. In this article, DWT-based pre-processing and ABC is used for optimization of features which helps to achieve better classification accuracy. It is utilized for initial diagnosis of abnormalities. The signals are taken from MIT-BIH arrhythmia database for the analysis. The aim of the research is to classification of six diseases; Normal, Atrial, Paced, PVC, LBBB, RBBB with an ABC optimization algorithm and an ANN classification algorithm on the basis of the extracted features. Various parameters, like FAR, FRR, and accuracy are measured for the execution. Comparative analysis is shown of the proposed and the existing work to depict the effectiveness of the work.

INTRODUCTION

Healthcare has always been a challenging frontier for new technological innovations. Artificial Intelligence (AI) is the latest technological advancement. Some healthcare systems are exploring the idea of using artificial intelligence.

DOI: 10.4018/978-1-6684-2408-7.ch043

Artificial intelligence is not trying to replace the doctors. It is not "man vs. machine". Instead, the future is about working with machines. USP of Artificial Intelligence:

1. Precision
2. Efficiency
3. Speed up process

Applications of AI technology can be panacea for real time diagnosis.
ECG (Electrocardiogram) is a diagnostic tool which is used for assessing:

1. Electrical function of heart;
2. Muscular function of heart (Berkaya et al., 2018).

As it is an easy test to execute, the analysis of ECG tracing needs considerable amount of training. The heart has two stages: electrical pumps with the electrical activity of heart that can be computed with the electrodes within skin.

ECG computes the rhythm and rate of heartbeat and provides indirect confirmation of blood flow towards heart's muscles (Agarwal et al., 2016). A uniform system was implemented for the placement of electrodes for conventional ECG. Ten electrodes are required for generating twelve heart's electrical views. Electrode wires/patches are placed on arms and legs and the remaining six are provided on the chest wall (Omer et al., 2017). Recording of signal received from every electrode is taken after that. Printed view for the records is Electrocardiogram. The monitoring does not comprise of absolute electrocardiogram (Francesca et al., 2018). ECG diagnosis is a challenging domain that require a system that acquire knowledge from examples and real time adaptation.

Big volumes of ECG data are available but the most challenging task is the analysis, interpretation & applications.

So, it is imperative to have system & process which can enhance the knowledge management & learning capabilities of existing systems.

The primary objective of this research work is extracting and analysing the valuable learning from the data to classify Heart disease using Artificial Neural Network on the basis of the knowledge acquisition.

Basic Knowledge About ECG Signal

Knowledge of the fundamental of ECG signal will lay solid groundwork for everything else that is to come.

There are different kind of signals, but ECG signal represents the electrically generated signal during the process of breath inhale and exhale by a human. There are several types of peaks formed such as P, Q, R, S and T.

To determine whether a normal heart rate or diseases is present requires the know-how to calculate the heart rate on the ECG.

Applications of these techniques to both the atrial rate, measured by the rate of the P wave, and the ventricular rate, measured by the rate of the QRS complex.

R-R intervals also play key role to find out the diseases using ECG signal basic knowledge in the medical science. Learning a normal sinus rhythm is based on the R-R intervals of an ECG signal in medical science system.

ECG Waveform

Each depicted heartbeat is a series of waves considered by peaks as well as valleys. It gives two types of information. Initial is the passage duration of waves via heart. It may determine while the electrical activity is usual or steady or uneven. This is followed by the quantity of electrical activity via heart muscle, which helps to discover if the heart is oversized or overworked. The ECG signals have a frequency range of 0.05 to 100 Hz with a dynamic range of 1-10 mV.

Figure 1. ECG wave form

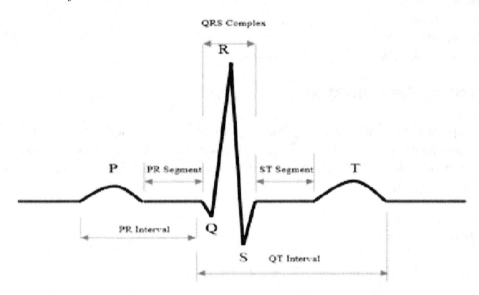

The characterization of ECG signals as shown in Figure 1, is into five peaks, named as P, Q, R, S and T (Francesca et al., 2018). Occasionally, U waves even exist. The ECG performance is dependent on precise and consistent QRS detection for QRS complexes (Acharya et al., 2017).

Optimization Techniques

It is the process of maximizing or minimizing the function with any of the constraints. Optimization techniques being cooperative for judging enhanced explanation or unconstrained maxima/continuous and minima of differentiable functions, which can be classified on optimization issue dependent on the existence of constraints, secondly, on the nature of equation involved thirdly permissible value of decision variables and last number of objective functions, which depends on three components:

- **Objective Function:** It reveals number of quantities which is optimized with a certain constraints and variables which are needed to be minimized or maximized using nonlinear programming technique;

- **Variable:** It may be utilized for describing the objective function and constraints which can be continuous, discrete or Boolean. Optimization problem can be solved by set of values of decision variable for which the objective function reaches its optimal value;
- **Constraints:** These are set that permits the unknown variable to obtain some values by excluding others. Moreover, collection of constraints can also restrict the value of decision variables.

The optimization problems may be resolved by various optimization techniques which are (Wang, Shi, & Xu, 2017):

1. Classical Type
2. Advanced Type
3. Simulated annealing
4. Evolutionary algorithm

Artificial Neural Network (ANN)

NN is an adaptive system with interesting features such as ability to adapt, learn and summarize. Because NN's parallel processing, self-organizing, fault-tolerant and adaptive capabilities make it capable of solving many complex problems, NN is also very accurate in the classification and prediction of outputs (Omer et al., 2017).

Figure 2. Artificial neural network

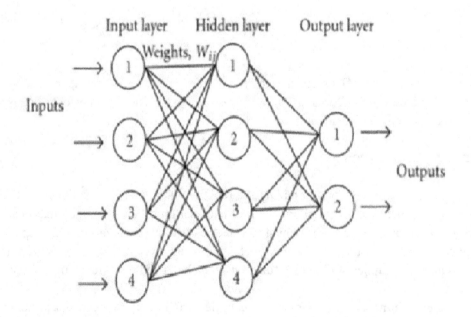

The neural network consists of number of layers; the initial layer has an association as of the system input. End layer gives the output of the network. Neural networks having hidden layers and sufficient neurons can be applied to any limited input-output mapping trouble. Figure 2 (Delrieu et al., 2017) depicts the neural network model, which consists of an input layer, the hidden layer, which takes 10 neurons, the last observation of an output.

RELATED WORK

In this section, the work performed by the various authors in the field of heart disease such as coronary artery disease, Arrhythmias, ventricular premature and "tachycardia beats are discussed. The proposed techniques along with the performance metrics is described in Table 1.

INFERENCE DRAWN FROM LITERATURE RIVIEW

Following gaps have been found from the study of previous work:

- Main issue in ECG interpretation is the elimination of unwanted noise and artefact. Cardiac monitor offers a means to filter the ECG signals. Therefore, it can be said that filters are mandatory for the ECG signals. In the previous work, only few of the researchers have used the concept of filters;
- The filters used in the previous works are directly used on the ECG signals. Though, the right criterion is to smooth the filters first and then to apply ECG signals;
- An optimization algorithm has not been used in the existing work. The usage of optimization is necessary to normalize the signals.

PROBLEM DEFFINITION

- Getting an ECG signal can be a simple job, but analysis by a specialist is a difficult job as it depends on domain knowledge, that's why automation of ECG signal analysis is required;
- Main issue in ECG interpretation is the elimination of unwanted noise and artefact. Therefore, it can be said that filters are mandatory to filter the ECG signals. In the previous work, only few of the researchers have used the concept of filters;
- The filters used in the previous work are directly used on the ECG signals. Though, the right criterion is to smooth the signals first and then to apply the filter;
- An optimization algorithm has not been used in the existing work. The usage of optimization is necessary to normalize the signals;
- The most important challenges faced by in previous work is selection of proper R-peaks and R-R intervals due to the lack of appropriate pre-processing steps like decomposition, smoothing, filtering etc.;
- So ECS analysis includes accurate feature extraction followed by training of the system so that it can classify the disease accurately.

Table 1. State-of-art of existing work in the field of ECG

References	Proposed Work	Proposed Techniques	Outcomes
Acharya et al., 2017	Proposed an automatic coronary artery disease detection system using continuous wavelet transform.	Improved binary particle swarm optimization algorithm has been used to optimize the features. Decision tree and K nearest neighbour are used as classification algorithms. The dataset has been taken from BIDMC &CHF	Has The system accuracy up to 99.55%
Acharya et al., 2017	Presented a CAD (computer aided diagnosis) model for detecting various ECG segments using convolution neural network (CNN) as a classification approach. The process has gone through different phases such as noise filtering, QRS detection, R-peak extraction and at last features have been formulated. The proposed system has been used to detect different kinds of Arrhythmias.	CNN that comprises of seven layers with four neurons at the output layer has been used.	The parameters such as accuracy, sensitivity, and efficiency are determined. The average values obtained for these parameters are 92.50%, 98.09% and 9313% respectively.
Wang, Shi, & Xu, 2017	Proposed an efficient approach for identifying ventricular premature and "tachycardia beats" on the basis of feature extraction techniques.	Fast Fourier transform method has been used to achieve characters of ventricular tachycardia. Also, SVM (support vector machine) along with optimization algorithm (GA) genetic algorithm have been utilized. MIT-BIH database has been used.	The accuracy of the proposed work measured for six and eight different feature vector space are 88% and 85%, respectively
Raghavendra et al., 2018	Presented a software detection technique to classify the coronary artery disease by using ECG images.	DD_DTDWT method has been used to subdivide the heart images into various frequency bands. Marginal fisher analysis has been used to decrease the dimension of feature set. The dataset has been created manually by using 129 total number of IHD ultrasound images.	The output in the form of accuracy, sensitivity and specificity have been determined and the values obtained for all these metrics are 96%, 96.12% and 96% respectively.
Kumar, Kumar, & Komaragiri, 2018	Proposed an integrated form of run length encoding along with bio-orthogonal wavelet transform in order to identifying the QRS complex wave and hence reducing the size of the ECG data.	bio-orthogonal wavelet transform comprises of three LPF (low pass filter) along in combination with single high pass filter. This arrangement decreases the hardware cost up to 50% of the total cost. The experiment has been performed on MIT_BIH arrhythmia dataset.	The value of sensitivity and predictivity obtained for this work are 99.75% and 99.98% respectively.
Raj et al., 2015	Proposed an automated ECG signal analysis scheme for long-term monitoring of non-stationary behaviour of the ECG signals is presented.	A new time–frequency-based feature extraction methodology is proposed. SVM classifier is used for classification and parameters of classifier are gradually tuned and optimized using PSO.	The proposed method yields an improved accuracy of 98.82%
Debnath, Hasan, & Biswas, 2016	Presented a method for analysis of ECG signal and classification of heart abnormalities using Artificial Neural Network	A back-propagation algorithm with feed forward neural network is used for classification of different heart classes e.g. normal, bradycardia, tachycardia and block had established.	Three conditions for heart such as normal, bradycardia, tachycardia is classified perfectly but block condition is not correctly identified.

PROPOSED METHODOLOGY AND ANALYSIS OF ECG SIGNALS

This work deals with the disease classification by ECG signals. The most important challenges faced in previous work is selection of proper R-peaks and R-R intervals due to the lack of appropriate pre-processing steps so in proposed work DWT based pre-processing is used with ABC Algorithm for feature optimization and Neural Network for classification purpose which helps to achieve better classification accuracy.

The database used for the computation is MIT-BIH arrhythmia database has two channels with 48 records of ECG signals (Sadhukhan et al., 2017).

In this work, 24 records are used that represents six types of classes such as Atrial, LBBB (Left bundle branch block), Normal, Paced, PVC (Preventricular contraction) and RBBB (Right bundle branch block). The proposed work has been designed by number of steps and the explanation for the same is defined below.

Step 1: Uploading Dataset

Upload ECG signal database of six classes: Normal, Arterial, PVC, LBBB, RBBB and Paced to train the system. The used database of ECG signals is taken from the "MIT-BIH Arrhythmia Database".

In the database, total category is 6 with 24 records of ECG signals (Kunjekar et al., 2018). This data set is used to construct the neural network model, which will be used for classification of heart disease.

Step 2: Pre-Processing

In proposed system, there may be one or more pre-processing steps as per the requirement. In pre-processing, ECG signal is processed in order to remove the noise and unwanted signal. The most common noise in ECG signal is the noise due to the power line (Banerjee et al., 2014). In this research work, the pre-processing comprises of smoothing of signal, De-noising of signal using DWT decomposition method and filtering of signal. The pre-processing steps are described below. Figure 2 shows the original ECG signal.

Smoothing Process

Smoothing is normally utilized to decrease noise within the signal and creates a signal with less bit value. The smoothing of ECG signal is shown in

From the Figure 3, it is clear that the noise in uploaded ECG signal is high and need to be removed before the peak analysis (Mporas et al., 2015).

So, smoothing process is used to estimate the level of noise which is presented in the signal. Algorithm1 is used for smoothening of ECG signal.

Algorithm 1: Smoothing

```
Input: ECG Signal (S) and Number of points to estimate noise (N)
Output: Smooth ECG Signal
Calculate size of S = S_z
For m = 1: S_z
```

```
        Frame = Divide signal in frame of N
        Calculate variation = Check connection between neighbour
        Estimate Noise Level = Maximum variation
End
```

Smooth *ECG* Signal = *S* – Estimated Noise Level   (1)

```
Return; Smooth ECG Signal
End
```

Figure 3. Original ECG signal

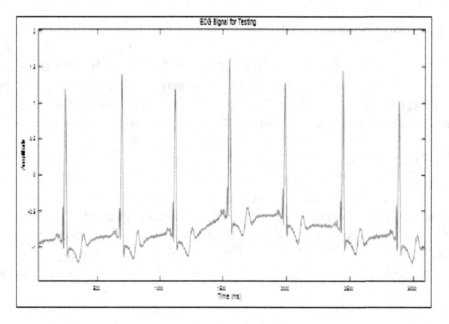

According to the smoothing algorithm 1, we have construct a smooth ECG signal as given in the Figure 4.

Figure 4 represents the signal which is obtained after applying smoothening process to original signal (Delrieju et al., 2015). In the figure, the X-axis denotes the time in milliseconds and the Y-axis denotes the amplitude of smooth ECG signal.

DWT (Discrete Wavelet Transform)

DWT process mainly uses two types of filters such as low pass filter and high pass filter to compute the approximation and details coefficients (Melgani et al., 2008). DWT is a wavelet transform in which the wavelets are sampled and in the proposed work, we have sampled the ECG signal by 2.

Figure 4. Smooth ECG signal

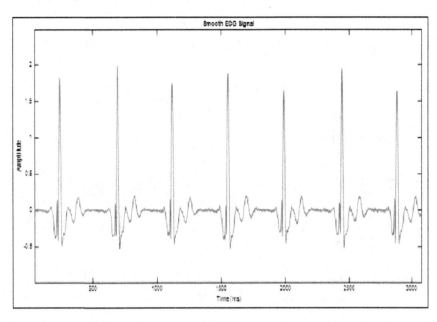

Algorithm 2: DWT

```
Input: Smooth ECG Signal (S ), Level (N) and Wavelet family (db4)
                         m
Output: Coefficients (C, L) of ECG Signal
Calculate size of S  = S
                    m     mz
For m = 1: S
            mz
        Initiate Low pass (LPF) and High Pass filter (HPF)
```

$$C = LFP(Sm, 2, N, db4) \tag{2}$$

$$L = HFP(Sm, 2, N, db4) \tag{3}$$

```
End
Return; Coefficients (C, L) of ECG Signal
End
```

According to the DWT decomposition algorithm 2, we have discovered the coefficients of a smooth ECG signal which helps to denoise the unwanted data from the signal. The coefficients of ECG signal is given in Figure 5 after applying DWT technique (Osowski et al., 2004). The DWT process is shown in the Figure 5.

As shown in the Figure 5, S is the input smooth ECG signal passed to the DWT process. In the figure, LPF is the Low pass filter and HPF is the high pass filter. The obtained filtered signal is down sampled by 2.

Figure 6 represents the coefficients of DWT which is derived after applying DWT decomposition technique on the ECG signal.

Figure 5. DWT decomposition of ECG signals

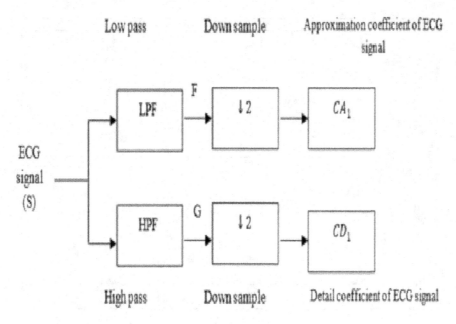

Figure 6. DWT coefficients of smooth ECG signal

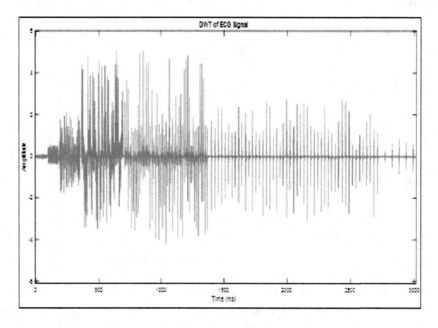

De-Noising

In ECG signal de-noising, process, we have used thresholding technique applied on smooth ECG signal with DWT coefficients (Raj et al., 2015). Here, the thresholding process is applied to calculate the threshold level of noise by the smooth ECG signal. Algorithm 3 is used for de-noising purposes.

Algorithm 3: De-noising

```
Input: Coefficients (C, L) of ECG Signal, Threshold level of noise (T, SH and,
App), Level (N) and Wavelet family (db4)
Output: Filtered ECG Signal
Calculate size of C = S_c
Calculate size of L = S_L
For m = 1: S_c
    For n = 1: S_L
```

Filtered *ECG* Signal = Filter (Global, *C, L,* '*db*4', *N, T, SH,* App)   (4)

```
    End
End
Return; Filtered ECG Signal
End
```

The Algorithm 4 is used to filter the uploaded ECG to simulate the proposed work. After de-noising, we have received a noise free ECG signal which is shown in Figure 7.

Figure 7 defines the signal obtained after applying the filtering technique in proposed simulator to classify the diseases from the ECG signals (Raghavendra et al., 2018). After this step, the features of filtered ECG signals are discovered using the peak analysis algorithm.

Figure 7. Pre-processed (filtered) ECG signal

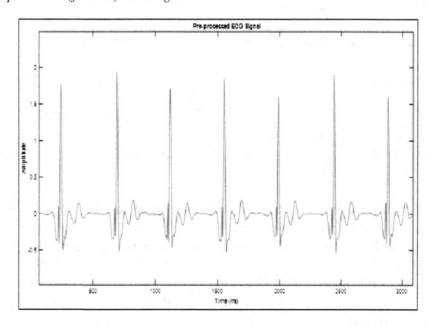

Step 3: Feature Extraction

Feature are used to train the system; wrong feature selection can degrade the performance of the system. Feature Acquisition is an important step in ECG signal diagnosis.

In this research work R-Peaks and R-R interval are used to train the ANN. Features are extracted from the filtered ECG signal based on the threshold value according to the R peaks and their intervals. To analyze the peaks, we have used Algorithm 4.

Algorithm 4: Peak analyzer

```
Input: Filtered ECG signal (ECG_F)
Output: R-peak of Signal with their intervals
Peaks with their locations = Find peaks (ECG_F)
Define maximum peak value
Max peak = max (Peaks)
```

$$Threshold\,of\,peaks\bigl(T\bigr)=\frac{\bigl(Max\,peak\,X\,75\bigr)}{100} \tag{5}$$

```
Count = 1
Create blank array to store R-peaks = [ ]
For i = 1to all Peaks
If Peaks (i) > T
```

$$R - peaks(1, Count) = \text{Location of Peaks} \tag{6}$$

$$R - peaks(2, Count) = \text{Value of Peaks} \tag{7}$$

```
Increment in array, Count=Count+1
End
End
R-R Intervals = Difference (Value of Peaks (Next) - Value of Peaks (Previous))
Return; R-peak of Signal (R-peaks) with their intervals (R-R Intervals)
End
```

With peak analyzer algorithm 4, we have found out the R-peak and their intervals in term of ECG features. The analysis of R-peak and their intervals are given in the figure 8 (Rodriguez et al., 2005).

In the Figure 8, the X-axis denotes the time in milliseconds and the Y-axis denotes the amplitude of ECG signal with peaks.

Figure 9 represents R-R interval of ECG signal and their value is given between the two R-peaks. The R-R intervals are calculated using the difference calculation between next R-peak and previous R-peak. After the determination of R-peaks and R-R interval, the optimal peaks have been found as a best feature, so we have used ABC optimization algorithm in proposed work to optimize the extracted feature sets (Martis et al., 2013).

Figure 8. R-peak of ECG signal

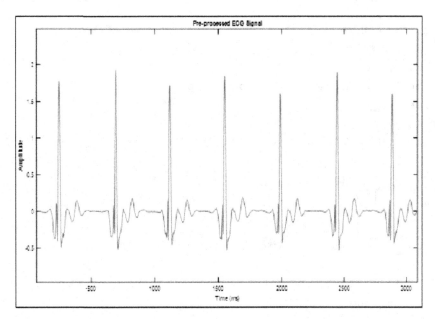

Figure 9. R-R intervals of ECG signal

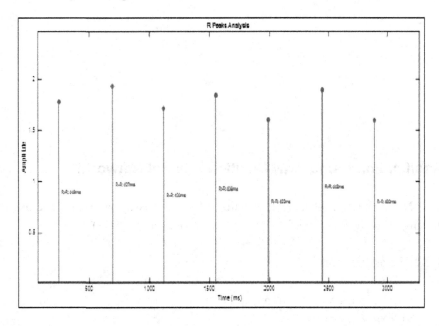

Step 4: Feature Optimization Using ABC (Artificial Bee Colony)

ABC optimization algorithm is used to optimize the features according to the fitness function of ABC algorithm. So, the management of the novel fitness functions in the ABC optimization algorithm should be considered. The ABC optimization is shown in Algorithm 5.

Algorithm 5: ABC optimization

`Input:` R-peak of Signal (R-peaks) with their intervals (R-R Intervals) as feature

`Output:` Optimized Features
Initialize the ABC with their function - Employ Bee (E_{bee})
- Onlooker Bee (O_{bee})
- Scout Bee (S_{bee})
Define the fitness function,

$$Fitness\,Function, fit\,(x) = \begin{cases} True\,\left(\mathrm{E}_{bee}\right), \mathrm{E}_{bee} > \mathrm{O}_{bee} \\ False\left(\mathrm{O}_{bee}\right), \mathrm{E}_{bee} \leq \mathrm{O}_{bee} \end{cases} \tag{8}$$

Create blank array to store optimized feature, ABC_{data} = []
Count = 0
Feature = R-peak of Signal (R-peaks) with their intervals (R-R Intervals)
Calculate rows (R) and columns (C) = Size (E_{bee})
For i = 1 to R
　　For j =1 to C
　　　　E_{bee} = Feature (i, j)
　　　　O_{bee} = Average (Feature)
　　　　Fit_bee = $fit\left(\mathrm{E}_{bee}, \mathrm{O}_{bee}\right)$
　　ABC_{data} (i, j) = Fit_bee
　　End
End
`Return;` ABC_{data} as optimized features
End

Step 5: Classification Using ANN (Artificial Neural Network)

Artificial Neural Network (ANN) has been initialized for the classification purpose using two phases, training and testing. The algorithm 6 of ANN is given as (Raj et al., 2017).

Algorithm 6: ANN classification

`Input:` Optimized Features as Training Data (T), Target (G) and Neurons (N)
`Output:` Trained ANN Structure
Initialize ANN with parameters;
- Epochs (E)
- Neurons (N)
- Performance parameters: MSE, Gradient, Mutation and Validation Points
- Training Techniques: Levenberg-Marquardt (Trainlm)
- Data Division: Random

```
For i=1 to all T
      If i <= Category (1)
         Target (1, i) = True
      Else if i <= Category (2)
         Target (2, i) = True
      Else if i <= Category (3)
         Target (3, i) = True
      Else if i <= Category (4)
         Target (4, i) = True
      Else if i <= Category (5)
         Target (5, i) = True
      Else if i <= Category (6)
         Target (6, i) = True
      Else
         Target (7, i) = True
      End
End
Initialized the ANN using Training data and Target
Net = Newff (T,G,N)
Set the training parameters according to the requirements and train the system
Net = Train (Net,T,G)
Return; Net as trained ANN structure
End
```

After the training of system, we have saved the trained structure which is used in the classification section to classify the diseases from the ECG signal. In the testing phase, the test ECG data is uploaded and iteration of the steps from 2 to 5 is taken. In the classification section, test ECG feature is matched with trained ANN structure and returns diseases type.

Step 6: Performance Evaluation

The performance metrics such as FAR, FRR, Accuracy are calculated to check proposed system efficiency. The explanation of the metrics is given below:

1. **False Acceptance Rate (FAR):** FAR is the type of error in the pattern recognition system which is measured by:

$$FRR = \frac{\text{Total Number of Features} - \text{Total Number of Falsely accepted Features}}{\text{Total Number of Features}} \tag{9}$$

2. **False Rejection Rate (FRR):** The FRR of the system is rate of falsely rejected feature with respect to the total feature. Its formula is given as:

$$FRR = \frac{\text{Total Number of Features} - \text{Total Number of Falsely Rejected Features}}{\text{Total Number of Features}} \quad (10)$$

3. **Accuracy:** Accuracy is a general term used to describe how accurate a system performs. Its formula is given as:

$$\text{Accuracy} = 100 - (FAR + FRR) \quad (11)$$

According to the above-mentioned steps, the model has been simulated and the results obtained after that are explained below in detail.

RESULT AND ANALYSIS

This section defines the result obtained after the simulation of the proposed work. The performance of the work has been calculated on the basis of parameters, viz. FAR, FRR, Execution time and accuracy. The comparison of proposed work with the current work is also presented in this section to depict the effectiveness of the proposed work.

MIT-BIH Arrhythmia Database

For calculating and authenticating the proposed work the experiments are carried out using the MIT-BIH arrhythmia database. Artificial Bee Colony is used as optimization algorithm and artificial neural network as a classifier. The database with two channel ambulatory ECG recordings of 47 different subjects comprises of 48 records studied by BIH Arrhythmia Laboratory. The database has 110109 beat labels whereas the data are band-pass filtered at 0.1H-100 Hz. The simulation has been computed on 24 records and the segments of heartbeat are computed with window in each R-peak. For the computation of the work, usage of class annotation is taken place in ground truth.

Table 2. Confusion matrix

		Correctly Classified Beats = 1151 Accuracy = 99.56 **Misclassified Beats = 5 Error Rate = 0.44**					
		Actual Beats					
	Class	**1**	**2**	**3**	**4**	**5**	**6**
Predicted Beats	**1**	175	1	0	0	0	1
	2	0	173	0	1	0	0
	3	0	0	183	0	0	1
	4	0	0	0	238	0	0
	5	1	0	0	0	203	0
	6	0	0	0	0	0	179

Here, in Table 2 of confusion matrix, the column defines the calculated beats being classified with proposed method using ABC optimization algorithm and ANN while the row represents the actual number of beats provided in the MIT-BIH Arrhythmia Database. The classification result for the proposed work is more than 90% with six different types of ECG signal categories.

Table 3. Performance parameters of proposed work

S. No.	FAR	FRR	Execution Time (S)	Accuracy (%)
1	0.934	0.989	3.92	99.99
2	0.934	0.882	4.42	99.12
3	0.945	0.938	6.44	99.83
4	0.885	0.984	4.23	99.47
5	0.956	0.963	3.34	99.43
6	0.835	0.964	4.34	99.45
7	0.928	0.992	2.55	99.42
8	0.947	0.883	3.66	99.43
9	0.988	0.837	3.88	99.81
10	0.973	0.972	3.95	99.74

The performance of the proposed system is checked with parameters such as FAR, FRR, Accuracy and execution time are calculated with ten samples to check proposed system efficiency, these are given in Table 3 and graphs are given in following section.

Figure 10 represents the results of FAR and FRR. As depicted, X-axis describes the number of samples considered for executing work and Y-axis defines values obtained after the simulation. Blue bar in the graph defines the values obtained of FAR and red bar defines the values of FRR being obtained. The average value of FAR is 0.9325 and the average value of FRR is 0.9404.

Figure 11 describes the execution time of the work while the testing of ECG signal. As depicted, X-axis describes the number of samples whereas Y-axis defines the obtained value of execution time. The work has taken execution time of 4.073 approximately for executing a sample of ECG signal.

Figure 12 defines how accurately the system has performed. As depicted, X-axis is for number of samples and Y-axis defines the value obtained after the evaluation. Accuracy defines how accurately the system executes. It has been seen that the research is 99.56 accurate.

Comparison of Proposed Work With the Existing Work

The research work has been compared with the existing work to depict the efficiency of the proposed work. Number of researches have been considered to execute the process using different techniques. The comparison has been shown in tabular form following the techniques used, number of classes with the accuracy respectively.

Figure 10. FAR and FRR evaluation

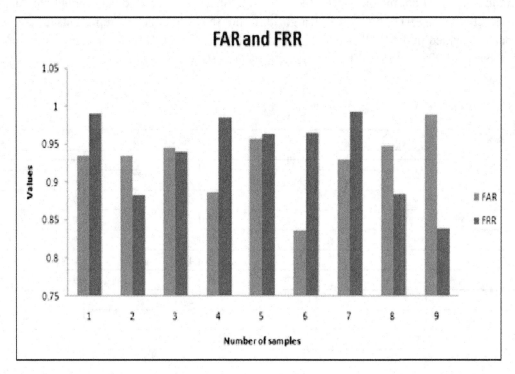

Figure 11. Evaluation of execution time

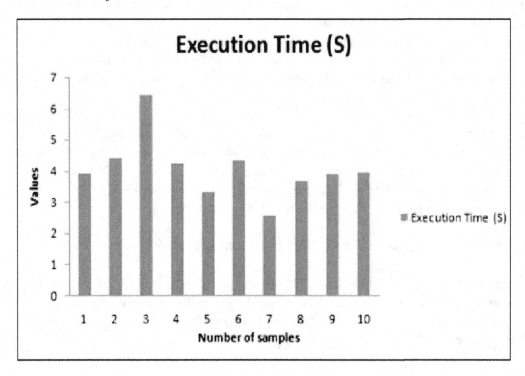

Figure 12. Evaluation of accuracy

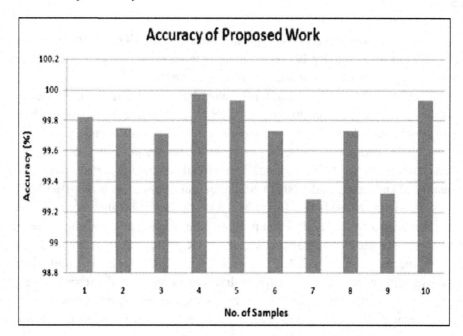

Table 4. Comparative analysis of existing and proposed work

Authors	Used Techniques	No. of Class	Accuracy (%)
Melgani et al., 2008	Morphology + PCA + SVM	6	91.67
Osowski at al., 2004	HOS + Hermite + SVM	13	95.91
Raj et. al et al., 2015	Wavelet + BPNN	8	97.4
Li et. al et al., 2016	PCA + K-ICA + SVM	5	97.78
Rodriguez et al., 2005	Morphology + Decision	16	96.13
Martis el al et al., 2013	PCA + LS-SVM	5	93.48
Sandeep Raj et al., 2018	DCT based DOST + SVM + PSO	16	98.82
Proposed	DWT + ABC + ANN	6	99.56

Table 4 represents the comparison of proposed work with existing work which is presented by different authors with different techniques. In previous work, ECG signal analysis using Support Vector Machine (SVM) along with DCT based Discrete Orthogonal Stockwell Transform (DOST) and Particle Swarm Optimization (PSO) algorithm is presented by Sandeep Raj et al. (2018). In their research, PSO is used as an optimization technique with SVM but used combination is more time-consuming process and the complexity is more as compare to the artificial neural network-based model. The most important challenges faced by Sandeep Raj are the selection of proper R-peaks and R-R intervals due to the lack of appropriate pre-processing steps like decomposition, smoothing, filtering etc. and in proposed work DWT based pre-processing is used which helps to achieve better classification accuracy. From Table 4 it is clear that the classification accuracy of proposed work is better than the existing work et al., 2018.

CONCLUSION

In disease diagnosis process knowledge is an important factor. Here ECG (Electrocardiogram) is utilized for recording heart's electrical activity. It's very important to know that the ECG signal is non-stationary by nature which makes the investigation and analysis very complex.

Efficient method for analysis ECG signal with the prediction of heart abnormalities using artificial neural network has been proposed in this paper. ANN is used as a classifier to facilitate knowledge management and decision-making system to improve disease diagnosis accuracy.

This work has considered six diseases, viz. tachycardia, bradycardia, Artial, Artificial Pace maker and Minor pace attack for the classification. ABC (Artificial bee colony) as an optimization method to improve the quality of knowledge and ANN (artificial neural network) as a classifier has been used for executing the research work. Novel fitness function in ABC optimization algorithm has been considered. ANN has been initialized for the classification purpose using testing and training phases. Performance of the work has been executed using parameters, like FAR, FRR and accuracy. The average value of FAR is 0.9325 and the average value of FRR is 0.9404. The work has taken execution time of 4.073 approximately for executing a sample of ECG signal. It has been seen that the research is 99.56 accurate. Comparison of proposed work with the existing work has been measured for the effectiveness of the work.

The most important challenges faced in previous work is knowledge acquisition that is selection of proper R-peaks and R-R intervals due to the lack of appropriate pre-processing steps like decomposition, smoothing, filtering etc. and in proposed work DWT based pre-processing is used which helps to achieve better classification accuracy. From the Table 4 it is clear that the classification accuracy of proposed work is better than the existing work.

FUTURE SCOPE

In the future work, a hybrid optimization technique will be used for the disease classification using ECG signals. We will classify the unique feature sets using the hybrid optimization technique from the extracted R peaks. More classes of heart disease can be used for classification and testing purpose.

REFERENCES

Acharya, U. R., Fujita, H., Lih, O. S., Hagiwara, Y., Tan, J. H., & Adam, M. (2017). Automated detection of arrhythmias using different intervals of tachycardia ECG segments with convolutional neural network. *Information Sciences*, *405*, 81–90. doi:10.1016/j.ins.2017.04.012

Acharya, U. R., Fujita, H., Sudarshan, V. K., Oh, S. L., Adam, M., Tan, J. H., ... Chua, K. C. (2017). Automated characterization of coronary artery disease, myocardial infarction, and congestive heart failure using contourlet and shearlet transforms of electrocardiogram signal. *Knowledge-Based Systems*, *132*, 156–166. doi:10.1016/j.knosys.2017.06.026

Agarwal, S., Krishnamoorthy, V., & Pratiher, S. (2016, September). ECG signal analysis using wavelet coherence and s-transform for classification of cardiovascular diseases. In *Proceedings of the 2016 International Conference on Advances in Computing, Communications and Informatics (ICACCI)* (pp. 2765-2770). IEEE.

Banerjee, S., & Mitra, M. (2014). Application of cross wavelet transform for ECG pattern analysis and classification. *IEEE Transactions on Instrumentation and Measurement*, *63*(2), 326–333. doi:10.1109/TIM.2013.2279001

Berkaya, S. K., Uysal, A. K., Gunal, E. S., Ergin, S., Gunal, S., & Gulmezoglu, M. B. (2018). A survey on ECG analysis. *Biomedical Signal Processing and Control*, *43*, 216–235. doi:10.1016/j.bspc.2018.03.003

Debnath, T., Hasan, M. M., & Biswas, T. (2016, December). Analysis of ECG signal and classification of heart abnormalities using Artificial Neural Network. In *Proceedings of the 2016 9th International Conference on Electrical and Computer Engineering (ICECE)* (pp. 353-356). IEEE.

Delrieu, A., Hoël, M., Phua, C. T., & Lissorgues, G. (2017). Multi physiological signs model to enhance accuracy of ECG peaks detection. In *Proceedings of the 16th International Conference on Biomedical Engineering* (pp. 58-61). Springer, Singapore. 10.1007/978-981-10-4220-1_12

Francesca, S., Carlo, C. G., Di Nunzio, L., Rocco, F., & Marco, R. (2018). Comparison of Low-Complexity Algorithms for Real-Time QRS Detection using Standard ECG Database. *International Journal on Advanced Science. Engineering and Information Technology*, *8*(2), 307–314.

Kumar, A., Kumar, M., & Komaragiri, R. (2018). Design of a Biorthogonal Wavelet Transform Based R-Peak Detection and Data Compression Scheme for Implantable Cardiac Pacemaker Systems. *Journal of Medical Systems*, *42*(6), 102. doi:10.100710916-018-0953-2 PMID:29675598

Kunjekar, P., & Desmukh, K. (2016). A Comparative Analysis on De-Noising of Bio-Medical Signal (ECG) Based on Multiple Filters. *Digital Signal Processing*, *8*(6), 163–167.

Li, H., Liang, H., Miao, C., Cao, L., Feng, X., Tang, C., & Li, E. (2016). Novel ECG signal classification based on KICA nonlinear feature extraction. *Circuits, Systems, and Signal Processing*, *35*(4), 1187–1197. doi:10.100700034-015-0108-3

Martis, R. J., Acharya, U. R., Mandana, K. M., Ray, A. K., & Chakraborty, C. (2013). Cardiac decision making using higher order spectra. *Biomedical Signal Processing and Control*, *8*(2), 193–203. doi:10.1016/j.bspc.2012.08.004

Melgani, F., & Bazi, Y. (2008). Classification of electrocardiogram signals with support vector machines and particle swarm optimization. *IEEE Transactions on Information Technology in Biomedicine*, *12*(5), 667–677. doi:10.1109/TITB.2008.923147 PMID:18779082

Mporas, I., Tsirka, V., Zacharaki, E. I., Koutroumanidis, M., Richardson, M., & Megalooikonomou, V. (2015). Seizure detection using EEG and ECG signals for computer-based monitoring, analysis and management of epileptic patients. *Expert Systems with Applications*, *42*(6), 3227–3233. doi:10.1016/j.eswa.2014.12.009

Omer, N., Granot, Y., Kähönen, M., Lehtinen, R., Nieminen, T., Nikus, K., ... Abboud, S. (2017). Blinded Analysis of an Exercise ECG Database Using High Frequency QRS Analysis. *Computing*, *44*, 1.

Osowski, S., Hoai, L. T., & Markiewicz, T. (2004). Support vector machine-based expert system for reliable heartbeat recognition. *IEEE Transactions on Biomedical Engineering*, *51*(4), 582–589. doi:10.1109/TBME.2004.824138 PMID:15072212

Raghavendra, U., Fujita, H., Gudigar, A., Shetty, R., Nayak, K., Pai, U., ... Acharya, U. R. (2018). Automated technique for coronary artery disease characterization and classification using DD-DTDWT in ultrasound images. *Biomedical Signal Processing and Control*, *40*, 324–334. doi:10.1016/j.bspc.2017.09.030

Raj, S., Chand, G. P., & Ray, K. C. (2015). Arm-based arrhythmia beat monitoring system. *Microprocessors and Microsystems*, *39*(7), 504–511. doi:10.1016/j.micpro.2015.07.013

Raj, S., & Ray, K. C. (2017). ECG signal analysis using DCT-based DOST and PSO optimized SVM. *IEEE Transactions on Instrumentation and Measurement*, *66*(3), 470–478. doi:10.1109/TIM.2016.2642758

Rodriguez, J., Goni, A., & Illarramendi, A. (2005). Real-time classification of ECGs on a PDA. *IEEE Transactions on Information Technology in Biomedicine*, *9*(1), 23–34. doi:10.1109/TITB.2004.838369 PMID:15787004

Sadhukhan, D., Pal, S., & Mitra, M. (2017, July). Automated ECG analysis using Fourier harmonic phase. In *2017 IEEE Region 10 Symposium (TENSYMP)* (pp. 1-5). IEEE.

Wang, T., Shi, R. X., & Xu, X. Y. (2017, August). Reliable classification of ventricular premature and tachycardia beats with novel feature extraction method and classifier ensembles. In *2017 IEEE 2nd International Conference on Signal and Image Processing (ICSIP)* (pp. 402-412). IEEE.

This research was previously published in the International Journal of Electronics, Communications, and Measurement Engineering (IJECME), 8(2); pages 67-86, copyright year 2019 by IGI Publishing (an imprint of IGI Global).

Chapter 44
Analysis of Precipitation Variability using Memory Based Artificial Neural Networks

Shyama Debbarma
Regent Education and Research Foundation Group of Institutions, India

Parthasarathi Choudhury
NIT Silchar, India

Parthajit Roy
NIT Silchar, India

Ram Kumar
Katihar Engineering College, Katihar, India

ABSTRACT

This article analyzes the variability in precipitation of the Barak river basin using memory-based ANN models called Gamma Memory Neural Network(GMNN) and genetically optimized GMNN called GMNN-GA for precipitation downscaling precipitation. GMNN having adaptive memory depth is capable techniques in modeling time varying inputs with unknown input characteristics, while an integration of the model with GA can further improve its performances. NCEP reanalysis and HadCM3A2 (a) scenario data are used for downscaling and forecasting precipitation series for Barak river basin. Model performances are analyzed by using statistical criteria, RMSE and mean error and are compared with the standard SDSM model. Results obtained by using 24 years of daily data sets show that GMNN-GA is efficient in downscaling daily precipitation series with maximum daily annual mean error of 6.78%. The outcomes of the study demonstrate that execution of the GMNN-GA model is superior to the GMNN and similar with that of the standard SDSM.

DOI: 10.4018/978-1-6684-2408-7.ch044

1. INTRODUCTION

Recently, climate change has attracted the attention of scientific community of multidisciplinary area due to its effects on human society and natural resources. Anthropologic activities have provoked the climate system causing significant changes in hydrologic cycle, ecosystem etc. Changes in hydrologic cycle have direct impact on human society due to changes in rainfall distribution, water availability, flood and drought (Gleick, 1987; Burn, 1994; Simonovic, 2001; Sivakumar, 2011). Water resource of a region is often affected due to changes in the precipitation pattern. Precipitation being a critical element speaking to atmosphere of a locale is viewed as the most vital variable for examining the effects of atmospheric changes, particularly on the water assets of an area. To study the climate change effects on water resources because of changes in precipitation, its changeability in the spatial and temporal domain is required to be assessed (Langousis and Kaleris, 2014). Global climate models (GCMs) are an important tool available for estimating the anticipated impacts of changing climate. GCMs are the numerical models that are normally used to simulate the response of the changing climate both in present and future climate based on the forcing by greenhouse gases and aerosols. GCM outputs are coarse in spatial resolution and often required to convert the outputs of GCMs into local climatological variables necessary for analysis of changes in the climate. A technique known as 'downscaling techniques' is used to convert the coarse GCM output into finer resolution.

Two major approaches of downscaling techniques are dynamical downscaling and statistical or empirical downscaling technique. Dynamic downscaling derives local-scale information through Regional Climate Model (RCM) while empirical downscaling is based on the principle that regional and local climates are the results of the interaction of the atmospheric and oceanic circulation as well as regional topography, land-sea distribution and land use, etc. (von Storch et al., 2000). Thus, empirical downscaling derives local climatic information from the larger scale through inference using stochastic or deterministic functions. Statistical downscaling models usually implement linear methods such as multiple linear regression, local scaling, canonical correlation analysis, or singular value decomposition (Salathe, 2003; Schubert and Henderson-Sellers, 1997; Conway et al., 1996). Statistical downscaling model (SDSM) is a well-recognized statistical downscaling tools to implements a regression based method (Wilby et al., 2002). Linear methods generally do not provide reliable information on various projected meteorological variables which includes rainfall and temperature (Xu, 1999; Schoof and Pryor, 2001). To overcome the situation, attempts were made to investigate the applicability of nonlinear methods such as artificial neural network (ANN) and analogue methods (Bishop, 1995; Zorita et al., 1995; Singh and Borah, 2013; Shao and Li, 2013). ANNs is recognized as one of the effective method in solving nonlinear and time-varying problems (Aziz et al., 2014; Jeong et al., 2012; Bhattacharjee et al., 2016). ANNs can approximate highly nonlinear relationships of input-output data series better than other nonlinear regression techniques due to their typical network structure and the nonlinear (Acharya and Nitha, 2017; Sharma and Virmani, 2017; Chatterjee et al., 2016). The performance of standard ANN models like Multilayer perceptron are comparable to that of the multiple regression downscaling methods (Weichert and Bürger, 1998; Cannon and Whitfield, 2002; Coulibaly, 2001). All things considered, a few studies have additionally demonstrated that the standard ANNs that are often utilized for hydrologic modeling are not appropriate to time varying problems, and often fail to yield optimal solution (Aksoy and Dahamsheh, 2009; Coulibaly et al., 2001; Lang, 1990).

Other classes of neural systems that incorporates memory structure to represent temporal features of input-output relationship which are found to be more appropriate for modeling complex nonlinear system (Coulibaly et al., 2001; Li et al., 2016; Li et al., 2016]. This memory can store the past information of a time series of input sequences. Memory may be incorporated in two in the neural network systems either by feed forward delays or feedback delays. Time Delay Neural Network (TDNN) is an example of feed forward memory which involves explicit inclusion of delays with a fixed memory resolution (Lang, 1990; Williams and Zipser, 1989; Principe, 1993). The drawback of TDNN is its inability to adjust the values of the time delays automatically. Recurrent neural network(RNN) is a feedback delays network that utilizes a trace of the previous states of the input series. One of the problems associated with RNN is that the training scales badly with both network and problem size (Williams and Zipser, 1989). To overcome these drawbacks, the research community started searching new types of memory. In literature, a special type of neural system based on gamma memory which includes properties of feed forward as well as feedback delays (Principe, 1993). This gamma memory based neural system has been suitably used for solving temporal problems in various fields (Lawrence, 1997; Choudhury and Roy, 2015). Studies have reported that ANN when trained with traditional learning algorithms such as gradient descent algorithm often fall into local minima and cannot reach the global optimal. Associated problems with this algorithm are the slow learning convergence and easily get trapped at local minima. There are various algorithms available in literatures (Kumar et al., 2016). Optimization techniques such as genetic algorithm is proved to be an efficient technique for optimizing the performance of ANN in various ways (Kumar et al., 2016; Chau et al., 2005). Integration of genetic algorithm with ANN models was found capable to improve the performance of the ANN models. Genetic algorithm being based on the survival of the fittest rule, potential global solution is easily obtained. In the present study applicability of gamma memory based ANN and genetically optimization of this technique in downscaling daily precipitation are investigated. The models are applied to the Barak basin in India. Performances of the proposed models are compared with the standard Statistical Downscaling Model (SDSM).

2. STUDY AREA AND DATA DESCRIPTION

The application of downscaling methods is made in the Barak river basin (Figure 1). The location of the basin lies between east longitudes 91° 10' to 95° 7' and north latitudes 21° 58' to 26° 24'. The river originates at the Japvo mountain of Manipur hills which passes through the southern part of Assam and meets in the Bay of Bengal. The drainage area of the river basin lying in India is 41,157 km2 out of which Assam shares 17.6%. The basin receives a mean annual rainfall of 2640 mm (Singh, Sharma & Ojha, 2011). The meteorological station at Laxmipur (latitude 24.7833° and longitude 93°) and Dholai (latitude 24.77° and longitude 92.85°) are selected for the study. One more dataset of precipitation has been prepared with the average value of Laxmipur and Dholai and called it as Mean (D+L) station. Therefore, three sets of daily observed precipitation data are used for downscaling experiments. 24 years (1978-2001) of daily total precipitation records representing the current climate were collected from the Regional Meteorological Centre, Guwahati and prepared for downscaling experiments. Corresponding daily observed data of large-scale predictor variables representing the current climate condition of the region are derived from NCEP_1961-2001 reanalysis. Climate variables corresponding to the future climate change scenario for the study area are extracted from HadCM3A2 (a) experiment. Both the GCM output data as shown in Table 1 are downloaded from Canadian Climate change scenario network

(CCCSN). The prediction data of HadCM3A2 are divided into three distinct periods, namely the current (1984-2013), the 2020s (2016-2045) and the 2050s (2046-2075) to facilitate trend analysis of the precipitation data.

Figure 1. Barak river system

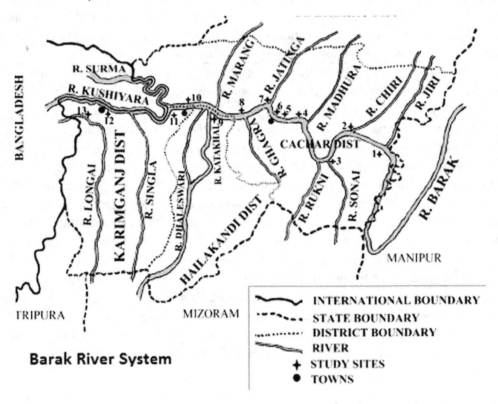

3. MODEL DESCRIPTION

In the present study, three downscaling techniques are chosen to downscale daily precipitation, which are described as follows:

3.1. Gamma Memory Neural Network (GMNN)

Gamma Memory Neural Network (GMNN) is an MLP extended with short term adaptable gamma memory. GMNN incorporates the properties of both feed forward and feedback delays due to which it is capable of adjusting memory depths depending on the temporal features of the input data series. GMNN when attached with memory in each input nodes are called focused GMNN which automatically selects the best set of depths. GMNN is better suited for applications where each input data series are characterized with different temporal patterns [Choudhury and P. Roy (2015)]. Memory elements have three important features such as memory order; memory depth; and memory resolution. Memory order (*P*) specifies the number of delay sections; memory depth (*D*) characterizes how far in the past the input signal is remembered; and memory resolution (μ) defines the level or fineness of the information content stored in the taps or it may also be viewed as the number of taps per unit time step. The memory depth-resolution product equals to the order of memory, P. In the case of time delay neural network (TDNN), memory resolution is fixed to unity as memory order (*P*) is equal to memory depth (*D*). But, in the case of gamma memory, the memory resolution (μ) is adapted through training and attains a value of $\mu = (P)/(D)$ depending on the patterns of the input series. As such, GMNN is supposed to perform better when input series of multiple patterns are to be modeled. Figure 2 shows a special type of focused gamma memory neural network GMNN model with one gamma memories at each node in the input layer that is used to process multiple time varying inputs using different memory depths. The output of the pth tap attached to the rt^{h} input node is given by:

$$x_{r,p}(t) = (1-\mu_r)x_{r,p}(t-1) + \mu_r x_{p-1}(t-1)$$ (1)

where *p*=1,2,3,...*P*, *r*=1,2,3,...(*N*+1) and, output of the first tap of the filter is given by

$$x_{r,p}(t) = I_r(t)$$ (2)

The activations, $x_{r,p}(t)$ representing the output of the taps at time (*t*) are fed to a feed forward MLP network. The output of a neuron, *i* in the first hidden layer receiving weighted outputs of the memory taps is given by:

$$y_i(t) = \sigma\left(\sum_{r=1}^{(N+1)}\sum_{p=0}^{P} w_{i,r,p}x_{r,p}(t) + b_i\right)$$ (3)

Here, $x_{r,p}(t)$ is the impulse response of the pth tap in the memory attached to the rth input node. $w_{i,r,p}$ is the synaptic weight of the connection joining p^{th} tap in the rth input node to the ith neuron in the hidden layer. σ = transfer function of the neuron i in the hidden layer. It is notable here that as given in Equation (1) the input layer in a focused GMNN is an recursive in nature involving the memory parameters μr_a special back-propagation through time procedure is required instead of the static back-propagation for adapting the parameter μr.

A quadratic performance index is used as given in Equation (4) to estimate the weights in a network through training:

$$E = \sum_{t=1}^{T}\frac{1}{2}[E(t)]^2 = \sum_{t=1}^{T}\frac{1}{2}[d(t)-y(t)]^2$$ (4)

where, *d(t)* is the desired output and *y(t)* are the corresponding network output. Figure 2 shows a topology of focused gamma memory neural network.

Figure 2. Focused Gamma Memory Neural Network

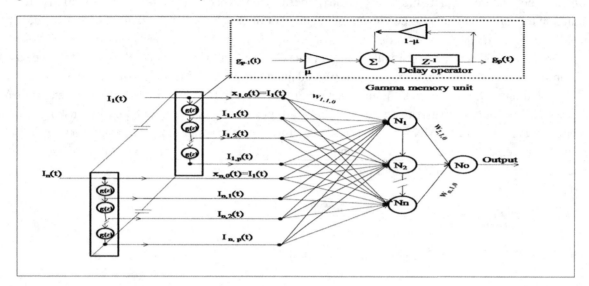

3.2. Gamma Memory Neural Network-Genetic Algorithm (GMNN-GA)

Genetic algorithms combined with artificial neural networks are implemented with an objective to optimize parameters of a neural network structure. Genetic Algorithms (GAs) works based upon the principles of evolutions observed in nature which are used as general-purpose search algorithms. Optimization of the network parameters of the ANNs using genetic algorithm is a commonly used efficient technique. In GA, optimal solutions are searched until a specified termination criterion is met. Genetic algorithm has been used successfully in various field (Kumar et al., 2016; Mirza et al., 2001; Song and Singh, 2010). A chromosome is the solution to a problem. A chromosome made up of a collection of genes is the neural network parameters to be optimized. Genetic algorithm creates an initial population and then evaluates this population through neural network training for each chromosome. Populations are then evolved through multiple generations using the genetic operators for the best network parameters. Evaluate the fitness of each potential solution is done by achieving the lowest cost during the training run. The crucial aspect of GMNN-GA system is the selection of the fitness function. The fitness is indirectly given by the ANN training using the error from the validation cases (Lee, 2009):

$$Fitness = \frac{1}{MSE_{va}} \tag{5}$$

$$MSE_{va} = \frac{1}{2}\sum_{t=1}^{n}\left(T_i - O_i\right)^2 \tag{6}$$

where T_i the target is output and O_i is the desired output.

Equation (7) id the objective function of GMNN-GA model used for initializing weights:

$$minJ\left(W\right) = \sum_{i=1}^{P} \left|Y_i - f\left(X_i, W\right)\right| \tag{7}$$

where W is the weight value, i is the data sequence, p is the total number of training data pairs, X_i is the ith input data, Y_i is the ith measured data, and $f(X_i, W)$ represents the simulated output. The goal of genetic algorithm model is to ascertain optimal parameters so that accumulative errors between the measured data and simulated data are minimal.

3.3. Statistical Downscaling Model (SDSM)

Statistical downscaling model (SDSM) is a hybrid model between a multivariate linear-regression method and a stochastic weather generator. SDSM has been used successfully by many researchers in downscaling climate variables due to its inherent facilities such as ability for rapid generation of multiple, low-cost, single-site simulations of daily weather variables under present and future climate forcings (Ghavidel and Montaseri, 2014; Neves and Cortez, 1998). Combining Genetic Algorithms, Neural Networks and Data Filtering for Time Series Forecasting., 1997; Wilby et al., 2000; Dibike and Coulibaly, 2005; Hassan et al., 2012; Tatsumi et al., 2014; Hashmi et al., 2011). SDSM needs two types of daily data i.e. local predictands (e.g. temperature, precipitation) and the data of large-scale predictors (NCEP and GCM) of a grid box closest to the study area. Few important steps of SDSM are the data quality control and transformation, selection of predictor variables, calibration, weather data generation, statistical analysis, graphing model output and scenario generation. SDSM has three steps of model operations between a user–specified predictand and a set of large-scale predictor variables, i.e. selection of optimization techniques selection of the model structure; and lastly selection of the process such as unconditional or conditional. In the weather generation, ensembles of synthetic daily weather series given observed (or NCEP re–analysis) atmospheric predictor variables are created which enables the verification of calibrated models (using independent data) and the synthesis of artificial time series representing current climate conditions. Data analysis compares both derived SDSM scenarios and observed climate data and produces the chosen statistics such as monthly/seasonal/annual means, maxima, minima, sums and variances. Graphical analysis is done in two ways of graphical analysis through the Compare Results screen and the Time Series Plot screen. The Compare Results screen enables the User to plot monthly statistics produced by the Analyze Data screen. The graphing option allows simultaneous comparison of two data sets and hence rapid assessment of downscaled versus observed, or current versus future climate scenarios. The Time Series Plot screen is used to produce a time series plot of the chosen data files in terms of monthly, seasonal, annual or water year periods for statistics such as Sum, Mean, Maximum, Winter/Summer ratios, Partial Duration Series, Percentiles and Standardized Precipitation Index. Lastly, the Generate Scenario operation is used to produces ensembles of synthetic daily weather series given atmospheric predictor variables supplied by a climate model (either for current or future climate experiments), rather than observed predictors.

4. RESULTS AND DISCUSSIONS

The results of the present study are discussed in three sub-sections. The firs sub-section discussed the calibration and validation of the downscaling models. The second sub-section discussed the generation of precipitation data for future and the last one discussed for detection of trends in both observed and simulated precipitation.

4.1. Model Calibration and Validation

The neural network models are developed using NeuroSolution-5 software. GMNN and GMNN-GA models are selected for downscaling daily total precipitation of Barak river basin purposes. These models are trained several times using 26 predictor variables derived from NCEP reanalysis as input and daily observed precipitation as desired output to the neural models to achieve the best network structure. Among these 26 variables, 12 predictor variables are selected using sensitivity analysis. The data considered here covers a period of 24 (1978-2001) years, out of which first 15 years data are considered for training, next 3 years data are considered for cross-validation and remaining 6 years data are considered for testing the models. Model parameters are adjusted during the calibration to get the best statistical agreement between the observed and simulated precipitation and the best performing network structure are selected for both the neural network models. In the case of downscaling precipitation with GMNN model, a time lag of 5 days and 9 neurons and the DeltaBarDelta learning rule gave the best performing network, whereas a time lag of 2 days, 6 neurons and Conjugate Gradient learning rule gave the best performance in GMNN-GA model. Hyperbolic tangent activation function is used at both the hidden and output layers in both the neural network models. In the case of SDSM, the best model performance is achieved with duplex optimization criteria at 12 variance inflations and 0.9 bias corrections. After the calibration, the models are validated using suitable data. The calibration and validation results of SDSM and ANN models are given in Table 1-Table 4. The calibration results indicate that the lowest mean squared error (MSE) of GMNN and GMNN-GA are 0.0055 and 0.0053 while the SDSM has lowest SE and R squared as 0.35 and 0.14. The validation results indicate that the lowest MSE for GMNN and GMNN-GA are 13.49 and 13.25 while the lowest SE and R squared errors for SDSM are 0.353 and 0.142.

Further. to assess the accuracy of the downscaling models, the model testing has been done with the data of the last six years (NCEP-1996-2001) in terms of model percentage error. From the test results, it is found that the maximum percentage error of GMNN, GMNN-GA and SDSM are 15.66%, 6.78% and 13.03%, while the minimum percentage error of GMNN, GMNN-GA and SDSM are 8.72%, 4.79% and 2.07% respectively. To investigate the variability in daily annual mean errors of observed and simulated precipitation of the test data series, year wise daily annual mean percentage errors are calculated for all the models and stations. Results showed that the maximum daily annual mean percentage error of GMNN, GMNN-GA and SDSM are 25.09% (2001), 18.62% (2001) and 16.01% (1997) while the minimum daily annual mean percentage error are 0.26% (1996), 0.56% (1998) and 0.84% (1996) respectively. These results indicate that GMNN-GA and the standard SDSM performances are found comparable with the observed data while GMNN model has the highest errors in simulating the daily precipitation of test data series.

Table 1 Calibration results of GMNN and GMNN-GA in MSE

Sl. No.	Station	Models	Training Results	
			Training	Cross Validation
1	Dholai	GMNN	0.0079	0.0113
		GMNN-GA	0.0099	0.0119
2	Laxmipur	GMNN	0.0055	0.0061
		GMNN-GA	0.0066	0.0066
3	Mean(D+L)	GMNN	0.0062	0.007
		GMNN-GA	0.0053	0.0062

Table 2 Calibration results of SDSM

	Dholai		Laxmipur		Mean(D+L)	
	R Squared	SE	R Squared	SE	R Squared	SE
SDSM	0.14	0.37	0.21	0.36	0.19	0.35

Table 3. The validation results of all the models and stations

Sl. No.	Station	Models	Testing results			
			MSE	NMSE	MAE	r
1	Dholai	GMNN	16.24	0.78	8.21	0.48
		GMNN-GA	16.17	0.77	8.23	0.49
2	Laxmipur	GMNN	15.10	0.78	7.93	0.49
		GMNN-GA	14.76	0.75	8.1	0.5
3	Mean(D+L)	GMNN	13.49	0.7	7.49	0.54
		GMNN-GA	13.25	0.68	7.15	0.57

Table 4. The validation results of all the models and stations

	Dholai		Laxmipur		Mean(D+L)	
	R Squared	SE	R Squared	SE	R Squared	SE
SDSM	0.14	0.37	0.217	0.36	0.19	0.35

4.2. Application of Models in Precipitation Projection

Once the downscaling models are calibrated and validated, the next step is to use these models to generate the precipitation scenario for future time series. In this case, the large-scale predictor variables derived from HadCM3A2 (a) scenario are used instead of NCEP large scale data. The projection period covers a period of 90 years (1984-2075), that is divided into three distinct periods, Current climate (1984-2013),

Future1 (2016-2045) and Future2 (2046-2075) respectively. To investigate the applicability of downscaling models in generating precipitation scenarios for future time series, climate scenario was generated first for the Current climate (1984-2013) and compared the performances of the downscaling models in terms of percentage mean errors and RMSE with the corresponding observed data and the results are presented in Table 5. From the results, it is observed that the standard SDSM performed best with the lowest RMSE and percentage mean error, followed by the GMNN-GA model and lastly the GMNN model in simulating daily precipitation data series.

Then precipitation scenarios for Future1 (2016-2045) and Future2 (2046-2075) are generated using SDSM, GMNN, and GMNN-GA models. In this case, the performances of GMNN and GMNN-GA models are compared with the SDSM. The model performances are measured in terms of percentage mean errors and RMSE and the results are presented in Table 6. The results indicate that GMNN-GA model has performed better than the GMNN model in generating precipitation scenarios in almost all the cases.

To investigate the annual and decadal variability in the projected precipitation scenarios generated by the models, annual mean mean of precipitation scenarios were calculated for the time period of 1984-2075 and presented in Figure 3-Figure 5. The maximum annual means of the GMNN, GMNN-GA and SDSM are 18.02 mm (Laxmipur), 16.79 mm (Laxmipur) and 15.74 mm (Laxmipur) while the corresponding minimum means are 6.53 mm (Dholai), 4.78 mm (Laxmipur) and 5.68 mm (Dholai) respectively. Though mean values of precipitations vary over time, the maximum annual and decadal means are detected to occur in the same year in 2065 in all the stations and models. It is clear from the plots of annual mean precipitation that the trend of precipitation is almost normal in the Current climate (1984-2013) and increases from the Future1 (2016-2045) and the highest increase is seen towards the past half of the Future2 (2046-2075) and then drops towards to the end of Future2 (2046-2075). The above results indicate that precipitation of significant magnitudes are likely to occur at the beginning of Future1 (2016-2056) and towards the end of Future2 (2075).

Table 5. RMSE and mean annual % error of precipitation scenarios generated using HadCM3A2 GCM outputs for the period of 1978-2001

Sl. No.	Stations	GMNN	GMNN-GA	SDSM
1	Dholai	1.54	1.58	1.53
2	Laxmipur	1.63	1.58	1.35
3	Mean(D+L)	1.54	1.44	1.29
Annual mean % errors				
1	Dholai	15.49	16.26	15.16
2	Laxmipur	16.39	16.16	14.25
3	Mean(D+L)	16.82	16.01	14.94

Table 6. RMSE and annual mean % error of precipitation scenarios of HadCM3A2 GCM outputs with respect to SDSM for Future1 (2016-2045) and Future2 (2046-2075)

	2016-2045		2046-2075	
RMSE				
Stations	**GMNN-GA**	**GMNN**	**GMNN-GA**	**GMNN**
Dholai	0.60	**0.65**	0.80	0.56
Laxmipur	0.79	1.12	0.70	0.98
Mean(D+L)	0.67	1.04	0.66	1.18
Annual mean % errors				
Dholai	5.34	6.12	6.58	4.09
Laxmipur	7.48	9.51	4.84	6.48
Mean(D+L)	4.64	8.06	3.52	7.77

Figure 3. Annual mean of precipitation scenario for Dholai station during 1984-2075

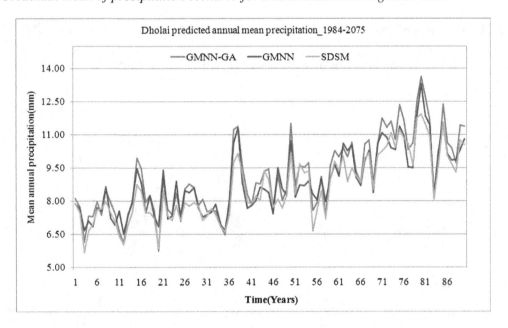

5. CONCLUSION

This study investigated the applicability of GMNN and GMNN-GA as downscaling model and compared the results of these models with that of the standard SDSM model. Study results showed that the GMNN-GA model is an effective method for downscaling daily precipitation. The main advantage of this downscaling model is its ability to incorporate both feed forward and feedback delays making it capable of adjusting memory depths depending the temporal features of the input sequences and its ability to optimize the network parameters simultaneously using genetic algorithm. The validation results showed that the GMNN-GA model is able to reproduce the observed precipitation comparable to that of SDSM.

Figure 4. Annual mean of precipitation scenario for Laxmipur station during 1984-2075

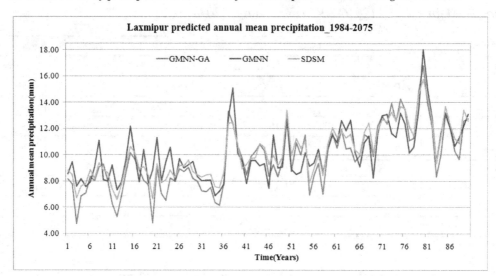

Figure 5. Annual mean of precipitation scenario for Mean (D+L) station during 1984-2075

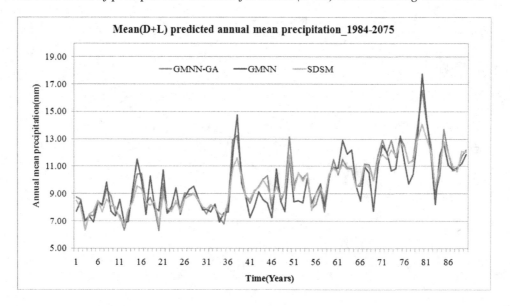

The downscaling results corresponding to the future 'HadCM3A2(a) experiment' climate change scenario indicated that GMNN-GA model was able to replicate the observed precipitation as that of the standard SDSM while the GMNN model was not efficient in simulating daily precipitation data during the year 1984-2103. GMNN-GA model was also found better in generating precipitation scenarios for Future1 (2016-2045) and Future2 (2046-2075) as compared to the GMNN model. It may be concluded here that GMNN-GA model has performed better than the GMNN model in generating precipitation scenarios in almost all the cases.

REFERENCES

Acharjya, D., & Anitha, A. (2017). A Comparative Study of Statistical and Rough Computing Models in Predictive Data Analysis. *International Journal of Ambient Computing and Intelligence*, 8(2), 32–51. doi:10.4018/IJACI.2017040103

Aksoy, H., & Dahamsheh, A. (2009). Artificial neural network models for forecasting monthly precipitation in Jordan. *Stochastic Environmental Research and Risk Assessment*, 23(7), 917–931. doi:10.100700477-008-0267-x

Aziz, K., Rahman, A., Fang, G., & Shrestha, S. (2014). Application of artificial neural networks in regional flood frequency analysis: A case study for Australia. *Stochastic Environmental Research and Risk Assessment*, 28(3), 541–554. doi:10.100700477-013-0771-5

Bhattacherjee, A., Roy, S., Paul, S., Roy, P., Kausar, N., & Dey, N. (2016). Classification Approach for Breast Cancer Detection Using Back Propagation Neural Network: A Study. In W. Karâa & N. Dey (Eds.), *Biomedical Image Analysis and Mining Techniques for Improved Health Outcomes* (pp. 210–221). Hershey, PA: IGI Global. doi:10.4018/978-1-4666-8811-7.ch010

Bishop, C. M. (1995). Neural Networks for Pattern Recognition. *Journal of the American Statistical Association*.

Burn, D. H. (1994). Hydrologic effects of climatic change in west-central Canada. *Journal of Hydrology (Amsterdam)*, 160(1–4), 53–70. doi:10.1016/0022-1694(94)90033-7

Cannon, A. J., & Whitfield, P. H. (2002). Downscaling recent streamflow conditions in British Columbia, Canada using ensemble neural network models. *Journal of Hydrology (Amsterdam)*, 259(1–4), 136–151. doi:10.1016/S0022-1694(01)00581-9

Chatterjee, S., Sarkar, S., Hore, S., Dey, N., Ashour, A. S., & Balas, V. E. (2017). Particle swarm optimization trained neural network for structural failure prediction of multistoried RC buildings. *Neural Computing & Applications*, 28(8), 2005–2016. doi:10.100700521-016-2190-2

Chau, K. W., Wu, C. L., & Li, Y. S. (2005). Comparison of several flood forecasting models in Yangtze River. *Journal of Hydrologic Engineering*, 10(852), 485–491. doi:10.1061/(ASCE)1084-0699(2005)10:6(485)

Choudhury, P., & Roy, P. (2014). Forecasting Concurrent Flows in a River System Using ANNs. *Journal of Hydrologic Engineering*, 20(8). doi:10.1061/(ASCE)HE.1943-5584.0001107

Conway, D., Wilby, R. L., & Jones, P. D. (1996). Precipitation and air flow indices over the British Isles. *Climate Research*, 7, 169–183. doi:10.3354/cr007169

Coulibaly, P., Anctil, F., Aravena, R., & Bobde, B. (2001). Artificial neural network modeling of water table depth fluctuations. *Water Resources Research*, 37(4), 885–896. doi:10.1029/2000WR900368

Coulibaly, P., Anctil, F., & Bobee, B. (2001). Multivariate reservoir inflow forecasting using artificial neural networks. *Journal of Hydrologic Engineering*, 6(October), 367–376.

Dibike, Y. B., & Coulibaly, P. (2005). Hydrologic impact of climate change in the Saguenay watershed: Comparison of downscaling methods and hydrologic models. *Journal of Hydrology (Amsterdam)*, *307*(1–4), 145–163. doi:10.1016/j.jhydrol.2004.10.012

Gleick, P. H. (1987). The development and testing of a water balance model for climate impact assessment: Modeling the Sacramento Basin. *Water Resources Research*, *23*(6), 1049–1061. doi:10.1029/WR023i006p01049

Hashmi, M. Z., Shamseldin, A. Y., & Melville, B. W. (2011). Comparison of SDSM and LARS-WG for simulation and downscaling of extreme precipitation events in a watershed. *Stochastic Environmental Research and Risk Assessment*, *25*(4), 475–484. doi:10.100700477-010-0416-x

Hassan, Z., Harun, S., & Malek, M. A. (2012). Application of ANNs Model with the SDSM for the Hydrological Trend Prediction in the Sub-catchment of Kurau River, Malaysia. *J. Environ. Sci. Eng. B*, *1*, 577–585.

Jeong, D. I., St-Hilaire, A., Ouarda, T. B. M. J., & Gachon, P. (2012). Comparison of transfer functions in statistical downscaling models for daily temperature and precipitation over Canada. *Stochastic Environmental Research and Risk Assessment*, *26*(5), 633–653. doi:10.100700477-011-0523-3

Kumar, R., Rajan, A., Talukdar, F. A., Dey, N., Santhi, V., & Balas, V. E. (2016). Optimization of 5.5-GHz CMOS LNA parameters using firefly algorithm. *Neural Computing & Applications*, *28*(12), 3765–3779. doi:10.100700521-016-2267-y

Kumar, R., Talukdar, F. A., Dey, N., & Balas, V. E. (2016). Quality Factor Optimization of Spiral Inductor using Firefly Algorithm and its Application in Amplifier. *International Journal of Advanced Intelligence Paradigms*.

Lang, K. J., Waibel, A. H., & Hinton, G. E. (1990). A time-delay neural network architecture for isolated word recognition. *Neural Networks*, *3*(1), 23–43. doi:10.1016/0893-6080(90)90044-L

Langousis, A., & Kaleris, V. (2014). Statistical framework to simulate daily rainfall series conditional on upper-air predictor variables. *Water Resources Research*, *50*(5), 3907–3932. doi:10.1002/2013WR014936

Lawrence, S., Back, A. D., Tsoi, A. C., & Giles, C. L. (1997). *The Gamma MLP – Using Multiple Temporal Resolutions for Improved Classification*. In Neural Networks Signal Process (pp. 362–367). doi:10.1109/NNSP.1997.622406

Lee, E. W. M. (2009). Application of an intelligent model developed from experimental data to building design for fire safety. Stoch. Environ. Res. Risk Assess., 23(4), 493-506.

Li, Z., Dey, N., Ashour, A. S., Cao, L., Wang, Y., Wang, D., ... Shi, F. (2017). Convolutional Neural Network Based Clustering and Manifold Learning Method for Diabetic Plantar Pressure Imaging Dataset. *Journal of Medical Imaging and Health Informatics*, *7*(3), 639–652.

Li, Z., Shi, K., Dey, N., Ashour, A. S., Wang, D., Balas, V. E., ... Sh, F. (2016). Rule-based back propagation neural networks for various precision rough set presented KANSEI knowledge prediction: A case study on shoe product form features extraction. *Neural Computing & Applications*, *28*(3), 613–663. doi:10.100700521-016-2707-8

Monirul Qader Mirza, M., Warrick, R. A., Ericksen, N. J., & Kenny, G. J. (2001). Are floods getting worse in the Ganges, Brahmaputra and Meghna basins? *Environmental Hazards*, *3*(2), 37–48.

Neves, J., & Cortez, P. (1998). *Combining Genetic Algorithms*. Neural Networks and Data Filtering for Time Series Forecasting.

Principe, J. C., de Vries, B., & de Oliveira, P. G. (1993). The Gamma Filter - a New Class of Adaptive IIR Filters with Restrictive Feed-back. *IEEE Transactions on Acoustics, Speech, and Signal Processing*, *41*(12), 649–656. doi:10.1109/78.193206

Salathe. (2003). Comparison of various precipitation downscaling methods for the simulation of streamflow in a rainshadow river basin. *Int. J. Climatol.*, *23*(8), 887-901.

Schoof, J. T., & Pryor, S. C. (2001). Downscaling temperature and precipitation: A comparison of regression-based and artificial neural networks. *International Journal of Control*, *21*, 773–790.

Schubert, S., & Henderson-Sellers, A. (1997). A statistical model to downscale local daily temperature extremes from synoptic-scale atmospheric circulation patterns in the Australian region. *Climate Dynamics*, *13*(3), 223–234. doi:10.1007003820050162

Shao, Q., & Li, M. (2013). An improved statistical analogue downscaling procedure for seasonal precipitation forecast. *Stochastic Environmental Research and Risk Assessment*, *27*(4), 819–830. doi:10.100700477-012-0610-0

Sharma, K., & Virmani, J. (2017). A Decision Support System for Classification of Normal and Medical Renal Disease Using Ultrasound Images: A Decision Support System for Medical Renal Diseases. *International Journal of Ambient Computing and Intelligence*, *8*(2), 52–69. doi:10.4018/IJACI.2017040104

Simonovic, S. P. (2001). *Assessment of the Impact of Climate Variability and Change on the Reliability*.

Singh, P., & Borah, B. (2013). Indian summer monsoon rainfall prediction using artificial neural network. *Stochastic Environmental Research and Risk Assessment*, *27*(7), 1585–1599. doi:10.100700477-013-0695-0

Sivakumar, B. (2011). Global climate change and its impacts on water resources planning and management: Assessment and challenges. *Stochastic Environmental Research and Risk Assessment*, *25*(4), 583–600. doi:10.100700477-010-0423-y

Song, S., & Singh, V. P. (2010). Frequency analysis of droughts using the Plackett copula and parameter estimation by genetic algorithm. *Stochastic Environmental Research and Risk Assessment*, *24*(5), 783–805. doi:10.100700477-010-0364-5

Tatsumi, K., Oizumi, T., & Yamashiki, Y. (2014). Assessment of future precipitation indices in the Shikoku region using a statistical downscaling model. *Stochastic Environmental Research and Risk Assessment*, *28*(6), 1447–1464. doi:10.100700477-014-0847-x

Singh, V. P., Sharma, N., & Ojha, C. S. P. (Eds.). (2013). The Brahmaputra basin water resources. Springer.

von Storch, H. (2000). Review of Empirical Downscaling Techniques. *Reg. Clim. Dev. under Glob. Warm.*, *8*(9), 29-46.

Weichert, A., & Bürger, G. (1998). Linear versus nonlinear techniques in downscaling. *Climate Research, 10*(2), 83–93. doi:10.3354/cr010083

Wilby, R. L., Dawson, C. W., & Barrow, E. M. (2002). Sdsm — a Decision Support Tool for the Assessment of Regional Climate Change Impacts. *Environmental Modelling & Software, 17*(2), 145–157. doi:10.1016/S1364-8152(01)00060-3

Wilby, R. L., Hay, L. E., Gutowski, W. J. Jr, Arritt, R. W., Takle, E. S., Pan, Z., ... Clark, M. P. (2000). Hydrological responses to dynamically and statistically downscaled climate model output. *Geophysical Research Letters, 27*(8), 1199–1202. doi:10.1029/1999GL006078

Williams, R. J., & Zipser, D. (1989). Experimental analysis of the real-time recurrent learning algorithm. Connection Science, *1*(1), 87–111.

Xu, C.Y. (1999). From GCMs to river flow: a review of downscaling methods and hydrologic modelling approaches. *Prog. Phys. Geogr., 23*(2), 229-249.

Zaman Zad Ghavidel, S., & Montaseri, M. (2014). Application of different data-driven methods for the prediction of total dissolved solids in the Zarinehroud basin. *Stochastic Environmental Research and Risk Assessment, 28*(8), 2101–2118. doi:10.100700477-014-0899-y

Zorita, E., Hughes, J. P., Lettemaier, D. P., & Von Storch, H. (1995). Stochastic characterization of regional circulation patterns for climate model diagnosis and estimation of local precipitation. *Journal of Climate, 8*(5), 1023–1042. doi:10.1175/1520-0442(1995)008<1023:SCORCP>2.0.CO;2

This research was previously published in the International Journal of Applied Metaheuristic Computing (IJAMC), 10(1); pages 29-42, copyright year 2019 by IGI Publishing (an imprint of IGI Global).

Chapter 45
Residual Life Estimation of Humidity Sensor DHT11 Using Artificial Neural Networks

Pardeep Kumar Sharma
https://orcid.org/0000-0001-9191-2731
Lovely Professional University, India

Cherry Bhargava
Lovely Professional University, India

ABSTRACT

Electronic systems have become an integral part of our daily lives. From toy to radar, system is dependent on electronics. The health conditions of humidity sensor need to be monitored regularly. Temperature can be taken as a quality parameter for electronics systems, which work under variable conditions. Using various environmental testing techniques, the performance of DHT11 has been analysed. The failure of humidity sensor has been detected using accelerated life testing, and an expert system is modelled using various artificial intelligence techniques (i.e., Artificial Neural Network, Fuzzy Inference System, and Adaptive Neuro-Fuzzy Inference System). A comparison has been made between the response of actual and prediction techniques, which enable us to choose the best technique on the basis of minimum error and maximum accuracy. ANFIS is proven to be the best technique with minimum error for developing intelligent models.

INTRODUCTION TO RELIABILITY AND LIFE ESTIMATION

Across the globe, every industry is trying to lure the customers for electronics and electrical items and for that they need to provide better performance, high quality and low cost. Another factor which comes into picture is the Time To Market (TTM) for these products(Barnes, 1971). As competition is increasing day by day every sector or industry tries to launch their product as soon as possible because there may be chances that likewise product may get launched and industry may face great loss economically.

DOI: 10.4018/978-1-6684-2408-7.ch045

Another factor which is most important now-a-days is the "Reliability" of any system. All the big brands, big industry with repute are moving forward to develop as reliable system as possible to contribute to-wards customer's safety as well as to maintain the quality. Higher the brand, higher the cost, high is the Reliability(Neri, Allen, & Anderson, 1979). Generally, a big trade-off is they're between the Reliability, Cost and Time. The overall Life of any product has been depicted by Bath-Curve shown in Figure 1,

Figure 1. Bath Tub Curve for Product Life

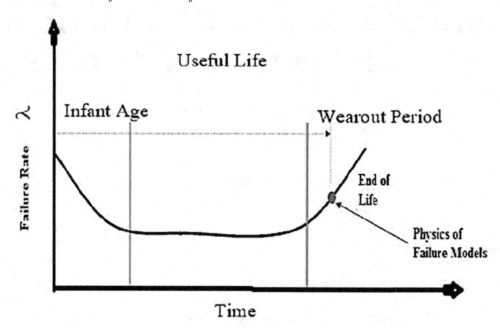

"Reliability" is the general term in our day-to-day life which means how much we can rely over that particular thing. Talking about electronics world than now-a-days this word has been a great buzz. This term is becoming so vast that we have one entire engineering stream with this name i.e. "Reliability Engineering". Now what is the meaning of term for an electronics Engineer. "It is the degree which tells how reliably a particular electronic system or component will work as it is expected to, in the specific or desired duration."

Now operational Reliability includes three parts:

1. Reliability, whether system is giving desired output or not.
2. Reliability, whether it's working fine under different environment.
3. Reliability, whether different conditions are not fluctuating the output.

If we go deeper in the Reliability then comes the term "Life Estimation or Prediction" Normally Prediction and Estimation are two different terms. Prediction is based on the historical observation or data available but Estimation is about the real time data available for that particular system. The data which we are using here is the data about that particular electronic component only that's why the topic recited as LIFE ESTIMATION. The meaning of this term is to estimate or observed the remaining useful Life (RUL) of that particular system under the various stressors we provide(Siddiqui & Çağlar, 1994).

Stressors are parameter, whose variation beyond the range could make the system fail. There are many categories of stressors i.e., Environmental stressors (Thermal Stressor), Electrical stressor (Voltage), Mechanical stressor (shock or vibration). More the stressor we select, more is the accuracy about failure or Life Estimation we get. If we talk about practical ground than it's very complicated to design the observation or experimental system to examine any component and more the parameters we add, more it get complicated. Mostly the big manufacturing companies only developed this kind of experiment setup because they want their selling product to be highly reliable and it is also the demand of the growing competition of the market. MTBF stands for Mean Time Between Failure, is the time duration for which the system is in operational state. In case of Repairable system, it is the total time component was active excluding the time for which it was under failure or under Maintenance and in case of Non-Repairable system, it is MTTF i.e., Mean Time to Failure as here we are not repairing. It is the time until which component meets its failure. 'Tool Life' or simple 'Life' of the component is the MTBF we calculate. Failure Rate is defined as the reciprocal of MTBF.

PARAMETERS AFFECTING RELIABILITY

There can be many parameters practically which tends to vary the Reliability graph. Factors affecting Reliability are mentioned below,

DESIGN FACTOR

Design plays major role in efficient operation of any system. Many time failures are observed not due to external changes but due to design faults such as voltage, current etc., these failures don't come under any prediction model and mostly it can't be handled at basic level since it needs changes in the design. Hence, careful designing must be done prior so to avoid any fault at design level(C Bhargava, Banga, & Singh, 2018).

COMPLEXITY

More complex the system less is its reliability as the operation becomes tough. A complete unit is a combination of many components, more the number of components, more complexes it becomes. Also, the reliability factor adds with increase in numbers of elements.

STRESS

One of the most prominent factors which affect the life of the component is stress. Factors for stress can be rise in current which tends to affect the temperature, vibration, voltage etc. Thermal stress is the parameter where special derating is needed as it tends to complete failure of the system as well. It this problem is quite prominent; coolers or fan should be used.

GENERIC (INHERENT) RELIABILITY

It involves selecting that component individually for which failure rate is very less. As the entire system is formed by individual components, it they would be having less failure rate, overall failure rate would reduce for the system(Lu & Christou, 2017). In case if we select high failure rate components, the overall reliability would decrease(Huston & Clarke, 1992).

DHT11 HUMIDITY SENSOR

The electronic component we have taken for observation is fabricated Humidity sensor cum Thermistor which is available in the market as DHT11. It's a resistive humidity sensor whose dielectric is made up of polymer. When the moisture level increase, the concentration of ions in the dielectric and in turn it decreases the resistance, which effect the voltage and hence these variation gives us relative Humidity and Temperature reading(Cherry Bhargava, Vijay kumar Banga, & Singh, 2018).

DHT11 is an Arduino compatible sensor hence we have used Arduino board for the experimental reading. The stressor parameter used here is temperature. The normal range if DHT11, is Humidity-[20-90] %RH, Temperature-[0-50] ^{0}celsius. That means this is the working range for this particular sensor(Korotcenkov, 2013). For checking the response, different temperatures have been provided to see the response as well the condition of the sensor until and unless it gets completely disfunction. Application of Humidity Sensor can be observed in many practical areas like soil-humidity detection, cold store monitoring, maintaining green-house, lie detector etc(Fei, Jiang, Liu, & Zhang, 2014).

CALCULATION OF TOOL LIFE

Calculation of DHT11 tool life is the main task we need to do. For calculating, Reliability, Failure Rate or MTBF we have many approaches shown in Figure 2,

EMPIRICAL METHOD

These methods are the one based on the analytical data collected from manufacturer, fields, Test laboratories etc. The most prominent set of such data is in MIL-HDBK-217, Bellcore, Prism etc. these are examples of Empirical method widely used by the Military purpose in twentieth century

Figure 2. Methods for Reliability Prediction

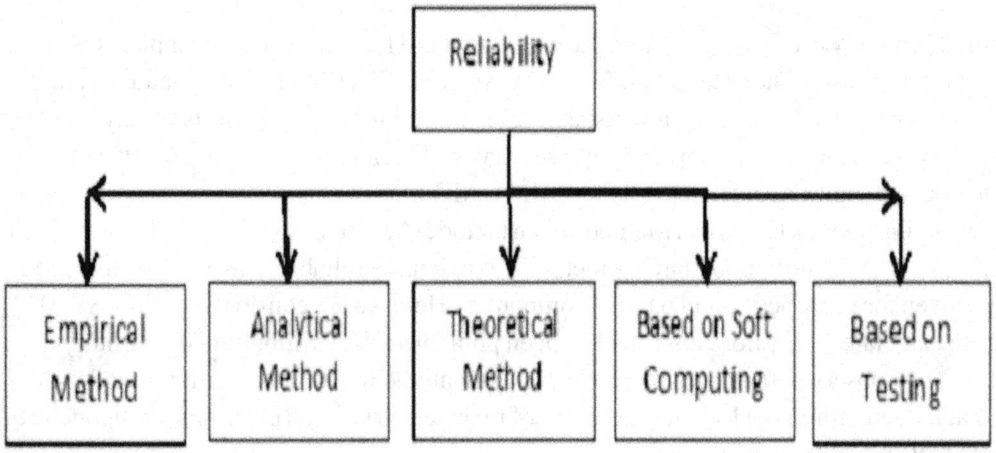

ANALYTICAL METHOD

Many numerical Models were developed for the prediction of Reliability or Failure rate which provides better results and this numerical Model comes under Analytical Methods for example FEM stands for Finite Element Methods where we look for the faulty characteristics of an element. Another one is Fault Tree Analysis (FTA), where in hierarchical ways we check for the faulty units in the entire system.

THEORETICAL MODEL

Normally, determining the failure of any model is tough and costly that's why we go for Physics of Failure approach which can deduce the reason of failure of any part by applying various models of physics to the data(Huston & Clarke, 1992). In real time application such as aeronautics where topology and environment changes abruptly, finding exact failure is very complexes hence there we can use theoretical Models.

APPROACH BASED ON SOFT COMPUTING MODELS

Here we used different Models or Intelligent Modelling techniques based on Artificial Intelligence like Artificial Neural Network, Adaptive Neuro-Fuzzy Inference System, Fuzzy Inference System Genetic Programming etc. Apart from this basic approach we have highly efficient approach like Monte Carlo Method, Naïve-Bayes etc. Along with this we can also apply hybrid approach which is a combination of two or more approaches(Gokulachandran & Mohandas, 2015).

BASED ON TESTING

This method is mainly used by big manufacturing unit where large number of samples or electrical units is subjected under tests. These tests can be environmental, Electrical, thermal and so on. For having reliable commercial product, better understanding of the failure mechanism is highly needed. Hence, thereby testing we get to know the exact failure reason or Model for any component. One of the examples of such testing is Highly Accelerated Life Testing (HALT).

For calculating we took Empirical Method which includes MIL-HDBK 217F, Bellcore, NTT Procedure etc. These all are Reliability book having methods to calculate reliability as well as directed reliability values are given for many active and passive component. Here we are considering MIL-HDBK217 F as a reference to calculate Tool Life. This book has been published by Washington D.C Military in year 1990 January, 2. They observed the data provided various manufacturers about the failure of the component and use that in predicting Tool Life or failure rate of many electrical and electronic component(Solomon, Sandborn, & Pecht, 2000).

For preparing an Intelligent Model we took Soft-computing approach using the various Artificial Intelligence techniques. Here we have taken Artificial Neural Network, Fuzzy Inference System and Adaptive Neuro-Fuzzy Inference System (ANFIS). Data set has been generated and feed to these techniques as an input and hence we get to know which technique is the most efficient(Wang, 2009).

NEED OF INTELLIGENT MODELLING

In today's world we need everything smart. Be it our vehicles, gadgets, home or surroundings(Venet, Perisse, El-Husseini, & Rojat, 2002). We want every system to be autonomous so that we could remove human intervention from their operation. This comfort leads to the basis of Intelligent Modelling, where we tend to developed intelligent model for every system(Wang, 2009). The basic terminology we required to understand for this id Artificial Intelligence. "Artificial Intelligence is the method or way where we try to provide intelligence or human like thinking capabilities to the machine or system through learning or any other method."

The approach to implement Artificial Intelligence is through Soft Computing where we have various algorithms that tend to make the system adaptive or intelligent or developed "Intelligent Model". The basic implementation approach one can take is Artificial Neural Network (ANN), Fuzzy Inference System (FIS), Adaptive Neuro-Fuzzy Inference System (ANFIS), Genetic Programming (GPs), Support Vector Machine (SVM) etc. In this work we have taken first three approaches to implement the Intelligent Model for our designed sensor(Chen, Zhang, Vachtsevanos, & Orchard, 2011).

MODELLING OF INTELLIGENT SYSTEM USING ARTIFICIAL NEURAL NETWORK (ANN)

As the world is getting modernized, we are moving more towards intelligent system which could work same way as human use to do. We are searching for method which could remove or reject human intervention by developing intelligent system. Here, our first method is Artificial Neural Network (ANN). Artificial Neural Network is an analogous system of human neural network which tries to mimic the functioning of actual brain. Input data along with target data has been fed to the network. Activation function has been provided to start the process where system learns by itself how output is coming(Cherry Bhargava & Handa, 2018). The system gets train with the number of epochs we specified. The system will train itself and reduce the error after every epoch and hence after specific number of epochs we get the best result(Rajeev, Dinakaran, & Singh, 2017). The ANN based figure is shown below,

Figure 3. Artificial Neural Network

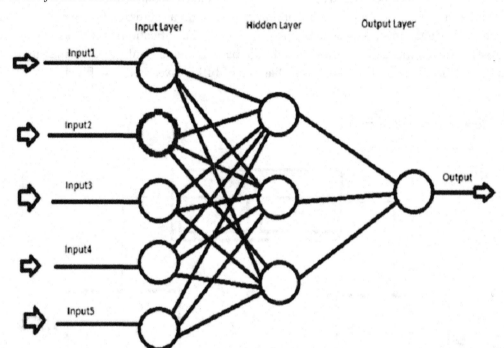

MODELLING THROUGH FUZZY INFERENCE SYSTEM

Fuzzy Inference System or Fuzzy Logic is used to handle Ambiguity and Uncertainty in Data(Lefik, 2013). As the complexity increases, we can't make exact statement about the behaviour of the system as in the traditional method we were using Binary Logic which says 0 or 1, i.e., YES or NO, but the real-world problems are beyond as it can't be TRUE or FALSE only(Hayward & Davidson, 2003). Taking water Problem than the possible answer could be hot, cold, slightly cold, slightly hot, extremely cold, extremely hot etc.(Hayward & Davidson, 2003)

For this purpose, we deal with Linguistic variables in fuzzy which are user understandable. Entire input set is known as Crisp Set which after fuzzification converts into fuzzy sets(Jiao, Lei, Pei, & Lee, 2004). Here we use the concept of Membership function, it defines the membership of particular input value in the fuzzy sets, and its range is from 0 to 1. If input value has complete membership, it is 1 otherwise it can be any value in this range(Kirby & Chen, 2007). If we have fuzzy set A than considering the Universal set, X can be defined as, **A= {(x, μ_A(x))|x$\in$ X},** where μ_A is known as A's Membership

Function. In FIS we defined certain rules for fuzzification to defines crisp relation into Fuzzy relation in IF, THEN, ELSE format e.g.

IF (f is x_1, x_2.....a_n) THEN (g is y_1, y_2....y_n) ELSE (g is z_1, z_2....z_n)

This fuzzified data goes to decision-making unit which decides about the membership function and hence attached the related linguistic Variable for that particular value(Aronson, Liang, & Turban, 2005). The fuzzy output from this block directly goes to defuzzifier Interface unit, which is reverse of Fuzzifier. And hence after this block we get proper output in Crisp set form as defuzzifier convert fuzzy set back to crisp set(Virk, Muhammad, & Martinez-Enriquez, 2008). Fuzzification as well as defuzzification unit are assisted by knowledge base which has design base as well as Rule base for making rules and modifying data(Chen et al., 2011). The Block Diagram of FIS is given below in Figure 4,

Figure 4. Block Diagram of Fuzzy Inference System

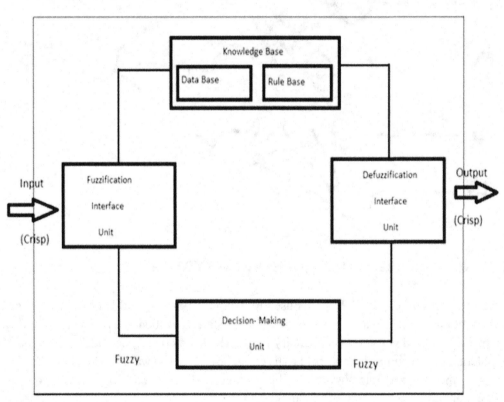

MODELLING THROUGH ADAPTIVE NEURO-FUZZY INFERENCE SYSTEM (ANFIS)

ANFIS is a hybrid technique comprises both ANN as well as Fuzzy Tool. It has advantage of both the technique as ANN has this self-learning mechanism but it doesn't know how the hidden process is following to reach the particular target and the disadvantage is that the output is not that user understandable also, need very precise and accurate(Manogaran, Varatharajan, & Priyan, 2018). It can't handle ambiguity(Chen et al., 2011). On the other hand, the advantage with Fuzzy logic is that it can handle uncertain data and also, we use linguistic variable to have better understanding but no self-learning is there(Jiao et al., 2004). Hence to omit each other advantages, these two techniques have been combined to formed third technique that is ANFIS (Adaptive neuro-fuzzy Inference system). Here the rules needed by fuzzy get self-updated through the self-learning mechanism possessed by ANN(Parler, 1999). That's why a smaller number of errors is shown by the predicted Data of ANFIS. The basic structure of ANFIS is shown in the figure 5 below,

Figure 5. Adaptive Neuro-Fuzzy Inference System

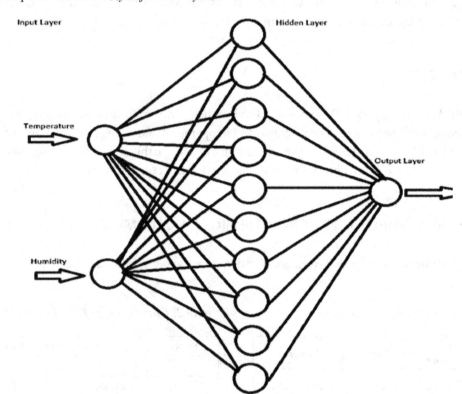

COMPONENTS AND TOOLS USED

Components Used

In this section, all the electrical equipment's, Chemicals, Lab instruments and components and software tools used for this work are mentioned,

TOOLS USED

Matlab

MATLAB stands for Matrix Laboratory, tools comprise Simulator as well as programming window, used for computation, integration, designing graphical user Interface(Simulink & Natick, 1993). It is highly used in the field like Communication, Machine Learning, Reliability Prediction, Digital Signal Processing etc. MATLAB Simulink is an in-built Window comprises many Interfaces like Neural Network, Fuzzy logic, Neuro- Fuzzy etc. The programming Interface has Editor Window to write the program, Command History stores all the related variables, matrix etc. Command Window is used for running the programming and Workspace is used load all the necessary matrix, xls. file etc. Here, are working on both Interfaces. ANN and ANFIS on MATLAB SIMULINK and MATLAB Programming Interface for Naïve-Bayes Classifier Algorithm.

ARDUINO 1.6.13

Arduino 1.6.13 is an Integrated Development Environment Tool with Java as basic for programming which is used to write basic programme related to the operation and to load it on Arduino-Board. Our digital sensor DHT11 is an Arduino compatible sensor. We can run this software on Windows OSX, Mac and Linux. We have used DHT library for programming to have compatible function to run the coding.

ELECTRICAL COMPONENTS AND CHEMICAL EQUIPMENT USED

Electrical components used for this work are mentioned in the table 1 and table 2 as below,

Table 1. Electrical Component Used

Sr. No.	Component Name	Numbers	Company
1.	DHT-11 sensor	3	D-robotics
2.	LCD	1	Blaze Display
3.	Resistor (2.2 K)	2	Reckon Electronics
4.	Connecting Wires	14	----------
5.	Arduino-Board	1	Bharthi Electronics
6.	PC	1	Personal computer

Table 2. Chemicals and Equipment Used

Sr. No.	Chemical or Equipment
1.	Zinc-Oxide
2.	Carbon Black
3.	Pottasium Bromide (KBr)
4.	Mortar Pestle
5.	Hydraulic Pelletizer
6.	Spatula
7.	Petri-Dish
8.	Hot air Oven

EXPERIMENTAL SETUP FOR DHT11

The experimental set up for calculating Data set of DHT11 comprises one computer system which has Arduino Library as well as software installed in it, an Arduino board, Bread –board, DHT11 sensor, LCD-Display, 2.2K resistors and connecting wires. For giving the overview of connection an image is shown below(Aggarwal & Bhargava, 2016),

Figure 6. DHT11 Experiment

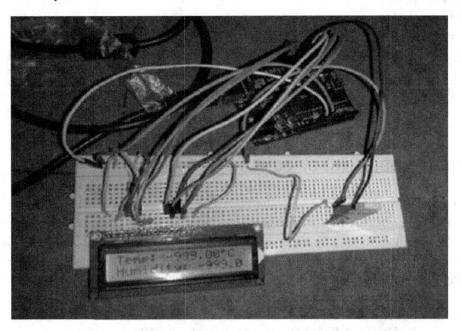

According to DHT11 commercial manual range its normal operating range is 0 to 50 degrees and for Humidity it is 20 to 90%RH, that's why for failure mechanism it was necessary to provide temperature more than this range. Behaviour of sensor has been keenly observed for entire range until and unless it's been immediately failed at 60%. Temperature has been increased through hot dryer and sample of sand whose temperature has been increased every time up to specified limit and their temperature has been measured through Hygrometer(Cherry Bhargava et al., 2018). In spite of having range up to 50-degree, sensor was working normally uptill 63 degree. It started showing deflection at 64 and completely failed at 68 degree. For checking the sensor at lower temperature, it has been kept in ice box keeping in mind that it didn't get drenched because of that.

Talking about Humidity which has been observed by keeping sensor in air-tight box along with calcium carbonate powder. More the concentration of the powder, more the humidity it absorbed. Like-wise, Humidity is increased through keeping the sensor in air-tight box having glass of ho6t water in it which increases the humidity level uptill 99%RH. Talking about effect of Humidity then only long exposure to high humidity can affect the health of sensor. If momentarily exposure is considered than it may not cause any harm unlike temperature. Long exposure can cause rusting to the contact pin of the sensor(Nazari, Kashanian, Moradipour, & Maleki, 2018).

TOOL LIFE CALCULATION

For Tool Life Calculation, Military Handbook i.e. MIL-HDBK217 F has been used to provide numerical model which gives equation for failure rate i.e.

$$\Lambda_p = \lambda_b \pi_T \pi_A \pi_Q \pi_E, \text{ Failure}/10^6 \text{ hours}$$

where, Λ_p = Overall Failure rate
λ_b = Base Failure Rate.
π_T = Temperature Factor.
π_Q = Quality Factor.
π_E = Environment factor.

None of the value has been given directly. Each of the above parameter involve numerical analysis and formula to predict exact value or tool Life at that particular Temperature(Kötz, Hahn, & Gallay, 2006).

INTELLIGENT MODELLING OF SENSOR

Since the era of Artificial Intelligence has started, every other observed system is there on its way to become smart or analogous to Human. Intelligent Modelling has become the base of every new upcoming technology. With Reliability also Manufacturers are moving towards developing an intelligent system that could sense its need, behaviour and it should be able to perform all the analysis required. Here also we are trying to utilize different Artificial Intelligence technique to develop successful model which could estimate the Life for the sensor we designed.

A Guide How To Use Artificial Neural Network (ANN)

Let us take a case of DHT 11 where input parameters are five, output parameter is single(Seth, 2014). An expert system is designed using following steps:

1. Right click on workspace---new----name it
    Three files will be created in workspace, one for input, one for sample (only one column of input), one for output
    Click on name, a workspace will be opened
    Paste the excel data (transpose form) into the worksheet
2. Function--->nntool
3. Click on input data---import
4. Click on input---import data (for sample)
5. Click on target—import data (output)
6. Click on networks--new
7. Click on network1---open
8. Train the sample
9. Simulate

Input---sample

Change name of output

Then simulate

10. Click on network1_output

Export—select all

11. Export and it will be in workspace

A GUIDE HOW TO USE FUZZY LOGIC (FL)

Let us take a case of DHT11 where input parameters are five, output parameter is single. An expert system is designed using fuzzy logic as per following steps:

1. Open MATLAB Toolbox
2. Open fuzzy using "Fuzzy" command in the command window of MATLAB toolbox.
3. Fuzzy editor window will get open.
4. Now, add the number of inputs as per the number of input variables using "Edit" menu. In the edit menu, go to "Add variable" and then select "input or output according to number of inputs and output.

   The selected number of inputs will be available on FIS editor window. Rename the inputs by changing the name in dialog box beyond the "Name" that is shown below the Fuzzy structure.

   In the same way, name of another input and output can be changed.
5. In the next step, the input data and the output data are loaded in the input variables and output variables in the form of linguistic variables by selecting the particular variable. The variable will be selected by double clicking that particular variable and the membership function editor window will get open(Manogaran et al., 2018).

   The membership function can be of any types such as triangular, Gaussian or trap etc and one of all these types will be selected according to the range of loaded data. The name of membership functions can also be changed using "Add MFs" from the edit menu.

   The name and range of membership functions is changed by selecting each membership function. The range of the input variables is also changed by editing the range in the edit box named as "Range" as shown below.

   In the same way, the range and name of the membership functions of all the inputs and output will be changed as per the range of data.
6. After editing all the input and output variables, the rules are defined using edit menu and then rules.

   A rule editor window gets open after selecting the rules by right click.

   Rules are defined for each combination of inputs with the output such as when both inputs (time and temperature) are at low range, the output (life) will be high.

   Similarly, rules will be defined for every combination of inputs and output such as if the input have 3 membership functions low, medium and high & if the output also have 3 membership functions the 3*3 = 9 rules will be formed.

7. Once all the rules are defined, the output is verified by viewing the rule viewer using view menu and then select "Rules".
    Rule viewer window gets open and from this window output is obtained by giving the input data ranges in the input dialog box(Mansouri, Gholampour, Kisi, & Ozbakkaloglu, 2018).

A GUIDE FOR ADAPTIVE NEURO FUZZY INFERENCE SYSTEM (ANFIS)

Let us take a case of DHT11 where input parameters are five, output parameter is single. An expert system is designed using ANFIS as per following steps:

1. Open MATLAB and ANFIS window by command anfisedit
2. Right side, workspace is there. Right click---new----name
    Double click- open excel
    Copy paste own data
    Close it.
3. After writing >>anfisedit
4. Load data----training--- wrksp--- click on load data
5. Generate FIS
    Select membership function ---gaussian
    MF type-linear
6. Train now---epochs-50
7. Test FIS
8. Click on Structure
9. Edit—FIS editor (to change name and range)
10. Edit—membership function
11. Edit---rules
12. View-surface
13. View-rule (for output values)

You can get new output, by changing input. Using intelligent modelling techniques, the failure of DHT11 can be very well pre-accessed and necessary replacement of the components can be done before the actual destruction of the whole system.

REFERENCES

Aggarwal, J., & Bhargava, C. (2016). Reliability Prediction of Soil Humidity Sensor using Parts Count Analysis Method. *Indian Journal of Science and Technology*, *9*(47).

Aronson, J. E., Liang, T.-P., & Turban, E. (2005). *Decision support systems and intelligent systems*. Pearson Prentice-Hall.

Barnes, F. (1971). *Component Reliability*. Springer.

Bhargava, Banga, & Singh. (2018). Failure prediction of humidity sensor DHT11 using various environmental testing techniques. *Journal of Materials and Environmental Sciences, 9*(7), 243-252.

Bhargava, C., Banga, V., & Singh, Y. (2018). Mathematical Modelling and Residual Life Prediction of an Aluminium Electrolytic Capacitor. *Pertanika Journal of Science & Technology, 26*(2), 785–798.

Bhargava, C., & Handa, M. (2018). An Intelligent Reliability Assessment technique for Bipolar Junction Transistor using Artificial Intelligence Techniques. *Pertanika Journal of Science & Technology, 26*(4).

Chen, C., Zhang, B., Vachtsevanos, G., & Orchard, M. (2011). Machine condition prediction based on adaptive neuro–fuzzy and high-order particle filtering. *IEEE Transactions on Industrial Electronics, 58*(9), 4353–4364. doi:10.1109/TIE.2010.2098369

Fei, T., Jiang, K., Liu, S., & Zhang, T. (2014). Humidity sensors based on Li-loaded nanoporous polymers. *Sensors and Actuators. B, Chemical, 190*, 523–528. doi:10.1016/j.snb.2013.09.013

Gokulachandran, J., & Mohandas, K. (2015). Comparative study of two soft computing techniques for the prediction of remaining useful life of cutting tools. *Journal of Intelligent Manufacturing, 26*(2), 255–268. doi:10.100710845-013-0778-2

Hayward, G., & Davidson, V. (2003). Fuzzy logic applications. *Analyst (London), 128*(11), 1304–1306. doi:10.1039/b312701j PMID:14700220

Huston, H. H., & Clarke, C. P. (1992). *Reliability defect detection and screening during processing-theory and implementation.* Paper presented at the IEEE 30th Annual Symposium on International Reliability Physics, San Diego, CA.

Jiao, Y., Lei, S., Pei, Z., & Lee, E. (2004). Fuzzy adaptive networks in machining process modeling: Surface roughness prediction for turning operations. *International Journal of Machine Tools & Manufacture, 44*(15), 1643–1651. doi:10.1016/j.ijmachtools.2004.06.004

Kirby, E. D., & Chen, J. C. (2007). Development of a fuzzy-nets-based surface roughness prediction system in turning operations. *Computers & Industrial Engineering, 53*(1), 30–42. doi:10.1016/j.cie.2006.06.018

Korotcenkov, G. (2013). Chemical Sensors: Simulation and Modeling: Vol. 5. *Electrochemical Sensors.* Momentum Press.

Kötz, R., Hahn, M., & Gallay, R. (2006). Temperature behavior and impedance fundamentals of supercapacitors. *Journal of Power Sources, 154*(2), 550–555. doi:10.1016/j.jpowsour.2005.10.048

Lefik, M. (2013). Some aspects of application of artificial neural network for numerical modeling in civil engineering. *Bulletin of the Polish Academy of Sciences. Technical Sciences, 61*(1), 39–50. doi:10.2478/bpasts-2013-0003

Lu, Y., & Christou, A. (2017). Lifetime Estimation of Insulated Gate Bipolar Transistor Modules Using Two-step Bayesian Estimation. *IEEE Transactions on Device and Materials Reliability, 17*(2), 414–421. doi:10.1109/TDMR.2017.2694158

Manogaran, G., Varatharajan, R., & Priyan, M. (2018). Hybrid recommendation system for heart disease diagnosis based on multiple kernel learning with adaptive neuro-fuzzy inference system. *Multimedia Tools and Applications*, *77*(4), 4379–4399. doi:10.100711042-017-5515-y

Mansouri, I., Gholampour, A., Kisi, O., & Ozbakkaloglu, T. (2018). Evaluation of peak and residual conditions of actively confined concrete using neuro-fuzzy and neural computing techniques. *Neural Computing & Applications*, *29*(3), 873–888. doi:10.100700521-016-2492-4

Nazari, M., Kashanian, S., Moradipour, P., & Maleki, N. (2018). A novel fabrication of sensor using ZnO-Al2O3 ceramic nanofibers to simultaneously detect catechol and hydroquinone. *Journal of Electroanalytical Chemistry*, *812*, 122–131. doi:10.1016/j.jelechem.2018.01.058

Neri, L., Allen, V., & Anderson, R. (1979). Reliability based quality (RBQ) technique for evaluating the degradation of reliability during manufacturing. *Microelectronics and Reliability*, *19*(1-2), 117–126. doi:10.1016/0026-2714(79)90369-X

Parler, S. G. (1999). *Thermal modeling of aluminum electrolytic capacitors*. Paper presented at the IEEE 34th Annual Meeting on Industry Applications Conference, Phoenix, AZ. 10.1109/IAS.1999.799180

Rajeev, D., Dinakaran, D., & Singh, S. (2017). Artificial neural network based tool wear estimation on dry hard turning processes of AISI4140 steel using coated carbide tool. *Bulletin of the Polish Academy of Sciences. Technical Sciences*, *65*(4), 553–559. doi:10.1515/bpasts-2017-0060

Seth, S. (2014). MExS A Fuzzy Rule Based Medical Expert System To Diagnose The Diseases. *IOSR Journal of Engineering*, *4*(7), 57–62. doi:10.9790/3021-04735762

Siddiqui, M., & Çağlar, M. (1994). Residual lifetime distribution and its applications. *Microelectronics and Reliability*, *34*(2), 211–227. doi:10.1016/0026-2714(94)90104-X

Solomon, R., Sandborn, P. A., & Pecht, M. G. (2000). Electronic part life cycle concepts and obsolescence forecasting. *IEEE Transactions on Components and Packaging Technologies*, *23*(4), 707–717. doi:10.1109/6144.888857

Venet, P., Perisse, F., El-Husseini, M., & Rojat, G. (2002). Realization of a smart electrolytic capacitor circuit. *IEEE Industry Applications Magazine*, *8*(1), 16–20. doi:10.1109/2943.974353

Virk, S. M., Muhammad, A., & Martinez-Enriquez, A. (2008). *Fault prediction using artificial neural network and fuzzy logic*. Paper presented at the IEEE Seventh Mexican International Conference on Artificial Intelligence (MICAI'08), Atizapan de Zaragoza, Mexico. 10.1109/MICAI.2008.38

Wang, X. (2009). *Intelligent modeling and predicting surface roughness in end milling*. Paper presented at the IEEE Fifth International Conference on Natural Computation (ICNC'09), Tianjin, China.

Chapter 46
Investigation of the Attitudes for Environment and Evaluation of Artificial Neural Networks

Semra Benzer
Education Faculty, Gazi University, Turkey

Recep Benzer
Cyber Security, Ostim Technical University, Turkey

Şule Bozkurt
Graduate School of Educational Science, Gazi University, Turkey

ABSTRACT

This study was conducted to evaluate the attitudes of the students in a secondary school in Aksaray towards the environment according to some variables. The research group of the study was constituted of 426 students who were attending in the 1st, 2nd, 3rd, and 4th grade at a secondary school in the academic year of 2015-2016. The research done by using environmental attitude scale concluded that the secondary students have a positive attitude towards the environment. It was found that there was a meaningful difference according to gender, age group, father profession status, mother profession status. It was also concluded that students did not differ according to mother education level, father education level, grade level, family income level, and number of siblings variables. Similar evaluations were made with artificial neural networks. In this study, it has been shown that artificial neural networks can be used in the studies conducted in the field of education.

INTRODUCTION

The concept of environment is a very wide and diverse concept. Keleş and Hamamcı (1998) defined the concept of environment as the total of physical, chemical, biological and social factors which directly or indirectly affect human activities and live assets immediately or in a certain time. Özey (2001) defined

DOI: 10.4018/978-1-6684-2408-7.ch046

the concept of environment as the environment in which human or any other living thing live. In another definition, it is stated that living beings are connected to and affected by vital ties and also affected by various ways (Güney, 2004).

Attitudes are not only a behavioural tendency or a feeling; they are also the integration of cognition, emotion and behaviour tendency. Attitude is a tendency attributed to an individual that regularly forms thoughts, feelings and behaviours about a psychological object (Kağıtçıbaşı, 2010).

The way to use the environment we live in more effectively and efficiently is to reveal a social structure of environmentally conscious individuals. This can be achieved by training in this context; environmental education is of great importance.

The aim of environmental education is to raise awareness of all segments of the society about the environment, to provide positive and lasting behavioural changes and to ensure the active participation of individuals. For this reason, an education method that will enable individuals to participate actively in environmental issues, react to negativity, understand the fact that individual interests cannot be considered apart from social interests, and the education system aiming at public participation will improve the thinking and decision-making power of the masses. Environmental education should not only provide information and a sense of responsibility, but also influence human behaviour. The aim of the efforts to protect, develop and improve the environment is to provide opportunities for living in a healthier and safer environment. The desired and successful results in terms of the environment are directly related to the human element. This is possible by educating and developing people in the environment. Human awareness and development can be achieved by providing the necessary knowledge and skills (Ministry of Environment and Forestry, 2004; Ünlü, 1995).

Secondary education provides the individual with a lot of cognitive skills such as literacy, problem solving and the basis for success in life. These are extremely important skills in the relationship between the environment and the individual. The knowledge, skills and values to be gained in secondary education constitute the basis for upper education steps. The aims of the secondary education were grouped under four headings: Personal, human relations, economic life and social life. When the sub-objectives under these four main topics are examined, it is seen that there are some goals related to ecological culture, environmental awareness, environmental attitudes and behaviours, cleanliness and thriftiness. Education in secondary education; It is aimed to educate individuals who love and respect the nature, protect plants and animals, are aware of the natural beauty around and endeavours to improve the environment, are sensitive to environmental problems, have environmental awareness (Vural, 2003).

Questionnaires also became useful tools for studies with low budget, helping them plan correctly the next semesters without excessive spending. It was very valuable to predict the next prefer that each student would choose, and it could be achieved by using questionnaires. In that direction the contribution of Artificial Neural Networks (ANNs) was remarkable (Matzavela et al., 2017). ANNs are directed graphs with weights and they are used, apart from education, in weather forecasting, predicting earthquakes, calculating the financial risk of a loan, in automatic pilots, in stock exchange.

The purpose of this research is to be able to make an effective prediction regarding the attitudes of the students in a secondary school in Aksaray towards the environment according to some variables with ANNs which is used as an effective prediction method in various sectors and as an alternative for traditional methods in the field of education.

BACKGROUND

Due to the increasing environmental problems, it has become necessary to identify the attitudes of individuals towards the environment and find solutions to solve the problems. Although the original studies in these areas will increase the sensitivity of the societies to the environment, they will provide important steps in minimizing the time spent on solving the problems and the environment. At the beginning of these steps, determining the attitudes towards the environment and giving the necessary training to the individuals are significant. Some research was conducted to examine the environmental attitudes of students studying in Turkey as secondary school level (Ayhan, 1999; İşyar, 1999; Morgil et al., 2002; Tuncer et al., 2004; Yılmaz et al., 2004; Atasoy, 2005; Kaya and Turan, 2005; Ürey, 2005; Alp et al., 2006; Gökçe et al., 2007; Tecer, 2007; Alp et al., 2008; Aslan et al., 2008; Atasoy and Ertürk 2008; Meydan and Doğu, 2008; Sağır et al., 2008; Ünal, 2009; Özpınar, 2009; Aslanyolu, 2010; Baş, 2010; Yaman et al., 2010, Aydın et al., 2011).

ANNs are mathematical models inspired by biological neural networks contained in human brain. Having similar characteristics to those of biological neural networks, these systems attempt to learn tasks and determine how they will react to new tasks by means of creating their own experiences through the data obtained by using the predetermined samples (Sagiroglu et al., 2003). The implementation of a user-friendly software tool based on neural network classifiers was described for predicting the student's performance in the course of Mathematics of the first year of Lyceum (Livieris et al., 2012). Neural networks were also used to predict MBA (Master of Business Administration) student success (Naik et al., 2004). The authors classified applicants to MBA program into successful and marginal student pools based on undergraduate GPA (Grade Point Average), undergraduate major, age, GMAT (Graduate Management Admission Test) score using a neural network with three layers. There is some educational research (Naik and Ragothaman, 2004; Lykourentzou et al., 2009; Paliwal et al., 2009; Livieris et al., 2012; Oancea et al., 2013; Kardan et al., 2013; Khan and Kulkarni, 2013; Naser et al., 2015; Yorek and Ugulu, 2015; Bahadır, 2016; Özdemir and Polat, 2017; Matzavela et al., 2017) related to artificial neural networks. The great advantage of neural networks is that they can be used to make predictions in several aspects in education. Using neural networks and analyzing parameters such as student satisfaction, can lead to high prediction accuracy (Kardan et al, 2013).

MAIN FOCUS OF THE CHAPTER

In general, the results obtained from the studies reveal the existence of important problems in environmental education. The disruption of environmental education and its ineffectiveness prevent the steps to be taken to protect the environment and solve the environmental problems. At the basis of raising individuals who have sufficient environmental awareness, individuals are expected to gain positive attitudes towards the environment. It is of great importance to determine the views, sensitivities, awareness and attitudes of the students in Aksaray, in which environmental problems are rare but this does not mean that they will not happen in the future. It is observed that the studies on the views of the students in Aksaray province are very few. As a result of the research, students' positive attitude towards the environment has emerged.

It has been found that there is no study evaluating the environmental attitudes of the secondary students in Aksaray when the literature is examined. The study is the first from this point of view. It has been accepted in the scientific world that the studies which evaluated the environmental attitudes of the students according to various independent variables have made important contributions to the environmental education which has gained importance with the increase in environmental problems.

This research is important in that it sheds light on a less studied subject in Turkey to contribute to increasing the awareness of secondary school students towards environment. This research was conducted to determine the attitudes of the students in a secondary school in the city center of Aksaray.

The purpose of this research is to be able to make an effective prediction regarding the attitudes of the students in a secondary school in Aksaray towards the environment according to some variables with ANNs which is used as an effective prediction method in various sectors and as an alternative to traditional methods in the field of education.

The following questions were asked in this study: (1) What are the attitudes of secondary school students towards the environment? (2) Do the environmental attitude scores of secondary school students in terms of

- Gender,
- Age group,
- Mother education level,
- Father education level,
- Mother profession status,
- Father profession status,
- Family income level,
- Number of siblings,

change according to its parameters?

METHODOLOGY

In the study, "Environmental Attitude Scale" which was developed by Atasoy (2005) was used to determine the attitudes of primary school students towards the environment. Survey model is based on the quantitative stage and it is convenient to general survey model. The qualitative research is based on the views of the participants or the interests, skills, abilities, attitudes, etc. of a topic or event which are usually based on larger samples than on other studies (Büyüköztürk et al., 2011).

Qualitative data obtained from student answers to open-ended questions were used to train and test the ANNs model. 70% of this data was used for training of the network and the remaining 30% was used for testing the network (Hagan et al., 1996).

Likert-scale survey is usually in a non-numeric form. For neural network training, responses were converted to the range of 0 to 1. The mapping shown in Table 1 was used. It was used for the traditional education approach by 1-5 numerical values for the Likert-scale.

The body of an artificial neuron then sums the weighted inputs, bias and "processes" the sum with a transfer function. In the end, an artificial neuron passes the processed information via output(s). the benefit of artificial neuron model (Krenker et al., 2011) simplicity can be seen in its mathematical description below:

Table 1. Likert-scala value

Value	Normalized for ANNs	Traditional Value
1	0.24	1
2	0.42	2
3	0.58	3
4	0.74	4
5	0.90	5

$$y\left(k\right) = F \cdot \left(\sum_{i=0}^{m} w_i\left(k\right) \cdot x_i\left(k\right) \right)$$

Where:

$w_i(k)$ is weight value in discrete time k where i goes from 0 to m,
$x_i(k)$ is input value in discrete time k where i goes from 0 to m,
F is a transfer function,
$y_i(k)$ is output value in discrete time k.

Neural network consists of three layers (Figure 1). The first layer has k input neurons which send data via connection links to the second layer of M hidden neurons, and then via more connection links to the third layer of output neurons. The number of neurons in the input layer is usually based on the number of features in a data set. The second layer is also called the hidden layer.

Figure 1. Artificial neural networks model diagram

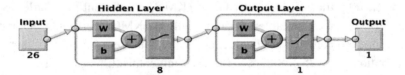

The supervised learning method trained with the network structure (Back-propagation Networks) will be used to solve the problems in this study. The transfer function, (VN is normalized data, VN is data to be normalized, Vmin is the minimum value of the data, Vmax is the maximum value of the data) mostly used as a sigmoid or a logistic function, gives values in the range of [0,1] and can be described as (normalization):

$$V_N = 0.8 \times \left(\frac{V_R - V_{min}}{V_{max} - V_{min}} \right) + 0.1$$

MATLAB is a multi-paradigm numerical calculation software and fourth generation programming language. Neural Network Toolbox of MATLAB was used for the ANNs calculations. The coefficient correlation (R2) was calculated by MATLAB.

The correlation between two variables numerically describes whether larger and smaller average values of one variable are related to larger or smaller than average values of the other variable. It measures the strength and direction of a linear relationship between two variables and can be described as:

$$r = \left(R^2\right) = cor\left(x, y\right) = \frac{\sum\left(x_i - \bar{x}\right)\left(y_i - \bar{y}\right)}{\sqrt{\left(x_i - \bar{x}\right)^2 \left(y_i - \bar{y}\right)^2}}$$

It has been determined the correlation coefficient into "weak," "moderate," or "strong" relationship. While researchers would agree that a coefficient of <0.1 indicates a negligible and >0.9 a very strong relationship. For example, a correlation coefficient of 0.65 could either be interpreted as a "good" or "moderate" correlation, depending on the applied rule of thumb.

Research Sample

The study group of the research consisted of male and female total 426 students who were studying on the 1st, 2nd, 3rd and 4th grade at one of the secondary schools in Aksaray, Turkey in 2015-2016 academic year. Random sampling method was used in the sample selection. The personal information of the students participating in the study is given in Table 2.

Data Collection Tool

In the study, "Environmental Attitude Scale" which was developed by Atasoy (2005) was used to determine the attitudes of primary school students towards the environment. Firstly, the data obtained from this study were checked by the Kaiser Meyer Olkin (KMO) coefficient and Barlett Sphericity test to determine whether the data were suitable for factor analysis (KMO coefficient .85 and Barlett test for significance = .000 p <.001) and it was concluded that the data were suitable for factor analysis.

When the distribution of the 25 problems in the environmental attitude scale is examined; 5 questions include animals and plants, 5 questions ecological problems and environmental pollution, 5 questions consumption and prudence, 5 questions human - environment relations and environmental sensitivity, and 5 questions include energy resources and energy use. Taking into account the calculation of the range of width of the scale with the formula of "sequence width / number of groups to be performed" (Tekin, 2002), the arithmetic mean intervals used in the evaluation of the research findings; "1.00-1.80 = Strongly Disagree", "1.81-2.60 = Disagree", "2.61-3.40 = Unstable", "3.41-4.20 = Agree" and "4.21-5.00 = Strongly Agree".

Table 2. Personal information of secondary school students participating in the study

Parameters	Demographic Properties	Number of Student (n=426)	Total (%100)
Gender	Male	204	48.2
	Female	221	51.8
Age Group	9-11 years old	157	37.0
	11-13 years old	163	38.4
	13-15 years old	102	24.0
	15-16 years old	2	0.47
Class	Fifth grade	154	36.2
	Sixth grade	99	23.2
	Seventh grade	79	18.5
	Eighth grade	93	21.8
Mother education level	Primary education	347	92.2
	Secondary education	26	6.9
	University	3	0.7
Father education level	Primary education	293	60.5
	Secondary education	91	23.0
	University	11	2.7
Mother profession status	Officer	4	0.9
	Worker	42	10.0
	Retired	2	0.4
	Housewife	395	94.7
Father profession status	Officer	12	2.9
	Worker	235	57.7
	Self-employment	140	34.3
	Retired	19	4.6
Family income level	< 1000 ₺	137	33.4
	1000 - 2000 ₺	211	51.5
	2000 - 3000 ₺	43	10.5
	> 3000 ₺	17	4.1
Number of siblings	<= 2 sibling	144	34.0
	2-4 sibling	182	43.0
	4-6 sibling	70	16.5
	6-8 sibling	22	5.2
	>= 8 sibling	5	1.18

Data Analysis

The data of the study was obtained by applying the environmental attitude scale to the students in a secondary school in the province of Aksaray in the second semester of the 2015/2016 academic year. The application took place in about 20 minutes, taking into account the principle of volunteering. Arithmetic mean and standard deviation values were used in the analysis of environmental attitudes of secondary school students.

It was determined by "t-test for Independent Samples" whether the attitudes of secondary school students towards the environment differed significantly by gender variable. One-Way Variance Analysis (ANOVA) was used to determine whether there is a significant difference between secondary school students' attitudes towards environment according to variables of age group, class level, mother education level, father education level, mother profession status, father profession status, family income level and number of siblings. Tukey HSD was used to determine the statistical differences between the two groups. The statistical significance of the scale was 0.05.

In this research, an effective prediction is made regarding the research data with ANNs approach. The Correlation ($R2$) is any statistical association, though in common usage it most often refers to how close two variables are to having a linear relationship with each other. The correlation values obtained by ANNs will be analysed and the existence of the relationship ($R2$) between the variables will be evaluated.

The correlation value ($R2$) obtained by the ANNs was compared with the statistical relationship value.

RESULTS

Table 3 shows the arithmetic averages and standard deviations of secondary school students' attitudes towards the environment for item-based scores.

As shown in Table 4, the arithmetic mean of the students' environmental attitude scale was found to be 3.94 (Agree) and the standard deviation was 1.12. According to this finding, students in this secondary school in Aksaray have positive attitudes towards environment.

A significant difference between the attitude scores and gender of secondary school students was determined by t-test for independent samples and the results are shown in Table 4.

There is a difference of 7.37 points between male and female students (Table 4). According to the results of t-test conducted to determine whether this difference is significant, environmental attitudes of secondary school students showed a significant difference by gender [$F_{(426)} = 4.627$; $p < 0.05$]. This result shows that gender is an important variable affecting environmental attitudes. The results of ANOVA according to the age group of the students' attitude towards environment in a middle school in Aksaray are given in Table 4.

It is seen that it is 99.6 in 9-11-year-old students, 96.72 in 11-13 years old students, 91.74 in 13-15 age group students and 96.00 in 15-17 years old students when the environmental attitude point average is examined (Table 5). Secondary school students' attitude towards environment showed a significant difference depending on the grade level [$F_{(3,420)} = 4.633$; $p < 0.05$]. The Tukey-HSD test was applied to determine the source of the difference between group averages. As a result of the analysis, a significant difference was found between the students in the 11-13 age group and 15-17 age group.

Table 3. Mean and standard deviations of students' attitudes on environmental attitude scale

Id	Expressions in the Environmental Attitude Scale	$\overline{X}$	SD
1	I turn off the lamps that are unnecessarily open at home or at school	4.30	1.07
2	I do not buy food products that cause harm to my health or the environment when shopping from grocery stores	3.85	1.16
3	When I go shopping with my parents, I tell them not to buy fruits and vegetables with hormones	3.52	1.31
4	One day when I buy my own car, I will buy the one polluting the environment least.	3.70	1.35
5	I would like my family to prefer those who consume less electricity while buying bulbs and household appliances.	3.96	1.24
6	The insensitivity of politicians and managers, to environmental problems worry me	3.78	1.28
7	I have to throw the waste to anywhere in places like picnic areas, beaches, forests where there is no bin.	2.25	1.54
8	I think there should be more flowers and green areas in my neighbourhood.	4.20	1.21
9	I don't burn fire in a woodland or picnic.	3.98	1.31
10	I use water and electricity at school and at home.	4.27	1.11
11	I feel sorry for the dogs that are hungry, injured, derelict on the streets.	4.28	1.06
12	It makes me sad that the camels, dogs, cocks fight, and bears are exploited in playgrounds.	3.98	1.27
13	I am very happy to be a member of an environmental foundation or association to protect plant and animal species.	4.08	1.12
14	Companies that try some food, medicine and weapons on animals should be closed.	4.22	2.65
15	I would be happy to feed and care for one of the animals in my house, such as cats, dogs and birds.	4.09	1.31
16	I think that water, electricity and energy should be saved in all houses and workplaces.	4.05	1.28
17	I do not pay attention to whether the products I buy have damaged the environment.	4.05	1.28
18	Natural gas should be used instead of wood and coal in the heating of houses.	3.67	1.34
19	I do not think that erosion and forest fires will cause serious environmental problems in our country.	4.55	0.68
20	I do not think that sufficient forestation works have been done for burnt, dry and cut forest lands.	4.14	1.09
21	I think people sometimes use energy unnecessarily by using cars.	3.72	1.37
22	The first nuclear power plant, which is expected to be established in our country in the coming years, worries me for the environment.	3.55	1.28
23	The use of energy sources wasted in Turkey worries me in terms of future	3.84	1.33
24	There are enough animals in Turkey, so I do not worry about the extinction of some species.	4.55	0.66
25	I am concerned that some factories work with energy that harms the environment.	3.96	1.28
Total		3.94	1.12

SD: Standard Deviation

Table 4. T-Test Results of gender in attitudes of environmental attitude scale scores

Parameter	n	$\overline{X}$	SD	t	p
Female	221	100.14	14.24	4.627	.000*
Male	204	92.77	19.24		

Table 5. ANOVA results of age group in attitudes of environmental attitude scale scores

Parameter	n	$\overline{X}$	SD
09-11	157	99.61	18.27
11-13	163	96.72	13.83
13-15	102	91.74	17.55
15-17	2	96.00	41.01
	Sum of Variance Squares	**Meaning of Variance Squares**	**F p**
Between Group (11-13) - (15-17)	3834.826	1278.2758	**4.633 .003***
Within Groups	115889.9466	275.928	

It is seen that it is 97.79 in the fifth class, 99.03 in the sixth class, 94.00 in the seventh class and 94.28 in the eighth class when the environmental attitude point average is examined (Table 6). Secondary school students' attitude towards environment showed a significant difference depending on the grade level [$F_{(3.421)}$ = 2.185; p <0.05].

Table 6. ANOVA results of class level in attitudes of environmental attitude scale scores

Parameter	n	$\overline{X}$	SD
5	154	97.79	19.30
6	99	99.03	12.14
7	79	94.00	17.60
8	93	94.28	15.57
	Sum of Variance Squares	**Meaning of Variance Squares**	**F p**
Between Group	1836.022	612.007	**2.185 .089**
Within Groups	117943.56	680.151	

It is seen that it is 102.73 in primary education level, 103.59 in secondary education level and 93.02 in university education level when the environmental attitude point average is examined (Table 7). Secondary school students' attitude towards environment showed a significant difference depending on the grade level [$F_{(3.373)}$=1.620; p>0.05].

Table 7. ANOVA results of mother education level in attitudes of environmental attitude scale scores

Parameter	n	$\overline{X}$	SD
Primary Education	444	102.73	10.94
Secondary Education	268	103.59	11.35
University Education	77	103.02	13.41
	Sum of Variance Squares	Meaning of Variance Squares	F p
Between Group	1417.644	472.548	1.620 .184
Within Groups	108772.727	291.616	

It is seen that it is 96.51 in primary education level, 97.70 in secondary education level and 106.36 in university education level when the environmental attitude point average is examined (Table 8). Secondary school students' attitude towards environment showed a significant difference depending on the grade level [$F_{(2.392)}$=2.159; p>0.05].

Table 8. ANOVA results of father education level in attitudes of environmental attitude scale scores

Parameter	n	$\overline{X}$	SD
Primary Education	293	96.51	15.90
Secondary Education	31	97.70	15.80
University Education	11	106.36	12.02
	Sum of Variance Squares	Meaning of Variance Squares	F p
Between Group	1077.799	538.900	2.159 .117
Within Groups	97824.743	249.553	

It is seen that it is 89.75 in officer, 89.71 in worker, 97.43 in housewife and 103.50 in retired when the environmental attitude point average is examined (Table 9). Secondary school students' attitude towards environment showed a significant difference depending on the grade level [$F_{(3.413)}$ = 3.067; p <0.05]. The Tukey-HSD test was applied to determine the source of the difference between group averages. As a result of the analysis, a significant difference was found between the students in the worker group and retired group.

It is seen that it is 87.25 in officer, 95.46 in worker, 98.93 in self-employment and 100.95 in retired when the environmental attitude point average is examined (Table 10). Secondary school students' attitude towards environment showed a significant difference depending on the grade level [$F_{(3.403)}$ = 2.934; p <0.05]. Tukey-HSD test was applied to determine the source of the difference between group averages. As a result of the analysis, a significant difference was found between the students in the worker group and retired group.

Table 9. ANOVA results of mother profession status in attitudes of environmental attitude scale scores

Parameter	n	$\overline{X}$	SD
Officer	4	89.75	20.30
Worker	42	89.71	24.35
Housewife	369	97.43	15.37
Retired	2	103.50	30.40
	Sum of Variance Squares	**Meaning of Variance Squares**	**F p**
Between Group (worker-retired)	2527.333	842.444	**3.060 .028**
Within Groups	113434.168	274.659	

Table 10. ANOVA results of father profession status in attitudes of environmental attitude scale scores

Parameter	n	$\overline{X}$	SD
Officer	12	87.25	26.95
Worker	235	95.46	17.45
Self-employment	141	98.93	14.87
Retired	19	100.95	12.91
	Sum of Variance Squares	**Meaning of Variance Squares**	**F p**
Between Group (worker-retired)	2473.905	824.635	**2.934 .033**
Within Groups	113286.931	281.109	

It is seen that it is 96.12 in < 1000 ₺ level, 96.83 in 1000 – 2000 ₺ level, 98.64 in 2000 - 3000 ₺ level and 97.06 in > 3000 ₺ level when the environmental attitude point average is examined (Table 11). Secondary school students' attitude towards environment showed a significant difference depending on the grade level [$F_{(3.405)}=.247; p>0.05$].

Table 11. ANOVA results of family income level in attitudes of environmental attitude scale scores

Parameter	n	$\overline{X}$	SD
< 1000 ₺	137	96.12	15.05
1000 - 2000 ₺	211	96.83	17.21
2000 - 3000 ₺	44	98.64	21.03
> 3000 ₺	17	97.06	16.84
	Sum of Variance Squares	**Meaning of Variance Squares**	**F p**
Between Group	213.708	71.236	**.247 .863**
Within Groups	116583.449	287.853	

It is seen that it is 95.43 in 0-2 siblings, 97.32 in 2-4 siblings, 97.84 in 4-6 siblings, 95.82 in 6-8 siblings and 97.20 in > 3000 ₺ level when the environmental attitude point average is examined (Table 12). Secondary school students' attitude towards environment showed a significant difference depending on the grade level [$F_{(4.418)}$=.369; p>0.05].

Table 12. ANOVA results of number of siblings in attitudes of environmental attitude scale scores

Parameter	n	$\overline{X}$	SD
0-2	144	95.41	17.07
2-4	182	97.32	17.09
4-6	70	97.84	15.67
6-8	22	95.82	16.23
> = 8	5	97.20	20.54
	Sum of Variance Squares	**Meaning of Variance Squares**	**F p**
Between Group	418.942	104.735	**.369 .831**
Within Groups	118789.687	284.186	

In that direction, the contribution of ANNs was remarkable. ANNs are graphs directed with weights and they are used, apart from education, in weather forecasting, predicting earthquakes, calculating the financial risk of a loan, in automatic pilots, in stock exchange. The disadvantage of questionnaires is that they are not dynamically adapted to each student. Thus, when someone takes an examination, s/he has to answer all questions, whether s/he is well prepared or not. The capabilities of ANNs can allow us to implement them in complicated problems and eliminate that disadvantage, minimizing time and cost.

Figure 2 depicts graphical presentation of the overlapping between the actual and predicted values for the results of the regression on learning, validation and test clusters in MATLAB *for gender, all questions – point (sums the weighted)*. Performance measurements of ANNs between predicted values for *gender, all questions – point (sums the weighted)* are shown in Figure 3.

Figure 2. Relationship between observed and forecast values

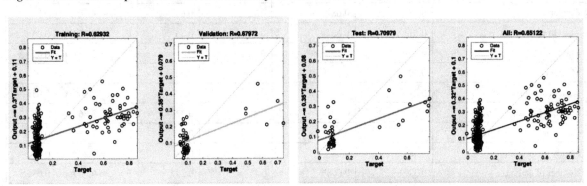

Figure 3. Performance of ANNs between observed and forecast values

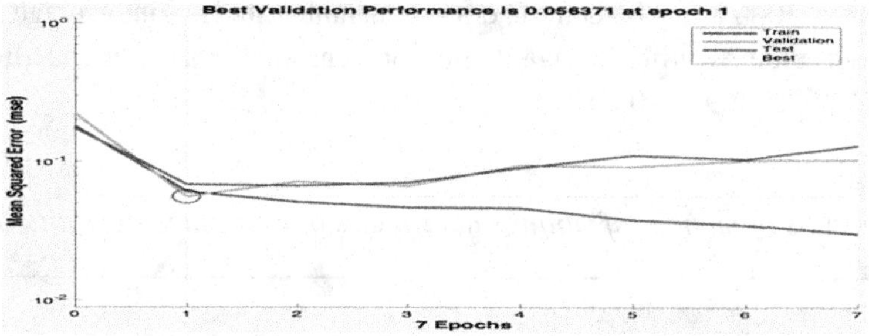

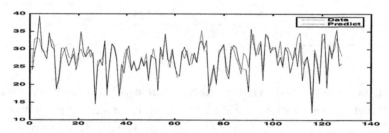

Figure 4 shows the distribution of the actual data with data predicted for the results in MATLAB. Figure 2-4 are drawn with MATLAB coding.

Figure 4. Observed and predicted data

The correlation value (R2) with parameters and of 25 questions of secondary school students' attitudes towards the environment values calculated by ANNs are presented in Table 13. This table is provided for the comparison of ANNs correlation value.

Table 13. Comparison results for ANNs and statistical

Parameter	ANNs Correlation Value (R^2)				Statistical Results
	Training	**Validation**	**Test**	**All**	
Gender	0.63	0.68	0.71	0.65	$t_{(426)} = 4.627; p < 0.05$
Age Group	0.51	0.62	0.66	0.56	$F_{(3,420)} = 4.633; p < 0.05$
Class	0.40	0.35	0.45	0.48	$F_{(3,421)} = 2.185; p < 0.05$
Mother education level	0.30	0.17	0.086	0.20	$F_{(3,373)} = 1.620; p > 0.05$
Father education level	0.31	0.32	0.029	0.27	$F_{(2,392)} = 2.159; p > 0.05$
Mother profession status	0.30	0.30	0.45	0.32	$F_{(3,413)} = 3.067; p < 0.05$
Father profession status	0.60	0.54	0.41	0.56	$F_{(3,403)} = 2.934; p < 0.05$
Family income level	0.48	0.07	0.25	0.37	$F_{(3,405)} = 0.247; p > 0.05$
Number of siblings	0.33	0.008	0.11	0.25	$F_{(4,418)} = 0.369; p > 0.05$

As a result of the analysis with ANNs; it is determined that there is a relationship between gender, age group and father profession status when the correlation values (R2) are examined. No relation was found in other parameters (class, mother education level, father education level, mother profession status, family income level and number of siblings). These findings are similar to the statistical results. Exceptionally; in the statistical results, the relationship with the ANNs was not determined while the relationship was found in the mother profession. It is considered that this result may be due to the fact that it is at the limit of p <0.05.

DISCUSSION AND CONCLUSION

It was tried to determine the attitudes of students towards environment in a secondary school in Aksaray with this research. In addition, it was examined whether students' environmental attitudes differed according to gender, age group, class level, mother's education level, father's education level, mother's professional status, father's professional status, family income level and number of siblings.

It can be said that the attitudes of the students in a secondary school in the city center of Aksaray towards the environment is positive when the arithmetical average of the attitude towards the environment of the students is examined. Some studies on different student groups support the same result (Kuhlemeier et al., 1999; Bonett & Williams, 1998; Ma & Bateson, 1999; Eagles & Demare, 1999; Jaus, 1982; Aydın & Kaya, 2011; Gökçe et al., 2007; Özpınar, 2009; Alp et al., 2007; Şahin & Erkal, 2010).

It is observed that secondary school students have low attitudes towards environment in their responses to some items (such as items 3, 4, 7, 18). In order to increase the environmental sensitivities of the second level students, it is possible to emphasize the environmental sensitivities in the subjects that the environmental subjects are taught in secondary education (Science, Social Studies etc.).

In this study, it was concluded that the arithmetic averages of female students' environmental attitude scores were higher than the male students. The environmental attitudes of the female students were found to be more positive than the male students. It was concluded that the female students' environmental attitude scores were higher than those of male students in some studies (Paraskevopoulos et al., 2003; Atasoy, 2005; Alp et al. 2006; Yılmaz et al., 2004). In this study, it was found that there was a statistically significant difference between the environmental attitude point averages of female and male students. Some studies on primary school students show that gender is effective on environmental attitudes.

The attitudes of the students in a secondary school in Aksaray towards the environment showed a significant difference according to age groups. The statistical difference shows that the age group is an important variable affecting environmental attitudes. Some studies on primary school students show that the age range is effective on environmental attitudes.

The attitudes towards the environment of secondary school students in Aksaray province did not show a significant difference according to their grade levels. This may be due to the fact that elementary school students are receiving similar courses for environmental education at each class level and there is no practical content for environmental education in the subject.

The attitudes of the students in a secondary school in Aksaray towards the environment showed no significant difference according to mother and father education level.

According to another result obtained in this study; the attitudes towards the environment of secondary students in Aksaray province showed a significant difference when examined in terms of mother professional status. A similar situation was obtained in the case of the father professional status.

Some researches on this subject (Özdemir, 2003; Baş, 2010; Özpınar, 2009) support this result. The professional status of the parents (professional status) shows the positive effect of the student's attitude towards the environment.

The attitudes towards the environment of secondary students in Aksaray province did not show a significant difference according to family income level. This finding shows that family income level is not an important variable affecting environmental attitudes.

The attitudes of secondary school students in Aksaray towards the environment did not show a significant difference according to the number of siblings. The number of siblings in the family indicates that there is no significant variable affecting the environmental attitude.

In general, it is of great importance for a secondary school student in Aksaray (n = 426) to have a positive attitude towards the environment, to prevent environmental problems and to create a liveable environment and point out that a successful environmental education has been carried out in secondary education. Also, it should be kept in mind that if environmental attitudes of the students are changed in a positive way with a conscious environmental education, environmental problems will decrease significantly. On the contrary, individuals with negative attitudes and behaviours towards the environment should be aware of the fact that their awareness and sensitivity towards the environment and environmental problems will be low. The level of knowledge, consciousness and attitude towards the environment of secondary school students should be determined and then developed. The more positive attitudes the students have towards the environment, the less environmental problems can occur. Therefore, educational practices that will change the attitudes of secondary school students towards their environment should be included.

Based on the research results, the following suggestions are given:

1. In this study, the province of Aksaray was chosen as the sample. The environmental attitudes of students in other settlements where environmental problems are felt in our country can be examined and the findings obtained can be compared.

2. In this study, it is concluded that female students have higher environmental attitudes than male students. The reasons for high environmental attitudes of female students can be investigated. In addition, practices should be included to change the environmental attitudes of male students positively. For example, learning environments where different methods and techniques are applied should be organized and seminars on environmental education should be given.

3. In order to create a society that respects the environmental values, it is necessary to ensure that the individuals who make up the society reach the right information and shape the training to be given accordingly. Environmental education should be shaped in such a way that people can take responsibility for environmental protection by providing information, consciousness, skills and values about the environment.

4. Environmental education is not only an element of the learning process but also an element of the whole life process of the individual. Therefore, environmental education should be considered and evaluated in the lifelong learning model.

5. There is great interest from researchers, in the field of dynamic questionnaires and with the help of ANNs we can predict the results, according to the profile of each student.

6. The design and implementation of the ANNs system can be designed to meet the need for automatic questioning as an expert questionnaire for future technology based measurement and evaluation activities.

ACKNOWLEDGMENT

This research received no specific grant from any funding agency in the public, commercial, or not-for-profit sectors.

REFERENCES

Alp, E., Ertepinar, H., Tekkaya, C., & Yilmaz, A. (2006). A statistical analysis of children's environmental knowledge and attitudes in Turkey. *International Research in Geographical and Environmental Education, 15*(3), 210–223. doi:10.2167/irgee193.0

Alp, E., Ertepınar, H., Tekkaya, C., & Yılmaz, A. (2008). A survey on Turkish elementary school students' environmental friendly behaviors and associated variables. *Environmental Education Research, 14*(2), 129–143. doi:10.1080/13504620802051747

Aslan, O., Sağır Uluçınar, S., & Cansaran, A (2008). The adaptation of environment attitude scala and determination of primary school students' environmental attitutes. Selçuk University Journal of Ahmet Keleşoğlu Education Faculty, 25, 283-295.

Atasoy, E. (2005). *Environmantal Education: A study for elementary school students' environmental attitude and knowledge* (PhD Thesis). Uludağ University, Social Science Institute, Bursa.

Atasoy, E., & Ertürk, H. (2008). A Field Study About Environmental Knowledge and Attitudes of Elementart School Students. Erzincan University Journal of Education Faculty, 10(1), 105-122.

Aydın, F., & Çepni, O. (2010). University students' attitudes towards environmental problems: A case study from Turkey. *International Journal of Physical Sciences, 5*(17), 2715–2720.

Aydın, F., & Çepni, O. (2012). Investigation of Primary Education Second Grade Students' Attitudes towards Environment in Terms of Various Variables (Karabük City Case). *Dicle University Journal of Ziya Gökalp of Education Faculty., 18*(190), 189–207.

Aydın, F., Coşkun, M., Kaya, H., & Erdönmez, İ. (2011). Gifted students' attitudes towards environment: A case study from Turkey. *African Journal of Agricultural Research, 6*(7), 1876–1883.

Aydın, F., & Kaya, H. (2011). Secondary education students' thoughts and behaviours towards environment (Karabuk Sample-Turkey). *American-Eurasian Journal of Agricultural & Environmental, 10*(2), 248–256.

Ayhan, F. N. (1999). *Factors affecting the wareness of immediate environment for students in the first three grades of primary education school* (MSc Thesis). Hacettepe University Social Science Institute, Ankara, Turkey.

Bahadır, E. (2016). Prediction of Prospective Mathematics Teachers' Academic Success in Entering Graduate Education by Using Back-propagation Neural Network. *Journal of Education and Training Studies, 4*(5), 113–122. doi:10.11114/jets.v4i5.1321

Baş Tarsus, M. (2010). *Evaluation of environmental school students* (MSc Thesis). Middle East Technical University (METU), Ankara, Turkey.

Bonnett, M., & Williams, J. (1998). Environmental education and primary children's attitudes towards nature and the environment. *Cambridge Journal of Education, 28*(2), 159–174. doi:10.1080/0305764980280202

Büyüköztürk, Ş. (2010). Manual of Data Analysis for Social Sciences. Ankara: Pegem A Press. (in Turkish)

Eagles, P. F. J., & Demare, R. (1999). Factors influencing children's environmental attitudes. *The Journal of Environmental Education, 30*(4), 33–37. doi:10.1080/00958969909601882

Gökçe, N., Kaya, E., Aktay, S., & Özden, M. (2007). Elementary Students' Attitudes Towards Environment. *Elementary Education Online, 6*(3), 452–468.

Güney, E. (2004). Environmental Problems Geography. Ankara: Gündüz Eğitim ve Yayıncılık. (in Turkish)

Hagan, M. T., Demuth, H. B., & Beale, M. (1996). *Neural network design.* Boston: PWS Pub.

İşyar, N. (1999). *The Evaluation of primary school childrens (3rd, 4th, 5th graders) positive environmental attitudes according to the age and socioeconomic status* (MSc Thesis). Uludağ University, Social Science Institute, Bursa, Turkey.

Jaus, H. H. (1982). The effect of environmental education instruction on children's attitudes toward the environment. *Science Education, 66*(5), 689–692. doi:10.1002ce.3730660504

Kağıtçıbaşı, Ç. (2010). People in today: Introduction to social psychology (12th ed.). İstanbul: Evrim Press. (in Turkish)

Kardan, A. A., Sadeghi, H., Ghidary, S. S., & Sani, M. R. F. (2013). Prediction of student course selection in online higher education institutes using neural network. *Computers & Education, 65,* 1–11. doi:10.1016/j.compedu.2013.01.015

Kasapoğlu, A., & Turan, F. (2008). Attitude-behavior relationship in environmental education: A case study from Turkey. *The International Journal of Environmental Studies, 65*(2), 219–231. doi:10.1080/00207230701502316

Kaya, N. Ç., & Turan, F. (2005). Sekizinci sınıf öğrencilerinin çevreye ilişkin bilgi ve duyarlılıkları: Ankara'da resmi ve özel ilköğretim okulları örneğinde bir çalışma. *Eurasian Journal of Educational Research, 21,* 103–112.

Keleş, R., & Hamamcı, C. (1998). Ecology. Ankara: İmge press. (in Turkish)

Khan, I., & Kulkarni, A. (2013). Knowledge extraction from survey data using neural networks. *Procedia Computer Science, 20,* 433–438. doi:10.1016/j.procs.2013.09.299

Kuhlemeier, H., Bergh, H. V. D., & Lagerweij, N. (1999). Environmental knowledge, attitudes, and behavior in Dutch secondary education. *The Journal of Environmental Education, 30*(2), 4–15. doi:10.1080/00958969909601864

Livieris, I. E., Drakopoulou, K., & Pintelas, P. (2012). Predicting students' performance using artificial neural networks. *8th PanHellenic Conference with International Participation Information and Communication Technologies in Education.*

Lykourentzou, I., Giannoukos, I., Mpardis, G., Nikolopoulos, V., & Loumos, V. (2009). Early and dynamic student achievement prediction in e-learning courses using neural networks. *Journal of the American Society for Information Science, 60*(2), 372–380. doi:10.1002/asi.20970

Ma, X., & Bateson, D. J. (1999). A multivariate analysis of the relationship between attitude toward science and attitude toward the environment. *The Journal of Environmental Education, 31*(1), 27–32. doi:10.1080/00958969909598629

Matzavela, V., Chrysafiadi, K., & Alepis, E. (2017). Questionnaires and artificial neural networks: A literature review on modern techniques in education. In *2017 IEEE Global Engineering Education Conference (EDUCON)* (pp. 1700-1704). IEEE.

Meydan, A., & Doğu, S. (2008). İlköğretim ikinci kademe öğrencilerinin çevre sorunları hakkındaki görüşlerinin bazı değişkenlere göre değerlendirilmesi. *Selçuk University Journal of Ahmet Keleşoğlu Education Faculty., 26*, 267–277.

Ministry of Environment and Forestry. (2004). *Turkey Environmental Map.* Ankara: Turkish.

Naik, B., & Ragothaman, S. (2004). Using Neural Network to Predict MBA Student Success. *College Student Journal, 38*(1), 1–4.

Naser, S. A., Zaqout, I., Ghosh, M. A., Atallah, R., & Alajrami, E. (2015). Predicting student performance using artificial neural network: In the faculty of engineering and information technology. *International Journal of Hybrid Information Technology, 8*(2), 221–228. doi:10.14257/ijhit.2015.8.2.20

Oancea, B., Dragoescu, R., & Ciucu, S. (2013). *Predicting students' results in higher education using a neural network.* MPRA Paper No. 72041. Retrieved from https://mpra.ub.uni-muenchen.de/72041/

Özdemir, A. (2003). *The Study of environmental knowledge and consciousness levels of eighth grade students* (PhD Thesis). Dokuz Eylül University, Education Science Institute, İzmir, Turkey.

Özdemir, I., & Polat, D. (2017). Forecasting With Artificial Neural Network Of Science Teachers' Professional Burnout Variables. *Int. J. Educ. Stud., 04*(03), 49–64.

Özey, R. (2001). Environmental problems. İstanbul: Aktif Press. (in Turkish)

Öznur, A. S. (2008). *The effect of cooperative learning approach on preservice science and technology teachers? attitude towards environment* (MSc Thesis). Abant İzzet Baysal University, Social Science Institute, Bolu, Turkey.

Özpınar, D. (2009). *Primary school's 4th and 5th class student's views to the environment problems (Afyonkarahisar sample)* (MSc Thesis). Afyon Kocatepe University, Social Science Institute, Afyonkarahisar, Turkey.

Paliwal, M., & Kumar, U. A. (2009). A study of academic performance of business school graduates using neural network and statistical techniques. *Expert Systems with Applications*, *36*(4), 7865–7872. doi:10.1016/j.eswa.2008.11.003

Paraskevopoulos, S., Padeliadu, S., & Zafiropoulos, K. (1998). Environmental knowledge of elementary school students in Greece. *The Journal of Environmental Education*, *29*(3), 55–60. doi:10.1080/00958969809599119

Sağır, Ş., Aslan, O., & Cansaran, A. (2008). The Examination of Elementary School Students' Environmental Knowledge and Environmental Attitudes with Respect to the Different Variables. *Elementary Education Online*, *7*(2), 496–511.

Sağiroglu, S., Beşdok, E., & Erler, M. (2003). *Muhendislikte Yapay Zeka Uygulamalari-I: Yapay Sinir Ağları*. Ufuk Press. (in Turkish)

Şahin, H., & Erkal, S. (2010). The attitudes of middle school students towards the environment. *Social Behavior and Personality*, *38*(8), 1061–1072. doi:10.2224bp.2010.38.8.1061

Tecer, S. (2007). *Education for environmental: A study on the level of determination of the primary students' environmental behaviour, knowledge, consciousness and active participation in Balıkesir city* (MSc Thesis). Zonguldak Karaelmas University, Science Institute, Zonguldak, Turkey.

Tekin, H. (2002). Measurement and Evaluation in Education. Ankara: Yargı Press. (in Turkish)

Tuncer, G., Sungur, S., Tekkaya, C., & Ertepınar, H. (2004). Environmental attitudes of the 6th grade students from Rural and Urban areas: A case study for Ankara. *Hacettepe Universitesi Eğitim Fakültesi Dergisi*, *26*, 167–175.

Ünal, F. T. (2009). *A study on the level of determination of the primary students? environmental behaviour, knowledge, consciousness and active participation in Çorlu* (MSc Thesis). Gazi University, Education Institute, Ankara, Turkey.

Ünlü, H. (1995). Local administration and environment. İstanbul: Ministry of Environment and Forestry Press. (in Turkish)

Ürey, M. (2005). *Primary school teacher' and students' attitudes and their sufficiency of knowledge about environment and regional differences in environmental education* (MSc Thesis). Kafkas University Science Institute, Kars, Turkey.

Uzun, N. (2007). *A study on the secondary school students' knowledge and attitudes towards the environment* (PhD Thesis). Hacettepe University, Science Institute, Ankara, Turkey.

Vural, M. (2003). Primary school program with the latest changes. Erzurum: Yakutiye Press. (in Turkish)

Worsley, A., & Skrzypiec, G. (1998). Environmental attitudes of senior secondary school students in South Australia. *Global Environmental Change*, *8*(3), 209225. doi:10.1016/S0959-3780(98)00016-8

Yaman, S., Deniz, M., & Akyiğit, G. (2010). *İlköğretim birinci kademe öğrencilerinin fen öğrenmeye yönelik motivasyonları ile çevreye ilişkin tutumları arasındaki ilişki. In IX. Ulusal Fen Bilimleri ve Matematik Eğitimi Kongresi. Dokuz Eylül Üniversitesi Buca Eğitim Fakültesi İzmir*. (in Turkish)

Yılmaz, Ö., Boone, W. J., & Andersen, H. O. (2004). Views of elementary and middle school Turkish students toward environmental issues. *International Journal of Science Education*, *26*(12), 1527–1546. doi:10.1080/0950069042000177280

Yorek, N., & Ugulu, I. (2015). A CFBPN Artificial Neural Network Model for Educational Qualitative Data Analyses: Example of Students' Attitudes Based on Kellerts' Typologies. *Educational Research Review*, *10*(18), 2606–2616. doi:10.5897/ERR2015.2370

KEY TERMS AND DEFINITIONS

Artificial Neural Network: An artificial neuron network (ANN) is a computational model based on the structure and functions of biological neural networks.

Environment: The sum total of all surroundings of a living organism, including natural forces and other living things, which provide conditions for development and growth as well as of danger and damage.

Environmental Attitude: Environmental attitudes are important because they often, but not always, determine behaviour that either increases or decreases environmental quality.

Environmental Attitude Scale: A crucial construct in environmental psychology, are a psychological tendency expressed by evaluating the natural environment with some degree of favour or disfavour.

Environmental Education: Environmental education is a process that allows individuals to explore environmental issues, engage in problem solving, and take action to improve the environment.

Lifelong Learning Model: All learning activity undertaken throughout life, with the aim of improving knowledge, skills and competences within a personal, civic, social, and/or employment-related perspective.

Questionnaire: A set of printed or written questions with a choice of answers, devised for the purposes of a survey or statistical study.

This research was previously published in Advanced MIS and Digital Transformation for Increased Creativity and Innovation in Business; pages 1-25, copyright year 2020 by Business Science Reference (an imprint of IGI Global).

Chapter 47
Applications of ANN for Agriculture Using Remote Sensed Data

Geetha M.
Bapuji Institute of Engineering and Technology, India

Asha Gowda Karegowda
Siddaganga Institute of Technology, India

Nandeesha Rudrappa
Siddaganga Institute of Technology, India

Devika G.
(iD) https://orcid.org/0000-0002-2509-2867
Government Engineering College, K. R. Pet, India

ABSTRACT

Ever since the advent of modern geo information systems, tracking environmental changes due to natural and/or manmade causes with the aid of remote sensing applications has been an indispensable tool in numerous fields of geography, most of the earth science disciplines, defense, intelligence, commerce, economics, and administrative planning. Remote sensing is used in science and technology, and through it, an object can be identified, measured, and analyzed without physical presence for interpretation. In India remote sensing has been using since 1970s. One among these applications is the crop classification and yield estimation. Using remote sensing in agriculture for crop mapping, and yield estimation provides efficient information, which is mainly used in many government organizations and the private sector. The pivotal sector for ensuring food security is a major concern of interest in these days. In time, availability of information on agricultural crops is vital for making well-versed decisions on food security issues.

DOI: 10.4018/978-1-6684-2408-7.ch047

INTRODUCTION

In India more than 60% of population is depending on agriculture. In agriculture, crop yield estimation before harvesting is a challenging task. Many models have been developed in Asia, USA, Europe and elsewhere in the country, but due to the complexity of agriculture ecosystem, yield prediction is still based on the traditional methods or the statistical methods. Artificial Neural Network (ANN) is one of the most powerful and self-adaptive model for crop yield estimation using remote sensing. This method employs a nonlinear response function that iterates many times in a special network structure in order to learn the complex functional relationship between input and output training data. Once trained, an ANN model can remember a functional relationship and be used for further calculation. For these reasons, the ANN concept has been widely used to develop models, especially in strongly nonlinear, complicated systems. Since Remote sensing provides the availability of large data in time with respect to the crop season would be combined with ANN to develop an efficient model for predicting the yield before harvesting. ANN and satellite remote sensing has got an unlimited scope in the sector of agriculture these days as it is being used for land resource mapping, weed detection, pesticide management, soil health mapping, crop yield estimation, and for assessment of natural calamities. In India the technology is being promoted by ministry of agriculture through MGNREGA scheme for rural area to assist farmers remotely.

The chapter is presented as follows. Section II covers overview of ANN, followed by detailed study of remote sensing in section III. Applications of ANN in agriculture using remote sensed data is briefed in section IV, followed by contribution to chapter, future scope for research and conclusions in the remaining sections.

Overview of ANN

Most of recent innovations and advances in statistical technology are conveyed through computational model artificial neural networks (ANN). ANN concept will be briefed in this section. The ANN model functions similar to nervous systems in human beings, where neurons are connected in complex patterns. It is not a new concept, but it has underwent gradual change because of which the current ANN does not certainly same as to that of its inception C. Stergiou (1996). As Howard Rheingold's explanation on ANN "The neural networks is these days technology is not an algorithm, it is a network that has weights on it, and you can adjust the weights so that it learns. You teach it through trails." ANN can be hardware or software that is carved of functioning to that of human brains. Few of researchers define ANN has a mathematical model of human neural network architecture with learning and generalization functions. The figure 1 gives comparison between actual neurons and synapses in human brain. The neurons are termed as perceptron in ANN during 1960 by McCulloch while presenting McCulloch –Pitt's neurons model V.S. Dave, K. Dutta (2014).

A typical ANN consist of large number of perceptrons, they operate parallel even though organized in the form of layers. As human brains receive information similarly in ANN first layer receives input, process and forward it to next layer, same sequencing happens until input reaches last layer T.J. Huang (2017). The working process is divided into three layers; input, hidden and output layers. ANN will consist of single and equal perceptron numbered input and output layer, and multiple hidden layers as in figure 2(a). Every perceptron in network will receive weighted input from its preceding perceptron known as synapses. The perceptron will process received inputs to generate output based on activation function of a perceptron. The single perceptron is shown in figure 2(b). The sum of weights and inputs

Figure 1. Comparison between actual neurons and synapses in human brain

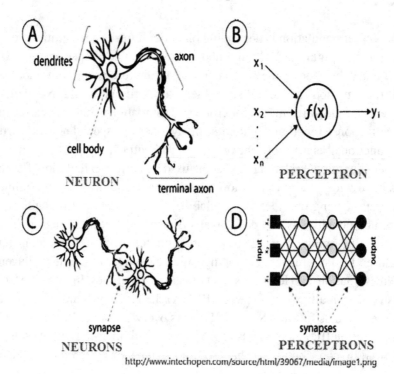

generates output in form of activation signal. The most commonly used activation functions are linear, step, sigmoid, tan and rectified linear unit (ReLu) functions as in figure 3. Each perceptron contribute in ANN for processing, as they are individually capable of contributing to ANN with their knowledge including rules that which has been programmed and learnt by itself. Each perceptron are extremely adaptive and learn quickly. Each perceptron will weight for its importance of input it receives from its preceding perceptrons based on it the current perceptron contribute towards the right output in order to give the highest weight. A specific layer can have an arbitrary number of nodes. This arbitrary number of nodes is called bias node. A bias major function is to provide node with a constant value that is trainable, in addition to the normal inputs received by the network node. Mainly, a bias value enables one to move the activation function either to the right or the left that can be analytical for ANN training success.

ANN can be applied for various tasks which include: Prediction and optimization, System modeling and design, Estimation, control, pattern recognition, forecasting, Implementing complex mapping and system identification, Signal processing, Application based on both linear and non-linear problem.

An ANN Application provides an alternative way to tackle complex problems as they are among the newest data and signal processing technologies. Neural network based solution is very efficient in terms of development, time and resources.

Types of ANN

The initial ANN models designed were biased perceptron, but then gradually moved on to multilayer perceptron to achieve better performance. The different types of ANN are discussed below:

Figure 2. (a) Layered structure of ANN; (b) Typical perceptron view

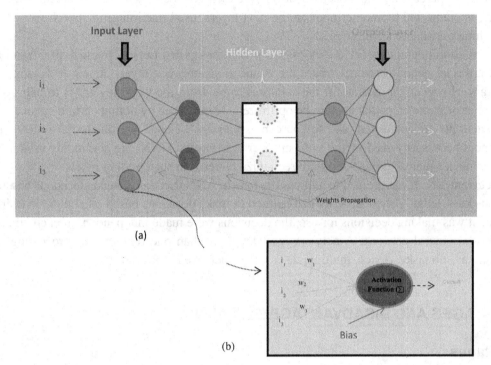

Figure 3. Activation function

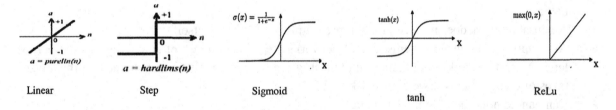

- Feed forward ANN: A feed-forward network is a simple neural network consisting of an input layer, an output layer and one or more layers of neurons. Through evaluation of its output by reviewing its input, the power of the network can be noticed base on group behavior of the connected neurons and the output is decided. The main advantage of this network is that it learns to evaluate and recognize input patterns.
- Feedback ANN: In this type of ANN, the output goes back into the network to achieve the best-evolved results internally. The feedback network feeds information back into itself and is well suited to solve optimization problems, according to the University of Massachusetts, Lowell Center for Atmospheric Research. Feedback ANNs are used by the internal system error corrections.
- Radial Basis ANN: In this type of ANN inner layer the featured are combined with the radial basis function. The output is taken into consideration in calculation of weights of next layer.

- Multilayer perceptron: Here the perceptron's are fully connected with more than three layers. Each node is connected to another node in the next layers, used maximum in speech recognition and machine translation technologies.
- Convolution neural network (CNN): CNN sometimes called LeNets (named after Yann LeCun), are artificial neural networks where the connections between layers appear to be somewhat arbitrary. However, the reason for the synapses to be setup the way they are is to help reduce the number of parameters that need to be optimized. This is done by noting certain symmetry in how the neurons are connected, and so you can essentially "re-use" neurons to have identical copies without necessarily needing the same number of synapses. CNNs are commonly used in working with images thanks to their ability to recognize patterns in surrounding pixels.
- Recurrent NN: It was created to address the flaw in ANN that didn't make decisions based on previous knowledge. A typical ANN had learned to make decisions based on context in training, but once it was making decisions for use, the decisions were made independent of each other.
- Modular Neural network: A network includes more than one function for processing independently as sub tasks. Hence, multiple tasks can be achieved at faster rate.

ADVANTAGES AND DISADVANTAGES OF ANN

Advantages

- A neural network can perform tasks in which a linear program cannot perform.
- When an element of the neural network fails, it can continue without any problem by their parallel nature.
- A neural network does not need to be reprogrammed as it learns itself.
- As adaptive, intelligent systems, neural networks are robust and excel at solving complex problems. Neural networks are efficient in their programming and the scientists agree that the advantages of using ANNs outweigh the risks.
- Can handle noisy and incomplete data.

Disadvantages

- The neural network requires training to operate.
- Requires high processing time for large neural networks.
- The architecture of a neural network is different from the architecture and history of microprocessors so they have to be emulated.

REMOTE SENSING

This section mainly covers the various remote sensing methodologies for agriculture related data acquisition. Remote sensing is defined as the science and technology using which specified objects properties, size, area, or it's a phenomenon that can be used to identify, measure, and analyze the objects without direct contact to provide useful decision making. With the development of computer technology, Geographical Information System (GIS), remote sensing and various satellite image processing tools a new era has been evolved since from 1970's. It is a phenomenon that has various applications which includes photography, geology, monitoring earth resources, forestry, change detection, surveying, flood assessment, droughts, fire in forest, and classification of crops in agriculture and many more.

The main source of remote sensing data is the electromagnetic radiations which are emitted or reflected by the object, which will helps in their identification and classification.

Figure 4. (a) Feed forward (b) Feedback (c) Radial basis function (d) Multi- layer (e) Recurrent (f) Convolution neural network (g) Modal network

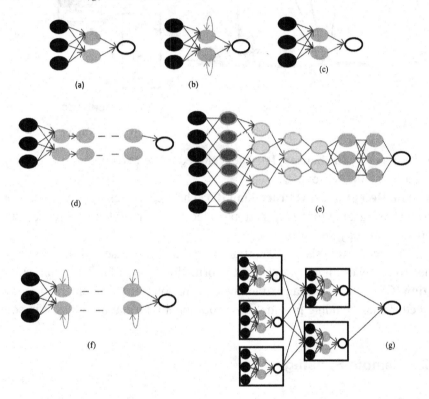

Components of Remote Sensing

In much of remote sensing, **the process** involves an interaction between incident radiation and the targets of interest.

- **Illumination or Source of Energy (A):** Is the basic requirement for remote sensing .It is the energy source which illuminates or provides electromagnetic energy to the target of interest.
- **Atmosphere and the Radiation (B):** As the electromagnetic energy travels from its source to the target, it will come in contact with and interact with the atmosphere as it passes through.
- **Interaction with the Target (C):** Once the energy from the source reaches its target through the atmosphere, it interacts with the target depending on the both target and radiation properties.

Figure 5. The Process of Remote Sensing (http1)

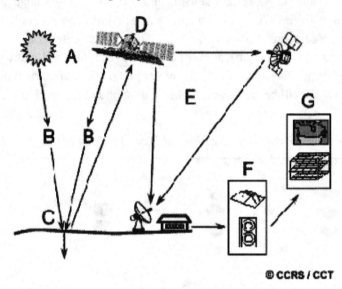

© CCRS / CCT

- **Footage of Energy by the Sensor (D)**: The scattered or emitted energy from the target is collected and recorded using the sensors.
- **Transmission, Reception, and Processing (E)**: The recorded energy by the sensor will be transmitted to a receiving and processing station in electronic form where the processed data will in an image format (hardcopy and/or digital).
- **Interpretation and Analysis (F)**: The transmitted and processed image is interpreted, visually and/or electronically or digitally, to extract information of the illuminated target.
- **Application (G)** – Finally we can extract the information from the element of remote sensing process, for better understanding provide some additional information or assist in solving a specific problem.

Platforms for Remote Sensing

- Platform: A Platform is defined as the carrier for remote sensing sensors. There are three major remote sensing platforms: ground-level platform (towers and cranes), aerial platforms (Helicopters, low altitude aircraft, high altitude aircraft), and space borne platforms (space shuttles, polar-orbiting satellites, and geostationary satellites).

Figure 6. Platforms for Remote sensing

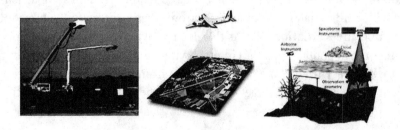

Types of remote sensing instruments are

- **Active sensor:** Active sensors provide their own energy in order to scan objects and areas whereupon a sensor then detects and measures the radiation that is reflected or backscattered from the target.

    Ex: RADAR and LiDAR (SAR or microwave data) Sentinel 2A, Awifis etc.

- **Passive sensor:** Passive sensors detect natural energy that is reflected by the object scene being observed (Optical Data).

    Ex: Photography, Charge-Coupled Devices and Radiometers, Landsat, sentinel-2B etc.

Figure 7. Difference between Active and Passive sensors
(www.nrcan.gc.ca)

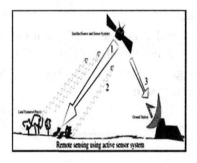 

- **Active sensing** sends the energy towards the object then measure and detects the radiation that is reflected or backscattered from the object.
- **Passive sensing** is a collection of energy that is reflected or emitted from the surface of the earth.
- **Optical Remote Sensing:** It makes use of visible, near infrared and short-wave infrared sensors to form images of the earth's surface by detecting the solar radiation reflected from targets on the ground. Different materials reflect and absorb differently at different wavelengths. Thus, the targets can be differentiated by their spectral reflectance signatures in the remotely sensed images. Optical remote sensing systems are classified into the following types, depending on the number of spectral bands used in the imaging process.
- **Panchromatic Imaging System:** The sensor is a single channel detector sensitive to radiation within a broad wavelength range. If the wavelength ranges coincide with the visible range, then the resulting image resembles a "black-and-white" photograph taken from space. The physical quantity being measured is the apparent brightness of the targets. The spectral information or "colour" of the targets is lost. Examples of panchromatic imaging systems are: IKONOS PAN,SPOT HRV-PAN

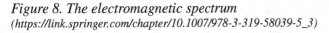

Figure 8. The electromagnetic spectrum
(https://link.springer.com/chapter/10.1007/978-3-319-58039-5_3)

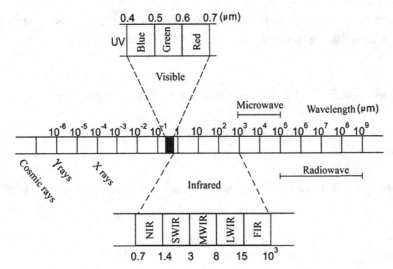

- **Multispectral Imaging System:** The sensor is a multichannel detector with a few spectral bands. Each channel is sensitive to radiation within a narrow wavelength band. The resulting image is a multilayer image which contains both the brightness and spectral (colour) information of the targets being observed. Examples of multispectral systems are:
  ◦ LANDSAT MSS
  ◦ LANDSAT TM
  ◦ SPOT HRV-XS
  ◦ IKONOS MS
  ◦ SENTINEL 2B
- **Super Spectral Imaging Systems:** A super spectral imaging sensor has many more spectral channels (typically >10) than a multispectral sensor. The bands have narrower bandwidths, enabling the finer spectral characteristics of the targets to be captured by the sensor. Examples of super spectral systems are: MODIS, MERIS
- **Hyperspectral Imaging Systems:** A hyperspectral imaging system is also known as an "imaging spectrometer". It acquires images in about a hundred or more contiguous spectral bands. The precise spectral information contained in a hyperspectral image enables better characterization and identification of targets. Hyperspectral images have potential applications in such fields as precision agriculture (e.g. monitoring the types, health, moisture status and maturity of crops), coastal management (e.g. monitoring of phyto planktons, pollution, bathymetry changes). An example of a hyperspectral system is: Hyperion on EO1 satellite (https://crisp.nus.edu.sg/).
- **Synthetic Aperture Radar** (SAR) image data provide information different from that of optical sensors operating in the visible and infrared regions of the electromagnetic spectrum. SAR data consist of high-resolution reflected returns of radar-frequency energy from terrain that has been illuminated by a directed beam of pulses generated by the sensor. The radar returns from the terrain are mainly determined by the physical characteristics of the surface features (such as surface roughness, geometric structure, and orientation), the electrical characteristics (dielectric constant,

moisture content, and conductivity), and the radar frequency of the sensor. By supplying its own source of illumination, the SAR sensor can acquire data day or night without regard to cloud cover. Characteristics of SAR are:

◦ The unique information of surface roughness, physical structure, and electrical conduction properties

◦ The high spatial resolution

◦ The 24-hour, all-weather data-acquisition capability; and

◦ The now-realizable long-term continuity of the data that enables repetitive (seasonal) coverage of major global land regions. (http://www.ciesin.org/TG/RS/sarsens.html).

Some of Indian satellite details of launching, characteristics of these satellites, along with tasks are given in table 1. Satellite launched by other countries is mentioned in table 2.

Table 1. Details of Indian satellites and its tasks

SN	Satellite	No. of Bands, Resolution and Revisit	Task
1.	Resourcesat-2A LISS III LISS IV AWiFs	4,23.5m,24 Days 3,5.8m,5 Days 4,56m,5 Days http://lps16.esa.int/ posterfiles/paper1213/[RD13]_ Resourcesat-2_Handbook.pdf	To provide multispectral images for inventory and management of natural resources, Crop production forecast, wasteland inventory, Land & Water Resources development, and Disaster Management Support. (https://directory.eoportal.org/web/eoportal/satellite-missions/r/ resourcesat-2)
2.	Cartosat-1	4,2.5m,5 Days(http://www.eotec. com/images/IRS_-_Current_and_ Future_-_Web.pdf)	To provide high resolution images for Cartographic mapping, Stereo data for Topographic Mapping & DEM, and host of DEM Applications – Contour, Drainage network, etc.
4.	RISAT-1	3-4,1-50m,5 Days http://www. eotec.com/images/IRS_-_Current_ and_Future_-_Web.pdf	To provide all weather imaging capability useful for agriculture, particularly paddy and jute monitoring in kharif season and management of natural disasters.
5.	Kalpana-1	3,2km, 16 Days https://nssdc.gsfc. nasa.gov/nmc/spacecraft/display. action?id=2002-043A	To provide meteorological data to enable weather forecasting services.

Table 2. Foreign satellite and its tasks

SN	Satellite	No. of Bands, Resolution and Revisit	Task
1	Sentinel 2	13 10,30,60 5 Days	The objective of SENTINEL-2 is land monitoring, and the mission will be composed of two polar-orbiting satellites providing high-resolution optical imagery. Vegetation, soil and coastal areas are among the monitoring objectives.(https://sentinel.esa.int)
2	MODIS	36, 250,500,1000 16 Days	MODIS is playing a vital role in the development of validated, global, interactive Earth system models able to predict global change accurately enough to assist policy makers in making sound decisions concerning the protection of our environment. (https://modis. gsfc.nasa.gov)
3	Landsat 8	8,30,16 Days	The objective of scheduling and data collection is to provide cloud-free coverage of the global landmass on a seasonal basis. (https://earth.esa.int)

Basic Steps Involved in Remote Sensing

- Data acquisition (energy propagation, platforms)
- Processing (conversion of energy pattern to images)
- Analysis (quantitative and qualitative analysis)
- Analysis (quantitative and qualitative analysis)
- Information distribution to users

IV Remote Sensing Applications

It is a phenomenon that has numerous applications including photography, surveying, geology, forestry, land-use land Cover Mapping, weather forecasting, environmental study, natural hazards study, and crop classification, yield monitoring and Estimation, monitoring earth resources, change detection, flood assessment, droughts, fire in forest and many more.

- Land Use Mapping: Remote sensing data is useful in obtaining up-to-date land use pattern of large areas at any given time and also monitor changes that occur from time to time. It can be used for updating road maps, asphalt conditions, and wetland delineation. This information is used by regional planners and administrators to frame policy matters for all-round development of the region.
- Weather Forecasting: Remote sensing is extensively used in India for weather forecasting. It is also used to warn people about impending cyclones.
- Environmental Study: It can be used to study deforestation, degradation of fertile lands, pollution in atmosphere, desertification, eutrophication of large water bodies and oil spillage from oil tankers.
- Study of Natural hazards: Remote sensing can be used to study damages caused by earthquakes, volcanoes, landslides, floods and melting of ice in polar regions. Many times remote sensing will be helpful to predict the occurrence of natural hazards.
- Resource exploration: Remote sensing data is helpful for updating existing geological maps, rapid preparation of lineament and tectonic maps, identifying the sites for quarrying the minerals and helpful in locating fossil fuel deposits.

Applications of Remote Sensing in Agricultural Sector

- **Crop Production Forecasting:** Remote sensing is used to forecast the expected crop production and yield over a given area and determine how much of the crop will be harvested under specific conditions. Researchers can be able to predict the quantity of crop that will be produced in a given farmland over a given period of time.
- **Assessment of Crop Damage and Crop Progress:** In the event of crop damage or crop progress, remote sensing technology can be used to penetrate the farmland and determine exactly how much of a given crop has been damaged and the progress of the remaining crop in the farm.
- **Horticulture, Cropping Systems Analysis:** Remote sensing technology has also been instrumental in the analysis of various crop planting systems. This technology has mainly been in use

in the horticulture industry where flower growth patterns can be analyzed and a prediction made out of the analysis.

- **Crop Identification:** Remote sensing has also played an important role in crop identification especially in cases where the crop under observation is mysterious or shows some mysterious characteristics. The data from the crop is collected and taken to the labs where various aspects of the crop including the crop culture are studied.

- **Crop Acreage Estimation:** Remote sensing has also played a very important role in the estimation of the farmland on which a crop has been planted. This is usually a cumbersome procedure if it is carried out manually because of the vast sizes of the lands being estimated.

- **Crop Condition Assessment and Stress Detection:** Remote sensing technology plays an important role in the assessment of the health condition of each crop and the extent to which the crop has withstood stress. This data is then used to determine the quality of the crop.

- **Identification of Planting and Harvesting Dates:** Because of the predictive nature of the remote sensing technology, farmers can now use remote sensing to observe a variety of factors including the weather patterns and the soil types to predict the planting and harvesting seasons of each crop.

- **Crop Yield Modeling and Estimation:** Remote sensing also allows farmers and experts to predict the expected crop yield from a given farmland by estimating the quality of the crop and the extent of the farmland. This is then used to determine the overall expected yield of the crop.

- **Identification of Pests and Disease Infestation:** Remote sensing technology also plays a significant role in the identification of pests in farmland and gives data on the right pests control mechanism to be used to get rid of the pests and diseases on the farm.

- **Soil Moisture Estimation:** Soil moisture can be difficult to measure without the help of remote sensing technology. Remote sensing gives the soil moisture data and helps in determining the quantity of moisture in the soil and hence the type of crop that can be grown in the soil.

- **Irrigation Monitoring and Management:** Remote sensing gives information on the moisture quantity of soils. This information is used to determine whether a particular soil is moisture deficient or not and helps in planning the irrigation needs of the soil.

- **Soil Mapping:** Soil mapping is one of the most common yet most important uses of remote sensing. Through soil mapping, farmers are able to tell what soils are ideal for which crops and what soil require irrigation and which ones do not. This information helps in precision agriculture.

- **Monitoring of Droughts:** Remote sensing technology is used to monitor the weather patterns including the drought patterns over a given area. The information can be used to predict the rainfall patterns of an area and also tell the time difference between the current rainfall and the next rainfall which helps to keep track of the drought.

- **Land Cover and Land Degradation Mapping:** Remote sensing has been used by experts to map out the land cover of a given area. Experts can now tell what areas of the land have been degraded and which areas are still intact. This also helps them in implementing measures to curb land degradation.

- **Identification of Problematic Soils:** Remote sensing has also played a very important role in the identification of problematic soils that have a problem in sustaining optimum crop yield throughout a planting season.

- **Crop Nutrient Deficiency Detection:** Remote sensing technology has also helped farmers and other agricultural experts to determine the extent of crop nutrients deficiency and come up with remedies that would increase the nutrients level in crops hence increasing the overall crop yield.

- **Reflectance Modeling:** Remote sensing technology is just about the only technology that can provide data on crop reflectance. Crop reflectance will depend on the amount of moisture in the soil and the nutrients in the crop which may also have a significant impact on the overall crop yield.

- **Determination of Water Content of field Crops:** Apart from determining the soil moisture content, remote sensing also plays an important role in the estimation of the water content in the field crops.

- **Crop Yield Forecasting:** Remote sensing technology can give accurate estimates of the expected crop yield in a planting season using various crop information such as the crop quality, the moisture level in the soil and in the crop and the crop cover of the land. When all of this data is combined it gives almost accurate estimates of the crop yield.

- **Flood Mapping and Monitoring**: Using remote sensing technology, farmers and agricultural experts can be able to map out the areas that are likely to be hit by floods and the areas that lack proper drainage. This data can then be used to avert any flood disaster in future.

- **Collection of Past and Current Weather Data**: Remote sensing technology is ideal for collection and storing of past and current weather data which can be used for future decision making and prediction.

- **Crop Intensification**: Remote sensing can be used for crop intensification that includes collection of important crop data such as the cropping pattern, crop rotation needs and crop diversity over a given soil.

- **Water Resources Mapping**: Remote sensing is instrumental in the mapping of water resources that can be used for agriculture over a given farmland. Through remote sensing, farmers can tell what water resources are available for use over a given land and whether the resources are adequate.

- **Precision Farming**: Remote sensing has played a very vital role in precision agriculture. Precision agriculture has resulted in the cultivation of healthy crops that guarantees farmers optimum harvests over a given period of time.

- **Climate Change Monitoring**: Remote sensing technology is important in monitoring of climate change and keeping track of the climatic conditions which play an important role in the determination of what crops can be grown where.

- **Compliance Monitoring:** For the agricultural experts and other farmers, remote sensing is important in keeping track of the farming practices by all farmers and ensuring compliance by all farmers. This helps in ensuring that all farmers follow the correct procedures when planting and when harvesting crops.

- **Soil Management Practices**: Remote sensing technology is important in the determination of soil management practices based on the data collected from the farms.

- **Air Moisture Estimation**: Remote sensing technology is used in the estimation of air moisture which determines the humidity of the area. The level of humidity determines the type of crops to be grown within the area.

- **Crop Health Analysis**: Remote sensing technology plays an important role in the analysis of crop health which determines the overall crop yield.

- **Land Mapping**: Remote sensing helps in mapping land for use for various purposes such as crop growing and landscaping. The mapping technology used helps in precision agriculture where specific land soils are used for specific purposes.https://grindgis.com/remote-sensing/remote-sensing-applications-in-agriculture#

Remote Sensing for Yield Estimation

Remote sensing is commonly used to monitor and estimating yield crops in large areas. K. Kuwataa, R. & Shibasakib (2016) have used MODIS data with daily input dataset and 5-days accumulation input dataset with surface reflectance from https://lpdaac.usgs.gov and calculated Enhanced Vegetation Index(EVI) using the following equation(1): EVI=G*NIR-R/NIR+C1*R-C2*B+L, where G=Gain Factor, R=MODIS band1,NIR= MODIS band2,B= MODIS band3, C1C2=Aerial resistance weights, L=the canopy background adjustment factor, with G=2.5, L=1,C1=6 &C2=7.5. They developed a model for estimation corn Yield using an Artificial Neural Network, Support Vector Machine (SVM) and deep Neural Network (DNN).The performance of crop yield estimation model was evaluated based on the Root Mean Square Error (RMSE) and the coefficient of determination (R^2). Nearly 80% of the dataset is used for training and the remaining 20% is used to evaluate the accuracy of the models. The comparison between the two models shows that the DNN with six hidden layers produce higher accuracy than SVM.

Yield estimation is very essential for decision making in food and agriculture economic growth of a country as well as for import and export of food grains. Mohammad Saleem Khan et.al (2019) acquired multispectral satellite Landsat8 OLI (Operational Land Imager) data for the month of May 2019 and derived different vegetation Indices like NDVI(Normalized Difference Vegetation Index), ENDVI(Enhanced Normalized Difference Vegetation Index), TNDVI(Transformed Normalized Difference Vegetation Index), GVI(Green Vegetation Index) etc., for the yield estimation of Menthol crops along with the Artificial Neural Network techniques of Multi-Layer Perceptron. This algorithm is used to optimize the dependent variables (field biomass) with respect to independent variables (Vegetation Indices). The figure 9 shows the ANN topology used for predicting Menthol mint crop biomass.

Figure 9. The architecture of ANN model used to estimate the Menthol mint crop biomass (Mohammad Saleem Khan et.al (2019))

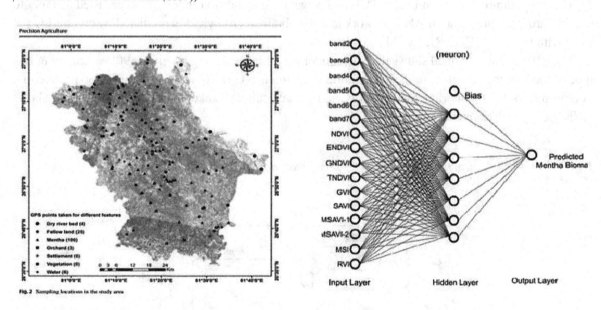

ANN was implemented to identify the important predictors from amongst spectral bands, indices and they collected field data for estimation of the crop biomass which has a good relationship (R2 = 0.785 and root mean square error (RMSE) = 2.74 t/ha) with field-measured biomass. Linear regression method was used further to calculate regression coefficients and the empirical equation thus developed was used to visualize biomass variability in the study area (Barabanki). The Artificial Neural Network model with the various vegetation Indices of satellite data coupled with collection of field sampling during crop maturity enabled the menthol mint yield estimation with high accuracy.

With the rapid development of Precision Agriculture (PA) promoted by high-resolution remote sensing, it makes significant sense in management and estimation of agriculture through crop classification of high-resolution remote sensing image. Due to the complex and fragmentation of the features and the surroundings in the circumstance of high-resolution, the accuracy of the traditional classification methods has not been able to meet the standard of agricultural problems. In this case, Yao Chunjing et.al(2017) proposed a classification method for high-resolution agricultural remote sensing images based on convolution neural networks (CNN). For training, a large number of training samples were produced by panchromatic images of GF-1 high-resolution satellite of China. In the experiment, through training and testing on the CNN under the toolbox of deep learning by MATLAB, the crop classification finally got the correct rate of 99.66% after the gradual optimization of adjusting parameter during training. Through improving the accuracy of image classification and image recognition, the applications of CNN provide a reference value for the field of remote sensing in Precision Agriculture.

Rice is a globally used staple food. Forecasting and yield estimation of Boro Rice in Bangladesh plays a crucial role in economy of agro departments. Due to rapid increase in population and reduction in agricultural land area has become a key issue in Bangladesh economy to maintain the food security for its large population. Kawsar Akhand et.al (2018) have developed a model for predicting Boro Rice crop using ANN and Advanced Very High Resolution radiometer(AVHRR) satellite data and calculated NDVI using the formula NDVI= (NIR-VIS) / (NIR+VIS) for vegetation health Indices.

The temperature Condition index (TCI) and Vegetation Condition Index (VCI) are used as input to the forward back propagation ANN network and the obtained crop yield is predicted by comparing the yield with the actual Boro Rice yield statistical data.

Thus, the results obtained shows that this model is highly promising by giving 90% accuracy & this type of models are important to the agricultural departments, Governments, Planning crop production, Policy makers for monitoring food security and for agricultural stake holders. The Figure 10 shows ANN yield prediction model.

Figure 10. NARX Neural network Boro rice yield prediction model simulated diagram (Kawsar Akhand et.al (2018))

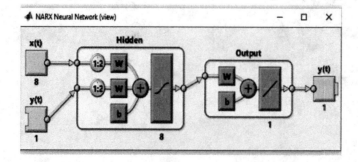

Machine Learning approaches such as ANN and Random Forest algorithms are used to develop a model for Kharif Rice yield prediction in Purulia and Bankura district, West Bengal. Aditi Chandrae.t. al(2019),have developed a model by integrating Non-weather variables at block level for the period from 2006 to 2015 with monthly NDVI. The correlation obtained from the model was 0.702 with MSE 0.01.

The various model like Weather Variables vs Yield Models, Weather Variables vs NDVI Models, NDVI vs Yield Models, Weather Variables & NDVI vs Yield, Weather Variables, Fertilizer and NDVI vs Yield. The study reveals that NDVI alone may not yield the desired model for rain fed kharif rice yield prediction, combining non-weather predictor variables improve the model accuracy up to 70%.

Now-a-days a growing number of applications of machine learning techniques in agriculture are required for which a large amount of data currently available from many resources can be analyzed to find the hidden knowledge. This is an advanced researched field and is expected to grow in the future. The integration of computer science with agriculture helps in forecasting agricultural crops. It is required to build on objective methodology for pre-harvest crop forecasting. Building up a suitable model will have certain merits over the traditional forecasting method. A detail about the study is which has been developed by Subhadra Mishra et.al(2016) is shown in table3.

Table 3. Applications of various models

Fusion Type	Application Area
Non Linear Regression	Forecasting Corn Yields
Markov Chain Approach	Forecasting Cotton Yields
Linear Regression	Estimating Grain Yield of Maturing Rice
Modified K-Means Clustering	Crop Prediction
Polynomial Regression	Factors Affecting the Yield of Winter Cereals in Crop Margins
Decision Tree	Soybean Productivity Modeling

(Subhadra Mishra et.al(2016))

Remote sensing plays a vital role in agricultural activities like yield estimation before harvesting, in Bangladesh due to increase in population and decrease in crop land, yield prediction before harvesting is very essential for food security. The aim of this paper is to develop a model for Wheat Yield Prediction in Bangladesh Advanced Very High-Resolution Radiometer (AVHRR) sensor data by considering Vegetation condition Index (VCI) and Temperature Condition Index (TCI) and Multilayer Perceptron Network (MLP) of ANN by training the model by Back Propagation algorithm, which reduces error using weights and bias adjustments. The obtained results are compared with the actual statistics of the yield, the predicted results shows the more than 90% accuracy.

Results in figure 11prove that Artificial Neural Network is a potential tool for wheat yield prediction model development using AVHRR satellite data by considering vegetation indices of crops health TCI and VCI characterizing thermal and moisture conditions respectively.

ANN has proved to be a powerful tool for yield estimation compared to simple non-linear and traditional linear analysis. This study demonstrated that it is possible to develop a yield estimation model using remote sensing images and ANN techniques. Kawsar Akhand et.al (2018) developed a model to predict winter wheat yield estimation in north China, during winter yield is affected by many factors like temperature, water stress, soil conditions and sunlight supply. Five Indices has been selected to represent the above factors such as NDVI, absorbed photosynthesis active radiation (APAR), surface temperature (Ts), water stress index and average crop yield over the last 10 years. 1 km*1 km resolution NOAA AVHRR dataset is used for yield estimation along with back propagation model as shown in below figure 12. Thus it has been confirmed from the survey that ANN yield estimation model with remote sensing plays a vital role in agriculture from several characteristics (1) capabilities of ANN itself, such as self-learning, compatibility and flexibility; (2) integrated use of remotely sensed data together with historical statistical information. Parameters retrieved from satellite images were coalesced by the main growing season of the crop; and (3) precise division of the study area based on agricultural knowledge and careful selection of sample data. This model has been implemented in the Nan province in 1999. The model has only been applied in the He Nan province in 1999. Further studies may focus on the test and calibration of this model in larger areas and over longer temporal scales.

Figure 11. Comparison graph of actual and predicted wheat yield in Bangladesh
(Subhadra Mishra et.al(2016))

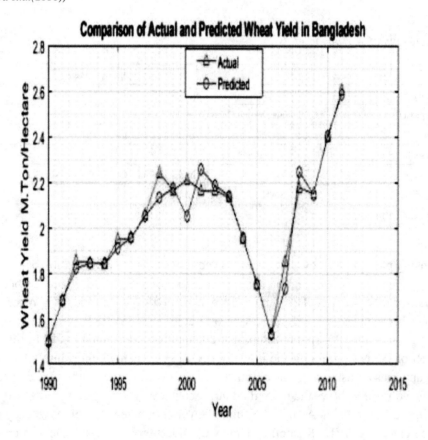

Figure 12 and 13 represents Spatial distribution of the sample countries in He Nan province and the structure of a back-propagation ANN model used for winter wheat yield estimation by using various indices like NDVI, NDWI etc.,as input layers.

Figure 12. Spatial distribution of the sample countries and the structure of a back-propagation ANN model (Kawsar Akhand et.al (2018))

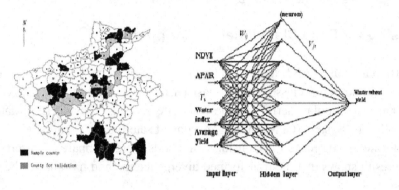

Figure 13. Yields per area unit of winter wheat estimated by ANN model (Kawsar Akhand et.al (2018))

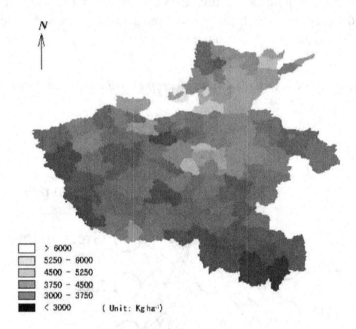

Table 4. Comparison of results of ANN model and multi-regression model

County name	NDVI	T_s (°C)	Water index	APAR (MJ m^{-2})	Average yield (kg ha^{-1})	Actual yield (kg ha^{-1})	Result of ANN	Result of MR	Relative error (ANN)	Relative error (MR)
Qi Xian	3329.1	3466.8	100.5	3664.2	3950.6	4807.1	5194.7	4742.0	−8.06	1.35
Luan Chuan	2121.7	3606.2	78.5	3460.8	2634.6	4215.9	4269.9	3466.8	−1.28	17.8
Lu Shan	1635.3	3974.1	57.6	2555.5	2483.0	3593.4	3414.9	2389.9	4.97	33.5
Jia Xian	2401.2	3852.8	83.5	3018.0	4087.2	4686.5	4482.6	3815.7	4.35	18.6
JunXian	2918.2	3495.9	117.3	3823.4	5202.1	5473.1	5570.0	5415.3	−1.77	1.06
Yan Jin	2426.0	3438.8	94.6	3272.9	4494.9	5220.3	5343.0	4804.8	−2.34	7.96
Qing Feng	2897.4	3551.5	106.9	3834.8	5498.1	5417.9	5557.9	5481.6	−2.59	−1.2
Chang Ge	3237.2	3642.4	130.2	4210.7	4855.7	5948.1	5612.9	5187.0	5.64	12.8
Fu Gou	2781.8	3549.3	97.7	3530.0	4764.6	5132.1	5296.7	4934.0	−3.21	3.86
Nan Zhao	1394.4	3772.0	46.2	2749.7	2698.0	3420.8	3394.8	2837.2	0.76	17.1

(Kawsar Akhand et.al (2018))

Table 4 represents the comparison results of ANN model and Multi-Regression model which shows that ANN model provides an better results in comparison with regression model.

Remote Sensing for Crop Classification/Cropping

P Kumar et al(2016) have used ANN algorithm for classification of corn, pigeon pea, rice, green gram, corn, other crops and non-crop classes in Varanasi District, UP, India using RISAT-1 with medium resolution of C-band, dual polarimertic temporal satellite datasets. Ground truth data were collected using Global Positioning System (GPS) on the same day of satellite data acquisition. Jefferies Matusita (JM) and Transformed Divergence (TD) distance methods were compared for separability analysis. The comparison result shows that the transformed divergence method has shown the better separation between the classes.

ANN is a mathematical model which is used for classification consisting of three input layers of satellite bands as neurons, a single hidden layer contains 8 neurons and one output layer contains 6 neurons of crop classes which are used for classification. ENVI 5.1 is used for supervised learning which uses back propagation and reduces the RMSE between desired actual outputs with the expected output. The figure 14 shows the three layers of ANN structure.

Figure 14. Three layer of ANN structure of multiple crop classification using various polarizations (P Kumar et al(2016))

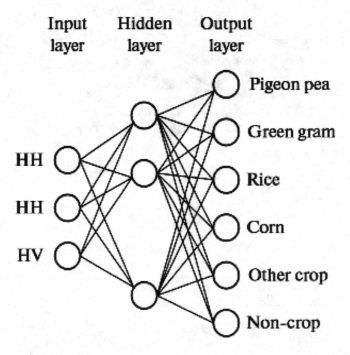

The result of classification shows the overall accuracy of 74.21 and 77.36 for the acquired satellite data on August 9th 2013 and Sept 28th 2013 respectively. The accuracy of September is better because of high reflection during crop maturity.

In this study Pradeep Kumar et.al (2015) have used Resourcesat-2, the Linear Imaging and Improved Self-Scanning (LISS IV) which is suitable satellite for crop classification which has a spatial resolution of 5.8 m was used for comparison of accuracies obtained by ANN, Support Vector Machine (SVM) and Spectral Angle Mapper (SAM) algorithms at UP, India. The overall accuracies of SVM, ANN and SAM were 93.45%, 92.32% and 74.99% respectively. The results obtained were validated using error matrix and the results were compared with the ground truth.

Rajendra Prasad et.al(2015) are classified various crops such as wheat, barley, mustard, lentil, pigeon pea, sugar cane and other no-crops such as water, sand, fallow, built up, dense vegetation, sparse vegetation using the comparison of Landsat 8 OLI multispectral satellite data with LISS-IV to evaluate the performance of Artificial Neural Network algorithm using various learning parameters.

The comparison study reveals that, larger the learning rates, high fluctuation and lower the classification accuracy LISS-IV, while less but consistent results were found using Landsat 8 OLI.

Crop Mapping using satellite images is a challenging task due to complexities within field, and having the similar spectral properties with other crops in the same region. R. Saini & S.K. Ghosh(2018), have used Sentinel-2 satellite that 13 thirteen spectral bands, 5 days revisit time and resolution at three different level (10m, 20m, 60m), also the free availability of data, makes it a correct choice for vegetation mapping. The aim of this paper is to classify crop using single date Sentinel-2 imagery in the Roorkee, Uttarakhand, India.

Most efficient machine learning algorithms namely Support Vector Machine (SVM) and Random Forest (RF) are used for classification of crops by considering four spectral bands i.e., Near Infra-Red (NIR), Red, Blue, Green of sentinel-2 data are stacked for the classification. The comparison study of RF and SVM shows the overall accuracy achieved is 84.22% and 81.22% respectively, which states that the RF with sentinel-2 yields better results. Table 5 and figure 15 provides the brief description of the comparison study.

Table 5. Class specific accuracy by RF and SVM for crop images

Class Name	RF (%)	SVM (%)
High Density Forest	92.93	90.66
Low Density Forest	85.05	82.6
Orchard	75.37	74.46
Sandy area	84.47	81.76
Water	89.76	89.32
Built-up	86.47	83.53
Fallow land	90.48	87.99
Wheat	82.11	78.55
Sugarcane	84.76	81.77
Fodder	61.22	59.21
Other crops	83.24	80.99

(R. Saini & S.K. Ghosh(2018))

Figure 15. Classified crop images by RF and SVM
(R.& Saini, S.K. Ghosh(2018))

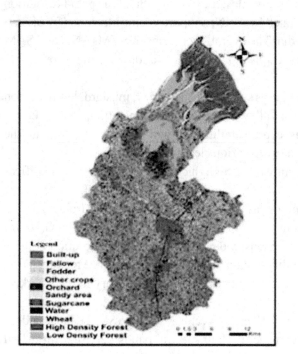 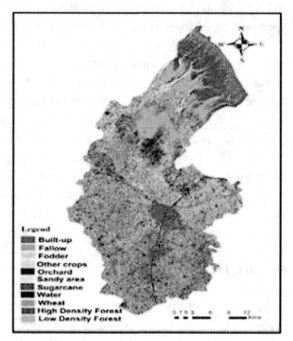

Contributions

The following are the contribution for the chapter.

- Provides an insight regarding various acquisition methods for remote sensed data.
- Introduction on ANN characteristics and functionalities
- Provide briefly an insight to various applications of ANN
- Provides applications of ANN for agriculture using remote sensed data in particular yield
- Prediction of crops and crop mapping/classification
- Future scope of research with other machine learning techniques deep learning and other domains for agriculture is covered

CHALLENGES AND FURTHER SCOPE

The existing challenges in this area will be presented. In addition future directions of research area for application agriculture using advance machine learning methods (deep learning) and suitable domains will be covered in this section.

Remote sensing plays an important role in future in agriculture. The different data can be taken in precise and high modeling of electromagnetic scattering and parameter extraction of crop and farm land images. In modern remote sensing application involves the implanting non-chips in plants and trees to monitor crop. The deep learning methodologies such as CNN, RNN and LSTM variants can be incorporated to extract and address spectral-spatial feature learning in various applications. Currently CNN is been used commonly for remote sensing. Further integration of CNN with other models like RNN, RBN might yield better temporal-spatial yields for remote image processing. Remote sensing future opportunities are listed below,

- Combination of deep learning methods for retrieval of images are structuring of part of images.
- Considering memory effects of climate and vegetation
- Classification of multi sensor data and any deep learning methods
- For damage estimation with high resolution UAV imagery
- RNN/LSTM for satellite imagery for reliable classification of land usage

CONCLUSION

Various ANN methods like Support Vector Machine, Random Forest algorithm, Decision tree, Back propagation method, K means clustering in combination with various satellites images like optical or microwave data in agriculture can be efficiently used for crop classification, Yield prediction, effect of soil in yield prediction, calculating Leaf area Index, NDVI to obtain accurate results. Forecasting of crop yield is helpful in food management and growth of a nation, which has specially agriculture based economy. In the last few decades, Artificial Neural Networks have been used successfully in different fields of agricultural remote sensing especially in crop type classification and crop area yield estimation.

REFERENCES

Akhand, K., Nizamuddin, M., & Roytman, L. (2018). An Artificial Neural Network-Based Model for Predicting Boro Rice Yield in Bangladesh Using AVHRR-Based Satellite Data. *International Journal of Agriculture and Forestry*, 8(1), 16–25. doi:10.5923/j.ijaf.20180801.04

Akhand, K., Nizamuddin, M., & Roytman, L. (2018). Wheat Yield Prediction in Bangladesh using Artificial Neural Network and Satellite Remote Sensing Data. *Global Journal of Science Frontier Research: D Agriculture and Veterinary, 18*(2).

Ayoubi. (2011). Application of Artificial Neural Network (ANN) to Predict Soil Organic Matter Using Remote Sensing Data in Two Ecosystems. In *Biomass and Remote Sensing of Biomass*. InTech.

Chandra, A., Mitra, P. S. K., Dubey, & Ray. (2019). *Machine Learning Approach For Kharif Rice Yield Prediction Integrating Multi-Temporal Vegetation Indices And Weather And Non-Weather Variables*. The International Archives of the Photogrammetry, Remote Sensing and Spatial Information Sciences, New Delhi, India.

Dave, V. S., & Dutta, K. (2014). Neural network-based models for software effort estimation: A review. *Artificial Intelligence Review*, 42(2), 295–307.

Huang. (2017). Imitating the brain with neurocomputer a "new" way towards artificial general intelligence. *Int. J. Autom. Comput., 14*(5), 520-531.

Jiang, Yang, Clinton, & Wang. (2004). An artificial neural network model for estimating crop yields using remotely sensed information. *International Journal of Remote Sensing*. http://www.tandf.co.uk/journals

Kumar, Gupta, Mishra, & Prasad. (2015). Comparison of support vector machine, artificial neural network, and spectral angle mapper algorithms for crop classification using LISS IV data. *International Journal of Remote Sensing, 36*(6).

Kumar, P., Prasad, R., Prashant, K., & Srivasta. (2015). Artificial neural network with different learning parameters for crop classification using multispectral datasets. In *International Conference on Microwave, Optical and Communication Engineering (ICMOCE)*. IEEE.

Kumara, P., Prasada, R., Mishraa, V. N., Guptaa, D. K., & Singhb, S. K. (2016). Artificial Neural Network for Crop Classification Using C-band RISAT-1 Satellite Datasets. *Russian Agricultural Sciences, 42*(3-4), 281–284.

Kuwataa, K. R., & Shibasakib. (2016), Estimating Corn Yield In The United States With Modis EVI And Machine Learning Methods. *ISPRS Annals Of The Photogrammetry, Remote Sensing And Spatial Information Sciences, 8*.

Manoj, Semwal, & Verma. (2019). *An Artificial Neural Network Model For Estimating Mentha Crop Biomass Yield Using Landsat 8 OLI*. Precision Agriculture. Https://Doi.Org/10.1007/S11119-019-09655-1

Mishra, S., Mishra, D., & Santra, G. H. (2016). Applications of Machine Learning Techniques in Agricultural Crop Production: A Review Paper. *Indian Journal of Science and Technology, 9*(38). doi:10.17485/ijst/2016/v9i38/95032

Mishra. (2016). Applications of Machine Learning Techniques in Agricultural Crop Production: A Review Paper. *Indian Journal of Science and Technology, 9*(38). www.indjst.org

Saini, R. S. K., & Ghosh. (2018). *Crop Classification On Single Date Sentinel-2 Imagery Using Random Forest And Suppor Vector Machine*. The International Archives of the Photogrammetry, Remote Sensing and Spatial Information Sciences, Dehradun, India.

Taşdemir & Wirnhardt. (2012). Neural network-based clustering for agriculture management. *EURASIP Journal on Advances in Signal Processing*, 200.

Yan, F., Gong, Y., & Feng, Z. (2015). Combination of Artificial Neural Network with Multispectral Remote Sensing Data as Applied in Site Quality Evaluation in Inner Mongolia. *Croatian Journal of Forest Engineering, 36*, 2.

Yao, C., Zhang, Y., Zhang, Y., & Liu, H. (2017). Application of convolutional Neural Network in classification of high resolution Agricultural Remote Sensing Images. The International archives of the photogrammetry, remote sensing and spatial information sciences, Wuhan, China.

Yao, C. (2017). *Application of convolutional Neural Network in classification of high resolution Agricultural Remote Sensing Images*. The International archives of the photogrammetry, remote sensing and spatial information sciences, Wuhan, China.

Index

A

Accuracy 24, 33, 45-47, 60-62, 72, 74-77, 88-94, 114, 133-136, 147, 151, 167, 172-175, 184, 189-190, 204-210, 220-221, 228, 231, 236, 243, 245, 250, 263, 267, 278, 283-285, 290, 293-295, 298, 300-301, 303, 307-310, 318, 329-330, 336, 338-339, 350, 356-357, 368-371, 380, 402-404, 406, 409, 412-413, 417, 421-422, 433, 499-500, 502-503, 509-511, 513, 516-520, 523, 527-532, 541, 555-556, 558-559, 561-565, 572, 578, 590, 600, 602, 604, 612, 614-615, 619, 621-626, 628, 630-631, 639, 641, 643, 645, 651, 671-672, 677, 685-686, 689, 698, 704-708, 710, 713, 717-723, 749, 751-754, 757, 762, 770-771, 777, 779, 804-805, 825, 827, 849, 853, 856, 859, 862, 868-869, 872-873, 876, 882, 895-902, 906, 909, 914, 933, 939, 947-949, 951-953, 962, 971, 973, 989, 1021-1023, 1026-1027, 1044-1045, 1056, 1068, 1077-1079, 1083, 1096, 1118-1119, 1122, 1126, 1131-1132, 1146-1147, 1151, 1156, 1170, 1174, 1176-1179, 1181, 1184-1189, 1208, 1220, 1233, 1247, 1249, 1253, 1255, 1260, 1263-1264, 1269-1271, 1278-1280, 1285, 1288-1290, 1309, 1330, 1348, 1354-1355, 1368, 1375-1377, 1382, 1404, 1414-1417, 1420, 1422-1423, 1428, 1433, 1435, 1444-1446, 1457, 1459, 1465-1466, 1469, 1471-1475, 1495-1496, 1505, 1511, 1533-1535, 1537, 1540-1541, 1551, 1555, 1565-1567, 1570-1572

Activation Function 8, 12, 24, 28, 59, 91, 100, 133, 153, 169, 173, 175, 202-203, 205-207, 209-211, 216, 220-221, 223, 225, 258-261, 284-286, 288, 299-300, 341, 362-365, 379-380, 382, 387, 393, 407, 410, 451, 519, 549-550, 554, 603, 636-637, 655-656, 661, 667, 688, 753, 757, 761, 807, 848, 852, 883-884, 887, 889, 898, 918, 962, 977, 1009-1011, 1063-1064, 1119, 1149-1150, 1166, 1182-1183, 1200, 1202, 1251-1252, 1268-1270, 1275, 1291, 1293, 1321, 1381, 1385-1386, 1388,

1391, 1393, 1396-1397, 1415, 1417-1418, 1422, 1433, 1441, 1457, 1471, 1482-1483, 1495, 1515, 1562-1563, 1565-1567, 1570, 1574

Active And Reactive Power 440-442, 445-446, 448, 450, 455, 462, 731

Agriculture 85, 138, 167, 1008-1009, 1012-1013, 1016, 1019-1024, 1028-1042, 1048-1050, 1077, 1102, 1116, 1130-1131, 1141, 1143, 1287-1288, 1299, 1311, 1358, 1533

airspace zone 1334, 1353

AlexNet 1559, 1566-1567, 1572

Analysis 29, 38-39, 42, 47, 49-50, 63, 65-66, 69, 73, 76, 78-80, 83, 89, 91, 102-103, 106, 113, 116-117, 137-146, 148, 151, 156, 163, 167, 173, 179-180, 184, 198, 204, 208, 219-220, 226, 228, 239, 241, 243, 245-246, 264-266, 281, 283-285, 290, 292-294, 297-300, 304-305, 309, 325, 328, 336-337, 339-340, 348, 356-357, 361, 365-366, 371-373, 378, 381, 391, 405, 422-424, 429-430, 437, 450, 465, 469, 473, 477, 487, 491, 494, 496-497, 499, 501, 503-504, 510-512, 515, 517-519, 521-522, 524-525, 527-528, 533-536, 538-539, 542-543, 545, 551-552, 555, 561-570, 572-577, 585-586, 588-589, 592-595, 599, 603, 607-608, 611-614, 620-621, 624-628, 631, 634-635, 646-647, 650, 664, 666, 670, 675, 677, 679, 681, 685, 698, 700, 704-705, 707-708, 725-726, 762, 770-771, 783-785, 787-789, 792-795, 797, 799-803, 813, 818, 821-822, 828-830, 839-841, 846, 849-850, 853, 857, 862-864, 867, 873, 876-877, 880-883, 885, 902, 908-912, 933-934, 937, 939, 943-944, 948, 951-956, 958, 961-962, 967, 969-970, 975, 982, 984, 992, 994, 997, 1001, 1003-1005, 1014, 1018-1020, 1023, 1026, 1035, 1043-1044, 1046-1047, 1052, 1055-1056, 1063, 1073-1075, 1080-1081, 1085, 1096, 1118-1119, 1131, 1135-1137, 1142-1143, 1146-1148, 1150, 1155-1156, 1168-1171, 1173, 1179-1181, 1189, 1191, 1195-1198, 1200, 1214-1216, 1218-1220, 1223-1224, 1226-1227,

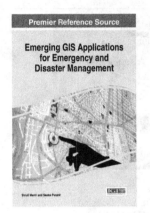

IGI Global Author Services

Providing a high-quality, affordable, and expeditious service, IGI Global's Author Services enable authors to streamline their publishing process, increase chance of acceptance, and adhere to IGI Global's publication standards.

Benefits of Author Services:

- **Professional Service:** All our editors, designers, and translators are experts in their field with years of experience and professional certifications.

- **Quality Guarantee & Certificate:** Each order is returned with a quality guarantee and certificate of professional completion.

- **Timeliness:** All editorial orders have a guaranteed return timeframe of 3-5 business days and translation orders are guaranteed in 7-10 business days.

- **Affordable Pricing:** IGI Global Author Services are competitively priced compared to other industry service providers.

- **APC Reimbursement:** IGI Global authors publishing Open Access (OA) will be able to deduct the cost of editing and other IGI Global author services from their OA APC publishing fee.

Author Services Offered:

 English Language Copy Editing
Professional, native English language copy editors improve your manuscript's grammar, spelling, punctuation, terminology, semantics, consistency, flow, formatting, and more.

 Scientific & Scholarly Editing
A Ph.D. level review for qualities such as originality and significance, interest to researchers, level of methodology and analysis, coverage of literature, organization, quality of writing, and strengths and weaknesses.

 Figure, Table, Chart & Equation Conversions
Work with IGI Global's graphic designers before submission to enhance and design all figures and charts to IGI Global's specific standards for clarity.

 Translation
Providing 70 language options, including Simplified and Traditional Chinese, Spanish, Arabic, German, French, and more.

Hear What the Experts Are Saying About IGI Global's Author Services

"Publishing with IGI Global has been *an amazing experience* for me for sharing my research. The *strong academic production* support ensures quality and timely completion." – **Prof. Margaret Niess, Oregon State University, USA**

"The service was *very fast, very thorough, and very helpful* in ensuring our chapter meets the criteria and requirements of the book's editors. I was *quite impressed and happy* with your service." – **Prof. Tom Brinthaupt, Middle Tennessee State University, USA**

Learn More or Get Started Here:

For Questions, Contact IGI Global's Customer Service Team at cust@igi-global.com or 717-533-8845

IGI Global's Transformative Open Access (OA) Model:
How to Turn Your University Library's Database Acquisitions Into a Source of OA Funding

Well in advance of Plan S, IGI Global unveiled their OA Fee Waiver (Read & Publish) Initiative. Under this initiative, librarians who invest in IGI Global's InfoSci-Books and/or InfoSci-Journals databases will be able to subsidize their patrons' OA article processing charges (APCs) when their work is submitted and accepted (after the peer review process) into an IGI Global journal.

How Does it Work?

Step 1: **Library Invests in the InfoSci-Databases:** A library perpetually purchases or subscribes to the InfoSci-Books, InfoSci-Journals, or discipline/subject databases.

Step 2: **IGI Global Matches the Library Investment with OA Subsidies Fund:** IGI Global provides a fund to go towards subsidizing the OA APCs for the library's patrons.

Step 3: **Patron of the Library is Accepted into IGI Global Journal (After Peer Review):** When a patron's paper is accepted into an IGI Global journal, they option to have their paper published under a traditional publishing model or as OA.

Step 4: **IGI Global Will Deduct APC Cost from OA Subsidies Fund:** If the author decides to publish under OA, the OA APC fee will be deducted from the OA subsidies fund.

Step 5: **Author's Work Becomes Freely Available:** The patron's work will be freely available under CC BY copyright license, enabling them to share it freely with the academic community.

Note: This fund will be offered on an annual basis and will renew as the subscription is renewed for each year thereafter. IGI Global will manage the fund and award the APC waivers unless the librarian has a preference as to how the funds should be managed.

Hear From the Experts on This Initiative:

"I'm very happy to have been able to make one of my recent research contributions *freely available* along with having access to the *valuable resources* found within IGI Global's InfoSci-Journals database."

– Prof. Stuart Palmer,
Deakin University, Australia

"Receiving the support from IGI Global's OA Fee Waiver Initiative *encourages me to continue my research work without any hesitation.*"

– Prof. Wenlong Liu, College of Economics and Management at Nanjing University of Aeronautics & Astronautics, China